Repetition in the

- Examines repetition
- Explores the form,
- Evaluates the text a
- Evidence for the authenticity of the original text
- Quotes more than 5,000 verses as evidence of repetition in the Bible
- Translates all repetition from the Greek and Hebrew for the lay reader
- Written for students of the Bible

The evident repetition by the New Testament Greek of the pattern established 15 centuries earlier in Moses' Hebrew gives further affirmation of the unity of Scripture - and in so doing, it establishes a corollary of verbal inspiration as well as a clear refutation of any attempt to classify the Bible as an accumulation of purely human writings. A must-read for anyone who does biblical study.
    Rev. Professor David P. Kuske, professor emeritus of New Testament Theology at Wisconsin Lutheran Seminary, Mequon, WI.

Cascione's research has taken a further step in identifying Hebraic meter first used in the Pentateuch and then carried through the rest of the Bible. This meter, like chiasm, has been virtually invisible until recent times. Few scholars such as Umberto Moshe David Cassuto, Eyal Rav-Noy, and Diana Jill Kirby, whose research Cascione has combined with his own, have ventured to investigate repetition in the Bible.
    Rev. Professor Robert A. Dargatz, former professor of Old Testament Studies and chairman of the Religion Division at Concordia University Irvine, California, and Pastor of Emmanuel Lutheran Church, Orange, CA, elected to the LCMS Commission on Theology and Church Relations.

Cascione utterly destroys the documentary hypothesis that has prevailed in academia for generations. He demonstrates the integrity of the biblical text from Hebraic meter within the text itself.
    Rev. Rolf Preus, theologian, pastor of Trinity Lutheran Church, Sidney, MT, and St. John Lutheran Church, Fairview, MT.

I highly recommend this book, as I also do Cascione's earlier "In Search of the Biblical Order." Anyone working with the text of the Bible should have both of these close-at-hand at all times.
    Rev. Professor James B. Jordan, Director, Biblical Horizons Ministries, and Scholar-in-Residence, Theopolis Institute.

Repetition in the Bible

by
Gioacchino Michael Cascione
edited by
David Kuske • Robert Dargatz • Rolf Preus

RedeemerPress.org
P.O. Box 89386
Tucson, AZ 85752

Copyright © 2016 by Gioacchino Michael Cascione

Published by
RedeemerPress.org
P.O. Box 89386
Tucson, AZ 85752

Copy Editors: Randi G. Vincent, Rev. John Preus
Typesetter: Sarah Carter
Designers: Scott Cain, Christina Westermeyer

Printed in the United States of America by The Missourian, Washington, MO.

Information about the book, author, and sales is available at:
www.RedeemerPress.org
ContactUs@RedeemerPress.org
Contact phone 586-553-0555

The original art, 5' by 4' oil on canvas by the author titled *Tucson Madonna*, Copyright © 2015 by Gioacchino Michael Cascione.

Quotations from Umberto Cassuto used by permission of Alexander Gendler of Varda Books.

Quotations from *Repetition in the Book of Revelation* used by permission of the author, Diana Jill Kirby.

All rights reserved. No part of this publication may be reproduced, stored in a retrieval system, or transmitted in any form or by any means, electronic, mechanical, photocopying, recording or otherwise, without the prior written permission of Gioacchino Michael Cascione.

ISBN 978-0-9966124-0-1

Library of Congress Control Number: 2015949675

ABOUT THE FRONT COVER
The raised Greek words from John 16 translate: *These things I have spoken to you.*

ABOUT THE BACK COVER
Tucson Madonna—5' by 4' oil on canvas portrait painted by the author in 2014. The subject is Brianna Galvez, a junior at Ironwoodridge High School in the Tucson area, posed as the Virgin Mary in front of the old stone ruin on Dove Mountain Blvd. The painting was purchased directly from the artist by "The University of Southern Indiana Art Collection." An explanation of the painting as a visual introduction to repetition as the key element of this book is found on page 300.

Dedication

To my wife Virginia, whose support helped make this book possible.

About the Author and the Editors

Gioacchino Michael Cascione is the author of *In Search of the Biblical Order* published in 1987 and an expanded edition in 2012. He earned a Master of Fine Arts degree from Southern Illinois University in Edwardsville and became a professor of art at the University of Southern Indiana University from 1974-77. He earned a Master of Divinity degree from Concordia Theological Seminary in Fort Wayne and served congregations from 1981-2012.

The author wishes to express his appreciation for the encouragement, guidance, and counsel from the excellent theologians who served as editors for this book. Without their assistance, and particularly that of David Kuske, who encouraged the author to write this book, it would not have been written.

Rev. Professor David P. Kuske is professor emeritus of New Testament Theology at Wisconsin Lutheran Seminary, Mequon, Wisconsin. As chairman of the editorial committee, Kuske had final approval on the contents of this book. He is the author of:

> *Biblical Interpretation: The Only Right Way*, Northwestern Publishing House, Milwaukee, 1997;
>
> *1, 2 Thessalonians (The People's Bible)*, Northwestern Publishing House, Milwaukee, 2000;
>
> *A Commentary on Romans 1-8*, Northwestern Publishing House, Milwaukee, 2007;
>
> *A Commentary on Romans 9-16*, Northwestern Publishing House, Milwaukee, 2014;
>
> *A Commentary on 1 & 2 Peter, Jude*, Northwestern Publishing House, Milwaukee, 2015.

Kuske served as an editor for the GWN and NET translations of the New Testament published in 1988 and 1990. He is currently a technical advisor for a new translation of the entire Bible known as the Wartburg Project (Wartburgproject.org), with more than 100 translators participating.

Rev. Professor Robert A. Dargatz served as a professor of Old Testament Studies at Concordia University Irvine, California, from 1977 to 1995, and as chairman of the Religion Division for most of his career there. He currently serves as pastor of Immanuel Lutheran Church, Orange, California, and as an elected member of the LCMS

Commission on Theology and Church Relations. He recently finished two terms on the Board of Regents at Concordia University Irvine. He graduated from Concordia Theological Seminary with a Master of Divinity degree in 1976 and a Master of Sacred Theology degree in 1985. Dargatz also completed extensive graduate work at UCLA in Near Eastern Languages and Cultures, and at Concordia Seminary, St. Louis, in Theological Studies.

Rev. Rolf Preus has 36 years of experience in parish ministry. Preus earned both his Master of Divinity degree and Master of Sacred Theology degree at Concordia Theological Seminary, Fort Wayne, Indiana. He is the author of *Justification: Am I Good Enough for God?*, published by Northwestern Publishing House. An expert on the Doctrine of Justification and the Doctrine of Inspiration, many of his papers can be viewed online at ChristForUs.org. He is currently serving Trinity Lutheran Church, Sidney, Montana, and St. John Lutheran Church, Fairview, Montana. He and his wife Dorothy have 12 children and 35 grandchildren. Preus's father, Dr. Robert Preus, is the author of *The Inspiration of Scripture*, published by Concordia Publishing House.

Comments by the Editors

"My investment of time and expense devoted to *Repetition in the Bible* by Gioacchino Cascione has paid me huge dividends. Cascione has spent three decades using sophisticated Bible software to study the original Greek and Hebrew texts of the Scriptures. He has discovered the use of "Hebraic meter" throughout the inspired writings of the prophets and apostles which he documents in detail in his book. Gioacchino Michael Cascione's research does not attempt to put forth new doctrines and teachings from the Scriptures, but it does confirm and amplify the teachings of God through His prophets and apostles. The chiastic structure found in many sections of the Bible has captured the attention of recent scholarship dealing with the text of Holy Writ. Cascione's research has taken a further step in identifying Hebraic meter first used in the Pentateuch and then carried through the rest of the Bible. This meter, like chiasm, has been virtually invisible until recent times. Few scholars such as Umberto Moshe David Cassuto, Eyal Rav-Noy, and Diana Jill Kirby, whose research Cascione has combined with his own, have ventured to investigate repetition in the Bible. Hebraic meter provides internal evidence of a divine signature authenticating the inspired text of the Bible. Cascione puts forth thought-provoking suggestions regarding Biblical genealogies, the use of numbers in the Bible, and the value of the Vulgate over and against the Septuagint in textual criticism. He also provides evidence for the literary connection between Song of Solomon and the Book of Revelation that may well leave the reader with a deeper appreciation and respect for both of these books. Any one of the above items will more than justify the investment in the book. While the book supplies the Greek and Hebrew for advanced Bible students, it also supplies the English translation of these texts to make it easy for the common reader to follow the argumentation and to see the evidence for the author's presentation of the Biblical patterns."

— **Rev. Professor Robert A. Dargatz**

"The author wrote two earlier books titled *In Search of the Biblical Order*, and in this third book he furthers the goal of those first two books. *Repetition in the Bible* is a significant advance both in the data he supplies, as well as the conclusions based on this data. One does not have to agree with every assertion Cascione makes to realize the evidence is overwhelming that there is a pattern of constant repetition woven into the fabric of many of the books of the Bible. The evident repetition by the New Testament Greek of the pattern established 15 centuries earlier in Moses' Hebrew gives further affirmation of the unity of Scripture - and in so doing, it establishes a corollary of verbal inspiration as well as a clear refutation of any attempt to classify the Bible as an accumulation of purely human writings. A must-read for anyone who does biblical study."

— **Rev. Professor David P. Kuske**

"We live in a day when what is crass and ugly is celebrated and what is pure and lovely is denigrated. The Church's precious heritage of beautiful hymns and liturgies is discarded in favor of crass, shallow, and sentimental 'Christianized' pop music. The Christian heart longs to gaze upon the beauty of the Lord in his temple. Traditional Christians have long argued that matters of aesthetics are not purely subjective. To their defense comes a remarkable book written by a theologian whose theological training was preceded by an education as an artist.

"Christians have always appreciated the literary beauty of God's written Word. What we have not appreciated, and what this book brings to our attention, is a beauty of verbal repetition in the Bible. With the help of computer technology, Rev. Cascione brings an artist's eye to the structure of the biblical text. He finds an amazing tapestry of repetition woven into the Scriptures. He discerns no new teaching. He discovers no secret code. He learns nothing of biblical teaching we did not already know. What he does find disproves the claims of the critics that the text of the Bible evolved over a period of time, being redacted by various editors. Repetition of words and phrases, especially in multiples of seven and ten, prove a deliberation that could not have occurred under the scenario contrived by the critics. Rev. Cascione utterly destroys the documentary hypothesis that has prevailed in academia for generations. He demonstrates the integrity of the biblical text from Hebraic meter within the text itself. He demonstrates a consistent numerical meter throughout the whole Bible. This book is an especially valuable tool for those engaged in textual criticism. Reliance on unprovable theories and speculation without evidence must give way to the evidence within the text itself of the text's authenticity."

—**Rev. Rolf Preus**

Table of Contents

PREFACE i

DATA IN THIS BOOK iv

CHAPTER ONE — *REPETITION IN THE GOSPEL OF MATTHEW* 1
Collecting the Data 2
Heptadic Phrases in Matthew 4
What Is a Greek Text? 11
How Many Ancient Greek Manuscripts Are There? 12
How Were Ancient Manuscripts Collated into 9 Greek Texts? 12
Who Assembled These Greek Texts? 13
Metered Introduction to Conversation: Anaphoric Phrases 15
Decadal Phrases in Matthew 22
Dodecadal Phrases in Matthew 31
Integration of Hebraic Meter in Matthew 10:24-42 35
Single Words Repeated 7, 10, and 12 Times in Matthew 37
Single Words in Heptadic Meter 37
Single Words in Decadal Meter 38
Single Words in Dodecadal Meter 39
Single Word Repeated 17 Times 40

CHAPTER TWO — *REPETITION IN THE GOSPEL OF MARK* 41
Heptadic Meter in Mark 43
Decadal Meter in Mark 47
Metered Introduction to Conversation: Anaphoric Phrases 49
Hebraic Meter Verifies Authenticity of Mark Chapter 16:9-20 58
Additional Metered Words in Mark 59

CHAPTER THREE — *REPETITION IN THE GOSPEL OF LUKE* 61
Heptadic Meter in Luke 62
Dodecadal Meter in Luke 68
Metered Introduction to Conversation: Anaphoric Phrases 71
Probability of Repetition in Numbers and Phrases in the Bible 77
Single Words in Heptadic Meter 78
Single Words in Decadal Meter 79
Single Words in Dodecadal Meter 79
Single Word Repeated 17 Times 80

CHAPTER FOUR — *REPETITION IN THE GOSPEL OF JOHN* 81
Eternal Life and Truth 82
Heptadic Meter in John 87

Metered Introduction to Conversation: Anaphoric Phrases.................97
Repetition in Conversation in the Four Gospels................103
Decadal Meter in John................104
Metered Words and Phrases within Accounts................106
Dodecadal Meter in John................121
Exceptions................122
Single Words in Heptadic Meter................122
Single Words in Decadal Meter................124
Single Words in Dodecadal Meter................125
Single Words Repeated 17 Times................126
The Woman Caught in Adultery................127
Hebraic Meter in Gospel Events................129

CHAPTER FIVE — *REPETITION IN THE BOOK OF REVELATION*................133
Heptadic Meter in Revelation................134
Activity in Heaven................140
God in Heptadic Meter................141
Blessing in Revelation................144
Signs in Revelation................144
Time in Revelation................147
Decadal Meter in Revelation................149
God in Decadal Meter................151
Activity on Earth................156
Metered Introduction to Conversation: Anaphoric Phrases................158
Dodecadal Meter in Revelation................161
Three Plus Four or Three Times Four................162
Single Words in Heptadic Meter................165
Single Words in Decadal Meter................169
Single Words in Dodecadal Meter................173
Word Stems in Revelation................175

CHAPTER SIX — *REPETITION: A CONTEMPORARY DEFINITION*................179
Important Authors on Repetition in Revelation................180
Forms of Repetition in the Book of Revelation................186
Repeated Phrases in Revelation................188
Sternberg's Research Applied to Revelation................191
The Function of Repetition................193
Applying Aesthetic Hermeneutics to the Text................195
Repetition versus Nestle-Aland's Greek Text................197

CHAPTER SEVEN — *SONG OF SOLOMON:*
A PATTERN FOR JESUS IN REVELATION................199
Revelation Repeats the Shape of the Old Testament................199
Song of Solomon and Revelation Employ Same Decadal Image................202
Metered Phrases and Words in Song of Solomon................210

CHAPTER EIGHT — *REPETITION IN GENESIS AND EXODUS* 213
Chiasm: A Form of Repetition...213
Cassuto: A Primary Source for This Chapter...217
The Documentary Hypothesis..218
Cassuto on Heptadic Repetition..219
Heptadic Repetition in the Creation Account..220
Heptadic Structure: An Eastern View of Order.....................................224
Heptadic Unity in the Creation Accounts..225
Heptadic Repetition in the Flood..228
Heptadic Blessings Given to Abraham, Isaac, and Jacob.....................231
Heptadic Events in Genesis...234
Heptadic Phrases in Genesis...235
Metered Introduction to Conversation: Anaphoric Phrases.................237
Cassuto on Exodus: Heptadic Meter in God's Call to Moses..............241
Heptadic Events in the 10 Plagues...244
Heptadic Repetition in the Sinai Desert...248
Single Words in Heptadic Meter in Genesis and Exodus.....................251
Seventy: An Expression of Heptadic Completion.................................253
Hebraic Meter Spanning Adjacent Books in the Bible.........................256
Decadal Meter in Genesis..263
Decadal Events in Genesis...272
Decadal Meter in Exodus...273
Nouns and Derivative Verbs in the Creation Account..........................277
Single Words in Decadal Meter in Genesis and Exodus......................278
Dodecadal Meter in Genesis..280
Single Words in Dodecadal Meter in Genesis.......................................283
Single Words Repeated 17 Times...284

CHAPTER NINE — *A DEEPER LOOK INTO GENESIS AND EXODUS*.............285
Hebraic Meter in Time..285
Origins of the Bible's Number System: Sexagesimal or Antediluvian?...................288
The Tabernacle..295
Order in the Bible...297
Cassuto on Perfection versus Blessing...300
Increased Complexity in Exodus..303
Decadal Meter in the *Waw* Consecutive (repetition of *and*s)...................312
Contemporary Authors' Views on Genesis 75 Years after Cassuto.............314

CHAPTER TEN — *REPETITION IN THE GENESIS GENEALOGY*.................323
Hebraic Meter in the Genesis Genealogy...323
Unity of Numbers in the Patriarchs..326
Genesis Mathematics Superior to Cuneiform Tablets..........................328
Additional Hebraic Meter in the Ages of the Patriarchs......................335
Dates for the Exodus, Abraham, and the Flood....................................336

Gaps in the Genealogy: Yes and No.. 337
How Genesis Records Numbers... 340
Questions about Terah's Age at Abraham's Birth.. 341
Genesis Genealogy Symbolized as World Government in Revelation...................... 343
Repetition of Prophetic Images... 344
Metered Genealogy in the Gospels... 345
Chronological Order Not a Priority in the Bible.. 346
Problem of the Second Cainan.. 348
Admin Missing from the Septuagint and the Old Testament..................................... 354
Hebraic Meter in Ezra and Nehemiah's Postexilic Records....................................... 355
Septuagint Inaccuracies in the Patriarchal Ages... 357
Repetition throughout the Genealogies.. 360
Repetition of Names in Genesis.. 362

CONCLUSION.. 363
Repetition in the Gnostic Gospels... 364
The Quackery of Q.. 369
How Was Meter Placed in the Text?... 372
Three Impossibilities... 377

APPENDIX A —
CALCULATIONS FROM A UNIVERSITY MATHEMATICIAN................................ 381

APPENDIX B —
CALCULATIONS FROM MATHEMATICIAN MATTHEW SWANSON..................... 384

WORKS CITED... 387

INDEX.. 397

PREFACE

The primary goal of this book is to document repetition in the writings of Moses, Matthew, Mark, Luke, John, and other biblical writers. Secondary goals are to learn the source, purpose, and configuration of this repetition. This is not a book about what the Bible says, but how it is written. It is hoped that the reader will gain an understanding and appreciation of the Bible's unique concept and application of repetition. This may be the first book to address the subject of repetition in both testaments of the Bible.

In many respects this is also a book about the aesthetics of repetition in the Bible. As an archeological artifact, the Bible employs repetition as a highly-developed Hebraic genre. In addition to analyzing the data, the reader has the opportunity to visualize the shape of repetition in the text.

In order to support the claims in this volume, approximately 5,000 Scripture verses are quoted herein, which may represent little more than 1% of the possible repetition. All Hebrew and Greek quotations are translated into English for the lay reader. However, publishing the actual Hebrew and Greek was essential for the purpose of documentation. Readers conversant with these languages will want to see concrete evidence.

Despite the significance and enormity of repetition in the Bible, there is scant study of the subject, particularly related to the 4 Gospels. The obscurity and paucity of information have even prevented agreement on a definition of repetition in the Bible. E. W. Bullinger's 1,004-page tome, *Figures of Speech Used in the Bible*, first published in 1898, catalogs 217 figures of speech in the Bible. For *Repetitio* (Latin for *repetition*) he lists 3½ pages of examples with nothing similar to the repetition in this volume.

The early church fathers do not make reference to the presence of repetition in the text. Therefore, ancient copyists must not have been aware that they were copying and preserving repetition in every scroll they reproduced.

Previous books by this author, titled *In Search of the Biblical Order*, were published in 1987 and 2012, the latter as a significantly expanded second edition. After 37 years of dealing with the subject, this volume arrives at an unexpected explanation for the data. The search for the biblical order was always a search for repetition in the Bible.

In 2008 James B. Jordan, book dealer and Bible chronologist, requested a reprint of the 1987 edition, and was asked to wait for a new and expanded second edition. As work on the second edition progressed, Rabbi Eyal Rav-Noy published his book, *Who Really Wrote the Bible?*, which defends, by use of pattern analysis, Mosaic authorship of the Pentateuch. His research was useful in proving that the source of metered words and chiasm in Revelation originates in Genesis.

After the second edition was completed in 2012, this author followed Rav-Noy's advice to research the works of the great rabbinic scholar Umberto Cassuto. In the late 1920s, Cassuto worked as the Vatican Archivist of Semitic scrolls. His four volumes identify the origin of Hebraic meter in the Bible with Moses.

James B. Jordan recommended books on chiasmus in the Bible by John Breck and David Dorsey, who also confirmed the presence and importance of repetition in the Bible.

In 2013 this writer discovered Dr. Diana Jill Kirby's 2009 dissertation, titled *Repetition in the Book of Revelation*, which proves that the repetition of phrases is a biblical genre. She has written the first book dedicated entirely to repetition in a book of the Bible. Kirby produced data similar to that of Cassuto's commentaries on Genesis and Exodus, published beginning in 1944. However, she was not aware that her data is based on Hebraic meter found by Cassuto.

The research of these authors, combined with the data from *In Search of the Biblical Order*, led to a search for Hebraic repetition in the Gospels. After reviewing some initial data on repetition in the Gospels, Professor David Kuske encouraged this writer to begin work on a new book. Without his further encouragement, scholarship, and guidance it would not have been written. Reverend Rolf Preus and Reverend Professor Robert Dargatz provided valuable assistance and direction—Preus through his expertise on the Doctrine of Inspiration, and Dargatz with his experience in Old Testament studies.

In addition to the primary editors, Reverend John Preus, Ukrainian Bible translator Roger Kovaciny, and mathematician Anne Betz provided much appreciated assistance in editing this book.

Professional proofreader and copy editor Randi Vincent provided excellent counsel and attention to detail. Sarah Carter, who has mastered the InDesign program, simultaneously set English, Greek, and Hebrew. Working together they produced a professional publication.

The full extent of repetition in the Bible is as yet unknown. The study of repetition first led to an investigation of the New and Old Testaments, the Septuagint (a 3rd-century B.C. translation of the Hebrew Bible into Greek), the Apocrypha, the Vulgate, the Pseudepigrapha (false writings), and the Gnostic Gospels. The abundance of data proves that the claims and research of those who promote the Documentary Hypothesis, J E P D, the Q source, higher criticism, and the Markan Priority are without foundation.

Kirby recommended *The Poetics of the Biblical Narrative* by the noted Hebrew Scholar Meir Sternberg. His insights confirm that there is no external source or explanation for repetition in the Hebrew Bible.

By utilizing training in the fine arts; experience teaching as an art professor at the University of Southern Indiana; and training in Hebrew and Greek exegesis, this author concludes that biblical repetition confirms the authenticity of the text. Altering, editing, adding, deleting, conflating, or redacting of the text would necessarily dismember the metered repetition of words and phrases in the text. The existence of undisturbed meter in the text necessarily means we possess the original text.

There is always the question of whether to publish or to continue the research. There are so many areas that require further study, and so much data to evaluate, such a task would extend beyond the life of this writer. Therefore the goal is not to master the subject, but to demonstrate its existence. Scholars with more knowledge than this writer will have more to contribute. Readers of this book are invited to join the expedition and explore repetition in the Bible for themselves.

Data in this Book

Meticulous effort was put forth in checking, rechecking, and cross-checking references in this book, which lists more than 5,000 verses; 400 examples of heptadic, decadal, and dodecadal Hebraic meter; and 300 individual words and word stems arranged in Hebraic meter. Most of the verses printed in English are accompanied by the original Greek and Hebrew text. Repetition in the New Testament was crosschecked with 9 different Greek Texts. Any questions or possible corrections may be sent to contactus@RedeemerPress.org, or to RedeemerPress.org, P.O. Box 89386, Tucson, AZ 85752.

Due to the abundance of numbers, and as a visual aid to the reader, the author regularly uses digits rather than word equivalents for numerals 1 through 9, in opposition to correct English usage. This also aids computer searches.

Many of the verses are quoted from the *King James Version* or the *New American Standard Bible* (1975 edition). These 2 widely-available translations were selected because they follow the Greek and Hebrew texts more closely than most modern translations. However, modifications were often necessary in order to preserve the meter, even if the translation became awkward. English-only readers are advised to cross-reference quotations between the KJV and the NASB. However, not all of the data in this book can be reproduced from English translations because many Hebrew and Greek words have more than one meaning in English, depending on context.

This volume presents a small fraction of the estimated repetition in the Bible. The enormity of data led the author to focus on the 4 Gospels, Revelation, Genesis, and Exodus, with a limited examination of Song of Solomon. There is also a brief examination of the Pentateuch, Joshua, Judges, Ruth, Numbers, Daniel, and Ezekiel. Word searches in the Hebrew were conducted without vowel points as they appeared in the original text. Genesis, the first 15 chapters of Exodus, John, Revelation, and the first 10 chapters of Matthew were given a far more thorough examination, which accounts for the disproportionate volume of data from these books of the Bible.

There are many portions of the Bible yet to be examined for repetition. Further research may prove that modifications and additions to the data are necessary as more examples of repetition become evident.

Chapter One
Repetition in the Gospel of Matthew

The study of repetition in the Bible leads to a study of how the Bible is written. What the Bible says versus how the Bible repeats what it says are two different subjects. Drivers do not need to understand combustion engines in order to drive a car, and readers do not need to know how the Bible is written or the origin of its ancient manuscripts in order to understand what it is saying. Yet, the ancient approach to communication is different from our Western thought process. The reader will be challenged to view the text in terms of its 3,500-year-old literary genre.

The primary question for this chapter is, "Does Matthew repeat lists of words and phrases in his Gospel according to Hebraic meter written by Moses?" In other words, "Does he purposely repeat key words and phrases in his Gospel?"

The Bible is a book of faith and it is also an archeological artifact. The Bible's standard of eloquence is so diverse from our own that what some mistake for primitive language is actually sacred and sublime articulation.

This book addresses 3 narrowly-defined aspects of repetition in the Bible:

1. The repetition of metered words and phrases as an aesthetic genre in the Hebrew and Greek texts;
2. An examination of how Moses' use of repetition is incorporated into the Old and New Testament texts; and
3. Establishment of the original wording of the text by selecting variant readings from manuscripts that complete Hebraic meter.

Each of these 3 areas of research leads to a broad range of study with significant implications for our understanding of how the Bible is written.

First, repetition in the Bible will be examined as an ancient and uniquely Hebraic literary device rather than a function of grammar or rhetoric. Evidence points to the antediluvian origin of this literary device that exhibits a correlation between the subject and the metered repetition in the text, as discussed in the first and second editions of *In Search of the Biblical Order*.[1]

Second, the study of repetition leads to a study of how the Bible is written. Repetition will be examined in phrases, words, and word stems in the Old and New Testament; the phenomenon of its symbolic meter; and the extent of repetition in the text. In 4 successive chapters there will be a comparison of how Matthew, Mark, Luke, and John repeat words and phrases while they exhibit their own style. Identifying Hebraic meter in the text sheds light on the selection of unique words or phrasing in the text. It also affirms the unity of the Bible in its adherence to Hebraic sacred style. Repetition in the Bible leads to the question of whether Matthew, Mark, Luke, and John were aware that they were writing repetition into the text, or if repetition is the nature of divine inspiration, or both.

Third, when comparing manuscripts that contain variant readings in metered words, word stems, or phrases, selecting the correct manuscript reading becomes rather self-evident. The correct variant or variants necessary to complete the meter are most likely the correct reading and thus affirm the authenticity of the manuscript. After a great deal of examination, it is apparent that copyists of ancient biblical manuscripts were either not aware of the repetition in the text or the extent of the repetition in the text.

Two approaches were considered on how to present the data: either lead the reader through an explanation of the data, or present the reader with the textual evidence and explain the process later. This book will present first, and explain later. Therefore, the reader is requested to view the data as a whole and refrain from arriving at any conclusions until the end of the book.

Collecting the Data

A significant expansion of data in the second edition of *In Search of the Biblical Order* (published in April of 2012, and hereafter referred to as the 2012 edition) led to more areas of investigation than anticipated. Beginning on December 26, 2010, a series of 4 meetings took place in Los Angeles with Israeli-born Rabbi Eyal Rav-Noy, author of *Who Really Wrote the Bible?*[2] He explained that his primary mentor was the

---

[1] Gioacchino Michael Cascione, *In Search of the Biblical Order*, RedeemerPress.org, Saint Clair Shores, MI, 2012.
[2] Eyal Rav-Noy and Gil Weinreich, *Who Really Wrote the Bible?*, Richard Vigilante Books, Minneapolis, 2010.

great Hebrew scholar Umberto Cassuto, Chief Rabbi of Florence, Chair at Hebrew University of Rome, archivist of the Vatican Semitic collection, and Chair at Hebrew University in Jerusalem. In October of 2012 there was time to follow Rav-Noy's recommendation and read Cassuto's 4 books on this subject.

In addition, Biblical Horizons book dealer and author James B. Jordan[3] recommended books by John Breck[4] and David Dorsey.[5] In 2013 an internet search led to a dissertation by Dr. Diana Jill Kirby titled, *Repetition in the Book of Revelation*.[6] Kirby references some of the same examples published in the 2012 edition. She has written the most thorough and fascinating study of repetition in Revelation attempted by any author. Kirby's definition of repetition will be addressed in Chapter Six. Her analysis of the data and scholarship reflect an approach similar to Rav-Noy's and Cassuto's work in the Old Testament.

An important aspect of research is finding new perspectives by comparing a variety of authors who worked independently from each other. The exegetical genius of Umberto Cassuto led to reexamination of the data in the 2012 edition. Cassuto's research demonstrates that Genesis is the unexpected source for the metered phrases in Revelation. Chapter Eight will explore this relationship in detail. Combining Cassuto's approach as a refinement to the 2012 edition, along with information from the above named authors, led to the development of a hybrid exegetical approach. After writing a few experimental chapters on the Gospels, it was the urging of Professor David Kuske in the summer of 2013 that convinced this writer to publish another book. Kuske is a retired professor of Wisconsin Lutheran Seminary, and the author of *Biblical Interpretation: The Only Right Way*, as well as commentaries on Romans, Thessalonians, 1 & 2 Peter, and Jude.[7]

---

[3] James B. Jordan, *A Chronological and Calendrical Commentary on the Pentateuch, Studies in Biblical Chronology No. 3*, Biblical Horizons, Niceville, FL, 2001.
[4] John Breck, *The Shape of Biblical Language: Chiasmus in the Scriptures and Beyond*, reprint of St. Vladimir's Seminary Press, Crestwood, NY, 1994, Kaloros Press, Wadmalaw Island, SC, 2008.
[5] David A. Dorsey, *The Literary Structure of the Old Testament: A Commentary on Genesis–Malachi*, Baker Academic, Grand Rapids, MI, 1999.
[6] Diana Jill Kirby, *Repetition in the Book of Revelation*, Ph.D. diss., ProQuest, Ann Arbor, MI, 2009.
[7] David P. Kuske, *Biblical Interpretation: The Only Right Way*, Northwestern Publishing House, Milwaukee, 1997;
1, 2 Thessalonians (*The People's Bible*), Northwestern Publishing House, Milwaukee, 2000;
A Commentary on Romans 1-8, Northwestern Publishing House, Milwaukee, 2007;

Chapter Fifteen of the 2012 edition explains that there is no agreement among scholars on the difference between apocalyptic and narrative literature in the Bible.[8] After reading Cassuto's 3 volumes on Genesis and Exodus[9] it became apparent that meter in the text is not unique to Revelation.

To our knowledge there are no books in print about repetition in the Gospels, let alone the entire Bible. However, according to the Doctrine of the Unity of Scripture and Cassuto's understanding of Genesis, locating numerically ordered phrases in the 4 Gospels is consistent with the rest of Scripture. In other words, the repetition in Genesis should also be in Matthew.

<u>Cassuto explains that the Hebrew Bible, beginning with Genesis, is filled with words, word stems, and phrases set in Hebraic meter based on the repetition and multiples of 7 (heptads), 10 (decads), and 12 (dodecads). The reader is advised to remember these 3 terms.</u>

If the entire Scripture is a unified communication, this meter should also appear in the 4 Gospels. Therefore, if there are words and phrases arranged in Hebraic meter in the Gospels, where are they?

The first attempt to test this theory about repetition in the Gospel of Matthew, with the assistance of the *BibleWorks 8* program, began with heightened anticipation followed by sudden amazement. There was an array of data on the screen. More attempts produced more results. There was the Hebraic meter woven into the text nearly 2,000 years ago.

Why is there meter in the text? Who put it there? How much is there? What does it mean? The answers to these questions could fill volumes.

Heptadic Phrases in Matthew

Heptadic repetition confirms intentional repetition by the author, or the guiding hand of the Holy Spirit. There is no expectation for the lay reader to follow the Greek and Hebrew words. All examples of Greek

---

A Commentary on Romans 9-16, Northwestern Publishing House, Milwaukee, 2014;
A Commentary on 1 & 2 Peter, Jude, Northwestern Publishing House, Milwaukee, 2015.
[8] Cascione, 2012, p. 215.
[9] Umberto Moshe David Cassuto, *A Commentary on the Book of Genesis: Part I from Adam to Noah, Genesis I-VI 8*, Jerusalem, 1944, translated by Israel Abrahams, Varda Books, Skokie, IL, 2005;
A Commentary on the Book of Genesis: Part II from Noah to Abraham, Genesis VI 9-XI 32, Jerusalem, 1949, translated by Israel Abrahams, Varda Books, Skokie, IL, 2005;
A Commentary on the Book of Exodus, Jerusalem, 1951, translated by Israel Abrahams, Varda Books, Skokie, IL, 2005.

and Hebrew are translated into English. However, claims made in this book must be substantiated for those who wish to investigate the original languages.

John the Baptist

The 3-word Greek phrase for *John the Baptist* appears 7 times in the Gospel of Matthew. The repetition in Matthew follows Cassuto's explanation of Hebraic meter, Kirby's analysis of repetition in Revelation, and more than a hundred examples of single words repeating in Hebraic meter in the 2012 edition. The repetition of this phrase is found by scanning the entire Gospel of Matthew in Greek for the phrase *John the Baptist*, which occurs exactly 7 times, with no variant readings.

In the following lists, a key word is bolded at times to highlight the repetition. In this case the key word is *Baptist*. Greek has numerous case endings not found in English; hence the last letters of *Baptist* are not always the same.

The best way for a reader to look up all these phrases in English translations is to use a *King James Version* and a *New American Standard Bible* at the same time, since these are the most literal translations. For the sake of clarity and the desire to translate the text into conversational English, many translations do not follow the same word order or include all the words that actually appear in the Greek text. There are no variant readings in the heptadic repetition of *John the Baptist*. In other words, all 9 recognized Greek texts of the New Testament in which this phrase was searched agree on the same wording, which is remarkable in itself.

The initials BNT stand for *Nestle-Aland's Greek New Testament*. Other texts could be chosen, but alphabetically BNT appears first on the screen out of a possible 9 choices. Since all 9 texts agree on the wording, it does not make any difference which text is chosen to illustrate the Hebraic meter in the text.

John the Baptist 7 times in the Gospel of Matthew

John the **Baptist**............Ἰωάννου ὁ **βαπτιστὴς** (Matt. 3:1 BNT)
John the **Baptist**............Ἰωάννου τοῦ **βαπτιστοῦ** (Matt. 11:11 BNT)
John the **Baptist**............Ἰωάννου τοῦ **βαπτιστοῦ** (Matt. 11:12 BNT)
John the **Baptist**............Ἰωάννης ὁ **βαπτιστής** (Matt. 14:2 BNT)
John the **Baptist**............Ἰωάννου τοῦ **βαπτιστοῦ** (Matt. 14:8 BNT)
John the **Baptist**............Ἰωάννην τὸν **βαπτιστήν** (Matt. 16:14 BNT)
John the **Baptist**............Ἰωάννου τοῦ **βαπτιστοῦ** (Matt. 17:13 BNT)

To Jerusalem

The phrase *to Jerusalem* appears 7 times in the Gospel of Matthew. It is a simple 2-word prepositional phrase, identical to English usage. There are no variant readings.

To Jerusalem 7 times in the Gospel of Matthew
To Jerusalem...............εἰς Ἱεροσόλυμα (Matt. 2:1 BNT)
To Jerusalem...............εἰς Ἱεροσόλυμα (Matt. 5:35 BNT)
To Jerusalem...............εἰς Ἱεροσόλυμα (Matt. 16:21 BNT)
To Jerusalem...............εἰς Ἱεροσόλυμα (Matt. 20:17 BNT)
To Jerusalem...............εἰς Ἱεροσόλυμα (Matt. 20:18 BNT)
To Jerusalem...............εἰς Ἱεροσόλυμα (Matt. 21:1 BNT)
To Jerusalem...............εἰς Ἱεροσόλυμα (Matt. 21:10 BNT)

In or *From that Hour*

A phrase of prophetic or apocalyptic significance, *in* or *from that hour* repeats 7 times in Matthew without variant readings. Notice the 3-4 division between the prepositions *in* and *from*. There will be many more examples of heptadic phrases exhibiting a 3-4 division, which is a division of 3 repetitions and 4 repetitions within a given series of metered texts. Translations often read *in that very hour*, or *from that selfsame hour*. There is one more phrase similar to these 7 that reads, *But that day and that hour*, δὲ τῆς ἡμέρας ἐκείνης καὶ ὥρας (Matthew 24:36 BNT); however, this phrase lacks a preposition and adds the word *day*. Thus the writer demonstrates a desire to use a preposition to distinguish the 7 phrases from similar arrangements of words such as, *The lord of **that** servant shall come **in** a day when he looketh not for him, and in an **hour** that he is not aware of* (Matthew 24:50). In other words, Matthew could easily have chosen different words to express the same thought rather than emphasize the following heptadic cadence.

In or *from that hour* 7 times in the Gospel of Matthew
In that **hour**.............ἐν τῇ **ὥρᾳ** ἐκείνῃ (Matt. 8:13 BNT)
From that **hour**..........**ἀπὸ** τῆς **ὥρας** ἐκείνης (Matt. 9:22 BNT)
In that **hour**.....ἐν ἐκείνῃ τῇ **ὥρᾳ** (Matt. 10:19 BNT)
From that **hour**..........**ἀπὸ** τῆς **ὥρας** ἐκείνης (Matt. 15:28 BNT)
From that **hour**..........**ἀπὸ** τῆς **ὥρας** ἐκείνης (Matt. 17:18 BNT)
In that **hour**.....**Ἐν** ἐκείνῃ τῇ **ὥρᾳ** (Matt. 18:1 BNT)
In that **hour**.....**Ἐν** ἐκείνῃ τῇ **ὥρᾳ** (Matt. 26:55 BNT)

My Father Who Is in the Heavens

This next phrase contains 6 Greek words. Some of the texts add brackets around *the*. A large number of variant readings in ancient manuscripts involve questions about the word *the*, which can be expressed 24 ways in Greek. Quite often the Greek article is not or cannot be translated into English. One would hardly say, *the Father of the me in the heavens* as a translation of Matthew 2:21.

The phrase *My Father who is in Heaven* repeats 7 times in the Gospel of Matthew. Some have attempted to explain the repetition of phrases in the Bible as a mnemonic device, something that aids memorization and recitation. However, this can hardly be the case when 7 repetitions of a phrase are spread out over 9 chapters.

The same 6 or 7 Greek words appearing together 7 times in the same order is hardly a random occurrence. Chapter Eight of this book quotes Cassuto's commentary in which he explains that the author of Genesis repeated words, word stems, and phrases, 7, 10, and 12 times, or multiples of these numbers, as a traditional Hebraic literary device. Therefore, Matthew, in keeping with traditional Hebraic syntax, intended to repeat this phrase 7 times. In other words, Matthew is incorporating the same Hebrew form of repetition found in Genesis and Revelation. Repetition in Hebrew syntax will be addressed in more detail in Chapters Eight and Nine.

The repetition of 7 phrases of significant length, with no variant readings, is remarkable to say the least. Why did Jesus say these words 7 times? Did Matthew turn back in his scroll to check his own writing and make sure he wrote the phrase correctly? Did Matthew know that he repeated this phrase 7 times? The words *Father my* and *in...heavens* have been bolded in Greek to aid visualization.

My Father who is in the heavens 7 times in the Gospel of Matthew
    My Father who is in the heavens (Matt. 7:21)
    My Father who is in the heavens (Matt. 10:32)
    My Father who is in the heavens (Matt. 10:33)
    My Father who is in the heavens (Matt. 12:50)
    My Father who is in the heavens (Matt. 16:17)
    My Father who is in the heavens (Matt. 18:10)
    My Father who is in the heavens (Matt. 18:19)

    τοῦ **πατρός** μου τοῦ ἐν τοῖς **οὐρανοῖς** (Matt. 7:21 BNT)
    τοῦ **πατρός** μου τοῦ ἐν [τοῖς] **οὐρανοῖς** (Matt. 10:32 BNT)
    τοῦ **πατρός** μου τοῦ ἐν [τοῖς] **οὐρανοῖς** (Matt. 10:33 BNT)
    τοῦ **πατρός** μου τοῦ ἐν   **οὐρανοῖς** (Matt. 12:50 BNT)
    ὁ **πατήρ** μου ὁ   ἐν τοῖς **οὐρανοῖς** (Matt. 16:17 BNT)
    τοῦ **πατρός** μου τοῦ ἐν   **οὐρανοῖς** (Matt. 18:10 BNT)
    τοῦ **πατρός** μου τοῦ ἐν   **οὐρανοῖς** (Matt. 18:19 BNT)
    (the father of me the in   heavens)

Woe to You, Scribes and Pharisees, You Hypocrites, Because

The following phrase, *woe to you, scribes and Pharisees, you hypocrites, because*, is a sequence of 7 Greek words that is repeated 7 times in Matthew. It is particularly interesting because Matthew 23:14 only appears in the *King James Version* which is following BYZ, GOC, SCR, and STE.

The letters BYZ[10] stand for *Majority Text*, primarily a Byzantine tradition. A small group of texts, or more accurately, a subgroup of manuscripts in the *Majority Text*, form the basis for the *King James Version* called Textus Receptus, while the BNT is the basis for more modern translations such as the *New American Standard, New International Version, English Standard Version,* and *Revised Standard Version*. If the reader has noticed a variation in the translation between the *King James Version* and more contemporary translations, the reason is that they are using slightly different Greek texts. The question is, "Which variant reading is the original?" "Which reading did Matthew write and which reading did someone else change?"

The phrase *woe to you, scribes and Pharisees, you hypocrites, because*, is found in BYZ at Matthew 23:14, and is missing from 5 of the 9 Greek texts. The fact that there is a 7th phrase that appears in some manuscripts suggests that in this particular case, BYZ is following the original Greek, and the other manuscripts are corrupted. This assumption is based on Matthew's intent to follow heptadic cadence, or the repeating of something 7 times. Chapters Five and Seven of the 2012 edition, and Cassuto in Chapter Eight of this book, explain this in detail.

Without 23:14 there are only 6 (not 7) statements about the scribes and Pharisees. There are only a few possible explanations for this discrepancy. Either some of the copyists were aware of Moses' heptadic meter, and decided to add one more phrase to the original manuscript in order to complete the meter, or the Alexandrian manuscripts that the modern translations are following are flawed because they omit these words. Nevertheless, more than half of the ancient manuscripts contain the 7th phrase. Is it or is it not the original text of the Holy Bible?

In any case, scholars today are unaware that the Gospel writers were following Hebrew meter as a literary device. Why would the 7th phrase just happen to be in the list of variant readings? According to Moses' heptadic cadence, and the proliferation of heptadic meter in Matthew, the phrase in 23:14 is part of the original text.

---

[10] See p. 13 for further explanation of BYZ and additional *BibleWorks* abbreviations.

Modern literary critics overlook the possibility of phrases ordered in Hebraic meter in the Gospels because they project the limitations and norm of Western literature onto the ancient oriental mind. The ancients neither thought nor reasoned exactly as we do. The text must be evaluated for what it is, not for what we think it should be according to 21st-century literary standards. Approaching the text from a position of magisterial omniscience, and demeaning the biblical writers to the status of primitive nomads, has led to significant oversight. Evaluating the Bible text by Western criteria obscures the transcendent qualities of an essentially Eastern text.

What if these people were actually more intelligent than we are today and mankind is devolving? What if the Gospels are not an anthology of myths about Jesus, as modern scholarship teaches, but each text is carefully constructed and metered by its author? Christ's declaration that the very hairs on our head are numbered may be an allusion to far more important matters than hairs on our head.

Woe to you, scribes and Pharisees, you hypocrites, because
7 times in the Gospel of Matthew
But woe to you, scribes and Pharisees, you hypocrites, because (Matt. 23:13)
   Woe to you, scribes and Pharisees, you hypocrites, because (Matt. 23:14)*
   Woe to you, scribes and Pharisees, you hypocrites, because (Matt. 23:15)
   Woe to you, scribes and Pharisees, you hypocrites, because (Matt. 23:23)
   Woe to you, scribes and Pharisees, you hypocrites, because (Matt. 23:25)
   Woe to you, scribes and Pharisees, you hypocrites, because (Matt. 23:27)
   Woe to you, scribes and Pharisees, you hypocrites, because (Matt. 23:29)

Οὐαὶ δὲ ὑμῖν, γραμματεῖς καὶ Φαρισαῖοι, ὑποκριταί, ὅτι (Matt. 23:13 BNT)
   Οὐαὶ ὑμῖν, γραμματεῖς καὶ Φαρισαῖοι, ὑποκριταί, ὅτι (Matt. 23:14 BYZ)*
   Οὐαὶ ὑμῖν, γραμματεῖς καὶ Φαρισαῖοι, ὑποκριταί, ὅτι (Matt. 23:15 BNT)
   Οὐαὶ ὑμῖν, γραμματεῖς καὶ Φαρισαῖοι, ὑποκριταί, ὅτι (Matt. 23:23 BNT)
   Οὐαὶ ὑμῖν, γραμματεῖς καὶ Φαρισαῖοι, ὑποκριταί, ὅτι (Matt. 23:25 BNT)
   Οὐαὶ ὑμῖν, γραμματεῖς καὶ Φαρισαῖοι, ὑποκριταί, ὅτι (Matt. 23:27 BNT)
   Οὐαὶ ὑμῖν, γραμματεῖς καὶ Φαρισαῖοι, ὑποκριταί, ὅτι (Matt. 23:29 BNT)
*Matt. 23:14 only in BYZ, GOC, SCR, STE, and missing from BNT, GNT, TIS, VST, and WHO.

Cast out Demons
   As in the above, the repetition of phrases can appear in machine-like order. However, they may also appear as 7 repeated concepts with varying word sequence. There is much conversation about casting out demons in Matthew, but the words *cast out* and the noun *demons* are only contiguous 7 times in Matthew. The Greek verb for *cast out* has been bolded below. Notice that the word for *demons* appears 3 times in

front of *cast out* and 4 times after *cast out*. Assuming that the author is conscious that he is using the verb *cast out* 7 times adjacent to *demons*, he apparently has no compulsion to maintain a specific word order as seen above. Repetition of words, but not necessarily word order, illustrates that the repetition of phrases is also a repetition of concepts. Also note that there are no variant readings.

Cast out demons 7 times in the Gospel of Matthew

cast out **demons** (Matt. 7:22)

And when the **demon** was cast out (Matt. 9:33)

He casts out **demons** (Matt. 9:34)

You cast out **demons** (Matt. 10:8)

He casts out **demons** (Matt. 12:24)

I cast out **demons** (Matt. 12:27)

I cast out **demons** (Matt. 12:28)

δαιμόνια **ἐξεβάλομεν** (Matt. 7:22 BNT)

Καὶ **ἐκβληθέντος** τοῦ δαιμονίου (Matt. 9:33 BNT)

τῶν δαιμονίων **ἐκβάλλει** (Matt. 9:34 BNT)

δαιμόνια **ἐκβάλλετε** (Matt. 10:8 BNT)

ἐκβάλλει τὰ δαιμόνια (Matt. 12:24 BNT)

ἐκβάλλω τὰ δαιμόνια (Matt. 12:27 BNT)

ἐκβάλλω τὰ δαιμόνια (Matt. 12:28 BNT)

Demon-Possessed

The Greek word for *demon-possessed* is actually a compound word in both Greek and English. Greek puts the word for *demon* together with the word for *the one who is living*, to mean a demon who is living inside the victim. The *King James Version* translates the word as *possessed with a devil*, and *New American Standard* translates it as *demon-possessed*.

An often-stated misconception is that 7 is the symbolic number for God, perfection, or completion. *Demons, demon-possession*, and *casting out demons* have nothing to do with divine perfection. The origin of this exegetical nonsense can be traced to Pythagoras in the 5th century B.C. It was popularized by Philo in the beginning of the 1st century at the time of Christ. It was established as early church doctrine by Eusebius circa 320 A.D., and was accepted into Lutheran and Reformed thinking from the Catholic Church with little examination. Furthermore, this would mean that 7 and 10 are the only 2 numerical symbols that mean the same thing. At this time we will only comment that 7 is the symbolic number for judgment, either blessing or damnation. A discussion of this subject can be found in Chapters Thirteen,

Fourteen, and Fifteen of the 2012 edition[11] and in Chapter Nine of this book.

If an English translation lacks all 7 of the following phrases, or any of the above phrases, it is simply because it is more paraphrastic (i.e., it restates the original text in simpler terms) than literal in these particular examples. There are no variant readings in the following:

Demon-possessed 7 times in the Gospel of Matthew
Demon-possessed..............δαιμονιζομένους (Matt. 4:24 BNT)
Demon-possessed..............δαιμονιζομένους (Matt. 8:16 BNT)
Demon-possessed..............δαιμονιζόμενοι (Matt. 8:28 BNT)
Demon-possessed..............δαιμονιζομένων (Matt. 8:33 BNT)
Demon-possessed..............δαιμονιζόμενον (Matt. 9:32 BNT)
Demon-possessed..............δαιμονιζόμενος (Matt. 12:22 BNT)
Demon-possessed..............δαιμονίζεται (Matt. 15:22 BNT)

What Is a Greek Text?

Before displaying more examples of Hebraic meter in Matthew, an explanation of how this data is collected may be helpful. We live in an era of amazing computer technological advancement. The *BibleWorks 8*[12] program, among many other functions, has the capability to simultaneously search in all 9 Greek texts for a word, syllable, or phrase.

For example, in order to scan Matthew for the phrase *great multitudes* (ὄχλοι πολλοὶ), the phrase is typed in Greek into the search window. After viewing the results, the phrase 'ὄχλ* πολλ* is typed in again (with asterisks in place of case endings in order to locate all possible variations of the same phrase). The following is what appears on the screen for Matthew 8:18 in all 9 Greek texts after making such an entry. In KJV this clause reads, *Now when Jesus saw great multitudes about him*, and in NASB it reads, *Now when Jesus saw a crowd around Him*.

Ἰδὼν δὲ ὁ Ἰησοῦς ὄχλον περὶ αὐτὸν (Matt. 8:18 BNT)
Ἰδὼν δὲ ὁ Ἰησοῦς **πολλοὺς ὄχλους** περὶ αὐτόν (Matt. 8:18 BYZ)
Ἰδὼν δὲ ὁ Ἰησοῦς ὄχλον περὶ αὐτὸν (Matt. 8:18 GNT)
Ἰδὼν δὲ ὁ Ἰησοῦς **πολλοὺς ὄχλους** περὶ αὐτόν (Matt. 8:18 GOC)
Ἰδὼν δὲ ὁ Ἰησοῦς **πολλοὺς ὄχλους** περὶ αὐτόν (Matt. 8:18 SCR)
Ἰδὼν δὲ ὁ Ἰησοῦς **πολλοὺς ὄχλους** περὶ αὐτόν (Matt. 8:18 STE)
Ἰδὼν δὲ ὁ Ἰησοῦς **πολλοὺς ὄχλους** περὶ αὐτόν (Matt. 8:18 TIS)
Ἰδὼν δὲ ὁ Ἰησοῦς ὄχλους περὶ αὐτὸν (Matt. 8:18 VST)
Ἰδὼν δὲ ὁ Ἰησοῦς **ὄχλον** περὶ αὐτὸν (Matt. 8:18 WHO)

---
[11] Cascione, 2012.
[12] *BibleWorks 8*, DVD-ROM, BibleWorks, LLC, Norfolk, VA, 2008.

The *BibleWorks 8* program also includes a list of how many times the phrase *great multitudes* appears in each of the 9 Greek texts. Matthew 8:18 was selected because the texts do not agree on the phrase *great multitudes* in this verse. Some texts indicate Matthew 8:18 is part of a Hebraic heptad, while others do not, as seen on page 14. Notice the phrase *great multitudes* is bolded in some texts as πολλοὺς ὄχλους, while other texts are missing *great* (πολλοὺς).

The reader may be asking, what are these Greek texts and where do they come from? A Greek text is a collation of the ancient Greek manuscripts of the New Testament.

How Many Ancient Greek Manuscripts Are There?
Parts of the New Testament have been preserved in more manuscripts than any other ancient work, having over 5,800 complete or fragmented Greek manuscripts, 10,000 Latin manuscripts and 9,300 manuscripts in various other ancient languages, including Syriac, Slavic, Gothic, Ethiopic, Coptic, Latin, and Armenian. The dates of these manuscripts range from c. A.D. 125 (the John Rylands manuscript, P52; oldest copy of John fragments) to the introduction of printing in Germany in the 15th century. The vast majority of these manuscripts are post-10th century. There are 14 fragments of Matthew dating from c. A.D. 200, and 2 complete copies of the New Testament dating from the 4th century.

How Were Ancient Manuscripts Collated into 9 Greek Texts?
Over the centuries there have been 9 significant attempts by scholars to collate the ancient manuscripts of the New Testament into texts thought to be in agreement with the originals written by Matthew, Mark, Luke, etc. Also, within the past 100 years more ancient manuscripts have been discovered.

It takes great skill, dedication, credentials, and courage for anyone or a committee to publish what he or they think is the original text of the Greek New Testament. Depending on the views, bias, and methodology of the scholars who collate manuscripts into texts, more or less importance is given to certain families of manuscripts than to others. Thus they have varying opinions as to what the original Greek New Testament actually looked like, and are subjective to a greater or lesser degree depending on the scholars' theories of manuscript transmission. In the more recent past there has been a tendency to use a more objective method that simply lists the witnesses to the text, and selects the preferred variant reading based on which was both the earliest and the most widespread in the various regions of the early church. Most often there are only 2 variants of a passage.

Some of the Greek texts say the correct reading of Matthew 8:18 is, "Now when Jesus saw *great multitudes* about him, he gave commandment to depart unto the other side" (KJV). Others say the correct reading is, "Now when Jesus saw a *crowd* around Him, He gave orders to depart to the other side" (NASB). The essential difference is in the phrase *great multitudes* versus *crowds*.

Who Assembled These Greek Texts?
BNT refers to Nestle-Aland's Greek New Testament, 27th edition, edited by Eberhard Nestle and Kurt Aland. It is considered the most comprehensive and authoritative of all Greek texts.

BYZ refers to the Majority or the Byzantine texts edited by Arthur Farstad and Zane C. Hodges. *Majority* means that 51% of the ancient manuscripts include a particular word regardless of manuscript pedigree.

GNT refers to the United Bible Society Greek Text edited by Kurt Aland, Matthew Black, Carlo Martini, Bruce Metzger, and Allen Wikgren.

GOC refers to the Greek Text of the Greek Orthodox Church.

SCR refers to F. H. A. Scrivener, who edited a less than satisfactory revision of STE in 1894.

STE refers to Stephanus, also known as Textus Receptus, a collection of manuscripts first edited by Erasmus in 1514, 1516, 1519, and 1522, later to form the basis of Luther's German Translation and the *King James Version*. Stephanus wrote the words Textus Receptus, "Received Text," in the beginning of his 1550 edition.

TIS refers to Lobegott Friedrich Constantin (von) Tischendorf (1815-1874), who in the 1840s deciphered Codex Ephraemi Rescriptus, a 5th-century Greek manuscript of the New Testament, and rediscovered Codex Sinaiticus, a 4th-century New Testament manuscript, in 1859.

VST refers to the text edited by the brilliant German exegete Hermann von Soden, first published in 1902.

WHO refers to editors Brooke Foss Westcott (1825–1901) and Fenton John Anthony Hort (1828–1892) who published their critical edition of the Greek New Testament in 1881.

Great Multitudes
The Matthew 8:18 listing of the phrase *great multitudes*, below, is followed by an asterisk which leads to a note that only 5 of the 9 Greek texts agree with the reading. Which are correct? According to Hebrew meter, in this particular case BYZ, GOC, SCR, STE, and TIS are correct. None of the scholars who assembled these 9 texts were aware that Matthew was following Mosaic heptadic cadence, and that he was liter-

ally counting (or that the Holy Spirit was guiding Matthew to use) the number of times his Gospel said, *great multitudes*.

Also notice that 8:18 inverts the word order, which is acceptable in Greek. Perhaps this is one of the reasons why some scholars think it does not belong in the text and some earlier copyists omitted it from their manuscripts. BNT is not sure that *multitudes* belongs in Matthew 13:2, so they put a bracket around it. As stated earlier, BNT appears first on the screen in a list of 9 texts. If all the others, bracket or no bracket, have the same reading, BNT is followed. Additional Greek words were included for the sake of context. Also notice that *Him* is included in every phrase, which is not a coincidence, and that *followed* appears 4 times for a 3-4 division.

Great multitudes 7 times in the Gospel of Matthew
    And **great multitudes** followed Him (Matt. 4:25)
      great multitudes followed Him (Matt. 8:1)
      great multitudes about Him (Matt. 8:18)*
    And **great multitudes** followed Him (Matt. 12:15)
And To Him gathered **great multitudes** (Matt. 13:2)
     And **great multitudes** came to Him (Matt. 15:30)
     And **great multitudes** followed Him (Matt. 19:2)

καὶ ἠκολούθησαν αὐτῷ **ὄχλοι πολλοὶ** (Matt. 4:25 BNT)
ἠκολούθησαν αὐτῷ **ὄχλοι πολλοί** (Matt. 8:1 BNT)
πολλοὺς ὄχλους περὶ αὐτόν (Matt. 8:18 BYZ)*
καὶ ἠκολούθησαν αὐτῷ [**ὄχλοι**] **πολλοί** (Matt. 12:15 BNT)
καὶ συνήχθησαν πρὸς αὐτὸν **ὄχλοι πολλοί** (Matt. 13:2 BNT)
καὶ προςῆλθον αὐτῷ **ὄχλοι πολλοί** (Matt. 15:30 BNT)
καὶ ἠκολούθησαν αὐτῷ **ὄχλοι πολλοί** (Matt. 19:2 BNT)

*_Great multitudes_ only in BYZ, GOC, SCR, STE, and TIS; *multitudes* in BNT, GNT, VST, and WHO.

The Kingdom of Heavens Is Like

The beautiful thought of what heaven is like repeats in the Gospel of Matthew exactly 7 times. The asterisk after Matthew 20:1 leads the reader to a note that Matthew 22:2 has a similar statement, but says the *Kingdom of heaven is compared to a man*, and does not use the Greek word for *like*. In other words, there was an intentional effort to create 7 phrases with the same wording. Also, Matthew 13:52 uses the same words, but places *is like* after *kingdom of heaven* instead of before it. These kinds of variations in the word order make it difficult to find some heptadic phrases without the aid of a computer.

The kingdom of heavens is like 7 times in the Gospel of Matthew
    The kingdom of heavens is **like** (Matt. 13:31)
    The kingdom of heavens is **like** (Matt. 13:33)
    The kingdom of heavens is **like** (Matt. 13:44)
    The kingdom of heavens is **like** (Matt. 13:45)
    The kingdom of heavens is **like** (Matt. 13:47)
    The kingdom of heavens is **like** (Matt. 13:52)
For the kingdom of heavens is **like** (Matt. 20:1)*

    ὁμοία ἐστὶν ἡ βασιλεία τῶν οὐρανῶν (Matt. 13:31 BNT)
    ὁμοία ἐστὶν ἡ βασιλεία τῶν οὐρανῶν (Matt. 13:33 BNT)
    ὁμοία ἐστὶν ἡ βασιλεία τῶν οὐρανῶν (Matt. 13:44 BNT)
    ὁμοία ἐστὶν ἡ βασιλεία τῶν οὐρανῶν (Matt. 13:45 BNT)
    ὁμοία ἐστὶν ἡ βασιλεία τῶν οὐρανῶν (Matt. 13:47 BNT)
        τῇ βασιλείᾳ τῶν οὐρανῶν **ὅμοιός** ἐστιν (Matt. 13:52 BNT)
    ὁμοία γάρ ἐστιν ἡ βασιλεία τῶν οὐρανῶν (Matt. 20:1 BNT)*
*Matt. 22:2 has verb *compared* (ὡμοιώθη) instead of adjective *like* (ὁμοία) and verb *is* (ἐστὶν), not included above.

Metered Introduction to Conversation: Anaphoric Phrases[13]
Then He Said to Him or Them

    The phrase *then He said to him* or *them* appears 7 times in the Gospel of Matthew, with no variants. There are 3 Greek words in the phrase, and care was taken that they appear exactly 7 times. The final word can be singular or plural, that is, *he said to him* or *he said to them*. In Greek it is the same word with the equivalent of *s* added to express the plural.

    Matthew chooses a select group of phrases for heptadic meter (7 repetitions). One of the surprising aspects of these numerically-repeated phrases is that they are often an introduction to mundane parlance technically called *anaphoric phrases*, or words that require another word in a particular sequence.[14] In other words, they are often found where you would not look for them. There are numerous examples of Hebraic meter in anaphoric phrases recorded in this book. They are also similar to the repetition of numerically-ordered mundane parlance found in Genesis and Revelation. The process of discovering which phrases were selected for heptadic meter requires more explanation that will be offered in succeeding chapters, particularly in Chapters Four and Eight. Note the 3-4 division of the singular and plural pronoun.

---

[13] Matthew S. Demoss, *Pocket Dictionary for the Study of New Testament Greek*, InterVarsity Press, Downer's Grove, IL, 2001, p. 18: "anaphora: a reference back to a previous context by the repetition or inclusion of a word or phrase....In rhetoric, anaphora occurs when successive clauses begin with the same word or group of words."
[14] Kirby, p. 71.

Then he said to him or *them* 7 times in the Gospel of Matthew
Then he said to him..........τότε λέγει αὐτῷ ὁ Ἰησοῦς (Matt. 4:10 BNT)
Then he said to them........τότε λέγει αὐτοῖς (Matt. 22:21 BNT)
Then he said to them........τότε λέγει αὐτοῖς ὁ Ἰησοῦς (Matt. 26:31 BNT)
Then he said to them........τότε λέγει αὐτοῖς ὁ Ἰησοῦς (Matt. 26:38 BNT)
Then he said to him..........τότε λέγει αὐτῷ ὁ Ἰησοῦς (Matt. 26:52 BNT)
Then he said to him..........τότε λέγει αὐτῷ ὁ Πιλᾶτος (Matt. 27:13 BNT)
Then he said to them........τότε λέγει αὐταῖς ὁ Ἰησοῦς (Matt. 28:10 BNT)
(*then he said to them the Jesus*)

Jesus Answered

The mundane phrase *But Jesus answered and said* is the longest anaphoric introduction to a conversation identified in Matthew. It repeats 7 times in machine-like order similar to those found in Genesis and Revelation. The asterisk indicates that GOC disagrees and is missing *and*. However, the following heptad is also a bit of an anomaly. In addition to 7 precisely repeated phrases, the computer highlighted 7 more irregular phrases that include the words *Jesus* and *answered*, but may be missing *and* or *said*.

At this point it is difficult to determine what is intended and what is unintended, especially in view of the next set of examples. It appears the author intentionally combined 2 heptads into the text using the same phrase, one regular and the other irregular. This is an aesthetic choice of concurrent asymmetry and symmetry identified in the 2012 edition, which will also appear in future examples. Also notice how many variant readings occur in the asymmetric or irregular example, indicating that copyists may have been confused by the irregularities of the expression. Some texts say Matthew 17:11 includes *Jesus* and others do not. The last example in the second list below (Matthew 26:63) has the cryptic words that Jesus remained silent and the High Priest answered for Him, but contains the same Greek words repeated in heptadic rhythm.

But Jesus answered and said 7 times in the Gospel of Matthew
But Jesus answered and said...ἀποκριθεὶς δὲ ὁ Ἰησοῦς εἶπεν (Matt. 3:15 BNT)
But Jesus answered and said...ἀποκριθεὶς δὲ ὁ Ἰησοῦς εἶπεν (Matt. 16:17 BNT)*
But Jesus answered and said...ἀποκριθεὶς δὲ ὁ Ἰησοῦς εἶπεν (Matt. 17:17 BNT)
But Jesus answered and said...ἀποκριθεὶς δὲ ὁ Ἰησοῦς εἶπεν (Matt. 20:22 BNT)
But Jesus answered and said...ἀποκριθεὶς δὲ ὁ Ἰησοῦς εἶπεν (Matt. 21:21 BNT)
But Jesus answered and said...ἀποκριθεὶς δὲ ὁ Ἰησοῦς εἶπεν (Matt. 21:24 BNT)
But Jesus answered and said...ἀποκριθεὶς δὲ ὁ Ἰησοῦς εἶπεν (Matt. 22:29 BNT)
*Jesus answered said...ἀποκριθεὶς ὁ Ἰησοῦς εἶπεν (Matt. 16:17 GOC).

Jesus and *Answered* irregular 7 times in the Gospel of Matthew
                And Jesus **answered** [and] said (Matt. 11:4)
                Jesus **answered** [and] said (Matt. 11:25)
                Jesus **answered** [and] said (Matt. 15:28)
                But Jesus **answered** [and] said (Matt. 17:11)*
                And Jesus **answered**   (Matt. 22:1)
                And Jesus **answered** [and] said (Matt. 24:4)
But Jesus was silent and the High Priest **answered**   (Matt. 26:63)**
                Καὶ **ἀποκριθεὶς** ὁ Ἰησοῦς εἶπεν (Matt. 11:4 BNT)
                ἀποκριθεὶς ὁ Ἰησοῦς εἶπεν (Matt. 11:25 BNT)
                ἀποκριθεὶς ὁ Ἰησοῦς εἶπεν (Matt. 15:28 BNT)
            Ὁ δὲ Ἰησοῦς **ἀποκριθεὶς** εἶπεν (Matt. 17:11 BYZ)*
                Καὶ **ἀποκριθεὶς** ὁ Ἰησοῦς (Matt. 22:1 BNT)
                Καὶ **ἀποκριθεὶς** ὁ Ἰησοῦς εἶπεν (Matt. 24:4 BNT)
Ὁ δὲ Ἰησοῦς ἐσιώπα. Καὶ **ἀποκριθεὶς** ὁ ἀρχιερεὺς εἶπεν (Matt. 26:63 BYZ)**
*BNT, GNT, TIS, VST, WHO missing *Jesus* and only have ὁ δὲ ἀποκριθεὶς εἶπεν (Matt. 17:11).
**BNT, GNT, WHO missing *answered* ὁ δὲ Ἰησοῦς ἐσιώπα. καὶ ὁ ἀρχιερεὺς εἶπεν (Matt. 26:63).

And He Said to Him / Jesus Said to Him / Jesus Said to Them
    The following are 3 heptadic phrases: *and he said to him, Jesus said to him, Jesus said to them*. Matthew 8:4, 7, and 20 overlap for a combined set of 10, a cadence that will be discussed shortly. There are two ways to express *said*, and half of the texts include the wrong Greek word at Matthew 4:9. It is a simple unintentional error. Yet Matthew's Gospel is so carefully written it exposes a slight alteration. Could this be part of the reason for incorporating Hebraic meter into the text? There were no photocopy machines. Who could tell if someone altered an original document except those who understood the function and presence of heptadic cadence in the text?

And he said to him 7 times in the Gospel of Matthew*
        And he said to him..............καὶ λέγει αὐτῷ (Matt. 4:6 BNT)
        And he said to him..............καὶ λέγει αὐτῷ (Matt. 8:4 BNT)
        And he said to him..............καὶ λέγει αὐτῷ (Matt. 8:7 BNT)**
        And he said to him..............καὶ λέγει αὐτῷ (Matt. 8:20 BNT)
        And he said to him..............καὶ λέγει αὐτῷ (Matt. 9:9 BNT)
        And he said to him..............καὶ λέγει αὐτῷ (Matt. 14:31 BNT)
        And he said to him..............καὶ λέγει αὐτῷ (Matt. 22:12 BNT)
**And he said to him*, καὶ λέγει αὐτῷ in Matthew 4:9 is missing in BNT, GNT, TIS, and WHO, which have καὶ εἶπεν αὐτῷ (Matt. 4:9 BNT) and therefore is not included in the above example.
**TIS and WHO have εἶπεν instead of λέγει at Matt. 8:7.

Jesus said to him 7 times in the Gospel of Matthew
  Jesus said to him............λέγει αὐτῷ ὁ Ἰησοῦς (Matt. 4:10 BNT)
  Jesus said to him............λέγει αὐτῷ ὁ Ἰησοῦς (Matt. 8:4 BNT)
  Jesus said to him............λέγει αὐτῷ ὁ Ἰησοῦς (Matt. 8:7 BYZ)*
  Jesus said to him............λέγει αὐτῷ ὁ Ἰησοῦς (Matt. 8:20 BNT)
  Jesus said to him............λέγει αὐτῷ ὁ Ἰησοῦς (Matt. 18:22 BNT)
  Jesus said to him............λέγει αὐτῷ ὁ Ἰησοῦς (Matt. 26:52 BNT)
  Jesus said to him............λέγει αὐτῷ ὁ Ἰησοῦς (Matt. 26:64 BNT)
Jesus only in BYZ, GOC, SCR, STE.

Jesus said to them 14 times in the Gospel of Matthew
  Jesus said to them.......ὁ Ἰησοῦς εἶπεν αὐτοῖς (Matt. 11:4 BNT)
  And Jesus said to them....ὁ δὲ Ἰησοῦς εἶπεν αὐτοῖς (Matt. 13:57 BNT)
  And Jesus said to them...ὁ δὲ [Ἰησοῦς] εἶπεν αὐτοῖς (Matt. 14:16 BNT)
  And Jesus said to them....ὁ δὲ Ἰησοῦς εἶπεν αὐτοῖς (Matt. 16:6 BNT)
  But Jesus said to them....δὲ ὁ Ἰησοῦς εἶπεν αὐτοῖς (Matt. 16:8 BYZ)*
  And Jesus said to them....ὁ δὲ Ἰησοῦς εἶπεν αὐτοῖς (Matt. 17:20 BYZ)*
  But Jesus said to them....δὲ ὁ Ἰησοῦς εἶπεν αὐτοῖς (Matt. 19:26 BNT)
  And Jesus said to them....ὁ δὲ Ἰησοῦς εἶπεν αὐτοῖς (Matt. 19:28 BNT)
  But Jesus said to them.....δὲ ὁ Ἰησοῦς εἶπεν αὐτοῖς (Matt. 21:21 BNT)
  But Jesus said to them.....δὲ ὁ Ἰησοῦς εἶπεν αὐτοῖς (Matt. 21:24 BNT)
  But Jesus said to them.....δὲ ὁ Ἰησοῦς εἶπεν αὐτοῖς (Matt. 22:29 BNT)
  And Jesus said to them....ὁ δὲ Ἰησοῦς εἶπεν αὐτοῖς (Matt. 24:2 BYZ)*
  ....Jesus said to them.......ὁ Ἰησοῦς εἶπεν αὐτοῖς (Matt. 24:4 BNT)
  But Jesus said to them....δὲ ὁ Ἰησοῦς εἶπεν αὐτοῖς (Matt. 26:10 BNT)
*Matt. 16:8, 17:20, and 24:2 missing *Jesus* in BNT, GNT, TIS, VST, WHO.

Notice that the above double heptad has 3 variants that are missing *Jesus*. Three texts, BYZ, SCR, and STE, repeat *Jesus* 130 times, while in GOC the name appears 129 times. BNT, GNT, TIS, VST, and WHO have significantly fewer occurrences, ranging from 108 to 111. If the 3 additions of *Jesus* (Matt. 16:8, 17:20, 24:2) were intentional, this may indicate that copyists were aware of meter in the text and were attempting to complete the meter. If these 3 are in the original text, it may indicate that some copyist, unaware of the intended use of repetition in the text, deleted some of the excessive repetition thinking it was poor Greek. Notice δὲ ὁ or ὁ δὲ is translated here as *but* or *and.* They each repeat 6 times for a subset total of 12. The numbers 7, 10, and 12, or their multiples, are the 3 major Hebraic cadences.

My or *Your Father Who Is in the Heavens*
The phrase *My Father who is in the heavens*, which repeats 7 times in the Gospel of Matthew, was printed earlier in this chapter. Matthew takes the same phrase and repeats it another 7 times with one small change: *my* into *your.* Notice in the note beneath the example that both

variants are missing the preposition *in*. It is hardly coincidental that exactly the right words needed to complete this heptadic cadence are found in some manuscripts.

This leads to 3 reasonable choices: 1) Matthew was counting out the number of times he used the phrase, *Your Father who is in the heavens*; 2) The Holy Spirit guided Matthew in how many times he used this phrase; or 3) Later copyists added the correct words because they wanted his Gospel to include heptadic cadence. The first or second option must be correct because the third option means the copyists were more aware of Hebraic meter than Matthew. Hebraic meter in the text guides us to the correct text when a choice must be made as to which copyist made a mistake in his manuscript. A copyist's failure to copy the meter correctly most likely means he was not aware of the Hebraic repetition in the text. It is interesting to note that this is the third time Matthew includes the word *heaven* in a heptadic phrase.

My Father who is in the heavens 7 times in the Gospel of Matthew
    My Father who is in the heavens (Matt. 7:21)
    My Father who is in the heavens (Matt. 10:32)
    My Father who is in the heavens (Matt. 10:33)
    My Father who is in the heavens (Matt. 12:50)
    My Father who is in the heavens (Matt. 16:17)
    My Father who is in the heavens (Matt. 18:10)
    My Father who is in the heavens (Matt. 18:19)

Your Father who is in the heavens 7 times in the Gospel of Matthew
    Your Father who is in the heavens (Matt. 5:16)
    Your Father who is in the heavens (Matt. 5:45)
    Your Father who is in the heavens (Matt. 5:48)*
    Your Father who is in the heavens (Matt. 6:1)
    Your Father who is in the heavens (Matt. 7:11)
    Your Father who is in the heavens (Matt. 18:14)
    Your Father who is in the heavens (Matt. 23:9)**

    τὸν **πατέρα ὑμῶν** τὸν ἐν τοῖς **οὐρανοῖς** (Matt. 5:16 BNT)
    τοῦ **πατρὸς ὑμῶν** τοῦ ἐν **οὐρανοῖς** (Matt. 5:45 BNT)
    ὁ **πατὴρ ὑμῶν** ὁ ἐν τοῖς **οὐρανοῖς** (Matt. 5:48 BYZ)*
    τῷ **πατρὶ ὑμῶν** τῷ ἐν τοῖς **οὐρανοῖς** (Matt. 6:1 BNT)
    ὁ **πατὴρ ὑμῶν** ὁ ἐν τοῖς **οὐρανοῖς** (Matt. 7:11 BNT)
    τοῦ **πατρὸς ὑμῶν** τοῦ ἐν **οὐρανοῖς** (Matt. 18:14 BNT)
    ὁ **πατὴρ ὑμῶν**, ὁ ἐν τοῖς **οὐρανοῖς** (Matt. 23:9 BYZ)**

*At Matt. 5:48 BNT, GNT, TIS, VST, WHO have *your heavenly father*, ὁ πατὴρ ὑμῶν ὁ οὐράνιος.
**At Matt. 23:9 BNT, GNT, TIS, VST, WHO have *your heavenly father*, ὑμῶν ὁ πατὴρ ὁ οὐράνιος.

The Father or *Mother* / *Father and/or Mother*

Quite often a longer phrase like the above will be a subset of a shorter phrase such as *My Father*. The following is an awkward translation in order to emphasize the Greek word order. Of the 9 Greek texts we are following, WHO incorrectly adds the phrase *My Father* to 18:14.

The Father of Me 10 Times in the Gospel of Matthew*
    The Father of Me..............τοῦ πατρός μου (Matt. 7:21 BNT)
    The Father of Me..............τοῦ πατρός μου (Matt. 10:32 BNT)
    The Father of Me..............τοῦ πατρός μου (Matt. 10:33 BNT)
    The Father of Me..............τοῦ πατρός μου (Matt. 11:27 BNT)
    The Father of Me..............τοῦ πατρός μου (Matt. 12:50 BNT)
    The Father of Me..............τοῦ πατρός μου (Matt. 18:10 BNT)
    The Father of Me..............τοῦ πατρός μου (Matt. 18:19 BNT)
    The Father of Me..............τοῦ πατρός μου (Matt. 20:23 BNT)
    The Father of Me..............τοῦ πατρός μου (Matt. 25:34 BNT)
    The Father of Me..............τοῦ πατρός μου (Matt. 26:29 BNT)
*The variant in WHO adds the phrase at 18:14, which is rejected.

Matthew's application of Hebraic meter with Jesus' *Father* led to an obvious search for meter referencing His *mother*. Jesus and His mother appear in the same phrase 7 times. Note the 3-4 division that incorporates *child*. There is a variant reading that adds *the mother of him* at 15:6 that is not speaking about Jesus and Mary, and is rejected. In either case there are 7 phrases that refer to Christ and His mother Mary. This is one of the most remarkable heptads in the 4 Gospels. It is the only known honor given to Jesus' mother in the Gospels outside of Luke chapter 1.

The mother of Him 7 times in the Gospel of Matthew*
        The mother of Him (Matt. 1:18)
        The mother of Him (Matt. 2:11)
    The Child and the mother of Him (Matt. 2:13)
    The Child and the mother of Him (Matt. 2:14)
    The Child and the mother of Him (Matt. 2:20)
    The Child and the mother of Him (Matt. 2:21)
        The mother of Him (Matt. 13:55)

        τῆς μητρὸς αὐτοῦ (Matt. 1:18 BNT)
        τῆς μητρὸς αὐτοῦ (Matt. 2:11 BNT)
  τὸ παιδίον καὶ τὴν μητέρα αὐτοῦ (Matt. 2:13 BNT)
  τὸ παιδίον καὶ τὴν μητέρα αὐτοῦ (Matt. 2:14 BNT)
  τὸ παιδίον καὶ τὴν μητέρα αὐτοῦ (Matt. 2:20 BNT)
  τὸ παιδίον καὶ τὴν μητέρα αὐτοῦ (Matt. 2:21 BNT)
        ἡ μήτηρ αὐτοῦ (Matt. 13:55 BNT)
*All 7 verses refer to Mary. However, BYZ, GOC, SCR, STE, and TIS add *the mother of him* (τὴν μητέρα αὐτοῦ) at 15:5 and 6. This is not a reference to Mary; thus the variant is rejected.

The next example has 7 repetitions of *father and/or mother*. This phrase would also have an extra repetition if the variant at 15:6 were followed.

Father and/or mother 7 times in the Gospel of Matthew*
    Father **or** mother………πατέρα **ἢ** μητέρα (Matt. 10:37 BNT)
    Father **and** mother…τὸν πατέρα **καὶ** τὴν μητέρα (Matt. 15:4 BNT)
    Father **or** mother………πατέρα **ἢ** μητέρα (Matt. 15:4 BNT)
    Father **or** mother……τῷ πατρὶ **ἢ** τῇ μητρί (Matt. 15:5 BNT)
    Father **and** mother…τὸν πατέρα **καὶ** τὴν μητέρα (Matt. 19:5 BNT)
    Father **and** mother…τὸν πατέρα **καὶ** τὴν μητέρα (Matt. 19:19 BNT)
    Father **or** mother………πατέρα **ἢ** μητέρα (Matt. 19:29 BNT)
*BYZ, GOC, SCR, STE, TIS, VST add *the mother of him* (τὴν μητέρα αὐτοῦ) at 15:6; thus the variant is rejected.

They or *He Followed Him*
    The phrase *they* or *he followed Him* appears in a double heptad. Within this double heptad, which consists of 14 phrases that include either *he* or *they*, there is also a decadal subset of phrases beginning with *they*.

They or *he followed Him* 14 times in the Gospel of Matthew
    They followed Him……**ἠκολούθησαν** αὐτῷ (Matt. 4:20 BNT)
    They followed Him……**ἠκολούθησαν** αὐτῷ (Matt. 4:22 BNT)
    They followed Him……**ἠκολούθησαν** αὐτῷ (Matt. 4:25 BNT)
    They followed Him……**ἠκολούθησαν** αὐτῷ (Matt. 8:1 BNT)
    They followed Him……**ἠκολούθησαν** αὐτῷ (Matt. 8:23 BNT)
      He followed Him……**ἠκολούθησεν** αὐτῷ (Matt. 9:9 BNT)
      He followed Him……**ἠκολούθησεν** αὐτῷ (Matt. 9:19 BNT)
    They followed Him……**ἠκολούθησαν** [αὐτῷ] (Matt. 9:27 BNT)*
    They followed Him……**ἠκολούθησαν** αὐτῷ (Matt. 12:15 BNT)
    They followed Him……**ἠκολούθησαν** αὐτῷ (Matt. 14:13 BNT)
    They followed Him……**ἠκολούθησαν** αὐτῷ (Matt. 19:2 BNT)
      He followed Him……**ἠκολούθησεν** αὐτῷ (Matt. 20:29 BNT)
    They followed Him……**ἠκολούθησαν** αὐτῷ (Matt. 20:34 BNT)
    He was following Him……**ἠκολούθει** αὐτῷ (Matt. 26:58 BNT)
*Matthew 9:27 missing from WHO.

Last…First
    Matthew repeats the antonyms *first* and *last* in Christ's dialogue. He uses the 2 words together 7 times. Matthew is the only Gospel writer to employ Mosaic cadence with this phrase. Seven is the symbolic number for judgment, and these 2 words are appropriate for these 7 judgments. There are no variants.

Last...first 7 times in the Gospel of Matthew
>And the **last** *state* of that man is
>>Worse than the **first** (Matt. 12:45)
>
>But many *who are* **first** will be **last** (Matt. 19:30)
>And *the* **last, first** (Matt. 19:30)
>Beginning from the **last** unto the **first** (Matt. 20:8)
>So the **last** shall be **first** (Matt. 20:16)
>And the **first last** (Matt. 20:16)
>So the **last** error shall be
>>Worse than the **first** (Matt. 27:64)

>καὶ γίνεται τὰ **ἔσχατα** τοῦ ἀνθρώπου ἐκείνου
>>χείρονα τῶν **πρώτων** (Matt. 12:45 BNT)
>
>πολλοὶ δὲ **ἔσονται πρῶτοι** ἔσχατοι (Matt. 19:30 BNT)
>καὶ **ἔσχατοι πρῶτοι** (Matt. 19:30 BNT)
>ἀπὸ τῶν **ἐσχάτων** ἕως τῶν **πρώτων** (Matt. 20:8 BNT)
>οὕτως **ἔσονται** οἱ ἔσχατοι **πρῶτοι** (Matt. 20:16 BNT)
>καὶ οἱ **πρῶτοι ἔσχατοι** (Matt. 20:16 BNT)
>καὶ ἔσται ἡ **ἐσχάτη** πλάνη
>>χείρων τῆς **πρώτης** (Matt. 27:64 BNT)

Decadal Phrases in Matthew

As stated earlier, Cassuto identifies 7, 10, and 12 as the basis for Hebraic meter. This is an examination of Matthew's use of Hebrew decadal cadence. According to more than a hundred examples of decads (a list of 10 phrases) published in the 2012 edition,[15] and many examples in Cassuto's writings, 10 is the symbolic number for completion or all of something.

That Which Was Fulfilled Spoken...through...the Prophet Saying

Hebraic repetition can take place in 2-word phrases or rather lengthy phrases such as *That which was fulfilled spoken...through...the prophet saying*. The first ellipsis allows for the alternate phrase, *by the Lord*, and the second ellipsis allows for the names of various prophets.

It is rather surprising to find so many Greek words that appear 10 times in the same phrase without any variant readings in the 9 Greek texts, except for the word *by* (ὑπὸ) instead of *through* (διά) in Matthew 2:17 and 3:3. The entire meter has remained undisturbed in the Greek manuscripts for nearly 2,000 years. BNT, GNT, TIS, VST, and WHO are followed at 2:17 and 3:3, as they maintain 10 repetitions of *through* (διά). This reverses the thought that the Byzantine texts were embellished to illustrate Hebraic meter. If the Byzantine copyists were trying

---

[15] Cascione, 2012, pp. 133-34, 207.

to embellish the text to maintain a given meter, they were not as skilled as were the Alexandrian copyists. In other words, Hebraic cadence in the text was written by Matthew and was not a later addition.

The bolded words in Greek, below, are *fulfilled* and *through*. Notice the column of 7 words bolded on the left, the Greek word for *fulfilled*. Quite often Mosaic cadence will include 7 as a subset of 10, as seen here. The longer expression of the phrase appears in a heptad, and the shorter expression appears in a decad.

Hebraic number symbolism regularly depicts a relationship between 7 and 10, such as 7 multiplied 10 times; 7 and 10 added together for 17; 7 and 10 appearing together as separate numbers; or 7 appearing as a subset in 10. The numeric expressions *seven, seventh* or *seventy* appear in the same verse of the Bible with *ten* or *tenth* at least 28 times. The Hebrew *twenty*, or *twentieth*, which is the plural of 10 when written in Hebrew, appears in the same verse with *seven, seventh*, or *seventy* at least 31 times. Visually, Revelation speaks about the 3 beasts with 7 heads and 10 horns 4 times. In Matthew *Son of David* repeats 10 times, and *David* (1:6 (x2), 17 (x2); 12:3; 22:43, 45) appears 7 more times, for a total of 17. *Christ* also repeats 17 times (excluding a variant rejected in GOC at 12:23 and a variant missing from BNT, GNT, TIS, VST, and WHO at 23:8). The names *Jesus* and *Christ* appear in the same verse 7 times (1:1, 16, 18; 16:20; 26:63; 27:17, 22).

Spoken...through...the prophet saying 10 times in the Gospel of Matthew
That which was fulfilled spoken...through...the prophet saying 7 times*

In order that **might be fulfilled** that which was spoken by the Lord **through** the prophet saying (Matt. 1:22)
In order that **might be fulfilled** that which was spoken by the Lord **through** the prophet saying (Matt. 2:15)
In order that **might be fulfilled** what was spoken **through** Isaiah the prophet, saying (Matt. 4:14)
    That it **might be fulfilled** which was spoken **through** Isaiah the prophet (Matt. 8:17)
In order that **might be fulfilled** what was spoken **through** Isaiah the prophet, saying (Matt. 12:17)
    That it **might be fulfilled** which was spoken **through** the prophet, saying (Matt. 13:35)
In order that **might be fulfilled** that which was spoken **through** the prophet saying (Matt. 21:4)
Then that which **was spoken through** Jeremiah the prophet was fulfilled, saying (Matt. 2:17)
For this is he that **was spoken** of **through** the prophet Isaiah, saying (Matt. 3:3)
Then that which **was spoken through** Jeremiah the prophet was fulfilled, saying (Matt. 27:9)

ἵνα **πληρωθῇ** τὸ ῥηθὲν ὑπὸ κυρίου **διὰ** τοῦ προφήτου λέγοντος (Matt. 1:22 BNT)
ἵνα **πληρωθῇ** τὸ ῥηθὲν ὑπὸ κυρίου **διὰ** τοῦ προφήτου λέγοντος (Matt. 2:15 BNT)
ἵνα **πληρωθῇ** τὸ ῥηθὲν **διὰ** Ἠσαΐου τοῦ προφήτου λέγοντος (Matt. 4:14 BNT)
ὅπως **πληρωθῇ** τὸ ῥηθὲν **διὰ** Ἠσαΐου τοῦ προφήτου λέγοντος (Matt. 8:17 BNT)
ἵνα **πληρωθῇ** τὸ ῥηθὲν **διὰ** Ἠσαΐου τοῦ προφήτου λέγοντος (Matt. 12:17 BNT)
ὅπως **πληρωθῇ** τὸ ῥηθὲν **διὰ** τοῦ προφήτου λέγοντος (Matt. 13:35 BNT)
ἵνα **πληρωθῇ** τὸ ῥηθὲν **διὰ** τοῦ προφήτου λέγοντος (Matt. 21:4 BNT)
τότε ἐπληρώθη τὸ ῥηθὲν **διὰ** Ἰερεμίου τοῦ προφήτου λέγοντος (Matt. 2:17 BNT)**
οὗτος γάρ ἐστιν ὁ ῥηθεὶς **διὰ** Ἠσαΐου τοῦ προφήτου λέγοντος (Matt. 3:3 BNT)***
τότε ἐπληρώθη τὸ ῥηθὲν **διὰ** Ἰερεμίου τοῦ προφήτου λέγοντος (Matt. 27:9 BNT)

*In order that might be fulfilled that which was spoken by the Lord through the prophet (ἵνα πληρωθῇ τὸ ῥηθὲν ὑπὸ τοῦ Matt. 27:35) appears to be a rather extensive

addition in SCR and STE. According to Hebraic cadence, modern translations are correct in removing most of 27:35 from the text.
The following have *by* (ὑπὸ) instead of *through* (διὰ).
**Τότε ἐπληρώθη τὸ ῥηθὲν ὑπὸ Ἰερεμίου τοῦ προφήτου, λέγοντος (Matt. 2:17 BYZ, GOC, SCR, STE).
***ὁ ῥηθεὶς ὑπὸ Ἡσαΐου τοῦ προφήτου, λέγοντος (Matt. 3:3 BYZ, GOC, SCR, STE).

At this point there might be more questions such as, "Do the other Gospels repeat this phrase in a Hebraic meter?" The answer is, "No, they do not." This and many other metered phrases in the 4 Gospels have led to the conclusion that there is no so-called Q source from which Matthew, Mark, and Luke's Gospels were copied. The Q source is the mythical text fabricated by higher critics on which Matthew, Mark, and Luke based their Gospels. It is discussed at length in the Conclusion. Also, there is no so-called Markan Priority. The Markan Priority is another higher critical myth that Matthew and Luke copied both Q and Mark. At this time it will only be stated that the evidence according to pattern theory, more technically termed aesthetic hermeneutics (see Chapter Fifteen of the 2012 edition), is that Matthew is the first Gospel and the other writers were using Matthew as their source. Stated more simply, paisley is not an accident. In any case, a few surprises are guaranteed when the meter in Matthew is compared with the meter in Mark, Luke, and John. Some of the evidence defies any known theory of contemporary textual criticism.

Notice how Matthew carefully follows his wording exactly 10 times. The phrase is of such a length that if Matthew was aware of this decadal meter, he may have turned back in his scroll to make sure the entire phrase was written as he intended. Thus we also have internal textual assurance that this is Matthew's original writing as it first appeared by his own hand.

Scribes and Pharisees

The following decad is a longer list of *scribes and Pharisees*, displayed earlier in a heptad of the lengthier phrase, *woe to you, scribes and Pharisees, you hypocrites, because*. Metered phrases often increase in number when the phrase is shorter. When Matthew 23:14 is added to the text and 15:1 is rejected because of reverse order in BNT, GNT, TIS, and WHO, there is a full decad. When one variant falls into place it often completes overlapping meters.

Scribes and Pharisees 10 times in the Gospel of Matthew*
Scribes and Pharisees........γραμματέων καὶ Φαρισαίων (Matt. 5:20 BNT)
Scribes and Pharisees........γραμματέων καὶ Φαρισαίων (Matt. 12:38 BNT)
Scribes and Pharisees...οἱ γραμματεῖς καὶ οἱ Φαρισαῖοι (Matt. 23:2 BNT)

Scribes and Pharisees.......γραμματεῖς καὶ Φαρισαῖοι (Matt. 23:13 BNT)
Scribes and Pharisees.......γραμματεῖς καὶ Φαρισαῖοι (Matt. 23:14 BYZ)**
Scribes and Pharisees.......γραμματεῖς καὶ Φαρισαῖοι (Matt. 23:15 BNT)
Scribes and Pharisees.......γραμματεῖς καὶ Φαρισαῖοι (Matt. 23:23 BNT)
Scribes and Pharisees.......γραμματεῖς καὶ Φαρισαῖοι (Matt. 23:25 BNT)
Scribes and Pharisees.......γραμματεῖς καὶ Φαρισαῖοι (Matt. 23:27 BNT)
Scribes and Pharisees.......γραμματεῖς καὶ Φαρισαῖοι (Matt. 23:29 BNT)
*Matt. 15:1 *Pharisees and scribes* reverse order in BNT, GNT, TIS, WHO is correct and rejected from above.
**Matt. 23:14 only in BYZ, GOC, SCR, STE, and missing from BNT, GNT, TIS, VST, WHO.

Came to Him / They Followed Him / Worshiped Him / To His Disciples

The following 4 decadal phrases exhibit the same mundane introduction to conversation found in heptads viewed earlier. The phrases *came to Him, they followed Him, worshiped Him,* and *to His disciples* would barely draw attention in any other setting, other than that they were all chosen to exhibit Hebraic decadal meter. There are no variants in the second example.

Came to Him 10 times in the Gospel of Matthew
    Came to Him...................προσῆλθον αὐτῷ (Matt. 5:1)*
    Came to Him...................προσῆλθον αὐτῷ (Matt. 9:28)
    Came to Him...................προσῆλθον αὐτῷ (Matt. 13:36)
    Came to Him...................προσῆλθον αὐτῷ (Matt. 14:15)
    Came to Him...................προσῆλθον αὐτῷ (Matt. 15:30)
    Came to Him...................προσῆλθον αὐτῷ (Matt. 19:3)
    Came to Him...................προσῆλθον αὐτῷ (Matt. 21:14)
    Came to Him...................προσῆλθον αὐτῷ (Matt. 21:23)
    Came to Him...................προσῆλθον αὐτῷ (Matt. 22:23)
    Came to Him...................προσῆλθον αὐτῷ (Matt. 24:3)
*BNT, GNT, TIS, VST, WHO have προσῆλθαν at 5:1.

They followed Him 10 times in the Gospel of Matthew
    They followed Him.........ἠκολούθησαν αὐτῷ (Matt. 4:20 BNT)
    They followed Him.........ἠκολούθησαν αὐτῷ (Matt. 4:22 BNT)
    They followed Him.........ἠκολούθησαν αὐτῷ (Matt. 4:25 BNT)
    They followed Him.........ἠκολούθησαν αὐτῷ (Matt. 8:1 BNT)
    They followed Him.........ἠκολούθησαν αὐτῷ (Matt. 8:23 BNT)
    They followed Him.........ἠκολούθησαν [αὐτῷ] (Matt. 9:27 BNT)
    They followed Him.........ἠκολούθησαν αὐτῷ (Matt. 12:15 BNT)
    They followed Him.........ἠκολούθησαν αὐτῷ (Matt. 14:13 BNT)
    They followed Him.........ἠκολούθησαν αὐτῷ (Matt. 19:2 BNT)
    They followed Him.........ἠκολούθησαν αὐτῷ (Matt. 20:34 BNT)

Worshiped Him 10 times in the Gospel of Matthew
    To worship Him..............προσκυνῆσαι αὐτῷ (Matt. 2:2 BNT)
    I may worship Him..............προσκυνήσω αὐτῷ (Matt. 2:8 BNT)
    They worshipped Him..........προσεκύνησαν αὐτῷ (Matt. 2:11 BNT)
    He was worshipping Him.........προσεκύνει αὐτῷ (Matt. 8:2 BNT)
    He was worshipping Him.........προσεκύνει αὐτω (Matt. 9:18 BNT)
    They worshipped Him...........προσεκύνησαν αὐτῷ (Matt. 14:33 BNT)
    He was worshipping Him.........προσεκύνει αὐτῷ (Matt. 15:25 BNT)
    He was worshipping Him.........προσεκύνει αὐτῷ (Matt. 18:26 BNT)
    They worshipped Him...........προσεκύνησαν αὐτῷ (Matt. 28:9 BNT)
    They worshipped Him............προσεκύνησαν αὐτῷ (Matt. 28:17 BYZ)*
*BYZ, GOC, SCR, STE, VST add 28:17; variant accepted.

To His disciples 10 times in the Gospel of Matthew*
    To His disciples..............τοῖς μαθηταῖς αὐτοῦ (Matt. 9:10 BNT)
    To His disciples..............τοῖς μαθηταῖς αὐτοῦ (Matt. 9:11 BNT)
    To His disciples..............τοῖς μαθηταῖς αὐτοῦ (Matt. 9:37 BNT)
    To His disciples..............τοῖς μαθηταῖς αὐτοῦ (Matt. 16:21 BNT)
    To His disciples..............τοῖς μαθηταῖς αὐτοῦ (Matt. 16:24 BNT)
    To His disciples..............τοῖς μαθηταῖς αὐτοῦ (Matt. 19:23 BNT)
    To His disciples..............τοῖς μαθηταῖς αὐτοῦ (Matt. 23:1 BNT)
    To His disciples..............τοῖς μαθηταῖς αὐτοῦ (Matt. 26:1 BNT)
    To His disciples..............τοῖς μαθηταῖς αὐτοῦ (Matt. 28:7 BNT)
    To His disciples..............τοῖς μαθηταῖς αὐτοῦ (Matt. 28:8 BNT)
*BYZ, GOC, SCR, STE add 15:36, 16:20, 28:9.

How many decadal phrases Matthew placed in his Gospel is anyone's discovery. The estimate is that this chapter reproduced about 20% of them, if that many.

Four of the 9 texts that repeat the phrase *came to Him* use a different spelling in Matthew 5:1 above. Either someone was aware that Matthew lacked a 10th phrase and added it, or a copyist did not record it properly. The latter likely occurred because the reverse is seen in *to His disciples*, where BYZ, GOC, SCR, and STE exceed decadal meter by 3 phrases, and so demonstrate no intent to preserve, let alone create, the decad.

There is a significant difference of 3 phrases (15:36, 16:20, 28:9) between BYZ, GOC, SCR, and STE; and BNT, GNT, TIS, VST, and WHO on *to His disciples*. If the copyists of BYZ, GOC, SCR, and STE were attempting to add the correct number of *came to Him* at Matthew 5:1, they overshot both decadal and dodecadal meter (a list of 12 phrases) when they added *to His disciples*, 3 times. All of this indicates the copyists were not keeping count and mistakes were made.

An excess of 1 repetition may indicate that this series was intended to be a dodecad instead of a decad. So is it 10 or 12? The lack of 3 repetitions in TIS is a significant factor. However, this writer is also influenced by the fact that Mark has the identical decadal meter in his Gospel, which is 12 chapters shorter than Matthew! Hence it appears that Mark observed the pattern in Matthew and used it in his own Gospel. Luke with 1 repetition and John with 4, do not use this phrase in Hebraic cadence. If there is a Q source, Luke and John did not have it. Imagine! Two documents on the same subject containing the identical decadal phrase, *to His disciples*. Future chapters will say more on the similarity of Hebraic meter in one or more of the Gospels.

There will be more similarities when phrases in the Gospels are compared to the Hebrew text. The Septuagint, a 3rd-century B.C. translation of the Hebrew Bible into Greek, is virtually useless on the subject of Hebraic meter. The translators from Hebrew to Greek show little, if any, awareness of duplicating the Hebraic meter found in the Hebrew text, or they chose not to copy it. However, the Septuagint translators may have introduced their own metered phrases not found in the Hebrew.

Claims by critics that Matthew is following the Septuagint and cannot read Hebrew ring a little hollow. Why would he not copy the established Septuagint text into his Gospel when he is writing in Greek? Today, authors regularly quote passages from recognized versions, just as the KJV and NASB are copied in this chapter. Matthew proves himself to be an absolute master of Mosaic repetition as defined by Umberto Cassuto, especially when Matthew copies metered phrases into his Gospel directly from the Hebrew text that are not found in the Septuagint.

He Said to Him

The simple anaphoric phrase *said to him* appears in a double decadal sequence of 20, a truly Hebraic repetition. When the meters get this long, there is a higher probability of variant readings. Matthew 4:9 is the primary disputed example with the odd division of BYZ, GOC, SCR, STE, and VST in favor, and BNT, GNT, TIS, and WHO opposed. The question is whether Matthew 4:9 is λέγει αὐτῷ, *said to him*, or εἶπεν αὐτῷ, another way of saying *said to him*.

Every action in the text causes a reaction. If BYZ is followed with λέγει αὐτῷ, this also creates 14 εἶπεν αὐτῷ in BYZ, a double heptad. The selection of Matthew 4:9 creates 2 metered sequences of 20 and 14 repetitions, instead of 19 and 15. Hence, we are led to follow Mosaic meter as a guide to textual criticism. If it is in the mind of the writer to maintain a cadence in a particular phrase, then the cadence becomes a rule in itself that determines which variant reading is selected.

Another odd occurrence is that BNT, GNT, TIS, VST, and WHO add λέγει αὐτῷ at Matthew 8:22, while BYZ, GOC, SCR, and STE add λέγει αὐτῷ at 17:26. Either one could complete the meter, but not both. However, following BYZ at 17:26 maintains a meter of 24 for the name *Peter* in BYZ, which must include λέγει αὐτῷ. It all gets a little complicated when dealing with multiple variants that impact other lists of phrases. However, if Matthew is keeping count of the phrases, we have some additional guidance at 17:26 in making the correct selection of variant readings to recreate the original wording of his Gospel.

He said to him 20 times in the Gospel of Matthew
    He said to him.................λέγει αὐτῷ (Matt. 4:6 BNT)
    He said to him....................λέγει αὐτῷ (Matt. 4:9 BYZ)*
    He said to him....................λέγει αὐτῷ (Matt. 4:10 BNT)
    He said to him....................λέγει αὐτῷ (Matt. 8:4 BNT)
    He said to him....................λέγει αὐτῷ (Matt. 8:7 BNT)
    He said to him....................λέγει αὐτῷ (Matt. 8:20 BNT)
    He said to him....................λέγει αὐτῷ (Matt. 9:9 BNT)
    He said to him....................λέγει αὐτῷ (Matt. 14:31 BNT)
    He said to him....................Λέγει αὐτῷ (Matt. 17:26 BYZ)**
    He said to him....................Λέγει αὐτῷ (Matt. 18:22 BNT)
    He said to him....................λέγει αὐτῷ (Matt. 18:32 BNT)
    He said to him....................Λέγει αὐτῷ (Matt. 19:18 BNT)***
    He said to him....................Λέγει αὐτῷ (Matt. 19:20 BNT)
    He said to him....................Λέγει αὐτῷ (Matt. 20:21 BNT)
    He said to him....................λέγει αὐτῷ (Matt. 22:12 BNT)
    He said to him....................Λέγει αὐτῷ (Matt. 26:25 BNT)
    He said to him....................Λέγει αὐτῷ (Matt. 26:35 BNT)
    He said to him....................Λέγει αὐτῷ (Matt. 26:52 BNT)
    He said to him....................Λέγει αὐτῷ (Matt. 26:64 BNT)
    He said to him....................λέγει αὐτῷ (Matt. 27:13 BNT)
*Only in BYZ, GOC, SCR, STE, VST.
**Only in BYZ, GOC, SCR, STE.
***TIS missing at 19:18.

Son of David / Son of God / Son of Man
    The phrase *Son of David* occurs exactly 10 times in the Gospel of Matthew. There are no variants. When compared with the previous phrase, the reader can understand why it is easier to keep track of *Son of David* when copying a manuscript. The Greek word for *David* jumps right out at the reader. Matthew likes to use names for repetition, as seen earlier in *John the Baptist*. He also uses the names *Abraham*, *Joseph*, *Sadducees*, and others 7 times. *David* and *Christ* each repeat 17 times.

According to BYZ, GOC, SCR, and STE (KJV) *Peter* repeats 24 times. In the last verse Jesus identifies Himself as the *Son of David* and lets the Pharisees finish the phrase. (This last line is doubled in the list below because it is too long for the page.)

As shown earlier, the repetition in *Son of David* is not a coincidence. Rather we are witnessing a carefully crafted and complex text that is hardly a collection of stories about Jesus. The entire text is woven together as a single unit. How long did it take Matthew to write his Gospel? How many times did he have to rewrite it before he had the finished product? We have barely uncovered the intricacy of his masterpiece. It takes 21st-century computing just to begin unraveling these mysteries. Notice the subset of 7 phrases without the article before *Son*.

Son of David 10 times in the Gospel of Matthew
    Son of David……………υἱοῦ Δαυὶδ (Matt. 1:1 BNT)
    Son of David……………υἱὸς Δαυίδ (Matt. 1:20 BNT)
    Son of David……………υἱὸς Δαυίδ (Matt. 9:27 BNT)
    The **Son** of David…………ὁ υἱὸς Δαυίδ (Matt. 12:23 BNT)
    Son of David……………υἱὸς Δαυίδ (Matt. 15:22 BNT)
    Son of David……………υἱὸς Δαυίδ (Matt. 20:30 BNT)
    Son of David……………υἱὸς Δαυίδ (Matt. 20:31 BNT)
    To the **Son** of David………τῷ υἱῷ Δαυίδ (Matt. 21:9 BNT)
    To the **Son** of David………τῷ υἱῷ Δαυίδ (Matt. 21:15 BNT)
    Whose **Son** is He? They said to Him of David
    …………τίνος **υἱός** ἐστιν; λέγουσιν αὐτῷ· τοῦ Δαυίδ (Matt. 22:42 BNT)

Not only does Matthew write about Christ 10 times as the *Son of David*, he uses the phrase *Son of God* 10 times. *Son of God* repeats in a variety of contexts, from questions to confessions and declarations. One of the repetitions in Matthew 5:9 is in a plural where Jesus calls us *sons of God*. *God* and *Son* are bolded in the Greek below.

Son of God 10 times in the Gospel of Matthew
    If you are the Son of God…………εἰ **υἱὸς** εἶ τοῦ **θεοῦ** (Matt. 4:3 BNT)
    If you are the Son of God…………εἰ **υἱὸς** εἶ τοῦ **θεοῦ** (Matt. 4:6 BNT)
    Sons of God……………**υἱοὶ θεοῦ** (Matt. 5:9 BNT)
    Thou Son of God……………**υἱὲ** τοῦ **θεοῦ** (Matt. 8:29 BNT)
    You are the Son of God……**θεοῦ υἱὸς** εἶ (Matt. 14:33 BNT)
    The Son of the living God…………ὁ **υἱὸς** τοῦ **θεοῦ** τοῦ ζῶντος (Matt. 16:16 BNT)
    The Son of God…………ὁ **υἱὸς** τοῦ **θεοῦ** (Matt. 26:63 BNT)
    If you are the Son of God…………εἰ **υἱὸς** εἶ τοῦ **θεοῦ** (Matt. 27:40 BNT)
    I am the Son of God…**θεοῦ** εἰμι **υἱός** (Matt. 27:43 BNT)
    This was the Son of God………**θεοῦ υἱὸς** ἦν οὗτος (Matt. 27:54 BNT)

As with *Son of David*, there are no variants in the above. Both decads are preserved perfectly as they were written 2,000 years ago. This decadal meter was carefully placed by Matthew throughout his Gospel. His method of keeping count and arranging these phrases is lost to history. There are no records of how this process was accomplished. However, his Gospel exhibits the same meter found in Genesis and Revelation.

One of the more remarkable lists of decadal meter in Matthew is *Son of Man*. After observing the Hebraic cadence in *Son of David* and *Son of God*, it seemed appropriate to check for a similar meter in the phrase *Son of Man*. There were not 10 or 20, but 30 repetitions! They are all found in BNT, GNT, TIS, VST, and WHO. Two additional variants that should be rejected were found in BYZ, GOC, SCR, and STE at Matthew 18:11 and 25:13. In BYZ, GOC, SCR, and STE Matthew 18:11 was copied by later copyists from Luke 19:10. Matthew 25:13 was copied into the text from Matthew 24:44. It seems reasonable to assume that the scholars who assembled BNT, GNT, TIS, VST, and WHO were not aware that their texts were preserving 30 identical phrases. Note that 20 of the phrases begin with the Greek nominative ὁ (*the*). In order to save space, the English was not included in the list below, nor the text initials BNT.

Son of Man 30 times in the Gospel of Matthew

ὁ δὲ υἱὸς τοῦ ἀνθρώπου (Matt. 8:20)   ὁ υἱὸς τοῦ ἀνθρώπου (Matt. 9:6)
ὁ υἱὸς τοῦ ἀνθρώπου (Matt. 10:23)   ὁ υἱὸς τοῦ ἀνθρώπου (Matt. 11:19)
ὁ υἱὸς τοῦ ἀνθρώπου (Matt. 12:8)   τοῦ υἱοῦ τοῦ ἀνθρώπου (Matt. 12:32)
ὁ υἱὸς τοῦ ἀνθρώπου (Matt. 12:40)   ὁ υἱὸς τοῦ ἀνθρώπου (Matt. 13:37)
ὁ υἱὸς τοῦ ἀνθρώπου (Matt. 13:41)   τὸν υἱὸν τοῦ ἀνθρώπου (Matt. 16:13)
ὁ υἱὸς τοῦ ἀνθρώπου (Matt. 16:27)   τὸν υἱὸν τοῦ ἀνθρώπου (Matt. 16:28)
ὁ υἱὸς τοῦ ἀνθρώπου (Matt. 17:9)   ὁ υἱὸς τοῦ ἀνθρώπου (Matt. 17:12)
ὁ υἱὸς τοῦ ἀνθρώπου (Matt. 17:22)   ὁ υἱὸς τοῦ ἀνθρώπου (Matt. 19:28)
ὁ υἱὸς τοῦ ἀνθρώπου (Matt. 20:18)   ὁ υἱὸς τοῦ ἀνθρώπου (Matt. 20:28)
τοῦ υἱοῦ τοῦ ἀνθρώπου (Matt. 24:27)   τοῦ υἱοῦ τοῦ ἀνθρώπου (Matt. 24:30)
τὸν υἱὸν τοῦ ἀνθρώπου (Matt. 24:30)   τοῦ υἱοῦ τοῦ ἀνθρώπου (Matt. 24:37)
τοῦ υἱοῦ τοῦ ἀνθρώπου (Matt. 24:39)   ὁ υἱὸς τοῦ ἀνθρώπου (Matt. 24:44)
ὁ υἱὸς τοῦ ἀνθρώπου (Matt. 25:31)   ὁ υἱὸς τοῦ ἀνθρώπου (Matt. 26:2)
υἱὸς τοῦ ἀνθρώπου (Matt. 26:24)   ὁ υἱὸς τοῦ ἀνθρώπου (Matt. 26:24)
ὁ υἱὸς τοῦ ἀνθρώπου (Matt. 26:45)   τὸν υἱὸν τοῦ ἀνθρώπου (Matt. 26:64)

Matthew's setting of *Son of David, Son of Man,* and *Son of God* in Moses' decadal meter is hardly a coincidence. New Testament scholars must come to the realization that the Gospels were written in Greek, but the format is clearly Hebraic. The criterion for evaluating the text must shift from Western textual criticism to Mosaic meter if there is going to be an accurate evaluation of the text. Hebraic meter is a significant tool in determining the correct reading of the original text.

Swears By

Matthew uses the simple phrase *swears by* 10 times in his Gospel. There are no variant readings. All the examples occur in one discourse found in Matthew 23:16-22. Locating these decads is one thing, but giving an adequate analysis of the data is another. Later it will be shown that John employs more numerically-ordered cadence within a discourse, as found here in Matthew 23:16-22, than the other Gospels.

Swears by 10 times in the Gospel of Matthew

Whoever **swears by** the temple (Matt. 23:16)

But whoever **swears by** gold in the temple (Matt. 23:16)

Whoever **swears by** the altar (Matt. 23:18)

But whoever **swears by** the gift (Matt. 23:18)

Therefore whoever **swears by** the altar (Matt. 23:20)

Swears by it (Matt. 23:20)

Whoever **swears by** the temple (Matt. 23:21)

Swears by it (Matt. 23:21)

Whoever **swears by** heaven (Matt. 23:22)

Swears by the throne of God (Matt. 23:22)

ὃς ἂν **ὀμόσῃ** ἐν τῷ ναῷ (Matt. 23:16 BNT)

ὃς δ' ἂν **ὀμόσῃ** ἐν τῷ χρυσῷ τοῦ ναοῦ (Matt. 23:16 BNT)

ὃς ἂν **ὀμόσῃ** ἐν τῷ θυσιαστηρίῳ (Matt. 23:18 BNT)

ὃς δ' ἂν **ὀμόσῃ** ἐν τῷ δώρῳ (Matt. 23:18 BNT)

ὁ οὖν **ὀμόσας** ἐν τῷ θυσιαστηρίῳ (Matt. 23:20 BNT)

ὀμνύει ἐν αὐτῷ (Matt. 23:20 BNT)

ὁ **ὀμόσας** ἐν τῷ ναῷ (Matt. 23:21 BNT)

ὀμνύει ἐν αὐτῷ (Matt. 23:21 BNT)

ὁ **ὀμόσας** ἐν τῷ οὐρανῷ (Matt. 23:22 BNT)

ὀμνύει ἐν τῷ θρόνῳ τοῦ θεοῦ (Matt. 23:22 BNT)

Dodecadal Phrases in Matthew

Then He Said

The simple phrase *then he said* occurs 12 times in Matthew in all 9 Greek texts without variant readings. Quite often repetitions of 12 include subsets of 10 and/or 7. This particular example repeats the entire meter with machine-like precision as is often found in Genesis and other books of the Old Testament.

It would not be possible for those reading English translations to find this phrase 12 times. For example, *New American Standard* records 6 repetitions of *then he said*, when the Greek clearly shows 12 with no variants. A translation that attempted to record exact Greek parlance into English would be stilted to say the least. The question is whether the Gospel writers actually spoke as they wrote. In other words, the precision of the writing necessary to incorporate Hebraic meter, and potentially many more literary devices than are currently known, may have resulted in a text that reflected the tradition of sacred communication.

Then he said 12 times in the Gospel of Matthew
Then he said..................τότε λέγει (Matt. 4:10 BNT)
Then he said..................τότε λέγει (Matt. 9:6 BNT)
Then he said..................τότε λέγει (Matt. 9:37 BNT)
Then he said..................τότε λέγει (Matt. 12:13 BNT)
Then he said..................τότε λέγει (Matt. 12:44 BNT)
Then he said..................τότε λέγει (Matt. 22:8 BNT)
Then he said..................τότε λέγει (Matt. 22:21 BNT)
Then he said..................τότε λέγει (Matt. 26:31 BNT)
Then he said..................τότε λέγει (Matt. 26:38 BNT)
Then he said..................τότε λέγει (Matt. 26:52 BNT)
Then he said..................τότε λέγει (Matt. 27:13 BNT)
Then he said..................τότε λέγει (Matt. 28:10 BNT)

Through the Prophet
The phrase *spoken...through...the prophet saying*, printed on page 23, repeats 10 times in Matthew with a subset of *In order that **might be fulfilled** that which was spoken...through...the prophet saying*, which repeats 7 times. There is also the shorter phrase *through...the prophet* that occurs 12 times in Matthew, which incorporates all 10 of these phrases and adds Matthew 2:5 and 24:15. Here is an example of all 3 major cadences, 7, 10, and 12, in one set of phrases. A subset with the names of the 7 prophets is bolded 7 times. Notice the 10 repetitions of *saying* (λέγοντος).

As in some of the examples of the Old Testament and Revelation, there is meter within meter within meter. It is in the mind of the writer to integrate a variety of meter within a larger, more complex art form. This could be compared to various melodies coordinated in a work by Bach. These are only examples. The full extent of this coordination in Matthew is not known.

Through…the prophet 12 times in the Gospel of Matthew
Through	the **prophet saying**	(Matt. 1:22)
Through	the **prophet**	(Matt. 2:5)
Through	the **prophet saying**	(Matt. 2:15)
Through **Jeremiah**	the **prophet saying**	(Matt. 2:17)
Through **Isaiah**	the **prophet saying**	(Matt. 3:3)
Through **Isaiah**	the **prophet saying**	(Matt. 4:14)
Through **Isaiah**	the **prophet saying**	(Matt. 8:17)
Through **Isaiah**	the **prophet saying**	(Matt. 12:17)
Through	the **prophet saying**	(Matt. 13:35)
Through	the **prophet saying**	(Matt. 21:4)
Through **Daniel**	the **prophet**	(Matt. 24:15)
Through **Jeremiah**	the **prophet saying**	(Matt. 27:9)

διὰ	τοῦ **προφήτου λέγοντος**	(Matt. 1:22 BNT)
διὰ	τοῦ **προφήτου**	(Matt. 2:5 BNT)
διὰ	τοῦ **προφήτου λέγοντος**	(Matt. 2:15 BNT)
διὰ **Ἰερεμίου**	τοῦ **προφήτου λέγοντος**	(Matt. 2:17 BNT)
διὰ **Ἡσαΐου**	τοῦ **προφήτου λέγοντος**	(Matt. 3:3 BNT)
διὰ **Ἡσαΐου**	τοῦ **προφήτου λέγοντος**	(Matt. 4:14 BNT)
διὰ **Ἡσαΐου**	τοῦ **προφήτου λέγοντος**	(Matt. 8:17 BNT)
διὰ **Ἡσαΐου**	τοῦ **προφήτου λέγοντος**	(Matt. 12:17 BNT)
διὰ	τοῦ **προφήτου λέγοντος**	(Matt. 13:35 BNT)
διὰ	τοῦ **προφήτου λέγοντος**	(Matt. 21:4 BNT)
διὰ **Δανιὴλ**	τοῦ **προφήτου**	(Matt. 24:15 BNT)
διὰ **Ἰερεμίου**	τοῦ **προφήτου λέγοντος**	(Matt. 27:9 BNT)

Right

The word *right* is also set in dodecadal meter with a heptadic subset of the phrase *on…right*. There are no variants.

Right 12 times / *on…right* 7 times in the Gospel of Matthew
The right	ὁ δεξιὸς	(Matt. 5:29 BNT)
Your right hand	ἡ δεξιά σου χεὶρ	(Matt. 5:30 BNT)
Into the right	εἰς τὴν δεξιὰν	(Matt. 5:39 BNT)
Your right	ἡ δεξιά σου	(Matt. 6:3 BNT)
On your right	ἐκ δεξιῶν σου	(Matt. 20:21 BNT)
On My right	ἐκ δεξιῶν μου	(Matt. 20:23 BNT)
On My right	ἐκ δεξιῶν μου	(Matt. 22:44 BNT)
On His right	ἐκ δεξιῶν αὐτοῦ	(Matt. 25:33 BNT)
On His right	ἐκ δεξιῶν αὐτοῦ	(Matt. 25:34 BNT)
On the right	ἐκ δεξιῶν	(Matt. 26:64 BNT)
In His right	ἐν τῇ δεξιᾷ αὐτου	(Matt. 27:29 BNT)
On the right	ἐκ δεξιῶν	(Matt. 27:38 BNT)

The integration of phrases in Hebraic meter is found throughout the Gospel of Matthew. Such coordination is far beyond a man simply sitting down and recording his recollections from 3½ years with Jesus.

As the next 3 chapters proceed to examine and compare Hebraic repetition in Mark, Luke, and John, it should be remembered how far removed our generation is from the mindset, culture, and presuppositions of the Gospel writers. The reader should also be aware that there are more examples of Hebraic repetition in Genesis than in any of the Gospels.

Our 21st-century Western civilization can hardly fathom a culture with its concepts of numbers, symbols, and word associations in which these writers were immersed. Current efforts to analyze the biblical text in terms of Western literary criticism may be as misguided as evaluating Egyptian scrolls by the literary standards of checkout-line tabloids. Is the goal to study the scrolls or use them as a pretext to exalt Western literary prowess?

The presence of Hebraic meter in the text demonstrates the amazing accuracy with which Matthew's Gospel has been preserved for us and the authenticity of the text. His document stands as a unique artifact of history without comparison to any composition in our world today.

In keeping with the phenomenon of divine communication, there are always intriguing anomalies such as the 7 repetitions of *righteousness* in Matthew, listed in the right-hand column below. More recent translations include Matthew 6:1, which is supported by BNT, GNT, TIS, VST, and WHO.

Genesis does not have a meter for the equivalent of *righteousness* צְדָקָה (*tsedaqah*, tsed-aw-kaw'). However, the Septuagint repeats the Greek word for *righteousness* 10 times in Genesis, as seen in the left-hand column. Based on the Hebrew text in the second column, this is a coincidence. There is no pattern in the Hebrew on which this pattern is based in the Greek. In fact, the Septuagint translates 3 different Hebrew words as *righteousness*, as seen in the third column. This may also indicate that the Septuagint translators understood that all 3 Hebrew words were used forensically. The anomaly is that the column on the left from the Septuagint contains a bolded subset of 7 occurrences of *righteousness*, δικαιοσύνην (*dikaiosune*, dik-ah-yos-oo'-nay), all with the same case ending. Thus there is a heptadic subset in the Septuagint list. Another anomaly for which we have no explanation is that 7 of the Hebrew words are based on *loving-kindness* חֶסֶד (*checed*, kheh'-sed), which the

Septuagint incorrectly translates as *righteousness*. Is it possible that the Septuagint was held in such high regard that Matthew copied its cadence for *righteousness* into his Gospel? A second possibility is that Matthew simply chose to set *righteousness* in heptadic meter. A third possibility, and a question, is "Did Matthew think of righteousness in terms of loving-kindness?"

Septuagint	Hebrew	Hebrew Translation	Matthew
δικαιοσύνην	צְדָקָה (Gen. 15:6)	Righteousness	δικαιοσύνην (Matt. 3:15 BNT)
δικαιοσύνην	צְדָקָה (Gen. 18:19)	Righteousness	δικαιοσύνην (Matt. 5:6 BNT)
δικαιοσύνην	חַסְדְּךָ (Gen. 19:19)	Loving-kindness	δικαιοσύνης (Matt. 5:10 BNT)
δικαιοσύνη	בְּנִקְיֹן (Gen. 20:5)	In innocence	δικαιοσύνη (Matt. 5:20 BNT)
δικαιοσύνην	חַסְדְּךָ (Gen. 20:13)	Loving-kindness	δικαιοσύνην (Matt. 6:1 BNT)*
δικαιοσύνην	בְּחֶסֶד (Gen. 21:23)	Loving-kindness	δικαιοσύνην (Matt. 6:33 BNT)
δικαιοσύνην	חַסְדּוֹ (Gen. 24:27)	Loving-kindness	δικαιοσύνης (Matt. 21:32 BNT)
δικαιοσύνην	חֶסֶד (Gen. 24:49)	Loving-kindness	
δικαιοσύνη	צִדְקָתִי (Gen. 30:33)	My righteousness	
δικαιοσύνης	הַחֲסָדִים (Gen. 32:11)	The loving-kindnesses	

*BNT, GNT, TIS, VST, WHO have δικαιοσύνην at 6:1.

The existence of Mosaic repetition in the Gospels opens further opportunities for examining the level of coordination between the Old and the New Testament. The Hebrew text may be more helpful in interpreting the New Testament than is currently appreciated.

The Gospel writers probably spoke Aramaic, wrote in Greek, but thought in Hebrew syntax. How else do we explain the intricacy and attention to detail in reproducing Genesis syntax in their Gospels?

Integration of Hebraic Meter in Matthew 10:24-42

The integration of heptadic, decadal, and dodecadal meter is woven together in the text as individual words, phrases, and statements. The following is a masterful integration of all 3 meters in one text.

Within the text are contrasting words and phrases such as *disciple-master*, *servant-Lord*, *covered-revealed*, *darkness-light*, etc., which are examples of Hebrew antithetic parallelism (opposite statements in pairs). More or different words could have been bolded or italicized to illustrate the point, but these will suffice. These patterns were isolated in the text by working back from verse 42 at the end of the chapter.

As you read Matthew 10:24-42, note the reversal of word order such as *body* and *soul* to *soul* and *body*, or *find* and *lose* to *lose* and *find*. Also note that the phrase *fear them not therefore* is repeated as a summation at the end of 10 statements. In fact, each of the 3 successive decadal motifs concludes with a summation. Was Matthew aware that the first sentence in each of the 3 major sections is followed by 3 decadal motifs? Did Christ actually speak in rhythmic patterns, or were His words reorganized by Matthew? We should not be surprised if He who sent the prophets spoke like the prophets without script or notes. This gives new perspective to the observation of the soldiers, "The officers answered, 'Never man spake like this man'" (John 7:46).

The text is divided into sections. The first has a dodecadal pattern in 6 pairs. The second section also has a dodecadal pattern in 6 pairs, set in 10 statements within a matrix of the word *fear*. The third pattern has a double heptad with 7 pairs set in 10 statements. The fourth section is a double decadal pattern with 10 pairs set in 10 statements.

The **disciple** is not above *his* **master**,
nor the **servant** above his **lord**.
It is enough for the **disciple** that he be as his **master**,
and the **servant** as his **lord**.
If they have called the **master of the house** Beelzebub,
how much more *shall they call* them of **his household**?
Fear them not therefore:
1. for there is nothing **covered**, that shall not be **revealed**;
2. and **hid**, that shall not be **known**.
3. What I tell you in **darkness**, that speak ye in **light**: and
4. what ye **hear** in the ear, that **preach** ye upon the housetops.
5. And **fear** not them which kill the **body**, but are not able to kill the **soul**:
6. but rather **fear** him which is able to destroy both **soul** and **body** in hell.
7. Are not two sparrows sold for a farthing? and
8. one of them shall not fall on the ground without your Father.
9. But the very hairs of your head are all numbered.
10. **Fear** ye not therefore, ye are of more value than many sparrows.

1. Whosoever therefore shall **confess** me before men,
2. him will I **confess** also before my Father which is in heaven.
3. But whosoever shall **deny** me before men,
4. him will I also **deny** before my Father which is in heaven.
5. Think not that I am come to send **peace** on earth:
6. I came not to send **peace**, but a sword.
7. For I am come to set a **man** at variance against his **father**,
8. and the **daughter** against her **mother**,
9. and the **daughter** in law against her **mother in law**.
10. And a **man's foes** shall be they of his own **household**.

1. He that loveth father or mother **more than me** is not **worthy of me**: and
2. he that loveth son or daughter **more than me** is not **worthy of me**. And
3. he that taketh not his cross, and followeth **after me** is not **worthy of me**.
4. He that **findeth** his life shall **lose** it: and
5. he that **loseth** his life for my sake shall **find** it.
6. He that **receiveth** you **receiveth** me, and

7. he that **receiveth** me **receiveth** him that sent me.
8. He that **receiveth** a prophet in the name of a prophet shall **receive** a prophet's reward; and
9. he that **receiveth** a righteous man in the name of a righteous man shall **receive** a righteous man's reward.
10. And whosoever **shall give** to drink unto one of these little ones a cup of cold water only in the name of a disciple, verily I say unto you, he shall in **no wise lose** his reward.

This chapter concludes with the thought that scholars have underestimated the amount of internal textual evidence that is currently available to them to establish the original autograph. However, there are no significant variant readings in Matthew 10:24-42.

Single Words Repeated 7, 10, and 12 Times in Matthew

Chapter Ten of the 2012 edition lists more than 110 examples of words in Revelation that repeat 7, 10, and 12 times and in multiples of these numbers. To our surprise Umberto Cassuto's commentaries listed more examples of this type in Genesis and Exodus. This led to the realization that numeric sequences in Revelation are actually Hebraic meter adapted into Greek. Therefore, this same Hebraic meter should be found in key words in the 4 Gospels. The following are some examples found in the Gospel of Matthew.

Single Words in Heptadic Meter

Abraham: 7, Ἀβραάμ (*Abraam*, ab-rah-am') 1:1, 2, 17; 3:9 (x2); 8:11; 22:32;

Anxious: 7, verb, μεριμνάω (*merimnao*, mer-im-nah'-o) 6:25, 27, 28, 31, 34 (x2); 10:19;

Baptism/Baptize: 7, Chapter 3, baptism, βάπτισμα (*baptisma*, bap'-tismah) 3:7; baptize, βαπτίζω (*baptizo*, bap-tid'-zo) 3:6, 3:11 (x2), 13, 14, 16;

Beyond: 7, πέραν (*peran*, per'-an) 4:15, 25; 8:18, 28; 14:22; 16:5; 19:1;

But the Chief Priests: 3, Οἱ δὲ ἀρχιερεῖς 26:59; 27:6, 20;

The Chief Priests: 7/10, οἱ ἀρχιερεῖς, ἀρχιερεύς (*archiereus*, ar-khee-er-yuce') 21:15, 23, 45; 26:3; 27:1, 41, 62;

Commandment: 7, ἐντολή (*entole*, en-tol-ay') 5:19; 15:3, 6; 19:17; 22:36, 38, 40; 15:6 missing from BNT, GNT, TIS, VIS, WHO;

Cup: 7, ποτήριον (*poterion*, pot-ay'-ree-on) 10:42; 20:22, 23; 23:25, 26, 27, 39; BYZ, GOC, SCR, STE add 27:42; variant rejected;

Demon-possessed: 7, δαιμονίζομαι (*daimonizomai*, dahee-mon-id'-zomahee) see list in phrases above;

Fruit: 7, Chapter 7:16-20 καρπός (*karpos*, kar-pos') 7:16, 17 (x2), 18 (x2), 19, 20;

Hell Fire: 7, γέεννα (*geenna*, gheh'-en-nah) 5:22, 29, 30; 10:28; 18:9; 23:15, 33;

Joseph: 7, (father of Jesus) Ἰωσήφ (*Ioseph*, ee-o-safe') 1:16, 18, 19, 20, 24; 2:13, 19;
Law: 7, νόμος (*nomos*, nom'-os) 5:18; 7:12; 11:13; 12:5; 22:36, 40; 23:23;
Moses: 7, Μωσεῦς (*Moseus*, mocè-yoos') 8:4; 17:3, 4; 19:7, 8; 22:24; 23:2;
People: 14, λαός (*laos*, lah-os') 1:21; 2:4, 6; 4:16, 23; 13:15; 15:8; 21:23; 26:3, 5, 47; 27:1, 25, 64; BYZ, GOC, SCR, STE add 9:35; variant rejected;
Persecute/Persecution: 7, διώκω (*dioko*, dee-o'-ko) 5:10, 11, 12, 44; 10:23; 23:34; διωγμός (*diogmos*, dee-ogue-mos') 13:21;
Repentance: 7, μετάνοια (*metanoia*, met-an'-oy-ah) 3:2, 8, 11; 4:17; 11:20, 21; 12:41; BYZ, GOC, SCR, STE add 9:13; variant rejected;
Righteousness: 7, δικαιοσύνη (*dikaiosune*, dik-ah-yos-oo'-nay) 3:15; 5:6, 10, 20; 6:1, 33; 21:32; BYZ, GOC, SCR, STE missing 6:1;
Sadducees: 7, Σαδδουκαῖος (*Saddoukaios*, sad-doo-kah'-yos) 3:7; 16:1, 6, 11, 12; 22:23, 34;
Sin: 7, ἁμαρτία (*hamartia*, ham-ar-tee'-ah) 1:21; 3:6; 9:2, 5, 6; 12:31; 26:28;
Spirit(s): 7, πνεῦμα (*pneuma*, pnyoo'-mah) 5:3; 8:16; 10:1; 12:18; 12:43, 45; 22:43;
Water: 7, ὕδωρ (*hudor*, hoo'-dore) 3:11, 16; 8:32; 14:28, 29; 17:15; 27:24;
Woe: 14, οὐαί (*ouai*, oo-ah'-ee) 11:21 (x2); 18:7 (x2); 23:13, 14, 15, 16, 23, 25, 27, 29; 24:19; 26:24; variant accepted in BYZ, GOC, SCR, STE at 23:14;
Worship: 14, προσκυνέω (*proskuneo*, pros-koo-neh'-o) 2:2, 8, 11; 4:9, 10; 8:2; 9:18; 14:33; 15:25; 18:26; 20:20; 27:60; 28:9, 17.

Single Words in Decadal Meter
Angel: 20, ἄγγελος (*aggelos*, ang'-el-os) 1:20, 24; 2:13, 19; 4:6, 11; 11:10; 13:39, 41, 49; 16:27; 18:10; 22:30; 24:31, 36; 25:31, 41; 26:53; 28:2, 5;
Blessed: 10, Μακάριοι (*makarioi*, mak-ar'-ee-oi) adjective nominative masculine plural, no degree from μακάριος (*makarios*, mak-ar'-ee-os), 5:3, 4, 5, 6, 7, 8, 9, 10, 11; 13:16;
Blind: 10/17, 10 τυφλοὶ (*tuphloi*, toof-loi') adjective nominative masculine plural, 9:27, 28; 11:5; 15:14; 20:30; 21:14; 23:16, 17, 19, 24; **7** all other cases; τυφλός (*tuphlos*, toof-los') 11:15; 12:22, 31; 15:4 (x3); 23:26; BYZ, GOC, SCR, STE add another at 12:22; variant rejected;
Child: 10, Chapter 2, παιδίον (*paidion*, pahee-dee'-on) 2:8, 9, 11, 13 (x2), 14, 16, 20 (x2), 21;
Child: 20, παιδίον (*paidion*, pahee-dee'-on) 2:8, 9, 11, 13 (x2), 14, 16, 20 (x2), 21; 11:16; 14:21; 15:38; 18:2, 3, 4, 5; 19:13, 14; 21:15;
Crucify: 7, Cross: 3 = 10, Chapter 27, σταυρόω (*stauroo*, stow-ro'-o) 27:22, 23, 26, 31, 35, 38; Cross, σταυρός (*stauros*, stow-ros') 27: 32, 40, 42; Crucify-with, συσταυρόω (*sustauroo*, soos-tow-ro'-o) 27:44;
Depart: 10, ἀναχωρέω (*anachoreo*, an-akh-o-reh'-o) 2:12, 13, 14, 22;

4:12; 9:24; 12:15; 14:13; 15:21; 27:5;
Face: 10, πρόσωπον (*prosopon*, pros'-o-pon) 6:16, 17; 11:10; 16:3; 17:2, 6; 18:10; 22:16; 26:39, 67;
I Came: 10, ἦλθον (*aylthon*, ayl'-thon) 5:17 (x2); 7:25, 27; 9:13; 10:34 (x2), 35; 14:34; 21:1;
Multitude: 50, ὄχλος (*ochlos*, okh'los) 4:25; 5:1; 7:28; 8:1, 18; 9:8, 23, 25, 33, 36; 11:7; 12:15, 23, 46; 13:2 (x2), 34, 36; 14:5, 13, 14, 15, 19 (x2), 22, 23; 15:10, 30, 31, 32, 33, 35, 36, 39; 17:14; 19:2; 20:29, 31; 21:8, 9, 11, 26, 46; 22:33; 23:1; 26:47, 55; 27:15, 20, 24; TIS, VST, WHO missing 12:15; variant rejected;
Pharisee: 30, Φαρισαῖος (*Pharisaios*, far-is-ah'-yos) 3:7; 5:20; 9:11, 14, 34; 12:2, 14, 24, 38; 15:1, 12; 16:1, 6, 11, 12; 19:3; 21:45; 22:15, 34, 41; 23:2, 13, 14, 15, 23, 25, 26, 27, 29; 27:62; BYZ, GOC, SCR, STE include 23:13; variant accepted; BYZ, GOC include 27:41; variant rejected;
Reward: 10, μισθός (*misthos*, mis-thos') 5:12, 46; 6:1, 2, 5, 16; 10:41, 42 (x2); 20:8;
Sabbath: 10, σάββατον (*sabbaton*, sab'-bat-on) 12:1, 2, 5 (x2), 8, 10, 11, 12; 24:20; 28:1; not including εἰς μίαν σαββάτων (28:1) *the first day of the Sabbath*, or Sunday;
Touch: 10, ἅπτω (*hapto*, hap-to') 8:3, 15; 9:20, 21, 29; 14:36 (x3); 17:7; 20:34;
Vineyard: 10, ἀμπελών (*ampelon*, am-pel-ohn') 20:1, 2, 4, 7, 8; 21:28, 33, 39, 40, 41;
Written: 10, γράφω (*grapho*, graf'-o) verb indicative perfect passive 3rd person singular **γέγραπται** 2:5; 4:4, 6, 7, 10; 11:10; 21:13; 26:24, 31; **γεγραμμένην** verb participle perfect passive accusative feminine singular 27:37.

Single Words in Dodecadal Meter
Become: 12, γίνομαι (*ginomai*, ghin'-om-ahee) It might become γένηται verb subjunctive aorist middle 3rd person singular, 5:18; 10:25; 18:12, 13; 21:19; 23:15, 26; 24:20, 21, 32, 34; 26:5;
Demon: 12, δαιμόνιον (*daimonion*, dahee-mon'-ee-on) 7:22; 8:31; 9:33, 34; 10:8; 11:18; 12:24, 27, 28; 17:18;
Elders: 12, πρεσβύτερος (*presbuteros*, pres-boo'-ter-os) 15:2; 16:21; 21:23; 26:3, 47, 57; 27:1, 3, 12, 20, 41; 28:12, BYZ, GOC, SCR, STE add 26:59; variant rejected;
Eye(s): 24, ὀφθαλμός (*ophthalmos*, of-thal-mos') BNT, GNT, TIS, VST, WHO use 2 ὄμμα (*omma*) at 20:34, and BYZ, GOC, SCR, STE have 26;
Fire: 12, πῦρ (*pur*, poor) 3:10, 11, 12; 5:22; 7:19; 13:40, 42, 50; 17:15; 18:8, 9; 25:41; BYZ missing at 3:11; variant rejected;
Peter: 24, Πέτρος (*Petros*, pet'-ros) 4:18; 8:14; 10:2; 14:28, 29; 15:15; 16:16, 18, 22, 23; 17:1, 4, 24, 26; 18:21; 19:27; 26:33, 35, 37, 40, 58, 69, 73, 75; BNT, GNT, TIS, VST, WHO missing at 17:26;
Scribe: 24, γραμματεύς (*grammateus*, gram-mat-yooce') 2:4; 5:20; 7:29; 8:19; 9:3; 12:38; 13:52; 15:1; 16:21; 17:10; 20:18; 21:15; 23:2, 13, 14, 15,

23, 25, 27, 29, 34; 26:3, 57; 27:41; BYZ, GOC, SCR, STE include 23:13 and 26:3; variants accepted;
(Holy) Spirit: 12, πνεῦμα (*pneuma*, pnyoo'-mah) 1:18, 20; 3:11, 16; 4:1; 10:20; 12:28, 31, 32; 26:41; 27:50; 28:19;
Tree: 12, δένδρον (*dendron*, den'-dron) 3:10 (x2); 7:17 (x2), 18 (x2), 19; 12:33 (x3); 13:32; 21:8.

Single Word Repeated 17 Times
Parable: 17, παραβολή (*parabole*, par-ab-ol-ay') 13:3, 10, 13, 18, 24, 31, 33, 34 (x2), 35, 36, 53; 15:15; 21:33, 45; 22:1; 24:32.

Chapter Two
Repetition in the Gospel of Mark

There are numerous opinions on the significance of repetition in the Bible. In his recent book titled *The Book of Genesis: a Biography*, University of California, Berkeley, Hebrew scholar Ronald Hendel writes:

> But a perfect text does not have repetitions that are merely literary or stylistic. To the early interpreters each word has its own special significance. God does not repeat himself or use rhetorical flourishes; his words must always reveal new meanings.[1]

Some may recall that the Bible speaks against repetition, as follows:

> And when you are praying, do not use meaningless repetition, as the Gentiles do, for they suppose that they will be heard for their many words (Matthew 6:7).

Hendel tends to skew the understanding of Genesis with false dichotomies. Here he misrepresents the biblical prohibition against repetition. Matthew 6:7 is speaking against the pagan view that repetition of sacred words gains God's favor.

First, the reader may have observed that the examples in the previous chapter are not doctrinal pronouncements or prayers.

Second, the separation of these phrases in the text hardly lends itself to a form of worship.

Third, the Bible is filled with literary and stylistic repetition that is not accurately defined by Hendel's "merely literary or stylistic."

Fourth, the verse says, "...do not use ***meaningless*** repetition, as the Gentiles do." None of the repetition displayed in this book resembles any repetition practiced by the heathen, or for that matter, practiced by anyone else. Rather, when something is repeated in the Bible there is a purpose.

---

[1] Ronald Hendel, *The Book of Genesis: a Biography*, Princeton University Press, Princeton, NJ, 2013, p. 57.

These Are the Generations

When Hendel brings up the well-known phrase *these are the generations*,[2] which occurs 10 times in Genesis, he leads the reader to believe that this repetition proves the text is not perfect. He establishes his own definition of a perfect text as a straw man which he then knocks down with his own criteria for repetition in the text. Just the opposite is true. In this case, the repetition proves the text is perfect. The text still preserves the phrase written by Moses in decadal meter 3,500 years ago, as follows:

These are the generations 10 times in Genesis
    These are the generations .... אֵלֶּה תוֹלְדוֹת (Gen. 2:4)
    These are the generations .... אֵלֶּה תּוֹלְדֹת (Gen. 6:9)
    And these are the generations .... וְאֵלֶּה תּוֹלְדֹת (Gen. 10:1)
    These are the generations .... אֵלֶּה תּוֹלְדֹת (Gen. 11:10)
    And these are the generations .... וְאֵלֶּה תּוֹלְדֹת (Gen. 11:27)
    And these are the generations .... וְאֵלֶּה תֹּלְדֹת (Gen. 25:12)
    And these are the generations .... וְאֵלֶּה תּוֹלְדֹת (Gen. 25:19)
    And these are the generations .... וְאֵלֶּה תֹּלְדוֹת (Gen. 36:1)
    And these are the generations .... וְאֵלֶּה תֹּלְדוֹת (Gen. 36:9)
    These are the generations .... אֵלֶּה תֹּלְדוֹת (Gen. 37:2)

The importance of this particular phrase in Genesis will be addressed again in Chapters Eight and Nine and the Conclusion. Hendel writes:

> "These are the generations of…" occurs roughly 10 times in Genesis, creating an internal structure within the book. The last clause, "when they were created," coming after "heaven and earth," echoes the initial sequence, "God created heaven and earth," in Genesis 1:1, thus framing the whole Creation account.

The reader should understand that when Hendel uses the word *God*, he is not acknowledging the possibility of divine communication in the text, or that Moses existed, or even the existence of God.

On the one hand, Hendel ridicules repetition as a flaw in what should be a perfect text, and on the other he recognizes repetition as a literary device that frames the text. He makes no mention of Moses' decadal cadence as identified by Cassuto in Genesis more than 70 years earlier.

---

[2] Ibid.

There is some unintended truth to Hendel's statement that, "God does not repeat himself...his words must always reveal new meanings." In terms of divine pronouncements, the 2 lists of the 10 commandments in Exodus and Deuteronomy, 3 accounts of creation in the beginning of Genesis, 2 histories of Israel, 4 formulas for the Lord's Supper, 2 formulas for the Lord's Prayer, 2 different accounts of Christ's temptation, 4 different Gospels, etc., do not repeat the same words. For example, even though there are 92 verses in the New Testament that contain the same form of the word for baptism, not one verse repeats the same words. Each statement is perfect and complete in itself.

This introduction is intended to give some perspective on what is taking place when the repetition in Mark is compared to that of Matthew. Repetition functions as its own unique genre in the Bible. Each writer adapts this genre to his own style. Exegetes more astute than this writer will be able to give a more complete explanation of the data we now present.

Heptadic Meter in Mark

The following sets of phrases appear in both Matthew and Mark, even though the contexts in which the phrases appear are different. One of these two Gospel writers is fully aware of the other writer's heptadic meter, and is copying it into his own Gospel, or at least that is what seems to be happening. There are no variants.

To Jerusalem

In Matthew we find the following heptadic pattern:

To Jerusalem 7 times in the Gospel of Matthew
    To Jerusalem............εἰς Ἱεροσόλυμα (Matt. 2:1 BNT)
    To Jerusalem............εἰς Ἱεροσόλυμα (Matt. 5:35 BNT)
    To Jerusalem............εἰς Ἱεροσόλυμα (Matt. 16:21 BNT)
    To Jerusalem............εἰς Ἱεροσόλυμα (Matt. 20:17 BNT)
    To Jerusalem............εἰς Ἱεροσόλυμα (Matt. 20:18 BNT)
    To Jerusalem............εἰς Ἱεροσόλυμα (Matt. 21:1 BNT)
    To Jerusalem............εἰς Ἱεροσόλυμα (Matt. 21:10 BNT)

In Mark we find the same pattern:

To Jerusalem 7 times in the Gospel of Mark
    To Jerusalem............εἰς Ἱεροσόλυμα (Mark 10:32 BNT)
    To Jerusalem............εἰς Ἱεροσόλυμα (Mark 10:33 BNT)
    To Jerusalem............εἰς Ἱεροσόλυμα (Mark 11:1 BNT)*
    To Jerusalem............εἰς Ἱεροσόλυμα (Mark 11:11 BNT)
    To Jerusalem............εἰς Ἱεροσόλυμα (Mark 11:15 BNT)

To Jerusalem............εἰς Ἱεροσόλυμα (Mark 11:27 BNT)
To Jerusalem............εἰς Ἱεροσόλυμα (Mark 15:41 BNT)
*BYZ, GOC, SCR, STE use Septuagint spelling for *Jerusalem* (Ἱερουσαλήμ).

How is it possible that 2 authors repeat the same phrase in heptadic meter? Contextually-speaking, Matthew and Mark differ as to where the verses with the phrase *to Jerusalem* appear. For example, Matthew 2:1 is speaking about the Wise Men, and Mark does not address the subject. Matthew 5:35 is a quote from the Sermon on the Mount, but Mark does not include this phrase in his account. The last 5 phrases in Matthew deal with events leading to the Passion. Mark's phrases address 6 events prior to the Passion and one during the Passion. Hence, the Hebraic meter is independent of context in these 2 Gospels. With 7 repetitions in both Gospels, obviously someone is copying someone, and for some reason. Does Mark know that Matthew wrote *to Jerusalem* 7 times, or is it vice-versa? From this example and others that follow, it appears in some instances that Mark is copying Matthew. Mark places his meter within chapters 10, 11, and 15, while Matthew takes 20 chapters to complete the same meter. Another possible solution will be offered later in this chapter.

As noted above, BYZ, GOC, SCR, and STE use the Septuagint spelling for *Jerusalem* (Ἱερουσαλήμ) in Mark 11:1. This will become important when we examine the Gospel of Luke. Luke uses the same phrase 12 times, but 7 of the phrases follow the Septuagint spelling for *Jerusalem*. Why would Luke do that unless he is trying to emphasize a heptad within dodecadal meter, as does Matthew? John, with only 4 repetitions, does not use this phrase in Hebraic cadence. All 4 Gospels contain a total of 30 repetitions. The change in spelling may indicate that the Byzantine manuscripts are more influenced by the Septuagint, or that the Western texts are inferior because they attempted to correct the spelling. However, there is still the enigma of 2 spellings for *Jerusalem* in Luke.

Cast out Demons
In Matthew we saw the following:

Cast out demons 7 times in the Gospel of Matthew
cast out **demons** (Matt. 7:22)
And when the **demon** was cast out (Matt. 9:33)
He casts out **demons** (Matt. 9:34)
You cast out **demons** (Matt. 10:8)
He casts out **demons** (Matt. 12:24)
I cast out **demons** (Matt. 12:27)
I cast out **demons** (Matt. 12:28)

In Mark we find the same meter with no variants:

Cast out demons 7 times in the Gospel of Mark
    And casting out **demons** (Mark 1:39)
    And to cast out **demons** (Mark 3:15)
    He casts out **demons** (Mark 3:22)
    He would cast out the **demon** (Mark 7:26)
    He was casting out **demons** (Mark 9:38)
    He had cast out seven **demons** (Mark 16:9)
    They shall cast out **demons** (Mark 16:17)

    καὶ τὰ **δαιμόνια** ἐκβάλλων (Mark 1:39 BNT)
    καὶ ἐκβάλλειν τὰ **δαιμόνια** (Mark 3:15 BNT)
    ἐκβάλλει τὰ **δαιμόνια** (Mark 3:22 BNT)
    τὸ **δαιμόνιον** ἐκβάλῃ (Mark 7:26 BNT)
    ἐκβάλλοντα **δαιμόνια** (Mark 9:38 BNT)
    ἐκβεβλήκει ἑπτὰ **δαιμόνια** (Mark 16:9 BNT)
    δαιμόνια ἐκβαλοῦσιν (Mark 16:17 BNT)

Mark adds 2 more examples that include the word *many*. Thus, Mark repeats the same phrase 9 times, but makes the distinction of a subset of 7 by changing 2 of the phrases (Mark 1:34 and 6:13) in a manner not seen in Matthew.

    And He cast out **many** demons (Mark 1:34)
    And they cast out **many** demons (Mark 6:13)

    καὶ δαιμόνια **πολλὰ** ἐξέβαλεν (Mark 1:34 BNT)
    καὶ δαιμόνια **πολλὰ** ἐξέβαλλον (Mark 6:13 BNT)

The Unclean Spirit(s)
    Where Matthew says *demon-possessed* 7 times, Mark repeats the phrase *the unclean spirit(s)* 7 times. The Greek word for *spirit* is bolded in the following:

The unclean spirit(s) 7 times in the Gospel of Mark
    The unclean spirit........τὸ **πνεῦμα** τὸ ἀκάθαρτον (Mark 1:26 BNT)
    The unclean spirits...τοῖς **πνεύμασι** τοῖς ἀκαθάρτοις (Mark 1:27 BNT)
    The unclean spirits......τὰ **πνεύματα** τὰ ἀκάθαρτα (Mark 3:11 BNT)
    The unclean spirit........τὸ **πνεῦμα** τὸ ἀκάθαρτον (Mark 5:8 BNT)
    The unclean spirit........τὰ **πνεύματα** τὰ ἀκάθαρτα (Mark 5:13 BNT)
    The unclean spirits...τῶν **πνευμάτων** τῶν ἀκαθάρτων (Mark 6:7 BNT)
    The unclean spirits.....τῷ **πνεύματι** τῷ ἀκαθάρτῳ (Mark 9:25 BNT)

This phrase is a subset of a larger group of 11. The point of differentiation is that Mark places an introductory article (*the*) before *spirit* and *unclean* in 7 of the phrases. Again Mark creates a heptadic subset within a longer list, as shown earlier.

John and *Baptism*

Both Matthew and Mark repeat 7 statements about *John* and *baptism*. As in the above, Matthew is more structured, and Mark's repetition is irregular. There are no variants.

John the Baptist 7 times in the Gospel of Matthew
    John the Baptist..........Ἰωάννου ὁ **βαπτιστὴς** (Matt. 3:1)
    John the Baptist.......Ἰωάννου τοῦ **βαπτιστοῦ** (Matt. 11:11)
    John the Baptist.......Ἰωάννου τοῦ **βαπτιστοῦ** (Matt. 11:12)
    John the Baptist..........Ἰωάννης ὁ **βαπτιστής** (Matt. 14:2)
    John the Baptist.......Ἰωάννου τοῦ **βαπτιστοῦ** (Matt. 14:8)
    John the Baptist.......Ἰωάννην τὸν **βαπτιστήν** (Matt. 16:14)
    John the Baptist.......Ἰωάννου τοῦ **βαπτιστοῦ** (Matt. 17:13)

John and *baptism* 7 times in the Gospel of Mark
    John the **Baptist** (Mark 1:4)
    And was **baptized** by John in the Jordan (Mark 1:9)
    That John the **Baptist** was risen (Mark 6:14)
    The head of John the **Baptist** (Mark 6:24)
    The head of John the **Baptist** (Mark 6:25)
    John the **Baptist** (Mark 8:28)
    The **baptism** of John (Mark 11:30)

    Ἰωάννης [ὁ] **βαπτίζων** (Mark 1:4 BNT)
    καὶ **ἐβαπτίσθη** εἰς τὸν Ἰορδάνην ὑπὸ Ἰωάννου (Mark 1:9 BNT)
    ὅτι Ἰωάννης ὁ **βαπτίζων** ἐγήγερται (Mark 6:14 BNT)
τὴν κεφαλὴν Ἰωάννου τοῦ **βαπτίζοντος** (Mark 6:24 BNT)
τὴν κεφαλὴν Ἰωάννου τοῦ **βαπτιστοῦ** (Mark 6:25 BNT)
    Ἰωάννην τὸν **βαπτιστήν** (Mark 8:28 BNT)
    τὸ **βάπτισμα** τὸ Ἰωάννου (Mark 11:30 BNT)

With no comparable examples of authors adopting each other's Hebraic cadence, we are witnessing a literary phenomenon, an explanation for which we can only offer as educated speculation, but speculation nonetheless.

The Kingdom of God

The first chapter noted that Matthew used the word *heaven* in at least 3 different heptadic repetitions. Mark prefers the phrase *the kingdom of God*, which Matthew does not use in Mosaic cadence. Although it has some similarities, Matthew has *the kingdom of heaven is like* in heptadic repetition, but Mark does not use the phrase. *The kingdom of heaven* in Matthew versus *the kingdom of God* in Mark shows no indication of the so-called Q source or Markan Priority. But they are both following Mosaic cadence.

There is a well-known variant in Mark 1:14 (*the kingdom of God*, τῆς βασιλείας τοῦ Θεοῦ) that is found in BYZ, GOC, SCR, and STE, which is rejected. Adding that variant would result in 15 and not 14 repetitions (or twice 7).

The kingdom of God 14 times in the Gospel of Mark
    The kingdom of God......ἡ βασιλεία τοῦ θεοῦ (Mark 1:15 BNT)
    The kingdom of God....τῆς βασιλείας τοῦ θεοῦ (Mark 4:11 BNT)
    The kingdom of God......ἡ βασιλεία τοῦ θεοῦ (Mark 4:26 BNT)
    The kingdom of God...τὴν βασιλείαν τοῦ θεοῦ (Mark 4:30 BNT)
    The kingdom of God...τὴν βασιλείαν τοῦ θεου (Mark 9:1 BNT)
    The kingdom of God...τὴν βασιλείαν τοῦ θεοῦ (Mark 9:47 BNT)
    The kingdom of God......ἡ βασιλεία τοῦ θεου (Mark 10:14 BNT)
    The kingdom of God...τὴν βασιλείαν τοῦ θεοῦ (Mark 10:15 BNT)
    The kingdom of God...τὴν βασιλείαν τοῦ θεοῦ (Mark 10:23 BNT)
    The kingdom of God...τὴν βασιλείαν τοῦ θεοῦ (Mark 10:24 BNT)
    The kingdom of God...τὴν βασιλείαν τοῦ θεοῦ (Mark 10:25 BNT)
    The kingdom of God...τῆς βασιλείας τοῦ θεοῦ (Mark 12:34 BNT)
    The kingdom of God.....τῇ βασιλείᾳ τοῦ θεου (Mark 14:25 BNT)
    The kingdom of God...τὴν βασιλείαν τοῦ θεοῦ (Mark 15:43 BNT)

The above meter appears to be Mark's response to *My* or *your Father who is in the heavens* that repeats 14 times in Matthew. Although they did not copy each other's words, they both copied the same meter. But whom were they copying?

Decadal Meter in Mark
Son of Man
Matthew repeats the phrase *Son of David* 10 times, whereas Mark repeats *Son of Man* 10 times. However, previously we saw that Mark separates 7 repetitions of *cast out demons* as a subset within 9 phrases. He also separates 10 repetitions of *Son of Man* (ὁ υἱὸς τοῦ ἀνθρώπου) as a subset within 16 phrases. The other 6 have different case endings. Perhaps this is Mark's particular technique when he incorporates Mosaic cadence in his Gospel. Perhaps he adjusted his Gospel to match the meter in Matthew. All 4 Gospels repeat their phrases in the 7, 10, or 12 meter Hebraic cadence, as identified by Cassuto and found in Revelation. These writers are all following the same genre that originates with Moses in Genesis. Observing how each writer applies Mosaic style becomes increasingly fascinating.

Son of Man 10 times in the Gospel of Mark
    Son of Man......ὁ υἱὸς τοῦ ἀνθρώπου (Mark 2:10 BNT)
    Son of Man......ὁ υἱὸς τοῦ ἀνθρώπου (Mark 2:28 BNT)
    Son of Man......ὁ υἱὸς τοῦ ἀνθρώπου (Mark 8:38 BNT)

Son of Man......ὁ υἱὸς τοῦ ἀνθρώπου (Mark 9:9 BNT)
Son of Man......ὁ υἱὸς τοῦ ἀνθρώπου (Mark 9:31 BNT)
Son of Man......ὁ υἱὸς τοῦ ἀνθρώπου (Mark 10:33 BNT)
Son of Man......ὁ υἱὸς τοῦ ἀνθρώπου (Mark 10:45 BNT)
Son of Man......ὁ μὲν υἱὸς τοῦ ἀνθρώπου (Mark 14:21 BNT)
Son of Man......ὁ υἱὸς τοῦ ἀνθρώπου (Mark 14:21 BNT)
Son of Man......ὁ υἱὸς τοῦ ἀνθρώπου (Mark 14:41 BNT)

They or *He Follow Him*

This phrase occurs 10 times in the Gospel of Mark, whereas it appears 14 times (a double heptad) in the Gospel of Matthew, and includes a decadal subset of phrases beginning with *they* (as shown in Chapter One).

As more data is examined in this study, it will become apparent that Matthew's Gospel has the widest range, the most unique examples, and more phrases in Hebraic meter than the other Gospels. Mark has the fewest.

This leads to the conclusion that the other Gospels are influenced by Matthew. If they were all copying from the mythical Q source (a rather humorous title for an imaginary text), what is the explanation for the variations and similarities in metered phrases from one Gospel to another? There must be another source rather than the imaginary Q source or the so-called Markan Priority.

They or *he follow Him* 10 times in the Gospel of Mark*
    They **followed** Him..........ἠκολούθησαν αὐτῷ (Mark 1:18 BNT)
    He **followed** Him..........ἠκολούθησεν αὐτῷ (Mark 2:14 BNT)
    They were **following** Him.........ἠκολούθουν αὐτῷ (Mark 2:15 BNT)
    He was **following** Him........ἠκολούθει αὐτῷ (Mark 5:24 BNT)
    They **follow** Him............ἀκολουθοῦσιν αὐτῷ (Mark 6:1 BNT)
    He was **following** Him.........ἠκολούθει αὐτῷ (Mark 10:52 BNT)**
    You **follow** Him............ἀκολουθήσατε αὐτῷ (Mark 14:13 BNT)
    He was **following** Him...συνηκολούθει αὐτῷ (Mark 14:51 BNT)
    He **followed** Him..........ἠκολούθησεν αὐτῷ (Mark 14:54 BNT)
    They were **following** Him.........ἠκολούθουν αὐτῷ (Mark 15:41 BNT)

*The Eastern and the Western texts each have 10 repetitions. Western texts were chosen. *Him* added in 3:7 BYZ, GOC, SCR, STE is rejected.
**He was following Jesus* in 10:52 BYZ, GOC, SCR, STE is rejected.

To His Disciples

Perhaps one of the most amazing similarities between Matthew and Mark is that both use the phrase *to His disciples* 10 times, as seen in the previous chapter. There is a variant reading at Mark 4:34. In this verse only BYZ, SCR, and STE have *to His disciples* instead of *to his own disciples* (τοῖς ἰδίοις μαθηταῖς). Notice that the Western texts have the longer and incorrect reading here. It is clear that Mark has a preference for this particular phrase; he is following Hebraic cadence, and a majority of the ancient manuscripts have the correct reading to complete the meter.

To His disciples 10 times in the Gospel of Mark
    To His disciples......τοῖς μαθηταῖς αὐτοῦ (Mark 2:15 BNT)
    To His disciples......τοῖς μαθηταῖς αὐτοῦ (Mark 2:16 BNT)
    To His disciples......τοῖς μαθηταῖς αὐτοῦ (Mark 3:9 BNT)
    To His disciples......τοῖς μαθηταῖς αὐτου (Mark 4:34 BYZ)*
    To His disciples......τοῖς μαθηταῖς [αὐτοῦ] (Mark 6:41 BNT)
    To His disciples......τοῖς μαθηταῖς αὐτοῦ (Mark 8:6 BNT)
    To His disciples......τοῖς μαθηταῖς αὐτοῦ (Mark 8:34 BNT)
    To His disciples......τοῖς μαθηταῖς αὐτοῦ (Mark 10:23 BNT)
    To His disciples......τοῖς μαθηταῖς αὐτοῦ (Mark 14:32 BNT)
    To His disciples......τοῖς μαθηταῖς αὐτοῦ (Mark 16:7 BNT)

*BYZ, SCR, STE have *to His disciples* at 4:34. Remaining (Western) texts have *to his own disciples* (τοῖς ἰδίοις μαθηταῖς), which is rejected.

Metered Introduction to Conversation: Anaphoric Phrases

The following sequences can be understood as traditional Hebraic metered introduction to conversation in Mark. The assumption is that Mark is intentionally writing in Hebraic meter; therefore the appropriate and felicitous variants are selected that complete the meter. Proportionally, Mark appears to contain more metered phrases as introductions to conversation than the 3 other Gospels.

And He Said to Him or *Them*

As in Matthew and Genesis, many of the Mosaic phrases in Mark are found in mundane communication (anaphoric phrases). In Matthew we observed *and he said to him* 7 times, and in Mark we find the identical heptadic phrase.

And he said to him 7 times in the Gospel of Matthew*
    And he said to him............καὶ λέγει αὐτῷ (Matt. 4:6 BNT)
    And he said to him............Καὶ λέγει αὐτῷ (Matt. 8:4 BNT)
    And he said to him............Καὶ λέγει αὐτῷ (Matt. 8:7 BNT)**
    And he said to him............Καὶ λέγει αὐτῷ (Matt. 8:20 BNT)
    And he said to him............καὶ λέγει αὐτῷ (Matt. 9:9 BNT)
    And he said to him............καὶ λέγει αὐτῷ (Matt. 14:31 BNT)
    And he said to him............καὶ λέγει αὐτῷ (Matt. 22:12 BNT)

**And he said to him*, καὶ λέγει αὐτῷ in Matthew 4:9 is missing in BNT, GNT, TIS, WHO, which have καὶ εἶπεν αὐτῷ, another way of saying *and he said to him*, and therefore is not included in the above example.

**TIS and WHO have εἶπεν (*he said*) instead of λέγει (*he said*) at Matt. 8:7.

And he said to him 7 times in the Gospel of Mark*
    And he said to him............καὶ λέγει αὐτῷ (Mark 1:41 BNT)**
    And he said to him............καὶ λέγει αὐτῷ (Mark 1:44 BNT)
    And he said to him............καὶ λέγει αὐτῷ (Mark 2:14 BNT)
    And he said to him............καὶ λέγει αὐτῷ (Mark 7:28 BNT)
    And he said to him............καὶ λέγει αὐτῷ (Mark 7:34 BNT)
    And he said to him............καὶ λέγει αὐτῷ (Mark 14:30 BNT)
    And he said to him............καὶ λέγει αὐτῷ (Mark 14:61 BNT)
*BYZ, GOC, SCR, STE are missing καὶ λέγει αὐτῷ at Mark 5:9; variant accepted.
**Only TIS is missing καὶ λέγει αὐτῷ at Mark 1:41.

A similar example in Mark of Hebraic metered introduction to conversation is the phrase *And he said to them*, shown here in heptadic (καὶ εἶπεν αὐτοῖς) and double heptadic (καὶ λέγει αὐτοῖς) meter. The phrase also occurs in dodecadal meter in Mark (καὶ ἔλεγεν αὐτοῖς), listed later in this section.

And he said to them 7 times in the Gospel of Mark*
    And he said to them......καὶ εἶπεν αὐτοῖς (Mark 1:17 BNT)
    And he said to them......καὶ εἶπεν αὐτοῖς (Mark 2:19 BNT)
    And he said to them......καὶ εἶπεν αὐτοῖς (Mark 4:40 BNT)
    And he said to them......καὶ εἶπεν αὐτοῖς (Mark 9:29 BNT)
    And he said to them......καὶ εἶπεν αὐτοῖς (Mark 10:14 BNT)
    And he said to them......καὶ εἶπεν αὐτοῖς (Mark 14:24 BNT)
    And he said to them......καὶ εἶπεν αὐτοῖς (Mark 16:15 BNT)
*BYZ, GOC, SCR, STE add 6:31 λέγει (*he said*) instead of εἶπεν (*he said*).

And he said to them 14 times in the Gospel of Mark*
    And he said to them.........καὶ λέγει αὐτοῖς (Mark 1:38 BNT)
    And he said to them.........καὶ λέγει αὐτοῖς (Mark 3:4 BNT)
    And he said to them.........καὶ λέγει αὐτοῖς (Mark 4:13 BNT)
    And he said to them.........καὶ λέγει αὐτοῖς (Mark 4:35 BNT)
    And he said to them.........καὶ λέγει αὐτοῖς (Mark 6:50 BNT)
    And he said to them.........καὶ λέγει αὐτοῖς (Mark 7:18 BNT)
    And he said to them.........καὶ λέγει αὐτοῖς (Mark 9:35 BNT)
    And he said to them.........καὶ λέγει αὐτοῖς (Mark 10:11 BNT)
    And he said to them.........καὶ λέγει αὐτοῖς (Mark 11:2 BNT)
    And he said to them.........καὶ λέγει αὐτοῖς (Mark 12:16 BNT)
    And he said to them.........καὶ λέγει αὐτοῖς (Mark 14:13 BNT)
    And he said to them.........καὶ λέγει αὐτοῖς (Mark 14:27 BNT)
    And he said to them.........καὶ λέγει αὐτοῖς (Mark 14:34 BNT)
    And he said to them.........καὶ λέγει αὐτοῖς (Mark 14:41 BNT)
*καὶ λέγει αὐτοῖς is also found in 2:25 and 6:31 in BNT, GNT, TIS, WHO. It should be Καὶ αὐτὸς ἔλεγεν αὐτοῖς as found in BYZ, GOC, SCR, STE, VST 2:25, and καὶ εἶπεν αὐτοῖς as found in BYZ, GOC, SCR, STE 6:31.

At times the variants appear to favor the Byzantine texts, but this is probably because Nestle–Aland and the United Bible Society were too aggressive in following the Alexandrian or Western manuscripts. However, in general, the range of variant readings in the 4 Gospels tends to show their occurrence is indiscriminant. BNT is a little more consistent in the Gospels. STE is superior in Revelation. TIS is often preferred in the Gospel of John. This will become more apparent in future chapters as variant preferences are examined. The copyists appear to be less cognizant of Mosaic meter in the Gospels than were the translators of the Septuagint when they translated the Hebrew Old Testament.

As shown above, Mark has the identical heptadic phrase *and he said to him* as Matthew. How is this humanly possible unless Mark is aware of Matthew's cadence and is copying the meter? According to Bruce M. Metzger, Westcott and Hort regarded Western Greek manuscripts as almost totally corrupt, and selected those readings which were shorter, or what they called 'Western non-interpolations.'[3] Nestle-Aland, or BNT, favors these shorter Western readings. Based on this methodology, the assumption is that contemporary translations such as NASB, NIV, and ESV presumably have shorter and more accurate readings than the Eastern texts of the KJV, which are assumed to be expanded by the editorial additions of copyists. This is true in a number of cases, but they ignore 'Eastern non-interpolations' in different places. Here the supposedly longer texts, BYZ, GOC, SCR, and STE, are actually shorter, and are missing the phrase *and he said to him* at Mark 5:9. Examples of longer texts in BNT occur throughout the first 5 chapters of this book.

Chapter Eight will more fully address Cassuto's understanding of Hebraic meter in Genesis. For the present, it is useful to note here that the following meter from Genesis is strikingly similar to the above in Matthew and Mark. The phrase *and he said to him* appears 17 times in Genesis. As stated in the first chapter, 17 is usually a combination of 10 and 7. In this particular sequence, God speaks 7 times and man speaks 10 times. The beautiful part about the Old Testament is that there are far fewer variant readings in the Hebrew than the Greek texts. In other words, the 3,500-year-old Hebrew text is more static because there are fewer copies and the Hebrew scribes took more care in reproducing their scrolls.

---

[3] Bruce M. Metzger, *The Text of the New Testament: Its Transmission, Corruption, and Restoration*, 2d ed., Oxford University Press, New York and Oxford, 1968.

It does not seem possible that Matthew and Mark were aware of the same numeric patterns in each other's texts, and that one copied the other, though such speculation was stated earlier. Yet, how do we explain the existence of the same metered phrases in the 2 Gospels? The answer must be that they were not copying each other, or the mythical Q source, but that they were copying Moses. Another possibility is that the same Holy Spirit who directed Moses also directed Matthew and Mark. In this case, when writing their Gospels, Matthew and Mark may or may not have been aware of the meter in their own or other Scriptural texts.

It appears that the Hebrew text was examined with such intensity at the time of Christ that the authors were aware that God spoke *and he said to him* 7 times in Genesis. Thus Matthew and Mark placed this heptadic pattern in their Gospels, independent of each other, as a traditional Hebraic genre. They could not have copied this pattern from the Septuagint because the Septuagint is not consistent in translating *and he said to him* from the Hebrew into Greek. The only source for this phrase in a heptad is the Genesis Hebrew. Of course we are told by higher critics that the apostles, except for Paul, could not read Hebrew.

The point is that Moses is the real Q source for this meter. In this study, the heptadic phrase *and he said to him* was first observed in Matthew. Then a search was made for the same phrase in Mark, followed by Genesis. This heptad and other numerically-ordered phrases were found in Genesis by first identifying them in Revelation and/or the Gospels.

There is no question about the meaning of the words in the text. However, the data assembled in this book will confirm again and again how far we are from understanding the manner in which the text of the Bible was assembled.

For the reader not familiar with Hebrew, the text reads from right to left. The first word ו (*and*), pronounced "wāw," or "vahv," looks like a candy cane. The next word אָמַר *'amar* is *he said*, and לוֹ (*lᵉô*) is actually 2 words, *to him*. Hebrew can be much more compact than English. Notice that the phrase appears 17 times with an internal division of 7 and 10. WTT stands for Codex Leningradensis, also known as the Masoretic Text. Every time this data is rechecked, there is a renewed sense of amazement.

And He said to him 7 times in Genesis (God speaking)
    And He said to him.......... וַיֹּאמֶר לוֹ (Gen. 3:9 WTT)
    And He said to him.......... וַיֹּאמֶר לוֹ (Gen. 4:15 WTT)
    And He said to him.......... וַיֹּאמֶר לוֹ (Gen. 15:5 WTT)
    And He said to him.......... וַיֹּאמֶר לוֹ (Gen. 20:3 WTT)
    And He said to him.......... וַיֹּאמֶר לוֹ (Gen. 31:24 WTT)

    And He said to him..........וַיֹּאמֶר־לוֹ (Gen. 35:10 WTT)
    And He said to him..........וַיֹּאמֶר־לוֹ (Gen. 35:11 WTT)

And he said to him 10 times in Genesis (man speaking)
    And he said to him.......... וַיֹּאמֶר לוֹ (Gen. 20:9 WTT)
    And he said to him.......... וַיֹּאמֶר לוֹ (Gen. 27:32 WTT)
    And he said to him.......... וַיֹּאמֶר לוֹ (Gen. 28:1 WTT)
    And he said to him.......... וַיֹּאמֶר לוֹ (Gen. 29:14 WTT)
    And he said to him.......... וַיֹּאמֶר לוֹ (Gen. 37:10 WTT)
    And he said to him.......... וַיֹּאמֶר לוֹ (Gen. 37:13 WTT)
    And he said to him.......... וַיֹּאמֶר לוֹ (Gen. 37:14 WTT)
    And he said to him.......... וַיֹּאמֶר לוֹ (Gen. 40:9 WTT)
    And he said to him.......... וַיֹּאמֶר לוֹ (Gen. 40:12 WTT)
    And he said to him.......... וַיֹּאמֶר לוֹ (Gen. 47:29 WTT)

Many examples from the Hebrew text will be introduced in Chapter Eight, but the primary focus of this chapter is the Gospel of Mark.

The following is the third Greek variation of the phrase *And he said to them* (καὶ ἔλεγεν αὐτοῖς), which demonstrates a dodecadal cadence in Mark.

And he said to them 12 times in the Gospel of Mark
    And he said to them.........καὶ ἔλεγεν αὐτοῖς (Mark 2:27 BNT)
    And he said to them.........καὶ ἔλεγεν αὐτοῖς (Mark 4:2 BNT)
    And he said to them.........καὶ ἔλεγεν αὐτοῖς (Mark 4:11 BNT)
    And he said to them.........Καὶ ἔλεγεν αὐτοῖς (Mark 4:21 BNT)
    And he said to them.........Καὶ ἔλεγεν αὐτοῖς (Mark 4:24 BNT)
    And he said to them.........καὶ ἔλεγεν αὐτοῖς (Mark 6:4 BNT)*
    And he said to them.........καὶ ἔλεγεν αὐτοῖς (Mark 6:10 BNT)
    And he said to them.........καὶ λεγεν αὐτοῖς (Mark 7:9 BNT)
    And he said to them.........καὶ ἔλεγεν αὐτοῖς (Mark 8:21 BNT)
    And he said to them.........Καὶ ἔλεγεν αὐτοῖς (Mark 9:1 BNT)
    And he said to them.........καὶ ἔλεγεν αὐτοῖς (Mark 9:31 BNT)
    And he said to them.........καὶ ἔλεγεν αὐτοῖς (Mark 11:17 BNT)**

*BYZ, GOC, SCR, STE have *But he said to them*, ἔλεγεν δὲ αὐτοῖς; variant rejected.
**BYZ, GOC, SCR, STE have *saying unto them*, λέγων αὐτοῖς; variant rejected.

Following BNT, GNT, TIS, VST, and WHO results in 12 phrases. The above meter leads to the importance of details such as the correct *and*, *the*, and *but* in the text that might otherwise seem insignificant. These details also reveal the precision with which the text was written and has come down to us nearly 2,000 years later.

And Jesus Answered and Said

    The following repetition of phrases also appears in both Matthew and Mark:

But Jesus answered and said 7 times in the Gospel of Matthew
    But Jesus **answered** and said (Matt. 3:15)
    But Jesus **answered** and said (Matt. 16:17)
    But Jesus **answered** and said (Matt. 17:17)
    But Jesus **answered** and said (Matt. 20:22)
    But Jesus **answered** and said (Matt. 21:21)
    But Jesus **answered** and said (Matt. 21:24)
    But Jesus **answered** and said (Matt. 22:29)

And Jesus answered and said 7 times in the Gospel of Mark
    And Jesus **answered** and said (Mark 10:5 BYZ)
    And Jesus **answered** and said (Mark 11:14 BYZ)
    And Jesus **answered** and said (Mark 11:29 BYZ)
    And Jesus **answered** and said (Mark 12:17 BYZ)
    And Jesus **answered** and said (Mark 12:24 BYZ)
    And Jesus **answered** and said (Mark 13:2 BYZ)
    And Jesus **answered** and said (Mark 14:48 BYZ)

    Καὶ **ἀποκριθεὶς** ὁ Ἰησοῦς εἶπεν αὐτοῖς (Mark 10:5 BYZ)
    Καὶ **ἀποκριθεὶς** ὁ Ἰησοῦς εἶπεν αὐτῇ (Mark 11:14 BYZ)
Ὁ δὲ Ἰησοῦς **ἀποκριθεὶς** εἶπεν αὐτοῖς (Mark 11:29 BYZ)
    Καὶ **ἀποκριθεὶς** ὁ Ἰησοῦς εἶπεν αὐτοῖς (Mark 12:17 BYZ)
    Καὶ **ἀποκριθεὶς** ὁ Ἰησοῦς εἶπεν αὐτοῖς (Mark 12:24 BYZ)
Καὶ ὁ Ἰησοῦς **ἀποκριθεὶς** εἶπεν αὐτῷ (Mark 13:2 BYZ)
    Καὶ **ἀποκριθεὶς** ὁ Ἰησοῦς εἶπεν αὐτοῖς (Mark 14:48 BYZ)

There are numerous variants in these phrases from Mark. The above complete heptad is only found in BYZ, SCR, and STE, which also represent the majority of existing ancient manuscripts. By comparison, Matthew is more structured and Mark changes the word order. As noted in the previous chapter, the number of variants increases when there is a change in word order. The word for *answered* is bolded above in Mark. Again Mark appears to follow Matthew's lead. Similar to the first example in this chapter, Mark's phrases are found within a 5-chapter span, but Matthew takes 19 chapters to complete his list.

Jesus Said to Them

    The following example, *and Jesus said to them*, has the same translation as the above, but contains a different verb for *he said*. Mark also has some irregular words, such as *answered* and *indignant* (italicized in the English list, below). These 10 phrases were found in the Gospel of Mark with a computer search in Greek for the words *Jesus said to them*. The following assumptions directed the search for metered phrases in the Greek text. First, we know in advance that Mosaic meter is repeated 7, 10, or 12 times. Second, mundane introductions to conversation (anaphoric phrases) are often set in Mosaic meter. Third, one of the first places to look for Mosaic meter is in anaphoric phrases. Thus, the assumption was that the phrase *and Jesus said to them* might be set in Hebraic meter. It is.

However, this meter is irregular and changes the word order, which is typical of Mark. Therefore, the question could be raised as to whether or not this particular example is coincidental. But what is the explanation for variant readings falling into place? Mark 11:29, below, has the word *answered* in Greek, and is a variant reading. It appears in BYZ, GOC, SCR, and STE, but is missing from BNT, GNT, TIS, VST, and WHO. Its inclusion also completes 7 repetitions of *and Jesus answered and said*, listed earlier in this chapter. In other words, it is necessary to follow the reading in BYZ, GOC, SCR, and STE in order to complete 2 overlapping meters. The reader is not expected to keep track of such details. The text is so tightly constructed with overlapping meter, that a change in one phrase effects a change in a series of related phrases. This is nearly the same format as a long word in a crossword puzzle that crosses 2 or 3 other words.

Assuming (based on the above) that Mark 11:29 is correct, there is the added inclination to follow BYZ, GOC, SCR, and STE at Mark 12:24, which read ὁ Ἰησοῦς εἶπεν αὐτοῖς (*Jesus said to them*), instead of BNT, GNT, TIS, VST, and WHO, which read ἔφη αὐτοῖς ὁ Ἰησοῦς, a different way of saying the same thing. How do such errors occur between manuscripts? The answer might be quite simple. Suppose there is a room with a number of scribes taking dictation in order to produce multiple copies. The words *Jesus said to them* are heard, and one of the scribes writes down the correct meaning with the wrong words. Considering that more than 5,800 ancient texts have survived, as stated in the previous chapter, there must have been a tremendous demand for copies of New Testament books in the early church. It is surprising that there were not more mistakes. Establishing the existence of Hebraic meter in the text leads us back to the original text.

As the reader may have noticed, many of these variant readings are innocuous, apparently unintentional, and most likely due to nothing more than inattention, weariness, or incompetence. In other words, it does not appear that anyone intended to corrupt the text in Mark 11:29 or 12:24. However, the Mosaic cadence in the text is clearly intentional. Note that the bold **καὶ** (*and*) in the Greek creates a 7-3 division.

And Jesus said to them 10 times in the Gospel of Mark
        And Jesus **said** to them (Mark 1:17)
        And Jesus **said** to them (Mark 2:19)

And Jesus **said** to them (Mark 10:5)
And Jesus *was indignant* and **said** to them (Mark 10:14)
And Jesus **said** to them (Mark 10:38)
And Jesus **said** to them (Mark 10:39)
And Jesus *answered* and **said** to them (Mark 11:29)*
And Jesus **said** to them (Mark 12:17)
Jesus **said** to them (Mark 12:24)**
Jesus **said** to them (Mark 14:48)

καὶ **εἶπεν** αὐτοῖς ὁ Ἰησοῦς (Mark 1:17 BNT)
καὶ **εἶπεν** αὐτοῖς ὁ Ἰησοῦς (Mark 2:19 BNT)
ὁ δὲ Ἰησοῦς **εἶπεν** αὐτοῖς (Mark 10:5 BNT)
δὲ ὁ Ἰησοῦς ἠγανάκτησεν καὶ **εἶπεν** αὐτοῖς (Mark 10:14 BNT)
ὁ δὲ Ἰησοῦς **εἶπεν** αὐτοῖς (Mark 10:38 BNT)
ὁ δὲ Ἰησοῦς **εἶπεν** αὐτοῖς (Mark 10:39 BNT)
Ο δὲ Ἰησοῦς ἀποκριθεὶς **εἶπεν** αὐτοῖς (Mark 11:29 BYZ)*
ὁ δὲ Ἰησοῦς **εἶπεν** αὐτοῖς (Mark 12:17 BNT)
ὁ Ἰησοῦς **εἶπεν** αὐτοῖς (Mark 12:24 BYZ)**
ὁ Ἰησοῦς **εἶπεν** αὐτοῖς (Mark 14:48 BNT)

*Answered missing from BNT, GNT, TIS, VST, WHO; thus variant rejected.
***Jesus said to them*, ἔφη αὐτοῖς ὁ Ἰησοῦς in BNT, GNT, TIS, VST, WHO is not the correct wording; thus variant rejected.

The question remains, "How many times do Matthew, Mark, Luke, and John incorporate these metered phrases in their Gospels?" This writer is not able to answer.

He Said to Him

Another example of overlapping meter is found in the comparison of *and he said to him*, above, with *he said to him*. The variant at Mark 5:9 is rejected because it would increase the repetitions of *and he said to him* from 7 to 8, and *he said to him*, below, from 12 to 13. Once again we have a heptad as a subset of a dodecad, just like the 7 prophet names listed in the 12 repetitions of *through the prophet* in Matthew.

He said to him 12 times in the Gospel of Mark*
And He said to him.....**καὶ** λέγει αὐτῷ (Mark 1:41 BNT)
And He said to him.....**καὶ** λέγει αὐτῷ (Mark 1:44 BNT)
And He said to him......**καὶ** λέγει αὐτῷ (Mark 2:14 BNT)
     He said to him..........λέγει αὐτῷ (Mark 5:19 BNT)
And He said to him......**καὶ** λέγει αὐτῷ (Mark 7:28 BNT)
And He said to him......**καὶ** λέγει αὐτῷ (Mark 7:34 BNT)
     He said to him..........λέγει αὐτῷ (Mark 8:29 BNT)
     He said to him..........λέγει αὐτῷ (Mark 10:51 BYZ)**
     He said to him..........λέγει αὐτῷ (Mark 11:21 BNT)

He said to him..........λέγει αὐτῷ (Mark 13:1 BNT)
And He said to him.....καὶ λέγει αὐτῷ (Mark 14:30 BNT)
And He said to him.....καὶ λέγει αὐτῷ (Mark 14:61 BNT)
*BYZ, GOC, SCR, STE, VST are missing λέγει αὐτῷ at Mark 5:9.
**BNT, GNT, TIS, VST, WHO are missing λέγει αὐτῷ at Mark 10:51.

The question may be raised as to how many times the phrase *and he said to him* appears in Luke and John. Most texts do not include the phrase in Luke, and others include it one time. However, the Gospel of John repeats it 7 times, just as in Matthew and Mark.

And he said to him 7 times in Matthew, Mark, John and Genesis

καὶ λέγει αὐτῷ (Matt. 4:6 BNT)   καὶ λέγει αὐτῷ (Mark 1:41 BNT)*
καὶ λέγει αὐτῷ (Matt. 8:4 BNT)   καὶ λέγει αὐτῷ (Mark 1:44 BNT)
καὶ λέγει αὐτῷ (Matt. 8:7 BNT)*   καὶ λέγει αὐτῷ (Mark 2:14 BNT)
καὶ λέγει αὐτῷ (Matt. 8:20 BNT)   καὶ λέγει αὐτῷ (Mark 7:28 BNT)
καὶ λέγει αὐτῷ (Matt. 9:9 BNT)   καὶ λέγει αὐτῷ (Mark 7:34 BNT)
καὶ λέγει αὐτῷ (Matt. 14:31 BNT)   καὶ λέγει αὐτῷ (Mark 14:30 BNT)
καὶ λέγει αὐτῷ (Matt. 22:12 BNT)   καὶ λέγει αὐτῷ (Mark 14:61 BNT)

*Only TIS is missing καὶ λέγει αὐτῷ at Mark 1:41.

καὶ λέγει αὐτῷ (John 1:41 BNT)   וַיֹּאמֶר לוֹ (Gen. 3:9 WTT)*
καὶ λέγει αὐτῷ (John 1:43 BNT)   וַיֹּאמֶר לוֹ (Gen. 4:15 WTT)
καὶ λέγει αὐτῷ (John 1:45 BNT)   וַיֹּאמֶר לוֹ (Gen. 15:5 WTT)
καὶ λέγει αὐτῷ (John 1:49 BYZ)*   וַיֹּאמֶר לוֹ (Gen. 20:3 WTT)
καὶ λέγει αὐτῷ (John 1:51 BYZ)   וַיֹּאמֶר לוֹ (Gen. 31:24 WTT)
καὶ λέγει αὐτῷ (John 2:10 BYZ)   וַיֹּאמֶר־לוֹ (Gen. 35:10 WTT)
καὶ λέγει αὐτῷ (John 13:6 BYZ)*   וַיֹּאמֶר לוֹ (Gen. 35:11 WTT)

*These are 7 phrases where God speaks to man in Genesis, as discussed above.

Another popular myth is that Matthew, Mark, and Luke all copied Q, but John did not. Mosaic meter unmasks the fallacies promoted by many contemporary exegetes about the so-called *Synoptic Problem*. The point is that there is no problem. Approximately 80% of John is not found in Matthew, Mark, or Luke; yet John contains the same repetition of *and he said to him* as Matthew and Mark. It is doubtful that John is copying Matthew or Mark, although it is possible. The plausible explanation is that John, like Mark, is copying the same meter from Genesis, as seen above.

University scholars will have difficulty understanding the 4 Evangelists' motivation to incorporate Mosaic repetition into their Greek Gospels. They tend to view the text as an academic exercise. But the apostles sacrificed their lives to produce their Gospels for the purpose of communicating eternal life to their readers through paper and ink. Instead of copying from a non-existent Q source, the apostles copied their repetition from Moses, whom the scholars consider non-existent. These scholars do not view the existence of a real prophet as necessary for the existence of a real Messiah. If they insist on viewing the text as an academic exercise, then they should at least give the text the same respect they would to any other ancient literature.

Hebraic Meter Verifies Authenticity of Mark Chapter 16:9-20
As found in Revelation, Genesis, and the 3 other Gospels, Mark includes a number of single words in Mosaic meter. Most scholars consider Mark 16:9-20 an addition to the text. However, there are words and phrases in Hebraic meter that run through the entire book, including Mark 16:9-20, suggesting that it is part of the original text, as found in BYZ, GOC, SCR, STE, and TIS, bolded below, such as:

> **Demon: 14**, δαιμόνιον (*daimonion*, dahee-mon'-ee-on) 1:34 (x2), 39; 3:15, 22 (x2); 5:12; 6:13; 7:26, 29, 30; 9:38; 16:9, BYZ, GOC, SCR, STE;
> **Preach: 14**, κηρύσσω (*kerusso*, kay-roos'-so) 1:4, 7, 14, 38, 39, 45; 3:14; 5:20; 6:12; 7:36; 13:10; 14:9; 16:8, 15; variant at 16:20 in BNT, GNT, and WHO is rejected;
> **Sign: 7**, σημεῖον (*semeion*, say-mi'-on) 8:11, 12 (x2); 13:4, 22; 16:17, 20;
> **Word: 24**, λόγος (*logos*, log'-os) 1:45; 2:2; 4:14, 15 (x2), 16, 17, 18, 19, 20, 33; 5:36; 7:13, 29; 8:32, 38; 9:10; 10:22, 24; 11:29; 12:13; 13:31; 14:39; 16:20; GOC add 4:34, variant rejected.

And he said to them 7 times in the Gospel of Mark*
> And he said to them...........καὶ εἶπεν αὐτοῖς (Mark 1:17 BNT)
> And he said to them...........καὶ εἶπεν αὐτοῖς (Mark 2:19 BNT)
> And he said to them...........καὶ εἶπεν αὐτοῖς (Mark 4:40 BNT)
> And he said to them...........καὶ εἶπεν αὐτοῖς (Mark 9:29 BNT)
> And he said to them...........καὶ εἶπεν αὐτοῖς (Mark 10:14 BNT)
> And he said to them...........καὶ εἶπεν αὐτοῖς (Mark 14:24 BNT)
> And he said to them...........καὶ εἶπεν αὐτοῖς (Mark 16:15 BNT)

*BYZ, GOC, SCR, STE add 6:31 λέγει instead of εἶπεν, which is alternative wording for *he said*; thus variant rejected.

Cast out demons 7 times in the Gospel of Mark
> And casting out **demons** (Mark 1:39 BNT)
> And to cast out **demons** (Mark 3:15 BNT)
> He casts out **demons** (Mark 3:22 BNT)
> He would cast out the **demon** (Mark 7:26 BNT)
> He was casting out **demons** (Mark 9:38 BNT)
> He had cast seven **demons** (Mark 16:9 BNT)
> They shall cast out **demons** (Mark 16:17 BNT)

Additional Metered Words in Mark

Heptadic

Amazed: 7, θαμβέω (*thambeo*, tham-beh'-o) 1:27; 9:15; 10:24, 32; 14:33; 16:5, 6;

Blessed: 7, εὐλογέω (*eulogeo*, yoo-log-eh'-o) 6:41; 8:7; 10:16; 11:9, 10; 14:22, 61;

Christ: 7, Χριστός (*Christos*, khris-tos') BNT, BYZ, GNT, SCR, STE, TIS, VST 1:1; 8:29; 9:41; 12:35; 13:21; 14:61; 15:32; GOC, WHO add 1:34; variant rejected;

David: 7, Δαυίδ (*Dauid*, dau-weed') 2:25; 10:47, 48; 11:10; 12:35, 36, 37;

Enter: 7, εἰσέρχομαι (*eiserchomai*, ice-er'-khom-ahee), εἰσελθεῖν infinitive 1:45; 9:43, 45, 47; 10:24, 25 (x2);

Holy: 7, ἅγιος (*hagios*, hag'-ee-os) 1:8, 24; 3:29; 6:20; 8:38; 12:36; 13:11;

The Spirit: 7, τὸ πνεῦμα (*pneuma*, pnyoo'-mah) 1:10, 12, 26; 3:29; 5:8; 9:20; 13:11;

Spirit: 7, πνεύματι (*pneuma*, pnyoo'-mah) 1:8, 23; 2:8; 5:2; 8:12; 9:25; 12:36;

It is written: 7, γράφω (*grapho*, graf'-o) indicative perfect passive 3rd person singular γέγραπται 1:2; 7:6; 9:12, 13; 11:17; 14:21, 27;

Decadal

Peter: 20, Πέτρος (*Petros*, pet'-ros) 3:16; 5:37; 8:29, 32, 33; 9:2, 5; 10:28; 11:21; 13:3; 14:29, 33, 37, 54, 66, 67, 70, 72; 15:46; 16:7;

Dodecadal

Spirit: 12, πνεῦμα (*pneuma*, pnyoo'-mah) 1:10, 12, 26; 3:29, 30; 5:8; 7:25; 9:17, 20, 25; 13:1; 14:38.

Chapter Three
Repetition in the Gospel of Luke

The comparison of repetition between Matthew, Mark, and Luke increases the complexity of meter integration in what are called the Synoptic Gospels. Matthew, Mark, and Luke share an approximate 80% similarity in their accounts about Christ, while John only recounts about 20% of the information in the first 3 Gospels. This division of 3 within the 4 Gospels is an interesting phenomenon. Numerous examples from Revelation in the 2012 edition exhibit a division of 3 parts within 4 parts that suggest an overlapping pattern of 7.

A similar progression is found in Proverbs 30:15, 18, 21, and 29, and in Amos 1:3, 6, 9, 11, 13, and 2:1, 4, and 6. For example, "Thus saith the LORD; For three transgressions of Israel, and for four, I will not turn away the punishment thereof; because they sold the righteous for silver, and the poor for a pair of shoes" (Amos 2:6). The progression may not be from 3 to 4, but 3 plus 4. We see the same sequence in Exodus 34:7 and similar verses (Exodus 20:5; Numbers 14:18; Deuteronomy 5:9): "…visiting the iniquity of the fathers upon the children, and upon the children's children, unto the third and to the fourth generation." This does not mean the 3rd or 4th generation, but 3 generations plus 4 generations. More will be said on this subject in Chapters Five and Eight.

The repetition in Luke is similar to Matthew and Mark. Luke contains similar key phrases and anaphoric expressions of conversation.

To Jerusalem

Luke contains phrases found in both Matthew and Mark, in addition to other phrases found in either Matthew or Mark. There are some phrases that appear in all 4 Gospels. The simple heptadic phrase *to Jerusalem* was identical in Matthew and Mark, as follows:

To Jerusalem 7 times in the Gospel of Matthew
    To Jerusalem…………...εἰς Ἱεροσόλυμα (Matt. 2:1 BNT)
    To Jerusalem…………...εἰς Ἱεροσόλυμα (Matt. 5:35 BNT)
    To Jerusalem…………...εἰς Ἱεροσόλυμα (Matt. 16:21 BNT)
    To Jerusalem…………...εἰς Ἱεροσόλυμα (Matt. 20:17 BNT)

To Jerusalem...............εἰς Ἱεροσόλυμα (Matt. 20:18 BNT)
To Jerusalem...............εἰς Ἱεροσόλυμα (Matt. 21:1 BNT)
To Jerusalem...............εἰς Ἱεροσόλυμα (Matt. 21:10 BNT)

To Jerusalem 7 times in the Gospel of Mark
To Jerusalem...............εἰς Ἱεροσόλυμα (Mark 10:32 BNT)
To Jerusalem...............εἰς Ἱεροσόλυμα (Mark 10:33 BNT)
To Jerusalem...............εἰς Ἱεροσόλυμα (Mark 11:1 BNT)*
To Jerusalem...............εἰς Ἱεροσόλυμα (Mark 11:11 BNT)
To Jerusalem...............εἰς Ἱεροσόλυμα (Mark 11:15 BNT)
To Jerusalem...............εἰς Ἱεροσόλυμα (Mark 11:27 BNT)
To Jerusalem...............εἰς Ἱεροσόλυμα (Mark 15:41 BNT)

*BYZ, GOC, SCR, STE use Septuagint spelling for *Jerusalem* (Ἱερουσαλήμ) at Mark 11:1.

Therefore, a search was made for the same meter in Luke. As stated in Chapter One, there are 3 major Hebraic cadences, 7, 10, and 12. Luke chooses the same phrase, but repeats it 12 times instead of 7 times.

To Jerusalem 12 times in the Gospel of Luke*
To Jerusalem...............εἰς Ἱεροσόλυμα (Luke 2:22 BNT)
To Jerusalem...............εἰς Ἱερουσαλὴμ (Luke 2:41 BNT)
To Jerusalem...............εἰς Ἱερουσαλὴμ (Luke 2:45 BNT)
To Jerusalem...............εἰς Ἱερουσαλὴμ (Luke 4:9 BNT)
To Jerusalem...............εἰς Ἱερουσαλὴμ (Luke 9:51 BNT)
To Jerusalem...............εἰς Ἱερουσαλὴμ (Luke 9:53 BNT)
To Jerusalem...............εἰς Ἱεροσόλυμα (Luke 13:22 BNT)
To Jerusalem...............εἰς Ἱερουσαλήμ (Luke 17:11 BNT)
To Jerusalem...............εἰς Ἱερουσαλήμ (Luke 18:31 BNT)
To Jerusalem...............εἰς Ἱεροσόλυμα (Luke 19:28 BNT)
To Jerusalem...............εἰς Ἱερουσαλὴμ (Luke 24:33 BNT)
To Jerusalem...............εἰς Ἱερουσαλὴμ (Luke 24:52 BNT)

*BYZ, GOC, SCR, STE add an additional phrase at Luke 2:42; thus variant rejected.

Heptadic Meter in Luke
Journey to Jerusalem

After finding 12 repetitions of the phrase *to Jerusalem*, the next thought was to keep looking for a subset of 7 phrases, or a heptad within this dodecad. However, everything does not always fit neatly in the prescribed categories. In addition to *to Jerusalem*, a search was made for a third word in Luke that may appear with this phrase 7 times. With no variants, the Greek word πορεύομαι (*poreuomai*, por-yoo'-om-ahee) appears in close proximity to the phrase *to Jerusalem* in 7 of the 12 verses, which is more than coincidental. However, whether this meets the criteria for a numerically-ordered phrase is a matter of judgment. According to context, πορεύομαι is broadly translated as *journey*, *go*, *went*, or *proceed*. In order to demonstrate the heptadic meter, *journey* is utilized in the list below. The key words are bolded in English and Greek. Notice that the computer also found *to* (εἰς) in each phrase, with the exception that *to* is separated from Jerusalem in Luke 24:13. The phrase appears more consistent in Greek than in English. The following is a literal, though awkward, translation.

Journey to Jerusalem 7 times in the Gospel of Luke
Now his parents **journeyed** every year **to Jerusalem** (Luke 2:41)
    to journey to Jerusalem (Luke 9:51)
    he was **journeying to Jerusalem** (Luke 9:53)
    and **journeying** on His way **to Jerusalem** (Luke 13:22)
    as he **journeyed to Jerusalem** (Luke 17:11)
    He was **journeying** on ahead, ascending **to Jerusalem** (Luke 19:28)
    journeyed to a village which is *about*
        sixty stadia from **Jerusalem** (Luke 24:13)

Καὶ **ἐπορεύοντο** οἱ γονεῖς αὐτοῦ κατ᾽
    ἔτος **εἰς Ἰερουσαλὴμ** (Luke 2:41 BNT)
    πορεύεσθαι εἰς Ἰερουσαλήμ (Luke 9:51 BNT)
    πορευόμενον εἰς Ἰερουσαλήμ (Luke 9:53 BNT)
    καὶ **πορείαν** ποιούμενος **εἰς Ἱεροσόλυμα** (Luke 13:22 BNT)
    ἐν τῷ **πορεύεσθαι εἰς Ἰερουσαλήμ** (Luke 17:11 BNT)
ἐπορεύετο ἔμπροσθεν ἀναβαίνων **εἰς Ἱεροσόλυμα** (Luke 19:28 BNT)
    πορευόμενοι εἰς κώμην ἀπέχουσαν
    σταδίους ἑξήκοντα ἀπὸ **Ἰερουσαλήμ** (Luke 24:13 BNT)

In the Temple / He Entered Into / They or *He Follow Him*
After discovering 7 repetitions of the phrase *journey to Jerusalem*, finding the phrase *in the temple* 7 times in Luke is not unexpected. There are no variants. Matthew, Mark, and Luke all set the phrase *follow Him* in Hebraic meter. John uses *follow Me*.

In the temple 7 times in the Gospel of Luke
    In the temple........................ἐν τῷ ἱερῷ (Luke 2:46 BNT)
    In the temple........................ἐν τῷ ἱερῷ (Luke 19:47 BNT)
    In the temple........................ἐν τῷ ἱερῷ (Luke 20:1 BNT)
    In the temple........................ἐν τῷ ἱερῷ (Luke 21:37 BNT)
    In the temple........................ἐν τῷ ἱερῷ (Luke 21:38 BNT)
    In the temple........................ἐν τῷ ἱερῷ (Luke 22:53 BNT)
    In the temple........................ἐν τῷ ἱερῷ (Luke 24:53 BNT)

He entered into 7 times in the Gospel of Luke (no variants)*
    He entered into.....................εἰσῆλθεν εἰς (Luke 1:40 STE)
    He entered into.....................εἰσῆλθεν εἰς (Luke 4:38 STE)

He entered into......................εἰσῆλθεν εἰς (Luke 6:4 STE)
He entered into......................εἰσῆλθεν εἰς (Luke 7:1 STE)
He entered into......................εἰσῆλθεν εἰς (Luke 8:30 STE)*
He entered into......................εἰσῆλθεν εἰς (Luke 8:33 STE)*
He entered into......................εἰσῆλθεν εἰς (Luke 10:38 STE)

*All the texts have the same word for *entered*, but this spelling is only found in SCR and STE (See word list for John in Chapter 4).

They or *he follow Him* 7 times in the Gospel of Luke (no variants)
    They **followed** Him..........ἠκολούθησαν αὐτῷ (Luke 5:11 BNT)
    He was **following** Him..........ἠκολούθει αὐτῷ (Luke 5:28 BNT)
    Who was **following** Him..........ἀκολουθοῦντι αὐτῷ (Luke 7:9 BNT)
    They **followed** Him..........ἠκολούθησαν αὐτῷ (Luke 9:11 BNT)
    He was **following** Him..........ἠκολούθει αὐτῷ (Luke 18:43 BNT)
    You **follow** Him................ἀκολουθήσατε αὐτῷ (Luke 22:10 BNT)
    Who were **following** Him....συνακολουθοῦσαι αὐτῷ (Luke 23:49 BNT)

Cast out Demons

In Matthew and Mark the phrase *cast out demons* appears 7 times, as follows:

Cast out demons 7 times in the Gospel of Matthew
    Many **demon**-possessed and he cast out (Matt. 8:16)
    And when the **demon** was cast out (Matt. 9:33)
    He casts out **demons** (Matt. 9:34)
    You cast out **demons** (Matt. 10:8)
    He casts out **demons** (Matt. 12:24)
    I cast out **demons** (Matt. 12:27)
    I cast out **demons** (Matt. 12:28)

Cast out demons 7 times in the Gospel of Mark
    And casting out **demons** (Mark 1:39)
    And to cast out **demons** (Mark 3:15)
    He casts out **demons** (Mark 3:22)
    He would cast out the **demon** (Mark 7:26)
    He was casting out **demons** (Mark 9:38)
    He had cast seven **demons** (Mark 16:9)
    They shall cast out **demons** (Mark 16:17)

The same pattern is found in Luke. There are no variants.

Cast out demons 7 times in the Gospel of Luke
    He was casting out **demons** (Luke 9:49)
    Casting out **demons** (Luke 11:14)
    He cast out **demons** (Luke 11:15)
    To cast out **demons** (Luke 11:18)
    I cast out **demons** (Luke 11:19)
    I cast out **demons** (Luke 11:20)

I cast out **demons** (Luke 13:32)

ἐκβάλλοντα **δαιμόνια** (Luke 9:49 BNT)
ἐκβάλλων **δαιμόνιον** (Luke 11:14 BNT)
ἐκβάλλει τὰ **δαιμόνια** (Luke 11:15 BNT)
ἐκβάλλειν με τὰ **δαιμόνια** (Luke 11:18 BNT)
ἐκβάλλω τὰ **δαιμόνια** (Luke 11:19 BNT)
ἐκβάλλω τὰ **δαιμόνια** (Luke 11:20 BNT)
ἐκβάλλω **δαιμόνια** (Luke 13:32 BNT)

The above is one of the most remarkable repetitions of phrases this writer has encountered. All 3 Gospel writers set the phrase *cast out demons* in Moses' heptadic meter, without variants. Luke's setting is the most pristine, with no variation in word order as seen in Matthew and Mark. It appears that Mark copied Matthew because Mark alters 2 of his 9 phrases by adding the word *many* to create a subset of 7, as shown in the previous chapter. It also appears that Luke decided to polish up their work and make it more orderly in his Gospel than the other two. The question is, "What tradition or source motivated this repetition by all 3 writers?" It certainly was not the mythological Q source. Matthew and Luke complete their pattern within 5 chapters, but Mark requires 16 chapters, which also confirms that Mark 16:9-20 is part of the original text, as discussed in Chapter Two.

The phrase or words *cast out demons*, *demons*, or *demon-possessed* do not appear in the Hebrew or the Septuagint. Job uses *Satan* in double heptadic meter 14 times, but the Septuagint is inaccurate, and is actually missing *Satan* at Job 2:9. Hence, the only precedent for heptadic meter with *Satan* is the Hebrew text of Job. There is no instance of the devil being cast out in the Old Testament except by inference in Genesis 3:14.

The Hebrew word for *serpent*, נָחָשׁ (*nachash*, naw-khawsh'), is found 6 times in Genesis 3:1, 2, 4, 13, 14, and 49:17. The Septuagint adds a 7th repetition in 3:1 instead of the Hebrew pronoun. There is no question that all of the Gospel writers, particularly Luke, were familiar with the Septuagint. The question then remains as to whether the Septuagint preserves the original Hebrew, or if its writers intentionally added a 7th repetition. We should also remember that the Septuagint is often more paraphrastic than literal. The 4th-century A.D. Vulgate follows the Hebrew and not the Septuagint. In any case, the Septuagint that Luke used repeats *serpent* in heptadic rhythm in Genesis 3.

Amen (Verily) I Say to You

Matthew, Mark, and Luke all say the same phrase with one *amen* (or *truly/verily*), while John doubles it by saying *Amen Amen*, or *truly truly*, or *verily verily*.

Verily I say to you 7 times in the Gospel of Luke
But verily **I say** to you........δέ· ἀμὴν λέγω ὑμῖν (Luke 4:24 BNT)
Verily **I say** to you.............ἀμὴν λέγω ὑμῖν (Luke 12:37 BNT)
But verily **I say** to you...........μὴν δὲ λέγω ὑμῖν (Luke 13:35 STE)*
Verily **I say** to you.............ἀμὴν λέγω ὑμῖν (Luke 18:17 BNT)
Verily **I say** to you.............ἀμὴν λέγω ὑμῖν (Luke 18:29 BNT)
Verily **I say** to you.............ἀμὴν λέγω ὑμῖν (Luke 21:32 BNT)
Verily **I say** to you.......ἀμήν σοι λέγω   (Luke 23:43 BNT)
*Only SCR and STE include *amen* at 13:35, a strange but necessary variant.

Chief Priests and Scribes

Matthew places *scribes* and *Pharisees* together 7 times. Luke places *chief priests* and *scribes*, Christ's primary opposition, together 7 times, as seen below. He also reverses the word order at 20:19, one of a number of instances noted in this study where a phrase set in heptadic meter is reversed.

Chief priests and scribes 7 times in the Gospel of Luke
And chief **priests** and scribes (Luke 9:22)
And the chief **priests** and scribes (Luke 19:47)
The chief **priests** and scribes (Luke 20:1)*
The scribes and chief **priests**   (Luke 20:19)
The chief **priests** and scribes (Luke 22:2)
Chief **priests** and scribes (Luke 22:66)
And the chief **priests** and scribes (Luke 23:10)

καὶ **ἀρχιερέων** καὶ γραμματέων (Luke 9:22 BNT)
οἱ δὲ **ἀρχιερεῖς** καὶ οἱ γραμματεῖς (Luke 19:47 BNT)
οἱ **ἀρχιερεῖς** καὶ οἱ γραμματεῖς (Luke 20:1 BNT)*
οἱ γραμματεῖς καὶ οἱ **ἀρχιερεῖς**   (Luke 20:19 BNT)
οἱ **ἀρχιερεῖς** καὶ οἱ γραμματεῖς (Luke 22:2 BNT)
ἀρχιερεῖς τε καὶ γραμματεῖς (Luke 22:66 BNT)
δὲ οἱ **ἀρχιερεῖς** καὶ οἱ γραμματεῖς (Luke 23:10 BNT)
*BYZ, GOC, TIS, VST have *priests* at 20:1 instead of *chief priests*; variant rejected.

In or *From that Hour*

Matthew has the following heptad with the word *hour*. This led to a search for a similar phrase in Mark, which does not use the phrase in Hebraic meter. However, it appears that Luke does use a similar phrase, *in that very hour*, with an intensive dative (indirect object), which adds the word *very*. There is a question about Luke 14:17, which uses a pronoun in the genitive case before *the hour*, but that pronoun modifies the noun that precedes it: *And sent the servant of him....* Luke arranges the Greek words to resemble the other patterns. These kinds of word arrangements are found in other books, including Revelation.

In or *from that hour* 7 times in the Gospel of Matthew
  In that hour...............ἐν τῇ **ὥρᾳ** ἐκείνῃ (Matt. 8:13 BNT)
  From that hour...........ἀπὸ τῆς **ὥρας** ἐκείνης (Matt. 9:22 BNT)
  In that hour.......ἐν ἐκείνῃ τῇ **ὥρᾳ** (Matt. 10:19 BNT)
  From that hour...........ἀπὸ τῆς **ὥρας** ἐκείνης (Matt. 15:28 BNT)
  From that hour...........ἀπὸ τῆς **ὥρας** ἐκείνης (Matt. 17:18 BNT)
  In that hour......Εν ἐκείνῃ τῇ **ὥρᾳ** (Matt. 18:1 BNT)
  In that hour......Εν ἐκείνῃ τῇ **ὥρᾳ** (Matt. 26:55 BNT)

In that very hour 7 times in the Gospel of Luke
  And that very hour..........καὶ αὐτῇ τῇ **ὥρᾳ** (Luke 2:38 BNT)
  In that very hour...........Ἐν αὐτῇ τῇ **ὥρᾳ** (Luke 10:21 BNT)
  In that very hour............ἐν αὐτῇ τῇ **ὥρᾳ** (Luke 12:12 BNT)
  In that very hour...........Ἐν αὐτῇ τῇ **ὥρᾳ** (Luke 13:31 BNT)*
  In that very hour..............αὐτοῦ τῇ **ὥρᾳ** (Luke 14:17 BNT)**
  In that very hour............ἐν αὐτῇ τῇ **ὥρᾳ** (Luke 20:19 BNT)
  That very hour.............αὐτῇ τῇ **ὥρᾳ** (Luke 24:33 BNT)
*BYZ, GOC, SCR, STE have *in the same day* at Luke 13:31; thus variant rejected.
**The pronoun modifies *servant*, followed by *the hour* at Luke 14:17.

And Jesus
 The following short heptad has no variant readings in the name *Jesus*. There are 7 verses in Luke that begin with the following:

  And Jesus....................ὁ δὲ Ἰησοῦς (Luke 7:6 BNT)
  And Jesus....................ὁ δὲ Ἰησοῦς (Luke 8:46 BNT)
  And Jesus....................ὁ δὲ Ἰησοῦς (Luke 8:50 BNT)
  And Jesus....................ὁ δὲ Ἰησοῦς (Luke 9:47 BNT)
  And Jesus....................ὁ δὲ Ἰησοῦς (Luke 18:16 BNT)
  And Jesus....................ὁ δὲ Ἰησοῦς (Luke 22:48 BYZ)*
  And Jesus....................ὁ δὲ Ἰησοῦς (Luke 23:34 BNT)
*BNT, GNT, TIS, VST, WHO lack the ὁ (*the*).

Son of God
 Like Matthew, but not Mark, Luke arranges *Son of God* with no variants in Mosaic cadence.

Son of God 10 times in the Gospel of Matthew
  If you are the **Son** of God.............εἰ **υἱὸς** εἶ τοῦ θεοῦ (Matt. 4:3 BNT)
  If you are the **Son** of God.............εἰ **υἱὸς** εἶ τοῦ θεοῦ (Matt. 4:6 BNT)
  Sons of God................**υἱοὶ** θεοῦ (Matt. 5:9 BNT)
  Thou **Son** of God.................**υἱὲ** τοῦ θεοῦ (Matt. 8:29 BNT)
  You are the **Son** of God.........θεοῦ **υἱὸς** εἶ (Matt. 14:33 BNT)
  The **Son** of the living God.............ὁ **υἱὸς** τοῦ θεοῦ τοῦ ζῶντος (Matt. 16:16 BNT)
  The **Son** of God.............ὁ **υἱὸς** τοῦ θεοῦ (Matt. 26:63 BNT)

If you are the **Son** of God............εἰ **υἱὸς** εἶ τοῦ θεοῦ (Matt. 27:40 BNT)
I am the **Son** of God...θεοῦ εἰμι **υἱός** (Matt. 27:43 BNT)
This was the **Son** of God.........θεοῦ **υἱὸς** ἦν οὗτος (Matt. 27:54 BNT)

Son of God 7 times in the Gospel of Luke

He shall be called the **Son** of God	(Luke 1:35)
If you are the **Son** of God	(Luke 4:3)
If you are the **Son** of God	(Luke 4:9)
You are the **Son** of God	(Luke 4:41)
Jesus, *thou* **Son** of God most high	(Luke 8:28)
And you are **sons** of God	(Luke 20:36)
Are you then the **Son** of God	(Luke 22:70)

κληθήσεται **υἱὸς** θεοῦ	(Luke 1:35 BNT)
εἰ **υἱὸς** εἶ τοῦ θεοῦ	(Luke 4:3 BNT)
εἰ **υἱὸς** εἶ τοῦ θεοῦ	(Luke 4:9 BNT)
σὺ εἶ ὁ **υἱὸς** τοῦ θεοῦ	(Luke 4:41 BNT)
Ιησοῦ **υἱὲ** τοῦ θεοῦ τοῦ ὑψίστου	(Luke 8:28 BNT)
καὶ **υἱοί** εἰσιν τοῦ θεοῦ	(Luke 20:36 BNT)
σὺ οὖν εἶ ὁ **υἱὸς** τοῦ θεοῦ	(Luke 22:70 BNT)

In Matthew 5:9 and Luke 20:36 Jesus tells the people they are *sons of God*. The phrase is the same spelling as *Son of God* but in a plural. Both phrases are necessary to complete their respective meters. Notice that Matthew uses the phrase *Son of God* in a decad, and Luke uses it in a heptad. Hence, Luke changes the meter in *Son of God*. The Septuagint rarely translates Moses' Hebraic meter correctly into the Greek. Tradition has it that Luke's Gospel, like Acts, is written under the direction of the Apostle Paul, who calls himself an expert of the law taught by Gamaliel (Acts 22:3). How else would Luke—a Greek Gentile—become a master of Hebraic cadence?

Dodecadal Meter in Luke
Son of Man

As in Matthew and Mark, Luke also uses the phrase *Son of Man* in Hebraic meter. Matthew repeats it 30 times, Mark repeats it 10 times, and Luke repeats it 24 times, 12 in the exact same phrase and 12 more in irregular word order.

Son of Man 30 times in the Gospel of Matthew

ὁ δὲ υἱὸς τοῦ ἀνθρώπου (Matt. 8:20)	ὁ υἱὸς τοῦ ἀνθρώπου (Matt. 9:6)
ὁ υἱὸς τοῦ ἀνθρώπου (Matt. 10:23)	ὁ υἱὸς τοῦ ἀνθρώπου (Matt. 11:19)
ὁ υἱὸς τοῦ ἀνθρώπου (Matt. 12:8)	τοῦ υἱοῦ τοῦ ἀνθρώπου (Matt. 12:32)
ὁ υἱὸς τοῦ ἀνθρώπου (Matt. 12:40)	ὁ υἱὸς τοῦ ἀνθρώπου (Matt. 13:37)
ὁ υἱὸς τοῦ ἀνθρώπου (Matt. 13:41)	τὸν υἱὸν τοῦ ἀνθρώπου (Matt. 16:13)

ὁ υἱὸς τοῦ ἀνθρώπου (Matt. 16:27)   τὸν υἱὸν τοῦ ἀνθρώπου (Matt. 16:28)
ὁ υἱὸς τοῦ ἀνθρώπου (Matt. 17:9)   ὁ υἱὸς τοῦ ἀνθρώπου (Matt. 17:12)
ὁ υἱὸς τοῦ ἀνθρώπου (Matt. 17:22)   ὁ υἱὸς τοῦ ἀνθρώπου (Matt. 19:28)
ὁ υἱὸς τοῦ ἀνθρώπου (Matt. 20:18)   ὁ υἱὸς τοῦ ἀνθρώπου (Matt. 20:28)
τοῦ υἱοῦ τοῦ ἀνθρώπου (Matt. 24:27) τοῦ υἱοῦ τοῦ ἀνθρώπου (Matt. 24:30)
τὸν υἱὸν τοῦ ἀνθρώπου (Matt. 24:30) τοῦ υἱοῦ τοῦ ἀνθρώπου (Matt. 24:37)
τοῦ υἱοῦ τοῦ ἀνθρώπου (Matt. 24:39) ὁ υἱὸς τοῦ ἀνθρώπου (Matt. 24:44)
ὁ υἱὸς τοῦ ἀνθρώπου (Matt. 25:31)   ὁ υἱὸς τοῦ ἀνθρώπου (Matt. 26:2)
υἱὸς τοῦ ἀνθρώπου (Matt. 26:24)   ὁ υἱὸς τοῦ ἀνθρώπου (Matt. 26:24)
ὁ υἱὸς τοῦ ἀνθρώπου (Matt. 26:45)   τὸν υἱὸν τοῦ ἀνθρώπου (Matt. 26:64)

Son of Man 10 times in the Gospel of Mark
- Son of Man...................ὁ υἱὸς τοῦ ἀνθρώπου (Mark 2:10 BNT)
- Son of Man...................ὁ υἱὸς τοῦ ἀνθρώπου (Mark 2:28 BNT)
- Son of Man...................ὁ υἱὸς τοῦ ἀνθρώπου (Mark 8:38 BNT)
- Son of Man...................ὁ υἱὸς τοῦ ἀνθρώπου (Mark 9:9 BNT)
- Son of Man...................ὁ υἱὸς τοῦ ἀνθρώπου (Mark 9:31 BNT)
- Son of Man...................ὁ υἱὸς τοῦ ἀνθρώπου (Mark 10:33 BNT)
- Son of Man...................ὁ υἱὸς τοῦ ἀνθρώπου (Mark 10:45 BNT)
- Son of Man..............ὁ μὲν υἱὸς τοῦ ἀνθρώπου (Mark 14:21 BNT)
- Son of Man...................ὁ υἱὸς τοῦ ἀνθρώπου (Mark 14:21 BNT)
- Son of Man...................ὁ υἱὸς τοῦ ἀνθρώπου (Mark 14:41 BNT)

Son of Man 12 times Nominative Case in the Gospel of Luke
- Son of Man...................ὁ υἱὸς τοῦ ἀνθρώπου (Luke 5:24 BNT)
- Son of Man...................ὁ υἱὸς τοῦ ἀνθρώπου (Luke 6:5 BNT)
- Son of Man...................ὁ υἱὸς τοῦ ἀνθρώπου (Luke 7:34 BNT)
- Son of Man...................ὁ υἱὸς τοῦ ἀνθρώπου (Luke 9:26 BNT)
- Son of Man...................ὁ υἱὸς τοῦ ἀνθρώπου (Luke 11:30 BNT)
- Son of Man...................ὁ υἱὸς τοῦ ἀνθρώπου (Luke 12:8 BNT)
- Son of Man...................ὁ υἱὸς τοῦ ἀνθρώπου (Luke 12:40 BNT)
- Son of Man...................ὁ υἱὸς τοῦ ἀνθρώπου (Luke 17:24 BNT)
- Son of Man...................ὁ υἱὸς τοῦ ἀνθρώπου (Luke 17:30 BNT)
- Son of Man...................ὁ υἱὸς τοῦ ἀνθρώπου (Luke 18:8 BNT)
- Son of Man...................ὁ υἱὸς τοῦ ἀνθρώπου (Luke 19:10 BNT)
- Son of Man...................ὁ υἱὸς τοῦ ἀνθρώπου (Luke 22:69 BNT)

Son of Man 12 times varied order in the Gospel of Luke*
- Of the **Son** of Man (Luke 6:22)
- Necessary that the **Son** of Man (Luke 9:22)
- For the **Son** of Man (Luke 9:44)
- But the **Son** of Man (Luke 9:58)
- To the **Son** of Man (Luke 12:10)
- Of the **Son** of Man (Luke 17:22)

Of the **Son** of Man (Luke 17:26)
To the **Son** of Man (Luke 18:31)
The **Son** of Man (Luke 21:27)
The **Son** of Man (Luke 21:36)
The **Son** of Man (Luke 22:48)
The **Son** of Man (Luke 24:7)

τοῦ **υἱοῦ** τοῦ ἀνθρώπου (Luke 6:22 BNT)
δεῖ τὸν **υἱὸν** τοῦ ἀνθρώπου (Luke 9:22 BNT)
ὁ γὰρ **υἱὸς** τοῦ ἀνθρώπου (Luke 9:44 BNT)
ὁ δὲ **υἱὸς** τοῦ ἀνθρώπου (Luke 9:58 BNT)
εἰς τὸν **υἱὸν** τοῦ ἀνθρώπου (Luke 12:10 BNT)
τοῦ **υἱοῦ** τοῦ ἀνθρώπου (Luke 17:22 BNT)
τοῦ **υἱοῦ** τοῦ ἀνθρώπου (Luke 17:26 BNT)
τῷ **υἱῷ** τοῦ ἀνθρώπου (Luke 18:31 BNT)
τὸν **υἱὸν** τοῦ ἀνθρώπου (Luke 21:27 BNT)
τοῦ **υἱοῦ** τοῦ ἀνθρώπου (Luke 21:36 BNT)
τὸν **υἱὸν** τοῦ ἀνθρώπου (Luke 22:48 BNT)
τὸν **υἱὸν** τοῦ ἀνθρώπου (Luke 24:7 BNT)

*BYZ, GOC, SCR, STE add 9:56 and 22:22; variants rejected.

Jesus is the subject of the Gospels, and it is no surprise that Matthew, Mark, and Luke all use the same phrase *Son of Man* in Mosaic cadence. Matthew and Mark use decadal meter, and Luke changes to dodecadal meter (rhythm of 12). The assumption is that the change in meter is a change in symbolic emphasis. Decadal meter emphasizes completion, the complete work of Christ, a complete account, or a complete person, as thoroughly explained in the 2012 edition. Dodecadal meter emphasizes Christ's relationship with Israel and the church. The fact that Luke doubles the phrases, 12 in order and 12 irregular, leaves little doubt that his emphasis is intentional.

Holy Spirit

Luke is the only Gospel that uses the phrase *Holy Spirit* or *Holy Ghost* in Hebraic meter. In this case, the shorter Eastern texts are preferred, and the longer Western texts, which add *holy* to Luke 10:21, are not followed. Luke also creates a subset of 10 by reversing the word order in the last 2 verses. The nominative (subject) *spirit* (πνεῦμα) is also found in Revelation 12 times. Luke and John are following the same meter. Obviously the Spirit of the Church is implied.

Holy Spirit 12 times in the Gospel of Luke*

Holy Spirit………………πνεύματος ἁγίου		(Luke 1:15 BNT)
Holy Spirit…………….….πνεῦμα ἅγιον		(Luke 1:35 BNT)
Holy Spirit……………....πνεύματος ἁγίου		(Luke 1:41 BNT)
Holy Spirit……………....πνεύματος ἁγίου		(Luke 1:67 BNT)

Holy Spirit............καὶ πνεῦμα ἦν ἅγιον		(Luke 2:25 BNT)
By the **Holy** Spirit...ὑπὸ τοῦ πνεύματος τοῦ ἁγίου		(Luke 2:26 BYZ)
In **Holy** Spirit...........ἐν πνεύματι ἁγίῳ		(Luke 3:16 BNT)
Holy Spirit..............τὸ πνεῦμα τὸ ἅγιον		(Luke 3:22 BNT)
Holy Spirit................πνεύματος ἁγίου		(Luke 4:1 BNT)
Holy Spirit...................πνεῦμα ἅγιον		(Luke 11:13 BNT)
Holy Spirit......................τὸ ἅγιον πνεῦμα		(Luke 12:10 BNT)
Holy Spirit.........................ἅγιον πνεῦμα		(Luke 12:12 BNT)

*BNT, GNT, TIS, WHO add τῷ πνεύματι τῷ ἁγίῳ at Luke 10:21; thus variant rejected.

In the Days

Luke chooses dodecadal meter for the phrase *in the days*, with no variants. However, many English translations of the Gospel of Luke do not exhibit this cadence because they substitute words like *years* or *time* for *days* in most of these phrases. Why Luke chose dodecadal meter for this phrase is speculation. If Cassuto were commenting here, he would suggest Babylonian influence in counting time, one day for each of the 12 hours of daylight. This writer prefers to view this as a panoramic view of church history, from the birth of John the Baptist to the end of the world.

In the days 12 times in the Gospel of Luke

In the days..................ἐν ταῖς ἡμέραις		(Luke 1:5 BNT)
In the days..................ἐν ταῖς ἡμέραις		(Luke 1:7 BNT)
In the days..................ἐν ταῖς ἡμέραις		(Luke 1:18 BNT)
In the days..................ἐν ταῖς ἡμέραις		(Luke 1:39 BNT)
In the days..................ἐν ταῖς ἡμέραις		(Luke 2:1 BNT)
In the days..................ἐν ταῖς ἡμέραις		(Luke 4:2 BNT)
In the days..................ἐν ταῖς ἡμέραις		(Luke 4:25 BNT)
In the days..................ἐν ταῖς ἡμέραις		(Luke 6:12 BNT)
In the days..................ἐν ταῖς ἡμέραις		(Luke 17:26 BNT)
In the days..................ἐν ταῖς ἡμέραις		(Luke 17:26 BNT)
In the days..................ἐν ταῖς ἡμέραις		(Luke 17:28 BNT)
In the days..................ἐν ταῖς ἡμέραις		(Luke 24:18 BNT)

Metered Introduction to Conversation: Anaphoric Phrases

As in Matthew and Mark, Luke follows the same approach to metered introductions to mundane conversation.

But Jesus Answered and Said

The repetition of *Jesus answered and said* in Matthew, Mark, and Luke, illustrates the truly Hebraic nature of the Gospels. Each writer adapts the phrase in heptadic meter right out of Genesis. Matthew uses the phrase 7 times with machine-like precision, and then repeats it 7 more times in scrambled word order. Mark also repeats it 7 times in irregular word order. Luke uses the phrase in a double heptad, but includes a subset of 10 pronouns as indirect objects or prepositions, bolded in the list below.

But Jesus answered and said 7 times in the Gospel of Matthew*
    But Jesus answered and said (Matt. 3:15 BNT)
    But Jesus answered and said (Matt. 16:17 BNT)
    But Jesus answered and said (Matt. 17:17 BNT)
    But Jesus answered and said (Matt. 20:22 BNT)
    But Jesus answered and said (Matt. 21:21 BNT)
    But Jesus answered and said (Matt. 21:24 BNT)
    But Jesus answered and said (Matt. 22:29 BNT)
*See Greek in Chapter One.

Jesus answered (irregular) 7 times in the Gospel of Matthew*
                        And Jesus **answered** [and] said (Matt. 11:4)
                              Jesus **answered** [and] said (Matt. 11:25)
                              Jesus **answered** [and] said (Matt. 15:28)
                    But Jesus **answered** [and] said (Matt. 17:11)**
                            And Jesus **answered**   (Matt. 22:1)
                        And Jesus **answered** [and] said (Matt. 24:4)
    But Jesus was silent and the High Priest **answered**   (Matt. 26:63)***
*See Greek in Chapter One.
**BNT, GNT, TIS, VST, WHO missing *Jesus* and only have ὁ δὲ ἀποκριθεὶς εἶπεν (Matt. 17:11).
***BNT, GNT, WHO missing *answered* ὁ δὲ Ἰησοῦς ἐσιώπα. καὶ ὁ ἀρχιερεὺς εἶπεν (Matt. 26:63).

And Jesus answered and said 7 times in the Gospel of Mark*
    And Jesus **answered** and said (Mark 10:5)
    And Jesus **answered** and said (Mark 11:14)
    And Jesus **answered** and said (Mark 11:29)
    And Jesus **answered** and said (Mark 12:17)
    And Jesus **answered** and said (Mark 12:24)
    And Jesus **answered** and said (Mark 13:2)
    And Jesus **answered** and said (Mark 14:48)
*See Greek in Chapter Two.

And answering Jesus said 14 times in the Gospel of Luke
    And answering Jesus said **to him**   (Luke 4:8)
    And answering Jesus said **to him**   (Luke 4:12)
        answering Jesus said **to them** (Luke 5:22)
    And answering Jesus said **to them** (Luke 5:31)
    And answering Jesus said **to them** (Luke 6:3)
    And answering Jesus said **to them** (Luke 7:22)
    And answering Jesus said **to him**   (Luke 7:40)
        answering Jesus said   (Luke 9:41)
        answering Jesus said **to her**   (Luke 10:41)

And answering Jesus said **to them** (Luke 13:2)
And answering Jesus said (Luke 14:3)
answering Jesus said (Luke 17:17)
And answering Jesus said **to them** (Luke 20:34)
answering Jesus said (Luke 22:51)

καὶ ἀποκριθεὶς ὁ Ἰησοῦς εἶπεν αὐτῷ (Luke 4:8 BNT)
καὶ ἀποκριθεὶς εἶπεν αὐτῷ ὁ Ἰησοῦς (Luke 4:12 BNT)
ὁ Ἰησοῦς...ἀποκριθεὶς εἶπεν πρὸς αὐτούς (Luke 5:22 BNT)
καὶ ἀποκριθεὶς ὁ Ἰησοῦς εἶπεν πρὸς αὐτούς (Luke 5:31 BNT)
καὶ ἀποκριθεὶς ὁ Ἰησοῦς πρὸς αὐτοὺς εἶπεν (Luke 6:3 BNT)
καὶ ἀποκριθεὶς ὁ Ἰησοῦς εἶπεν αὐτοῖς (Luke 7:22 BYZ)*
καὶ ἀποκριθεὶς ὁ Ἰησοῦς εἶπεν πρὸς αὐτόν (Luke 7:40 BNT)
ἀποκριθεὶς δὲ ὁ Ἰησοῦς εἶπεν (Luke 9:41 BNT)
ἀποκριθεὶς δὲ εἶπεν αὐτῇ ὁ Ἰησοῦς (Luke 10:41 BYZ)*
καὶ ἀποκριθεὶς ὁ Ἰησοῦς εἶπεν αὐτοῖς (Luke 13:2 BYZ)*
καὶ ἀποκριθεὶς ὁ Ἰησοῦς εἶπεν (Luke 14:3 BNT)
ἀποκριθεὶς δὲ ὁ Ἰησοῦς εἶπεν (Luke 17:17 BNT)
καὶ ἀποκριθεὶς εἶπεν αὐτοῖς ὁ Ἰησοῦς (Luke 20:34 BYZ)*
ἀποκριθεὶς δὲ ὁ Ἰησοῦς εἶπεν (Luke 22:51 BNT)

*Jesus missing from BNT, GNT, TIS, WHO at 7:22, 10:41, 13:2, 20:34.

There is a wide spread of variants in Luke's double heptad between BYZ, GOC, SCR, and STE, and BNT, GNT, TIS, and WHO. BNT, GNT, TIS, and WHO are all missing the name *Jesus* at 7:22, 10:41, 13:2, and 20:34. Therefore BYZ, GOC, SCR, and STE produce 14 phrases, and BNT, GNT, TIS, and WHO produce 10. However, notice the use of a pronoun 10 times, which indicates the presence of a decadal meter subset.

The name *Jesus* repeats 100 times in the *King James Version* of Luke. *New American Standard* and other contemporary translations repeat *Jesus* 89 times because they are relying on different Greek texts or use a pronoun in place of the name. The manuscripts that support the translation of the KJV may have more repetitions than those found in the original autographs, but it is doubtful that the number is as few as 89. The longer readings in BYZ, GOC, SCR, and STE were preferred because the short readings in BNT, GNT, TIS, and WHO remove the decadal subset of pronouns. This arrangement may be more speculative, but the precedent for heptadic meter is established in Matthew and Mark, the correct variants are present, and there is a decadal subset.

But He Said

Luke sets the same mundane introduction to dialogue in Hebraic meter as do Matthew and Mark. However, he also sets some phrases in his own unique style. The simple words *but he said*, using the Greek words εἶπεν δὲ, appear in the Gospels about 60 times, but only once in Matthew, never in Mark, and 5 times in John. All the rest are in Luke. The same phrase is only found outside the Gospels in Acts, 15 or 16 times with no apparent meter. The point is that this is one of Luke's signature phrases. The following are 3 examples of Hebraic meters with Luke's particular phrasing.

But he said unto him or *them* 10 times in the Gospel of Luke
    But he said unto him......εἶπεν δὲ πρὸς αὐτὸν (Luke 1:13 BNT)
    But he said unto them.....εἶπεν δὲ πρὸς αὐτούς (Luke 9:13 BNT)
    But he said unto him......εἶπεν δὲ πρὸς αὐτὸν (Luke 9:50 BNT)
    But he said unto him......εἶπεν δὲ [πρὸς αὐτὸν] (Luke 9:62 BNT)*
    But he said unto him......εἶπεν δὲ πρὸς αὐτούς (Luke 12:15 BNT)
    But he said unto him......εἶπεν δὲ πρὸς αὐτούς (Luke 15:3 BNT)
    But he said unto him......εἶπεν δὲ πρὸς αὐτὸν (Luke 19:9 BNT)
    But he said unto them.....εἶπεν δὲ πρὸς αὐτούς (Luke 20:41 BNT)
    But he said unto them.....εἶπεν δὲ πρὸς αὐτούς (Luke 24:17 BNT)
    But he said unto them.....εἶπεν δὲ πρὸς αὐτούς (Luke 24:44 BNT)**
*BYZ and GOC have a different word order at 9:62.
**BYZ, GOC, SCR, STE have the dative plural in place of the preposition at Luke 24:44.

But he said unto him 7 times in the Gospel of Luke*
    But he said unto him.........εἶπεν δὲ αὐτῷ (Luke 4:3 BNT)
    But he said unto him.........εἶπεν δὲ αὐτῷ (Luke 9:60 BNT)
    But he said unto him.........εἶπεν δὲ αὐτῷ (Luke 10:28 BNT)
    But he said unto him.........εἶπεν δὲ αὐτω (Luke 10:37 BNT)
    But he said unto him.........εἶπεν δὲ αὐτῷ (Luke 12:20 BNT)
    But he said unto him.........εἶπεν δὲ αὐτῷ (Luke 16:31 BNT)
    But he said unto him.........εἶπεν δὲ αὐτῷ (Luke 18:19 BNT)
*BYZ, GOC, SCR, STE, TIS add 12:41 and 15:21 and are missing 4:3 and 10:37; thus variants rejected.

But said the Lord 7 times in the Gospel of Luke*
    But said the Lord..........εἶπεν δὲ ὁ Κύριος (Luke 7:31 STE)
    But said the Lord..........εἶπεν δὲ ὁ κύριος (Luke 11:39 STE)
    But said the Lord..........εἶπεν δὲ ὁ κύριος (Luke 12:42 STE)
    But said the Lord..........εἶπεν δὲ ὁ κύριος (Luke 17:6 STE)
    But said the Lord..........εἶπεν δὲ ὁ κύριος (Luke 18:6 STE)
    But said the Lord..........εἶπεν δὲ ὁ κύριος (Luke 20:13 STE)
    But said the Lord..........εἶπεν δὲ ὁ Κύριος (Luke 22:31 STE)
*Missing from Luke 7:31, 12:42, and 22:31 in some or all of the other texts.

Each Gospel writer follows some of the same meter, and each has his own unique contribution. The phrase *but said the Lord*, seen above, has 3 possible variants. This makes it rather difficult to establish whether this particular phrase is actually set in Hebraic meter. In addition, it is only found in heptadic repetition in Textus Receptus (KJV/STE), which means roughly 90% of the texts do not agree with Textus Receptus' repetition on this phrase. However, it is obvious that Luke does employ Mosaic cadence in some phrases. It is also interesting that whoever is adding the phrase *But said the Lord* to the text, as many as 3 times (if they are indeed added), is following Luke's unique style. In other words, the copyist(s) who wrote the variants understood exactly how Luke would have written the phrase, not like Matthew, Mark, or John. Therefore, even with meager textual support, this heptad is published above for the reader's consideration.

And He Said to Him

The simple phrase *and he said to him*, is found in all 4 Gospels in Mosaic cadence. It is as if each Gospel writer knows that this particular phrase must be set in Hebraic meter. How is such coordination possible when each Gospel writer is working independently? The assumption is that each writer is aware that he is writing in the sacred style of the Torah under the guidance of the Holy Spirit, and knows the required rubrics of the genre. Again the 7 statements from Genesis are presented, where God speaks to man and the text says, *And He said to him*. Note that Luke uses the same phrase, but changes the Greek verb.

And He said to him 7 times in Genesis (God speaking)
    And He said to him................ וַיֹּאמֶר לוֹ (Gen. 3:9 WTT)
    And He said to him................ וַיֹּאמֶר לוֹ (Gen. 4:15 WTT)
    And He said to him................ וַיֹּאמֶר לוֹ (Gen. 15:5 WTT)
    And He said to him................ וַיֹּאמֶר לוֹ (Gen. 20:3 WTT)
    And He said to him................ וַיֹּאמֶר לוֹ (Gen. 31:24 WTT)
    And He said to him................ וַיֹּאמֶר־לוֹ (Gen. 35:10 WTT)
    And He said to him................ וַיֹּאמֶר לוֹ (Gen. 35:11 WTT)

And he said to him 7 times in the Gospel of Matthew*
    And he said to him.................καὶ λέγει αὐτῷ (Matt. 4:6 BNT)
    And he said to him.................καὶ λέγει αὐτῷ (Matt. 8:4 BNT)
    And he said to him.................καὶ λέγει αὐτῷ (Matt. 8:7 BNT)**
    And he said to him.................καὶ λέγει αὐτῷ (Matt. 8:20 BNT)
    And he said to him.................καὶ λέγει αὐτῷ (Matt. 9:9 BNT)
    And he said to him.................καὶ λέγει αὐτῷ (Matt. 14:31 BNT)
    And he said to him.................καὶ λέγει αὐτῷ (Matt. 22:12 BNT)

*And he said to him, καὶ λέγει αὐτῷ in Matthew 4:9 is missing in BNT, GNT, TIS, WHO, which have καὶ εἶπεν αὐτῷ, another way of saying *and he said to him*, and therefore is not included in the above example.
**TIS and WHO have εἶπεν (*he said*) instead of λέγει (*he said*) at Matt. 8:7.

And he said to him 7 times in the Gospel of Mark*
    And he said to him.................καὶ λέγει αὐτῷ (Mark 1:41 BNT)**

And he said to him................καὶ λέγει αὐτῷ (Mark 1:44 BNT)
And he said to him................καὶ λέγει αὐτῷ (Mark 2:14 BNT)
And he said to him................καὶ λέγει αὐτῷ (Mark 7:28 BNT)
And he said to him................καὶ λέγει αὐτῷ (Mark 7:34 BNT)
And he said to him................καὶ λέγει αὐτῷ (Mark 14:30 BNT)
And he said to him................καὶ λέγει αὐτῷ (Mark 14:61 BNT)

*BYZ, GOC, SCR, STE are missing καὶ λέγει αὐτῷ at Mark 5:9 which is why it is not listed.
**Only TIS is missing καὶ λέγει αὐτῷ at Mark 1:41.

And he said to him 7 times in the Gospel of Luke*

And he said to him.................καὶ εἶπεν αὐτῷ (Luke 4:6 BNT)
And he said to him.................καὶ εἶπεν αὐτῷ (Luke 4:9 BNT)
And he said to him.................καὶ εἶπεν αὐτῷ (Luke 5:27 BNT)
And he said to him.................καὶ εἶπεν αὐτῷ (Luke 9:58 BNT)
And he said to him.................καὶ εἶπεν αὐτῷ (Luke 17:19 BNT)
And he said to him.................καὶ εἶπεν αὐτῷ (Luke 19:17 BNT)
And he said to him.................καὶ εἶπεν αὐτῷ (Luke 23:43 BNT)

*BYZ, GOC, SCR, STE add 4:3, 10:35, 16:6; variants rejected.

As noted just above, the exact phrase in Luke is found 3 more times in BYZ, GOC, SCR, and STE at 4:3, 10:35, and 16:6. This presents an interesting choice between 7 and 10. Which is it? As seen in the previous chapter, Genesis uses this phrase in both a heptad and a decad, the first for God speaking, and the second for man speaking. There are also a surprising number of variants between the Eastern and Alexandrian texts. The spread from 7 to 10 almost appears to be intentional. In this case 7 is chosen because that is the same meter found in Matthew and Mark, and it is doubtful that in this case the text would have been reduced from 10 to 7.

The criteria for these heptadic and decadal phrases are not evident in Greek literature. The only other known source is Moses. Therefore, knowledge of Hebrew syntax is helpful if one wishes to gain a deeper understanding of New Testament textual criticism. Chapter Six will discuss Meir Sternberg's opinion on repetition.

Having come to the end of this chapter, the thought occurred that a search might be made in the Septuagint for the phrase *and he said to him* (Καὶ εἶπεν αὐτῷ). It appears in Genesis 30 times, a number this writer finds rather remarkable, which is not consistent with the Hebrew text. Did the Septuagint translators unintentionally copy Mosaic decadal cadence, or did the writers plan to meter their translation? In view of the Septuagint's inconsistency in translating the Hebrew text, the latter may be the case.

And he said to him 30 times in Genesis (Septuagint)

καὶ εἶπεν αὐτω (Gen. 3:9)	καὶ εἶπεν αὐτῷ (Gen. 3:10)
καὶ εἶπεν αὐτῷ (Gen. 3:11)	καὶ εἶπεν αὐτῷ (Gen. 4:15)
καὶ εἶπεν αὐτῷ (Gen. 12:7)	καὶ εἶπεν αὐτῷ (Gen. 15:5)
καὶ εἶπεν αὐτῷ (Gen. 17:1)	καὶ εἶπεν αὐτῷ (Gen. 19:21)
καὶ εἶπεν αὐτῷ (Gen. 20:9)	καὶ εἶπεν αὐτῷ (Gen. 21:26)
καὶ εἶπεν αὐτῷ (Gen. 22:11)	καὶ εἶπεν αὐτῷ (Gen. 24:24)
καὶ εἶπεν αὐτῷ (Gen. 24:25)	καὶ εἶπεν αὐτῷ (Gen. 24:31)
καὶ εἶπεν αὐτῷ (Gen. 25:33)	καὶ εἶπεν αὐτῷ (Gen. 26:9)
καὶ εἶπεν αὐτῷ (Gen. 27:1)	καὶ εἶπεν αὐτῷ (Gen. 27:26)
καὶ εἶπεν αὐτῷ (Gen. 27:32)	καὶ εἶπεν αὐτῷ (Gen. 27:42)
καὶ εἶπεν αὐτῷ (Gen. 29:14)	καὶ εἶπεν αὐτῷ (Gen. 30:31)
καὶ εἶπεν αὐτῷ (Gen. 31:24)	καὶ εἶπεν αὐτῷ (Gen. 31:32)
καὶ εἶπεν αὐτῷ (Gen. 31:46)	καὶ εἶπεν αὐτῷ (Gen. 32:27)
καὶ εἶπεν αὐτῷ (Gen. 35:10)	καὶ εἶπεν αὐτω (Gen. 37:10)
καὶ εἶπεν αὐτῷ (Gen. 40:12)	καὶ εἶπεν αὐτῷ (Gen. 47:29)

Probability of Repetition in Numbers and Phrases in the Bible

Just as the Bible selects its own unique meter for repeating phrases, it also repeats certain numbers in the text. For example, the phrase *40 days* appears 22 times in the Bible, but 31, 32, 34, 35, 36, 37, 38, 39, 41, 42, 43, 44, 45, 46, 47, 48, and 49 days never appear in the Bible. The repeated selection of 40 literal days is not a statistical coincidence. The Bible's preference for the numbers 1, 2, 3, 4, 5, 6, 7, 8, 10, 12, 17, 20, 30, 40, 42, 50, 70, 72, 100, and 1,000 lies far beyond the realm of statistical probability. There are also many numbers that appear only once in the Bible, such as 27, and others, such as 26, which never appear in the Bible. The primary numbers for Hebraic cadence, 7, 10, and 12, occur respectively more than 380, 190, and 170 times in the Bible, not counting their hundreds of multiples, such as 14, 21, 28, 20, 30, 40, 70, 100, 1,000, 24, 120, and 144. Chapter Thirteen in the 2012 edition includes a more thorough discussion of this topic.

Metered words are an important source for locating metered phrases. In other words, there is a higher probability that a metered word will also be part of a metered phrase. Based on Cassuto's 3 primary cadences found in Genesis and Exodus, 7, 10, 12, and their multiples, there is a 25% probability that any particular word will exhibit Hebraic cadence when repeated 7 or more times. However, metered phrases with as many as 10 words exhibit a much lower probability of Hebraic meter than individual words. The longer the phrase is, the lower the probability.

Another step in the process of establishing the existence of Hebraic cadence is locating the same metered phrase in other books of the Bible, such as Revelation, Genesis, and multiple Gospels. The existence of identical metered phrases that originate in Genesis and are found in 3 or 4 Gospels is beyond the realm of statistical probability. The possibility of subsets of Hebraic cadence, such as a heptad within a decad, or a heptad and a decad within a dodecad, is particularly intriguing. Possible reasons for employing these metered phrases in the 4 Gospels include tradition, genre, literary device, subject, aesthetics, cultus, ritual, symbolism, and as a means of identifying an authentic text, among other, as yet unknown, reasons.

Numbers in the Bible are often selected under the Spirit's influence in order to emphasize a symbolic connotation, unless we are to believe that the selection of 12 tribes and 12 apostles is another coincidence.

As in all of the Gospels, Luke includes a number of single words in Mosaic cadence. The following words were selected because of their relationship to repetition in other books of the Bible and their importance for determining correct variant readings. Words that are often selected for cadence are names, places, numbers, titles, things, *amen*, *forever*, *spirit*, and *bless*. After conducting similar searches in Revelation and Genesis, these are the words most likely chosen for Hebraic metering. One of the reasons Matthew and John appear to have more individual words set in Hebraic meter is because this writer spent more time searching those 2 books.

Single Words in Heptadic Meter
Amen: 7, ἀμήν (*amen*, am-ane') 4:24; 12:37; 13:35; 18:17, 29; 21:32; 23:43; 13:35 in GOC, SCR, STE is accepted and 24:53 in BYZ, GOC, SCR, STE is rejected;

Fish/Fishes: 7, ἰχθύς (*ichthus*, ikh-thoos') 5:6, 9; 9:13, 16; 11:11 (2x); 24:42;

John (the Apostle): 7, Ἰωάννης (*Ioannes*, ee-o-an'-nace) 5:10; 6:14; 8:51; 9:28, 49, 54; 22:8;

Passover: 7, πάσχα (*pascha*, pas'-khah) 2:41; 22:1, 7, 8, 11, 13, 15;

Peter: 14, Πέτρος (*Petros*, pet'-ros) nominative 5:8; 8:45; 9:20, 32, 33; 12:41; 18:28; 22:54, 55, 58, 60, 61, 62; 24:12; BYZ, GOC, SCR, STE;

Seven: 7, ἑπτά (*hepta*, hep-tah') 2:36; 8:2; 11:26; 17:4; 20:29, 31, 33;

Spirit: 7, Πνεύματος (*pneumatos*, pnyoo'-mah-tos) BYZ, GOC, SCR, STE 1:15, 41, 67; 2:26; 4:1, 14; 9:55;

Stone: 7, λίθον (*lithon*, lee'-thon) accusative 4:11; 11:11; 19:44 (x2); 20:17, 18; 24:2; longer reading in 11:11 is correct in BYZ, GOC, SCR, STE, TIS, VST and KJV.

Single Words in Decadal Meter

Abraham/Lazarus: 10, Chapter 16, Ἀβραάμ (*Abraam*, ab-rah-am') 16:22, 23, 24, 25, 29, 30; Λάζαρος (*Lazaros*, lad'-zar-os) 16:20, 23, 24, 25;

Blessed: 30, 16 μακάριος (*makarios*, mak-ar'-ee-os) 1:45, 48; 6:20, 21 (x2), 23; 7:23; 10:23; 11:27, 28; 12:37, 38, 43; 14:14; 23:29; 14 εὐλογέω, 1:42 (x2), 64, 68; 2:28, 34; 6:28; 9:16; 13:35; 19:38; 24:30, 50, 51, 53; 1:28 in BYZ, GOC, SCR, STE rejected (see Lord); Revelation has 7 μακάριος and 3 εὐλογέω for a total of 10;

High priests: 10, ἀρχιερεῖς (*archiereus*, ar-khee-er-yuce') nominative plural 19:47; 20:1, 19; 22:2, 52, 66; 23:4, 10, 13; 24:20;

Lord: 30, κύριος (*kurios*, koo'-ree-os) nominative singular 1:25, 28, 32, 58, 68; 2:11, 15; 6:5; 7:13; 10:1; 11:39; 12:37, 42 (x2), 43, 45, 46; 13:15; 14:23; 16:3, 8; 17:6; 18:6; 19:31, 34; 20:13, 15, 42; 22:61; 24:34; BNT, GNT, TIS, VST, WHO remove 1:28; BYZ, GOC, SCR, STE remove 10:41 and replace it with *Jesus* (see Blessed); Lord is in Revelation 24 times;

Moses: 10, Μωσεῦς (*Moseus*, moce-yoos') 2:22; 5:14; 9:30, 33; 16:29, 31; 20:28, 37; 24:27, 44; Moses' name is also associated with the 10 Commandments;

Peter: 20, Πέτρος (*Petros*, pet'-ros) 5:8; 6:14; 8:45, 51; 9:20, 28, 32, 33; 12:41; 18:28; 22:8, 34, 54, 55, 58, 60, 61 (x2), 62; 24:12; BNT, GNT, BYZ, GOC, SCR, STE, VST include 24:12; Peter is also in Mark 20 times;

Pharisees: 10, Φαρισαῖος (*Pharisaios*, far-is-ah'-yos) nominative plural 5:17, 21, 30; 6:7; 7:30; 11:39, 53; 13:31; 15:2; 16:14; BYZ, GOC, SCR, STE add 11:44; variant rejected;

Sabbath: 20, σάββατον (*sabbaton*, sab'-bat-on) 4:16, 31; 6:1, 2, 5, 6, 7, 9; 13:10, 14 (x2), 15, 16; 14:1, 3, 5; 18:12; 23:54, 56; 24:1;

Third: 10, τρίτος (*tritos*, tree'-tos) 9:22; 12:38; 13:32; 18:33; 20:12, 31; 23:22; 24:7, 21:46;

Zacharias: 10, (*Ζαχαρίας*, dzakh-ar-ee'-as) 1:5, 12, 13, 18, 21, 40, 59, 67; 3:2; 11:51.

Single Words in Dodecadal Meter

Boat, Net, Fish: 12, Chapter 5:1-11;
Boat, πλοῖον (*ploion*, ploy'-on) 5:2, 3 (x2), 7 (x2), 11;
Fish, ἰχθύς (*ichthus*, ikh-thoos') 5:6, 9;
Net, δίκτυον (*diktuon*, dik'-too-on) 5:2, 4, 5, 6;

Christ: 12, Χριστός (*Christos*, khris-tos') 2:11, 26; 3:15; 4:41; 9:20; 20:41; 22:67; 23:2, 35, 39; 24:26, 46; BYZ, GOC, SCR, STE add 4:41 which is rejected; Christ is in Revelation 10 times;

David: 12/13, Δαυίδ (*Dauid*, dau-weed') 1:27, 32, 69; 2:4 (x2), 11; 3:31; 6:3; 18:38, 39; 20:41, 42, 44; the meter is probably 12 because 3:31 is in the genealogy;

Heart: 24, καρδία (*kardia*, kar-dee'-ah) 1:17, 51, 66; 2:19, 35, 51; 3:15; 4:18; 5:22; 6:45; 8:12, 15; 9:47; 10:27; 12:34, 45 (x3); 16:15; 21:14, 34; 24:25, 32, 38; BNT, GNT, TIS, VST, WHO lack 4:18; 6:45;

John the Baptist: 24, 1:13, 60, 63; 3:2, 15, 16, 20; 5:33; 7:18, 19, 20, 22, 24 (x2), 28, 29, 33; 9:7, 9, 19; 11:1; 16:16; 20:4, 6;
Mary: 12, Μαριάμ (*Mariam*, mar-ee-am') 1:27, 30, 34, 38, 39, 41, 46, 56; 2:5, 16, 19, 34;
Pilate: 12, Πιλᾶτος (*Pilatos*, pil-at'-os) 3:1; 13:1; 23:1, 3, 4, 6, 11, 12, 13, 20, 24, 52;
Twelve: 12, δώδεκα (*dodeka*, do'-dek-ah) 2:42; 6:13; 8:1, 42, 43; 9:1, 12, 17; 18:31; 22:3, 30, 47; BYZ, GOC, SCR, STE add 22:14; variant rejected; twelve and twelfth are in Revelation 24 times.

Single Word Repeated 17 Times
Simon: 17, Σίμων (*Simon*, see'-mone) 16 *Simon Peter*, and 1 *Simon of Cyrene,* 4:38 (x2); 5:3, 4, 5, 8, 10 (x2); 6:14, 15; 7:40, 43, 44; 22:31 (x2); 23:26; 24:34.

Chapter Four
Repetition in the Gospel of John

Repetition in the Gospel of John presents some rather unique features:

First, there is the opportunity to compare John with the 3 previous Gospels.

Second, there are similarities between the repetition in John and Revelation, a challenge to those who question John's apostolic authorship of Revelation.

Third, John incorporates more repetition within specific chapters or accounts than the other Gospels. Cassuto finds many examples of meter within accounts, as will be shown in Chapters Eight and Nine.

An examination of John verifies the continuity of Hebraic meter as a literary device in all 4 Gospels. Even though approximately 80% of John's Gospel is new information about Jesus, John follows Mosaic cadence with the same genre as found in Matthew, Mark, and Luke. In a number of cases he repeats the same phrases or metered words found in one or more of the other Gospels. Such an observation refutes numerous theories and speculation about which Gospel writer copied another Gospel writer or another source. We are led to the following possibilities:

1. All 4 Gospel writers met together and coordinated everything they wrote.

2. All 4 Gospels were edited by an unknown writer or committee of writers, who destroyed all previous copies.

3. All 4 Gospel writers independently employed traditional Hebraic meter, as identified in the writings of Umberto Cassuto in Chapters Eight and Nine.

4. The entire process of repetition in the Gospels is directed by the Holy Spirit. To whatever extent, the Gospel writers became aware of the repetition by examining their own writing.

After reviewing the data in the previous 3 chapters on the Gospels, let the reader come to the conclusion that best fits one of these possibilities.

Eternal Life and Truth

All 4 Gospels focus on eternal life and eternal truth, but John speaks about *everlasting life* and *life* more than the other 3 Gospels combined. Where the other 3 Gospels emphasize God's eternal truth with *verily*, John says *verily verily*, and repeats *amen* as many times as Matthew, Mark, and Luke combined.

Everlasting Life / The Ages of Ages / Forever

Only John uses the phrase *everlasting life* in Hebraic meter, which he repeats 14 times—a double heptad—in his Gospel. Using a similar phrase, *the ages of ages* (almost always translated as *forever and ever*), he then repeats the identical meter in Revelation. Daniel, which appears to be the source for the phrase, has 7 repetitions, or one heptad, of the word *forever*. Revelation is not only a book of mysteries, but the manner in which it repeats phrases in Genesis, Daniel, and the Gospel of John raises new mysteries.

Everlasting life 14 times in the Gospel of John (no variants)
Everlasting life......................ἔχῃ ζωὴν αἰώνιον (John 3:15 BNT)
Everlasting life...............ἀλλ᾽ ἔχῃ ζωὴν αἰώνιον (John 3:16 BNT)
Everlasting life......................ἔχει ζωὴν αἰώνιον (John 3:36 BNT)
Everlasting life........................εἰς ζωὴν αἰώνιον (John 4:14 BNT)
Everlasting life........................εἰς ζωὴν αἰώνιον (John 4:36 BNT)
Everlasting life......................ἔχει ζωὴν αἰώνιον (John 5:24 BNT)
Everlasting life..............ἐν αὐταῖς ζωὴν αἰώνιον (John 5:39 BNT)
Everlasting life........................εἰς ζωὴν αἰώνιον (John 6:27 BNT)
Everlasting life........................εἰς ζωὴν αἰώνιον (John 6:40 BNT)
Everlasting life......................ἔχει ζωὴν αἰώνιον (John 6:47 BNT)
Everlasting life......................ἔχει ζωὴν αἰώνιον (John 6:54 BNT)
Everlasting life..................αὐτοῖς ζωὴν αἰώνιον (John 10:28 BNT)
Everlasting life........................εἰς ζωὴν αἰώνιον (John 12:25 BNT)
Everlasting life..................αὐτοῖς ζωὴν αἰώνιον (John 17:2 BNT)

The ages of ages 14 times in Revelation*
The ages of ages, amen...τοὺς αἰῶνας τῶν αἰώνων, ἀμήν (Rev. 1:6 BNT)
The ages of ages, amen...τοὺς αἰῶνας τῶν αἰώνων, ἀμήν (Rev. 1:18 BNT)
The ages of ages...............τοὺς αἰῶνας τῶν αἰώνων (Rev. 4:9 BNT)
The ages of ages...............τοὺς αἰῶνας τῶν αἰώνων (Rev. 4:10 BNT)
The ages of ages...............τοὺς αἰῶνας τῶν αἰώνων (Rev. 5:13 BNT)
The ages of ages...............τοὺς αιωνας τῶν αἰώνων (Rev. 5:14 SCR, STE)**
The ages of ages, amen...τοὺς αἰῶνας τῶν αἰώνων, ἀμήν (Rev. 7:12 BNT)
The ages of ages...............τοὺς αἰῶνας τῶν αἰώνων (Rev. 10:6 BNT)

The ages of ages	τοὺς αἰῶνας τῶν αἰώνων	(Rev. 11:15 BNT)
To ages of ages	εἰς αἰῶνας αἰώνων	(Rev. 14:11 BNT)
The ages of ages	τοὺς αἰῶνας τῶν αἰώνων	(Rev. 15:7 BNT)
The ages of ages	τοὺς αἰῶνας τῶν αἰώνων	(Rev. 19:3 BNT)
The ages of ages	τοὺς αἰῶνας τῶν αἰώνων	(Rev. 20:10 BNT)
The ages of ages	τοὺς αἰῶνας τῶν αἰώνων	(Rev. 22:5 BNT)

*Almost always translated as *forever and ever*, but is really *the ages of ages*.
**Rev. 5:14 only in SCR, STE; variant accepted.

Forever 7 times in Daniel

Forever	לְעָלְמִין	(Dan. 2:4)
Forever	לְעָלְמִין	(Dan. 2:44)
Forever	לְעָלְמִין	(Dan. 3:9)
Forever	לְעָלְמִין	(Dan. 5:10)
Forever	לְעָלְמִין	(Dan. 6:7)
Forever	לְעָלְמִין	(Dan. 6:22)
Forever	לְעָלְמִין	(Dan. 6:27)

Amen, Amen or *Verily, Verily*

In addition to *eternal life*, John is the only Gospel that doubles the word *amen*, commonly translated as *verily, verily* or *truly, truly*. The Hebrew phrase אָמֵן אָמֵן (pronounced aw-mane›) first appears in Numbers 5:22 in the Law of Jealousy. In other words, the unrepentant will be judged and the faithful will be blessed when Christ speaks these words. In Nehemiah 8:6 the people pledged their faithfulness to God with a double *amen*. In Revelation, John uses a single *amen* 10 times. There are no variant readings for the phrase *verily, verily, I say unto you* in any of the texts. However, there is a subset heptad with *that* (ὅτι) if BYZ, GOC, SCR, and STE are followed at 16:23.

Verily, verily, I say unto you 20 times in the Gospel of John

Verily, verily, I say unto you	ἀμὴν ἀμὴν λέγω ὑμῖν	(John 1:51)
Verily, verily, I say unto you	ἀμὴν ἀμὴν λέγω ὑμῖν	(John 5:19)
Verily, verily, I say unto you that	ἀμὴν ἀμὴν λέγω ὑμῖν ὅτι	(John 5:24)
Verily, verily, I say unto you that	ἀμὴν ἀμὴν λέγω ὑμῖν ὅτι	(John 5:25)
Verily, verily, I say unto you that	ἀμὴν ἀμὴν λέγω ὑμῖν	(John 6:26)
Verily, verily, I say unto you	ἀμὴν ἀμὴν λέγω ὑμῖν	(John 6:32)
Verily, verily, I say unto you	ἀμὴν ἀμὴν λέγω ὑμῖν	(John 6:47)
Verily, verily, I say unto you	ἀμὴν ἀμὴν λέγω ὑμῖν	(John 6:53)
Verily, verily, I say unto you that	ἀμὴν ἀμὴν λέγω ὑμῖν ὅτι	(John 8:34)
Verily, verily, I say unto you	ἀμὴν ἀμὴν λέγω ὑμῖν	(John 8:51)
Verily, verily, I say unto you	ἀμὴν ἀμὴν λέγω ὑμῖν	(John 8:58)
Verily, verily, I say unto you	ἀμὴν ἀμὴν λέγω ὑμῖν	(John 10:1)
Verily, verily, I say unto you	ἀμὴν ἀμὴν λέγω ὑμῖν ὅτι	(John 10:7)
Verily, verily, I say unto you	ἀμὴν ἀμὴν λέγω ὑμῖν	(John 12:24)
Verily, verily, I say unto you	ἀμὴν ἀμὴν λέγω ὑμῖν	(John 13:16)

Verily, verily, I say unto you............ἀμὴν ἀμὴν λέγω ὑμῖν (John 13:20)
Verily, verily, I say unto you that.....ἀμὴν ἀμὴν λέγω ὑμῖν ὅτι (John 13:21)
Verily, verily, I say unto you............ἀμὴν ἀμὴν λέγω ὑμῖν (John 14:15)
Verily, verily, I say unto you that.....ἀμὴν ἀμὴν λέγω ὑμῖν ὅτι (John 16:20)
Verily, verily, I say unto you that.....ἀμὴν ἀμὴν λέγω ὑμῖν ὅτι (John 16:23)*
*That (ὅτι) is missing from BNT, GNT, TIS, VST, WHO in 16:23.

With 20 phrases and no variants, a number of subsets are expected. The shorter phrase *verily, verily, I say* is found 25 times in John. The longer phrase above, *verily, verily, I say unto you* (plural *you*; in Greek, ὑμῖν), repeats 20 times. This makes a total of 50 *amen* in John without a variant. Imagine a word so important, that there are no variants out of 50 repetitions. *Amen* may be the most accurately copied word in the Gospel of John. The *amens* at the end of the Gospels in Eastern texts were all added, and are also out of context. The question remains as to why the context for *amen* in John's Gospel is so different from Revelation. In Revelation it would not be possible to translate *amen* as *verily*, or *truly*. Without sorting through the variants, there are a total of 100 repetitions of the shorter phrase *verily, I say* (ἀμὴν λέγω) in the 4 Gospels.

In the Gospel of John there are 10 repetitions of the longer phrase, *Jesus answered* and/or *said, Verily, verily, I say unto you* (singular and plural *you*; in Greek, σοι and ὑμῖν, respectively). Surprisingly, there are no variant readings. A possible 11th phrase is found in 13:38, but the phrase is interrupted with Jesus asking a question. The 10th phrase in this Hebraic meter (John 13:21) incorporates a comment on Jesus' emotion before He speaks. Note that while Jesus' statement, *Verily, verily, I say unto you*, is arranged in mechanical repetition, the forepart of the longer phrase is irregular. It is an interesting combination of concurrent asymmetric and symmetric order. Notice the bolded Greek ὁ (*the*) before Ἰησοῦς (*Jesus*) 7 times.

Jesus answered and/or *said, Verily, verily, I say unto you* 10 times in the Gospel of John

Jesus answered and said unto him, Verily, verily, I say unto thee (John 3:3)
Jesus answered, Verily, verily, I say unto thee (John 3:5)
Then answered Jesus and said unto them, Verily, verily, I say unto you (John 5:19)
Jesus answered them and said, Verily, verily, I say unto you (John 6:26)
Then Jesus said unto them, Verily, verily, I say unto you (John 6:32)
Then Jesus said unto them, Verily, verily, I say unto you (John 6:53)
Jesus answered them, Verily, verily, I say unto you (John 8:34)
Jesus said unto them, Verily, verily, I say unto you (John 8:58)
Then said Jesus unto them again, Verily, verily, I say unto you (John 10:7)
When Jesus had thus said…Verily, verily, I say unto you (John 13:21)*
*Full text without ellipsis: "When Jesus had thus said, he was troubled in spirit, and testified, and said, Verily, verily, I say unto you" (John 13:21).

ἀπεκρίθη Ἰησοῦς καὶ εἶπεν αὐτῷ, ἀμὴν ἀμὴν λέγω σοι (John 3:3 BNT)
ἀπεκρίθη Ἰησοῦς, ἀμὴν ἀμὴν λέγω σοι (John 3:5 BNT)
Ἀπεκρίνατο οὖν ὁ Ἰησοῦς καὶ εἶπεν αὐτοῖς, ἀμὴν ἀμὴν λέγω ὑμῖν (John 5:19 BNT)
Ἀπεκρίθη αὐτοῖς ὁ Ἰησοῦς καὶ εἶπεν, ἀμὴν ἀμὴν λέγω ὑμῖν (John 6:26 BNT)
εἶπεν οὖν αὐτοῖς ὁ Ἰησοῦς, ἀμὴν ἀμὴν λέγω ὑμῖν (John 6:32 BNT)
εἶπεν οὖν αὐτοῖς ὁ Ἰησοῦς, ἀμὴν ἀμὴν λέγω ὑμῖν (John 6:53 BNT)
ἀπεκρίθη αὐτοῖς ὁ Ἰησοῦς, ἀμὴν ἀμὴν λέγω ὑμῖν (John 8:34 BNT)
εἶπεν αὐτοῖς Ἰησοῦς, ἀμὴν ἀμὴν λέγω ὑμῖν (John 8:58 BNT)
Εἶπεν οὖν πάλιν ὁ Ἰησοῦς, ἀμὴν ἀμὴν λέγω ὑμῖν (John 10:7 BNT)
Ταῦτα εἰπὼν [ὁ] Ἰησοῦς…ἀμὴν ἀμὴν λέγω ὑμῖν (John 13:21 BNT)*

*Full text without ellipsis: "Ταῦτα εἰπὼν [ὁ] Ἰησοῦς ἐταράχθη τῷ πνεύματι καὶ ἐμαρτύρησεν καὶ εἶπεν ἀμὴν ἀμὴν λέγω ὑμῖν" (John 13:21 BNT).

The same phrase, *verily, I say to you*, is found in Matthew 24 times, Mark 14 times, and Luke 7 times, except that they only use one *amen*, or *verily*. None of the English translations say *amen*, even though it has a more emphatic tone of divine pronouncement.

In Matthew, a number of the texts contain the phrase *verily, I say to you* at 18:19, which would make 25 repetitions, the identical number in John. However, BNT, GNT, and WHO place it in brackets, which means they are not sure. BYZ and GOC add it to the text, while the strange mix of Receptus (SCR, STE), TIS and VST omit it. Rarely do variants in TIS and STE agree. The question is, "Did some of the copyists add the 25th example at Matthew 18:19 in order to match John's meter? Or was it in the original text, but omitted by other copyists in order to create an even 100 repetitions in all 4 Gospels?" If the correct variants are selected, we even find the same subset of 7 *that* (ὅτι) in Matthew as found in John. However, with so many variants of *that* (ὅτι), it is difficult to decide about removing 6:5 or 6:16. In this case, SCR, STE, TIS, and VST are the shorter texts.

Verily, I say to you 24 times in the Gospel of Matthew*
Verily, I say to you………ἀμὴν λέγω ὑμῖν (Matt. 6:2 BNT)
Verily, I say to you **that**…ἀμὴν λέγω ὑμῖν ὅτι (Matt. 6:5 BNT)**
Verily, I say to you **that**…ἀμὴν λέγω ὑμῖν ὅτι (Matt. 6:16 BNT)***
Verily, I say to you………ἀμὴν λέγω ὑμῖν (Matt. 8:10 BNT)
Verily, I say to you………ἀμὴν λέγω ὑμῖν (Matt. 10:15 BNT)
Verily, I say to you………ἀμὴν λέγω ὑμῖν (Matt. 10:42 BNT)
Verily, I say to you………ἀμὴν λέγω ὑμῖν (Matt. 11:11 BNT)
Verily, I say to you………ἀμὴν λέγω ὑμῖν (Matt. 16:28 BNT)
Verily, I say to you………ἀμὴν λέγω ὑμῖν (Matt. 18:3 BNT)
Verily, I say to you **that**…ἀμὴν λέγω ὑμῖν ὅτι (Matt. 18:13 BNT)
Verily, I say to you………ἀμὴν λέγω ὑμῖν (Matt. 18:18 BNT)
Verily, I say to you **that**…ἀμὴν λέγω ὑμῖν ὅτι (Matt. 19:23 BNT)
Verily, I say to you **that**…ἀμὴν λέγω ὑμῖν ὅτι (Matt. 19:28 BNT)
Verily, I say to you………ἀμὴν λέγω ὑμῖν (Matt. 21:21 BNT)

Verily, I say to you **that**...ἀμὴν λέγω ὑμῖν ὅτι (Matt. 21:31 BNT)
Verily, I say to you.........ἀμὴν λέγω ὑμῖν (Matt. 23:36 BNT)
Verily, I say to you.........ἀμὴν λέγω ὑμῖν (Matt. 24:2 BNT)
Verily, I say to you **that**...ἀμὴν λέγω ὑμῖν ὅτι (Matt. 24:34 BNT)
Verily, I say to you.........ἀμὴν λέγω ὑμῖν (Matt. 24:47 BNT)
Verily, I say to you.........ἀμὴν λέγω ὑμῖν (Matt. 25:12 BNT)
Verily, I say to you.........ἀμὴν λέγω ὑμῖν (Matt. 25:40 BNT)
Verily, I say to you.........ἀμὴν λέγω ὑμῖν (Matt. 25:45 BNT)
Verily, I say to you.........ἀμὴν λέγω ὑμῖν (Matt. 26:13 BNT)
Verily, I say to you **that**...ἀμὴν λέγω ὑμῖν ὅτι (Matt. 26:21 BNT)

*BNT, GNT, WHO question *amen* [ἀμὴν] at 18:19; BYZ and GOC include *amen*, but missing from SCR, STE, TIS, VST; variant rejected.
**That (ὅτι, *hoti*) at 6:5 only in BYZ, GOC, SCR, STE, VST; variant accepted.
***That (ὅτι, *hoti*) at 6:16 only in BYZ, GOC, SCR, STE, VST; variant accepted.

Verily, I say to you 14 times in the Gospel of Mark

Verily, I say to you...........ἀμὴν λέγω ὑμῖν (Mark 3:28 BNT)
Verily, I say to you.........ἀμὴν λέγω ὑμῖν (Mark 6:11 BYZ)*
Verily, I say to you.........ἀμὴν λέγω ὑμῖν (Mark 8:12 BNT)
Verily, I say to you...........ἀμὴν λέγω ὑμῖν (Mark 9:1 BNT)
Verily, I say to you.........ἀμὴν λέγω ὑμῖν (Mark 9:41 BNT)
Verily, I say to you.........ἀμὴν λέγω ὑμῖν (Mark 10:15 BNT)
Verily, I say to you.........ἀμὴν λέγω ὑμῖν (Mark 10:29 BNT)
Verily, I say to you...........ἀμὴν λέγω ὑμῖν (Mark 11:23 BNT)**
Verily, I say to you...........ἀμὴν λέγω ὑμῖν (Mark 12:43 BNT)
Verily, I say to you...........ἀμὴν λέγω ὑμῖν (Mark 13:30 BNT)
Verily, I say to you.........ἀμὴν δὲ λέγω ὑμῖν (Mark 14:9 BNT)
Verily, I say to you...........ἀμὴν λέγω ὑμῖν (Mark 14:18 BNT)
Verily, I say to you..........ἀμὴν λέγω ὑμῖν (Mark 14:25 BNT)
Verily, I say to you.........ἀμὴν λέγω σοι (Mark 14:30 BNT)

*The entire sentence in Mark 6:11, "Verily I say unto you, it shall be more tolerable for Sodom and Gomorrah in the day of judgment, than for that city," is not found in BNT, GNT, TIS, VST, WHO, and is deleted from the NASB and the NIV. The assumption is that it was copied from Luke 10:12, and the phrase *verily I say unto you* was added to Mark 6:11. The longer reading of Mark 6:11, as found in BYZ, GOC, SCR, and STE, is necessary for 14 repetitions of *verily I say unto you*. The question is, "Was it added to the text?" There is another possibility. Mark 14:30 has the only plural pronoun, and Mark has the habit of making differentiations in phrases. Removing both 14:30 and 6:11 would make 12 repetitions. At this writing, it is difficult to decide which is the original meter because none of the other words of the longer version of 6:11 complete any other Hebraic meter in Mark.
**BYZ, GOC, SCR, STE read, *For verily I say to you* (Ἀμὴν γὰρ λέγω ὑμῖν) at Mark 11:23; variant rejected.

Luke includes a 3-4 subset with *that* (ὅτι). Why each Gospel writer uses the same phrase in Mosaic cadence is a mystery. For reasons known only to the Biblical writers, certain words or phrases are selected as a literary device for Hebraic meter. In total, 5 examples of heptadic phrases with *amen,* including 3 subsets, are displayed. With 100 repetitions of *amen* in the 4 Gospels, 50 of them in John, the assumption is that there are more sets and subsets than these. The 51st *amen* at the end of John is an obvious out-of-context copyist's addition. It is the only *amen* in John that cannot be translated as *verily.*

Verily, I say to you 7 times in the Gospel of Luke
    Verily, I say to you that…ἀμὴν λέγω ὑμῖν ὅτι (Luke 4:24 BNT)
    Verily, I say to you that…ἀμὴν λέγω ὑμῖν ὅτι (Luke 12:37 BNT)
    Verily, I say to you……….ἀμὴν δὲ λέγω ὑμῖν (Luke 13:35 STE)*
    Verily, I say to you……….ἀμὴν λέγω ὑμῖν (Luke 18:17 BNT)
    Verily, I say to you that…ἀμὴν λέγω ὑμῖν ὅτι (Luke 18:29 BNT)
    Verily, I say to you that…ἀμὴν λέγω ὑμῖν ὅτι (Luke 21:32 BNT)
    Verily, I say to you……….ἀμὴν λέγω σοι (Luke 23:43 BYZ)**
*Amen at 13:35 is only in Receptus (SCR, STE) and also lacks *that* (ὅτι) in BNT, GNT, TIS, VST, WHO, to make a 3-4 subset.
**BYZ, GOC, SCR, STE are followed at 23:43 for the preferred word order, though all have *amen.*

Heptadic Meter in John
World / Temple / In You / In…and I In
    Another phrase without variants is Jesus coming *into the world,* which appears in John in a double heptad.

Into the world 14 times in the Gospel of John
    Into the world……εἰς τὸν κόσμον (John 1:9 BNT)
    Into the world……εἰς τὸν κόσμον (John 3:17 BNT)
    Into the world……εἰς τὸν κόσμον (John 3:19 BNT)
    Into the world……εἰς τὸν κόσμον (John 6:14 BNT)
    Into the world……εἰς τὸν κόσμον (John 8:26 BNT)
    Into the world……εἰς τὸν κόσμον (John 9:39 BNT)
    Into the world……εἰς τὸν κόσμον (John 10:36 BNT)
    Into the world……εἰς τὸν κόσμον (John 11:27 BNT)
    Into the world……εἰς τὸν κόσμον (John 12:46 BNT)
    Into the world……εἰς τὸν κόσμον (John 16:21 BNT)
    Into the world……εἰς τὸν κόσμον (John 16:28 BNT)
    Into the world……εἰς τὸν κόσμον (John 17:18 BNT)
    Into the world……εἰς τὸν κόσμον (John 17:18 BNT)
    Into the world……εἰς τὸν κόσμον (John 18:37 BNT)

    Like the above, the phrase *of the world* also appears 14 times in the Gospel of John. BYZ, GOC, SCR, STE, and TIS have the correct word order at 8:23, ἐκ τοῦ κόσμου τούτου, *out of this world*, while BNT, GNT, VST, and WHO have ἐκ τούτου τοῦ κόσμου, which says the same thing. The inclusion of this error in BNT, GNT, VST, and WHO illustrates the excessive rubrics that lead some scholars to regard the correct reading as being the only variant of this phrase by John out of 14 repetitions. If it is different, they think that means it is correct. John wrote ἐκ τοῦ κόσμου τούτου, not ἐκ τούτου τοῦ κόσμου. Sometimes the over-glamorized *electos difficilior* (the more difficult reading) is nothing more than an obvious copyist's error.

Of the world 14 times in the Gospel of John
    Of the world........ἐκ τοῦ κόσμου (John 8:23 BNT)
    Of the world........ἐκ τοῦ κόσμου (John 8:23 BYZ)*
    Of the world......ἐκ τοῦ κόσμου (John 13:1 BNT)
    Of the world......ἐκ τοῦ κόσμου (John 15:19 BNT)
    Of the world........ἐκ τοῦ κόσμου (John 15:19 BNT)
    Of the world......ἐκ τοῦ κόσμου (John 15:19 BNT)
    Of the world......ἐκ τοῦ κόσμου (John 17:6 BNT)
    Of the world......ἐκ τοῦ κόσμου (John 17:14 BNT)
    Of the world......ἐκ τοῦ κόσμου (John 17:14 BNT)
    Of the world......ἐκ τοῦ κόσμου (John 17:15 BNT)
    Of the world......ἐκ τοῦ κόσμου (John 17:16 BNT)
    Of the world......ἐκ τοῦ κόσμου (John 17:16 BNT)
    Of the world......ἐκ τοῦ κόσμου (John 18:36 BNT)
    Of the world......ἐκ τοῦ κόσμου (John 18:36 BNT)
*BNT, GNT, VST, WHO have a longer phrase, *out of this world*, ἐκ τούτου τοῦ κόσμου, which is rejected.

Originally, it was thought that *in the temple* was unique to John. However, when the first 3 Gospels were rechecked, the phrase *in the temple* was also found in Luke 7 times. Thus, the phrase was added to the previous chapter after typing the information below.

In the temple 7 times in the Gospel of John (no variants)
    In the temple......ἐν τῷ ἱερῷ (John 2:14 BNT)
    In the temple......ἐν τῷ ἱερῷ (John 5:14 BNT)
    In the temple......ἐν τῷ ἱερῷ (John 7:28 BNT)
    In the temple......ἐν τῷ ἱερῷ (John 8:20 BNT)
    In the temple......ἐν τῷ ἱερῷ (John 10:23 BNT)
    In the temple......ἐν τῷ ἱερῷ (John 11:56 BNT)
    In the temple......ἐν τῷ ἱερῷ (John 18:20 BNT)

In you 7 times in the Gospel of John*
    And you do not have His word abiding **in you** (John 5:38)
    Because My words have no place **in you** (John 8:37)
    And is **in you** (John 14:17)

And is also **in you** (John 14:20)
And is also **in you** (John 15:4)
And the words of me **in you** (John 15:7)
In order that My joy abide **in you** (John 15:11)

καὶ τὸν λόγον αὐτοῦ οὐκ ἔχετε **ἐν ὑμῖν** (John 5:38 BNT)
...ὅτι ὁ λόγος ὁ ἐμὸς οὐ χωρεῖ **ἐν ὑμῖν** (John 8:37 BNT)
καὶ **ἐν ὑμῖν** ἔσται (John 14:17 BNT)
κἀγὼ **ἐν ὑμῖν** (John 14:20 BNT)
κἀγὼ **ἐν ὑμῖν** (John 15:4 BNT)
καὶ τὰ ῥήματά μου **ἐν ὑμῖν** (John 15:7 BNT)
ἵνα ἡ χαρὰ ἡ ἐμὴ **ἐν ὑμῖν** (John 15:11 BNT)

*In 12:35 (not included above) instead of *yet a little while the light is with you*, BNT, GNT, TIS, VST, and WHO have *yet a little while the light is in you* (ἔτι μικρὸν χρόνον τὸ φῶς ἐν ὑμῖν ἐστιν). In addition to breaking the heptadic meter, in the context of the above this is also false doctrine. Believers never lose the light of Christ dwelling in them. Some recent translations soften the meaning of this incorrect variant added to 12:35, and read *among you* instead of *in you*.

In...and I in 7 times in the Gospel of John
abides **in Me, and I in** him (John 6:56)
that the Father is **in Me, and I in** the Father (John 10:38)
and you **in Me, and I in** you (John 14:20)
Abide **in Me, and I in** you (John 15:4)
He who abides **in Me, and I in** him (John 15:5)
even as Thou, Father, *art* **in Me, and I in** Thee (John 17:21)
Thou didst love **Me** may be **in them, and I in** them (John 17:26)*

*Full quotation: *that the love wherewith Thou didst love Me may be **in them, and I in** them* (John 17:26).

ἐν ἐμοὶ μένει **κἀγὼ ἐν** αὐτῳ (John 6:56 BNT)
ὅτι **ἐν ἐμοὶ** ὁ πατὴρ **κἀγὼ ἐν** τῷ πατρί (John 10:38 BNT)
καὶ ὑμεῖς **ἐν ἐμοὶ κἀγὼ ἐν** ὑμῖν (John 14:20 BNT)*
μείνατε **ἐν ἐμοί, κἀγὼ ἐν** ὑμῖν (John 15:4 BNT)
ὁ μένων **ἐν ἐμοὶ κἀγὼ ἐν** αὐτῷ (John 15:5 BNT)
καθὼς σύ, πάτερ, **ἐν ἐμοὶ κἀγὼ ἐν** σοί (John 17:21 BNT)
με **ἐν αὐτοῖς** ᾗ **κἀγὼ ἐν** αὐτοῖς (John 17:26 BNT)**

*BYZ separates the Greek conjunction *andI* (κἀγὼ) to *and I* (καὶ ἐγὼ) at 14:20.
Full quotation: ἵνα ἡ ἀγάπη ἣν ἠγάπησάς **με ἐν αὐτοῖς ᾗ **κἀγὼ ἐν** αὐτοῖς (John 17:26 BNT).

John loves to speak about Christ indwelling the believer and His *perichoresis*[1] with the Father. He uses the same phrase 7 times. In the last verse, instead of *in Me* he says *in them*. There are no variants except for BYZ separating the conjunction at 14:20. In either case, the transla-

---

[1] *Perichoresis* refers to the mutual intersecting or interpenetration of the 3 Persons of the Godhead, and may help clarify the concept of the Trinity.

tion is the same. Jesus refers to Himself as *Me* 7 times in these verses. Note that there are 2 overlapping verses in the 2 heptads above (14:20, 15:4).

The Hour Is Coming / The Last Day / Seeking to Kill [Christ] / You ...Seek Me

In this section there are 5 heptads on judgment. They deal with the end of the world and Christ's Passion and death.

Matthew and Luke include the heptadic phrases *in* or *from that hour*, and *in that very hour*. This finding led to a search for a similar phrase in John. Where Matthew implies an apocalyptic event, John is clearly apocalyptic, and has the most striking adaptation of the phrase. There are no variants with 7 identical verbs for *coming* (ἔρχεται); however, 16:32 begins with *but* in some texts. Also note that there are 7 more irregular phrases that say the same thing, for a total of 14. Thus, there are 7 phrases with the same verb tense, and 7 that are different.

The hour is coming 7 times in the Gospel of John (no variants)
  Because **the hour** is coming........ὅτι ἔρχεται **ὥρα** (John 4:21 BNT)
  But **the hour** is coming...ἀλλὰ ἔρχεται **ὥρα** (John 4:23 BNT)
  Because **the hour** is coming........ὅτι ἔρχεται **ὥρα** (John 5:25 BNT)
  Because **the hour** is coming.......ὅτι ἔρχεται **ὥρα** (John 5:28 BNT)
  But **the hour** is coming....ἀλλ' ἔρχεται **ὥρα** (John 16:2 BNT)
  But **the hour** is coming....ἀλλ' ἔρχεται **ὥρα** (John 16:25 BYZ)*
  Behold **the hour** is coming.....ἰδοὺ ἔρχεται **ὥρα** (John 16:32 BNT)

*There are no variant readings in the phrase; however, BYZ, GOC, SCR, STE add *but* at 16:25.

The hour is come irregular 7 times in the Gospel of John (no variants)
  Because His **hour** had not yet come (John 7:30)
  Because His **hour** had not yet come (John 8:20)
  The **hour** has come (John 12:23)
  Because His **hour** had come (John 13:1)
  In order that when their **hour** comes (John 16:4)
  Because her **hour** has come (John 16:21)
  The **hour** has come (John 17:1)

  ὅτι οὔπω ἐληλύθει ἡ **ὥρα** αὐτοῦ (John 7:30 BNT)
  ὅτι οὔπω ἐληλύθει ἡ **ὥρα** αὐτοῦ (John 8:20 BNT)
  ἐλήλυθεν ἡ **ὥρα** (John 12:23 BNT)
  ὅτι ἦλθεν αὐτοῦ ἡ **ὥρα** (John 13:1 BNT)
  ἵνα ὅταν ἔλθῃ ἡ **ὥρα** αὐτῶν (John 16:4 BNT)
  ὅτι ἦλθεν ἡ **ὥρα** αὐτῆς (John 16:21 BNT)
  ἐλήλυθεν ἡ **ὥρα** (John 17:1 BNT)

Again, there is a division between regular and irregular heptads on *the hour is coming*. This reinforces the theory of intentional concurrent symmetric and asymmetric design. This genre was not introduced in Western European art until the 20th century, where it first appeared in German Expressionism, which later developed into Abstract Expressionism. In other words, the writer planned order and disorder within the same motif. Such a practice would be forbidden in ancient pagan, oriental, Islamic, and Indian art. Notice the 3-4 division of *because* in both heptads, with a total of 7 *because*. Without variants, this is indeed a remarkable art form. It almost appears that the text has been edited to create this pattern, but the lack of variants invalidates such speculation.

The last day 7 times in the Gospel of John (no variants)
    In the last day.......[ἐν] τῇ **ἐσχάτῃ** ἡμέρᾳ (John 6:39)
    In the last day.......[ἐν] τῇ **ἐσχάτῃ** ἡμέρᾳ (John 6:40)
    In the last day.........ἐν τῇ **ἐσχάτῃ** ἡμέρᾳ (John 6:44)
    the last day...............τῇ **ἐσχάτῃ** ἡμέρᾳ (John 6:54)
    And in the last day....Εν δὲ τῇ **ἐσχάτῃ** ἡμέρᾳ (John 7:37)
    In the last day.........ἐν τῇ **ἐσχάτῃ** ἡμέρᾳ (John 11:24)
    In the last day.........ἐν τῇ **ἐσχάτῃ** ἡμέρᾳ (John 12:48)

Seeking to kill [Christ] 7 times in the Gospel of John*
    The Jews were seeking **to kill** Him (John 5:18 BNT)
    The Jews were seeking **to kill** Him (John 7:1 BNT)
    Why do you seek **to kill** Me (John 7:19 BNT)
    Who is seeking **to kill** You (John 7:20 BNT)
    Whom they are seeking **to kill** (John 7:25 BNT)
    But you seek **to kill** Me (John 8:37 BNT)
    But you seek **to kill** Me (John 8:40 BNT)

    ἐζήτουν αὐτὸν οἱ Ἰουδαῖοι **ἀποκτεῖναι** (John 5:18 BNT)
    ἐζήτουν αὐτὸν οἱ Ἰουδαῖοι **ἀποκτεῖναι** (John 7:1 BNT)
    τί με ζητεῖτε **ἀποκτεῖναι** (John 7:19 BNT)
    τίς σε ζητεῖ **ἀποκτεῖναι** (John 7:20 BNT)
    ὃν ζητοῦσιν **ἀποκτεῖναι** (John 7:25 BNT)
    ἀλλὰ ζητεῖτέ με **ἀποκτεῖναι** (John 8:37 BNT)
    δὲ ζητεῖτέ με **ἀποκτεῖναι** (John 8:40 BNT)
**And sought to slay him* (John 5:16) missing from BNT, GNT, TIS, VST, WHO.

You...seek Me 7 times in the Gospel of John (no variants)*
    You seek Me.........ζητεῖτέ με (John 6:26 BNT)
    You will seek Me.......ζητήσετέ με (John 7:34 BNT)
    You will seek Me.......ζητήσετέ με (John 7:36 BNT)
    You will seek Me.......ζητήσετέ με (John 8:21 BNT)
    You seek Me.........ζητεῖτέ με (John 8:37 BNT)
    You seek Me.........ζητεῖτέ με (John 8:40 BNT)

You will seek Me……..ζητήσετέ με (John 13:33 BNT)
*Note that John 8:37 and 8:40 overlap in the above 2 heptads. Also note the 3-4 division with *you seek Me*.

Betray Him

Another meter related to the above example is the phrase, *betray Him*. There are 7 phrases referring to Judas betraying Christ before the betrayal takes place, which include the verb *betray* and a pronoun for Christ. The only variants are in the word order of *Him* and *betray*. If the variant word order in BYZ, GOC, SCR, and STE at 6:71 and 13:2 is followed, there is a 3-4 division in the arrangement of *Him* (αὐτόν). It is interesting that TIS follows the variant word order at 6:71. The theory for this variation in word order is that some copyists attempted to correct what they thought was poor Greek by placing the pronoun before the verb. Western texts tend to correct what appear to be errors in the Eastern texts.

Betray Him 7 times in the Gospel of John
Who would **betray** Him (John 6:64)
To **betray** Him (John 6:71)*
Who was about to **betray** Him (John 12:4)
In order to **betray** Him (John 13:2)**
Who was **betraying** Him (John 13:11)
Who was **betraying** Him (John 18:2)
Who was **betraying** Him (John 18:5)

παραδώσων αὐτόν (John 6:64 BNT)
αὐτόν **παραδιδόναι** (John 6:71 BYZ)*
ὁ μέλλων αὐτὸν **παραδιδόναι** (John 12:4 BNT)
ἵνα αὐτὸν **παραδῷ** (John 13:2 BYZ)**
τὸν **παραδιδόντα** αὐτόν (John 13:11 BNT)
ὁ **παραδιδοὺς** αὐτὸν (John 18:2 BNT)
ὁ **παραδιδοὺς** αὐτὸν (John 18:5 BNT)

*BYZ, GOC, SCR, STE, TIS reverse the word order; variant accepted.
**BYZ, GOC, SCR, STE reverse the word order; variant accepted.

Follow Me / Sent Me / Hear Voice

There are occasions when the question arises as to whether variants were added to the text in order to complete a pattern. The classic phrase, *follow Me*, or a similar 2-word Greek phrase, appears 7 times in John. *Me* was added to the end of 13:36 (see note) with no apparent awareness that this phrase is set in a heptadic pattern. Once again, TIS proves to be a reliable text in John.

Follow Me 7 times in the Gospel of John
>follow Me (John 1:43)
>The one following Me (John 8:12)
>They follow Me (John 10:27)
>Let him follow Me (John 12:26)
>Not able to follow Me now (John 13:36)*
>follow Me (John 21:19)
>You follow Me (John 21:22)

>>ἀκολούθει μοι (John 1:43 BNT)
>>ὁ ἀκολουθῶν ἐμοὶ (John 8:12 BNT)
>>ἀκολουθοῦσίν μοι (John 10:27 BNT)
>>ἐμοὶ ἀκολουθείτω (John 12:26 BNT)
>>οὐ δύνασαί μοι νῦν ἀκολουθῆσαι (John 13:36 BNT)*
>>ἀκολούθει μοι (John 21:19 BNT)
>>σύ μοι ἀκολούθει (John 21:22 BNT)

*Me (μοι) added to the end of John 13:36 in BYZ, GOC, SCR, STE; variant rejected.

That He has or *You have sent Me* 7 times in the Gospel of John (no variants)
>That He has sent Me...κἀκεῖνός με ἀπέστειλεν (John 7:29 BNT)
>That He has sent Me.....ἐκεῖνός με ἀπέστειλεν (John 8:42 BNT)
>That You have sent Me......ὅτι σύ με ἀπέστειλας (John 11:42 BNT)
>That You have sent Me......ὅτι σύ με ἀπέστειλας (John 17:8 BNT)
>That You have sent Me......ὅτι σύ με ἀπέστειλας (John 17:21 BNT)
>That You have sent Me......ὅτι σύ με ἀπέστειλας (John 17:23 BNT)
>That You have sent Me......ὅτι σύ με ἀπέστειλας (John 17:25 BNT)

Hear voice 7 times in the Gospel of John (no variants)
>You hear the voice (John 3:8)
>They will hear the voice of the Son (John 5:25)
>They will hear His voice (John 5:28)
>He hears His voice (John 10:3)
>They will hear My voice (John 10:16)
>He hears My voice (John 10:27)
>He hears My voice (John 18:37)

>>τὴν φωνὴν αὐτοῦ ἀκούεις (John 3:8 BNT)
>>ἀκούσουσιν τῆς φωνῆς τοῦ υἱοῦ (John 5:25 BNT)
>>ἀκούσουσιν τῆς φωνῆς αὐτοῦ (John 5:28 BNT)
>>τῆς φωνῆς αὐτοῦ ἀκούει (John 10:3 BNT)
>>τῆς φωνῆς μου ἀκούσουσιν (John 10:16 BNT)
>>τῆς φωνῆς μου ἀκούει (John 10:27 BNT)
>>ἀκούει μου τῆς φωνῆς (John 18:37 BNT)

Notice that there are 4 verbs in the present tense and 3 in the future tense. Also note the 3-4 division with *My voice*. *Voice* and *hear* are separated by 4 words in 3:29, which is not listed because John the Baptist is speaking, not Jesus. Also, 5:37 is not included because Jesus is telling people they have never heard the voice of God, and, unlike the others, the verb *hear* is in the perfect tense, and there is no article in front of the noun *voice*.

Love Me / You Do Not Know / Other Disciple
In John, the 44 verbs (ἀγαπάω, *agapao*) and 7 nouns for *love* repeat a total of 51 times. The accuracy of this list is quite amazing. It is the largest set of verbs encountered in the Gospels with no variants. There are 7 phrases of *love Me* in the present or present subjunctive tense, which speak about believers loving Jesus. There are an additional 5 phrases in the aorist tense (similar to the English past tense), for a total of 12. However, there is a 6th example with *Me* before the verb *love* instead of after it. Perhaps John is making a distinction, but the 5 verbs in the aorist tense are nonetheless not included in the following example.

Love Me 7 times in the Gospel of John (no variants)
    If you **love** Me.......Ἐὰν **ἀγαπᾶτέ** με (John 14:15 BNT)
    The one who **loves** Me.........ὁ **ἀγαπῶν** με (John 14:21 BNT)
    The one who **loves** Me...........**ἀγαπῶν** με (John 14:21 BNT)
    If anyone **loves** Me...ἐάν τις **ἀγαπᾷ** με (John 14:23 BNT)
    The one who **loves** Me............**ἀγαπῶν** με (John 14:24 BNT)
    Do you **love** Me.............**ἀγαπᾷς** με (John 21:15 BNT)
    Do you **love** Me.............**ἀγαπᾷς** με (John 21:16 BNT)

You do not know 7 times in the Gospel of John (no variants)
    One whom you do not **know** (John 1:26)
    You worship what you do not **know** (John 4:22)
    Which you do not **know** (John 4:32)
    One whom you do not **know** (John 7:28)
    But you do not **know** (John 8:14)
    That you do not **know** (John 9:30)
    You do not **know** anything (John 11:49)

    ὃν ὑμεῖς οὐκ **οἴδατε** (John 1:26 BNT)
    ὑμεῖς προσκυνεῖτε ὃ οὐκ **οἴδατε** (John 4:22 BNT)
    ἣν ὑμεῖς οὐκ **οἴδατε** (John 4:32 BNT)
    ὃν ὑμεῖς οὐκ **οἴδατε** (John 7:28 BNT)
    ὑμεῖς δὲ οὐκ **οἴδατε** (John 8:14 BNT)
    ὅτι ὑμεῖς οὐκ **οἴδατε** (John 9:30 BNT)
    ὑμεῖς οὐκ **οἴδατε** οὐδέν (John 11:49 BNT)

Other disciple 7 times in the Gosple of John*
    other disciple............ ἄλλος μαθητής (John 18:15 BNT)
    other disciple............ ἄλλον μαθητὴν (John 20:2 BNT)
    other disciple............ ἄλλος μαθητὴς (John 20:3 BNT)
    other disciple............ ἄλλος μαθητὴς (John 20:4 BNT)

other disciple............ ἄλλος μαθητὴς (John 20:8 BNT)
other disciples.......... ἄλλοι μαθηταί (John 20:25 BNT)
other disciples.......... ἄλλοι μαθηταὶ (John 21:8 BNT)
*All citations include the Apostle John.

Son of God / Son of Man / Son of David

The phrases *Son of God*, *Son of Man*, and *Son of David* are all set in Hebraic meter: the first in 3 of the Gospels, the second in all 4 of the Gospels, and the third only in John. *Son of Man*—a Hebraism—is another way of saying *Son of Adam*. *Son of David* refers to Christ's prophetic office. *Son of God* and *Son of Man* deal with the 2 natures of Christ, divine and human. At times the variant readings exchange one for the other. For example, in order to maintain *Son of Man* in a dodecad and *Son of God* in a decad, the variant reading at John 9:35 must be rejected in BYZ, GOC, SCR, STE, and VST. Otherwise there are 13 *Son of Man* and 9 *Son of God*.

Notice the heptadic subset of the Greek article τὸν (*the*) bolded in *Son of Man*. Also notice the heptadic subset of Greek articles in *Son of God*. There is order within order. Not even one *the* is missing.

Son of God 10 times in the Gospel of John*
  Son of God....................ὁ υἱὸς τοῦ θεοῦ (John 1:34 BNT)
  Son of God....................ὁ υἱὸς τοῦ θεοῦ (John 1:49 BNT)
  Son of God......................υἱοῦ τοῦ θεοῦ (John 3:18 BNT)
  Son of God................τοῦ υἱοῦ τοῦ θεοῦ (John 5:25 BNT)
  Son of God................τὸν υἱὸν τοῦ Θεοῦ (John 9:35 BYZ)**
  Son of God......................υἱὸς τοῦ θεοῦ (John 10:36 BNT)
  Son of God....................ὁ υἱὸς τοῦ θεοῦ (John 11:4 BNT)
  Son of God....................ὁ υἱὸς τοῦ θεου (John 11:27 BNT)
  Son of God........................υἱὸν θεοῦ (John 19:7 BNT)
  Son of God....................ὁ υἱὸς τοῦ θεοῦ (John 20:31 BNT)
Son of the Living God at 6:69 missing from BNT, GNT, TIS, VST, WHO; variant accepted.
**Son of God* at John 9:35 is correct according to BYZ, GOC, SCR, STE, VST; the variant in BNT, GNT, TIS, WHO should be rejected.

Son of Man 12 times in the Gospel of John
  Son of Man..............**τὸν** υἱὸν τοῦ ἀνθρώπου (John 1:51 BNT)
  Son of Man..................ὁ υἱὸς τοῦ ἀνθρώπου (John 3:13 BNT)
  Son of Man..............**τὸν** υἱὸν τοῦ ἀνθρώπου (John 3:14 BNT)
  Son of Man..........................υἱὸς ἀνθρώπου (John 5:27 BNT)
  Son of Man..................ὁ υἱὸς τοῦ ἀνθρώπου (John 6:27 BNT)
  Son of Man..............**τοῦ** υἱοῦ τοῦ ἀνθρώπου (John 6:53 BNT)
  Son of Man..............**τὸν** υἱὸν τοῦ ἀνθρώπου (John 6:62 BNT)
  Son of Man..............**τὸν** υἱὸν τοῦ ἀνθρώπου (John 8:28 BNT)
  Son of Man..................ὁ υἱὸς τοῦ ἀνθρώπου (John 12:23 BNT)

Son of Man..............τὸν υἱὸν τοῦ ἀνθρώπου (John 12:34 BNT)
Son of Man..............τὸν υἱὸν τοῦ ἀνθρώπου (John 12:34 BNT)
Son of Man..............ὁ υἱὸς τοῦ ἀνθρώπου (John 13:31 BNT)

The following chart gives an overview of the above 2 phrases in the 4 Gospels, in addition to *Son of David*. *Christ*, *David*, and *Peter* were also included in the interest of comparison.

	Son of God	Son of Man	Son of David	Christ	David	Peter
Matthew	10	30	10	17	7	24*
Mark		10		7**	7	20***
Luke	7	24 (12 +12)		12	10	20+
John	10	12		20++		34 (2x17)

*BYZ, GOC, SCR, STE add *Peter* at Matthew 17:26, which completes 24 repetitions; variant accepted.
**GOC, WHO add Mark 1:34; variant rejected.
***BNT, GNT, WHO rejected at Mark 16:20; GOC at 14:31 accepted.
+BYZ, GOC, SCR, STE add Luke 22:62; variant accepted.
++BYZ, GOC, SCR, STE add *Christ* at John 4:42 and 6:69, for a total of 21; however, including 6:69 would also increase the number of repetitions for *Son of God*; therefore 4:42 is preferred, and 6:69 is rejected.

The above table demonstrates that every number exhibits Mosaic cadence. Mark repeats *Son of God* only 2 times. Luke and John each repeat *Son of David* 3 times, and *David* is only found in one verse in John. When each of the Gospel writers repeats these 3 phrases about Jesus more than 3 times they all follow Hebraic literary genre. How is such orchestration between 4 separate writers possible? From the above data one could hardly prove that any of them are copying another Gospel writer. However, it is clear that Matthew has the most complete meter.

Simon Peter

The phrase *Simon Peter* appears 17 times in the Gospel of John, with no variants. This is the same repetition found in Matthew for *Christ* and *David*, if *David* and *Son of David* are combined in the above table.

Simon Peter 17 times in the Gospel of John
   Simon Peter.......Σίμωνος Πέτρου (John 1:40 BNT)
   Simon Peter.......Σίμωνος Πέτρου (John 6:8 BNT)
   Simon Peter.......Σίμων Πέτρος (John 6:68 BNT)
   Simon Peter.......Σίμωνα Πέτρον (John 13:6 BNT)
   Simon Peter.......Σίμων Πέτρος (John 13:9 BNT)
   Simon Peter.......Σίμων Πέτρος (John 13:24 BNT)
   Simon Peter.......Σίμων Πέτρος (John 13:36 BNT)
 Then Simon Peter.......Σίμων οὖν Πέτρος (John 18:10 BNT)
   Simon Peter.......Σίμων Πέτρος (John 18:15 BNT)

Simon Peter.......Σίμων Πέτρος (John 18:25 BNT)
Simon Peter.......Σίμωνα Πέτρον (John 20:2 BNT)
Simon Peter.......Σίμων Πέτρος (John 20:6 BNT)
Simon Peter.......Σίμων Πέτρος (John 21:2 BNT)
Simon Peter.......Σίμων Πέτρος (John 21:3 BNT)
Then Simon Peter.......Σίμων οὖν Πέτρος (John 21:7 BNT)
Simon Peter.......Σίμων Πέτρος (John 21:11 BNT)
Simon Peter.......Σίμωνι Πέτρῳ (John 21:15 BNT)

The last column in the table above lists Peter's name, which is identified more than any of the other apostles' names in the 4 Gospels. Matthew repeats Peter's name 24 times, if his name is included in 17:26 according to BYZ, SCR, STE, and GOC. Mark repeats Peter's name 20 times, if the obscure variant in GOC is followed at 14:31, and the specious addition of *Peter* at 16:20 in BNT, GNT, and WHO is rejected. Luke repeats Peter's name 20 times. John repeats Peter's name 34 times, the only doubling of 17 encountered thus far. John states Peter's name as *Simon Peter* 17 times, and as *Peter* 17 times, thus verifying the intentional doubling of 17 with no variant. This is indeed a remarkable example of Hebrew meter and the accuracy of the text.

The conclusion is that the Evangelists were keenly aware of Moses' repetition of key figures, or, under the direction of the Holy Spirit, they are all copying Moses and his literary device, a rubric of sacred Hebrew writing. It is reasonable to assume that Moses' repetition of key figures in Genesis was well known to the Gospel writers. The following are some examples of this literary device in Genesis:

LORD God, 20;
Abraham, 133 + Sarah, 37 = 170;
Abram/Abraham, 14 in chapter 17;
Egypt, 100 (search *מִצְרַיִ*);
Hagar, 12;
Ishmael, 17;
Isaac, 80;

Jacob, 180 (not including 27:36b);
Judah 28;
Leah, 33 + Zilphah, 7 = 40;
Lot, 30;
Rebecca, 30;
Rachel, 44 + Leah, 33 = 77;
Rachel, 44 + Bilhah, 9 + Zilphah, 7 = 60.

Metered Introduction to Conversation: Anaphoric Phrases
After these Things

As in the first 3 Gospels, John employs metered phrasing in mundane introduction to conversation. The phrase *after these things* appears 7 times in John and 10 times in Revelation. This phrase only appears 3 times in Luke, and is not found in Matthew or Mark. This is another one of the phrases that identifies John as the author of Revelation. He is the only one of the Gospel writers to use it in Hebraic meter, just as was seen in the phrase *everlasting life* earlier in this chapter.

After these things 7 times in the Gospel of John*
    After these things............μετὰ ταῦτα (John 3:22 BNT)
    After these things............μετὰ ταῦτα (John 5:1 BNT)
    After these things............μετὰ ταῦτα (John 5:14 BNT)
    After these things............μετὰ ταῦτα (John 6:1 BNT)
    After these things............μετὰ ταῦτα (John 7:1 BNT)
    After these things............μετὰ ταῦτα (John 13:7 BNT)
    After these things............μετὰ ταῦτα (John 21:1 BNT)
*BYZ adds μετὰ ταῦτα at John 19:38, but all the other texts have μετὰ δὲ ταῦτα.

Jesus Said to Them or *Him / And He Said to Him / They Therefore Said to Him*
Rather than describe each example separately, the following 4 examples will be presented as a group. There doesn't seem to be anything unique about these phrases in comparison to the other Gospels. The genre appears to be established by Moses in Genesis, and the Evangelists continue the tradition.

Jesus said to them 7 times in the Gospel of John
    Jesus said to them........λέγει αὐτοῖς ὁ Ἰησοῦς (John 2:7 BNT)
    Jesus said to them........λέγει αὐτοῖς ὁ Ἰησοῦς (John 4:34 BNT)
    Jesus said to them........λέγει αὐτοῖς ὁ Ἰησοῦς (John 8:39 BNT)
    Jesus said to them........λέγει αὐτοῖς ὁ Ἰησοῦς (John 11:44 BNT)
    Jesus said to them........λέγει αὐτοῖς ὁ Ἰησοῦς (John 18:5 BYZ)*
    Jesus said to them........λέγει αὐτοῖς ὁ Ἰησοῦς (John 21:10 BNT)
    Jesus said to them........λέγει αὐτοῖς ὁ Ἰησοῦς (John 21:12 BNT)
*BNT, GNT, TIS, WHO missing at 18:5, and TIS adds 7:6; perhaps TIS is correct.

Jesus said to him 10 times in the Gospel of John*
    Jesus said to him..........λέγει αὐτῷ ὁ Ἰησοῦς (John 1:43 BNT)**
    Jesus said to him..........λέγει αὐτῷ ὁ Ἰησοῦς (John 4:50 BNT)
    Jesus said to him..........λέγει αὐτῷ ὁ Ἰησοῦς (John 5:8 BNT)
    Jesus said to him..........λέγει αὐτῷ ὁ Ἰησοῦς (John 13:10 BNT)***
    Jesus said to him..........λέγει αὐτῷ [ὁ] Ἰησοῦς (John 13:29 BNT)***
    Jesus said to him..........λέγει αὐτῷ [ὁ] Ἰησοῦς (John 14:6 BNT)***
    Jesus said to him..........λέγει αὐτῷ ὁ Ἰησοῦς (John 14:9 BNT)
    Jesus said to him..........λέγει αὐτῷ ὁ Ἰησοῦς (John 20:29 BNT)
    Jesus said to him..........λέγει αὐτῷ [ὁ Ἰησοῦς] (John 21:17 BNT)***
    Jesus said to him..........λέγει αὐτῷ ὁ Ἰησοῦς (John 21:22 BNT)
*Rarely do we see BNT, GNT, BYZ, VST agree on the above.
**GOC, SCR, STE missing at 1:43; variant rejected.
***TIS, WHO missing at 13:10, 13:29, 14:6, 21:17; variant rejected.

And he said to him 7 times in the Gospel of John*
    And he said to him..........καὶ λέγει αὐτῷ (John 1:41 BNT)
    And he said to him..........καὶ λέγει αὐτῷ (John 1:43 BNT)
    And he said to him..........καὶ λέγει αὐτῷ (John 1:45 BNT)

And he said to him..........καὶ λέγει αὐτῷ (John 1:49 BYZ)**
And he said to him..........Καὶ λέγει αὐτῷ (John 1:51 BNT)
And he said to him..........καὶ λέγει αὐτῷ (John 2:10 BNT)
And he said to him..........καὶ λέγει αὐτῷ (John 13:6 BYZ)***
*BNT, GNT, TIS add 21:17; variant rejected.
**BYZ, GOC, SCR, STE, VST add 1:49; variant accepted.
***BYZ, GOC, SCR, STE add 13:6; variant accepted.

They therefore said to him 7 times in the Gospel of John
    They therefore said to him...εἶπον οὖν αὐτω (John 4:52 TIS)
    They therefore said to him...εἶπον οὖν αὐτῷ (John 6:30 TIS)
    They therefore said to him...εἶπον οὖν αὐτῷ (John 8:13 TIS)
    They therefore said to him...εἶπον οὖν αὐτῷ (John 9:26 TIS)
    They therefore said to him...εἶπον οὖν αὐτῷ (John 11:12 TIS)
    They therefore said to him...εἶπον οὖν αὐτῷ (John 18:25 TIS)
    They therefore said to him...εἶπον οὖν αὐτῷ (John 18:31 TIS)

There are so many variants in the other texts on the above heptad, they will not be listed. One might conclude that there is no meter. However, this pattern in John is preserved by TIS (and VST that must be following TIS). Tischendorf (TIS) has some surprisingly accurate readings in Luke and John.

Said to Him or *Them*

The following 4 phrases are a classic progression of shorter to longer phrases using the same core phrase, *said to him*, from the above example. The third phrase has a variety of pronouns. The progression of Hebraic cadence moves from 20 to 14 to 7. Each time the phrase lengthens, the repetitions decrease, as one metered phrase is placed inside another.

Said to him 20 times in the Gospel of John
    Said to him......εἶπεν αὐτῷ (John 1:46 BNT)
    Said to him......εἶπεν αὐτῷ (John 1:48 BNT)
    Said to him......εἶπεν αὐτῷ (John 1:50 BNT)
    Said to him......εἶπεν αὐτῷ (John 3:2 BNT)
    Said to him......εἶπεν αὐτῷ (John 3:3 BNT)
    Said to him......εἶπεν αὐτῷ (John 3:9 BNT)
    Said to him......εἶπεν αὐτῷ (John 3:10 BNT)
    Said to him......εἶπεν αὐτῷ (John 4:50 BNT)
    Said to him......εἶπεν αὐτῷ (John 4:53 BNT)
    Said to him......εἶπεν αὐτῷ (John 5:14 BNT)
    Said to him......εἶπεν αὐτῷ (John 9:7 BNT)
    Said to him......εἶπεν αὐτῷ (John 9:35 BYZ)*
    Said to him......εἶπεν αὐτῷ (John 13:7 BNT)
    Said to him......εἶπεν αὐτῷ (John 13:28 BNT)
    Said to him......εἶπεν αὐτῷ (John 14:23 BNT)
    Said to him......εἶπεν αὐτῷ (John 18:33 BNT)

Said to him......εἶπεν αὐτῷ (John 20:28 BNT)
Said to him......εἶπεν αὐτῷ (John 21:17 BNT)
Said to him......εἶπεν αὐτῷ (John 21:17 BYZ)**
Said to him......εἶπεν αὐτῷ (John 21:23 BYZ)***
*BNT, GNT, TIS, WHO missing at 9:35; variant rejected.
**BNT, GNT, TIS missing second occurrence at 21:17; variant rejected.
***21:23 has additional δὲ (*but* or *and*) in BNT, GNT, WHO.

Jesus answered and said 14 times in the Gospel of John
    Jesus answered and said to him (John 1:49)
    Jesus answered and said to him αὐτῷ (John 1:51)
    Jesus answered and said to them (John 2:19)
    Jesus answered and said to him (John 3:3)
    Jesus answered and said to him (John 3:10)
    Jesus answered and said to her (John 4:10)
    Jesus answered and said to her (John 4:13)
    Jesus answered and said to them (John 6:29)
    Jesus answered and said to them (John 6:43)
    Jesus answered and said to them (John 7:21)
    Jesus answered and said to them (John 8:14)
    Jesus answered and said (John 12:30)
    Jesus answered and said to him (John 13:7)
    Jesus answered and said to him (John 14:23)

    ἀπεκρίθη Ἰησοῦς καὶ εἶπεν αὐτῷ (John 1:49 TIS)
    ἀπεκρίθη Ἰησοῦς καὶ εἶπεν αὐτῷ (John 1:51 TIS)
    ἀπεκρίθη Ἰησοῦς καὶ εἶπεν αὐτοῖς (John 2:19 TIS)
    ἀπεκρίθη Ἰησοῦς καὶ εἶπεν αὐτῷ (John 3:3 TIS)
    ἀπεκρίθη Ἰησοῦς καὶ εἶπεν αὐτῷ (John 3:10 TIS)
    ἀπεκρίθη Ἰησοῦς καὶ εἶπεν αὐτῇ (John 4:10 TIS)
    ἀπεκρίθη Ἰησοῦς καὶ εἶπεν αὐτῇ (John 4:13 TIS)
    ἀπεκρίθη Ἰησοῦς καὶ εἶπεν αὐτοῖς (John 6:29 TIS)
    ἀπεκρίθη Ἰησοῦς καὶ εἶπεν αὐτοῖς (John 6:43 TIS)
    ἀπεκρίθη Ἰησοῦς καὶ εἶπεν αὐτοῖς (John 7:21 TIS)
    ἀπεκρίθη Ἰησοῦς καὶ εἶπεν αὐτοῖς (John 8:14 TIS)
    ἀπεκρίθη Ἰησοῦς καὶ εἶπεν (John 12:30 TIS)
    ἀπεκρίθη Ἰησοῦς καὶ εἶπεν αὐτῷ (John 13:7 TIS)
    ἀπεκρίθη Ἰησοῦς καὶ εἶπεν αὐτῷ (John 14:23 TIS)

Tischendorf (TIS) was selected for the above heptadic phrase because the first 4 Greek words are so perfectly arranged that it appears someone tried to make all the phrases identical, or else TIS is the most superior copy of John we possess.[2] An untranslatable article is added before Jesus' name in BNT 6:29; BYZ 3:3, 6:43; GNT 6:29; GOC 3:3,

---

[2] Some verse numbers in TIS do not match verse numbers in English translations.

6:43, 12:30; SCR and STE 2:19, 3:3, 3:10, 4:13, 6:29, 6:43, 7:21, 12:30, 14:23; VST 3:10, 6:29; and WHO 6:29, 12:30. SCR and STE add *therefore* (οὖν) at 6:43. If *therefore* is rejected at 6:43, which it should be, the total repetition of *therefore* in STE would be 200, which would also agree with BNT and GNT.

And said to him 14 times in the Gospel of John*
    And said to him....καὶ εἶπεν αὐτῷ (John 1:46 BNT)
    And said to him....καὶ εἶπεν αὐτῷ (John 1:48 BNT)
    And said to him....καὶ εἶπεν αὐτῷ (John 1:50 BNT)
    And said to him....καὶ εἶπεν αὐτῷ (John 3:2 BNT)
    And said to him....καὶ εἶπεν αὐτῷ (John 3:3 BNT)
    And said to him....καὶ εἶπεν αὐτῷ (John 3:9 BNT)
    And said to him....καὶ εἶπεν αὐτῷ (John 3:10 BNT)
    And said to him....καὶ εἶπεν αὐτῷ (John 5:14 BNT)
    And said to him....καὶ εἶπεν αὐτῷ (John 9:7 BNT)
    And said to him....καὶ εἶπεν αὐτῷ (John 13:7 BNT)
    And said to him....καὶ εἶπεν αὐτῷ (John 14:23 BNT)
    And said to him....καὶ εἶπεν αὐτῷ (John 18:33 BNT)
    And said to him....καὶ εἶπεν αὐτῷ (John 20:28 BNT)
    And said to him....καὶ εἶπεν αὐτῷ (John 21:17 BNT)
*BNT, GNT, VST, WHO add 4:17; variant rejected. The absence of this phrase from BYZ, GOC, SCR, STE, and surprisingly, TIS shows impressive accuracy in John.

Answered and said to them 7 times in the Gospel of John
    Jesus answered and **said** to them (John 2:19)
    Jesus answered and **said** to them (John 6:29)
    Jesus answered and **said** to them (John 6:43)
    Jesus answered and **said** to them (John 7:21)
    Jesus answered and **said** to them (John 8:14)
    The man answered and **said** to them (John 9:30)
    Jesus knew...and **said** to them (John 16:19)

    ἀπεκρίθη Ἰησοῦς καὶ **εἶπεν** αὐτοῖς (John 2:19 TIS)
    ἀπεκρίθη [ὁ] Ἰησοῦς καὶ **εἶπεν** αὐτοῖς (John 6:29 TIS)
    ἀπεκρίθη Ἰησοῦς καὶ **εἶπεν** αὐτοῖς (John 6:43 TIS)
    ἀπεκρίθη Ἰησοῦς καὶ **εἶπεν** αὐτοῖς (John 7:21 TIS)
    ἀπεκρίθη Ἰησοῦς καὶ **εἶπεν** αὐτοῖς (John 8:14 TIS)
    ἀπεκρίθη ὁ ἄνθρωπος καὶ **εἶπεν** αὐτοῖς (John 9:30 TIS)
    Ἔγνω [ὁ] Ἰησοῦς... καὶ **εἶπεν** αὐτοῖς (John 16:19 TIS)

The above heptad is another anomaly in Tischendorf. The other texts repeat the same phrase 8 (BNT, GNT, VST, WHO), 10 (BYZ, SCR, STE), or 11 (GOC) times. Only Tischendorf repeats this phrase 7 times. The phrase *said to them*, εἶπεν αὐτοῖς (not printed below), repeats 20 times in Tischendorf. All the other texts have 23 or 24 repetitions. Why does Tischendorf exhibit such precision in the Gospel of John?

Jesus and said to him 7 times in the Gospel of John (no variants)
    Answered Jesus and said to him (John 1:48)
    Answered Jesus and said to him (John 1:50)
    Answered Jesus and said to him (John 3:3)
    Answered Jesus and said to him (John 3:10)
    Answered Jesus and said to him (John 13:7)
    Answered Jesus and said to him (John 14:23)
        Jesus and said to him (John 18:33)

    ἀπεκρίθη Ἰησοῦς καὶ εἶπεν αὐτῷ (John 1:48 BNT)
    ἀπεκρίθη Ἰησοῦς καὶ εἶπεν αὐτῷ (John 1:50 BNT)
    ἀπεκρίθη Ἰησοῦς καὶ εἶπεν αὐτῷ (John 3:3 BNT)
    ἀπεκρίθη Ἰησοῦς καὶ εἶπεν αὐτῷ (John 3:10 BNT)
    ἀπεκρίθη Ἰησοῦς καὶ εἶπεν αὐτῷ (John 13:7 BNT)
    ἀπεκρίθη Ἰησοῦς καὶ εἶπεν αὐτῷ (John 14:23 BNT)
        Ιησοῦν καὶ εἶπεν αὐτῷ (John 18:33 BNT)

The phrase *answered and said* is repeated in Hebraic meter in Matthew, Mark, Luke, and John. Two Hebrew words for *answered and said* appear together exactly 7 times in Genesis. This repetition in Genesis (shown below) was found simply by isolating the 2 words and scanning the Hebrew text. It is obviously a Hebrew figure of speech that Moses repeats 7 times in the text. All 4 Gospel writers use this phrase. If TIS above is followed, then all 4 Gospel writers use this phrase in heptadic meter, just as in Genesis.

How is this possible? The higher critics will tell us this is proof of the Q source, but who told the Gospel writers that this is the part of Q they would all have to copy? John is not supposed to be following Q. There was no committee meeting where the 4 Gospel writers sat down together and decided who was going to use a particular phrase in Hebraic meter, and who was not. Each Gospel writer incorporated the repetition of this phrase in his Gospel according to the genre consistent with sacred writing. They were not copying each other. Rather, they were following Moses' Hebrew text. They could not be following the Septuagint because this phrase is not translated consistently from the Greek to the Hebrew. It appears 11 times in the Septuagint translation of Genesis (Genesis 18:9, 27; 23:10; 27:37, 39; 31:31, 36, 43; 40:18; 41:16; 42:22). This means the Septuagint translators either had lost track of nearly all the Hebrew meter in Genesis, or they purposely did not copy it. Therefore, each Gospel writer was keenly aware that he was adding another book to Holy Scripture in the tradition of Moses and not the Septuagint.

And answered...and said 7 times in Genesis
    And answered Abraham and said (Gen. 18:27)
    And answered Isaac and said (Gen. 27:37)
    And answered Isaac his father and said (Gen. 27:39)
    And answered Jacob and said (Gen. 31:31)
    And answered Jacob and said (Gen. 31:36)
    And answered Laban and said (Gen. 31:43)
    And answered Joseph and said (Gen. 40:18)

    וַיַּעַן אַבְרָהָם וַיֹּאמַר...........(Gen. 18:27)
    וַיַּעַן יִצְחָק וַיֹּאמֶר..........(Gen. 27:37)
    וַיַּעַן יִצְחָק אָבִיו וַיֹּאמֶר.....(Gen. 27:39)
    וַיַּעַן יַעֲקֹב וַיֹּאמֶר..........(Gen. 31:31)
    וַיַּעַן יַעֲקֹב וַיֹּאמֶר..........(Gen. 31:36)
    וַיַּעַן לָבָן וַיֹּאמֶר............(Gen. 31:43)
    וַיַּעַן יוֹסֵף וַיֹּאמֶר...........(Gen. 40:18)

There are so many examples of mundane introductions to conversation in all 4 Gospels that, rather than turning back to see what each writer contributed, the following lists are provided for the convenience of the reader and this writer. During the compiling process it was observed that Luke had only 3 sets of repetition in this genre. A search was made for the Greek word εἶπεν (*he said*) in all 4 Gospels. It was observed that Luke had the unique habit of writing this word as εἶπεν δὲ (*but he said*), as described earlier. In this manner, 3 more sets of repetitions were found in Luke, as seen below: *but he said unto him/them, but he said unto him,* and *but said the Lord*. They were added to the previous chapter.

Repetition in Conversation in the Four Gospels
Matthew
    He said to him, 20......................λέγει αὐτῷ
    And he said to him, 7....................καὶ λέγει αὐτῷ
    Then he said to him, 7...................τότε λέγει αὐτῷ
    Then he said, 12.........................τότε λέγει
    Jesus said to him, 7......................λέγει αὐτῷ ὁ Ἰησοῦς
    But Jesus answered and said, 7 + 7...ἀποκριθεὶς δὲ ὁ Ἰησοῦς εἶπεν
    And Jesus answered [and] said, 20....καὶ ἀποκριθεὶς ὁ Ἰησοῦς εἶπεν
    Verily, I say to you, 14..................ἀμὴν λέγω ὑμῖν
    Jesus said to them, 14...................ὁ Ἰησοῦς εἶπεν αὐτοῖς
Mark
    And he said to him, 7.....................καὶ λέγει αὐτῷ
    And he said to them, 7.................... καὶ εἶπεν αὐτοῖς
    And he said to them, 14...................καὶ λέγει αὐτοῖς
    And he said to them, 10...................καὶ ἔλεγεν αὐτοῖς
    And Jesus said to them, 10............... καὶ εἶπεν αὐτοῖς ὁ Ἰησοῦς

And Jesus answered and said, 7
................Καὶ ἀποκριθεὶς ὁ Ἰησοῦς εἶπεν αὐτοῖς
Verily, I say to you that, 14...............Ἀμὴν λέγω ὑμῖν ὅτι

Luke
And he said to him, 7.......................Καὶ εἶπεν αὐτῷ
But he said unto him/them, 10............εἶπεν δὲ πρὸς αὐτὸν
But he said unto him, 7....................εἶπεν δὲ αὐτῷ
But said the Lord, 7........................εἶπεν δὲ ὁ Κύριος
And answering Jesus said, 14
.................................καὶ ἀποκριθεὶς ὁ Ἰησοῦς εἶπεν
But verily I say to you, 7............... δέ ἀμὴν λέγω ὑμῖν

John
And he said to him, 7...............................καὶ λέγει αὐτῷ
Jesus said to him, 10..........................λέγει αὐτῷ ὁ Ἰησοῦς
Jesus said to them, 7..........................λέγει αὐτοῖς ὁ Ἰησοῦς
Said to him, 20..............................εἶπεν αὐτῷ
And said to him, 14..........................καὶ εἶπεν αὐτῷ
And said to them, 7.........................καὶ εἶπεν αὐτοῖς
Jesus answered and said, 14.................ἀπεκρίθη Ἰησοῦς καὶ εἶπεν
Jesus and said to him, 7....................Ἰησοῦς καὶ εἶπεν αὐτῷ
Verily, verily, I say unto you, 20..............ἀμὴν ἀμὴν λέγω ὑμῖν
Jesus answered and said unto him, Verily, verily, I say unto thee, 10
.................ἀπεκρίθη Ἰησοῦς καὶ εἶπεν αὐτῷ ἀμὴν ἀμὴν λέγω σοι
They therefore said to him, 7................εἶπον οὖν αὐτω

Decadal Meter in John
Commandment / Therefore the Jews / I Am Coming / Of the or *His Disciples*

Most people are aware that God gave Moses the 10 Commandments. The Greek word for *commandment* is ἐντολή (*entole*). John repeats this Greek word 10 times in his Gospel, as follows. This is not a phrase but a single word. However, it illustrates the symbolic relationship between text and numbers. There are no variants.

Commandment 10 times in the Gospel of John (no variants)

This **commandment** have I received (John 10:18)
had given a **commandment** (John 11:57)
He gave me a **commandment** (John 12:49)
And I know that His **commandment** is eternal life (John 12:50)
A new **commandment** I give unto you (John 13:34)
Keep my **commandments** (John 14:15)
He that hath my **commandments** (John 14:21)
If ye keep my **commandments** (John 15:10)
Have kept my Father's **commandments** (John 15:10)
This is my **commandment** (John 15:12)

ταύτην τὴν **ἐντολὴν** ἔλαβον παρὰ (John 10:18 BNT)
ἐδώκεισαν δὲ ...**ἐντολὰς** (John 11:57 BNT)
αὐτός μοι **ἐντολὴν** (John 12:49 BNT)
καὶ οἶδα ὅτι ἡ **ἐντολὴ** αὐτοῦ ζωὴ αἰώνιός ἐστιν (John 12:50 BNT)
ἐντολὴν καινὴν δίδωμι ὑμῖν (John 13:34 BNT)
τὰς **ἐντολὰς** τὰς ἐμὰς τηρήσετε (John 14:15 BNT)
ὁ ἔχων τὰς **ἐντολάς** μου (John 14:21 BNT)
ἐὰν τὰς **ἐντολάς** μου τηρήσητε (John 15:10 BNT)
ἐγὼ τὰς **ἐντολὰς** τοῦ πατρός μου τετήρηκα (John 15:10 BNT)
Αὕτη ἐστὶν ἡ **ἐντολὴ** (John 15:12 BNT)

Therefore the Jews 10 times in the Gospel of John
Therefore the Jews.........οὖν οἱ Ἰουδαῖοι (John 2:18 BNT)
Therefore the Jews.........οὖν οἱ Ἰουδαῖοι (John 2:20 BNT)
Therefore the Jews.........οὖν οἱ Ἰουδαῖοι (John 5:10 BNT)
Therefore the Jews.........οὖν οἱ Ἰουδαῖοι (John 6:41 BNT)
Therefore the Jews.........οὖν οἱ Ἰουδαῖοι (John 7:15 BNT)*
Therefore the Jews.........οὖν οἱ Ἰουδαῖοι (John 7:35 BNT)
Therefore the Jews.........οὖν οἱ Ἰουδαῖοι (John 8:22 BNT)
Therefore the Jews.........οὖν οἱ Ἰουδαῖοι (John 8:57 BNT)
Therefore the Jews.........οὖν οἱ Ἰουδαῖοι (John 9:18 BNT)
Therefore the Jews.........οὖν οἱ Ἰουδαῖοι (John 11:36 BNT)
*BNT, GNT, TIS, VST, WHO are missing *the* (οἱ) at 8:48, and are missing *therefore* (οὖν) at 7:15. The other texts all appear to be following TIS at 7:15 and 8:48.

I am coming 10 times in the Gospel of John
I am coming...................ἔρχομαι (John 4:15 BYZ)*
I am coming...................ἔρχομαι (John 5:7 BNT)
I am coming...................ἔρχομαι (John 8:14 BNT)
I am coming...................ἔρχομαι (John 14:3 BNT)
I am coming...................ἔρχομαι (John 14:18 BNT)
I am coming...................ἔρχομαι (John 14:28 BNT)
I am coming...................ἔρχομαι (John 17:11 BNT)
I am coming...................ἔρχομαι (John 17:13 BNT)
I am coming...................ἔρχομαι (John 21:22 BNT)
I am coming...................ἔρχομαι (John 21:23 BNT)
*At 4:15 BYZ, GOC, VST have *I am coming* (ἔρχομαι); BNT, GNT, TIS, WHO have *I come all the way* (διέρχωμαι); SCR, STE have *I come* (ἔρχωμαι); variant preferred in BYZ, GOC, VST.

Of the disciples 10 times in the Gospel of John*
Two of his disciples...ἐκ τῶν μαθητῶν αὐτοῦ δύο (John 1:35 BNT)
  Of the disciples...ἐκ τῶν μαθητῶν (John 3:25 BNT)
  Of His disciples...ἐκ τῶν μαθητῶν αὐτοῦ (John 6:8 BNT)
  Of His disciples...ἐκ τῶν μαθητῶν αὐτοῦ (John 6:60 BNT)
   Of His disciples..[ἐκ] τῶν μαθητῶν αὐτοῦ (John 12:4 BNT)**
  Of His disciples...ἐκ τῶν μαθητῶν αὐτοῦ (John 13:23 BNT)***

Of His disciples...ἐκ τῶν μαθητῶν αὐτοῦ (John 16:17 BNT)
Of the disciples...ἐκ τῶν μαθητῶν (John 18:17 BNT)
Of His disciples...ἐκ τῶν μαθητῶν αὐτοῦ (John 18:25 BNT)
Two of His disciples...ἐκ τῶν μαθητῶν αὐτοῦ δύο (John 21:2 BNT)
*Of (ἐκ) added at John 6:66 in BNT, GNT, WHO; variant rejected.
**Of (ἐκ) at John 12:4 missing from WHO; variant rejected.
***Of (ἐκ) at John 13:23 missing from BYZ, SCR, STE; variant rejected.

The question of 10 or 11 repetitions is difficult in the above series. John 6:66 was rejected because TIS and VST did not agree. Note that 1:35 refers to John's and not Jesus' disciples. Therefore there are 7 repetitions of *His disciples* in this decad, creating a heptadic subset. Also note that both the first and the last example include the word *two*, bracketing the decad, a style similar to Song of Solomon, shown in Chapter Seven.

The range of repetition in the Gospels is so varied that it is apparent that one Gospel writer was not copying another. A rhythmic motif may appear in Luke and John, but not Matthew and Mark; or in Matthew and John, but not Luke and Mark. There is clearly another source on which these writers are relying. As stated before, the only choice for that source is Moses.

Assuming each Evangelist is incorporating traditional Hebraic meter, the data also shows that each Evangelist approaches the tradition of sacred writing with a different emphasis. Matthew appears to take the most comprehensive or ordered approach. Mark prefers to create meter by making differentiations within unmetered lists. Luke often changes vocabulary and spelling. Rather than a narrative, John's Gospel is structured more like a series of separate accounts that often involve whole chapters with metered words inside each account. For example, the first chapter of John is an introduction to Jesus Christ; the second, the Wedding at Cana; the third, an interview with Nicodemus; the fourth, the woman at the well, etc.

Metered Words and Phrases within Accounts

Cassuto, as will be shown in Chapters Eight and Nine, identifies hundreds of metered words, as well as some phrases within paragraphs and individual accounts of Genesis. Matthew has some of the same structure, as shown earlier, but not to the extent as found in John. John mirrors Genesis so closely that an argument could be made that his Gospel is following Genesis chapter by chapter. For example, John begins his Gospel with words similar to Genesis 1:1, *in the beginning*. Genesis 1 is the creation account, with the Spirit hovering over the waters, and John 1 talks about the new creation, with the Spirit given in Baptism.

Genesis 2 is about the first marriage, and John 2 is about the wedding at Cana. The Wedding at Cana begins *on the third day* (2:1). This is in addition to the 4 days that John records in chapter 1, which makes 7 days. In Genesis God rested on the 7th day, and in John He goes to a wedding on the 7th day. The concept of the 7th day is not reported until the beginning of the 2nd chapter in Genesis, just as it is not recorded until the beginning of the 2nd chapter in John. Genesis 3 is about the fall into sin and the first Gospel (3:15), and John 3 is an explanation of the first Gospel with a crescendo at 3:15-16. Both chapters introduce a serpent in a tree or on a pole. Genesis 4-7 is about fallen man, with Noah saved by water. John 4 is about the fallen woman at the well who is saved by living water, and John 5 tells of a paralytic cured beside the pool at Bethesda. More could be said.

Become or *Come into Being*
Note how John incorporates Mosaic cadence within the parameters of separate accounts. The same Greek word in the same verb tense for *become* or *come into being*, the essence of creation itself, appears 7 times in John chapter 1 with 5 different meanings.

Become or *come into being* 7 times in the Gospel of John Chapter 1 (no variants)
  All things **were made** by him (John 1:3)
  And without him was not any thing **made** (John 1:3)
  There was a man sent from God (John 1:6)
  And the world **was made** by him (John 1:10)
  And the Word **was made** flesh (John 1:14)
  Truth **came** by Jesus Christ (John 1:17)
  These things **took place** in Bethany (John 1:28)

$$\pi\acute{\alpha}\nu\tau\alpha\ \delta\iota'\ \alpha\mathrm{\dot{\upsilon}}\tau o\tilde{\upsilon}\ \textbf{ἐγένετο}\ (\text{John 1:3 BNT})$$
$$\chi\omega\rho\grave{\iota}\varsigma\ \alpha\mathrm{\dot{\upsilon}}\tau o\tilde{\upsilon}\ \textbf{ἐγένετο}\ o\mathrm{\mathring{\upsilon}}\delta\grave{\epsilon}\ \mathrm{\ddot{\epsilon}}\nu\ (\text{John 1:3 BNT})$$
$$\textbf{ἐγένετο}\ \mathrm{\ddot{\alpha}}\nu\theta\rho\omega\pi o\varsigma\ (\text{John 1:6 BNT})*$$
$$\kappa\alpha\grave{\iota}\ \mathrm{\acute{o}}\ \kappa\acute{o}\sigma\mu o\varsigma\ \delta\iota'\ \alpha\mathrm{\dot{\upsilon}}\tau o\tilde{\upsilon}\ \textbf{ἐγένετο}\ (\text{John 1:10 BNT})$$
$$\mathrm{K}\alpha\grave{\iota}\ \mathrm{\acute{o}}\ \lambda\acute{o}\gamma o\varsigma\ \sigma\grave{\alpha}\rho\xi\ \textbf{ἐγένετο}\ (\text{John 1:14 BNT})$$
$$\mathrm{\dot{\eta}}\ \mathrm{\dot{\alpha}}\lambda\acute{\eta}\theta\epsilon\iota\alpha\ \delta\iota\grave{\alpha}\ \mathrm{'I}\eta\sigma o\tilde{\upsilon}\ X\rho\iota\sigma\tau o\tilde{\upsilon}\ \textbf{ἐγένετο}\ (\text{John 1:17 BNT})$$
$$\tau\alpha\tilde{\upsilon}\tau\alpha\ \mathrm{\dot{\epsilon}}\nu\ B\eta\theta\alpha\nu\acute{\iota}\mathrm{\mathord{\text{\usefont{U}{fav}{m}{n}\char 0}}}\ \textbf{ἐγένετο}\ (\text{John 1:28 BNT})$$

*Full text: there was a man sent from God, ἐγένετο ἀπεσταλμένος παρὰ θεοῦ. The English above could all be literally translated as *came into being* or *happened.*

The following are 3 more examples of repetition in the first chapter of John:

God: 12, Chapter 1, John 1:1 (x2), 2, 6, 12, 13, 18, 29, 34, 36, 49, 51, if the variant for a second *God* is rejected at BNT, GNT, TIS, VST, WHO at 1:18;

Jesus: 12, Chapter 1, John 1:17, 29, 36, 37, 38, 42 (x2), 43, 45, 47, 48, 50;
John: 10, Chapter 1, John 1:6, 15, 19, 26, 28, 29, 32, 35, 40, 42; BYZ, GOC, SCR, STE add 1:29, and BNT, GNT, TIS, VST add *John* instead of *Jona* at 42.

The repetition of key words in Hebraic meter, as found in the first chapter of John, is characteristic of Moses repeating key words in the first chapter of Genesis. Some of the examples are as follows:

And God said: 10, Chapter 1, וַיֹּאמֶר אֱלֹהִים Gen. 1:3, 6, 9, 11, 14, 20, 24, 26, 28, 29;
And there was: 20, Chapter 1, וַיְהִי Gen. 1:3, 5 (x2), 6, 7, 8 (x2), 9, 11, 13 (x2), 15, 19 (x2), 23 (x2), 24, 30, 31 (x2);
God saw that it was good: 7, Chapter 1, וַיַּרְא אֱלֹהִים כִּי־טוֹב Gen. 1:4, 10, 12, 18, 21, 25, 31;
Good: 7, Chapter 1, טוֹב Gen. 1:4, 10, 12, 18, 21, 25, 31;
Day: 10, Chapter 1, יוֹם Gen. 1:5 (x2), 8, 13, 14, 16, 18, 19, 23, 31;
Earth: 20, Chapter 1, אֶרֶץ Gen. 1:1, 4, 10, 11 (x2), 12, 15, 17, 20, 22, 24 (x2), 25, 26 (x2), 28 (x2), 29, 30 (x2);
Heaven(s): 7, Chapter 1, שָׁמַיִם Gen. 1:1, 8, 9, 14, 15, 17, 20;
Kind: 10, Chapter 1, Gen. 1:11, 12 (x2), 21 (x2), 24 (x2), 25 (x3);
Light: 10, Chapter 1, אוֹר Gen. 1:3 (x2), 4 (x2), 5, 15, 16 (x2), 17;
Over the earth: 7, Chapter 1, עַל־הָאָרֶץ Gen. 1:11, 15, 17, 20, 26, 28, 30.

Water or *Wine*

In John chapter 2 the words *water* and *wine* appear 10 times with no variants. Both words repeat 5 times to combine into one metered sequence. More examples of subject-related words linked in Hebraic meter will be observed in Chapters Five and Eight.

Water or *wine* 10 times in the Gospel of John Chapter 2
    And when they wanted **wine** (John 2:3)
        They have no **wine** (John 2:3)
            that was made **wine** (John 2:9)
                the good **wine** first (John 2:10)
                the good **wine** until now (John 2:10)
            six stone **water**pots (John 2:6)
        Fill the **water**pots (John 2:7)
        water (John 2:7)
the headwaiter tasted the **water** (John 2:9)
    who had drawn the **water** (John 2:9)

        καὶ ὑστερήσαντος **οἴνου** (John 2:3 BNT)
            οἶνον οὐκ ἔχουσιν (John 2:3 BNT)
            οἶνον γεγενημένον (John 2:9 BNT)
    πρῶτον τὸν καλὸν **οἶνον** (John 2:10 BNT)
        τὸν καλὸν **οἶνον** ἕως ἄρτι (John 2:10 BNT)

λίθιναι **ὑδρίαι** ἓξ (John 2:6 BNT)
γεμίσατε τὰς **ὑδρίας** (John 2:7 BNT)
ὕδατος (John 2:7 BNT)
ἐγεύσατο ὁ ἀρχιτρίκλινος τὸ **ὕδωρ** (John 2:9 BNT)
οἱ ἠντληκότες τὸ **ὕδωρ** (John 2:9 BNT)

Believe

In his dialogue with Nicodemus, Christ repeats the word *believe* 7 times. What is expressed as a single word in Greek, requires a verb phrase of 2 or more words (depending on the context) for the English translation. There are no variants.

Believe 7 times in conversation with Nicodemus in the Gospel of John Chapter 3
    And you do not **believe** (John 3:12)
        how shall ye **believe**, if I tell you *of* heavenly things? (John 3:12)
    That whosoever **believeth** in him (John 3:15)
        that whosoever **believeth** in him (John 3:16)
            He that **believeth** on him is not condemned (John 3:18)
            but he that **believeth** not is condemned already (John 3:18)
because he hath not **believed** (John 3:18)

καὶ οὐ **πιστεύετε** (John 3:12 BNT)
πῶς ἐὰν εἴπω ὑμῖν τὰ ἐπουράνια **πιστεύσετε** (John 3:12 BNT)
ἵνα πᾶς ὁ **πιστεύων** ἐν αὐτῷ (John 3:15 BNT)
ἵνα πᾶς ὁ **πιστεύων** εἰς αὐτὸν (John 3:16 BNT)
ὁ **πιστεύων** εἰς αὐτὸν οὐ κρίνεται (John 3:18 BNT)
ὁ δὲ μὴ **πιστεύων** ἤδη κέκριται (John 3:18 BNT)
ὅτι μὴ **πεπίστευκεν** (John 3:18 BNT)

In John chapter 20 Christ speaks about *believe* or *believing* 7 times in the closed room after His resurrection.

Believe 7 times in conversation with disciples in the Gospel of John 20:19-31
        I will not **believe** (John 20:25 BNT)
        And be not **unbelieving** (John 20:27 BNT)
            But **believing** (John 20:27 BNT)
    Because you have seen me you have **believed** (John 20:29 BNT)
            And *yet* have **believed** (John 20:29 BNT)
        In order that you might **believe** (John 20:31 BNT)
            That **believing** you might have life
                (John 20:31 BNT)

οὐ μὴ **πιστεύσω** (John 20:25 BNT)
μὴ γίνου **ἄπιστος** (John 20:27 BNT)
ἀλλὰ **πιστός** (John 20:27 BNT)
ὅτι ἑώρακάς με **πεπίστευκας** (John 20:29 BNT)
καὶ **πιστεύσαντες** (John 20:29 BNT)

ἵνα **πιστεύσητε** (John 20:31 BNT)
ἵνα **πιστεύοντες** ζωὴν ἔχητε (John 20:31 BNT)

There are no variants in the above dialogue. The verb for *believe* and all its tenses appears 100 times in John if BYZ, GOC, SCR, and STE are followed at John 10:38 and 12:47. The other texts repeat *believe* 98 times.

In the entire Gospel, John uses the phrase *the one who believes in Me* 7 times. This phrase was found by scanning all 100 examples of *believe* in John's Gospel. This chapter does not look for meter in all the vocabulary in John's Gospel, but key words in phrases that already exhibit meter. This phrase was included in this section because of its relationship to the 2 previous heptads. Notice that it spans 9 chapters, while the 2 previous heptads are found in individual accounts.

The one who believes in Me 7 times in the Gospel of John
    The one who believes in Me (John 6:35)
    The one who believes in Me (John 6:47)*
    The one who believes in Me (John 7:38)
    The one who believes in Me (John 11:25)
    The one who believes in Me (John 12:44)
    The one who believes in Me (John 12:46)
    The one who believes in Me (John 14:12)

    ὁ πιστεύων εἰς ἐμὲ (John 6:35 BNT)
    ὁ πιστεύων εἰς ἐμέ (John 6:47 BYZ)*
    ὁ πιστεύων εἰς ἐμέ (John 7:38 BNT)
    ὁ πιστεύων εἰς ἐμὲ (John 11:25 BNT)
    ὁ πιστεύων εἰς ἐμὲ (John 12:44 BNT)
    ὁ πιστεύων εἰς ἐμὲ (John 12:46 BNT)
    ὁ πιστεύων εἰς ἐμὲ (John 14:12 BNT)

*BYZ, GOC, SCR, STE have *in Me* (εἰς ἐμέ) at John 6:47. BYZ, GOC, SCR, STE have 12 repetitions of *in Me* (εἰς ἐμέ) because they include John 6:47. John 11:26 is not in the above because it is missing the article *the*. *In Me* (εἰς ἐμέ) is found 12 times in John 6:35, 47; 7:38; 11:25, 26; 12:44 (x2), 46; 14:1, 12; 16:9; 17:20.

Worship

The account of the woman at the well centers on the subject of true worship. The Greek word for *worship* appears 10 times in Christ's dialogue with the woman at the well. There are no variants.

Worship 10 times, Woman at the well in the Gospel of John Chapter 4
    Our fathers **worshipped** in this mountain (John 4:20)
    The place where men ought to **worship** (John 4:20)
    Shall you **worship** the Father (John 4:21)
    You **worship** that which you do not know (John 4:22)

We know what we **worship** (John 4:22)
When the true **worshippers** (John 4:23)
Shall **worship** the Father (John 4:23)
Worship him (John 4:23)
And they that **worship** him (John 4:24)
Must **worship** in spirit and truth (John 4:24)

ἐν τῷ ὄρει τούτῳ **προσεκύνησαν** (John 4:20 BNT)
τόπος ὅπου **προσκυνεῖν** δεῖ (John 4:20 BNT)
προσκυνήσετε τῷ πατρι (John 4:21 BNT)
ὑμεῖς **προσκυνεῖτε** ὃ οὐκ οἴδατε (John 4:22 BNT)
προσκυνοῦμεν ὃ οἴδαμεν (John 4:22 BNT)
ὅτε οἱ ἀληθινοὶ **προσκυνηται** (John 4:23 BNT)
προσκυνήσουσιν τῷ πατρὶ (John 4:23 BNT)
προσκυνοῦντας αὐτόν (John 4:23 BNT)
καὶ τοὺς **προσκυνοῦντας** αὐτὸν (John 4:24 BNT)
ἐν πνεύματι καὶ
ἀληθείᾳ δεῖ **προσκυνεῖν** (John 4:24 BNT)

From Heaven

In John chapter 6, Jesus says 7 times that He is the living bread which came down from heaven.

Come down from heaven 7 times in the Gospel of John Chapter 6
cometh down from heaven (John 6:33)
For I **came down** from heaven (John 6:38)*
which **came down** from heaven (John 6:41)
I **came down** from heaven (John 6:42)
which **cometh down** from heaven (John 6:50)
which **came down** from heaven (John 6:51)
which **came down** from heaven (John 6:58)*

ὁ **καταβαίνων** ἐκ τοῦ οὐρανοῦ (John 6:33 BNT)
τι **καταβέβηκα** ἐκ τοῦ οὐρανοῦ (John 6:38 BYZ)*
ὁ **καταβὰς** ἐκ τοῦ οὐρανοῦ (John 6:41 BNT)
ὅτι ἐκ τοῦ οὐρανοῦ **καταβέβηκα** (John 6:42 BNT)
ὁ ἐκ τοῦ οὐρανοῦ **καταβαίνων** (John 6:50 BNT)
ὁ ἐκ τοῦ οὐρανοῦ **καταβάς** (John 6:51 BNT)
ὁ ἐκ τοῦ οὐρανοῦ **καταβάς** (John 6:58 BYZ)*

*BNT, GNT, TIS, VST, WHO include *from* (ἀπὸ) and *out of* (ἐξ) at 6:38 and 6:58, which are rejected.

Note the 3-4 division on both sides of the bold Greek words above, with οὐρανοῦ (*heaven*) following and then preceding the bold word in Greek. As stated in the above note, the 2 variants in John 6:38 and 6:58 include the prepositions *from* (ἀπὸ) and *out of* (ἐξ) in BNT, GNT, TIS, VST, and WHO, which should be rejected. When they are rejected, there is a complete double heptadic phrase, *from heaven*, as shown below. Also note that there are 10 repetitions in John 6.

From heaven 14 times in the Gospel of John
    From heaven.........ἐκ τοῦ οὐρανοῦ (John 3:13 BNT)
    From heaven.........ἐκ τοῦ οὐρανοῦ (John 3:27 BNT)
    From heaven.........ἐκ τοῦ οὐρανοῦ (John 3:31 BNT)
    From heaven.........ἐκ τοῦ οὐρανοῦ (John 6:31 BNT)
    From heaven.........ἐκ τοῦ οὐρανοῦ (John 6:32 BNT)
    From heaven.........ἐκ τοῦ οὐρανου (John 6:32 BNT)
    From heaven.........ἐκ τοῦ οὐρανοῦ (John 6:33 BNT)
    From heaven.........ἐκ τοῦ οὐρανοῦ (John 6:38 BYZ)*
    From heaven.........ἐκ τοῦ οὐρανοῦ (John 6:41 BNT)
    From heaven.........ἐκ τοῦ οὐρανοῦ (John 6:42 BNT)
    From heaven.........ἐκ τοῦ οὐρανοῦ (John 6:50 BNT)
    From heaven.........ἐκ τοῦ οὐρανοῦ (John 6:51 BNT)
    From heaven.........ἐκ τοῦ οὐρανοῦ (John 6:58 BYZ)**
    From heaven.........ἐκ τοῦ οὐρανοῦ (John 12:28 BNT)

*BNT, GNT, TIS, VST, WHO at 6:38 have ἀπὸ (*from*) instead of ἐκ (*from*); variant rejected.

**BNT, GNT, TIS, VST, WHO at 6:58 have ἐξ (*out of*) instead of ἐκ (*from*); variant rejected.

Open Eyes

John chapter 9 repeats the phrase *open eyes* 7 times, which is in contrast to the religious leaders who could see, but whose eyes were closed to the truth.

Open eyes 7 times in the Gospel of John Chapter 9 (no variants)
    How were your **eyes** opened (John 9:10)*
    And opened his **eyes** (John 9:14)
    That he opened your **eyes** (John 9:17)
    Or who hath opened his **eyes** (John 9:21)
    How did He open your **eyes** (John 9:26)
    And yet He opened my **eyes** (John 9:30)
    That anyone opened **eyes** (John 9:32)

    Πῶς ἀνεῴχθησάν σου οἱ **ὀφθαλμοί** (John 9:10 BNT)*
    καὶ ἀνέῳξεν αὐτοῦ τοὺς **ὀφθαλμούς** (John 9:14 BNT)
    ὅτι ἠνέῳξέν σου τοὺς **ὀφθαλμούς** (John 9:17 BNT)
    ἢ τίς ἤνοιξεν αὐτοῦ τοὺς **ὀφθαλμούς** (John 9:21 BNT)
    πῶς ἤνοιξέν σου τοὺς **ὀφθαλμούς** (John 9:26 BNT)
    καὶ ἤνοιξέν μου τοὺς **ὀφθαλμούς** (John 9:30 BNT)
    ὅτι ἠνέῳξέν τις **ὀφθαλμοὺς** (John 9:32 BNT)

*No variants except in verb tense.

There are more examples of key words or phrases than are printed in this chapter. In John chapter 10, Christ the good shepherd speaks about *shepherd* and *flock* 7 times. The Greek word for *shepherd* is ποιμήν (*poimen*, poy-mane'), which repeats 6 times in 10:2, 11 (x2), 12, 14, and 16. The nearly identical Greek word for *flock*, ποίμνη (*poimne*, poym'-nay), is found once in 10:16.

The Greek word for *sheep*, πρόβατον (*probaton*, prob'-at-on), appears 17 times in John 10. The significance of this number was discussed in Chapter One on page 23. Usually it is subdivided into 10 and 7. If the 2 variant readings from BYZ, GOC, SCR, and STE are included at 10:4 and 10:12, πρόβατα (nominative plural) repeats 10 times and προβάτων (genitive plural) repeats 7 times in John 10:1, 2, 3 (x2), 4 (x2), 7, 8, 11, 12 (x3), 13, 15, 16, 26, 27. Such precision and dedication to literary device is remarkable, to say the least.

Wash Feet

The phrase *wash feet* appears 7 times in John 13. Perhaps the Protestant and Lutheran churches have not given this account due emphasis. This is not a suggestion for any ritual reenactment, but hymnody and the church calendar have virtually ignored the importance of this event.

Wash feet 7 times in the Gospel of John Chapter 13 (no variants)
                Wash the **feet** of disciples (John 13:5 BNT)
                Lord, you wash my **feet** (John 13:6 BNT)
                You will not ever wash my **feet** (John 13:8 BNT)
                Only has need to wash **feet** (John 13:10 BNT)
                After He washed their **feet** (John 13:12 BNT)
                If then I wash your **feet** (John 13:14 BNT)
                Wash one another's **feet** (John 13:14 BNT)

              νίπτειν τοὺς **πόδας** τῶν μαθητῶν (John 13:5 BNT)
κύριε, σύ μου νίπτεις τοὺς **πόδας** (John 13:6 BNT)
οὐ μὴ νίψῃς μου τοὺς **πόδας** εἰς τὸν αἰῶνα (John 13:8 BNT)
οὐκ ἔχει χρείαν εἰ μὴ τοὺς **πόδας** νίψασθαι (John 13:10 BNT)
    Ότε οὖν ἔνιψεν τοὺς **πόδας** αὐτῶν (John 13:12 BNT)
εἰ οὖν ἐγὼ ἔνιψα ὑμῶν τοὺς **πόδας** (John 13:14 BNT)
           ἀλλήλων νίπτειν τοὺς **πόδας** (John 13:14 BNT)

In My Name / You Ask / These Things I Have Spoken to You / A Little While / Which You Have Given to Me

The following are 5 sets of Hebraic meter found in Christ's farewell discourse, which is exclusive to John's Gospel. Only one of the 5 examples has a variant.

In my name 7 times in the Gospel of John
> In my name............ ἐν τῷ ὀνόματί μου (John 14:13 BNT)
> In my name............ ἐν τῷ ὀνόματί μου (John 14:14 BNT)
> In my name............ ἐν τῷ ὀνόματί μου (John 14:26 BNT)
> In my name............ ἐν τῷ ὀνόματί μου (John 15:16 BNT)
> In my name............ ἐν τῷ ὀνόματί μου (John 16:23 BNT)
> In my name............ ἐν τῷ ὀνόματί μου (John 16:24 BNT)
> In my name............ ἐν τῷ ὀνόματί μου (John 16:26 BNT)

The following heptad is not as consistent as other heptads in this chapter. It is a list of the verb *to ask* repeated 7 times in Christ's farewell discourse. Although the words are not repeated consistently in the heptad, the thought of asking God for anything in Christ's name is repeated 7 times. Each phrase also contains the word *name*, except 15:7, which says *abide in me* instead of *in my name*. The 7th repetition of *in my name*, above, is found in 16:26. Thus, there is an overlapping heptad of *in my name* and *you ask* within the farewell discourse. It should also be noted that the word stem in the verb *to ask* (αἰτ-) repeats 7 times, and the verb is always in the second person plural. This invitation to ask Christ for anything is repeated 7 times. KJV is quoted here because *ye* is the old English plural of *you*, which is no longer used in modern English, unless one follows the southern *you all* or *y'all*. There is no variant.

You ask 7 times in the Gospel of John
> And whatsoever ye shall **ask** in my **name** (John 14:13)
> If ye shall **ask** any thing in my **name** (John 14:14)
> If ye **abide in me**…ye shall **ask** what ye will (John 15:7)*
> That whatsoever ye shall **ask** of the Father in my **name** (John 15:16)
> Whatsoever ye shall **ask** the Father in my **name** (John 16:23)
> Ye asked nothing in my **name**: **ask**, and ye shall receive (John 16:24)
> At that day ye shall **ask** in my **name** (John 16:26)

*Full quotation: If ye **abide in me,** and my words abide in you, ye shall **ask** what ye will (John 15:7).

> καὶ ὅ τι ἂν **αἰτήσητε** ἐν τῷ **ὀνόματί** μου (John 14:13 BNT)
> ἐάν τι **αἰτήσητέ** με ἐν τῷ **ὀνόματί** μου (John 14:14 BNT)
> ἐὰν **μείνητε ἐν ἐμοὶ**…ὃ ἐὰν θέλητε **αἰτήσασθε** (John 15:7 BNT)*
> ἵνα ὅ τι ἂν **αἰτήσητε** τὸν πατέρα ἐν τῷ **ὀνόματί** μου (John 15:16 BNT)
> ἄν τι **αἰτήσητε** τὸν πατέρα ἐν τῷ **ὀνόματί** μου (John 16:23 BNT)
> οὐκ ᾐτήσατε οὐδὲν ἐν τῷ **ὀνόματί** μου· **αἰτεῖτε** καὶ λήμψεσθε (John 16:24 BNT)
> ἐν ἐκείνῃ τῇ ἡμέρᾳ ἐν τῷ **ὀνόματί** μου **αἰτήσεσθε** (John 16:26 BNT)

*Full quotation: ἐὰν **μείνητε ἐν ἐμοὶ** καὶ τὰ ῥήματά μου ἐν ὑμῖν μείνῃ, ὃ ἐὰν θέλητε **αἰτήσασθε** (John 15:7 BNT).

The following lengthy phrase is found 7 times in Christ's farewell discourse after the Lord's Supper. All texts agree with this Mosaic meter, which is further evidence that it is the original wording and number of repetitions planned and written by John. Also notice *in order that* (ἵνα) is written as a 3-4 division within the heptad. These 7 phrases may indicate 7 divisions in the discourse. The verb for *I have spoken to you* has a musical quality to it. It is pronounced *ley-la-lay-ka*, and fits very well with the word before it, which is pronounced *taŭ-tah*. It means *these things*. *Taŭ-tah ley-la-lay-ka hey-min* has an endearing quality to its tone as well as its meaning. There are no variants.

These things I have spoken to you 7 times in the Gospel of John
    These things I have **spoken** to you (John 14:25)
    These things I have **spoken** to you in order that (John 15:11)
    These things I have **spoken** to you in order that (John 16:1)
    But these things I have **spoken** to you in order that (John 16:4)
    But because these things I have **spoken** to you (John 16:6)
    These things I have **spoken** to you in parables (John 16:25)
    These things I have **spoken** to you in order that (John 16:33)

    Ταῦτα **λελάληκα** ὑμῖν (John 14:25 BNT)
    Ταῦτα **λελάληκα** ὑμῖν ἵνα (John 15:11 BNT)
    Ταῦτα **λελάληκα** ὑμῖν ἵνα (John 16:1 BNT)
    ἀλλὰ ταῦτα **λελάληκα** ὑμῖν ἵνα (John 16:4 BNT)
    ἀλλ' ὅτι ταῦτα **λελάληκα** ὑμῖν (John 16:6 BNT)
    Ταῦτα ἐν παροιμίαις **λελάληκα** ὑμῖν (John 16:25 BNT)
    ταῦτα **λελάληκα** ὑμῖν ἵνα (John 16:33 BNT)

Another heptad in Christ's farewell discourse is the phrase *a little while*, spoken by Christ and the disciples. There are no variants.

A little while 7 times in the Gospel of John Chapter 16
    A little while and you will not see Me (John 16:16)
    And again **a little while** and you will see Me (John 16:16)
    A little while and you will not see Me (John 16:17)
    A little while and you will not see Me (John 16:17)
    He says **a little while** (John 16:18 BNT)*
    A little while and you will not see Me (John 16:19)
    A little while and you will not see Me (John 16:19)
*Full quotation: What is this that He says **a little while** (John 16:18).

    Μικρὸν καὶ οὐκέτι θεωρεῖτέ με (John 16:16 BNT)
    καὶ πάλιν **μικρὸν** καὶ ὄψεσθέ με (John 16:16 BNT)
    μικρὸν καὶ οὐ θεωρεῖτέ με (John 16:17 BNT)
    καὶ πάλιν **μικρὸν** καὶ ὄψεσθέ με (John 16:17 BNT)

λέγει, τὸ **μικρόν** (John 16:18 BNT)*
μικρὸν καὶ οὐ θεωρεῖτέ με (John 16:19 BNT)
καὶ πάλιν **μικρὸν** καὶ ὄψεσθέ με (John 16:19 BNT)
*Full quotation: Τοῦτο τί ἐστιν ὃ λέγει, τὸ **μικρόν** (John 16:18 BNT).

The gift of God to Christ is those who believe in Him, a thought repeated 10 times.

Which You have given to Me 10 times in the Gospel of John
Which You have **given** to Me (John 17:4)
Whom You have **given** to Me (John 17:6)*
Everything You have **given** to Me (John 17:7)
Which You have **given** to Me (John 17:8)*
Which You have **given** to Me (John 17:9)
Which You have **given** to Me (John 17:11)
Which You have **given** to Me (John 17:12)
Which You have **given** to Me (John 17:22)
Which You have **given** to Me (John 17:24)
Which You have **given** to Me (John 17:24)**

ὃ **δέδωκάς** μοι (John 17:4 BNT)
οὓς **δέδωκάς** μοι (John 17:6 BYZ)*
ὅσα **δέδωκάς** μοι (John 17:7 BNT)
ἃ **δέδωκάς** μοι (John 17:8 BYZ)*
ὧν **δέδωκάς** μοι (John 17:9 BNT)
ᾧ **δέδωκάς** μοι (John 17:11 BNT)
ᾧ **δέδωκάς** μοι (John 17:12 BNT)
ἣν **δέδωκάς** μοι (John 17:22 BNT)
ὃ **δέδωκάς** μοι (John 17:24 BNT)
ἣν **δέδωκάς** μοι (John 17:24 BNT)**

*BYZ, GOC, SCR, STE have *you have given* (δέδωκάς) instead of *you gave* (ἔδωκάς); variant accepted.
**BNT, GNT, GOC, TIS, VST, WHO have *you have given* (δέδωκάς) instead of *you gave* (ἔδωκάς); variant accepted.

Examples of repetition within the discourses from John's Gospel follow the same repetition that originates with Moses. The 4 Gospels are clearly following a pre-established literary genre.

The ancients did not have printing presses, photocopy machines, and digitized text that could identify every error. Therefore, authentication of the text was more important and a greater challenge for them than it is for scholars today. Embedding key syllables, words, and phrases with numeric cadence into the text provides a means of verifying the origin, accuracy, and authenticity of a text. This made it possible, without considerable effort, to detect variants in words like *the*, and *and*. Of course, those engaged in the process of authentication would need prior knowledge of the genre and the meter that was employed.

Father

While checking in the Gospel of John for repetition of the Greek word κἀγώ (kag-o), a conjunction of *and* and *I*, this writer noticed that πατήρ (pat-ayr), Greek for *Father*, and κἀγώ appear together 10 times. The only variant is in BYZ, which is missing κἀγώ at 14:20. The key words are bolded below, and *Father* always precedes *and I* in the Greek, whereas none of the translations are consistent for the English reader. There are no variants.

Father…and I 10 times in the Gospel of John
My **Father** worketh hitherto, **and I** work (John 5:17)
except the **Father** which hath sent me draw him: **and I** (John 6:44)*
As the living **Father** hath sent me, **and I** live (John 6:57)
As the **Father** knoweth me, **and I** know the Father (John 10:15)
that the **Father** *is* in me, **and I** in him (John 10:38)
that I *am* in my **Father**, and ye in me, **and I** in you (John 14:20)
loved of my **Father**, **and I** will love him (John 14:21)**
As the **Father** hath loved me, **and I** have I loved you (John 15:9)
as thou, **Father**, *art* in me, **and I** in thee (John 17:21)
as *my* **Father** hath sent me, **and I** send you (John 20:21)

*Full quotation: except the **Father** which hath sent me draw him: **and I** will raise him up (John 6:44).
*Full quotation: and he that loveth me shall be loved of my **Father**, **and I** will love him (John 14:21).

ὁ **πατήρ** μου ἕως ἄρτι ἐργάζεται **κἀγὼ** ἐργάζομαι (John 5:17 BNT)
ἐὰν μὴ ὁ **πατὴρ** ὁ πέμψας με ἑλκύσῃ αὐτόν, **κἀγὼ** (John 6:44 BNT)*
με ὁ ζῶν **πατὴρ κἀγὼ** (John 6:57 BNT)
καθὼς γινώσκει με ὁ **πατὴρ κἀγὼ** γινώσκω τὸν πατέρα (John 10:15 BNT)
ὅτι ἐν ἐμοὶ ὁ **πατὴρ κἀγὼ** ἐν τῷ πατρι (John 10:38 BNT)
ὅτι ἐγὼ ἐν τῷ **πατρί** μου καὶ ὑμεῖς ἐν ἐμοὶ **κἀγὼ** ἐν ὑμῖν (John 14:20 BNT)
ὑπὸ τοῦ **πατρός** μου, **κἀγὼ** ἀγαπήσω αὐτόν (John 14:21 BNT)**
Καθὼς ἠγάπησέν με ὁ **πατήρ**, **κἀγὼ** ἠγάπησα ὑμᾶς (John 15:9 BNT)
καθὼς σύ, **πάτερ**, ἐν ἐμοὶ **κἀγὼ** ἐν σοί (John 17:21 BNT)
καθὼς ἀπέσταλκέν με ὁ **πατήρ**, **κἀγὼ** πέμπω ὑμᾶς (John 20:21 BNT)

*Full quotation: ἐὰν μὴ ὁ **πατὴρ** ὁ πέμψας με ἑλκύσῃ αὐτόν, **κἀγὼ** ἀναστήσω αὐτὸν (John 6:44 BNT).
Full quotation: ὁ δὲ ἀγαπῶν με ἀγαπηθήσεται ὑπὸ τοῦ **πατρός μου, **κἀγὼ** ἀγαπήσω αὐτὸν (John 14:21 BNT).

After rechecking the data, this writer noticed that the Greek word for *Father* was set in additional Hebraic patterns. After sorting it all out, it was observed that *My Father* repeats 7 times in the nominative (subject) case, 10 times in the genitive (possessive) case, 7 times in the dative (indirect object) case, and 7 times in the accusative (object) case. There are no variants in the dative case. BNT, GNT, TIS, VST, and WHO contain all 31 repetitions. The key text in this repetition reaffirms the astonishing accuracy of TIS in John. Thus John places *God the Father* in Hebraic cadence in all 4 Greek cases, a remarkable arrangement of Greek grammar, to say the least, and rather clever for an unschooled fisherman.

My Father 7 times in the Gospel of John (Subject)*
My Father.....................ὁ πατήρ μου (John 5:17 BNT)
My Father.....................ὁ πατήρ μου (John 6:32 BNT)
My Father.....................ὁ πατήρ μου (John 8:54 BNT)
My Father.....................ὁ πατήρ μου (John 10:29 BNT)
My Father.....................ὁ πατήρ μου (John 14:23 BNT)
My Father.....................ὁ πατήρ μου (John 15:1 BNT)
My Father.....................ὁ πατήρ μου (John 15:8 BNT)
*BYZ, GOC, SCR, STE add John 8:28 and 14:28; variants rejected.

My Father 10 times in the Gospel of John (Possessive)*
My Father.....................τοῦ πατρός μου (John 2:16 BNT)
My Father.....................τοῦ πατρός μου (John 5:43 BNT)
My Father.....................τοῦ πατρός μου (John 6:40 BNT)**
My Father.....................τοῦ πατρός μου (John 10:18 BNT)
My Father.....................τοῦ πατρός μου (John 10:25 BNT)
My Father.....................τοῦ πατρός μου (John 10:37 BNT)
My Father.....................τοῦ πατρός μου (John 14:2 BNT)
My Father.....................τοῦ πατρός μου (John 14:21 BNT)
My Father.....................τοῦ πατρός μου (John 15:10 BNT)
My Father.....................τοῦ πατρός μου (John 15:15 BNT)
*BYZ, GOC, SCR, STE add John 6:65, 10:29, and 10:32; variants rejected.
**BYZ, GOC, SCR, STE missing 6:40; variant rejected.

To or *In the Father* 7 times in the Gospel of John (Indirect Object)
To the Father..................τῷ πατρί (John 4:21 BNT)
To the Father..................τῷ πατρὶ (John 4:23 BNT)
To the Father..................τῷ πατρὶ (John 8:38 BNT)
In the Father...............ἐν τῷ πατρί (John 10:38 BNT)
In the Father...............ἐν τῷ πατρὶ (John 14:10 BNT)
In the Father...............ἐν τῷ πατρὶ (John 14:11 BNT)
In the Father...............ἐν τῷ πατρί (John 14:20 BNT)

My Father 7 times in the Gospel of John (Object)*
My Father.....................τὸν πατέρα μου (John 8:19 BNT)
My Father.....................τὸν πατέρα μου (John 8:19 BNT)
My Father.....................τὸν πατέρα μου (John 8:49 BNT)
My Father.....................τὸν πατέρα μου (John 14:7 BNT)
My Father.....................τὸν πατέρα μου (John 15:23 BNT)

My Father..................τὸν πατέρα μου (John 15:24 BNT)
My Father..................τὸν πατέρα μου (John 20:17 BNT)**
*BYZ, GOC, SCR, STE add 14:12 and 16:10; variants rejected.
**BYZ, GOC, SCR, STE add a second repetition in 20:17; variant rejected.

A subsequent search was made for all cases of the phrase *My Father* by typing (με πατ*), which appeared 7 times, and was accompanied by a little surprise. The participle for *sent* appears in front of *My Father* 7 times, resulting in the phrase *the Father who sent Me*, and creating an internal 3-4 division. This is one of those occurrences that lead to speculation that the copyists of BYZ, GOC, SCR, and STE added *Father* to 5:30 and 6:39 in order to arrive at 7 phrases. Of course, when there are patterns that appear to be contrived, this is exactly what one would expect to find when phrases are intentionally repeated in Hebraic meter. The fact that the manuscripts do not agree also indicates that copyists did not know they had made an error when copying a text. In other words, how could some copyists know there was meter in the text while others did not? How could some copyists keep the repetition in the text a secret from other copyists? Amidst all this conjecture, in the voluminous writings of the early church fathers there is no record of the apostles employing metered phrases. With all their fascination for allegory and numbers, this writer is not aware of any reference to the existence of Hebraic meter in the Greek text.

The Father who sent Me 7 times in the Gospel of John
    Of the Father who **sent** Me....τοῦ **πέμψαντός** με πατρός (John 5:30 BYZ)*
      The Father who **sent** Me......ὁ **πέμψας** με πατήρ (John 5:37 BNT)
    Of the Father who **sent** Me....τοῦ **πέμψαντός** με πατρός (John 6:39 BYZ)**
      The Father who **sent** Me......ὁ **πέμψας** με πατήρ (John 8:16 BNT)
      The Father who **sent** Me......ὁ **πέμψας** με πατήρ (John 8:18 BNT)
      The Father who **sent** Me......ὁ **πέμψας** με πατήρ (John 12:49 BNT)
    Of the Father who **sent** Me...τοῦ **πέμψαντός** με πατρός (John 14:24 BNT)
*BNT, GNT, TIS, VST, WHO are missing *Father* at 5:30; variant rejected.
**BNT, GNT, TIS, VST, WHO are missing *Father* at 6:39; variant rejected.

A search was then made for similar phrases in the 3 other Gospels. Mark and Luke do not employ these phrases in Mosaic cadence. However, Matthew has heptadic repetition of the phrases *Your Father who is in heaven* and *My Father who is in heaven*. Matthew also repeats the heptad *My Father who is in heaven* within the decad *My Father*, which is identical to the decad found above in John. This decad was added to the first chapter. The reader is only aware of this late addition to the first chapter after reading this paragraph.

The Father of Me 10 times in the Gospel of Matthew*
    The Father of Me.........τοῦ πατρός μου (Matt. 7:21 BNT)
    The Father of Me.........τοῦ πατρός μου (Matt. 10:32 BNT)
    The Father of Me.........τοῦ πατρός μου (Matt. 10:33 BNT)
    The Father of Me.........τοῦ πατρός μου (Matt. 11:27 BNT)
    The Father of Me.........τοῦ πατρός μου (Matt. 12:50 BNT)
    The Father of Me.........τοῦ πατρός μου (Matt. 18:10 BNT)
    The Father of Me.........τοῦ πατρός μου (Matt. 18:19 BNT)
    The Father of Me.........τοῦ πατρός μου (Matt. 20:23 BNT)
    The Father of Me.........τοῦ πατρός μου (Matt. 25:34 BNT)
    The Father of Me.........τοῦ πατρός μου (Matt. 26:29 BNT)
*WHO adds this phrase at 18:14, which is rejected.

These 2 Gospel writers are following a pre-established figure of speech that apparently has its source in the Old Testament. Therefore, a search was made in Genesis for *my father*, which produced no significant results with 41 repetitions. However, when the phrase was lengthened to *my father's house*, similar to *My Father who is in heaven*, the phrase was found in a heptad, as follows:

My father's house 7 times in Genesis
    From the house of my father..... מִבֵּית אָבִי (Gen. 20:13)
    From the house of my father..... מִבֵּית אָבִי (Gen. 24:7)
    To the house of my father..... אֶל־בֵּית־אָבִי (Gen. 24:38)
    And from the house of my father..... וּמִבֵּית אָבִי (Gen. 24:40)
    To the house of my father..... אֶל־בֵּית אָבִי (Gen. 28:21)
    All the house of my father...... כָּל־בֵּית אָבִי (Gen. 41:51)
    And the house of my father...... וּבֵית־אָבִי (Gen. 46:31)

Perhaps the above phrase is the inspiration for the introduction to the 2 heptads in Matthew, *your Father who is in heaven* and *My Father who is in heaven*. However, there may be another poetic form from which this genre originates. Christ tells us, "In My Father's house there are many mansions…" (John 14:2).

Some experimentation was attempted with the phrase *my father* in the entire Old Testament. The following phrase appears 10 times in 2 Chronicles, and nowhere else in the Bible. Notice the 3-7 division in the phrases.

My father David 10 times in 2 Chronicles
    With my father David.......... עִם־דָּוִיד אָבִי (2 Chron. 1:8)
    With my father David.......... עִם דָּוִיד אָבִי (2 Chron. 1:9)
    With my father David.......... עִם־דָּוִיד אָבִי (2 Chron. 2:2)
    My father David.......... דָּוִיד אָבִי (2 Chron. 2:6)
    My father David.......... דָּוִיד אָבִי (2 Chron. 6:4)
    My father David.......... דָּוִיד אָבִי (2 Chron. 6:7)

To my father David..........	אֶל־דָּוִיד אָבִי	(2 Chron. 6:8)
My father David..........	דָּוִיד אָבִי	(2 Chron. 6:10)
My father David..........	דָּוִיד אָבִי	(2 Chron. 6:15)
My father David..........	דָוִיד אָבִי	(2 Chron. 6:16)

One would hardly know where to look for these figures of speech unless given some direction. Following the rhythms in Matthew and John led this writer on a journey through the Old Testament. This entire process draws attention to a long-neglected element of Hebrew poetry, with no known comparable forms in other languages.

Dodecadal Meter in John
I Am

While tracking down the repetitions of *My Father* in all 4 Greek cases, repetition of the phrase *I am He*, also translated *I am* (if there is a predicate noun), became obvious. A scan for the phrase *I am He* (ἐγώ εἰμι) produced exactly 24 repetitions with no variants. That is one of the most remarkably preserved patterns in the entire New Testament. The phrase is preserved perfectly in 9 different Greek texts in double dodecadal meter. The word *that* or *because* (ὅτι, *hoti*), bolded in Greek below, appears 7 times, if BYZ, GOC, SCR, and STE are followed at 18:6. Anyone familiar with the Gospel of John will recognize the well-known *I am* passages. These comprise a subset of 14 phrases (a double heptad) where Christ refers to Himself with a metaphor, bolded in English, below.

I am He 24 times in the Gospel of John (no variants)
I am He, the one speaking to you…ἐγώ εἰμι, ὁ λαλῶν σοι (John 4:26)
I am He, do not be afraid………….ἐγώ εἰμι·μὴ φοβεῖσθε (John 6:20)
I am the bread of life…………….ἐγώ εἰμι ὁ ἄρτος τῆς ζωῆς (John 6:35)
I am the bread that……………..ἐγώ εἰμι ὁ ἄρτος (John 6:41)*
I am the bread of life…………….Εγώ εἰμι ὁ ἄρτος τῆς ζωῆς (John 6:48)
I am the living bread……………..ἐγώ εἰμι ὁ ἄρτος ὁ ζῶν (John 6:51)
I am the light of the world………ἐγώ εἰμι τὸ φῶς τοῦ κόσμου (John 8:12)
I am the one who bears witness…ἐγώ εἰμι ὁ μαρτυρῶν (John 8:18)
That I am He………………….**ὅτι** ἐγώ εἰμι (John 8:24)
That I am He………………….**ὅτι** ἐγώ εἰμι (John 8:28)
I am He……………………….....ἐγὼ εἰμί (John 8:58)
That I am He………………….**ὅτι** ἐγώ εἰμι (John 9:9)
That I am the door…………….**ὅτι** ἐγώ εἰμι ἡ θύρα (John 10:7)
I am the door……………….....ἐγώ εἰμι ἡ θύρα (John 10:9)
I am the good shepherd………….ἐγώ εἰμι ὁ ποιμὴν ὁ καλός (John 10:11)
I am the good shepherd………….ἐγώ εἰμι ὁ ποιμὴν ὁ καλὸς (John 10:14)
I am the resurrection…………….ἐγώ εἰμι ἡ ἀνάστασις καὶ ἡ ζωή (John 11:25)
That I am He………………….**ὅτι** ἐγώ εἰμι (John 13:19)
I am the way……………………ἐγώ εἰμι ἡ ὁδὸς (John 14:6)
I am the vine……………..…….ἐγώ εἰμι ἡ ἄμπελος (John 15:1)

I am the vine............................ἐγώ εἰμι ἡ ἄμπελος (John 15:5)
I am He................................ἐγώ εἰμι (John 18:5)
That I am He.......................ὅτι ἐγώ εἰμι (John 18:6)
That I am He.......................ὅτι ἐγώ εἰμι (John 18:8)
*Full quotation: I am the bread that came from heaven....ἐγώ εἰμι ὁ ἄρτος ὁ καταβὰς ἐκ τοῦ οὐρανοῦ (John 6:41).

Exceptions

As stated previously, the major Hebraic meters are 7, 10, and 12. There are also some repetitions of 17, usually a compound meter of 7 and 10. However, there are some exceptions that depict what are understood as minor Hebraic meters of 2, 3, 4, 5, 6, and 8. These repetitions were covered rather extensively as individual words or concepts in the 1987 and 2012 editions of *In Search of the Biblical Order*. The following example is a repetition of 8, the symbolic number for eternity, as seen in circumcision required on the 8th day, and 8 people saved by water in the Ark according to Genesis and 1 Peter, a symbol of baptism.[3] A clear indication that the following phrase is intentionally repeated 8 times is that it repeats 8 times as a phrase and 8 more times apart from the phrase, for a total of 16 repetitions.

To the tomb 8 times in the Gospel of John
To the tomb..................εἰς τὸ μνημεῖον (John 11:31 BNT)
To the tomb..................εἰς τὸ μνημεῖον (John 11:38 BNT)
To the tomb..................εἰς τὸ μνημεῖον (John 20:1 BNT)
To the tomb..................εἰς τὸ μνημεῖον (John 20:3 BNT)
To the tomb..................εἰς τὸ μνημεῖον (John 20:4 BNT)
To the tomb..................εἰς τὸ μνημεῖον (John 20:6 BNT)
To the tomb..................εἰς τὸ μνημεῖον (John 20:8 BNT)
To the tomb..................εἰς τὸ μνημεῖον (John 20:11 BNT)

Tomb: 16, μνημεῖον (*mnemeion*, mnay-mi'-on) John 5:28; 11:17, 31, 38; 12:17; 19:41, 42; 20:1 (x2), 2, 3, 4, 6, 8, 11 (x2).

The following are examples of proper names, places, things, and actions that were selected for Hebraic meter in the Gospel of John.

Single Words in Heptadic Meter
After: 7, ὀπίσω (*opiso*, op-is'-o) 1:15, 27, 30; 6:66; 12:19; 18:6; 20:14;
Ask: 7, αἰτέω (*aiteo*, ahee-teh'-o), farewell discourse after Lord's Supper, second person plural, 14:13, 14; 15:7, 16; 16:23, 24, 26;
Bear or Carry: 7, Chapter 15, φέρω (*phero*, fer'-o), 15:2 φέρον, φέρῃ, φέρον; 15:4 φέρειν; 15:5 φέρει; 15:8 φέρητε; 15:16 φέρητε;
Become: 7, Chapter 1, ἐγένετο (*egeneto*, eg'-en-etŏ), verb indicative aor-

---
[3] Cascione, 2012, p. 230.

ist middle deponent 3rd person singular from γίνομαι, 1:3 (x2), 6, 10, 14, 17, 28;
Become: 7, γενέσθαι (infinitive) (*genesthai*, gen'-esth-ahee) 1:12; 3:9; 5:6; 8:58; 9:27; 13:19; 14:29;
Believe: 7, Chapter 20, πιστεύω (*pisteuo*, pist-yoo'-o) 20:8, 25, 29 (x2), 31 (x2); πιστός (*pistos*, pis-tos') 20:27; unbelief, ἄπιστος (*apistos*, ap'-istos) 20:27 would make 7 in diaolgue with Thomas;
Chief Priest: 21, ἀρχιερεύς (*archiereus*, ar-khee-er-yuce') 7:32, 45; 11:47, 49, 51, 57; 12:10; 18:3, 10, 13, 15 (x2), 16, 19, 22, 24, 26, 35; 19:6, 15, 21;
The Crowd: 7, ὄχλος (*ochlos*, okh'los) 6:22, 24; 7:20, 49; 12:17, 18, 34; only in BYZ, GOC, SCR, STE;
Darkness: 7, σκοτία (*skotia*, skot-ee'-ah) noun nominative feminine singular common, 1:5 (x2); 6:17; 8:12; 12:35 (x2), 46;
Demon: 7, δαιμόνιον (*daimonion*, dahee-mon'-ee-on) 7:20; 8:48, 49, 52; 10:20, 21 (x2); 6 nouns, 1 verb;
Entered: 7, εἰσῆλθεν, (*eisailthen*, eis'-ail-then) 13:27; 18:1, 33; 19:9; 20:5, 6, 8;
Feast: 7, ἑορτή (*heorte*, heh-or-tay') noun accusative feminine singular, 2:23; 4:45; 7:8, 10; 11:56; 12:12; 13:29;
Feast: 7, Chaper 7, ἑορτή (*heorte*, heh-or-tay') 7:2, 8 (x2), 10, 11, 14, 37;
Feast: 7, Chaper 7, ἑορτή (*heorte*, heh-or-tay') noun dative feminine singular, 2:23; 4:45; 5:1; 6:4; 7:2, 11; 12:20;
Hate: 7, Chapter 15, μισέω (*miseo*, mis-eh'-o) 15:18 (x2), 19, 23 (x2), 24, 25;
Jesus: 7, Chapter 20:19-31, Ἰησοῦς (*Iesous*, ee-ay-sooce') 20:19, 21, 24, 26, 29, 30, 31;
Judea: 7, Ιουδαία (*Ioudaia*, ee-oo-dah'-yah) 3:22; 4:3, 47, 54; 7:1, 3; 11:7;
Life: 7, ζωή (*zoe*, dzo-ay') noun nominative feminine singular common, 1:4 (x2); 6:63; 11:25; 12:50; 14:6; 17:3;
Love: 7, ἀγάπη (*agape*, ag-ah'-pay) 5:42; 13:35; 15:9, 10 (x2), 13; 17:26;
Night: 7, νύξ (*nux*, noox) 3:2; 7:50; 9:4; 11:10; 13:30; 19:39; 21:3; BNT, GNT, TIS, VST, WHO missing 9:4;
Remain: 14, farewell discourse after Lord's Supper, μένω (*meno*, men'-o) 14:10, 17, 25; 15:4 (x3), 5, 6, 7 (x2), 9, 10 (x2), 16;
Stone: 7 (nouns), λίθος (*lithos*, lee'-thos) 8:7, 59; 10:31; 11:38, 39, 41; 20:1;
Stone(s) (throw *or* made of stone): **7**, (5 verbs) λιθάζω; (2 adjectives) λιθόστρωτος, λίθινος, 2:6; 8:5; 10:31, 32, 33; 11:8; 19:13. However, the count for the 14 nouns, adjectives, and verbs would be 12, or 6 + 6, if 8:5 and 8:7 are excluded from the account of the woman caught in adultery;
In the Temple: 7, 2:14; 5:14; 7:28; 8:20; 10:23; 11:56; 18:20;
They May Be: 7, Chapter 17, ὦσιν (*osin*, o-sin) verb subjunctive present active 3rd person plural from εἰμί, 17:11, 19, 21 (x2), 22, 23, 24;
Thus: 14, οὕτω (*houto*, hoo'-to) 3:8, 14, 16; 4:6; 5:21, 26; 7:46; 11:48; 12:50; 13:25; 14:31; 15:4; 18:22; 21:1; BYZ, GOC, SCR, STE add 8:58;

GOC, SCR, STE missing 13:25;
Truth: 7, Chapter 8, ἀλήθεια (*aletheia,* al-ay'-thi-a) 8:32 (x2), 40, 44 (x2), 45, 46;
Vine/Branch: 7, Chapter 15, vine, ἄμπελος (*ampelos,* am'-pel-os) 15:1, 4, 5; branch, κλῆμα (*klema,* kaly'-mah) 15:2, 4, 5, 6;
Wash: 14, (verb) νίπτω (*nipto,* nip'-to) 9:7 (x2), 11(x2), 15; 13:5, 6, 8 (x2), 10, 12, 14 (x2); (noun) νιπτήρ (*nipter,* nip-tare') 13:5;
Whole: 7, ὑγιής (*hugies,* hoog-ee-ace') 5:4, 6, 9, 11, 14, 15; 7:23; only BYZ, GOC, SCR, STE have verse 5:4;
Worship/Worshipers: 14, προσκυνέω (*proskuneo,* pros-koo-neh'-o) 4:20 (x2), 21, 22 (x2), 23 (x3), 24 (x2); 9:38; 11:9, 10; 12:20;
Written: 14, γράφω (*grapho,* graf'-o) γέγραφα, verb indicative perfect, 7 of the 14 are γεγραμμένον, verb participle perfect passive nominative neuter singular, 2:17; 6:31, 45; 8:17; 10:34; 12:14, 16; 15:25; 19:19 (x2), 20, 22; 20:30, 31.

Single Words in Decadal Meter
Crowd: 20, ὄχλος (*ochlos,* okh'los) 5:13; 6:2, 5, 22, 24; 7:12 (x2), 20, 31, 32, 40, 43, 49; 11:42; 12:9, 12, 17, 18, 29, 34;
Day: 30, ἡμέρα (*hemera,* hay-mer'-ah) 1:39; 2:1, 12, 19, 20; 4:40, 43; 5:9; 6:39, 40, 44, 54; 7:37; 8:56; 9:4; 11:6, 9 (x2), 17, 24, 53; 12:1, 7, 48; 14:20; 16:23, 26; 19:31; 20:19, 26; BNT, GNT, TIS, WHO add 9:14, which is an obvious expansion of the text;
Eat: 10, Chapter 6:23-58, φάγω, φάγομαι (*phago,* fag'-o) 6:23, 26, 31 (x2), 49, 50, 51, 52, 53, 58;
Fruit: 10, καρπός (*karpos,* kar-pos') 4:36; 12:24; 15:2 (x3), 4, 5, 8, 16 (x2);
Fufilled: 10, fullness, πλήρωμα (*pleroma,* play'-ro-mah) 1:16; πληρωθῇ (*plerothay,* play-ro'-thay) 12:38; 13:18; 15:11, 25; 17:12; 18:9, 32; 19:24, 36;
Go Out: 20, ἐξέρχομαι (*exerchomai,* ex-er'-khom-ahee) ἐξῆλθες, verb indicative aorist active singular, 4:43; 8:59; 10:39; 11:31, 44; 13:3, 30, 31; 16:30; 18:1, 4, 16, 29, 38; 19:4, 5, 17, 34; 20:3; 21:23; BYZ, GOC, SCR, STE missing at 18:4; variant rejected;
Hands, Side, Finger: 10, Chapter 20, hand, χείρ (*cheir,* khire) 20:20, 25 (x2), 27 (x2); side, πλευρά (*pleura,* plyoo-rah') 20:20, 25, 27; finger, δάκτυλος (*daktulos,* dak'-too-los) 20:25, 27;
Heaven: 20, οὐρανός (*ouranos,* oo-ran-os') 1:32, 52; 3:5, 13 (x3), 27, 31; 6:31, 32 (x2), 33, 38, 41, 42, 50, 51, 58; 12:28; 17:1 only in TIS;
Keep: 10, infinitive ζητεῖτε (*zeteitay,* dzay-tei'-tay) verb indicative present active 2nd person plural from ζητέω (*zeteo,* dzay-teh'-o) 1:38; 5:44; 6:26; 7:19; 8:37, 40; 16:19; 18:4, 7, 8;
Manifest: 10, φανερόω (*phaneroo,* fan-er-o'-o) 1:31; 2:11; 3:21; 7:4, 10; 9:3; 17:6; 21:1 (x2), 14;
Passover: 10, πάσχα (*pascha,* pas'-khah) 2:13, 23; 6:4; 11:55 (x2); 12:1; 13:1; 18:28, 39; 19:14;

Pharisees: 20, Φαρισαῖος (*Pharisaios*, far-is-ah'-yos) 1:24; 3:1; 4:1; 7:32 (x2), 45, 47, 48; 8:3, 13; 9:13, 15, 16, 40; 11:46, 47, 57; 12:19, 42; 18:3; this word may not be in decadal cadence because 8:3 is found in the account of the woman caught in adultery;
Pilate: 20, Πιλᾶτος (*Pilatos*, pil-at'-os) 18:29, 31, 33, 35, 37, 38; 19:1, 4, 6, 8, 10, 12, 13, 15, 19, 21, 22, 31, 38 (x2);
Scripture: 10, γραφή (*graphe*, graf-ay') (this form only) 2:22; 7:38, 42; 10:35; 13:18; 17:12; 19:24, 28, 36, 37;
Sign or miracle: 20, σημεῖον (*semeion*, say-mi'-on) (17 nouns and 3 verbs) 2:11, 18, 23; 3:2; 4:48, 54; 6:2, 14, 26, 30; 7:31; 9:16; 10:41; 11:47; 12:18, 33, 37; 18:32; 20:30; 21:19;
The Spirit: 10, τὸ πνεῦμα (*to pneuma*, pnyoo'-mah) 1:32, 33; 3:8, 34; 6:63; 14:17, 26; 15:26; 16:13; 19:30;
Temple: 10, ἱερόν (*hieron*, hee-er-on') 2:14, 15; 5:14; 7:14, 28; 8:20, 59; 10:23; 11:56; 18:20; meter is present if 8:2 is excluded from the account of the woman caught in adultery;
Temple: 3, ναός (*naos*, nah-os') 2:19, 20, 21 (possible trinitarian reference to Jesus' body); plus 7 of the phrase *in the temple*, ἐν τῷ ἱερῷ = 10;
True: 10, ἀληθής (*alethes*, al-ay-thace') adjective normal nominative masculine singular, 3:33; 5:31, 32; 7:18; 8:13, 14, 16, 17, 26; 21:24; only in BYZ, GOC, SCR, STE if 8:16 is included, and in BNT, GNT, TIS, VST, WHO if 6:55 (x2) is rejected;
True: 10, ἀληθῶς (*alethos*, al-ay-thoce') 1:47; 4:42; 6:14, 55 (x2); 7:26 (x2), 40; 8:31; 17:8; only if variants 6:55 (x2) and second 7:26 missing in BNT, GNT, TIS, VST, WHO are accepted;
Water: 10, Chapter 4, ὑδρία (*hudria*, hoo-dree-ah') 4:7, 10, 11, 13, 14 (x3), 15, 28, 46;
Wine/Water: 10, Chapter 2:1-11, (wine 5) οἶνος (*oinos*, oy'-nos) 2:3 (x2), 9, 10 (x2); (waterpot 2) ὑδρία (*hudria*, hoo-dree-ah') 2:6, 7; (water 3) ὕδωρ (*hudor*, hoo'-dore) 2:7, 9 (x2);
Word: 40, λόγος (*logos*, log'-os) 1:1 (x3), 14; 2:22; 4:37, 39, 41, 50; 5:24, 38; 6:60; 7:36, 40; 8:31, 37, 43, 51, 52, 55; 10:19, 35; 12:38, 48; 14:23, 24 (x2); 15:3, 20 (x2), 25; 17:6, 14, 17, 20; 18:9, 32; 19:8, 13; 21:23; however, BNT, GNT, TIS, VST, WHO add 11:50;
Word: 10, accusative neuter plural, ῥῆμα (*rhema*, hray'-mah) 3:34; 6:63, 68; 8:20, 47; 10:21; 12:48; 14:10; 15:7; 17:8 (see dodecadal);
Works: 20, ἔργα (*erga*, er'-ga) nominative masculine or neuter plural, 3:19, 20, 21; 5:20, 36 (x2); 6:28; 7:3, 7; 8:39, 41; 9:3, 4; 10:25, 32, 37; 14:10, 11, 12; 15:24.

Single Words in Dodecadal Meter

Call 12, φωνέω (*phoneo*, fo-neh'-o) 1:48; 2:9; 4:16; 9:18, 24; SCR, STE, 11:28 (x2); 12:17; 13:13, 38; 18:27, 33; BYZ, GOC, SCR, STE have *call*, καλέω (*kaleo*, kal-eh'-o) at 10:3 instead of φωνέω;
Crowd: 12, ὄχλος (*ochlos*, okh'los) nominative case, 6:2, 5, 22, 24; 7:20, 49; 12:9, 12, 17, 18, 29, 34;

Crucify 12, Chapter 19, σταυρόω (*stauroo*, stow-ro'-o) 19:6 (x3), 10, 15 (x2), 16, 18, 20, 23, 41; συσταυρόω (*sustauroo*, soos-tow-ro'-o) 19:32;
Hate: 12, μισέω (*miseo*, mis-eh'-o) 3:20; 7:7 (x2); 12:25; 15:18 (x2), 19, 23 (x2), 24, 25; 17:14;
Light: 24, φῶς (*phos*, foce) 1:4, 5, 7, 8 (x2), 9; 3:19 (x2), 20 (x2), 21; 5:35; 8:12 (x2); 9:5; 11:9, 10; 12:35 (x2), 36 (x3), 46; φωτίζω (*photizo*, fo-tid'-zo) 1:9; the verb for *enlighten* only appears once in John;
Moses: 12, Μωσεῦς (*Moseus*, moce-yoos') 1:17, 45; 3:14; 5:45, 46; 6:32; 7:19, 22 (x2), 23; 9:28, 29; meter is present if 8:5 is excluded from account of the woman caught in adultery;
Scripture: 12, γραφή (*graphe*, graf-ay') 2:22; 5:39; 7:38, 42; 10:35; 13:18; 17:12; 19:24, 28, 36, 37; 20:9;
Spirit: 24, πνεῦμα (*pneuma*, pnyoo'-mah) 1:32, 33 (x2); 3:5, 6 (x2), 8 (x2), 34; 4:23, 24 (x2); 6:63 (x2); 7:39 (x2); 11:33; 13:21; 14:17, 26; 15:26; 16:13; 19:30; 20:22;
True/Truth: 12, Chapter 8 (adjective) ἀληθής (*alethes*, al-ay-thace') 8:13, 14, 16, 17, 26; (noun) ἀλήθεια (*aletheia*, al-ay'-thi-a) 8:32 (x2), 40, 44 (x2), 45, 46;
Woman: 12, Chapter 4, γυνή (*gune*, goo-nay') 4:7, 9 (x2), 15, 17, 19, 21, 25, 27, 28, 39, 42; meter is present if variant in 4:11 is rejected, which is questioned by BNT, GNT, and removed from WHO; most important is that it is missing from manuscript P75;
Word: 12, ῥῆμα (*rhema*, hray'-mah) 3:34; 5:47; 6:63, 68; 8:20, 47; 10:21; 12:47, 48; 14:10; 15:7; 17:8; (10 accusative).

Single Words Repeated 17 Times

Become: 17, ἐγένετο verb indicative aorist middle 3rd person singular from γίνομαι (*ginomai*, ghin'-om-ahee) 1:3 (x2), 6, 10, 14, 17, 28; 2:1; 3:25; 5:9; 6:16, 21; 7:43; 10:19, 22, 35; 19:36;
Feast: 17, ἑορτή (*heorte*, heh-or-tay') (7/10; 7 accusative), 2:23; 4:45 (x2); 5:1; 6:4; 7:2, 8 (x2), 10, 11, 14, 37; 11:56; 12:12, 20; 13:1, 29;
Sin: 17, ἁμαρτία (*hamartia*, ham-ar-tee'-ah) 1:29; 8:21, 24 (x2), 34 (x2), 46; 9:34, 41 (x2); 15:22 (x2), 24; 16:8, 9; 19:11; 20:23;
Woman: 17, γυνή (*gune*, goo-nay') 2:4; 4:7, 9 (x2), 15, 17, 19, 21, 25, 27, 28, 39, 42; 16:21; 19:26; 20:13, 15; meter is present if 4 or 5 references are excluded from the account of the woman caught in adultery in 8:1-11.

Some observations on the above are noteworthy. John's use of *logos* (*word*) appears 40 times, which is the number of completion (10) times humanity (4), a rather appropriate symbol for the Word became flesh. Numerous symbolic uses of 40, beginning with Genesis, illustrate completion of significant human events.

The Woman Caught in Adultery

As much as the account of the woman caught in adultery is appreciated by this writer, the data does not support it being part of the Gospel written by John. The only word in this account that shows a significant list of repetition is *Pharisees*. However, if *Pharisees* in this account is rejected, *Pharisee(s)* and *Chief Priest(s)* combine for a total of 40. If words such as *woman, stone,* and *stoned* were removed from this account, their repetition would exhibit a different Hebraic meter in John.

Some of the other words and phrases that are not found in Greek outside this account in the Gospel of John are: *but Jesus went* (8:1), *the Mount of Olives* (8:1), *early in the morning* (8:2), *came again* (8:2), *all the people* (8:2), *and he sat down* (8:2), *scribes* (8:3), *in the midst* (8:3), *adultery* (8:3, 4), *Moses commanded* (8:5), *persisted* (8:7), *condemned* (8:10), etc. The more words and phrases that are unique to this account, the more indication that these are not John's words.

There are also a number of Hebraic meters that fall into place when the account is removed from John, such as *Moses* (12), *stone, stones, throw stones* (12), *woman* (17), and *temple* (10). Of the more than 30 examples from the Gospel of John of metered phrases displayed in this chapter, not one of the repetitions from any phrase is found in the account of the woman caught in adultery. The account most likely took place and became a part of the oral tradition of the church, which Luke speaks about in the first 2 verses of his Gospel. Eventually it was added to John's Gospel. If this scenario is correct, it means that this account is not part of the original text, but was a historical event in Christ's ministry that was added to the text at a later date. The pattern of repetition in the Gospels suggests that this is the case.

The following are words that exhibit Hebraic meter in John when the account of the woman caught in adultery is removed from the text.

> **Alone: 14**, μόνον (*monon*, mon'-on) 5:18, 44; 6:15, 22; 8:16, 29; 11:52; 12:9, 24; 13:9; 16:32 (x2); 17:3, 20; meter is present if 8:9 is excluded from the account of the woman caught in adultery; 8:9 also missing from GOC;
> **Chief Priest: 21** and **Pharisees: 19 = 40**, ἀρχιερεύς (*archiereus*, ar-khee-er-yuce') 7:32 (x2), 45; 11:47, 49, 51, 57; 12:10; 18:3, 10, 13, 15 (x2), 16, 19, 22, 24, 26, 35; 19:6, 15, 21; Φαρισαῖος (*Pharisaios*, far-is-ah'-yos) 1:24; 3:1; 4:1; 7:32, 45, 47, 48; 8:13; 9:13, 15, 16, 40; 11:46, 47, 57; 12:19, 42; 18:3; meter is present when 8:3 is removed from account of the woman caught in adultery;
> **First: 14**, πρῶτος (*protos*, pro'-tos) 1:15, 30, 41; 2:10; 5:4; 7:51; 10:40;

12:16; 15:18; 18:13; 19:32, 39; 20:4, 8; BYZ, GOC, SCR, STE add 5:4; variant accepted; BYZ, GOC, SCR, STE use πρότερον (*proteron*, prot'-er-on) instead of πρῶτος at 7:51; variant rejected; meter is present if 8:7 is excluded from the account of the woman caught in adultery;

Law: 14, νόμος (*nomos*, nom'-os) 1:17, 45; 7:19 (x2), 23, 49, 51; 8:17; 10:34; 12:34; 15:25; 18:31; 19:7 (x2); meter is present if 8:5 is excluded from the account of the woman caught in adultery;

Lead: 7, ἄγω (*ago*, ag'-o) 1:42; 7:45; 9:13; 10:16; 18:13, 28; 19:13; meter is present if 8:3 is excluded from the account of the woman caught in adultery;

Moses: 12, Μωσεῦς (*Moseus*, moce-yoos') 1:17, 45; 3:14; 5:45, 46; 6:32; 7:19, 22 (x2), 23; 9:28, 29; meter is present if 8:5 is excluded from the account of the woman caught in adultery;

Sin/Sinful/To Sin: 24, sin, ἁμαρτία (*hamartia*, ham-ar-tee'-ah) 1:29; 8:21, 24 (x2), 34 (x2), 46; 9:34, 41 (x2); 15:22 (x2), 24; 16:8, 9; 19:11; 20:23; sinful, ἁμαρτωλός (*hamartolos*, ham-ar-to-los') 9:16, 24, 25, 31; to sin, ἁμαρτάνω (*hamartano*, ham-ar-tan'-o) 5:14; 9:2, 3; meter is present if 8:7 and 11 are excluded from the account of the woman caught in adultery;

Stone: 7 (nouns), λίθος (*lithos*, lee'-thos) 8:7, 59; 10:31; 11:38, 39, 41; 20:1;

Stones(s) (throw *or* made of stone):**7**, (5 verbs) λιθάζω; (2 adjectives) λιθόστρωτος, λίθινος, 2:6; 8:5; 10:31, 32, 33; 11:8; 19:13. However, the count for the 14 nouns, adjectives, and verbs would be 12, or 6 + 6, if 8:5 and 8:7 are excluded from the account of the woman caught in adultery;

Woman: 12, Chapter 4, γυνή (*gune*, goo-nay') 4:7, 9 (x2), 15, 17, 19, 21, 25, 27, 28, 39, 42; meter is present if variant in 4:11 is rejected, which is questioned by BNT, GNT, and removed from WHO; most important is that it is missing from manuscript P75;

Woman: 17, γυνή (*gune*, goo-nay') 2:4; 4:7, 9 (x2), 15, 17, 19, 21, 25, 27, 28, 39, 42; 16:21; 19:26; 20:13, 15; meter is present if 4 or 5 references are excluded from the account of the woman caught in adultery;

Teacher: 7, διδάσκαλος (*didaskalos*, did-as'-kal-os) 1:38; 3:2, 10; 11:28; 13:13, 14; 20:16; meter is present if 8:4 is excluded from the woman caught in adultery;

Temple: 10, ἱερόν (*hieron*, hee-er-on') 2:14, 15, 5:14; 7:14, 28; 8:20, 59; 10:23; 11:56; 18:20; meter is present if 8:2 is excluded from the account of the woman caught in adultery;

Temple: 3, ναός (*naos*, nah-os') 2:19, 20, 21 (possible trinitarian reference to Jesus' body); plus 7 of the phrase *in the temple*, ἐν τῷ ἱερῷ = 10;

Throw: 24, βάλλω (*ballo*, bal'-lo) 2:15; 3:24; 5:7; 6:37; 7:30, 44; 8:59; 9:34, 35; 10:4; 12:6, 31; 13:2, 5; 15:6 (x2); 18:11; 19:24; 20:25 (x2), 27; 21:6 (x2), 7; meter is present if 8:7 is excluded from the account of the woman caught in adultery;

Write: 20, γράφω (*grapho*, graf'-o) 1:45; 2:17; 5:46; 6:31, 45; 8:6, 8, 17; 10:34; 12:14, 16; 15:25; 19:19 (x2), 20, 21, 22 (x2); 20:30, 31; 21:25 (x2); meter is present if 8:6 and 8:8 are excluded from the woman caught in adultery.

Hebraic Meter in Gospel Events

Hebraic meter becomes another means to identify and verify the original text. The ancients were obviously using this process. It is time to acknowledge their work.

Now that the reader has observed Hebraic meter in Matthew, Mark, Luke, and John, it should be noted that exegetes in the past have observed examples of repetition in the 4 Gospels. These observations usually deal with repeated events, actions, or things, and not repeated words. The following are quotations by William Barclay and Martin H. Franzmann. Both exegetes came to the conclusion that the Gospels include heptadic and/or decadal events:

In his exposition of Luke 14:1-6, *Jesus heals the man with dropsy*, Barclay writes:

> In the gospel story there are seven incidents in which Jesus healed on the Sabbath day. In Luke we already studied the story of the healing of Simon's mother-in-law (4:38); of the man with the withered hand (6:6); and of the woman who was bent for eighteen years (13:13). To these John adds the story of the healing of the paralytic at the pool Bethesda (John 5:9), and of the man born blind (John 9:14). Mark adds one more – the healing of the demon-possessed man in the synagogue at Capernaum (Mark 1:21).[4]

Jesus heals 7 Times on the Sabbath
Simon's mother-in-law healed of her fever (Luke 4:38)
Man with withered hand restored (Luke 6:6)
Woman bent over healed (Luke 13:13)
Man healed from dropsy (Luke 14:1-6)
Paralytic by the pool of Bethesda healed (John 5:9)
Man born blind given sight (John 9:14)
Demon cast out of man in the Synagogue (Mark 1:21)

In his book, *Follow Me: Discipleship According to Saint Matthew*, Franzmann writes:

> It is certainly significant that the sending of the Twelve is prefaced, not by an account of the maturation of the disciples nor by a disquisition on the principles or the ethics or the methods of the missions, but by an account of Messianic revelation. Again the disciple's life is characterized as wholly dominated by the Christ. The narrative of the ten miracles in chapters eight and nine is the record of a full and comprehensive Messianic revelation. It is marked as

---

[4] William Barclay, *The Gospel of Luke,* 3rd ed., The Westminster Press, Philadelphia, 1977, p. 187.

characteristically Messianic by the inclusion of two interludes in the narrative which recorded words and nonmiraculous deeds of Jesus which are, as will be seen, charged with Messianic meaning (8:18-22; 9:9-17). It is marked as full and comprehensive revelation by the fact that just ten miracles are recorded. The symbolism of numbers in the Bible should not be exaggerated; the men who were moved by the Holy Spirit to speak from God, were not interested in number speculation, they do not play with numerals. But neither can it be overlooked that numbers do signify. The number ten for example, does play a role in Scripture as the number expressive of completeness: ten commandments express the will of God in its completeness (Ex. 20); ten plagues reveal, climactically, the power of God who says, "Let My people go!" (Ex. 7-11). That significance was felt in Judaism: the rabbis spoke of ten words of God which created the world and of ten trials by which Abraham was made perfect in obedience. Jewish apocalyptic divided the world's history into ten epochs, the tenth being the age of the Messiah. And it is probably not accidental that in the New Testament Paul enumerates just ten vices which exclude a man from the inheritance of the Kingdom (1 Cor. 6:9ff.) and mentions just ten hostile powers when he wants to assert fully and emphatically that the love of God in Christ makes men more than conquerors over *all* opposition (Rom. 8:35ff.). And if Matthew selects just ten miracles in this massed account of Jesus' mighty deeds, he is telling the attentive reader that he is thereby giving a rounded and comprehensive account of the "deeds of the Christ" (11:2).[5]

When this study of the 4 Gospels began, this writer was of the opinion that Matthew probably contains the most Hebraic meter of all the Gospels. However, as time progressed, far more effort was made in searching for Hebraic meter in John because he is also the author of Revelation. The challenge was to discover how closely John repeated similar meter in both books. Thus, more data was collected from John than the other Gospels. At this writing, the opinion is still held that Matthew contains the most repetition. If the same amount of time invested in John had been spent on Matthew, Matthew would probably produce more metered words and phrases than John. Perhaps the opportunity for future study will prove this opinion correct.

After identifying literally thousands of examples of Hebraic repetition in the texts of the Bible from Genesis to Revelation, this writer concludes that the order and structure of this repetition is more closely

---

[5] Martin H. Franzmann, *Follow Me: Discipleship According to Saint Matthew,* Concordia Publishing House, St. Louis, 1961, pp. 66-67.

related to aesthetics than mathematics. The choice of words and phrases, their arrangement, positioning of subsets within sets, and the juxtaposition and counterbalance of linguistic symmetry and asymmetry are aesthetic choices illustrating a highly refined and elaborate art form.

The following chapters will deal with repetition in Revelation, and look for further confirmation of the origin of this literary genre in Genesis and Exodus.

Chapter Five
Repetition in the Book of Revelation

Repetition in the Book of Revelation is similar to repetition found in the Gospels and Genesis. It also contains repetition unique to apocalyptic symbolism. There is a direct relationship in Revelation between numbers in the text and Hebraic meter in the text.

The initial observation of repetition in phrases was published in the first edition of *In Search of the Biblical Order* in 1987,[1] followed by a few more examples in the second edition published in 2012.[2] But their function was not understood. The assumption was that heptadic, decadal, and dodecadal repetition in phrases was coincidental with the repetition of individual words, and not a genre in itself. This writer was not aware of Dr. Diana Jill Kirby's dissertation, *Repetition in the Book of Revelation*, until 2013. Kirby confirmed that numerically-ordered phrases are an integral part of repetition in Revelation.

Kirby's insight led to a reexamination of the data in the first 2 editions. She identified a number of repeated phrases, but she did not know that John's repetition is following the ancient tradition of Hebraic meter. Nearly 70 years earlier, Umberto Cassuto published his discovery of Hebraic meter, but did not understand it or define it as repetition. Kirby unknowingly confirmed Cassuto's research in her analysis of repetition in Revelation. Cassuto's observation of repetition in Mosaic literature is clearly evident in Revelation. If the assumptions found in Cassuto, Kirby, and the 2012 edition are correct, there should be more data to substantiate these theories. By combining Cassuto's concept of Hebraic meter, Kirby's understanding of repetition, and the data from the first and second editions, numerous phrases in Hebraic meter were located in Revelation.

In the process of collecting data, it became apparent that Nestle-Aland's text (BNT) is more reliable in the search for Hebraic cadence in the Gospels than it is in Revelation. In Revelation the Eastern texts, BYZ, GOC, SCR, and particularly STE, are more reliable. Even though Receptus (SCR and STE) adds more than 35 Greek *and*s (*kai,* καὶ) and

---

[1] J. M. Cascione, *In Search of the Biblical Order*, Biblion, Fairview Park, OH, 1987.
[2] Cascione, 2012.

a few longer readings, Receptus contains remarkable readings that often complete complex Hebraic meter. Receptus also contains some important readings that are shorter than those found in Nestle-Aland. Either a knowledgeable copyist intentionally completed or enhanced Hebraic meter in the text of Receptus, or one of the 24 manuscripts of Revelation in Receptus is closer to the original autograph than any other manuscript.

In the first chapter of Revelation, 7 letters are sent to 7 churches, and 7 is repeated 10 or 11 times, including 7 lampstands, 7 stars, and 7 spirits.

As the last book in the Bible, Revelation serves as a primer for understanding the Hebraic style that begins in Genesis and continues through every book in the Bible. The obvious heptads, decads, and dodecads in Revelation lead to more complicated and intricate meter in the text. The very structure of the book leads to the inevitable observation of numerically-ordered phrases. The wedding of numbers, words, and repetition permeates the text. After decades of research, it became apparent that Moses and not John is the one who first recorded this genre. Revelation could be described as *Mosaic style made easy*.

Heptadic Meter in Revelation

The following heptadic phrases in Revelation illustrate similarities with phrases in the Gospels, as well as differences. The first 2 examples, *And to the angel of the church in...write these things*, and *He that hath an ear, let him hear what the Spirit says to the churches*, are the longest metered phrases found in Revelation. Each phrase has 10 Greek words. This 7-10 relationship is not coincidental. John is counting Greek words, numbers, and phrases in traditional Hebraic meter. These 2 phrases are a rather obvious selection because they begin and conclude each of the 7 letters. There is no need to include the English translation for each phrase. There are no variants.

And to the angel of the church in...write these things 7 times in Revelation

 Τῷ ἀγγέλῳ τῆς ἐν Ἐφέσῳ ἐκκλησίας γράψον· Τάδε λέγει (Rev. 2:1 BNT)
 Καὶ τῷ ἀγγέλῳ τῆς ἐν Σμύρνῃ ἐκκλησίας γράψον· Τάδε λέγει (Rev. 2:8 BNT)
 Καὶ τῷ ἀγγέλῳ τῆς ἐν Περγάμῳ ἐκκλησίας γράψον· Τάδε λέγει (Rev. 2:12 BNT)
 Καὶ τῷ ἀγγέλῳ τῆς ἐν Θυατείροις ἐκκλησίας γράψον· Τάδε λέγει (Rev. 2:18 BNT)
 Καὶ τῷ ἀγγέλῳ τῆς ἐν Σάρδεσιν ἐκκλησίας γράψον· Τάδε λέγει (Rev. 3:1 BNT)
 Καὶ τῷ ἀγγέλῳ τῆς ἐν Φιλαδελφείᾳ ἐκκλησίας γράψον· Τάδε λέγει (Rev. 3:7 BNT)
 Καὶ τῷ ἀγγέλῳ τῆς ἐν Λαοδικείᾳ ἐκκλησίας γράψον· Τάδε λέγει (Rev. 3:14 BNT)

He that hath an ear let him hear what the Spirit saith unto the churches
7 times in Revelation
    Ὁ ἔχων οὖς ἀκουσάτω τί τὸ πνεῦμα λέγει ταῖς ἐκκλησίαις (Rev. 2:7 BNT)
    Ὁ ἔχων οὖς ἀκουσάτω τί τὸ πνεῦμα λέγει ταῖς ἐκκλησίαις (Rev. 2:11 BNT)
    Ὁ ἔχων οὖς ἀκουσάτω τί τὸ πνεῦμα λέγει ταῖς ἐκκλησίαις (Rev. 2:17 BNT)
    Ὁ ἔχων οὖς ἀκουσάτω τί τὸ πνεῦμα λέγει ταῖς ἐκκλησίαις (Rev. 2:29 BNT)
    Ὁ ἔχων οὖς ἀκουσάτω τί τὸ πνεῦμα λέγει ταῖς ἐκκλησίαις (Rev. 3:6 BNT)
    Ὁ ἔχων οὖς ἀκουσάτω τί τὸ πνεῦμα λέγει ταῖς ἐκκλησίαις (Rev. 3:13 BNT)
    Ὁ ἔχων οὖς ἀκουσάτω τί τὸ πνεῦμα λέγει ταῖς ἐκκλησίαις (Rev. 3:22 BNT)

Jesus Christ / Jesus

    The name *Jesus Christ*, the most significant 2 words in the Bible, has more than 30 variants in the New Testament, and at least 3 in Revelation. According to Textus Receptus, *Jesus Christ* repeats 7 times. The question is, "Was the text altered to arrive at 7, or is Receptus surprisingly accurate here?" Because Receptus exhibits many inaccuracies, the notion of a copyist's contrived scheme to create repetition in Revelation is rejected.

Jesus Christ 7 times in Revelation
    Jesus Christ...................... Ἰησοῦ Χριστοῦ (Rev. 1:1 BNT)
    Jesus Christ...................... Ἰησοῦ Χριστοῦ (Rev. 1:2 BNT)
    Jesus Christ...................... Ἰησοῦ Χριστοῦ (Rev. 1:5 BNT)
    Jesus Christ...................... Ἰησοῦ Χριστοῦ (Rev. 1:9 STE)*
    Jesus Christ...................... Ἰησοῦ Χριστοῦ (Rev. 1:9 STE)*
    Jesus Christ...................... Ἰησοῦ Χριστοῦ (Rev. 12:17 STE)**
    Jesus Christ...................... Ἰησοῦ Χριστοῦ (Rev. 22:21 STE)***
*Christ missing in 1:9 in BNT, GNT, TIS, VST, WHO.
**Christ missing in 12:17 in BNT, BYZ, GNT, GOC, TIS, VST, WHO.
***Christ missing in 22:21 in BNT, GNT, TIS, VST.

    Unlike the Gospels, Revelation is a tightly-constructed form of acrostic, combined with aspects of a crossword puzzle and a numerically-based game of 9s called Sudoku. The introduction found in Wikipedia provides an excellent definition of acrostic, as follows:

> An acrostic is a poem or other form of writing in which the first letter, syllable or word of each line, paragraph or other recurring feature in the text spells out a word or a message. The word comes from the French *acrostiche* from post-classical Latin *acrostichis*, from Koine Greek ἀκροστιχίς, from Ancient Greek ἄκρος "highest, topmost" and στίχος "verse". As a form of constrained writing, an acrostic can be used as a mnemonic device to aid memory retrieval.

> Relatively simple acrostics may merely spell out the letters of the alphabet in order; such an acrostic may be called an 'alphabetical acrostic' or Abecedarius. These acrostics occur in the first four of

the five songs that make up the Book of Lamentations, in the praise of the good wife in Proverbs 31, 10-31, and in Psalms 9, 10, 25, 34, 37, 111, 112, 119 and 145 of the Hebrew Bible. Notable among the acrostic Psalms are the long Psalm 119, which typically is printed in subsections named after the letters of the Hebrew alphabet, each of which is featured in that section; and Psalm 145, which is recited three times a day in the Jewish services. Acrostics prove that the texts in question were originally composed in writing, rather than having existed in oral tradition before being put into writing.[3]

The above definition provides numerous examples from the Hebrew text, which are the oldest examples from this rather lengthy definition. Unless additional sources are found to show otherwise, it appears that the acrostic may have originated with the Hebrew Bible. Psalm 119 is usually printed in 22 sections with 8 verses in each section, which is called an octet. There are 22 letters in the Hebrew alphabet. The first letter in each line of the first octet begins with the same letter from the Hebrew alphabet. There are 22 octets corresponding to the 22 letters of the Hebrew alphabet in Psalm 119. For example, in English each line in the first octet would begin with words such as *apple, aphid, allergy, anchor, animal, angel, Alabama,* and *Atlantic*. The next section or octet also begins with 8 words with the letter B, and so forth. With 176 verses in all, Psalm 119 is an eloquent hymn of metered praise, prayer, and profound theological wisdom.

The point with the above is that numbers and words were seamlessly woven into the fabric of biblical Hebrew unlike any Western text. Rather than an acrostic in the sense of Psalm 119, Revelation is an acrostic of numbers, words, phrases, and word stems. If one letter is altered at the beginning of a line in Psalm 119's 176 verses, the entire psalm is out of rhythm. Likewise, if one phrase, such as *Jesus Christ*, is altered, a related chain of words and phrases in Revelation is affected.

Jesus Christ Rev. 1:1	**Jesus** Rev. 14:12	**Christ** Rev. 11:15
Jesus Christ Rev. 1:2	**Jesus** Rev. 17:6	**Christ** Rev. 12:10
Jesus Christ Rev. 1:5	**Jesus** Rev. 19:10	**Christ** Rev. 20:4
Jesus Christ Rev. 1:9	**Jesus** Rev. 19:10	**Christ** Rev. 20:6
Jesus Christ Rev. 1:9	**Jesus** Rev. 20:4	**Son of man** Rev. 1:13
Jesus Christ Rev. 12:17	**Jesus** Rev. 22:16	**Son of God** Rev. 2:18
Jesus Christ Rev. 22:21	**Jesus** Rev. 22:20	**Son of man** Rev. 14:14[4]

---

[3] Acrostic. (2015, June 3). In *Wikipedia, The Free Encyclopedia*. Retrieved 22:32, June 25, 2015, from https://en.wikipedia.org/w/index.php?title=Acrostic&oldid=665325247.
[4] Cascione, 2012, p. 120.

The 7 repetitions of *Jesus Christ* in Revelation leave a corresponding remainder of 7 *Jesus* for a total of 14, or a double heptad. When one phrase is set in its proper order, additional patterns also fall into place.

John uses the phrase *Son of Man* 12 times and *Son of God* 10 times in his Gospel, but only writes *Son of Man* 2 times and *Son of God* once in Revelation. By combining these phrases with *Christ* (4 times) the total is also 7. Most of the heptads in Revelation exhibit a 3-4 division.

There was no intent to search for metered Hebraic phrases in Revelation in the 2012 edition. Even being aware of the heptad *Jesus Christ* did not raise curiosity to look for more words before or after the phrase. It was Cassuto's and Kirby's approach that led to further areas of inquiry. The inclusion of 1:9, found in BYZ, GOC, SCR, and STE, completes a 3-4 division in the heptadic phrase, *the witness of Jesus*. Note that the following heptad is a subset of the previous example.

The witness of Jesus 7 times in Revelation
    The **witness** of Jesus Christ...τὴν **μαρτυρίαν** Ἰησοῦ Χριστοῦ (Rev. 1:2 BNT)
    The **witness** of Jesus Christ...τὴν **μαρτυρίαν** Ἰησου Χριστοῦ (Rev. 1:9 STE)*
    The **witness** of Jesus Christ...τὴν **μαρτυρίαν** Ἰησου Χριστοῦ (Rev. 12:17 STE)**
    The **witnesses** of Jesus..........τῶν **μαρτύρων** Ἰησοῦ (Rev. 17:6 BNT)
    The **witness** of Jesus..............τὴν **μαρτυρίαν** Ἰησοῦ (Rev. 19:10 BNT)
For the **witness** of Jesus..........ἡ γὰρ **μαρτυρία** Ἰησοῦ (Rev. 19:10 BNT)
    The **witness** of Jesus..............τὴν **μαρτυρίαν** Ἰησου (Rev. 20:4 BNT)
Christ missing in 1:9 in BNT, GNT, TIS, VST, WHO.
**Christ* missing in 12:17 in BNT, BYZ, GNT, GOC, TIS, VST, WHO.

I Know

In the beginning of Revelation, Jesus says 7 times that He knows something about the people in the 7 churches—either their works, tribulation, or where they dwell. There are 3 more related phrases for a 7-10 division, as seen earlier, with no variants.

I know thy works, or *tribulation*, or *where you dwell* 7 times in Revelation – also *know* 10 times (no variants)
    I **know** thy works.................**οἶδα** τὰ ἔργα σου (Rev. 2:2 BNT)
    I **know** thy tribulation...........**οἶδά** σου τὴν θλῖψιν (Rev. 2:9 BNT)
    I **know** where you dwell.......**οἶδα** ποῦ κατοικεῖς (Rev. 2:13 BNT)
    I **know** thy works.................**οἶδά** σου τὰ ἔργα (Rev. 2:19 BNT)
    I **know** thy works.................**οἶδά** σου τὰ ἔργα (Rev. 3:1 BNT)
    I **know** thy works.................**οἶδά** σου τὰ ἔργα (Rev. 3:8 BNT)
    I **know** thy works.................**οἶδά** σου τὰ ἔργα (Rev. 3:15 BNT)

    And you do not **know**...................καὶ οὐκ **οἶδας** (Rev. 3:17 BNT)
    My lord, you **know**..........κύριέ μου, σὺ **οἶδας** (Rev. 7:14 BNT)
    Which no one **knows**.............ὃ οὐδεὶς **οἶδεν** (Rev. 19:12 BNT)

Book

The phrase *the open book* is difficult to follow at Revelation 10:2 and 10:8. They are reverse variants. Two verses show the same phrase as a variant reading. If both are wrong, there are 6 phrases; and if both are correct, there are 8 phrases. If one or the other is correct, there are 7 phrases. One or the other is *the little book which is open*, which should not be in the following list of 7. Revelation 10:8 seems to be the best choice to complete a heptad, because it has more texts that agree with it than 10:2.

The open book 7 times in Revelation
    To open the **book** (Rev. 5:2)
    To open the **book** (Rev. 5:3)
    To open the **book** (Rev. 5:4)
    To open the **book** (Rev. 5:5)
      To take the **book** and to open (Rev. 5:9)
        The **book** which is open (Rev. 10:8)*
      And **books** were opened (Rev. 20:12)

    ἀνοῖξαι τὸ **βιβλίον** (Rev. 5:2 BNT)
    ἀνοῖξαι τὸ **βιβλίον** (Rev. 5:3 BNT)
    ἀνοῖξαι τὸ **βιβλίον** (Rev. 5:4 BNT)
    ἀνοῖξαι τὸ **βιβλίον** (Rev. 5:5 BNT)
      λαβεῖν τὸ **βιβλίον** καὶ ἀνοῖξαι (Rev. 5:9 BNT)
        βιβλίον ἀνεῳγμένον (Rev. 10:8 BNT)*
      καὶ **βιβλία** ἠνοίχθησαν (Rev. 20:12 BNT)

*At Rev. 10:2, only BYZ, GOC have *book which is open*, versus *little book which is open* in BNT, GNT, SCR, STE, TIS, VST, WHO; at Rev. 10:8, BNT, GNT, VST, WHO have *book which is open*, versus *little book which is open* in BYZ, GOC, SCR, STE, TIS.

Another heptadic phrase in Revelation that includes the word *book* is *the book of life*. At 22:19, the reading in Receptus (SCR and STE), as found in the KJV, is *book of life*, which completes this heptad. The remaining Greek texts have *tree of life* at 22:19. The second part of the phrase—*of life*—has no variants. The question is whether the proper word should be *book* or *tree* in 22:19. The 2 words do not look or sound similar in Greek. It is difficult to explain how there could be such discrepancy in the text.

The book of life 7 times in Revelation
    Out of the **book of life** (Rev. 3:5)
      In the **book of life** (Rev. 13:8)
      On the **book of life** (Rev. 17:8)
        Another **book** opened, which is **of life** (Rev. 20:12)
      In the **book of life** (Rev. 20:15)
      In the **book of life** (Rev. 21:27)
    From the **book of life** (Rev. 22:19)*

ἐκ τῆς **βίβλου** τῆς ζωῆς (Rev. 3:5 BNT)
ἐν **βίβλῳ** τῆς ζωῆς (Rev. 13:8 BNT)
ἐπὶ τὸ **βιβλίον** τῆς ζωῆς (Rev. 17:8 BNT)
βιβλίον ἄλλο ἠνεῴχθη, ὅ ἐστι τῆς ζωῆς (Rev. 20:12 BNT)
ἐν τῇ **βίβλῳ** τῆς ζωῆς (Rev. 20:15 BNT)
ἐν τῷ **βιβλίῳ** τῆς ζωῆς (Rev. 21:27 BNT)
ἀπὸ **βίβλου** τῆς ζωῆς (Rev. 22:19 STE)*
*At 22:19, BNT, BYZ, GNT, GOC, TIS, VST, WHO have *tree of life*, versus *book of life* in SCR, STE.

At Revelation 3:5, instead of *written in the book*, that text states, *I will not erase his name out of the book*, implying the name is already written in the book. Notice 3 negatives that create a subset of 7 repetitions. There are no variants.

Written in the book 10 times in Revelation
        Write in a book (Rev. 1:11)
        I will not erase his name out of the book (Rev. 3:5)
        A book **written** inside and outside (Rev. 5:1)
Name has not been **written** in the book (Rev. 13:8)
Name has not been **written** in the book (Rev. 17:8)
        Written in the books (Rev. 20:12)
        Written in the book of life (Rev. 20:15)
        Written in the book (Rev. 21:27)
        Written in this book (Rev. 22:18)
        Written in this book (Rev. 22:19)

        γράψον εἰς βιβλίον (Rev. 1:11 BNT)
        οὐ **μὴ ἐξαλείψω** τὸ ὄνομα αὐτοῦ ἐκ τῆς βίβλου (Rev. 3:5 BNT)
        βιβλίον **γεγραμμένον** ἔσωθεν καὶ ὄπισθεν (Rev. 5:1 BNT)
        οὐ **γέγραπται** τὸ ὄνομα ἐν τῷ βιβλίῳ (Rev. 13:8 BNT)
        οὐ **γέγραπται** τὸ ὄνομα ἐπὶ τὸ βιβλίον (Rev. 17:8 BNT)
        γεγραμμένων ἐν τοῖς βιβλίοις (Rev. 20:12 BNT)
ἐν τῇ **βίβλῳ** τῆς ζωῆς **γεγραμμένος** (Rev. 20:15 BNT)
        γεγραμμένοι ἐν τῷ βιβλίῳ (Rev. 21:27 BNT)
        γεγραμμένας ἐν τῷ βιβλίῳ τούτῳ (Rev. 22:18 BNT)
        γεγραμμένων ἐν τῷ βιβλίῳ τούτῳ (Rev. 22:19 BNT)

I Am or *He Is Coming*

There is an interesting relationship between the phrases *I am coming quickly*, and *behold I am coming*. All 10 phrases contain the word *coming*. But these are actually 2 overlapping heptads, 7 phrases beginning with *behold* and 7 phrases ending with *quickly*. At first, the thought was to write about 2 separate heptads. Not until the occasion of this writing was there recognition that these are not 2 separate heptads but one decad that contains 2 overlapping heptads. If it sounds confusing, it was also confusing to this writer. But look for yourself. On the left there are 7 *behold*, and on the right there are 7 *quickly*. Hence, there is a double heptad inside a decad. Also, careful observation of the Greek word for *coming* will reveal 7 ἔρχομαί (*erchomai*, er'-khom-ahee) bolded, which makes 3 overlapping heptads in one decad. Beyond cadence, this is a literary art form woven into the text, and a beautiful arrangement of words. Jesus says He is coming, and He gives us an ornate preview of the event.

I am or *He is coming* 10 times in Revelation
    Behold He is coming......................Ἰδοὺ ἔρχεται (Rev. 1:7 BNT)
        I am coming **quickly** to you........ἔρχομαί σοι ταχύ (Rev. 2:5 BYZ)*
        I am coming **quickly** to you.......ἔρχομαί σοι ταχύ (Rev. 2:16 BNT)
    Behold I am coming **quickly**..........ἰδού ἔρχομαι ταχύ (Rev. 3:11 STE)**
    Behold He is coming...................ἰδοὺ ἔρχεται (Rev. 9:12 BNT)
    Behold He is coming **quickly**........ἰδού ἔρχεται ταχύ (Rev. 11:14 BYZ)***
    Behold I am coming........................ἰδού ἔρχομαι (Rev. 16:15 BNT)
    Behold I am coming **quickly**.........ἰδού ἔρχομαι ταχύ (Rev. 22:7 BNT)
    Behold I am coming **quickly**...........ἰδού ἔρχομαι ταχύ (Rev. 22:12 BNT)
        I am coming **quickly**...............ἔρχομαι ταχύ (Rev. 22:20 BNT)
*Rev. 2:5 in BYZ, GOC, SCR, STE, VST.
**3:11 only in SCR, STE.
***All texts have these words, but this word order in 11:14 is only found in BYZ, GOC.

Also note that the Gospel of John repeats *I am coming*, ἔρχομαι, 10 times according to BYZ, GOC, and VST, thus indicating that John and Revelation are by the same author. This repetition further establishes the apostolic authorship of Revelation.

Activity in Heaven
Living Beings and Elders

The elders and the 4 living creatures appear together 7 times. They fall down and worship 3 times in 5:14, 7:11, and 19:4, creating a 3-4 division. With all the care seen in following the same word order in some examples, not one of the following 7 quotations is in the same order. No pattern could be established with the phrases *24 elders*, which repeats 6 times, or *4 living beings*, which repeats 11 times. However, together they make 17, a significant number. When the search was made for both *living beings* and *elders* together, it resulted in 7 repetitions. The assumption is that the 2 phrases are not to be counted separately. The endless variety of pattern arrangements is a constant source of amazement. The limitations of page width prevent displaying some of the Greek lines without wrapping the text.

Living beings and elders 7 times in Revelation (no variants)*
    And the four living **beings** and in the midst of the **elders** (Rev. 5:6)
        The four living **beings** and the 24 **elders** (Rev. 5:8)
        And the living **beings** and the **elders** (Rev. 5:11)
    And the four living **beings** saying amen, and the 24 **elders** (Rev. 5:14)**

And the **elders** and the four living **beings** (Rev. 7:11)
        The four living **beings** and the **elders** (Rev. 14:3)
The 24 **elders** and the four living **beings** (Rev. 19:4)
καὶ τῶν τεσσάρων ζῴων καὶ ἐν μέσῳ τῶν **πρεσβυτέρων** (Rev. 5:6 BNT)
    τὰ τέσσαρα ζῷα καὶ οἱ εἴκοσι τέσσαρες **πρεσβύτεροι** (Rev. 5:8 BNT)
    καὶ τῶν ζῴων καὶ τῶν **πρεσβυτέρων** (Rev. 5:11 BNT)
καὶ τὰ τέσσαρα ζῷα ἔλεγον Ἀμήν
        καὶ οἱ εἰκοσιτέσσαρες **πρεσβύτεροι** (Rev 5:14 STE)**
καὶ τῶν **πρεσβυτέρων** καὶ
    τῶν τεσσάρων ζῴων (Rev. 7:11 BNT)
    τῶν τεσσάρων ζῴων καὶ τῶν **πρεσβυτέρων** (Rev. 14:3 BNT)
καὶ ἔπεσαν οἱ **πρεσβύτεροι** οἱ εἴκοσι τέσσαρες
    καὶ τὰ τέσσαρα ζῷα (Rev 19:4 BNT)
*At 5:14, 7:11 and 19:4, the key words in Greek appear on separate lines due to page width limitations.
**Only SCR, STE have 24 at 5:14, for a 3-4 division.

Poured Out His Bowl / In Midst
The 7 angels pour their 7 bowls of wrath onto the world. There is a 3-4 division in the prepositions *onto* and *on*, with no variants.

Poured out his bowl 7 times in Revelation (no variants)
    poured out his bowl onto…ἐξέχεεν τὴν φιάλην αὐτοῦ **εἰς** (Rev. 16:2 BNT)
    poured out his bowl onto…ἐξέχεεν τὴν φιάλην αὐτοῦ **εἰς** (Rev. 16:3 BNT)
    poured out his bowl onto…ἐξέχεεν τὴν φιάλην αὐτοῦ **εἰς** (Rev. 16:4 BNT)
    poured out his bowl on……ἐξέχεεν τὴν φιάλην αὐτοῦ **ἐπὶ** (Rev. 16:8 BNT)
    poured out his bowl on……ἐξέχεεν τὴν φιάλην αὐτοῦ **ἐπὶ** (Rev. 16:10 BNT)
    poured out his bowl on……ἐξέχεεν τὴν φιάλην αὐτοῦ **ἐπὶ** (Rev. 16:12 BNT)
    poured out his bowl on……ἐξέχεεν τὴν φιάλην αὐτοῦ **ἐπὶ** (Rev. 16:17 BNT)

In midst 7 times in Revelation*
    In midst................ ἐν μέσῳ (Rev. 1:13 BNT)
    In midst................ ἐν μέσῳ (Rev. 2:1 BNT)
    In midst................ ἐν μέσῳ (Rev. 4:6 BNT)
    In midst................ ἐν μέσῳ (Rev. 5:6 BNT)
    In midst................ ἐν μέσῳ (Rev. 5:6 BNT)
    In midst................ ἐν μέσῳ (Rev. 6:6 BNT)
    In midst................ ἐν μέσῳ (Rev. 22:2 BNT)
In midst (ἐν μέσῶ) found in Rev. 2:7 in SCR, STE is rejected to make 12 repetitions of μέσ.

God in Heptadic Meter
The One Sitting On
Five of the 7 repetitions below refer to God. *God*, as in the phrase, *Word of God*, is usually in a repetition of 7.

The one sitting on 7 times in Revelation (no variants)
        And **the one sitting** on him (Rev. 6:2)
        And **the one sitting** on him (Rev. 6:5)

And **the one sitting** on him (Rev. 6:8)
And **the one sitting** on (Rev. 7:15)
    the one sitting on (Rev. 14:16)
And **the one sitting** on him (Rev. 19:11)
And I saw **the one sitting** on (Rev. 21:5)

    καὶ ὁ **καθήμενος** ἐπ᾽ αὐτὸν (Rev. 6:2 BNT)
    καὶ ὁ **καθήμενος** ἐπ᾽ αὐτὸν (Rev. 6:5 BNT)
    καὶ ὁ **καθήμενος** ἐπάνω αὐτοῦ (Rev. 6:8 BNT)
    καὶ ὁ **καθήμενος** ἐπὶ (Rev. 7:15 BNT)
       ὁ **καθήμενος** ἐπὶ (Rev. 14:16 BNT)
    καὶ ὁ **καθήμενος** ἐπ᾽ αὐτὸν (Rev. 19:11 BNT)
καὶ εἶπεν ὁ **καθήμενος** ἐπὶ (Rev. 21:5 BNT)

The Word(s) of God

The phrase *the Word(s) of God* contains a 3-4 division with the article τὸν, as seen in the Greek. This particular arrangement was found in Kirby's dissertation as an example of repetition. Kirby was not aware that John is following Mosaic meter in Revelation.

The word(s) of God 7 times in Revelation (no variants)
    The word of God...............**τὸν** λόγον τοῦ θεοῦ (Rev. 1:2 BNT)
    The word of God.............. **τὸν** λόγον τοῦ θεοῦ (Rev. 1:9 BNT)
    The word of God.............. **τὸν** λόγον τοῦ θεου (Rev. 6:9 BNT)
    The words of God.................οἱ λόγοι τοῦ θεοῦ (Rev. 17:17 BNT)
The true words of God....οἱ λόγοι ἀληθινοὶ τοῦ θεοῦ (Rev. 19:9 BNT)
    The word of God...................ὁ λόγος τοῦ θεοῦ (Rev. 19:13 BNT)
    The word of God...............**τὸν** λόγον τοῦ θεοῦ (Rev. 20:4 BNT)

Before God / Lord God Almighty / Wrath of God / God and Jesus

The following phrases, *before God, Lord God Almighty, wrath of God,* and *God* associated with *Jesus*, are all in heptadic meter. This heptadic repetition with *God* originates with Genesis. All 7 phrases with *God* and *Jesus* include words about *witness, commandment,* or *testimony*, shown underlined in English, with no variants.

Before God 7 times in Revelation*
    Before God......................ἐνώπιον τοῦ θεοῦ (Rev. 3:2 BNT)
    Before God......................ἐνώπιον τοῦ θεου (Rev. 8:2 BNT)
    Before God......................ἐνώπιον τοῦ θεοῦ (Rev. 8:4 BNT)
    Before God......................ἐνώπιον τοῦ θεοῦ (Rev. 9:13 BNT)
    Before God......................ἐνώπιον τοῦ θεοῦ (Rev. 11:4 STE)**
    Before God......................ἐνώπιον τοῦ θεοῦ (Rev. 12:10 BNT)
    Before God......................ἐνώπιον τοῦ θεοῦ (Rev. 16:19 BNT)

*Variant at 11:16 in BYZ, GOC is necessary for the phrase *before the throne*, below.
**SCR, STE have *before God* at 11:4; variant accepted.

Lord God Almighty 7 times in Revelation
    Lord God Almighty......κύριος ὁ θεός...ὁ παντοκράτωρ (Rev. 1:8 BNT)*
    Lord God Almighty......κύριος ὁ θεὸς ὁ παντοκράτωρ (Rev. 4:8 BNT)
    Lord God Almighty......κύριε ὁ θεὸς ὁ παντοκράτωρ (Rev. 11:17 BNT)
    Lord God Almighty......κύριε ὁ θεὸς ὁ παντοκράτωρ (Rev. 15:3 BNT)
    Lord God Almighty......κύριε ὁ θεὸς ὁ παντοκράτωρ (Rev. 16:7 BNT)
    Lord God Almighty......κύριος ὁ θεὸς ὁ παντοκράτωρ (Rev. 19:6 BNT)
    Lord God Almighty......κύριος ὁ θεὸς ὁ παντοκράτωρ (Rev. 21:22 BNT)
*The shorter reading at Rev. 1:8 in BNT, BYZ, GNT, GOC, TIS, VST, WHO is correct; SCR, STE are missing *God*.

Wrath of God 7 times in Revelation (no variants)
    Out of wine of **wrath** of God (Rev. 14:10)
    Into wine press of **wrath** of God (Rev. 14:19)
        wrath of God is finished (Rev. 15:1)
    Full of **wrath** of God (Rev. 15:7)
    Seven bowls of the **wrath** of God (Rev. 16:1)
Before God, to give her...His...**wrath**   (Rev. 16:19)
    Wine of **wrath** of God (Rev. 19:15)

    ἐκ τοῦ οἴνου **τοῦ θυμοῦ** τοῦ θεου (Rev. 14:10 BNT)
    εἰς τὴν ληνὸν **τοῦ θυμοῦ** τοῦ θεου (Rev. 14:19 BNT)
    ἐτελέσθη **ὁ θυμὸς** τοῦ θεοῦ (Rev. 15:1 BNT)
    γεμούσας **τοῦ θυμοῦ** τοῦ θεοῦ (Rev. 15:7 BNT)
    τὰς ἑπτὰ φιάλας **τοῦ θυμοῦ** τοῦ θεου (Rev. 16:1 BNT)
ἐνώπιον τοῦ θεοῦ δοῦναι αὐτῇ...**τοῦ θυμοῦ**...αὐτοῦ (Rev. 16:19 BNT)
    τοῦ οἴνου **τοῦ θυμοῦ** τῆς ὀργῆς τοῦ θεοῦ (Rev. 19:15 BNT)

God and *Jesus* 7 times in Revelation (no variants)
The <u>Revelation</u> of **Jesus Christ**, which **God** gave unto him (Rev. 1:1)
Who bare <u>record</u> of the <u>word</u> of **God**, and of the <u>testimony</u> of **Jesus Christ** (Rev. 1:2)
Or the <u>word</u> of **God**, and for the <u>testimony</u> of **Jesus Christ** (Rev. 1:9)
Which keep the <u>commandments</u> of **God**, and have the <u>testimony</u> of **Jesus Christ** (Rev. 12:17)
Here *are* they that keep the <u>commandments</u> of **God**, and the <u>faith</u> of **Jesus** (Rev. 14:12)
And of thy brethren that have the <u>testimony</u> of **Jesus**: worship **God** (Rev. 19:10)
Beheaded for the <u>witness</u> of **Jesus**, and for the <u>word</u> of **God** (Rev. 20:4)

Ἀποκάλυψις **Ἰησοῦ Χριστοῦ** ἣν ἔδωκεν αὐτῷ ὁ **θεὸς** (Rev. 1:1 BNT)
τὸν λόγον τοῦ **θεοῦ** καὶ τὴν μαρτυρίαν **Ἰησοῦ χριστοῦ** (Rev. 1:2 BNT)
διὰ τὸν λόγον τοῦ **θεοῦ** καὶ τὴν μαρτυρίαν **Ἰησοῦ** (Rev. 1:9 BNT)
τὰς ἐντολὰς τοῦ **θεοῦ** καὶ ἐχόντων τὴν μαρτυρίαν **Ἰησοῦ** (Rev. 12:17 BNT)
τὰς ἐντολὰς τοῦ **θεοῦ** καὶ τὴν πίστιν **Ἰησοῦ** (Rev. 14:12 BNT)
τῶν ἐχόντων τὴν μαρτυρίαν **Ἰησοῦ**· τῷ **θεῷ** προσκύνησον (Rev. 19:10 BNT)
διὰ τὴν μαρτυρίαν **Ἰησοῦ** καὶ διὰ τὸν λόγον τοῦ **θεου** (Rev. 20:4 BNT)

Blessing in Revelation
Blessed

Becker and a few other commentaries have noted the appearance of the 7 blessings, or beatitudes, in Revelation.[5] Notice the 3-4 division with *are* and *is*.

Blessed 7 times in Revelation
Blessed *is* he that readeth (Rev. 1:3)
Blessed *are* the dead (Rev. 14:13)
Blessed *is* he that watcheth (Rev. 16:15)
Blessed *are* they which are called (Rev. 19:9)
Blessed and holy *is* he that hath part (Rev. 20:6)
Blessed *is* he that keepeth the sayings of the prophecy of this book (Rev. 22:7)
Blessed *are* they that do His commandments (Rev. 22:14)

μακάριος ὁ ἀναγινώσκων (Rev. 1:3 BNT)
μακάριοι οἱ νεκροί (Rev. 14:13 BNT)
μακάριος ὁ γρηγορῶν (Rev. 16:15 BNT)
μακάριοι οἱ…κεκλημένοι (Rev. 19:9 BNT)
μακάριος καὶ ἅγιος ὁ ἔχων μέρος (Rev. 20:6 BNT)
μακάριος ὁ τηρῶν τοὺς λόγους τῆς προφητείας τοῦ βιβλίου τούτου (Rev 22:7 BNT)
μακάριοι οἱ ποιοῦντες τὰς ἐντολὰς αὐτοῦ (Rev. 22:14 BYZ)*

*Commandments in BYZ, GOC, SCR, STE at 22:14; variant accepted.

Blessed them 7 times in Genesis
And God blessed them….. וַיְבָרֶךְ אֹתָם אֱלֹהִים (Gen. 1:22 WTT)
And God blessed them….. וַיְבָרֶךְ אֹתָם אֱלֹהִים (Gen. 1:28 WTT)
And blessed them………… וַיְבָרֶךְ אֹתָם (Gen. 5:2 WTT)
And blessed them………… וַיְבָרֶךְ אֶתְהֶם (Gen. 32:1 WTT)
And he blessed them……………… וַיְבָרֲכֵם (Gen. 48:20 WTT)
And he blessed them………… וַיְבָרֶךְ אוֹתָם (Gen. 49:28 WTT)
He blessed them…………. בֵּרַךְ אֹתָם (Gen. 49:28 WTT)

Signs in Revelation
Mark

The following example stretches the concept of heptadic phrasing because it is more of a repetition of 7 concepts than 7 phrases. This could be the basis for another book, which would indicate that sections of the Bible are outlined in heptads. On this subject, David A. Dorsey's *Literary Structure of the Old Testament* is recommended. Evidence can be offered to show that Revelation is written in 7 sections, as addressed in the 2012 edition[6] and in the next chapter. The following 7 phrases were found by searching

---
[5] Siegbert W. Becker, *Revelation: The Distant Triumph Song*, Northwestern Publishing House, Milwaukee, WI, 1985, p. 313.
[6] Cascione, 2012, p. 142.

for the word *mark*. It was then observed that each of them is in a lengthy statement about the same subject.

Mark 7 times in Revelation (no variants)
    To receive a **mark** in their right hand (Rev. 13:16)
    Save he that had the **mark**, or the name of the beast (Rev. 13:17)
    and receive *his* **mark** in his forehead, or in his hand (Rev. 14:9)
    whosoever receiveth the **mark** of his name (Rev. 14:11)
    Which had the **mark** of the beast (Rev. 16:2)
    That had received the **mark** of the beast (Rev. 19:20)
    neither had received *his* **mark** upon their foreheads (Rev. 20:4)

    ἵνα δῶσιν αὐτοῖς **χάραγμα** ἐπὶ τῆς χειρὸς αὐτῶν τῆς δεξιᾶς (Rev. 13:16 BNT)
    εἰ μὴ ὁ ἔχων τὸ **χάραγμα** τὸ ὄνομα τοῦ θηρίου (Rev. 13:17 BNT)
    αὐτοῦ καὶ λαμβάνει **χάραγμα** ἐπὶ τοῦ μετώπου αὐτοῦ (Rev. 14:9 BNT)
    εἴ τις λαμβάνει τὸ **χάραγμα** τοῦ ὀνόματος αὐτοῦ (Rev. 14:11 BNT)
    ἔχοντας τὸ **χάραγμα** τοῦ θηρίου (Rev. 16:2 BNT)
    τοὺς λαβόντας τὸ **χάραγμα** τοῦ θηρίου (Rev. 19:20 BNT)
    καὶ οὐκ ἔλαβον τὸ **χάραγμα** ἐπὶ τὸ μέτωπον (Rev. 20:4 BNT)

Saw, and Behold
The phrase *saw, and behold* is typical of phrasing in Genesis.

Saw, and behold 7 times in Revelation*
    After these things **I saw,** and behold (Rev. 4:1)
    And **I saw,** and behold (Rev. 6:2)
    And **I saw,** and behold (Rev. 6:5)
    And **I saw,** and behold (Rev. 6:8)
    After these things **I saw,** and behold (Rev. 7:9)
    And **I saw,** and behold (Rev. 14:1)
    And **I saw,** and behold (Rev. 14:14)

    Μετὰ ταῦτα **εἶδον**, καὶ ἰδοὺ (Rev. 4:1 BNT)
    καὶ **εἶδον**, καὶ ἰδοὺ (Rev. 6:2 BNT)
    καὶ **εἶδον**, καὶ ἰδοὺ (Rev. 6:5 BNT)
    καὶ **εἶδον**, καὶ ἰδοὺ (Rev. 6:8 BNT)
    Μετὰ ταῦτα **εἶδον**, καὶ ἰδοὺ (Rev. 7:9 BNT)
    Καὶ **εἶδον**, καὶ ἰδοὺ (Rev. 14:1 BNT)
    Καὶ **εἶδον**, καὶ ἰδοὺ (Rev. 14:14 BNT)

*SCR, STE add *and behold*, καὶ ἰδοὺ at 5:6 and 15:5; variants rejected.

Ten Horns
Ten horns also has no variants. However, 13:1 places the words together even though the context is divided. Nonetheless, it does imply 10 horns. There is also a 3-4 division in the arrangement of the Greek. *Ten* and *horns* are bolded.

Ten horns 7 times in Revelation (no variants)
    Ten horns........................ **κέρατα δέκα** (Rev. 12:3 BNT)
    Ten horns........................ **κέρατα δέκα** (Rev. 13:1 BNT)

Of his horns ten..**κεράτων αὐτοῦ δέκα** (Rev. 13:1 BNT)
Ten horns........................ **κέρατα δέκα** (Rev. 17:3 BNT)
Ten horns...........................**δέκα κέρατα** (Rev. 17:7 BNT)
Ten horns....................................**δέκα κέρατα** (Rev. 17:12 BNT)
Ten horns.......................................**δέκα κέρατα** (Rev. 17:16 BNT)

Revelation adapts or copies heptads not only from Genesis, but also from other books of the Old Testament, such as Daniel. The following figure lists 7 four-part phrases from Revelation. All of the lists from Revelation are in a different order, another example of concurrent asymmetry and symmetry. However, liberty was taken to unscramble the lists from Revelation in order to place them in the same order as they are found in Daniel. The 3 bolded words in each Revelation list are those that John copied from Daniel into Revelation. John scrambled the lists, thus changing them from the pagan rote order in which Daniel quoted the Babylonians, to the asymmetric order found in divine communication in the Bible. Perhaps this list means that Nebuchadnezzar's people in the world become God's people. The words in the top line that are not bolded are found in the Greek Septuagint, in or adjacent to the verses in Daniel. In other words, John took the lists from Daniel and added a word from the Septuagint to increase his list from 3 to 4 words. When the words from Daniel are placed beneath the lists from Revelation, the final list is 7 down and 7 across, or 49 repetitions, an apocalyptic sign of the eternal Jubilee. More information on these lists is published in the 2012 edition.[7]

Unscrambled list from Revelation, revealing list copied from Daniel

Rev. 5:9	Rev. 7:9	Rev. 10:11	Rev. 11:9	Rev. 13:7	Rev. 14:6	Rev. 17:15
tribe	tribes	kings	tribes	tribe	Tribe	multitudes
people	**peoples**	**peoples**	**peoples**	**people**	**people**	**peoples**
nation	**nation**	**nations**	**nations**	**nation**	**nation**	**nations**
language	**languages**	**languages**	**languages**	**language**	**language**	**languages**
peoples	peoples	people	peoples	peoples	peoples	peoples
nations	nations	nation	nations	nations	nations	nations
languages	languages	language	languages	languages	languages	languages
Dan. 3:4	Dan. 3:7	Dan. 3:29	Dan. 4:1	Dan. 5:19	Dan. 6:25	Dan. 7:14

In view of the above lists, what influence does the Septuagint have on Revelation? When quoting from Daniel, the Septuagint writes *tribe* instead of *nation*. Revelation uses both *tribe* and *nation*, the former appearing in the top line of the figure. *Kings* and *multitudes* are also found in the Septuagint translation of these verses from Daniel. All of this shows an even greater awareness of Daniel and the Septuagint in

---

[7] Cascione, 2012, p. 123. Also see index for 23 references to asymmetry.

Revelation. It is amazing to see what a 90-year-old man, exiled to a desert island, can accomplish from memory. The other possibility is that John did not need to recall anything. He simply wrote down the vision as God gave it to him.

Time in Revelation
Day and Night

The phrase *day and night*, with no variants, corresponds directly to the same set of phrases in Genesis from which it obviously originates. More will be said about this relationship in Chapter Eight.

Day and night 7 times in Revelation (no variants)
    Day and night (Rev. 4:8)
    Day and night (Rev. 7:15)
    Day shone not for a third part of it, and the night (Rev. 8:12)
    Day and night (Rev. 12:10)
    Day nor night (Rev. 14:11)
    Day and night (Rev. 20:10)
    Day: for there shall be no night there (Rev. 21:25)

    ἡμέρας καὶ νυκτὸς (Rev. 4:8 BNT)
    ἡμέρας καὶ νυκτὸς (Rev. 7:15 BNT)
    ἡμέρα μὴ φάνῃ τὸ τρίτον αὐτῆς καὶ ἡ νὺξ (Rev. 8:12 BNT)
    ἡμέρας καὶ νυκτὸς (Rev. 12:10 BNT)
    ἡμέρας καὶ νυκτὸς (Rev. 14:11 BNT)
    ἡμέρας καὶ νυκτὸς (Rev. 20:10 BNT)
    ἡμέρας, νὺξ (Rev. 21:25 BNT)

Day 7 times in Genesis
    And the **evening** and the **morning** were the first **day** (Gen. 1:5)
    And the **evening** and the **morning** were the second **day** (Gen. 1:8)
    And the **evening** and the **morning** were the third **day** (Gen. 1:13)
    And the **evening** and the **morning** were the fourth **day** (Gen. 1:19)
    And the **evening** and the **morning** were the fifth **day** (Gen. 1:23)
    And the **evening** and the **morning** were the sixth **day** (Gen. 1:31)
    And God blessed the **seventh day**, and sanctified it (Gen. 2:3)

The Ages of Ages

Daniel places *forever* in a heptad, and Revelation places *the ages of ages* (almost always translated as *forever and ever*) in a double heptad. Only SCR and STE preserve 14 repetitions, with the inclusion of Revelation 5:14. It is true that copyists have added *and*s and names of God to Receptus in Revelation. However, beneath these additions are some startlingly accurate readings that lead to the opinion that one of the manuscripts of Revelation in Receptus may be a copy of the original autograph.

Forever 7 times in Daniel
    Forever................................ לְעָלְמִין (Dan. 2:4)
    Forever................................ לְעָלְמִין (Dan. 2:44)
    Forever................................ לְעָלְמִין (Dan. 3:9)
    Forever................................ לְעָלְמִין (Dan. 5:10)
    Forever................................ לְעָלְמִין (Dan. 6:7)
    Forever................................ לְעָלְמִין (Dan. 6:22)
    Forever................................ לְעָלְמִין (Dan. 6:27)

The ages of ages 14 times in Revelation*
    The ages of ages, amen...τοὺς αἰῶνας τῶν αἰώνων, ἀμήν (Rev. 1:6 BNT)
    The ages of ages, amen...τοὺς αἰῶνας τῶν αἰώνων, ἀμήν (Rev. 1:18 BNT)
    The ages of ages...............τοὺς αἰῶνας τῶν αἰώνων (Rev. 4:9 BNT)
    The ages of ages...............τοὺς αἰῶνας τῶν αἰώνων (Rev. 4:10 BNT)
    The ages of ages...............τοὺς αἰῶνας τῶν αἰώνων (Rev. 5:13 BNT)
    The ages of ages...............τοὺς αἰωνας τῶν αἰώνων (Rev. 5:14 SCR, STE)**
    The ages of ages, amen...τοὺς αἰῶνας τῶν αἰώνων, ἀμήν (Rev. 7:12 BNT)
    The ages of ages...............τοὺς αἰῶνας τῶν αἰώνων (Rev. 10:6 BNT)
    The ages of ages...............τοὺς αἰῶνας τῶν αἰώνων (Rev. 11:15 BNT)
    The ages of ages..................εἰς αἰῶνας   αἰώνων (Rev. 14:11 BNT)
    The ages of ages...............τοὺς αἰῶνας τῶν αἰώνων (Rev. 15:7 BNT)
    The ages of ages...............τοὺς αἰῶνας τῶν αἰώνων (Rev. 19:3 BNT)
    The ages of ages...............τοὺς αἰῶνας τῶν αἰώνων (Rev. 20:10 BNT)
    The ages of ages...............τοὺς αἰῶνας τῶν αἰώνων (Rev. 22:5 BNT)

*Almost always translated as *forever and ever* is really *the ages of ages*.
**Rev. 5:14 only in SCR, STE; variant accepted.

There is an obvious progression from Daniel to the Gospel of John to Revelation on the concept of eternity.

Everlasting life in the Gospel of John 14 times
    Everlasting life..............ἔχῃ ζωὴν αἰώνιον (John 3:15 BNT)
    Everlasting life......ἀλλ᾽ ἔχῃ ζωὴν αἰώνιον (John 3:16 BNT)
    Everlasting life..............ἔχει ζωὴν αἰώνιον (John 3:36 BNT)
    Everlasting life................εἰς ζωὴν αἰώνιον (John 4:14 BNT)
    Everlasting life................εἰς ζωὴν αἰώνιον (John 4:36 BNT)
    Everlasting life..............ἔχει ζωὴν αἰώνιον (John 5:24 BNT)
    Everlasting life....ἐν **αὐταῖς** ζωὴν αἰώνιον (John 5:39 BNT)
    Everlasting life................εἰς ζωὴν αἰώνιον (John 6:27 BNT)
    Everlasting life................εἰς ζωὴν αἰώνιον (John 6:27 BNT)
    Everlasting life..............ἔχει ζωὴν αἰώνιον (John 6:47 BNT)
    Everlasting life..............ἔχει ζωὴν αἰώνιον (John 6:54 BNT)
    Everlasting life.........**αὐτοῖς** ζωὴν αἰώνιον (John 10:28 BNT)
    Everlasting life................εἰς ζωὴν αἰώνιον (John 12:25 BNT)
    Everlasting life.........**αὐτοῖς** ζωὴν αἰώνιον (John 17:2 BNT)

Note again that John follows the identical meter with the same word for *everlasting* in both his Gospel and in Revelation, further proof of Revelation's apostolic authorship. Establishing the apostolic authorship of Revelation makes the presence of Hebraic meter in the Gospels and the Pentateuch a virtual certainty.

John is not the only Gospel that speaks about eternal life in heptadic cadence, although no other Gospel has such machine-like repetition in using the phrase *eternal life*. Notice that there are no variants, which is rather remarkable for such a key phrase. This is Hebraic tradition. Mark and Matthew use the same Greek word stem *age*, which in context may mean *age*, *eternal*, or *forever*. In Mark it is found 7 times, and in Matthew 14 times for a double heptad, following the same repetition in John and Revelation. Hence, Matthew, Mark, and John copy the same motif from Daniel, not from each other or the mythical Q source. Notice that the first 4 letters in each bolded Greek word in the following 2 lists are the same.

Age or *Eternal* or *Forever* 7 times in the Gospel of Mark*
    Into the **age**............εἰς τὸν **αἰῶνα** (Mark 3:29 BNT)
        Eternal sin............**αἰωνίου** ἁμαρτήματος (Mark 3:29 BNT)
    Of the **age**...............τοῦ **αἰῶνος** (Mark 4:19 BNT)
        Eternal life....ζωὴν **αἰώνιον** (Mark 10:17 BNT)
    In the coming **age**..............ἐν τῷ **αἰῶνι** τῷ ἐρχομένῳ (Mark 10:30 BNT)
        Eternal life....ζωὴν **αἰώνιον** (Mark 10:30 BNT)
    For ever.......εἰς τὸν **αἰῶνα** (Mark 11:14 BNT)

*Mark 16:8 in BNT, GNT, WHO is rejected. Note the variety of English translations of the same Greek word.

Age or *Eternal* or *Forever* 14 times in the Gospel of Matthew
    Neither in this **age**...............οὔτε ἐν τούτῳ τῷ **αἰῶνι** (Matt. 12:32 BNT)
    Of the **age**............................τοῦ **αἰῶνος** (Matt. 13:22 BNT)
    End of the **age**...............συντέλεια **αἰῶνός** (Matt. 13:39 BNT)
    Of the **age**............................τοῦ **αἰῶνος** (Matt. 13:40 BNT)
    Of the **age**............................τοῦ **αἰῶνος** (Matt. 13:49 BNT)
    To **eternal** fire...........εἰς τὸ πῦρ τὸ **αἰώνιον** (Matt. 18:8 BNT)
        Eternal life...................ζωὴν **αἰώνιον** (Matt. 19:16 BNT)
        Eternal life...................ζωὴν **αἰώνιον** (Matt. 19:29 BNT)
        Forever......................εἰς τὸν **αἰῶνα** (Matt. 21:19 BNT)
    Of the **age**............................τοῦ **αἰῶνος** (Matt. 24:3 BNT)
    To **eternal** fire...........εἰς τὸ πῦρ τὸ **αἰώνιον** (Matt. 25:41 BNT)
    To **eternal** punishment...εἰς κόλασιν **αἰώνιον** (Matt. 25:46 BNT)
    To **eternal** life................εἰς ζωὴν **αἰώνιον** (Matt. 25:46 BNT)
    Of the **age**............................τοῦ **αἰῶνος** (Matt. 28:20 BNT)

Decadal Meter in Revelation

In addition to the above heptadic phrases, Revelation also has many decadal phrases. The longer a meter is, the higher the probability of variant readings.

And He Opened

This particular decad with a heptad subset was observed while assembling the list at the end of this chapter. The key verb *to open*, ἀνοίγω (*anoigo*, an-oy'-go) repeats 27 times, but BYZ has one extra repetition at Revelation 3:7, which makes 28, a quadruple heptad. Which one is it, 28 repetitions or 27, a number which has no observable symbolic significance? It was then noticed that the past tense *he opened* (ἤνοιξεν) repeats 10 times, which creates a 10-17 division for a total of 27. Within the decad there is a longer heptad, *and when he opened*, which creates a 7-20 division. This led to the selection of *when* (ὅτε) instead of *whenever* (ὅταν) at Revelation 8:1. Notice that *when* (ὅτε) repeats 7 times. Hence, the selection of one adverb, *when*, completes the Mosaic meter of 4 interlocking patterns, not including a heptad with *open book*, displayed earlier in this chapter.

And he opened 10 times in Revelation
    And I saw **when he opened**…Καὶ εἶδον **ὅτε ἤνοιξεν** (Rev. 6:1 BNT)
        And **when he opened**………Καὶ **ὅτε ἤνοιξεν** (Rev. 6:3 BNT)
        And **when he opened**………Καὶ **ὅτε ἤνοιξεν** (Rev. 6:5 BNT)
        And **when he opened**………Καὶ **ὅτε ἤνοιξεν** (Rev. 6:7 BNT)
        And **when he opened**………Καὶ **ὅτε ἤνοιξεν** (Rev. 6:9 BNT)
    And I saw **when he opened**…Καὶ εἶδον **ὅτε ἤνοιξεν** (Rev. 6:12 BNT)
        And **when he opened**………Καὶ **ὅτε ἤνοιξεν** (Rev. 8:1 BYZ)*
        And **he opened**……………καὶ **ἤνοιξεν** (Rev. 9:2 BNT)
        And **he opened**……………καὶ **ἤνοιξεν** (Rev. 12:16 BNT)
        And **he opened**……………καὶ **ἤνοιξεν** (Rev. 13:6 BNT)
*Rev. 8:1 BYZ, GOC, SCR, STE have *when* (ὅτε); BNT, GNT, TIS, VST, WHO have *whenever* (ὅταν).

Another Angel

The phrase *another angel* also includes a double 3-7 division. There are 3 verses that begin with *and I saw*, and 3 verses that end with *came out*. An exact count of 10 for the word *another*, ἄλλος (*allos*, al'-los) is also required to maintain a total of 20 repetitions, a double decad, as listed at the end of this chapter. Thus, *another* repeats 10 times with *angel*, and 10 more times without *angel*.

Another angel 10 times in Revelation
    And I saw another **angel** (Rev. 7:2)
    ………And another **angel** (Rev. 8:3)
    And I saw another **angel** (Rev. 10:1)*
    And I saw another **angel** (Rev. 14:6)*
    ………And another **angel** (Rev. 14:8)
    ………And another **angel** (Rev. 14:9)**
        Another **angel** came out (Rev. 14:15)

Another **angel** came out (Rev. 14:17)
Another **angel** came out (Rev. 14:18)
........I saw another **angel** (Rev. 18:1)
Καὶ εἶδον ἄλλον **ἄγγελον** (Rev. 7:2 BNT)
Καὶ ἄλλος **ἄγγελος** (Rev. 8:3 BNT)
Καὶ εἶδον ἄλλον **ἄγγελον** (Rev. 10:1 BNT)*
Καὶ εἶδον ἄλλον **ἄγγελον** (Rev. 14:6 BNT)*
Καὶ ἄλλος **ἄγγελος** (Rev. 14:8 BNT)
Καὶ ἄλλος **ἄγγελος** (Rev. 14:9 BNT)**
ἄλλος **ἄγγελος** ἐξῆλθεν (Rev. 14:15 BNT)
ἄλλος **ἄγγελος** ἐξῆλθεν (Rev. 14:17 BNT)
ἄλλος **ἄγγελος** [ἐξῆλθεν] (Rev. 14:18 BNT)
εἶδον ἄλλον **ἄγγελον** (Rev. 18:1 BNT)

*Rev. 10:1, 14:6 *another angel* in all texts except BYZ with *angel*.
**Rev. 14:9 *another angel* in all texts except SCR, STE with *angel*.

God in Decadal Meter
Lord God

God is set with less frequency in decadal than in heptadic meter in Revelation. In Chapter Eight we will see that the phrase *Lord God* repeats 20 times in Genesis. The following decad of *Lord God* has a heptadic subset of *the Almighty*. Surprisingly, SCR and STE are missing *God* at Revelation 1:8, and incorrectly add *the beginning and the end* to Revelation 21:6 and 22:13.

Lord God 10 times in Revelation, 7 with *almighty*, 3 without *almighty*
Lord God Almighty...κύριος ὁ θεός...ὁ παντοκράτωρ (Rev. 1:8 BNT)*
Lord God Almighty...κύριος ὁ θεὸς ὁ παντοκράτωρ (Rev. 4:8 BNT)
Lord God Almighty...κύριε ὁ θεὸς ὁ παντοκράτωρ (Rev. 11:17 BNT)
Lord God Almighty...κύριε ὁ θεὸς ὁ παντοκράτωρ (Rev. 15:3 BNT)
Lord God Almighty...κύριε ὁ θεὸς ὁ παντοκράτωρ (Rev. 16:7 BNT)
Lord God Almighty...κύριος ὁ θεὸς ὁ παντοκράτωρ (Rev. 19:6 BNT)
Lord God Almighty...κύριος ὁ θεὸς ὁ παντοκράτωρ (Rev. 21:22 BNT)
Lord God....................κύριος ὁ θεὸς (Rev. 18:8 BNT)
Lord God....................κύριος ὁ θεὸς (Rev. 22:5 BNT)
Lord God..................ὁ κύριος ὁ θεὸς (Rev. 22:6 BNT)

*The shorter reading in BNT, BYZ, GNT, GOC, TIS, VST, WHO is correct, and SCR, STE are missing *God*.

The One Who Sits on the Throne

There are 10 repetitions of *the One who sits on the throne* in Revelation, with no variants. This decad is introduced in Revelation 4:2 with a different word order that reads, *and behold a throne set in heaven, and on the throne one who was sitting* (καὶ ἰδοὺ θρόνος ἔκειτο ἐν τῷ οὐρανῷ καὶ ἐπὶ τὸν θρόνον καθήμενος). This is followed by 10 phrases in identical order, as seen below. After nearly 2,000 years, the entire decad, with 5 words in each Greek phrase, is found as John originally wrote it, including each verb in the same tense with no variants.

The One who sits on the throne 10 times in Revelation
    To the **One who sits** on the **throne** (Rev. 4:9)
    The **One who sits** on the **throne** (Rev. 4:10)
    The **One who sits** on the **throne** (Rev. 5:1)
    The **One who sits** on the **throne** (Rev. 5:7)
    To the **One who sits** on the **throne** (Rev. 5:13)
    The **One who sits** on the **throne** (Rev. 6:16)
    To the **One who sits** on the **throne** (Rev. 7:10)
    The **One who sits** on the **throne** (Rev. 7:15)
    To the **One who sits** on the **throne** (Rev. 19:4)
    To the **One who sits** on the **throne** (Rev. 21:5)

    τῷ **καθημένῳ** ἐπὶ τῷ **θρόνῳ** (Rev. 4:9 BNT)
    τοῦ **καθημένου** ἐπὶ τοῦ **θρόνου** (Rev. 4:10 BNT)
    τοῦ **καθημένου** ἐπὶ τοῦ **θρόνου** (Rev. 5:1 BNT)
    τοῦ **καθημένου** ἐπὶ τοῦ **θρόνου** (Rev. 5:7 BNT)
    τῷ **καθημένῳ** ἐπὶ τῷ **θρόνῳ** (Rev. 5:13 BNT)
    τοῦ **καθημένου** ἐπὶ τοῦ **θρόνου** (Rev. 6:16 BNT)
    τῷ **καθημένῳ** ἐπὶ τῷ **θρόνῳ** (Rev. 7:10 BNT)
    ὁ **καθήμενος** ἐπὶ τῷ **θρόνῳ** (Rev. 7:15 BNT)
    τῷ **καθημένῳ** ἐπὶ τῷ **θρόνῳ** (Rev. 19:4 BNT)
    ὁ **καθήμενος** ἐπὶ τῷ **θρόνῳ** (Rev. 21:5 BNT)

God Almighty

The phrase *God Almighty* appears 7 times in the entire Old Testament, and the phrase *to the Almighty* 3 more times in Job. Just as John was aware of 7 phrases in Daniel that he repeats in Revelation, we assume that Jewish scholars of John's day were aware that *God Almighty* repeated 7 times in the Old Testament. John's repetition cannot be based on the Septuagint, where the Hebrew *El Shaddai* (אֵל שַׁדַּי) is only translated twice as παντοκράτωρ (*pantokrator*, pan-tok-rat'-ore), as it is always translated in Revelation. Thus, either the Septuagint writers were not aware that *El Shaddai* appears 7 times in the Hebrew Old Testament, or they intentionally varied their translation. The only way for John to know of this repetition is through knowledge of Hebrew. Therefore, John's writing is hardly the work of an unschooled fisherman, but of one who is keenly aware of differences between the Hebrew and the Septuagint.

God Almighty (*El Shaddai*) 7 times in the Old Testament
    I am God Almighty............אֲנִי־אֵל שַׁדַּי (Gen. 17:1 WTT)
    And God Almighty............וְאֵל שַׁדַּי (Gen. 28:3 WTT)

I am God Almighty	אֲנִי אֵל שַׁדַּי	(Gen. 35:11 WTT)
And God Almighty	וְאֵל שַׁדַּי	(Gen. 43:14 WTT)
God Almighty	אֵל שַׁדָּי	(Gen. 48:3 WTT)
By God Almighty	בְּאֵל שַׁדָּי	(Exod. 6:3 WTT)
God Almighty	אֵל־שַׁדָּי	(Ezek. 10:5 WTT)
And to the Almighty	וְאֶל־שַׁדַּי	(Job 8:5 WTT)
To the Almighty	אֶל־שַׁדַּי	(Job 13:3 WTT)
And to the Almighty	וְאֶל־שַׁדַּי	(Job 15:25 WTT)

There is a recurring pattern of nominative (subject) singular articles referring to Christ or God the Father in the text. Those not familiar with Greek should notice *the* (ὁ, the Greek article, nominative case, pronounced like *hot* without the *t*), which has been bolded below. After a rather lengthy search, it was discovered that this curious repetition of *the* (ὁ) refers to Christ or God the Father 10 times in Revelation. These phrases were selected because they exhibit a triadic repetition of the nominative Greek article. There are 3 or more articles in sequence referring to Christ or God the Father in each of the 10 phrases. The entire sequence is shown, but it is rather obvious that 1:8 and 4:8 contain a triadic subset. Thus, all 10 phrases contain a sequence of 3 articles, for a total of 30 Greek articles in the nominative case that visibly illustrate triplicity in the one God, which we call the Trinity. In context, Revelation 1:4, 4:8, 11:17, and 16:5 refer to God the Father. There is a full discussion of this repetition in the 2012 edition. The variant reading at 6:10 in SCR and STE, which would add an 11th phrase, is rejected. Even KJV avoids translating the additional article at 6:10.

[Christ] or *God [the Father]* in article sequence 10 times in Revelation
  The One who is and **the** One who was and **the** One who will be (Rev. 1:4)
  The Witness **the** Faithful, **the** Almighty (Rev. 1:5)
  The One who is and **the** One who was and **the** One who will be (Rev. 1:8)*
  The First and **the** Last, and **the** One who is living (Rev. 1:17-18)
  The Holy, **the** True, **the** One has the Key of David (Rev. 3:7)
  The Amen, **the** Witness **the** Faithful (Rev. 3:14)
  The God, **the** Almighty, **the** One who was (Rev. 4:8)**
  The God, **the** Almighty, **the** One who is and **the** One who was (Rev. 11:17)
  The One who is and **the** One who was, **the** One who is holy (Rev. 16:5)
  The Star **the** Bright **the** Morning (Rev. 22:16)
*Verse continues: *the Almighty* (Rev. 1:8).
Verse continues: *and **the One who is and **the** One who will be* (Rev. 4:8).

The spaces were added to help visualize the Greek *the* (ὁ).

ὁ ὢν καὶ	ὁ ἦν καὶ	ὁ ἐρχόμενος	(Rev. 1:4 BNT)
ὁ μάρτυς	ὁ πιστός,	ὁ πρωτότοκος	(Rev. 1:5 BNT)
ὁ ὢν καὶ	ὁ ἦν καὶ	ὁ ἐρχόμενος, ὁ παντοκράτωρ	(Rev. 1:8 BNT)
ὁ πρῶτος καὶ ὁ ἔσχατος, καὶ	ὁ ζῶν		(Rev. 1:17-18 BNT)

ὁ ἅγιος,	ὁ ἀληθινός,	ὁ ἔχων τὴν κλεῖν τοῦ Δαυίδ	(Rev. 3:7 BNT)
ὁ Ἀμήν,	ὁ μάρτυς	ὁ πιστὸς	(Rev. 3:14 BNT)
ὁ θεὸς	ὁ παντοκράτωρ, ὁ ἦν καὶ ὁ ὢν καὶ ὁ ἐρχόμενος		(Rev. 4:8 BNT)
ὁ θεὸς	ὁ παντοκράτωρ, ὁ ὢν καὶ ὁ ἦν		(Rev. 11:17 BNT)
ὁ ὢν καὶ	ὁ ἦν,	ὁ ὅσιος	(Rev. 16:5 BNT)
ὁ ἀστὴρ	ὁ λαμπρὸς	ὁ πρωϊνός	(Rev. 22:16 BNT)

These 10 phrases about God from Revelation repeat the triadic repetition that is found in Moses' encounter with God at the burning bush. As stated in the 2012 edition,[8] God proclaims His name to Moses 3 times in Exod. 3:14 when Moses asks Who it is that is sending him to free Israel from Pharaoh: *And God said unto Moses, I AM THAT I AM: and he said, Thus shalt thou say unto the children of Israel, I AM hath sent me unto you.* The figure below presents this verse in Hebrew, along with a translation. The verb אֶהְיֶה (הָיָה, *hayâ*, to be, become, exist, happen), pronounced *ê-hi-yêh*, is translated in KJV as *I AM*. Gleason Archer writes, "Most likely the name should be translated something like 'I am he who is,' or 'I am he who exists' as reflected by the LXX's ἐγώ εἰμι ὁ ὤν [I am the One who is]. The echo of this is found surely in the NT, Rev. 1:8. More than anything perhaps, the 'is-ness' of God is expressive both of his presence and his existence. Neither concept can be said to be more important than the other."[9]

(read English from right to left)

וַיֹּאמֶר אֱלֹהִים אֶל־מֹשֶׁה **אֶהְיֶה**
אֶהְיֶה אֲשֶׁר
וַיֹּאמֶר כֹּה תֹאמַר לִבְנֵי יִשְׂרָאֵל **אֶהְיֶה**
שְׁלָחַנִי אֲלֵיכֶם

AM-I Moses to God said And
AM-I that
AM-I, Israel of sons the to say shall you Thus, said He And
    you to me sent has
Exod. 3:14

God and the Lamb

Phrases about God or Jesus often repeat in multiples of 10, as seen above. *God* repeats in Revelation 100 times, and *Lamb* (if the variant at Revelation 6:9 from BYZ and GOC is included) repeats 30 times. If the phrasing, *on account of the witness of the lamb which they held*, at Revelation 6:9 in BYZ and GOC is followed, instead of *on account*

---

[8] Cascione, 2012, pp. 27-28.
[9] *Theological Word Dictionary of the Old Testament*, Ed. by Harris, Archer, and Waltke, Moody Bible Institute, Chicago, 1980, pp. 213-14.

of the witness which they held, then *Lamb* and *God* appear together 10 times. Here again is an example of a particular variant completing multiple patterns. Also note that the repetition of a word often results in the repetition of concepts.

God and the Lamb 10 times in Revelation
Slain for the word of **God**, and for the testimony **of the Lamb** (Rev. 6:9)*
Salvation to our **God** which sitteth upon the throne, **and unto the Lamb** (Rev. 7:10)
For the **Lamb**...shall feed them...and **God** shall wipe away all tears (Rev. 7:17)
Being the firstfruits unto **God and to the Lamb** (Rev. 14:4)
Moses the bond-servant of **God** and the song **of the Lamb** (Rev. 15:3)
Called to the marriage supper **of the Lamb**....These are the true sayings of **God** (Rev. 19:9)
For the Lord **God** Almighty **and the Lamb** are the temple of it (Rev. 21:22)
For the glory of **God** did lighten it, **and the Lamb** *is* the light thereof (Rev. 21:23)
Proceeding out of the throne of **God and of the Lamb** (Rev. 22:1)
And the throne of **God and of the Lamb** shall be in it (Rev. 22:3)

διὰ τὸν λόγον τοῦ **θεοῦ**, καὶ διὰ τὴν μαρτυρίαν τοῦ **ἀρνίου** ἣν εἶχον (Rev. 6:9 BYZ)*
ἡ σωτηρία τῷ **θεῷ** ἡμῶν τῷ καθημένῳ ἐπὶ τῷ θρόνῳ καὶ τῷ **ἀρνίῳ** (Rev. 7:10 BNT)
ὅτι τὸ **ἀρνίον**...ποιμανεῖ αὐτούς...καὶ ἐξαλείψει ὁ **θεὸς** πᾶν δάκρυον (Rev. 7:17 BNT)
ἀπαρχὴ τῷ **θεῷ** καὶ τῷ **ἀρνίῳ** (Rev. 14:4 BNT)
Μωϋσέως τοῦ δούλου τοῦ **θεοῦ** καὶ τὴν ᾠδὴν τοῦ **ἀρνίου** (Rev. 15:3 BNT)
τοῦ **γάμου** τοῦ ἀρνίου κεκλημένοι....Οὗτοι οἱ λόγοι ἀληθινοὶ τοῦ **θεοῦ** εἰσιν (Rev. 19:9 BNT)
ὁ γὰρ κύριος ὁ **θεὸς** ὁ παντοκράτωρ ναὸς αὐτῆς ἐστιν καὶ τὸ **ἀρνίον** (Rev. 21:22 BNT)
ἡ γὰρ δόξα τοῦ **θεοῦ** ἐφώτισεν αὐτήν, καὶ ὁ λύχνος αὐτῆς τὸ **ἀρνίον** (Rev. 21:23 BNT)
ἐκπορευόμενον ἐκ τοῦ θρόνου τοῦ **θεοῦ** καὶ τοῦ **ἀρνίου** (Rev. 22:1 BNT)
καὶ ὁ θρόνος τοῦ **θεοῦ** καὶ τοῦ **ἀρνίου** (Rev. 22:3 BNT)
*Only BYZ, GOC have *Lamb* at Rev. 6:9.

Open...the Seal(s)

The phrase *open...the seal(s)* repeats 10 times in Revelation. In the first 3, the Lamb, who is Christ, is identified as the One who is qualified to open the seals, and in the following 7 He has completed the action. The word *open* appears as an infinitive 3 times with *seal*, and then in the past tense 7 times. At first the thought was to place the heptad, which has no variants, at the beginning of the chapter after the heptad, *He that hath an ear, let him hear what the Spirit saith unto the churches*. Upon further examination there were 3 infinitives, thus making a decad. The variant reading in BYZ at Revelation 5:5, which has a participle for *open* instead of an infinitive, is rejected.

Open...the seal(s) 10 times in Revelation
Who is worthy to **open** the book, and to loose the **seals** thereof? (Rev. 5:2)
    to **open** the book, and to loose the seven **seals** thereof (Rev. 5:5)*
  and to **open** the **seals** thereof (Rev. 5:9)

And I saw when the Lamb **opened** one of the **seals** (Rev. 6:1)
And when he had **opened** the second **seal** (Rev. 6:3)
And when he had **opened** the third **seal** (Rev. 6:5)

And when he had **opened** the fourth **seal** (Rev. 6:7)
And when he had **opened** the fifth **seal** (Rev. 6:9)
And I beheld when he had **opened** the sixth **seal** (Rev. 6:12)
And when he had **opened** the seventh **seal** (Rev. 8:1)

τίς ἄξιος **ἀνοῖξαι** τὸ βιβλίον καὶ λῦσαι τὰς **σφραγῖδας** αὐτου (Rev. 5:2 BNT)
ἀνοῖξαι τὸ βιβλίον καὶ τὰς ἑπτὰ **σφραγῖδας** αὐτου (Rev. 5:5 BNT)*
καὶ **ἀνοῖξαι** τὰς **σφραγῖδας** αὐτοῦ (Rev. 5:9 BNT)

Καὶ εἶδον ὅτε **ἤνοιξεν** τὸ ἀρνίον μίαν ἐκ τῶν ἑπτὰ **σφραγίδων** (Rev. 6:1 BNT)
Καὶ ὅτε **ἤνοιξεν** τὴν **σφραγῖδα** τὴν δευτέραν (Rev. 6:3 BNT)
Καὶ ὅτε **ἤνοιξεν** τὴν **σφραγῖδα** τὴν τρίτην (Rev. 6:5 BNT)
Καὶ ὅτε **ἤνοιξεν** τὴν **σφραγῖδα** τὴν τετάρτην (Rev. 6:7 BNT)
Καὶ ὅτε **ἤνοιξεν** τὴν πέμπτην **σφραγῖδα** (Rev. 6:9 BNT)
Καὶ εἶδον ὅτε **ἤνοιξεν** τὴν **σφραγῖδα** τὴν ἕκτην (Rev. 6:12 BNT)
Καὶ ὅταν **ἤνοιξεν** τὴν **σφραγῖδα** τὴν ἑβδόμην (Rev. 8:1 BNT)

*The participle *The one who is opening* (ὁ ἀνοίγων) in BYZ at 5:5 is rejected.

Activity on Earth
The Great City / On the Sea

The phrase *the great city* appears 10 times in some of the Greek manuscripts, and less in others. All 10 are in the KJV, while modern translations only have 8. In this particular case, the KJV translation is preferred. As stated earlier, the Eastern texts, BYZ, GOC, SCR, and STE, are generally more accurate in Revelation. There is also a subset of 7 not preceded by the phrase *woe, woe*.

The great city 10 Times in Revelation
  The **great city**............τῆς **πόλεως** τῆς **μεγάλης** (Rev. 11:8 BNT)
  The **great city**............ἡ **πόλις** ἡ **μεγάλη** (Rev. 14:8 STE)*
  The **great city**............ἡ **πόλις** ἡ **μεγάλη** (Rev. 16:19 BNT)
  The **great city**............ἡ **πόλις** ἡ **μεγάλη** (Rev. 17:18 BNT)
  Woe, woe, the **great city**...Οὐαὶ οὐαί, ἡ **πόλις** ἡ **μεγάλη** (Rev. 18:10 BNT)
  Woe, woe, the **great city**...Οὐαὶ οὐαί, ἡ **πόλις** ἡ **μεγάλη** (Rev. 18:16 BNT)
  The **great city**............τῇ **πόλει** τῇ **μεγάλῃ** (Rev. 18:18 BNT)
  Woe, woe, the **great city**.....οὐαὶ οὐαί, ἡ **πόλις** ἡ **μεγάλη** (Rev. 18:19 BNT)
  The **great city**........ἡ **μεγάλη πόλις** (Rev. 18:21 BNT)
  The **great city**............ἡ **πόλις** ἡ **μεγάλη** (Rev. 21:10 BYZ)**

*Only SCR, STE have *the great city* at Rev. 14:8.
**Only BYZ, SCR, STE have *the great city* at Rev. 21:10.

On the sea 7 times in Revelation (no variants)
  On the sea............ἐπὶ τῆς θαλάσσης (Rev. 5:13 BNT)
  On the sea............ἐπὶ τῆς θαλάσσης (Rev. 7:1 BNT)
  On the sea............ἐπὶ τῆς θαλάσσης (Rev. 10:2 BNT)
  On the sea............ἐπὶ τῆς θαλάσσης (Rev. 10:5 BNT)
  On the sea............ἐπὶ τῆς θαλάσσης (Rev. 10:8 BNT)
  On the sand of the sea...ἐπὶ τὴν ἄμμον τῆς θαλάσσης (Rev. 13:1 BNT)
  On the sea............ἐπὶ τὴν θάλασσαν (Rev. 15:2 BNT)

To the Earth / Those Who Dwell on Earth

The phrase *to the earth* could be arranged as 10 or 12 phrases, depending on which variants are selected. The majority of texts support 12 phrases; however, the context does not support this repetition. The phrase is found in repeated accounts of the earth's destruction. If the 2 variants are not followed, there is a shorter list of 10, which would signify a more appropriate complete destruction resembling the 10 plagues. Ten is the symbolic number of completion, as explained in the 2012 edition.

To the earth 10 times in Revelation*
> To the earth............εἰς τὴν γῆν (Rev. 6:13 BNT)
> To the earth............εἰς τὴν γῆν (Rev. 8:5 BNT)
> To the earth............εἰς τὴν γῆν (Rev. 8:7 BNT)
> To the earth............εἰς τὴν γῆν (Rev. 9:1 BNT)
> To the earth............εἰς τὴν γῆν (Rev. 9:3 BNT)
> To the earth............εἰς τὴν γῆν (Rev. 12:4 BNT)
> To the earth............εἰς τὴν γῆν (Rev. 12:9 BNT)
> To the earth............εἰς τὴν γῆν (Rev. 12:13 BNT)
> To the earth............εἰς τὴν γῆν (Rev. 14:19 BNT)
> To the earth............εἰς τὴν γῆν (Rev. 16:1 BNT)

*To the earth missing from BYZ at Rev. 13:13, and from SCR, STE at Rev. 16:2; variants preferred.

Those who dwell on earth 10 times in Revelation
> Those who dwell upon earth (Rev. 3:10)
> Those who dwell on earth (Rev. 6:10)
> To those who dwell on earth (Rev. 8:13)
> Those who dwell on earth (Rev. 11:10)
> Those who dwell on earth (Rev. 11:10)
> Those who dwell on earth (Rev. 13:8)
> Those who dwell on earth (Rev. 13:14)
> Those who dwell on earth (Rev. 13:14)
> To those who dwell on earth (Rev. 14:6)*
> Those who dwell on earth (Rev. 17:8)

> τοὺς κατοικοῦντας ἐπὶ τῆς γῆς (Rev. 3:10 BNT)
> κατοικούντων ἐπὶ τῆς γῆς (Rev. 6:10 BNT)
> τοῖς κατοικοῦσιν ἐπὶ τῆς γῆς (Rev. 8:13 BNT)
> οἱ κατοικοῦντες ἐπὶ τῆς γῆς (Rev. 11:10 BNT)
> τοὺς κατοικοῦντας ἐπὶ τῆς γῆς (Rev. 11:10 BNT)
> οἱ κατοικοῦντες ἐπὶ τῆς γῆς (Rev. 13:8 BNT)
> τοὺς κατοικοῦντας ἐπὶ τῆς γῆς (Rev. 13:14 BNT)
> τοῖς κατοικοῦσιν ἐπὶ τῆς γῆς (Rev. 13:14 BNT)
> τοὺς κατοικοῦντας ἐπὶ τῆς γῆς (Rev. 14:6 STE)*
> οἱ κατοικοῦντες ἐπὶ τῆς γῆς (Rev. 17:8 BNT)

*SCR, STE have *dwell* (κατοικοῦντας). BNT, BYZ, GNT, GOC, TIS, VST, WHO have *those who sit on the earth* (καθημένους); variant rejected. Including 14:6 in SCR, STE also results in 48 repetitions of *sit* and *dwell*, as seen in lists below.

Metered Introduction to Conversation: Anaphoric Phrases
After these Things

As in Genesis and all 4 Gospels, Revelation employs Mosaic cadence in mundane parlance. There is a rather odd variant at Revelation 7:1. Only SCR and STE have *after these things*, while all the other texts read *after this*. As is seen below, there is a consistent use of the plural, and just the right plural is found in SCR and STE.

After these things 10 times in Revelation
    After these things..........μετὰ ταῦτα (Rev. 1:19 BNT)
    After these things..........Μετὰ ταῦτα (Rev. 4:1 BNT)
    After these things..........μετὰ ταῦτα (Rev. 4:1 BNT)
    After these things..........μετὰ ταῦτα (Rev. 7:1 SCR, STE)*
    After these things..........Μετὰ ταῦτα (Rev. 7:9 BNT)
    After these things..........μετὰ ταῦτα (Rev. 9:12 BNT)
    After these things..........μετὰ ταῦτα (Rev. 15:5 BNT)
    After these things..........Μετὰ ταῦτα (Rev. 18:1 BNT)
    After these things..........Μετὰ ταῦτα (Rev. 19:1 BNT)
    After these things..........μετὰ ταῦτα (Rev. 20:3 BNT)
*Μετὰ τοῦτο at Rev. 7:1 in BNT, BYZ, GNT, GOC, TIS, VST, WHO rejected; μετὰ ταῦτα in SCR, STE accepted.

And He Said

John repeats the phrase *and he said to him* 10 times in his Gospel. In Revelation he uses the same phrase again 10 times, but changes the pronoun from *him* to *me*. One of the reasons Luther did not like Revelation is because the author praises his own book more than other books of the Bible, which Luther did not think was appropriate for an apostle.[10] In reply, one would ask, "What about Paul's numerous references to himself?" Once again, the only translation with all 10 examples is the KJV.

And he said to me 10 times in Revelation
    And....he said to me.........Καὶ...λέγει μοι (Rev. 10:9 BNT)
    and he said to me.............καὶ λέγει μοι (Rev. 10:11 SCR, STE)*
    and he said to me.............Καὶ λέγει μοι (Rev. 17:15 BNT)
    and he said to me.............Καὶ λέγει μοι (Rev. 19:9 BNT)
    and he said to me.............Καὶ λέγει μοι (Rev. 19:9 BNT)
    and he said to me.............καὶ λέγει μοι (Rev. 19:10 BNT)

---

[10] *Luther's Works, Vol. 35, Word and Sacrament I*, translated by E. Theodore Bachmann, Muhlenberg Press, Philadelphia, 1960, p. 398.

and he said to me..............Καὶ λέγει μοι (Rev. 21:5 BYZ)**
and he said to me..............Καὶ λέγει μοι (Rev. 22:6 BNT)
and he said to me..............Καὶ λέγει μοι (Rev. 22:9 BNT)
and he said to me..............Καὶ λέγει μοι (Rev. 22:10 BNT)
*Only in SCR, STE at Rev. 10:11; variant accepted.
**Rev. 21:5 only in BYZ, GOC, SCR, STE; variant accepted.

I Heard a Voice / With Me / Out of the Mouth

I heard a voice appears 20 times in Revelation, which comprises a double decad. There is remarkable accuracy in this list, considering that only one of the 9 manuscripts (BYZ), in one out of 20 verses, lists a variant reading. This means that BNT, GNT, GOC, SCR, STE, TIS, VST, and WHO are all in agreement on these 20 phrases. This phrase exhibits the prophetic nature of Revelation in that John hears a voice 20 times. Actually he hears a voice more than 20 times, but 20 verses use the same phrase. Note the 3-17 division with *which I heard*.

I heard a voice 20 times in Revelation
And I **heard** a voice......................καὶ **ἤκουσα** φωνὴν (Rev. 1:10 BNT)
And the first voice which I **heard**...καὶ ἡ φωνὴ ἡ πρώτη ἣν **ἤκουσα** (Rev. 4:1 BNT)
And I **heard** as a voice...................καὶ **ἤκουσα** ὡς φωνὴν (Rev. 5:11 BNT)
And I **heard** as a voice...................καὶ **ἤκουσα**...ὡς φωνὴ (Rev. 6:1 BNT)
And I **heard** as a voice...................καὶ **ἤκουσα** ὡς φωνὴν (Rev. 6:6 BNT)
I **heard** a voice.........................**ἤκουσα** φωνὴν (Rev. 6:7 BNT)*
And I **heard** a great voice............καὶ **ἤκουσα**...φωνῇ μεγάλῃ (Rev. 8:13 BNT)
And I **heard** a voice......................καὶ **ἤκουσα** φωνὴν (Rev. 9:13 BNT)
And I **heard** a voice......................καὶ **ἤκουσα** φωνὴν (Rev. 10:4 BNT)
And the voice which I **heard**.........καὶ ἡ φωνὴ ἣν **ἤκουσα** (Rev. 10:8 BNT)
And I **heard** a voice......................καὶ **ἤκουσα** φωνὴν (Rev. 11:12 BNT)
And I **heard** a voice......................καὶ **ἤκουσα** φωνὴν (Rev. 12:10 BNT)
And I **heard** a voice......................καὶ **ἤκουσα** φωνὴν (Rev. 14:2 BNT)
And the voice which I **heard**..........καὶ ἡ φωνὴ ἣν **ἤκουσα** (Rev. 14:2 BNT)
And I **heard** a voice......................καὶ **ἤκουσα** φωνῆς (Rev. 14:13 BNT)
And I **heard** a great voice..............καὶ **ἤκουσα** μεγάλης φωνῆς (Rev. 16:1 BNT)
And I **heard** another voice.............καὶ **ἤκουσα** ἄλλην φωνὴν (Rev. 18:4 BNT)
I **heard** as a great voice................**ἤκουσα** ὡς φωνὴν μεγάλην (Rev. 19:1 BNT)
And I **heard** as a voice...................καὶ **ἤκουσα** ὡς φωνὴν (Rev. 19:6 BNT)
And I **heard** a great voice..............καὶ **ἤκουσα** φωνῆς μεγάλης (Rev. 21:3 BNT)
*BYZ missing *voice* at 6:7, variant rejected.

Within the above double decad there is a subset of 10 phrases, *I heard a voice out of* or *in heaven*, shown below. The key word *heard* is bolded in both lists. Note the 3-7 division with *a great voice*, bolded in English, below.

I heard a voice out of or in heaven 10 times in Revelation
In heaven, and first voice which I **heard** (Rev. 4:1)
And I **heard** a voice out of heaven (Rev. 10:4)
And I **heard** a voice which was out of heaven (Rev. 10:8)

And I **heard a great voice** out of heaven (Rev. 11:12)
And I **heard a great voice** in heaven (Rev. 12:10)
And I **heard** a voice out of heaven (Rev. 14:2)
And I **heard** a voice out of heaven (Rev. 14:13)
And I **heard** another voice out of heaven (Rev. 18:4)
    I **heard** as a voice a great multitude in heaven (Rev. 19:1)
And I **heard a great voice** out of heaven (Rev. 21:3)*

ἐν τῷ οὐρανῷ, καὶ ἡ φωνὴ ἡ πρώτη ἣν **ἤκουσα** (Rev. 4:1 BNT)
    καὶ **ἤκουσα** φωνὴν ἐκ τοῦ οὐρανοῦ (Rev. 10:4 BNT)
καὶ ἡ φωνὴ ἣν **ἤκουσα** ἐκ τοῦ οὐρανοῦ (Rev. 10:8 BNT)
    καὶ **ἤκουσα** φωνὴν μεγάλην ἐκ τοῦ οὐρανοῦ (Rev. 11:12 BNT)
    καὶ **κουσα** φωνὴν μεγάλην ἐν τῷ οὐρανῷ (Rev. 12:10 BNT)
    καὶ **ἤκουσα** φωνὴν ἐκ τοῦ οὐρανοῦ (Rev. 14:2 BNT)
    καὶ **ἤκουσα** φωνῆς ἐκ τοῦ οὐρανοῦ λεγούσης (Rev. 14:13 BNT)
    καὶ **ἤκουσα** ἄλλην φωνὴν ἐκ τοῦ οὐρανοῦ (Rev. 18:4 BNT)
    ἤκουσα ὡς φωνὴν μεγάλην ὄχλου πολλοῦ ἐν τῷ οὐρανῷ (Rev. 19:1 BNT)
    καὶ **ἤκουσα** φωνῆς μεγάλης ἐκ τοῦ οὐρανοῦ (Rev. 21:3 BYZ)*
*Rev. 21:3 only in BYZ, GOC, SCR, STE; variant accepted.

With me 10 times in Revelation (no variants)
    Speaking with me.................ἐλάλει μετ' ἐμοῦ (Rev. 1:12 BNT)
        Walk with Me...περιπατήσουσιν μετ' ἐμοῦ (Rev. 3:4 BNT)
            He with Me....................αὐτὸς μετ' ἐμοῦ (Rev. 3:20 BNT)
            Sit with Me..................καθίσαι μετ' ἐμοῦ (Rev. 3:21 BNT)
    Speaking with me..............λαλούσης μετ' ἐμοῦ (Rev. 4:1 BNT)
    Speaking with me..............λαλοῦσα μετ' ἐμοῦ (Rev. 10:8 BNT)
        Spoke with me...............ἐλάλησεν μετ' ἐμοῦ (Rev. 17:1 BNT)
        Spoke with me...............ἐλάλησεν μετ' ἐμοῦ (Rev. 21:9 BNT)
    One speaking with me.................ὁ λαλῶν μετ' ἐμοῦ (Rev. 21:15 BNT)
    My reward is with Me..........ὁ μισθός μου μετ' ἐμοῦ (Rev. 22:12 BNT)

Out of the mouth 10 times and 7 pronouns in Revelation
    Out of the **mouth** of Him...ἐκ τοῦ **στόματος** αὐτοῦ (Rev. 1:16 BNT)
    Out of the **mouth** of Me.....ἐκ τοῦ **στόματός** μου (Rev. 3:16 BNT)
    Out of the **mouth** of them..ἐκ τοῦ **στόματος** αὐτῶν (Rev. 11:5 BNT)
    Out of the **mouth** of him....ἐκ τοῦ **στόματος** αὐτου (Rev. 12:15 BNT)
    Out of the **mouth** of him....ἐκ τοῦ **στόματος** αὐτου (Rev. 12:16 BNT)
    Out of the **mouth**................ἐκ τοῦ **στόματος** (Rev. 16:13 BNT)
    Out of the **mouth**................ἐκ τοῦ **στόματος** (Rev. 16:13 BNT)
    Out of the **mouth**................ἐκ τοῦ **στόματος** (Rev. 16:13 BNT)
    Out of the **mouth** of Him....ἐκ τοῦ **στόματος** αὐτοῦ (Rev. 19:15 BNT)
    Out of the **mouth** of Him....ἐκ τοῦ **στόματος** αὐτοῦ (Rev. 19:21 BNT)

Notice the 3-7 division with a pronoun. The above examples survived the juggernaut of copyist errors. Isolated copyists do not make the same errors. Therefore it is expected that some errors conflict with Hebraic meter. In such cases the probability of finding the exact reading that completes a decadal cadence is hardly accidental.

Dodecadal Meter in Revelation
It Was Given to Him / Before the Throne / Seven or *Seventh Angel(s)*

The following are examples of dodecadal rhythms, or repetitions of 12. Why some phrases appear in decadal rhythm and others in dodecadal is not clear. The assumption is that dodecadal meter is related to the church, either in a positive or a negative sense. In the first example, half of the phrases apply to the anti-Christ and those in league with him. In the second example, none of the 9 Greek texts have all 12 phrases, and the original text is being reassembled on the basis of Hebraic meter. The second example is also coordinated with the 48 repetitions of the word *throne* that are listed at the end of this chapter. These 12 phrases are necessary to complete the repetition of 48 *thrones*.

It was given to him 12 times in Revelation*
>It was given to him.................ἐδόθη αὐτῷ (Rev. 6:2 BNT)
>It was given to him.................ἐδόθη αὐτῷ (Rev. 6:4 BNT)
>It was given to him.................ἐδόθη αὐτῷ (Rev. 6:4 BNT)
>It was given to him.................ἐδόθη αὐτῷ (Rev. 8:3 BNT)
>It was given to him.................ἐδόθη αὐτῷ (Rev. 9:1 BNT)
>It was given to him.................ἐδόθη αὐτῷ (Rev. 13:5 BNT)
>It was given to him.................ἐδόθη αὐτῷ (Rev. 13:5 BNT)
>It was given to him.................ἐδόθη αὐτῷ (Rev. 13:7 BNT)
>It was given to him.................ἐδόθη αὐτῷ (Rev. 13:7 BNT)
>It was given to him.................ἐδόθη αὐτῷ (Rev. 13:14 BNT)
>It was given to him.................ἐδόθη αὐτῷ (Rev. 13:15 BNT)
>It was given to him.................ἐδόθη αὐτῷ (Rev. 16:8 BNT)

*ἐδόθη αὐτῷ found in Rev. 6:8 in BYZ, GOC is rejected.

Before the throne 12 times in Revelation
>Before the throne.....................ἐνώπιον τοῦ θρόνου (Rev. 1:4 BNT)
>Before the throne.....................ἐνώπιον τοῦ θρόνου (Rev. 4:5 BNT)
>Before the throne.....................ἐνώπιον τοῦ θρόνου (Rev. 4:6 BNT)
>Before the throne.....................ἐνώπιον τοῦ θρόνου (Rev. 4:10 BNT)
>Before the throne.....................ἐνώπιον τοῦ θρόνου (Rev. 7:9 BNT)
>Before the throne.....................ἐνώπιον τοῦ θρόνου (Rev. 7:11 BNT)
>Before the throne.....................ἐνώπιον τοῦ θρόνου (Rev. 7:15 BNT)
>Before the throne.....................ἐνώπιον τοῦ θρόνου (Rev. 8:3 BNT)
>Before the throne.....................ἐνώπιον τοῦ θρόνου (Rev. 11:16 BYZ)*
>Before the throne.....................ἐνώπιον τοῦ θρόνου (Rev. 14:3 BNT)
>Before the throne.....................ἐνώπιον τοῦ θρόνου (Rev. 14:5 STE)**
>Before the throne.....................ἐνώπιον τοῦ θρόνου (Rev. 20:12 BNT)***

(See *throne* in list at end of chapter. *Throne* repeats 48 times with the following variants.)
*11:16 only in BYZ, GOC; all others read *before God*.
**14:5 only in SCR, STE.
***20:12 missing from SCR, STE.

Seven or *seventh angel(s)* 12 times in Revelation
And I saw **seven** angels (Rev. 8:2)
And the **seven** angels (Rev. 8:6)
The voice of the **seventh** angel (Rev. 10:7)
And the **seventh** angel (Rev. 11:15)
Seven angels (Rev. 15:1)
And came the **seven** angels (Rev. 15:6)
To the **seven** angels (Rev. 15:7)
Of the **seven** angels (Rev. 15:8)
Saying to the **seven** angels (Rev. 16:1)
And the **seventh** angel (Rev. 16:17)*
One of the **seven** angels (Rev. 17:1)
One of the **seven** angels (Rev. 21:9)

καὶ εἶδον τοὺς **ἑπτὰ ἀγγέλους** (Rev. 8:2 BNT)
καὶ οἱ **ἑπτὰ ἄγγελοι** (Rev. 8:6 BNT)
τῆς φωνῆς τοῦ **ἑβδόμου ἀγγέλου** (Rev. 10:7 BNT)
καὶ ὁ **ἕβδομος ἄγγελος** (Rev. 11:15 BNT)
ἀγγέλους ἑπτὰ (Rev. 15:1 BNT)
καὶ ἐξῆλθον οἱ **ἑπτὰ ἄγγελοι** (Rev. 15:6 BNT)
τοῖς **ἑπτὰ ἀγγέλοις** (Rev. 15:7 BNT)
τῶν **ἑπτὰ ἀγγέλων** (Rev. 15:8 BNT)
λεγούσης τοῖς **ἑπτὰ ἀγγέλοις** (Rev. 16:1 BNT)
καὶ ὁ **ἕβδομος ἄγγελος** (Rev. 16:17 STE)*
εἷς ἐκ τῶν **ἑπτὰ ἀγγέλων** (Rev. 17:1 BNT)
εἷς ἐκ τῶν **ἑπτὰ ἀγγέλων** (Rev. 21:9 BNT)

Angels at 16:17 only in SCR, STE. There are so many variants with *angel* that it is difficult to decide whether the variant includes the assumed noun at 16:17 without agreement from the *Apocryphon of John*. See further discussion in Chapter Nine.

Three Plus Four or Three Times Four

The subject of heptadic phrases exhibiting 3-4 divisions was discussed earlier in this chapter. The relationship between 3 and 4, either added or multiplied, permeates the book of Revelation.

There are matching patterns of 3, 4, and 7 in Revelation and Daniel, displayed below.

glory	glory	power	blessing	blessing	salvation	salvation
honor	honor	riches	praise	glory	strength	glory
thanks	power	wisdom	glory	wisdom	kingdom	honor*
		strength	power	thanksgiving	power	power
		honor		power		
		glory		honor		
		blessing		might		
Rev. 4:9	**Rev. 4:11**	**Rev. 5:12**	**Rev. 5:13**	**Rev. 7:12**	**Rev. 12:10**	**Rev. 19:1**
kingdom	might	blessed	glory	praise	kingdom	dominion
power	power	praised	kingdom	extol	glory	glory
strength	honor	honored	honor	honor	majesty	kingdom
glory	majesty		splendor		honor	
Dan. 2:37	**Dan. 4:30**	**Dan. 4:34**	**Dan. 4:36**	**Dan. 4:37**	**Dan. 5:18**	**Dan. 7:14**

*_Honor_ (τιμή) appears 7 times if we include the variant at 19:1 as in SCR, STE, and exclude the variant at Rev. 21:24 in BYZ, GOC, SCR, STE. Removing this variant also results in a 7-10 division with _glory_.

The *living beings* and the *elders* in heaven praise God in 3s, while the multitudes from the earth (whether in heaven or on the earth) praise God in 4s. When they join together they praise God in 7s. In Daniel, we find a similar arrangement of 3s and 4s with the same pattern, subject, and vocabulary. Daniel 2:37; 4:30, 36; and 5:18 speak of praise to Nebuchadnezzar in 4s, while Daniel 4:34, 37, and 7:14 reference praise to God in 3s. None of the lists above are in the same order. Again we see an example of concurrent symmetry and asymmetry unique to biblical literature.

Coordinated Meter of 3, 4, and 7 in Revelation and Daniel

Revelation, as in all the Bible's visions, communicates doctrine through symbols. There is nothing to indicate that God's blessings must literally take place in 7s, just as there is no reason to believe that the bones of the 7 fat cows in Pharaoh's dream will ever be exhumed.

As more macro-patterns were compared, it became evident that 3-4 divisions are the dominant pattern of Revelation, and are pervasive in numbers, images, events, and words. For example, the 7 seals in chapter 6 begin with 4 horsemen. The first horseman, who does no harm, appears to represent Christ conquering with the Gospel. He appears again on a white horse in 19:11. His bow and crown may symbolize Law and Gospel. The singular form of the word ἵππος (*hippos, horse*) occurs 7 times in Revelation (4 times in Revelation 6[11] and 3 more times in Revelation 19,[12] for a 3-4 division), and the plural form appears 10 times[13] for a 7-10 division[14] and a total of 17. The patterns are like a wheel within a wheel. The first 4 of the 7 trumpets in chapter 8 are followed by 3 *woes*. The 7 vials in chapter 16 also form a 3-4 division, with the first 4 vials completing the destruction (3 *woes*) initiated by the first 4 trumpets.

Revelation describes the progressive destruction of 1/3 of the earth 12 times[15] within the first 4 trumpets. Notice the relationship between

---

[11] Rev. 6:2, 4, 5, 8.

[12] Rev. 19:11, 19, 21 (BYZ, GOC have ἱππικός (*horsemen*) at 9:16).

[13] Rev. 9:7, 9, 16, 17 (x2), 19; 14:20; 18:13; 19:14, 18.

[14] BNT, BYZ, GNT, GOC, TIS, VST, WHO have ἵππος *horse(s)* 17 times; SCR, STE missing ἵππος at Rev. 9:19.

[15] SCR, STE have τρίτος (*tritos, third*) only once in Rev. 8:7 for a total of 12 in chapter 8, and 22 in Revelation, while BNT, BYZ, GNT, GOC, TIS, VST, WHO have τρίτον twice in 8:7 for a total of 23.

3 and 4 that may either add up to 7 or multiply to 12. This is a progressive spiritual destruction, so that a portion of the earth, and ultimately the entire earth, is completely cut off from the Gospel. The symbolic number for the Church is 12. Therefore, the removal of the Gospel in 12 *1/3*s, for a total of 4, from the entire earth would also symbolize the removal of the Church.

Just as there is a 3-4 division between the trumpets and woes, the same relationship is found between the fraction *1/3* and the 4 trumpets. This is visionary mathematics! The numbers are symbolic concepts, not literal. Yes, 12 *1/3*s equals 4, but the *1/3*s are not evenly distributed among the 4 trumpets. As we examine the globe today, approximately 1/3 of the earth is cut off from the Gospel, that is, they have no Bibles, preachers, or churches. However, we should not look for an exact 1/3, but for a symbolic portion of the earth, 1/3 representing a divine curse. The time will come in the 7 vials of Revelation 16 when the entire earth, not just 1/3 of it, will be cut off from the Gospel.

Each of the first 10 cardinal numbers in Revelation has its own unique macro-pattern. Fractions are symbolic of whole numbers. Therefore 1/3, 3, 30, or 33 are closely related symbols. There are 12 *1/3*s in the 4 trumpets, and 10 more *1/3*s outside the description of the 4 trumpets, for a total of 22 in a 12-10 division. Negative 12s are rare. However, in this context, the 12-10 division would indicate the Church being completely eliminated in 1/3 of the earth, which is what the text states.

In itself, a total of 22 *1/3*s in Revelation has no known symbolic significance. However, there are also 11 *3*s in Revelation. When the 22 *1/3*s are added to the 11 *3*s, they total 33, which is a symbolic number for 3. The words and the numbers in visionary literature become interchangeable. The same kind of relationship is seen between 1/4, 4, 40, and 44. The concept of *1/4*, τέταρτος (*tetartos*, tet'-ar-tos) appears 7 times in Revelation, which leads to the symbolic, unstated *1/3* joined with *1/4* resulting in 1/7, a symbol for divine judgment. Incidentally, in Revelation the fractions *1/4* and *1/3* appear in the same verse 3 times.[16] In visionary literature, 1/4 + 1/3 = 1/7 or 7, which symbolizes man + God = judgment. In reality 1/4 + 1/3 = 7/12.

Another example of a verse integrating numbers, events, images, words, and text in a 3-4 division is Revelation 7:1, *And after these things I saw **four** angels standing on the **four** corners of the earth, holding the*

---

[16] Rev. 4:7; 8:12; 21:19.

four winds of the earth, that the wind should not blow on the **earth**, nor on the **sea**, nor on any **tree**. In this verse *four* is in a 3-4 division with *earth*, *sea*, and *tree*, and is repeated 3 times. The relationship between 3 and 4 appears in subtle minutiae and patterns covering the expanse of Revelation to the point that 4 is listed 30 times in Revelation.[17]

This kind of relationship is repeated in the 6th trumpet beginning at Revelation 9:13-18, where 4 angels from the 4 horns of the altar prepare for the hour, day, month, and year to slay 1/3 of mankind. They unleash 200,000,000 false witnesses to destroy men's souls. They have 3 colors—red, blue, and yellow—and they breathe out 3 things—fire, smoke and brimstone—and by these 3, 1/3 of mankind is killed, that is, they are spiritually dead and damned to hell. Notice the balance in these verses between 4 horns, 4 angels, and 4 divisions of time, intended to kill 1/3 of mankind with 3-colored creatures, with 3 kinds of breath repeated twice, for a numerical 4-3 division, and with a reverse of 3 and 4 parts. This is a classic example of the biblical order in a full apocalyptic mode. Similar patterns are listed in Chapter Four—*On 7* in the 2012 edition.[18]

The symbolic application of numbers shows again and again that Revelation requires a visionary and spiritual interpretation, and references to current events must be avoided. More information on this subject is found in Chapter Ten of the 2012 edition.

The search for repeated phrases in Revelation also led to the observation of additional repeated words in Hebraic meter, about 110 of which were listed in the 2012 edition,[19] and about 40 more are listed here. These words repeat 7, 10, and 12 times in Revelation, and in multiples of these numbers.

Single Words in Heptadic Meter

Abyss: 7, ἄβυσσος (*abussos*, ab'-us-sos) 9:1, 2, 11; 11:7; 17:8; 20:1, 3;

Around: 7, adverb 3, κυκλόθεν (*kuklothen*, koo-kloth'-en) 4:3, 4, 8; preposition 3, κύκλῳ (*kuklo*, koo'-klo) 4:6; 5:11; 7:11; verb 1, κυκλόω (*kukloo*, koo-klo'-o) 20:9;

Authority: 21, ἐξουσία (*exousia*, ex-oo-see'-ah) 2:26; 6:8; 9:3 (x2), 10, 19; 11:6 (x2); 12:10; 13:2, 4, 5, 7, 12; 14:18; 16:9; 17:12, 13; 18:1; 20:6; 22:14;

Become: 7, ἐγένοντο (*egenonto*, eg'-en-on-to) verb indicative aorist middle deponent 3rd person plural from γίνομαι, 8:5; 11:13, 15 (x2), 19; 16:18

---

[17] Rev. 4:4 (x2), 6, 8, 10; 5:6, 8 (x2), 14 (x2); 6:1, 6; 7:1 (x3), 2, 4, 11; 9:13, 14, 15; 11:16; 14:1, 3 (x2); 15:7; 19:4 (x2); 20:8; 21:17 in SCR, STE if 5:8 and 5:14 are included.
[18] Cascione, 2012.
[19] Ibid., pp. 133-35.

(x2); only SCR, STE have 7, most have 5;
Blessed: 7, μακάριος (*makarios*, mak-ar'-ee-os) 3 singular, 4 plural, 1:3; 14:13; 16:15; 19:9; 20:6; 22:7, 14;
Blood: 21, αἷμα (*haima*, hah'-ee-mah) 1:5; 5:9; 6:10, 12; 7:14; 8:7, 8; 11:6; 12:11; 14:20; 16:3, 4, 6 (x2); 17:6 (x2); 18:24; 19:2, 13; + 2 acrostic, 9:4 καὶ ἐρρέθη αὐταῖς ἵνα μὴ ἀδικήσωσιν τὸν χόρτον and 9:5 καὶ ἐδόθη αὐταῖς ἵνα μὴ ἀδικήσωσιν;
Bright: 7, 5 bright, λαμπρός (*lampros*, lam-pros') 15:6; 18:14; 19:8; 22:1, 16; + 2 lamp, λαμπάς (*lampas*, lam-pas') 4:5; 8:10;
Brimstone: 7, θεῖον (*theion*, thi'-on) 9:17 (x2), 18; 14:10; 19:20; 20:10; 21:8 (2 forms at 9:17);
Call/Called: 7, καλέω (*kaleo*, kal-eh'-o) 1:9; 11:8; 12:9; 16:16; 19:9, 11, 13;
Cast down: 7, ἐβλήθη, verb indicative aorist passive 3rd person singular, *was cast down*, from βάλλω (*ballo*, bal'-lo) 8:7, 8; 12:9 (x2), 13; 20:10, 15, only in SCR, STE; all the others add 12:10;
Child Give Birth: 7, Chapter 12, noun, τέκνον (*teknon*, tek'-non) 12:4, 5; verb, τίκτω (*tikto*, tik'-to) 12:2, 4 (x2), 5, 13; 8th noun occurs in 2:23;
Church: 7, ἐκκλησία, singular (*ekklesia*, ek-klay-see'-ah) 2:1, 8, 12, 18; 3:1, 7, 14;
City: 28, πόλις (*polis*, pol'-is) 3:12; 11:2, 8, 13; 14:8, 20; 16:19 (x2); 17:18; 18:10 (x2), 16, 18, 19, 21; 20:9; 21:2, 10, 14, 15, 16 (x2), 18, 19, 21, 23; 22:14, 19; we count 14:8 only in SCR, STE; 7 τὴν πόλιν, 11:2; 20:9; 21:2, 10, 15, 16; 22:14;
Clean: 7, καθαρός (*katharos*, kath-ar-os') 15:6; 19:8, 14; 21:18 (x2), 21; 22:1; BYZ, SCR, STE followed at 22:1;
Cloud: 7, νεφέλη (*nephele*, nef-el'-ay) 1:7; 10:1; 11:12; 14:14 (x2), 15, 16;
Come: 35, ἔρχομαι (*erchomai*, er'-khom-ahee) command line to search verb forms for /ερχ* ηρχ* ελεύ* ηλθ* εληλ*, 1:4, 7, 8; 2:5, 16; 3:10, 11; 4:8; 5:7; 6:1, 3, 5, 7, 17; 7:13, 14; 8:3; 9:12; 11:14, 18; 14:7, 15; 16:15; 17:1, 10; 18:10; 19:7; 21:9; 22:7, 12, 17 (x3), 20 (x2); 11:17 in GOC, SCR, STE; variant rejected;
Come: 7, imperative ἔρχου from ἔρχομαι (*erchomai*, er'-khom-ahee) 6:1, 3, 5, 7; 22:17 (x2), 20;
I come: 7, ἔρχομαι, 2:5, 16; 3:11; 16:15; 22:7, 12, 20;
Conquer: 7, νικάω (*nikao*, nik-ah'-o), νικῶν, *the one who overcomes*, 2:11, 26; 3:5, 12, 21; 6:2; 21:7;
Day: 21, ἡμέρα (*hemera*, hay-mer'-ah) 1:10; 2:10, 13; 4:8; 6:17; 7:15; 8:12; 9:6, 15; 10:7; 11:3, 6, 9, 11; 12:6, 10; 14:11; 16:14; 18:8; 20:10; 21:25. BYZ, GOC at 11:13 have *day* rather than *hour*;
Depart: 7, ἀπέρχομαι (*aperchomai*, ap-erkh'-om-ahee) 9:12; 10:9; 11:14; 12:17; 16:2; 18:14; 21:4; double variant SCR, STE have 2 repetitions at 18:14 and missing at 21:1. SCR, STE παρέρχομαι (*parerchomai*, parer'-khom-ahee) at 21:1 rejected, which results in 10 words beginning or containing παρ*, if ἀπαρτί, only found in SCR, STE, TIS, VST at 14:13, is

rejected. Only SCR, STE are missing παρ* at 22:11. The lack of παρ* at 22:11 supports SCR, STE text on justification. This also makes 7 ἀπέρχομαι and 10 with παρ*;

Each/Every: 7, ἕκαστος (*hekastos*, hek'-as-tos) 2:23; 5:8; 6:11; 20:13; 21:21; 22:2, 12;

Fill: 7, γέμω (*gemo*, ghem'-o) 4:6, 8; 5:8; 15:7; 17:3, 4; 21:9;

Fire: 7, πῦρ (*pur*, poor), πυρὶ noun dative neuter singular common from πῦρ, 8:8; 14:10; 15:2; 16:8; 17:16; 18:8; 21:8;

First: 21, 18 πρῶτος (*protos*, pro'-tos) 1:17; 2:4, 5, 8, 19; 4:1, 7; 8:7; 13:12 (x2); 16:2; 20:5, 6; 21:1 (x2), 4, 19; 22:13; + first born, πρωτότοκος, 1:11; + 2 morning, πρωϊνόν, 2:28; 22:16; variant πρῶτος rejected at 1:11, SCR, STE; variant καὶ ὀρθρινός rejected at 22:16, SCR, STE;

First: 7, πρῶτος (*protos*, pro'-tos) 1:17; 2:8; 8:7; 16:2; 21:1, 19; 22:13;

Five/Fifth: 7, 3 five, πέντε (*pente*, pen'-the) 9:5, 10; 17:10; + 4 fifth, πέμπτος (*pemptos*, pemp'-tos) 6:9; 9:1; 16:10; 21:20;

Fourth: 7, τέταρτος (*tetartos*, tet'-ar-tos) 4:7; 6:7 (x2), 8; 8:12; 16:8; 21:19;

Gather together: 7, συναγωγή (*sunagoge*, soon-ag-o-gay') συνάγω (*sunago*, soon-ag'-o) 2:9; 3:9; 16:14, 16; 19:17, 19; 20:8; 2 nouns (synagogue) and five verbs; SCR, STE add 13:10; variant rejected;

Go out: 14, ἐξέρχομαι (*exerchomai*, ex-er'-khom-ahee) 3:12; 6:2, 4; 9:3; 14:15, 17, 18, 20; 15:6; 16:17; 18:4; 19:5, 21; 20:8; SCR, STE missing at 19:21; variant rejected;

Here: 7, ὧδε (*hode*, ho'-deh) adverb, 4:1; 11:12; 13:10, 18; 14:12 (x2); 17:9; only SCR, STE add 14:12b;

Holy: 14, (same word as *saint* in context) ἅγιος (*hagios*, hag'-ee-os) 3:7; 4:8 (x3), 11; 6:10; 11:2; 14:10; 15:4; 20:6; 21:2, 10; 22:11, 19; variant in BYZ, VST at 4:11 accepted; variant in BYZ at 15:4 accepted; variant in SCR, STE at 22:11 accepted;

Honor: 7, τιμή (*time*, tee-may) 4:9, 11; 5:12, 13; 7:12; 21:24, 26; if we exclude variant at 19:1 in SCR, STE, and maintain variant at 21:24 as found in BYZ, GOC, SCR, STE;

Jesus: 14, Ἰησοῦς (*Iesous*, ee-ay-sooce') 1:1, 2, 5, 9 (x2); 12:17; 14:12; 17:6; 19:10 (x2); 20:4; 22:16, 20, 21; BYZ at 14:4 rejected;

Kingdom: 7, βασιλεία (*basileia*, bas-il-i'-ah) SCR, STE 1:9; 11:15; 12:10; 16:10; 17:12, 17, 18; BNT, BYZ, GNT, GOC, TIS, VST, WHO have *kingdom* rather than *kings* at 1:6, and BNT, GNT, TIS, WHO have *kingdom* rather than *kings* at 5:10. Becker makes no distinction in meaning between *kings* and *kingdom*. He writes: "He is described as...the one who made us kings and priests."[20] *They will be priests...and reign*, 5:10; 20:4, 6; 22:5; also *royal priesthood*, 1 Pet. 2:9. *Kings* is preferred to *Kingdom* at 1:6 and 5:10;

Know: 7, 5 γινώσκω (*ginosko*, ghin-oce'-ko) 2:17, 23, 24; 3:3, 9; + 2 read

---

[20] S. Becker, pp. 30-31.

ἀναγινώσκω (*anaginosko*, an-ag-in-oce'-ko) 1:3; 5:4; SCR, STE only have 2:17 and 5:4;
Lamp: 7, λαμπρας, 2 λαμπάς (*lampas*, lam-pas') 4:5; 8:10; bright, λαμπρός, 15:6; 18:14; 19:8; 22:1, 16;
Lampstand(s): 7, λυχνία (*luchnia*, lookh-nee'-ah) λυχνίαι, 1:12, 13, 20 (x2); 2:1, 5; 11:4;
Measure: 7, 5 verbs μετρέω (*metreo*, met-reh'-o) 11:1, 2; 21:15, 16, 17 (SCR, STE missing at 21:15); 2 nouns μέτρον, a measure, 21:15, 17;
Much/Many: 14, πολύς (*polus*, pol'-oos) 1:15; 5:4, 11; 7:9; 8:3, 11; 9:9; 10:11; 14:2; 17:1; 19:1, 6 (x2), 12;
Patience: 7, ὑπομονή (*hupomone*, hoop-om-on-ay') 1:9; 2:2, 3, 19; 3:10; 13:10; 14:12;
Prophecy: 7, προφητεία (*propheteia*, prof-ay-ti'-ah) 1:3; 11:6; 19:10; 22:7, 10, 18, 19;
Quickly: 7, adverb ταχύ (*tachu*, takh-oo') 2:5, 16; 3:11; 11:14; 22:7, 12, 20; 2:5 only in BYZ, GOC, SCR, VST;
Reign: 7, βασιλεύω (*basileuo*, bas-il-yoo'-o) 5:10; 11:15, 17; 19:6; 20:4, 6; 22:5;
Saint: 14, (same word as *holy* in context) ἅγιος (*hagios*, hag'-ee-os) 5:8; 8:3, 4; 11:18; 13:7, 10; 14:12; 16:6; 17:6; 18:20, 24; 19:8; 20:9; 22:21; variant in BYZ, GOC, and VST at 22:21 accepted;
Saying: 7, λέγοντος (*legantos*, leg-an-toos') participle from λέγω (*lego*, leg'-o) 6:1, 3, 5, 7; 8:13; 16:5, 7;
Saying: 7, Chapter 18, λέγων, λέγουσαν, λέγοντες, participles from λέγω (*lego*, leg'-o) 18:2, 4, 10, 16, 18, 19, 21;
Second: 14, 13 δεύτερος (*deuteros*, dyoo'-ter-os) 2:11; 4:7; 6:3; 8:8; 11:14; 14:8; 16:3; 19:3, 17; 20:6, 14; 21:8, 19; + Δεῦτε (come) adverb, 19:17; SCR, STE missing at 14:8;
Servant/Slave: 14, δοῦλος (*doulos*, doo'-los) 1:1 (x2); 2:20; 6:15; 7:3; 10:7; 11:18; 13:16; 15:3; 19:2, 5, 18; 22:3, 6;
Sharp: 7, ὀξύς (*oxus*, oz-oos') 1:16; 2:12; 14:14, 17, 18 (x2); 19:15;
Show: 7/8, δείκνυμι (*deiknumai*, dike-noo'-mahee) 1:1; 4:1; 17:1; 21:9, 10; 22:1, 6, 8 (the last one is a participle);
Sickle: 7, δρέπανον (*drepanon*, drep'-an-on) 14:14, 15, 16, 17, 18 (x2), 19;
Sign: 7, noun σημεῖον (*semeion*, say-mi'-on) 12:1, 3; 13:13, 14; 15:1; 16:14; 19:20; could be 8 if we add verb signified, ἐσήμανεν, 1:1;
Soul: 7, ψυχή (*psuche*, psoo-khay') 6:9; 8:9; 12:11; 16:3; 18:13, 14; 20:4;
Spirits: 7, πνεῦμα (*pneuma*, pnyoo'-mah) 1:4; 3:1; 4:5; 5:6; 16:13, 14; 22:6;
Star: 14, ἀστήρ (*aster*, as-tare') (2 in nominative case) 2+12=14; 1:16, 20 (x2); 2:1, 28; 3:1; 6:13; 8:10, 11, 12; 9:1; 12:1, 4; 22:16;
Tabernacle: 7, σκηνή (*skene*, skay-nay') 3 nouns, 4 verbs, 7:15; 12:12; 13:6 (x2); 15:5; 21:3 (x2);
Testimony: 7, μαρτυρία (*marturia*, mar-too-ree'-ah), μαρτυρίαν nominative or accusative feminine singular, 1:2, 9; 6:9; 11:7; 12:17; 19:10; 20:4;

Testimony, bear witness, witness: 14, μαρτυρία (*marturia*, mar-too-ree'-ah), μάρτυς (*martus*, mar'-toos), μαρτύριον (*marturion*, mar-too'-ree-on), μαρτυρῶ (*marturo*) 1:2, 9; 6:9; 11:7; 12:11, 17; 15:5; 17:6; 19:10 (x2); 20:4; 22:16, 18, 20;
There: 7, ἐκεῖ (*ekei*, ek-i') 1:12; 2:14; 12:6 (x2), 14; 21:25; 22:5; BYZ, GOC add 1:12; BYZ, SCR, STE add 22:5; SCR, STE missing second 12:6;
Time: 7, καιρός (*kairos*, kahee-ros') 1:3; 11:18; 12:12, 14 (x3); 22:10;
Tree: 7, ξύλον (*xulon*, xoo'-lon) 2:7; 9:20; 18:12 (x2); 22:2, 14; only SCR, STE have *book of life* instead of *tree of life* at 22:19, which makes 7 phrases for *book of life* above, and 7 *tree(s)*;
Trumpet, Trumpeter: 7, σάλπιγξ (*salpigx*, sal'-pinx) 1:10; 4:1; 8:2, 6, 13; 9:14; 18:22;
Twenty: 7, εἴκοσι (*eikosi*, i'-kos-ee) 4:4 (x2), 10; 5:8; 11:16; 19:4 + SCR, STE 5:14 εἴκοσιτέσσαρες;
Twenty four: 7, εἴκοσι (*eikosi*, i'-kos-ee) τέσσαρες (*tessares*, tes'-sar-es) 4:4 (x2), 10; 5:8; 11:16; 19:4; + SCR, STE 5:14 εἴκοσιτέσσαρες;
Under: 7, 3 ὑπό (*hupo*, hoop-o') 6:8, 13; 9:18, only in SCR, STE; and 4 ὑποκάτω (*hupokato*, hoop-ok-at'-o) 5:3, 13; 6:9; 12:1;
Us: 7, ἡμᾶς (*haymas, hey'-mas*) 1:5 (x2), 6; 5:9, 10; 6:16 (x2); 5:9 only in BYZ, GOC, SCR, and 5:10 only in SCR, STE;
Woe: 14, οὐαί (*ouai*, oo-ah'-ee) 8:13 (x3); 9:12 (x2); 11:14 (x2); 12:12; 18:10 (x2), 16 (x2), 19 (x2);
Wonder: 7, θαυμάζω (*thaumazo*, thou-mad'-zo) 13:3; 15:1, 3; 17:6 (x2), 7, 8;
Worthy: 7, ἄξιος (*axios*, ax'-ee-os) 3:4; 4:11; 5:2, 4, 9, 12; 16:6;
Year(s): 7, ἐνιαυτόν (*eniauton*, en-ee-ow-ton') 9:15; ἔτος (*etos*, et'-os) 20:2, 3, 4, 5, 6, 7.

Single Words in Decadal Meter
Amen: 10, ἀμήν (*amen*, am-ane') 1:6, 7, 18; 3:14; 5:14; 7:12 (x2); 19:4; 22:20, 21; BYZ, SCR, STE add *Amen* at 1:18; BYZ at 5:13 is rejected;
Angel: 70, ἄγγελος (*aggelos*, ang'-el-os) probably 70 if we include 8:13 *angel* rather than *eagle* in SCR, STE; 16:3 in BYZ, GOC, SCR, STE; and 16:8 in BYZ, SCR, STE. There are 67 in BNT, GNT, TIS, VST, WHO. SCR, STE add 8 more variants for a total of 75, and SCR adds 1 more for a total of 76;
Beast(s): 50, life, living, life (ζωή, ῆς, ἡ, *life*), live (ζάω contracted ζῶ, *live*), living being (ζῷον, ου, τό, *animal*) 1:18 (x2); 2:7, 8, 10; 3:1, 5; 4:6, 7 (x4), 8, 9 (x2), 10; 5:6, 8, 11, 14 (x2); 6:1, 3, 5, 6, 7; 7:2, 11, 17; 10:6; 11:11; 13:8, 14; 14:3; 15:7 (x2); 16:3; 17:8; 19:4, 20; 20:4, 5, 12, 15; 21:6, 27; 22:1, 2, 14, 17, 19; SCR, STE add 5:14 and missing at 20:5; variants accepted; this can only be done with a computer;
Become: 30, I became, ἐγενόμην; he became, ἐγένοντο; they became, ἐγένοντο; verb indicative aorist; all forms from γίνομαι (*ginomai*, ghin'-om-ahee) 1:9, 17, 18; 2:8; 4:2; 6:12 (x2); 8:1, 5, 7, 8, 11; 11:13 (x2), 15

(x2), 19; 12:7, 10; 16:2, 3, 4, 10, 18 (x4), 19; 18:2; SCR, STE missing at 8:11 with different form; variant rejected;
Behold: 30, ἰδού (*idou*, id-oo') too many variants: 30 possible if we follow SCR, STE at 3:11 and 6:12. BYZ adds one at 6:8 that interferes with ὁράω (see); SCR, STE at 5:6 remove 7th ἐν μέσῳ, and 15:5 adds an extra καὶ ἰδού to 7 καὶ εἶδον καὶ ἰδού; therefore we follow ἰδὼν (17:6 BNT) and ἴδω (18:7 BNT) instead of ἰδοὺ SCR, STE at 5:6 and 15:5;
Book: 30, βιβλίον (*biblion*, bib-lee'-on) 1:11; 3:5; 5:1, 2, 3, 4, 5, 7, 8, 9; 6:14; 10:2, 8, 9, 10; 13:8; 17:8; 20:12 (x3), 15; 21:27; 22:7, 9, 10, 18 (x2), 19 (x3), if we follow SCR, STE at 5:7 and 22:19;
Cast down: 30, 28 βάλλω (*ballo*, bal'-lo) (SCR, STE have καταβάλλω at 12:10) 2:10, 14, 22, 24; 4:10; 6:13; 8:5, 7, 8; 12:4, 9 (x3), 10, 13, 15, 16; 14:16, 19 (x2); 18:19, 21 (x2); 19:20; 20:3, 10, 14, 15; + ἐκβάλλω, 11:2; + ἀποβάλλω (*apoballo*, ap-ob-al'-lo) in BYZ and GOC, 3:2;
Christ: 10, Χριστός (*Christos*, khris-tos') 1:1, 2, 5, 9 (x2); 11:15; 12:10, 17; 20:6; 22:21;
1:9 and 22:21 in BYZ, GOC, SCR, STE; 12:17 only in SCR, STE;
Church(es): 20, ἐκκλησία (*ekklesia*, ek-klay-see'-ah) 1:4, 11, 20 (x2); 2:1, 7, 8, 11, 12, 17, 18, 23, 29; 3:1, 6, 7, 13, 14, 22; 22:16;
Conquer: 10, more of the same verb νικάω (*nikao*, nik-ah'-o) 2:7, 17; 3:21; 5:5; 6:2; 11:7; 12:11; 13:7; 15:2; 17:14;
Do/Make: 30, ποιέω (*poieo*, poy-eh'-o) 1:6; 2:5; 3:9, 12; 5:10; 11:7; 12:15, 17; 13:5, 7, 12 (x2), 13 (x2), 14 (x2), 15, 16; 14:7; 16:14; 17:16, 17 (x2); 19:19, 20; 21:5, 27; 22:2, 14, 15; BYZ, GOC missing at 13:13; BYZ adds 17:16; SCR, STE missing at 22:11; BYZ, GOC, SCR, STE add 22:14; Kirby also finds 30;[21]
Do/Make: 10, Chapter 13, according to BNT, GNT, SCR, STE, TIS, VST, WHO ποιῆσαι (13:5), ποιῆσαι (13:7), ποιεῖ (13:12), ποιεῖ, ποιῇ (13:13), ποιῆσαι, ποιῆσαι (13:14), ποιήσῃ (13:15), ποιεῖ (13:16);
Eye(s): 10, ὀφθαλμός (*ophthalmos*, of-thal-mos') 1:7, 14; 2:18; 3:18; 4:6, 8; 5:6; 7:17; 19:12; 21:4;
Face(s): 10, πρόσωπον (*prosopon*, pros'-o-pon) 4:7; 6:16; 7:11; 9:7; 10:1; 11:16; 12:14; 20:11; 22:4;
Fall: 20, πίπτω (*pipto*, pip'-to) all verb forms, 1:17; 4:10; 5:8, 14; 6:13; 7:11; 8:10 (x2); 11:11, 13, 16; 14:8 (x2); 16:19; 17:10; 18:2 (x2); 19:4, 10; 22:8;
Fear: 10, φοβέω (*phobeo*, fob-eh'-o) 1:17; 2:10; 11:11, 18; 14:7; 15:4; 18:10, 15; 19:5; + fearful/timid, δειλός (*deilos*, di-los') 21:8;
Feet: 10, πούς (*pous*, pooce) 1:15, 17; 2:18; 3:9; 10:1, 2; 11:11; 12:1; 13:2; 19:10; 22:8; 12 if we add 1:13 (long robe), 10:2 (foot);
Fire: 30, πῦρ (*pur*, poor); fiery red, πυρρός (*purrhos*, poor-hros'); fiery, πύρινος (*purinos*, poo'-ree-nos); burning, πύρωσις (*purosis*, poo'-ro-sis) 1:14; 2:18; 3:18; 4:5; 6:4; 8:5, 7, 8; 9:17 (x2), 18; 10:1; 11:5; 12:3; 13:13;

---

[21] Kirby, p. 86.

14:10, 18; 15:2; 16:8; 17:16; 18:8, 9, 18; 19:12, 20; 20:9, 10, 14, 15; 21:8, if the second repetition is removed at 20:14 according to BYZ, GOC, SCR, STE;
First: 20, πρῶτος (*protos*, pro'-tos) 1:17; 2:4, 5, 8, 19; 4:1, 7; 8:7; 13:12 (x2); 16:2; 20:5, 6; 21:1 (x2), 4, 19; 22:13; + firstborn, πρωτότοκος at 1:5; + firstfruits, ἀπαρχή (*aparche*, ap-ar-khay') at 14:4;
Fornication: 20, 5 to fornicate (πορνεῦσαι), 7 fornication (πορνεία), 5 prostitute (πόρνη), 2 fornicator (πόρνος), 2:14, 20, 21; 9:21; 14:8; 17:1, 2 (x2), 4, 5, 15, 16; 18:3 (x2), 9; 19:2 (x2); 21:8; 22:15; 1 adultery (μοιχεύω), 2:22;
Four: 30, τέσσαρες (*tessares,* tes'-sar-es) 4:4 (x2), 6, 8, 10; 5:6, 8 (x2), 14 (x2); 6:1, 6; 7:1 (x3), 2, 4, 11; 9:13, 14, 15; 11:16; 14:1, 3 (x2); 15:7; 19:4 (x2); 20:8; 21:17, if we follow SCR, STE at 5:8 and 5:14, and if we follow BNT, BYZ, GNT, GOC, TIS, VST, WHO at 7:4. We are amazed that SCR, STE read *100,000* rather than *144,000* at 7:4, when all other texts read *144,000* and the total of the elect is 144,000. Not even KJV follows Textus Receptus at 7:4!
Give: 10, I will give, δώσω (*doso*, do'-so) 2:7, 10, 17 (x2), 23, 26, 28; 3:21; 11:3; 21:6;
Given: 20, ἐδόθη (*edothay*, e'-do-thāy) was given, 6:2, 4 (x2), 8; 7:2; 8:3; 9:1, 3, 5; 11:1, 2; 13:5 (x2), 7 (x2), 14, 15; 16:8; 19:8; 20:4; if 6:11 is ἐδόθησαν according to SCR, STE;
God: 100, θεός (*theos*, theh'-os) if we follow all the correct variants;
Grasp/Dominion: 10, κρατέω (*krateo*, krat-eh'-o) 2:1, 13, 14, 15, 25; 3:11; 7:1; 20:2; κράτος (*kratos*, krat'-os) 1:6; 5:13;
Great: 80, μέγας (*megas*, meg'-as), including 18:2 in SCR, STE, and 21:10 in BYZ, SCR, STE;
Horn: 10, κέρας (*keras*, ker'-as) 5:6; 9:13; 12:3; 13:1, 11; 14:10; 17:3, 7, 12, 16; 18:6;
Hour: 10, ὥρα (*hora*, ho'-rah) 3:3, 10; 9:15; 11:13; 14:7, 15; 17:12; 18:10, 17, 19; BYZ, GOC at 11:13 have *day* rather than *hour*;
Image: 10, εἰκών (*eikon*, i-kone') 13:14, 15 (x3); 14:9, 11; 15:2; 16:2; 19:20; 20:4; notice that twenty and image are very close and could be 10 + 7 = 17;
Judge: 10, κρίνω (*krino*, kree'-no) 6:10; 11:18; 16:5, 7; 18:8, 20; 19:2, 11; 20:12, 13;
Key/Shut: 10, 4 key, κλείς (*kleis*, klice) + 6 close, κλείω (*kleio*, kli'-o) 1:18; 3:7 (x3), 8; 9:1; 11:6; 20:1, 3; 21:25;
King(s)/Kingdom(s): 30, 4 king, BNT, βασιλεύς (*basileus*, bas-il-yooce') 9:11; 15:3; 17:14; 19:16; 1 queen, βασίλισσα (*basilissa,* bas-il'-is-sah) 18:17; 19 kings, 1:5, 6; 5:10; 6:15; 10:11; 16:12, 14; 17:2 (x2), 10, 12, 14, 18; 18:3, 9; 19:16, 18, 19; 21:24; 6 kingdom, 1:9; 11:15; 12:10; 16:10; 17:12, 17, if we follow SCR, STE with kings at 1:6 instead of kingdom; and BYZ, GOC, SCR, STE, VST with kings at 5:10 instead of kingdom;
Lamb: 30, ἀρνίον (*arnion*, ar-nee'-on) 5:6, 8, 12, 13; 6:1, 9, 16; 7:9, 10, 14, 17; 12:11; 13:8, 11; 14:1, 4, 10; 15:3; 17:14; 19:7, 9; 21:9, 14, 22, 23,

27; 22:1, 3, if BYZ, GOC at 6:9 is included, which is also necessary for God and Lamb 10 times above;

Lampstands/Lamps: 10, 7 lampstands, λυχνίαι (*luchnia*, lookh-nee'-ah) 1:12, 13, 20 (x2); 2:1, 5; 11:4; 3 lamps, λύχνος (*luchnos*, lookh'-nos) 18:23; 21:23; 22:5;

Lead astray: 10, πλανάω (*planao*, plan-ah'-o) 2:20; 3:2, 17; 12:9; 13:14; 18:23; 19:20; 20:3, 8, 10; BYZ, GOC add 20:2;

Life/Living: 30, 15 of each, if SCR, STE variant added at 5:14 (see **Beasts(s)** above);

Living Being: 20, ζῷον (*zoon*, dzo'-on), ου, τό; 4:6, 7 (x4), 8, 9; 5:6, 8, 11, 14; 6:1, 3, 5, 6, 7; 7:11; 14:3; 15:7; 19:4 (see **Beasts(s)** above);

Love: 10, noun, 2 ἀγάπη (*agape*, ag-ah'-pay) 2:4, 19; verb, 4 ἀγαπάω (*agapao*, ag-ap-ah'-o) 1:5; 3:9; 12:11; 20:9; 2 Philadelphia, Φιλαδέλφεια (*Philadelpheia*, fil-ad-el'-fee-ah) 1:11; 3:7; 2 φιλέω (*phileo*, fil-eh'-o) 3:19; 22:15;

Mouth/Language: 30, 22 mouth, στόμα (*stoma*, stom'-a) 1:16; 2:16; 3:16; 9:17, 18, 19; 10:9, 10; 11:5; 12:15, 16 (x2); 13:2 (x2), 5, 6; 14:5; 16:13 (x3); 19:15, 21; 8 language, γλῶσσα (*glossa*, gloce-sah') 5:9; 7:9; 10:11; 11:9; 13:7; 14:6; 16:10; 17:15;

Name: 40, ὄνομα (*onoma*, on'-om-ah) 2:3, 13, 17; 3:1, 4, 5 (x2), 8, 12 (x3); 6:8; 8:11; 9:11 (x2); 11:13, 18; 13:1, 6, 8, 17 (x2); 14:1 (x2), 11; 15:2, 4; 16:9; 17:3, 5, 8; 19:12 (x2), 13, 16; 21:12 (x2), 14; 22:4; + acrostic at 2:11, ὁ νικῶν οὐ μὴ ἀδικηθῇ; STE, SCR missing ὄνομα at 14:1; BYZ, GOC add 1 at 19:12; SCR, STE, TIS, VST, WHO missing 1 at 21:12;

Number: 10, ἀριθμός (*arithmos*, ar-ith-mos') 7:4; 9:16 (x2); 13:17, 18 (x3); 15:2; 20:8; plus verb at 7:9; BYZ has 1 more at 14:1; only STE is missing 1 at 5:11, all others have 10;

Open: 10, ἤνοιξεν, ἀνοίγω (*anoigo*, an-oy'-go), he opened, 6:1, 3, 5, 7, 9, 12; 8:1; 9:2; 12:16; 13:6; (see **Key/Shut** =10 above);

Open: 20/7=27, ἀνοίγω (*anoigo*, an-oy'-go) 3:7 (x2), 8, 20; 4:1; 5:2, 3, 4, 5, 9; 6:1, 3, 5, 7, 9, 12; 8:1; 9:2; 10:2, 8; 11:19; 12:16; 13:6; 15:5; 19:11; 20:12 (x2); BYZ adds 1 at 3:7; variant rejected; **20/7** with the phrase ὅτε ἤνοιξεν, *when he opened*, 6:1, 3, 5, 7, 9, 12; 8:1; BYZ, GOC, SCR, STE variant accepted at 8:1 (see above); also see *book opened* 7 times in examples above;

Plagues: 10, πληγή (*plege*, play-gay'), plural, 9:18, 20; 15:1, 6, 8; 16:9; 18:4, 8; 21:9; 22:18; 6 singular, 11:6; 13:3, 12, 14; 16:21 (x2); SCR, STE missing πληγή at 9:18;

River: 10, 8 ποταμός (*potamos*, pot-am-os') 8:10; 9:14; 12:15, 16; 16:4, 12; 22:1, 2; 1 sweep away by a river, ποταμοφόρητος (*potamophoretos*, pot-am-of-or'-ay-tos) 12:15; 1 drink, ποτίζω (*potizo*, pot-id'-zo) 14:8, the only use of this verb; 8+1+1=10;

Saying: 20, λεγούσ* in SCR, STE;

Sitting: 10, καθήμενος, verb participle from κάθημαι (*kathemai*, kath'-ay-mahee) 4:2, 3; 6:2, 5, 8; 7:15; 14:14, 16; 19:11; 21:5; BYZ, GOC missing at 4:3; variant rejected;

Sword: 10, 4 μάχαιρα (*machaira*, makh'-ahee-rah) 6:4; 13:10 (x2), 14; 6 ρομφαία (*rhomphaia*, hrom-fah'-yah) 1:16; 2:12, 16; 6:8; 19:15, 21;
Ten: 10, δέκα (*deka*, dek'-ah) 2:10; 12:3; 13:1 (x2); 17:3, 7, 12 (x2), 16; + acrostic at 11:4 (BNT), οὗτοί εἰσιν αἱ **δύο ἐλαῖαι καὶ αἱ δύο λυχνίαι**;
Thousand: 30, χιλιάς (*chilias*, khil'-ee-as) no variants, 29 plus χιλίαρχος at 6:15, *commander of a thousand men*, says Friberg, Liddell & Scott, *Vocabulary of the Greek New Testament*, as in John 18:12, *captain*;
Thunders: 10, βροντή (*bronte*, bron-tay') 4:5; 6:1; 8:5; 10:3, 4 (x2); 11:19; 14:2; 16:18; 19:6;
True: 10, ἀληθινός (*alethinos*, al-ay-thee-nos') 3:7, 14; 6:10; 15:3; 16:7; 19:2, 9, 11; 21:5; 22:6;
Trumpeted: 10, σαλπίζω (*salpizo*, sal-pid'-zo) 8:6, 7, 10, 12, 13; 9:1, 13, 14; 10:7; 11:15;
Two: 10, δύο (*duo*, doo'-o) 9:12, 16; 11:2, 3, 4 (x2), 10; 12:14; 13:5, 11; 19:20; GOC, SCR, STE have δύο μυριάδες at 9:16; variant rejected; all others have δισμυριάδες;
Witness, Testimony, Testify, Martyr, Confess: 20, 1:2 (x2), 5, 9; 2:13; 3:5, 14; 6:9; 11:3, 7; 12:11, 17; 15:5; 17:6; 19:10 (x2); 20:4; 22:16, 18, 20; SCR, STE have συμμαρτυρέω (to confirm, testify) at 22:18 rather than μαρτυρέω (*martureo*, mar-too-reh'-o) 1:2; 22:16, 18, 20; μαρτυρία (*marturia*, mar-too-ree'-ah) 1:2; 1:9; 6:9; 11:7; 12:11, 17; 19:10 (x2); 20:4; μαρτύριον (*marturion*, mar-too'-ree-on) 15:15; μάρτυς (*martus*, mar'-toos) 1:5; 2:13; 3:14; 11:3; 17:6; confess, ὁμολογήσω (*homologayso*, ho-mo-lo-gay'-so) 3:5.

Single Words in Dodecadal Meter

After: 24, μετὰ (*meta*, met-ah') 1:7, 19; 3:21; 4:1 (x2); 7:1, 9; 9:12; 11:11; 12:7, 17; 13:7; 14:4; 15:5; 17:12, 14; 18:1; 19:1, 19 (x2); 20:3, 4; 21:3; 22:21; SCR, STE missing at 12:7, but adds 19:20;
Before: 36, ἐνώπιον (*enopion*, en-o'-pee-on) 1:4; 2:14; 3:2, 5 (x2), 8, 9; 4:5, 6, 10 (x2); 5:8; 7:9 (x2), 11, 15; 8:2, 3, 4; 9:13; 11:4, 16; 12:4, 10; 13:12, 13, 14; 14:3 (x2), 5, 10 (x2); 15:4; 16:19; 19:20; 20:12; SCR, STE add 14:5 for 36, necessary for multiple patterns with throne;
Bowl: 12, φιάλη BNT (*phiale*, fee-al'-ay) 5:8; 15:7; 16:1, 2, 3, 4, 8, 10, 12, 17; 17:1; 21:9 (5 plural, 7 singular);
But: 12, ἀλλὰ (*alla*, al-lah') 2:4, 6, 9 (x2), 14, 20; 3:9; 9:5; 10:7, 9; 17:12; 20:6; SCR, STE missing at 3:4; variant rejected;
Clothed: 12, περιβάλλω (*periballo*, per-ee-bal'-lo) 3:5, 18; 4:4; 7:9, 13; 10:1; 11:3; 12:1; 17:4; 18:16; 19:8, 13;
Come down/Come up: 24, 11 come down, καταβαίνω (*katabaino*, kat-ab-ah'-ee-no) 3:12; 10:1; 12:12; 13:8, 13; 16:21; 18:1; 20:1, 9; 21:2, 10; + 13 come up, ἀναβαίνω (*anabaino*, an-ab-ah'-ee-no) 4:1; 7:2; 8:4; 9:2; 11:7, 12 (x2); 13:1, 11; 14:11; 17:8; 19:3; 20:9;
Crown/Diadem/Give over power: 12, 2:10; 3:11; 4:4, 10; 6:2; 9:7; 12:1, 3; 13:1; 14:14; 17:3; 19:12; 8 crown, Στέφανος (*stephanos,* stef'-an-os), 3 diadem, διάδημα (*diadema,* dee-ad'-ay-mah), 1 give over, διαδίδωμι (*dia-*

didomi, dee-ad-id'-o-mee); only in SCR, STE at 17:3;

Cry: 12, 11 verbs, κράζω (*krazo*, krad'-zo) 6:10; 7:2, 10; 10:3 (x2); 12:2; 14:15; 18:2, 18, 19; 19:17; 1 noun, κραυγή (*krauge*, krow-gay') 21:4; BYZ, GOC, SCR, STE, VST add 14:18, which removes pattern of 20 for great voice; variant rejected;

Dead: 12, νεκρός (*nekros*, nek-ros') only GOC has nation, ἔθνος at 11:18 to make 12; all others have 13; GOC has 24 ἔθνος with 11:18; GOC variant completes 2 macro-patterns;

Dwell/Sit: 48, 16 dwell, κατοικέω (*katoikeo*, kat-oy-keh'-o) 2:13 (x2); 3:10; 6:10; 8:13; 11:10 (x2); 13:8, 12, 14 (x2); 17:2, 8; noun at 18:2; SCR, STE add 12:12; 14:6; 32 sit, κάθημαι (*kathemai*, kath'-ay-mahee) 4:2, 3, 4, 9, 10; 5:1, 7, 13; 6:2, 4, 5, 8, 16; 7:10, 15; 9:17; 11:16; 14:14, 15, 16; 17:1, 3, 9, 15; 18:7; 19:4, 11, 18, 19, 21; 20:11; 21:5; BNT, BYZ, GNT, GOC, TIS, VST, WHO add 14:6; variant rejected; notice 16/32 division;

Elders: 12, πρεσβύτερος (*presbuteros*, pres-boo'-ter-os) 4:4, 10; 5:5, 6, 8, 11, 14; 7:11, 13; 11:16; 14:3; 19:4; phrase *24 elders* appears 6 times according to SCR, STE at 5:14;

Harm: 12, ἀδικέω (*adikeo*, ad-ee-keh'-o) 2:11; 6:6; 7:2, 3; 9:4, 10, 19; 11:5 (x2); 18:5; 22:11 (x2);

Keep: 12, τηρέω (*tereo*, tay-reh'-o) 1:3; 2:26; 3:3, 8, 10 (x3); 12:17; 14:12; 16:15; 22:7, 9;

Like: 24, 21 ὅμοιος (*homoios*, hom'-oy-os) 1:13, 15; 2:18; 4:3 (x2), 6, 7 (x3); 9:7 (x2), 10, 19; 11:1; 13:2, 4, 11; 14:14; 18:18; 21:11, 18; 1 ὁμοίωμα (*homoioma*, hom-oy'-o-mah) 9:7; 2 ὁμοίως (*homoios*) 2:15; 8:12; rejected variants are BYZ missing at 9:7, and SCR, STE *hate*, μισέω (*miseo*, mis-eh'-o) rather than *likewise* at 2:15;

Lord: 24, κύριος (*kurios*, koo'-ree-os) 1:8, 10; 4:8, 11; 7:14; 11:8, 15, 17; 14:13; 15:3, 4; 16:7; 17:14 (x2); 18:8; 19:1, 6, 16 (x2); 21:22; 22:5, 6, 20, 21; SCR, STE, add 16:5, 19:1; BYZ adds 11:4, 19; BNT, GNT, SCR, STE, TIS, VST, WHO have *God* instead of *Lord* at 14:7; there are so many variant readings for *Lord* that a meter must be followed to determine the count;

Midst: 12, μέσος (*mesos*, mes'-os) 1:13; 2:1, 7; 4:6; 5:6 (x2); 6:6; 7:17; 22:2; μεσουρανήματι, mid-heaven, 8:13; 14:6; 19:17; SCR 7:17 has ἀναμέσον; all others have ἀνα μέσον; variant rejected; SCR, STE at 2:7; variant rejected;

Nation: 24, ἔθνος (*ethnos*, eth'-nos) 2:26; 5:9; 7:9; 10:11; 11:2, 9, 18; 12:5; 13:7; 14:6, 8; 15:3, 4; 16:19; 17:15; 18:3, 23; 19:15; 20:3, 8; 21:24 (x2), 26; 22:2; BNT, BYZ, GNT, GOC, TIS at 15:3 have *nation*, while SCR, STE, WHO have *saints*; BYZ adds *of the nations* at 21:24; GOC variant rejected, which has *nation* rather than *dead* at 11:18;

See: 12, βλέπω (*blepo*, blep'-o) 1:11, 12; 3:18; 5:3, 4; 9:20; 11:9; 16:15; 17:8; 18:9; 22:8 (x2); SCR, STE at 6:1, 3, 5, 7; variants rejected;

Smoke: 12, καπνός (*kapnos*, kap-nos') 8:4; 9:2 (x3), 3, 17, 18; 14:11; 15:8; 18:9, 18; 19:3;

Spirit: 24, πνεῦμα (*pneuma*, pnyoo'-mah) as Holy Spirit, 1:4, 10; 2:7, 11,

17, 29; 3:1, 6, 13, 22; 4:2, 5; 5:6; 11:11; 14:13; 17:3; 19:10; 21:10; 22:17, plus 5 other uses of spirit at 11:8; 13:15; 16:13, 14; 18:2; BNT, BYZ, GNT, GOC, TIS, VST, WHO add spirit at 22:6, but holy required according to SCR, STE to make 28 with holy/saints;

Spirit: 12, πνεῦμα nominative singular, 2:7, 11, 17, 29; 3:6, 13, 22; 11:11; 13:15; 14:13; 19:10; 22:17;

Stone: 12, 8 λίθος (*lithos*, lee'-thos) 4:3; 17:4; 18:12, 16, 21; 21:11 (x2), 19; 1 λίθινος (*lithinos*, lith-ee'-nos) *of stone* adjective, 9:20; 1 ψηφίζω (*psephizo*, psay-fid'-zo) *count with pebbles*, 13:18; 2 ψῆφος (*psephos*, psay'-fos) *smooth stone*, 2:17; no variants;

Strong: 12, adjective ἰσχυρός (*ischuros*, is-khoo-ros'), verb ἰσχύω (ischuo, is-khoo'-o), strength, to be strong, 5:2, 12; 6:15; 7:12; 10:1; 12:8; 18:2, 8, 10, 21; 19:6, 18; SCR, STE missing at 6:15; variant rejected;

Throne: 48, θρόνος (*thronos*, thron'-os) 1:4; 2:13; 3:21 (x2); 4:2 (x2), 3, 4 (x3), 5 (x2), 6 (x3), 9, 10 (x2); 5:1, 6, 7, 11, 13; 6:16; 7:9, 10, 11 (x2), 15 (x2), 17; 8:3; 11:16 (x2); 12:5; 13:2; 14:3, 5; 16:10, 17; 19:4, 5; 20:4, 11, 12; 21:5; 22:1, 3; maintains 12 *before the throne of God* above; 2x24 if we follow BYZ, GOC at 11:16, SCR, STE at 14:5, and reject BNT, GNT, TIS, VST, WHO at 21:3;

Twelve: 24, 23 δώδεκα (*dodeka*, do'-dek-ah) 7:5 (x3), 6 (x3), 7 (x3), 8 (x3); 12:1; 21:12 (x3), 14 (x3), 16, 21 (x2), 22; 22:2; plus 1 twelfth, δωδέκατος (*dodekatos*, do-dek'-at-os) 21:20. Notice **12** repetitions in chapter 7, and **10** repetitions in chapter 21;

Waters: 12, ὕδωρ (*hudor*, hoo'-dore), genitive plural, 1:15; 7:17; 8:10, 11 (x2); 11:6; 14:2, 7; 16:4, 5; 17:1; 19:6;

Word Stems in Revelation

To our knowledge, Umberto Cassuto, in his commentaries published beginning in 1944, is the first to write about Hebraic meter found in word stems or roots in the Torah.[22] The 1987 edition of *In Search of the Biblical Order* focused on the number of adjacent words coordinated with particular subjects, and in the 2012 edition the scope widened to include metered repetition of nonadjacent words. There was no awareness of repetition in word stems until reading Cassuto's books in 2013. Cassuto's reasoning is rather obvious. There are no vowels in Hebrew; therefore repetition of consonants with various prefixes and suffixes associated with prepositions, pronouns, declensions, conjugations, etc., is an integral part of Hebraic repetition. Applying Cassuto's theory is how much of the repetition in Genesis and Exodus was located. The same approach was adapted to the New Testament Greek. Rather than word stems without vowels, the Greek stems are actually syllables. The rep-

---

[22] Cassuto, *Genesis: Part I*, p. 94; *Genesis: Part II*, p. 32; and *Exodus*, pp. 12, 32, 52, 75, 389, 392, 395, 441.

etition of syllables in Revelation makes a rather amazing display that may incorporate 4 or 5 words with the same syllable. There is a surprising amount of accuracy in these stems, perhaps because copyists were not influenced by whole words.

There are numerous stems that bridge different words to make lists of 7s, 10s, and 12s. The lists become the key to variant readings. They encompass so much data that their presence significantly improves the possibility of helping to reconstruct the original autograph based on internal evidence, and identifying which are the most accurate manuscripts. The placement of an asterisk (*) before and/or after the stems below indicates how the word search was conducted. Those familiar with Greek will be able to follow the accuracy of these lists. A few of the syllables below include a list of all the words containing the stem. An asterisk following the stem indicates the word stem that was searched on a computer.

ἀλλή* 7 6:4; 11:10; 18:4; 19:1; 3, 4, 6
  ἀλλήλους (6:4 BNT)
  ἀλλήλοις (11:10 BNT)
  ἄλλην (18:4 BNT)
  ἀλληλουϊά (19:1 BNT)
  ἀλληλουϊά (19:3 BNT)
  ἀλληλουϊά (19:4 BNT)
  ἀλληλουϊά, (19:6 BNT);

ἀνά* 20 only as prefix, not counting 3 ἀνά, plus variant at SCR, STE 5:4, which is also needed for 7 *to know* in Revelation;
βάλ 20 (if proper names *Balaam* and *Balak* are not included with verbs); 40 with following verb scan. /ἐβλ* *βάλ* *βεβλ* ἐβέβ* 2:10, 14 (x3) Βαλαάμ, Βαλὰκ, 22, 24; 3:2 ἀποβάλλειν BYZ, 5 περιβαλεῖται, 18 περιβάλῃ; 4:10; 6:13; 8:5, 7, 8; 11:2; 12:4, 9 (x3), 10, 12, 13, 15, 16; 14:16, 19 (x2); 16:9 ἐβλασφήμησαν, 11 ἐβλασφήμησαν, 21 ἐβλασφήμησαν; 18:19, 21; 19:8 περιβάληται, 20; 20:3, 9, 10, 14, 15; 22:8 ἔβλεψα;
πρῶ* 21 BNT, GNT, GOC, BYZ, TIS, VST, WHO;

πᾶς* πᾶν* 70 SCR, STE;
περὶ* 20 all but TIS;
παρ 10 follow SCR, STE, TIS, VST at 14:3, SCR, STE at 22:11, reject SCR, STE at 21:1;
Πεπ 10 1:15; 2:5; 3:2, 17, 18; 9:1; 11:11; 14:8; 18:3; 20:4; BYZ, SCR, STE missing at 11:11;
Ποδ 12 1:13, 15, 17; 2:18; 3:9; 10:1, 2; 11:11; 12:1; 13:2; 19:10; 22:8;
Πορ* 20 2:14, 20, 21; 9:21; 14:8; 17:1, 2, 4 (x2), 5, 15, 16; 18:3, 9, 12, 16; 19:2 (x2); 21:8; 22:15;
πυρ* 30 SCR, STE, GOC;
πότ* 14 6:10; 8:10; 9:14; 12:15 (x2), 16; 14:10; 16:4, 12, 19; 17:4; 18:6; 22:1, 2;
ῥήμ 7 SCR, STE;
λιμ* 7 SCR, STE, GOC;
ἐλάλ* 7 no variants;
λάλ 12 no variants;
εἰρ 30 BYZ replaces εἴρηκα at 7:14 with εἶπον (7:14 BYZ), GOC, SCR, STE add χείρ at 1:17, BYZ, GOC, SCR, STE, TIS misspell σάπφειρος at 21:19;
ἐγέν* 30 SCR, STE have γίνεται 8:1, BYZ missing ἐγένετο at 16:18; 1:9,

10, 18; 2:8; 4:2; 6:12 (x3); 8:1, 5, 7, 8, 11; 11:13 (x2), 15 (x2), 19; 12:7, 10; 16:2, 3, 4, 10, 18 (x4), 19; 18:2; **χάλ*** 10 no variant; *hail* 4, *burnished bronze* 2, *brass* 1, *horse's bridle* 1, *brass money* 1, *chalcedony* 1;
Θυμ* 14 no variant, 10 *wrath*, 4 *incense*;
Θυς 10 θυσιαστήριον 6:9; 8:3, 5; 9:13; 11:1; 14:18; 16:7; 17:2 ἐμεθύσθησαν; 21:20 ἀμέθυστος;
κέρ 14 10 *horn(s)* plus 1 *potter*, 3 *mix*;
Κρατ 20 no variants;
κατὰ* 24 in SCR, STE;
Κρι* 12 no variants; *judgment* 3, *judge* 8, *barley* 1 = 12; in context *barley* is a wordplay on *judgment*;
κριθῶν *barley* (6:6)
κρίνεις *judgment* (6:10)
κριθῆναι *judge* (11:18)
κρίσεως *judgment* (14:7)
κρίσεις *judge* (16:7)
κρίμα *judgment* (17:1)
κρίνας *judge* (18:8)
κρίσις *judgment* (18:10)
κρίμα *judgment* (18:20)
κρινεν *judge* (19:2)
κρίνει *judge* (19:11)
κρίμαν *judgment* noun (20:4);
Κατε* 10
κατεσφραγισμένον (5:1 BNT)
κατεκάη (x2) (8:7 SCR, STE)
κατέφαγον (10:10 BNT)
κατεσθίει (11:5 BNT)
κατεβλήθη (12:10 SCR, STE only)
κατέβη (12:12 BNT)
κατέπιεν (12:16 BNT)
καὶ κατέβη, κατέφαγεν (x2) (20:9 BNT);
Κρι 20 no variants;
οἶδ* 10 in SCR, STE;
μέσ 12 BNT, BYZ, GNT, GOC, TIS, VST, WHO;
Πλη 36 BNT, BYZ, GNT, GOC, TIS, VST, WHO;

δεῖ 36 BYZ, GOC, SCR, STE, TIS, VST, WHO;
Θερ 10 no variants;
ἐλεύθερος *free* (6:15 BNT)
ἐθεραπεύθη *heal* (13:3 BNT)
ἐθεραπεύθη *heal* (13:12 BNT)
ἐλευθέρους *free* (13:16 BNT)
θέρισον *reap* (14:15 BNT)
θερίσαι *reap* (14:15 BNT)
θερισμὸς *harvest* (14:15 BNT)
ἐθερίσθη *reap* (14:16 BNT)
ἐλευθέρων *free* (19:18 BNT)
θεραπείαν *heal* (22:2 BNT);
Ψυχ* 10 no variants;
μαρ 30 all except BYZ, which adds ἁμαρτωλοῖς at 21:8;
νόμ 10 law νόμος (*nomos*, nom'-os) (1 Cor. 9:19-23) verse 20 ἐγενόμην, νόμον, νόμον, νόμον, 21 ἀνόμοις, ἄνομος, ἄνομος, ἔννομος, ἀνόμους, 22 ἐγενόμην BYZ, GOC, SCR, STE;
ὑπο* 14 *by*, *under*, 6:8, 13; 9:18 (only SCR, STE); *below* 5:3, 13; 6:9; 12:1; *patience* 1:9; 2:2, 3, 19; 3:10; 13:10; 14:12;
τρί 30 according to SCR, STE, 1:14; 4:7; 6:5 (x2), 12; 8:7, 8, 9 (x2), 10 (x2), 11, 12 (x5), 13; 9:8 (x2), 15, 18 (x2); 11:14; 12:4; 14:9; 16:4, 13, 19; 21:19; SCR, STE missing at 8:7; variant accepted, thus 12 *thirds* τρίτος (*tritos*, tree'-tos);
τρε 10 (however BYZ missing at 12:6) 6:6; 9:9; 11:9, 11; 12:6, 14; 21:13 (x4);
Σημ* 20 Gospel of John Σημεῖον (*semeion*, say-mi'-on), σημαίνω (*semaino*, say-mah'-ee-no);
ὧδ* 12 BYZ, GOC, SCR, STE add at 14:12 (problem: 7 ὧδε if we add 14:12 in SCR, STE);
ὧδ looks like 40.

CHAPTER SIX
REPETITION: A CONTEMPORARY DEFINITION

The first chapter states that a presentation of the data will be followed by an explanation of the data. The reader who has progressed to this point in the book has viewed sufficient examples of New Testament Hebraic meter to become familiar with the genre. This chapter also serves as a bridge between the New Testament and Genesis. Two authors are selected for an explanation and definition of this repetition in the Bible—Dr. Diana Jill Kirby in this chapter, and Umberto Cassuto in Chapters Eight and Nine. After considerable research, the only book available that is dedicated to the study of repetition in the Bible is Kirby's dissertation, which limits the subject to Revelation. Thus, her book is the most comprehensive study of repetition in Revelation or any other book of the Bible. It should also be observed that this subject is rarely researched, because the premise of intentional repetition in the Bible runs counter to numerous higher critical theories on the origin of biblical texts. Committees or redactors do not create repetition in heptads, decads, and dodecads.

Kirby completed and published her doctoral dissertation on *Repetition in the Book of Revelation* at Catholic University of America in 2009. Located in Washington, D.C., the University's School of Theology and Religious Studies, with 45 full-time faculty members, is one of the largest schools of its kind in the United States.

A review of Kirby's thesis is important for this book because it:

1. Is the only book in print on repetition in Revelation.
2. Encompasses the entire range of repetition in Revelation, much of which is also found throughout the Bible.
3. Records the most comprehensive taxonomy (nomenclature) of repetition.
4. Analyzes the commentaries of important authors on repetition in Revelation.
5. Gives perspective on how this book relates to the broader range of repetition in the Bible.

The standard critical view is that most books of the Bible, beginning with Genesis, are not written by the names attached to the books, but are collections of oral traditions, myths, and stories that have been edited, rewritten, and redacted. For example, among many other conclusions, the *Jesus Seminar* (a group of 150 scholars meeting from 1985-2005) decided by vote that only 20% of the words attributed to Jesus were actually spoken by Him. It was followed by the *Jesus Project*, 2007-09, which concluded that there is no reliable data to support the existence of Jesus Christ. With this level of skepticism about the text, one would hardly look for metered repetition in the Bible. The presence of metered repetition in the text implies a single author for each book of the Bible.

In her dissertation, Kirby presents opposing views on recapitulation, a form of repetition which is the retelling of the same account. This is not the same as repetition that repeats words or phrases, which is a primary focus in her research. The accepted view of recapitulation and repetition in the text among many critics today is that they result from various sources being edited into one document. According to the *Handbook of Biblical Criticism*, "In the OT [Old Testament], doublets (or three- and fourfold parallels) are evidence of multiple traditions...."[1] The suggestion is that biblical redactors did a sloppy job compiling various traditions into the biblical narratives, and thus created repetition in the text. However, the first 5 chapters of *Repetition in the Bible* demonstrate that repeated phrases in the text are not the result of sloppy collation, but are, in fact, a highly developed linguistic genre. Kirby takes a major step away from the *sloppy collation theory*, and credits the repetition of words and phrases in Revelation to John's unique approach to apocalyptic literature. Kirby does not address repetition outside of Revelation, nor does she suggest that there are heptadic, decadal, or dodecadal phrases in Revelation or in any other ancient literature. The questions she investigates include, "Why is there repetition in Revelation?" and "What does it mean?"

Important Authors on Repetition in Revelation

Kirby reviews 6 commentaries that address repetition in Revelation:[2]

A Critical and Exegetical Commentary on the Revelation of St. John by R. H. Charles[3]

L'Apocalypse by M. E. Boismard[4]

---

[1] Richard N. Soulen and R. Kendall Soulen, *Handbook of Biblical Criticism*, 3d ed., revised and expanded, Westminster John Knox Press, Louisville, KY, 2001, p. 50.
[2] Kirby, pp. 9-60.
[3] R. H. Charles, *A Critical and Exegetical Commentary on the Revelation of St. John*, Scribner's, New York, 1920.
[4] M. E. Boismard, "'L'Apocalypse', ou 'les Apocalypses' de S. Jean," *Revue Biblique*, 56, 1949.

The Combat Myth in the Book of Revelation by Adela Yarbro Collins[5]
The Book of Revelation: Justice and Judgment by Elizabeth Schussler-Fiorenza[6]
Revelation, 3 vols., by David E. Aune[7]
The Book of Revelation by Gregory K. Beale[8]

Kirby lists the taxonomy, or nomenclature, of repetition in the Bible in 4 categories:

1. **Sound and Linguistic**: alliteration, morphological, lexical, and phrasal repetition
2. **Plot**: characterization, sequence of action repetition, type scenes and recapitulation
3. **Thematic**: motifs and themes
4. **Generic**: genre, form[9]

She reports, "Because there is so much repetition in Revelation, the challenge is not to find enough repetition to support a given structural form, theory of composition, or narrative recapitulation, but to discern the most likely candidates from among a rather significant number of proposals. The debate has become increasingly sophisticated over time but there is as yet no consensus."[10] Recapitulation in this context means a retelling of the same account in the same or altered form, such as the 3 accounts of creation in the beginning of Genesis, 2 histories of Israel in the Old Testament, or the 4 Gospels, a point Kirby does not address.

Kirby quotes Charles' view that repetition in Revelation is Semitic. He writes, "In the sections of chapter 8 [of Revelation] that do not deal with the first 4 trumpets, the word order is almost entirely Semitic, that is, the verb precedes the subject."[11] Yet, Charles ignores repetition in Genesis as a theoretical basis for repetition in Revelation. Applying the

---

[5] Adela Yarbro Collins, *The Combat Myth in the Book of Revelation*, Scholars Press, Missoula, MT, 1976.
[6] Elizabeth Schussler-Fiorenza, *The Book of Revelation: Justice and Judgment*, Fortress Press, Philadelphia, 1985.
[7] David E. Aune, *Revelation*, 3 vols., Word Biblical Commentary 52, Thomas Nelson, Nashville, 1997.
[8] Gregory K. Beale, *The Book of Revelation*, Eerdmans, Grand Rapids, MI, 1999.
[9] Meir Sternberg, *The Poetics of Biblical Narrative: Ideological Literature and the Drama of Reading*, Indiana University Press, Bloomington, 1985, p. 365, quoted by Kirby, p. 6.
[10] Kirby, p. 8.
[11] Charles, p. 221, quoted by Kirby, pp. 14-15.

same conclusion to Genesis would inevitably debunk J E P D and the Documentary Hypothesis, which will be discussed in Chapters Eight and Nine.

Charles' view that repetition indicates a single author is a position Kirby adopts throughout her book. On this issue Kirby is in agreement with Cassuto, of whom she appears to be unaware. Charles believed that the repetition of 7 beatitudes scattered across the entire text, as displayed in Chapter Five, is additional evidence that Revelation was written by a single author.[12] This is the same pattern of random heptadic phrases found in the first 4 chapters of this book.

However, Charles also believed that variations in the word order of repeated phrases in Revelation, such as: *to show his servants what must soon happen* (1:1, 22:6); *I was in the spirit* (1:10, 4:2); *I am the first and the last* (1:17, 22:18); and *and the whole earth* (3:10, 12:9, 16:14), are evidence that someone else expanded the repetition of these phrases in John's text.[13] Therefore, Charles held the rather strange view that John wrote Revelation, but variations in repeated phrases are the result of someone adding words to the text. He did not consider that variations in repeated phrases are evidence that John was following the Hebraic genre of concurrent symmetry and asymmetry initiated by Moses. In other words, Charles viewed repetition of identical phrases in Revelation as examples of mechanical pagan rote, and variations of these phrases as evidence of later editing. This writer's response is, "How did these supposed editors know which key phrases in John's text to repeat in the wrong order?" Pagan style is to maintain order, not change it. Later in this book it will be shown that the author of *The Apocryphon of John* was meticulous in copying exact phrases from Revelation in his Gnostic apocalypse.

Kirby observes that Charles was so convincing in his argument that instances of identical repetition in the text prove one man wrote the entire book of Revelation, that he persuaded subsequent authors to agree with him. "[Charles'] close attention to the repetition of John's grammatical peculiarities and other striking phrases or words, which convinced him that Revelation had only one author, has also convinced those who followed him of the same thing."[14]

---

[12] Kirby, pp. 17-18.
[13] Ibid., p. 19.
[14] Ibid., p. 22.

When reviewing Adela Yarbro Collins' *The Combat Myth in the Book of Revelation*, Kirby notes that Collins sees repetition in Revelation as a matter of style. Kirby writes, "Based upon her perception of a unity of style, Collins rejected the extensive use of sources in favor of intentional repetition as a matter of style on the part of a single author."[15] Notice that Collins concludes the repetition is intentional.

Collins reads the 2 great cycles in Revelation (1:9-11:19 and 12:1-22:5) as classical recapitulation, that is, a retelling of the same events.[16]

Collins believes that John was "…consciously attempting to be international by incorporating and fusing traditional elements from a variety of cultures…."[17] Here she appears to be projecting contemporary views on multiculturalism onto Revelation.

Collins notes that there are numbered visionary sequences featuring overt lexical repetition in the count of seals, trumpets, bowls, etc., and unnumbered visionary sequences separated by repeated phrases of perception, such as *and I saw* or *and I heard*, or a combination of the 2.[18] With further research Collins would have found the source for these phrases in Genesis.

Kirby summarizes Collins' view, stating, "…it is clear that the repetition of seven is a major and deliberate organizing principle in Revelation,"[19] which is entirely accurate, and which Cassuto proves has its source in Genesis. David E. Aune dissents from Collins' position on 3 points:[20]

1. Why would John combine unnumbered elements when he clearly numbers others?
2. Collins' claim of 7 unnumbered visions lacks clear delineation.
3. He objects to Collins' designation of "appendix" for the visions of Babylon (17:1-19:10) and the New Jerusalem (21:9-22:5) that do not fit in her structural scheme.

In reply to Aune: Collins is attempting to build a theory based on what she actually sees in the text, while Aune does not address the obvious integration of numbered and unnumbered sequences in Revelation as evidence of concurrent asymmetry and symmetry. Like Charles,

---

[15] Ibid., p. 26.
[16] Ibid., p. 30.
[17] Collins, p. 58, quoted by Kirby, p. 33.
[18] Kirby, pp. 34-35.
[19] Ibid., pp. 36-37.
[20] Ibid.

Aune holds the Bible to the criteria of pagan rote instead of Hebraic genre.

Kirby quotes Schussler-Fiorenza's interesting chiastic order for the structure of Revelation: "Following John's central intention to repeat the themes he wished to convey to his readers in order to emphasize them, Schussler-Fiorenza found the surface structure of Revelation to be concentric:

A		1:1-8	Epistolary opening
	B	1:9-3:22	The inaugural vision and the letter septet
		C 4:1-9:21; 11:15-19	The seven-sealed scroll
		D 10:1-15:4	The small prophetic scroll
		C' 15:1, 5-19:10	The seven-sealed scroll
	B'	19:11-22:9	The visions of judgment and salvation
A'		22:10-21	Epistolary closing"[21]

Kirby analyzes Schussler-Fiorenza, stating, "The ordering principles that inform the sub-structure of Revelation are likewise thematically rather than temporally ordered."[22] Cassuto makes a similar observation about Eastern deviation from historical sequence in the Pentateuch, as will be discussed in Chapter Eight. In other words, those who read Revelation as a single historical narrative about the future have misinterpreted the book.

Schussler-Fiorenza finds a conical spiral of intensity in Revelation, a characteristic of chiasm.[23] John Breck observes this same phenomenon in John 1 and 21, which he describes as a "rhetorical helix."[24]

Aune observes uneven concentration of repetition of certain words and phrases.[25] He blames this unevenness on different editions of Revelation penned by John. By contrast, this author's contention is that asymmetric genre is Mosaic style, not the result of editorial accidents. Western critics cannot imagine biblical writers thinking in terms of asymmetry. Collins wrestles with the same issue in her category of unnumbered elements, which is quite accurate. The phenomenon is that the Hebrew mind regularly integrated abstraction and order. In Chapter Five, the example of *every nation, tribe, people, and tongue* reordered 7 different ways is a classic example of the so-called "unevenness" de-

---

[21] Schussler-Fiorenza, p. 175, quoted by Kirby, p. 40.
[22] Kirby, p. 41.
[23] Ibid., p. 43.
[24] Breck, pp. 49-51.
[25] Kirby, p. 50.

scribed by Aune that Collins accepts as John's style. Collins is not afraid to say what she sees on the page. More examples from the Old Testament will be shown in Chapter Eight.

Kirby observes that Beale is more interested in the structure and recapitulation of repetition in Revelation than in its composition history. She writes,

> This follows from Beale's purpose, which is to "trace in a more trenchant manner the flow of thought within the paragraphs of Revelation and from paragraph to paragraph, to summarize the main points of paragraphs and larger segments, and especially, to analyze the use of the OT in the book and to trace the treatment in Jewish exegetical tradition of passages alluded to in Revelation and the bearing of the tradition on those references."[26]

On this point Beale's approach is similar to Cassuto, who sees metered phrases and words within Genesis' paragraphs, chapters, and sections, as will be seen in Chapter Eight.

Kirby says, "…a significant part of Beale's argument [is] that Revelation is composed in imitation of the Book of Daniel."[27] According to the paradigm of *every nation, people, tribe, and tongue* in Chapter Five, Beale's approach is more correct than he realizes.

As with the other authors, Kirby explains that Beale believes repetition in Revelation proves recapitulation and must therefore be the work of a single author. "This repetition at crucial narrative junctions and in major sections of the book makes Revelation 'a tightly woven, though complex literary unity.'"[28] Note that the same must be said of Genesis, thus further establishing that Genesis also is written by a single author. How could repetition in one book prove to be evidence of a single author and not prove the same thing in another book?

Beale observes, "…repeated sections that concern past, present, and future occur throughout the book."[29] The 5 central visions in Revelation are patterned after the 5 central visions of Daniel.[30] According to Kirby, "His key insight is that Revelation is composed in imitation of the prophetic literature in the OT, and, in particular, the Book of Daniel."[31]

---

[26] Beale, p. 3, quoted by Kirby, p. 54.
[27] Kirby, p. 55.
[28] Beale, p. 108, quoted by Kirby, pp. 56, 61.
[29] Beale, p. 141, quoted by Kirby, pp. 57-58.
[30] Kirby, p. 58.
[31] Ibid., p. 60.

In support of Beale, Chapters Four and Five of this book have already shown repetition of meter from Daniel found in the Gospel of John and Revelation, particularly in the example on page 146 of 7 repetitions of *every nation, language, tribe, and tongue*, and the example on pages 162-63 of 7 repetitions of *glory, honor, power*, etc., in Revelation. The variation within ordered lists is a paradigm for the variation in the order of sections of the entire Book of Revelation.

Forms of Repetition in the Book of Revelation

In her second chapter, titled *Forms of Repetition in the Book of Revelation*, Kirby expends considerable effort defining and categorizing the taxonomy of repetition in Revelation. Her encyclopedic approach is a valuable resource to the subject.[32] She writes,

> Repetition as a rhetorical device falls under style. Style is divided into two parts: diction (*lexis*) and synthesis. Diction deals with the choice of words. The "proper" word is the most precise word in common usage, but new, unusual, or even foreign words may be used to achieve a desired effect. Synthesis covers the way in which words are put together. Repetition is part of synthesis. To examine repetition as a rhetorical device is therefore to explore how an author uses repetition to persuade and entertain an audience.[33]

Here, Kirby gives the accepted purpose of repetition as defined by Western higher critics. She reasons that the Greeks and Romans wrote in a rhetorical style. Revelation was written 1,900 years ago in Greek; therefore, Revelation is following the rhetorical style of the Greeks and Romans. This is the standard academic view taught in universities. The challenge is for these academics to identify in any ancient Greek or Roman literature, the literary devices (not rhetorical devises) found in the previous 5 chapters of this book. Why would the author of Revelation use repetition to persuade and entertain his audience if he is spreading the repetition, let us say, of 7 different phrases over 21 chapters? This is a major oversight in Kirby's thesis, which reflects the erroneous view held by the advisors who signed her dissertation, and the entire academic community, some of whom Kirby quotes. They hold to a Darwinian-based assumption that the genre of repetition in the Bible originated audibly and not visually.[34] One can hardly imagine Moses or the Gospel

---

[32] Ibid., p. 68.
[33] Ibid., pp. 68-69.
[34] Ibid., p. 70.

writers employing repetition for the sake of entertainment, or intending to confuse their readers with abstract order as a rhetorical device. But then, why let facts interfere with the canonized holy writ of academia?

Some of the most significant research of Kirby's dissertation involves a lengthy and well-organized list of definitions and categories for repetition in Revelation. It is Kirby's taxonomy that inspired the title of this book. However, the list does not include the form of repetition displayed in the first 5 chapters of this book.

Kirby lists 5 categories of repetition, as identified by Paul J. Achtemeier:

> ***Inclusio,*** as it plays out in narrative intercalation [to insert, in this case words or phrases, at regular intervals];
> ***Anaphoric phrases*** [being a word or phrase that takes its reference from another word or phrase and especially from a preceding word or phrase], such as, "he said to them";
> ***Adjacent words***;
> ***Variations*** in either repeated word or sound patterns;
> ***Parallelism*** [in Revelation it would be Hebraic Parallelism];
> ***Contact*** (adjacent) repetition as compared to repetition over extended textual space.[35]

Achtemeier's term *contact* is equivalent to the concepts of *adjacent* or *contiguous* as they are used in this book. Kirby's concept of *intermittent repetition*, repetition over extended textual space, is the same as this author's use of the term *noncontiguous repetition*.[36]

Following Achtemeier's categories, Kirby displays her outline of repetition. Kirby also relies on the well-known 1,000-page tome, *Figures of Speech Used in the Bible* by Ethelbert Bullinger.[37]

I. Repetition at the Level of Sound and Sense
  1. Introduction to repetition at the level of sound and sense
  2. Examples of repetition at the level of sound and sense
     a. equivalent repetition
        1) contact repetition
        2) parenthetical repetition

---

[35] Paul J. Achtemeier, "*Omne Verbum Sonat*: The New Testament and the Oral Environment of Late Western Antiquity," *Journal of Biblical Literature*, Vol. 109, No. 1, 1990, pp. 3-27 (esp. p. 3), quoted by Kirby, pp. 71-72.
[36] Kirby, p. 72.
[37] Ethelbert William Bullinger, *Figures of Speech Used in the Bible*, reprint of Eyre and Spottiswoode, London, 1898, Baker Book House, Grand Rapids, MI, 1968.

3) intermittent repetition
  b. loose repetition
    1) phonological variation [paronomasia]
    2) inflectional variation
    3) lexical variation
    4) sensible variation
  c. semantic repetition across extended textual space
    1) single words
    2) formulae

III. Repetition at the Level of Plot[38]
  1. Introduction to repetition at the level of plot
  2. Examples of repetition at the level of plot
    a. Sequence of action repetition
    b. Repetition in characterization
      1) synonymous and antithetical repetition
      2) synonymous repetition
    c. Repetition in scenes
      1) syntactic repetition
      2) type scenes
      3) reversing scenes
      4) accumulation scenes

IV. Repetition at the Level of Theme and Motif
  1. Introduction to repetition at the level of theme and motif
  2. An example of the repetition of theme and motif

V. Repetition at the Level of Form and Genre
  1. Introduction to repetition at the level of form and genre
  2. Examples of reception of form and genre
    a. Repetition of form
      1) beatitudes
      2) liturgical forms
      3) vice lists[39]

Repeated Phrases in Revelation

According to Kirby's taxonomy, the hundreds of examples listed in this book should be narrowly labeled under the heading of "I. 2. c. semantic repetition across extended textual space." This includes "1) single words" and "2) formulae." *Formulae* is the same as *repeated phrases*. In the following quotation Kirby describes the numerous examples of phrases and words appearing in the previous 5 chapters. However, her definition does not recognize that these *single words* and

---

[38] For some reason there is no Roman Numeral II in Kirby's outline.
[39] Kirby, pp. 72-74.

formulae are also set in Hebraic meter, namely, heptads, decads, and dodecads.

Kirby defines *formulae* as follows:

> **Formulae.** In contrast with the previous section, which dealt with the repetition of single words across an extended length of narrative, this section addresses the repetition of longer lexical elements. *These elements, called formulae, also occur at irregular intervals across the entire text.*
>
> Two issues distinguish the repetition of formulae from the repetition of single words. The first is a consideration of the length of the repeated element. I have arbitrarily set the lower limit of the number of words for this study at four [Greek] words. I have included shorter expressions that seem striking, or otherwise likely to catch the attention of a listener or reader.[70] The second is the matter of verbatim and near verbatim repetition. I have included as instances of repetition those variations in which the changes are matters of inflection, word order, and the addition or deletion of words.[71]
>
> Finally, I have not attempted to capture every instance of the repetition of formulae in Revelation. Instead I have opted for a table showing fifteen examples and a second table laying out the possible changes in form.[72]

---

[70] In setting these criteria, I have loosely followed the work of Anderson, *Matthew's Narrative Web*, 23-25.

[71] Bauckham, *Climax of Prophecy*, 22-23, argues that those formulae used as structural markers remained unchanged. Formulae that change do so because of deliberate intent on John's part.

[72] Additional lists of formulae, some of which overlap, may be found in Swete (*Apocalypse*, xlii-xliv), Charles (*Revelation*, lxxxviii), and Bauckham (*Climax of Prophecy*, 23-29).[40]

Her 15 examples give some insight into how Kirby, and the numerous scholars she has researched on repetition in Revelation, view the data.

The academic community is not aware that much of the repetition cited by Kirby is set in Hebraic meter identified by Umberto Cassuto as heptads, decads, and dodecads 70 years earlier. Kirby also makes the

---

[40] Ibid., pp. 97-98. Italics in the first paragraph added for emphasis.

important observation that these examples of deliberate repetition encompass the entire length of the document at irregular intervals. Therefore, John's repetition of single words and phrases is not accidental.

Kirby cites 15 examples of formulae (repeated phrases), 6 of which are only 2 or 3 repetitions. She does not recognize that some phrases are set in Hebraic meter and others are not, so her list combines metered phrases (formulae) and non-metered phrases (formulae) in the same category. Here is another example of concurrent symmetry and asymmetry, or *unevenness* as she described it earlier. Seven of her 15 examples also appear in Chapter Five, as they are clearly set in Hebraic meter, as described below.[41] The first example includes 2 separate phrases that actually form 1 decad. It is difficult to recognize these metered phrases in the Greek text without a familiarity with Hebrew syntax.

1. Kirby states that the phrase *to show to his servants what must happen soon*, δεῖξαι τοῖς δούλοις αὐτοῦ ἃ δεῖ γενέσθαι ἐν τάχει, appears twice in Revelation 1:1 and 22:6, and *I come to you quickly* appears 4 times. However, the related phrase *behold I am coming quickly* actually repeats 10 times in Revelation.
2. Kirby lists the phrase *the word of God* 7 times, which was copied and placed in Chapter Five.
3. Kirby lists *the witness of Jesus Christ* 5 times, but she missed 2 more repetitions which total 7.
4. Kirby lists 8 occurrences of *the inhabitants of the earth*. There are actually 10 repetitions of this phrase.
5. Kirby claims *day and night* repeat 2 times in 4:8 and 14:11, but these 2 words actually repeat 7 times.
6. Kirby lists 7 repetitions of *the one who sits upon the throne*, but it is found 10 times with no variants.

When the repetitions she did not include are added to her data, the above 7 phrases repeat in Hebraic meter. According to Kirby's criteria, Chapter Five lists at least 25 more phrases set in Hebraic meter, repeating 7, 10, or 12 times. This does not include phrases with only 2 words, and the nearly 200 examples of single words and word stems at the end of Chapter Five.

Why is there such a discrepancy in the amount of data? Perhaps the constraints of Kirby's dissertation committee prevented her from taking a broader and historic view of repetition in the Bible. Kirby, like many of the writers she quotes, does not work with Hebrew, and:

---

[41] Ibid., pp. 98-99.

1. Does not recognize John is following Mosaic meter in Revelation;
2. Does not investigate similar repetition in Genesis;
3. Does not refer to the genre of Hebraic meter; and
4. Limits herself to repetition found only in Nestle-Aland's Greek text, which does not consider repetition a criterion for selecting the correct variant reading.

Yet, more important than the above, the primary concern is not Kirby's accuracy in locating repeated phrases. Rather, of greater importance is her stated goal to find repeated phrases in Revelation. In this she has clearly succeeded. Kirby's dissertation is the only known or available source for a definition of repetition in Revelation or any other book in the New Testament. Thus, she has rendered significant service to biblical research. She and the theological faculty that signed her dissertation have agreed that there is repetition in Revelation written by one author, which is an affirmation of this book's primary thesis. However, despite even greater evidence supporting the theory that books of the Old Testament, such as Genesis, were also each written by one author, the theological faculty and Kirby do not arrive at this conclusion.

Sternberg's Research Applied to Revelation

Although Kirby does not work directly with the Hebrew text, she draws on excellent research by Meir Sternberg, and applies it to Revelation. As stated earlier, this book only addresses a narrow range of repetition in the Bible. Sternberg, a noted Hebrew scholar, addresses numerous poetic Hebrew devices, including repetition. He covers a wide range of repetition from which Kirby develops much of her taxonomy. Particularly interesting is her application of Sternberg's categories of expansion, truncation, reordering, transformation, and substitution in repetition.[42] Kirby locates examples of repetition in Revelation that fit all 5 of Sternberg's categories, an achievement worthy of a doctorate.

Sternberg's example of *reordering* is the same category this book identifies as *asymmetry*; which Collins and Aune identify as *unevenness*; and which Cassuto identifies as *variation* and *diversification*. This will be discussed in Chapter Nine. Sternberg cites Cassuto more than a dozen times. He is well aware of Cassuto's research on repetition in the Pentateuch, but he does not reference Cassuto's observations of heptadic, decadal, or dodecadal meter in the Hebrew text. If he had, most likely Kirby would have arrived at much of the information in this book.

---
[42] Ibid., p. 100.

Sternberg has a high regard for the Hebrew Bible, and views many of the accounts as historical events. He writes:

> The Bible's verbal artistry, without precedent in literary history and unrivaled since, operates by passing off its art for artlessness, its sequential linkages and supra-sequential echoes for unadorned parataxis, its density of evocation for chronicle-like thinness and transparency.[43]

With this high view of the Scripture, Sternberg astutely observes that there is no explanation for the apparently spontaneous appearance of Mosaic genre in the midst of pagan culture. He writes, "...the Bible's poetics appears to have sprung full-blown. And if anything can account for such a radical break in aesthetics, this is I believe the coincident break with pagan metaphysics."[44]

Sternberg addresses a primary thesis of this book, namely, that the Septuagint does not translate the repetition found in the Masoretic Text. He offers no explanation for this oversight that will be addressed in Chapters Eight and Nine. "Insofar as the Samaritan and Septuagint reading follow a version independent of the Masoretic, they establish a poetics of their own, whose compulsive tidiness bespeaks a form of narrative neurosis."[45]

Cassuto repeatedly describes this *narrative neurosis* as the Septuagint's obsession to smooth out and paraphrase difficult Hebrew passages. This indicates the Septuagint translators and the Masoretes were working with the same text. Why would the Masoretes make the Hebrew more difficult?

Again Sternberg correctly recognizes the anomaly of intentional variation within repeated phrases, as was illustrated in the first 5 chapters, and identified as concurrent symmetry and asymmetry. "One must then recognize the principle of semantic variation in all its forms and degrees, from a near-equivalence to head-on collision and mutual incompatibility."[46]

The reader will find significant context for Sternberg's insights in the ensuing chapters, but these issues must be discussed at this time because of his influence on Kirby.

---

[43] Sternberg, p. 53.
[44] Ibid., p. 232.
[45] Ibid., pp. 373-74.
[46] Ibid., p. 387.

Sternberg confronts the same frustration this writer encountered, when he notes that there is nothing in the Bible that comments on the manner in which repetition is incorporated in the text. "In the absence of an overall binding norm, then, not even a single case of biblical repetition is self-explanatory."[47]

Sternberg is a brilliant writer. His book has a great deal to teach about the Hebrew text; he recognizes its aesthetic nature, and often adopts aesthetic terminology germane to the fine arts. Yet, he does not draw the aesthetic conclusions that such terminology necessarily implies. If one is going to talk about the text in terms of the visual arts, the elements of art must be present, observable, and justifiably subject to art criticism.

The Function of Repetition

Probably at the urging of an advisor, Kirby makes an effort to explain why there is repetition in Revelation, but her explanation has nothing to do with Moses, meter, or Hebrew tradition. Her list of reasons could easily have been borrowed from a contemporary course on creative writing, drama, or grocery-store tabloids.

Kirby lists 7 functions of repetition in Revelation.[48]
1. First Function: To Highlight or Draw Attention
2. Second Function: To Establish or Fix Something in the Mind of the Reader
3. Third Function: To Emphasize the Importance of Something
4. Fourth Function: To Create Expectations, Increasing Predictability, and Assent (Anticipation)
5. Fifth Function: To Cause Review and Assessment (Retrospection)
6. Sixth Function: To Unify Disparate Elements, Sometimes Creating a Background Pattern Against Which Other Elements Can Be Understood
7. Seventh Function: To Build Patterns of Association or Draw Contrasts

These 7 functions are well thought-out, and Kirby supplies examples that she believes support her views. These 7 functions also represent the opinions of a wide range of scholars, and demonstrate academia's skewed view of the biblical text. The first part of Kirby's 7th function, *To Build Patterns of Association*, is the most accurate, though

---
[47] Ibid.
[48] Kirby, pp. 148-76.

still inadequate. She has done excellent work in collating and organizing the available information on the subject, in addition to communicating her own insights. However, in comparison to repetition in the first 5 chapters of this book, Kirby's outlined taxonomy of repetition in Revelation does not highlight the importance of the presence of Hebraic meter in the text.

The entire genre of biblical repetition is rooted in Hebraic meter, not Roman or Greek culture. Greek and Roman rhetoric are as distant from the sacred Hebrew poetics as Egyptian tomb paintings are from the frescoes of the Sistine Chapel. Once the parameters of the genre were understood, hundreds of these patterns in repetitions of 7, 10, 12, and their multiples were found in Genesis, Exodus, the Gospels, and Revelation. One of the important aspects of Kirby's thorough research is that she reveals how little is actually known about repetition in the Bible. She also exposes the error of those who deny the existence of recapitulation. In this chapter, and particularly Chapters Eight and Nine, the reader is introduced to the fundamentals of Hebraic repetition identified 70 years ago by Umberto Cassuto.

Chapters Eight, Nine and Ten will demonstrate that the function of Hebraic meter is fundamental to:

1. Antediluvian number symbolism,
2. Prophetic and apocalyptic literary genre,
3. Old Testament ceremonial law,
4. Hebrew parallelism, including chiasm,
5. Manuscript authentication,
6. The division of sections, chapters, accounts, and paragraphs, and
7. Concurrent asymmetry and symmetry.

Randomly dispersing 10, 20, 40, or 70 phrases throughout 50 chapters of Genesis is hardly intended to entertain the reader. Nothing in Cicero reads like repetition in Revelation. In fact, these repetitions may have been purposely camouflaged and are not intended to draw the readers' attention, or they would have been identified millennia ago. Manuscript authentication was even more important to the ancients than it is in our day.

The exact meaning and purpose of repetition in the Bible is as yet unknown. These 7 functions were drawn from the observation of the biblical text, not external sources. Kirby's list actually separates repetition from its prophetic intent of Revelation. In other words, she does not state that repetition is the signet of divine communication.

Applying Aesthetic Hermeneutics to the Text

The elements of art are an integral part of writing, painting, sculpture, music, architecture, etc. For all of the marvelous nomenclature and categories she lists, Kirby does not address the aesthetic selection process in which anyone engages when intentionally choosing to repeat something.

In order to bridge the gap between Western literary criticism and ancient Hebraic literary tradition, this writer employed aesthetic hermeneutics. *Aesthetics* applies to the principles governing the creation and perception of art. *Hermeneutics* means rules of interpretation. Aesthetic hermeneutics views the arrangement of thoughts, words, and phrases as an art form. It interprets the shape of the text according to aesthetic analysis. Viewing repetition as a genre is a concept higher critics have borrowed from the fine arts. One is not going to find theologians writing about repetition in the Bible as a genre prior to the late 1800s. The word *genre* did not even exist prior to 1770. Kirby employs a number of aesthetic terms common to the fine arts in her taxonomy above, such as *genre, repetition, form, space, motif, sequence, contact, intermittent,* and *adjacent*. The goal of aesthetic hermeneutics is to view ancient biblical texts in the aesthetic terms that theologians are currently using, but are not actually applying according to their proper definitions. It is counterintuitive for Kirby to apply these terms exegetically without also applying them aesthetically, just as it is not reasonable to speak about music without addressing sound. If a work of art has a particular appearance, then let us not just talk about it. Let us see what it looks like, or stop describing it in visual terms.

Kirby describes the text as a work of art. No object or artifact can rise above its own existence and the criteria that created it, whether it is an engine block, a toy in a cereal box, or a Hebrew scroll. If it exists, its form must display aesthetic qualities. Such an approach begins with questions, such as: "What does it look like?" "Why does it look the way it does?" "How can it be reproduced?" These are all aesthetic choices. *Genre*, or less accurately, *style*, is paramount. Impressionists paint like Impressionists, or they would not be Impressionists, and so forth. When aesthetic analysis is applied to the text, genre is preeminent, and an object must be evaluated on its own terms. A painting is not an Impressionist painting because someone says it is, but because anyone can see that it is impressionistic.

This approach is an aesthetic appeal to the first law of identity. In logic, the law of identity is the first of the 3 classical laws of thought. It states that "each thing is the same with itself and different from another." By this it is meant that each thing (be it a universal or a particular) is composed of its own unique set of characteristic qualities or features, which the ancient Greeks called its essence. Consequently, things that have the same essence are the same thing, while things that have different essences are different things.[49]

Thus, when one applies a string of aesthetic terms to describe the biblical text, evaluation of the text must be unimpeded by a veil of predetermined higher critical rubrics. Are we allowed to say what we see, or only what others tell us we are supposed to see? Therefore, if the repetition in Genesis is the same as found in the Gospels and Revelation, it is the same repetition, the same essence, the same genre, the same aesthetic, and the same tradition, regardless of hallucinatory higher critics.

An example of enshrined academic myth can be found in the entrenched bias that for centuries kept Western Europe from viewing Stonehenge as a giant astronomical computer, which it is currently understood to be. In an article for London's paper *The Guardian*, Mike Pitts writes, "By interpreting Stonehenge as a giant prehistoric observatory, [Gerald] Hawkins' work re-assessed what had previously been seen as a primitive temple. The archaeological community was skeptical and his theories were criticized by such noted historians as Richard Atkinson, who denounced the book as being '...tendentious, arrogant, slipshod, and unconvincing."[50] The experts condemned Hawkins' findings out of hand based on canonized academic legalism. Those who disagree are crackpots and charlatans militating against established truth.

In the last 150 years biblical criticism was mainly directed by liberal German Lutherans and some Reformed scholars, who spun their wheels explaining why the text is written and rewritten the way it is – and in many cases, we might add, with extreme prejudice. If one hates the object being analyzed, then analyze something else. Why become an art critic, if one hates art?

A thing is what it is, which includes line, texture, color, form, value and design, or it could not exist. As much as critics object, the evidence

---

[49] "Two things are called one, when the definition which states the essence of one is indivisible from another definition which shows us the other (though in itself every definition is divisible)" (Aristotle's *Metaphysics*, Book VI, Part 4 (c), translated by W. D. Ross).

[50] M. Pitts, "Gerald Hawkins: Astronomer who claimed Stonehenge was a computer," *The Guardian*, London, July 24, 2003. http://www.theguardian.com/news/2003/jul/24/guardianobituaries.highereducation (7/2015).

shows that the biblical writers intended to incorporate Mosaic repetition in their texts, and hardly for the reasons dictated by contemporary Western literary criticism.

Repetition versus Nestle-Aland's Greek Text

There is a contradiction between Kirby's conclusion that repetition in Revelation is intentional, and her sole reliance on Nestle-Aland's Greek text. If the repetition is intentional, all variant readings that complete the metered repetition, including those not found in Nestle-Aland, should be considered as part of the original text. Kirby also does not present any data to support the notion that ancient copyists were aware that John's repetition was intentional. Therefore, apparently accidental variant readings that complete intentional repetition should be given more credence as the preferred reading. Otherwise, the repetition is unintentional and there is no purpose for Kirby to write her dissertation.

Of the 150 extant ancient manuscripts of Revelation published in the New Gregory and Hoskier Table of Manuscripts,[51] Nestle-Aland's Greek New Testament relies only on a minority of these manuscripts. Kirby claims there is intentional repetition in Revelation. However, she does not apply the implications of this intentionality as a hermeneutic that might challenge the accuracy of Nestle-Aland's Greek Text. Nestle-Aland does not recognize the importance of intentional repetition as a factor that might determine the selection of one variant reading over another. In other words, Nestle-Aland views repetition in the text as accidental. Hence, Kirby's data is limited to a minority of the ancient manuscripts, and her work is not representative of all the manuscripts that incorporate the repetition she claims John intentionally included in the text of Revelation. In this matter Kirby's methodology contradicts her own research by claiming that repetition is intentional, but drawing conclusions from Nestle-Aland's Greek text that regards repetition as unintentional. There is also the likely possibility that Kirby's advisors would not allow her to investigate any text but Nestle-Aland, the "Received Text" from German higher critics.

Kirby has made an important aesthetic observation about Revelation: namely that intentional repetition throughout Revelation indicates the hand of one author. The same must be said of Genesis. One is hardly going to find examples of early American reproductions in Ethan Allen

---

[51] Arthur L. Farstad and Zane C. Hodges, *The Greek New Testament According to the Majority Text*, Thomas Nelson, Nashville, 1982, p. xlv.

furniture stores without a source for this style. An objective reading of the Bible requires that the text be evaluated on the basis of its own aesthetic.

Kirby's book is highly recommended for anyone seeking to examine the scope of repetition in Revelation, and is worthy of being a textbook on the subject. She covers a much wider review of repetition in Revelation that is outside the scope of this book. Her taxonomy, alone, is worth reading, not to mention her examples. This book relied on Kirby's research and scholarship as a benchmark on which to evaluate the current study and definition of repetition in the Bible. Her work would receive wider recognition if it were not for the bias and incomprehension of the academic community.

For one who has taught graphic design to more than a thousand high school and university students, it is obvious to this author that repetition is an aesthetic choice. It is not possible for 2 artists to follow the same genre without both of them copying a third artist or one copying the other. Egyptian art doesn't look like Aztec art. It does not matter if an ancient Greek vase is discovered in Tunisia; it is still a Greek vase and not Carthaginian. Hebraic meter in Revelation can only have one source, namely the Pentateuch.

CHAPTER SEVEN
SONG OF SOLOMON: A PATTERN FOR JESUS IN REVELATION

Finding a correlation between the Book of Revelation and the Song of Solomon is unexpected, to say the least. Yet both books are visionary and symbolic. Song of Solomon, the most obscure book in the Old Testament, appears to be the source for Revelation's image of Christ. Luther made a heroic effort in his commentary to show the relevance of Song of Solomon[1] to the New Testament church. At the same time he questioned Revelation's canonicity, and didn't number its pages in his first translation of the Bible.[2]

Revelation Repeats the Shape of the Old Testament

As generations pass, the Book of Revelation continues to convince scholars that it offers a more profound application of the Old Testament than has been previously recognized. In many respects, Revelation reveals as much about the past as it does the future. For example, Revelation contains numerous references from the Old Testament that not only speak about the past as events in the future, but also repeat the same poetic forms. A comparison of Isaiah 22:22 and Revelation 3:7 illustrates the point.

Figure 1
    And the **key** of the house of **David** will I lay upon his shoulder;
        so he shall **open**,
            and none shall **shut**;
            and he shall **shut**,
        and none shall **open**. (Isa. 22:22)

Figure 2
    And to the angel of the church in Philadelphia write;
    These things saith
        he that is holy,
        he that is true,
        he that hath the **key** of **David**,
            he that **openeth**,

---

[1] *Luther's Works, Vol. 15, Ecclesiastes, Song of Solomon, Last Words of David, 2 Samuel 23:1-7*, Concordia Publishing House, St. Louis, 1972, pp. 191-264.
[2] R. C. H. Lenski, *The Interpretation of St. John's Revelation*, Wartburg Press, 1943, Augsburg Publishing House, Minneapolis, 1963, p. 14.

       and no man **shutteth**;
       and **shutteth**,
    and no man **openeth** (Rev. 3:7)

Notice in Figure 2 how John not only repeats the same information from Isaiah in Figure 1, but also repeats the same chiastic form in which Isaiah writes it. In other words, John associates form with meaning. Some Hebrew chiasms restate a series of events in reverse order, as seen in Figure 3.

Figure 3

    A he that openeth,
      B and no man shutteth;
      B' and shutteth,
    A' and no man openeth (Rev. 3:7c)

This is a simple chiasm: A open, B shut, B' shut, and A' open. As shown in Figure 4, in addition to following the same form, John adds a 3-part trinitarian introduction from Isaiah 22:22, which presents Jesus as God. The 4 lines (Figure 3) and the 3 lines (Figure 4) total 7.

Figure 4

    he that is holy,
    he that is true,
    he that hath the key of David (Rev. 3:7b)

Lest the reader be given the impression that John always repeats the form with the text, in Revelation 18:21b-23a, John combines 2 quotations from Jeremiah, and adds *the voice of harpers, and musicians, and of pipers, and trumpeters, shall be heard no more at all in thee; and no craftsman...shall be found no more in thee* (Figure 5). Notice the repetition of tetradic (4-part) cadence from Jeremiah 16:9 in the first line of Revelation 18:22. Also notice the duplication of hexadic (6-part) structure between Jeremiah 25:10 and the phrase *no more* in Revelation 18:21b-23a. In this context a hexad symbolizes deconstruction or un-creation, a chiastic event juxtaposed with Genesis 1. John describes Jeremiah's prophecy of the end of *mirth* and *gladness* by naming the *harpers, musicians, pipers,* and *trumpeters* who will be taken away from Babylon. How did this fisherman become such an observant poet?

Figure 5

    For thus saith the LORD of hosts, the God of Israel; Behold,
    I **will cause to cease** out of this place in your eyes,
    and in your days,
        the voice of **mirth**,

and the voice of **gladness**,
the voice of the **bridegroom**,
and the voice of the **bride**. (Jer. 16:9)

I will take from them
the voice of **mirth**,
and the voice of **gladness**,
the voice of the **bridegroom**,
and the voice of the **bride**,
the sound of the **millstones**,
and the light of the **candle**. (Jer. 25:10)

Thus with violence shall that great city Babylon be thrown down,
and shall be found **no more** at all.
And the voice of **harpers**, and **musicians**, and of **pipers**, and **trumpeters**,
shall be heard **no more** at all in thee;
and **no craftsman**, of whatsoever craft *he be*,
shall be found *no* **more** in thee;
and the *voice* of a **millstone**
shall be heard **no more** at all in thee;
And the light of a **candle**
shall shine **no more** at all in thee;
and the voice of the **bridegroom** and of the **bride**
shall be heard **no more** at all in thee (Rev. 18:21b-23a)

Another example of John's awareness of form in Old Testament structure is his incorporation of 7 cryptic lists from Daniel into Revelation, as discussed in Chapter Five. As shown in Figure 6, John copies and expands the 7 lists from Daniel into Revelation, as follows:

Figure 6

Rev. 5:9	Rev. 7:9	Rev. 10:11	Rev. 11:9	Rev. 13:7	Rev. 14:6	Rev. 17:15
tribe	nation	peoples	peoples	tribe	nation	peoples
language	tribes	nations	tribes	people	tribe	multitudes
people	peoples	languages	languages	language	language	nations
nation	languages	kings	nations	nation	people	languages
peoples	peoples	people	peoples	peoples	peoples	peoples
nations	nations	nation	nations	nations	nations	nations
languages	languages	language	languages	languages	languages	languages
Dan. 3:4	Dan. 3:7	Dan. 3:29	Dan. 4:1	Dan. 5:19	Dan. 6:25	Dan. 7:14

It should also be remembered that the Bible is not restricted as to word order. Cassuto writes, "...the fact that a given writer once uses the word-sequence *the heavens and the earth* does not exclude the possibility that another writer may also employ this order of words, which is assuredly not a unique character nor does it imply that the former is never permitted to reverse the word-order and say, *the earth and the heavens.*"[3] The change of order from symmetric in Daniel to asymmetric in Revelation shows John reordering Babylonian pagan rote with divine asymmetry. The nadir of Nebuchadnezzar's pagan culture is transformed by Jesus Christ into God's nations, peoples, tribes, and languages.

Song of Solomon and Revelation Employ Same Decadal Image

This writer has long regarded Luther's 1531 commentary on Song of Solomon as little more than Luther falling off the wagon of allegorical sobriety. Luther claims Song of Solomon is not a sensual pagan love poem, but that Solomon made the groom a symbol of Christ, and the bride a symbol of the church. Yes, it was a valiant effort, but seems to stretch the limits of textual support. Luther's closing words tell of his own doubts: "In this way I understand this book to be about Solomon's state. If I am wrong about this, this first effort deserves lenience. The musings of others have a much larger share of absurdity!"[4] His candor and insight are disarming. On the other hand, Revelation, written by the Apostle John, and 3 times longer than Song of Solomon, was not worthy of his exegetical heroics.

After searching the Bible for numerically-ordered lists, published in the 1987 and 2012 editions, Song of Solomon was the only book in the Bible that failed to reveal similar poetic forms found in every other book. This raised further doubts about Song of Solomon's canonicity; that is, until reading David A. Dorsey's, *The Literary Structure of the Old Testament.*[5] Dorsey makes the startling observation that there are 10 body parts listed in the description of the groom (Song of Solomon 5:11-16, Figure 7) and the bride (7:1-6, Figure 8). If this is true, it means there is verifiable Hebraic meter supporting the allegorical assumptions many have made about Song of Solomon. It also means that Luther could have found textual support for his opinion about Song of Solomon from, of all places, the Book of Revelation.

Although Dorsey discovered the 2 decadal (10-part) patterns, his book shows no awareness that they share the same symbolic meaning and form found in the 3 decadal descriptions of Christ in Revelation (Figure 9), as published in the 1987 and 2012[6] editions of *In Search of the Biblical Order.*

---

[3] Cassuto, *Genesis: Part I*, p. 98.
[4] *Luther's Works, Vol. 15*, p. 264.
[5] Dorsey, p. 208.
[6] Cascione, 2012, p. 99.

Upon reading Dorsey's book, the first goal was to verify his claim. After hours of review it was apparent that Dorsey was correct in his count, but did not show how Solomon isolates these lists from the text by bracketing them with identical phrases, as shown in Figures 7 and 8.

Figure 7
> I charge you, **O daughters of Jerusalem**,
> > if ye find my **beloved**, that ye tell him, that I *am* sick of love.
> 1. His **head** *is as* the most fine gold,
> 2. His **locks** *are* bushy, *and* black as a raven.
> 3. His **eyes** *are* as *the eyes* of doves by the rivers of waters,
>   washed with milk, *and* fitly set.
> 4. His **cheeks** *are* as a bed of spices, *as* sweet flowers:
> 5. His **lips** *like* lilies, dropping sweet smelling myrrh.
> 6. His **hands** *are as* gold rings set with the beryl:
> 7. His **belly** *is as* bright ivory overlaid *with* sapphires.
> 8. His **legs** *are as* pillars of marble, set upon sockets of fine gold:
> 9. His **countenance** *is* as Lebanon, excellent as the cedars.
> 10. His **mouth** *is* most sweet: yea, he *is* altogether lovely.
>
> This is my **beloved**, and this *is* my friend, **O daughters of Jerusalem**.
> (Song 5:8, 11-16 KJV)

This numbered list in Figure 7 is quoted verbatim from the KJV. Notice how Solomon sets off his list with an A B B' A' chiasm:

> A *O daughters of Jerusalem*,
> > B *my beloved*,
> > B' *my beloved*,
>
> A' *O daughters of Jerusalem*.

The list about the bride (7:1-6, Figure 8) has the same arrangement.

Figure 8
> **How beautiful** are
> 1. thy **feet** with shoes, O prince's daughter!
> 2. the joints of thy **thighs** *are* like jewels,
>   the work of the hands of a cunning workman.
> 3. Thy **navel** *is like* a round goblet, *which* wanteth not liquor:
> 4. thy **belly** *is like* an heap of wheat set about with lilies.
> 5. Thy two **breasts** *are* like two young roes *that are* twins.
> 6. Thy **neck** *is* as a tower of ivory;
> 7. thine **eyes** *like* the fishpools in Heshbon, by the gate of Bathrabbim:
> 8. thy **nose** *is* as the tower of Lebanon which looketh toward Damascus.
> 9. Thine **head** upon thee *is* like Carmel,
> 10. and the **hair** of thine head like purple; the king *is* held in the galleries.
>
> **How** [*beautiful*] and how pleasant art thou, O love, for delights!
> (Song 7:1-6 KJV)

Solomon frames the second list by beginning with the phrase *How beautiful*, and ending with the phrase *How beautiful and how pleasant*. Unlike the *King James Version*, which begins 7:6 with the phrase *How fair*, *New American Standard* correctly translates יָפָה (*yaphah*, yaw-faw') as *beautiful* in Song of Solomon because it is the same Hebrew word at the beginning of 7:1. Therefore, the list begins and ends with *How beautiful*. We might wonder how many women would appreciate being told their neck and nose look like towers, and their head looks like a mountain. It appears the reason for these unusual compliments is that Solomon is speaking about the church and describing the walls of Jerusalem, Mount Zion, and Mount Moriah.

In addition to 10 parts in each list, Dorsey points out similarities in terminology, with words such as *head*, *eyes*, *hair*, *belly*, and *ivory* used in both lists.[7] Dorsey astutely observes that the lists from Song of Solomon in Figures 7 and 8 are in reverse order. The groom's list begins with the head and the bride's list begins with the feet, which is another chiastic arrangement in itself. Revelation's 3 physical descriptions of Christ in Figure 9 likewise include decadal lists, with terms similar to those in Song of Solomon's lists.

Figure 9
1. one like unto the **Son of man**, clothed with a garment down to the foot,
2. and girt about the **paps** with a golden girdle.
3. His **head** and
4. his **hairs** were white like wool, as white as snow;
5. and his **eyes** were as a flame of fire;
6. And his **feet** like unto fine brass, as if they burned in a furnace;
7. and his **voice** as the sound of many waters.
8. And he had in his right **hand** seven stars:
9. and out of his **mouth** went a sharp two-edged sword:
10. and his **countenance** was as the sun shineth in his strength.

And when I saw him, I fell at his feet as dead.
And he laid his right hand upon me, saying unto me,
Fear not; I am the first and the last (Rev. 1:12-17)

1. And I saw another **mighty angel** come down from heaven,
2. **clothed** with a cloud:
3. and a rainbow was upon his **head**,
4. and his **face** was as it were the sun,
5. and his **feet** as pillars of fire:
6. And he had in his **hand** a little book open:
7. and he set his right **foot** upon the sea,

---

[7] Dorsey, p. 208.

8. and his left **foot** on the earth,
9. And cried with a loud **voice**, as when a lion roareth:
10. and when he had cried, seven thunders uttered their **voices**.
And when the seven thunders had uttered their voices, I was about to write:
and I heard a voice from heaven saying unto me,
Seal up those things which the seven thunders uttered,
and write them not. (Rev. 10:1-4)

1. His **eyes** were as a flame of fire,
2. and on his **head** were many crowns;
3. and he had a **name** written, that no man knew, but he himself.
4. And he was **clothed** with a vesture dipped in blood:
5. and his name is called The **Word of God**.
6. And the armies which were in heaven followed him upon **white horses**,
    clothed in fine linen, white and clean.
7. And out of his **mouth** goeth a sharp sword,
    that with it he should smite the nations:
8. and he shall **rule** them with a rod of iron:
9. and he treadeth the **winepress** of the fierceness and wrath of Almighty God.
10. And he hath on his vesture and on his **thigh** a name written,
    KING OF KINGS, AND LORD OF LORDS. (Rev. 19:12-16)

The 3 decadal lists from Revelation describe Christ as *the Son of Man*, *a Mighty Angel*, and *the Word of God*. The greatest similarity is between the description of the groom in Song of Solomon 5:11-16 and that of Christ in Revelation 1:13b-16. The other lists from Revelation, though in 10 parts, have less similarity.

The next goal was to check Mitchell's 1,300-page commentary on the Song of Solomon, published by Concordia Publishing House. Mitchell does not mention the number of body parts in the lists. However, he spends no less than 50 pages explaining how Song of Solomon 5:9-16 is about Christ, under the subheading *Christ Prefigured by the Lover: Human as His Bride, Exalted as Priest and King*.[8] With all this research, Mitchell is not able to find a direct quote from Song of Solomon in the New Testament.

The unity in subject and number of parts in these lists from Revelation and Song of Solomon does, in fact, support Luther's and Mitchell's interpretations. The table in Figure 10 displays the 2 lists about the groom and bride in Song of Solomon adjacent to the 3 lists about Christ in Revelation.

---

[8] Christopher Mitchell, *Concordia Commentary, The Song of Songs*, Concordia Publishing House, St. Louis, 2003, pp. 915-65.

Figure 10

head	Son of Man	feet	Mighty Angel	eyes-flame
locks	breast-girded	thighs	clothed-cloud	head-crown
eyes	head-wool	navel	rainbow-head	clothed-blood
cheeks	hair-snow	belly	countenance	Word of God
lips	eyes-flame	breasts	feet-fire	white horse
hands	feet-bronze	neck	hand-book	mouth-sword
belly	voice-waters	eyes	foot-sea	rule-iron rod
legs	hand-stars	nose	foot-earth	winepress-God
countenance	mouth-sword	head	voice-lion	winepress-wrath
mouth	countenance	hair	spoke-voices	thigh-name
Song 5:11-16	**Rev. 1:13b-16**	**Song 7:1-6**	**Rev. 10:1-4**	**Rev. 19:12-16**

Figure 11 rearranges the lists in Figure 10 in order to illustrate the repetition among the 5 lists. Similar terms, where possible, are placed in the same row.

Figure 11

head	head	head	head	head
locks	hair	hair	foot	rule
eyes	eyes	eyes	foot	eyes
legs	feet	thighs	feet	thigh
mouth	mouth	nose	voice	mouth
cheeks	Son of Man	breasts	Mighty Angel	Word of God
hands	hand	feet	hand	winepress
countenance	countenance	neck	countenance	winepress
belly	breast-girded	belly	clothed	clothed
lips	voice	navel	voices	white horse
Song 5:11-16	**Rev. 1:13b-16**	**Song 7:1-6**	**Rev. 10:1-4**	**Rev. 19:12-16**

Luther would have been amazed to learn that pattern analysis corroborates his allegorical approach to the symbolism about Christ and His church in Song of Solomon. His 62-page commentary by Concordia Publishing House is well worth reading.

According to all available sources there are no other 10-part lists in the Bible describing Christ or any other individual except the lists in Song of Solomon and Revelation. This example, along with those from Isaiah (Figures 1 and 2) and Daniel (Figure 6), clearly demonstrate that John repeats the words and meter from the Old Testament in Revelation. He obviously uses Solomon's symbolic description of the groom as a paradigm for his symbolic description of Christ. There is a self-evident match between 8 of the 10 words in Song of Solomon 5:11-16 and Revelation 1:13b-16. This means John regarded Song of Solomon as a canonical source, and Solomon's description about the groom is actually a description of Christ in the Old Testament. It also indicates a key factor that commentators have overlooked, namely, repeating the form or the genre is nearly as significant as repeating the words. Not only are the words the inspired word of God, the form is the inspired form of God.

Near the end of his 50-page discussion on Song of Solomon 5:9-16, Mitchell writes:

> This commentary believes that the depiction of Solomon in 5:9-16 may be viewed as a type of the vision of Christ on the mount of transfiguration (Mt 17:1-8 and parallels), when "his face shone like the sun" (Mt 17:2), "his garment became white as lightning" (Lk 9:29), and the Father said, "This is my Son my chosen one" (ἐκλελεγμένος, Lk 9:35; cf. "chosen" in Song 5:15). The Shulammite's frequent appellation for Solomon דּוֹדִי, "my lover" (e.g., 5:10; דּוֹד, "love," also occurs four times in 5:9), may well be part of the OT background for the designation of Jesus Christ as the "beloved," as in Eph 1:6 (ἠγαπημένῳ) and in the Father's word at Christ's Baptism and transfiguration (e.g. ἀγαπητός in Mat 3:17; 17:5; Mk 1:11; 9:7). Relevant too are the hymnic descriptions of Christ in passages such as Phil 2:5-11; Col 1:15-20; 1Tim 3:16 and the portraits of the exalted Christ in Revelation 1 (cf. Revelation 10). Even if there are few precise verbal parallels between Song 5:9-16 and these NT passages, the commonality is that the portraits depict a man (Solomon, Jesus) as possessing extraordinary qualities that connote divine authority and splendor.[9]

Mitchell references the list in Revelation 10, but makes little mention of the list with more similarities in Revelation 1. He offers some marvelous comparisons between the Song of Solomon and Christ in the New Testament, but he has to admit, "...there are few precise verbal parallels." He cannot find any quote from Song of Solomon in the New Testament on this subject. He has allusions, "may be(s)," "may well be(s)," "background," "hymnic descriptions," "portraits," "commonality," and "connotation," but no quotations.

Mitchell's study does not consider the possibility of counting the number of parts in the lists as shown in Figures 7-11, above. Each list is decadal.

Mitchell quotes Brighton's commentary on *The Book of Revelation*, which states that there are no lists about Christ in the Bible that are comparable to those found in Revelation.[10] However, Brighton does

---

[9] Ibid., p. 961.

[10] Louis Brighton, *Concordia Commentary, Revelation*, Concordia Publishing House, St. Louis, 1999, p 261.

not believe Revelation 10:1-4 is about Christ,[11] even though Mitchell attempts to make it appear as if he does.[12]

There is a debate among scholars about the identity of the Mighty Angel in Revelation 10. Brighton gives a lengthy discourse on why the angel is not Christ: "The probability, however, is the angel is not Jesus Christ himself but rather an angel appointed by God to act on behalf of the Lord Christ."[13] Lenski agrees.[14] However, Becker says the angel is Christ. He writes, "While we therefore cannot insist that this strong angel is the Lord Jesus, there is good biblical evidence for making this identification, and in our comments we will assume this is correct."[15] On the basis of pattern analysis in Figures 10 and 11, the Mighty Angel clearly is Christ.

Rarely do commentaries on Daniel, Song of Solomon, and Revelation offer any information on the obvious literary forms (as seen in Figures 1-6) found in Old Testament literature that John incorporates into Revelation. Authors such as David Dorsey, John Breck, Eyal Rav-Noy, Umberto Cassuto, James Jordon, Diana Kirby, Meir Sternberg, and others publish marvelous books on form and structure in the Bible. However, the thinking of some appears to be that if Revelation may not be canonical, cannot be used for doctrinal support, and may not be the word of God, then research on Revelation's unique structure need not draw their attention.

Most significant is that all of the lists contain symbolic decadal descriptions. This is not coincidental. Decadal rhythm is further internal evidence that Revelation and Song of Solomon are canonical. The definition of canonicity may one day be expanded to include the form in which the Bible is written. The study of God's word without consideration of the form is like contemplating a quart of milk without the container. Our faith is not in paper and ink, but without paper and ink there would not be any way to quote the source of our faith. The Bible itself references ink with paper or books 4 times, and pen or stylus 6 times. Not only does the Bible present a unique message, it has an equally unique way of presenting the message. There is no literature from the ancient world that communicates in the same manner as the Bible.

---

[11] Ibid., p. 277.
[12] Mitchell, p. 961.
[13] Brighton, p. 277.
[14] Lenski, *The Interpretation of St. John's Revelation*, p. 311.
[15] S. Becker, p. 156.

Mitchell sees *my beloved* in Song of Solomon as a reference to Christ. This may be true, but this phrase is also applied to other individuals more than a dozen times in the New Testament. However, if the first list in Song of Solomon is about Christ (Figure 7), the second list must be about the church (Figure 8). The second list begins with the phrase, *How beautiful are thy feet.* Here is a direct quote from Song of Solomon in the New Testament. It appears that Mitchell doesn't associate this phrase with "How beautiful are the feet of them that preach the gospel of peace, and bring glad tidings of good things..." (Romans 10:15); "How beautiful upon the mountains are the feet of him that bringeth good tidings!" (Isaiah 52:7); and "Behold, on the mountains the feet of him who brings good news, who announces peace!" (Nahum 1:15). Three verses in the Old Testament speak about *beautiful feet*, which appears just once in the New Testament. This is a more direct correlation than is found with the word *beloved*. Mitchell goes so far as to identify the bride's navel as a symbol of the cup holding wine for the Lord's Supper, and her stomach as a symbol of the bread of the Lord's Supper on the altar.[16] "Your navel is like a round goblet which never lacks mixed wine; your belly is like a heap of wheat fenced about with lilies" (Song 7:2 NASB).

Rather than the Sacrament, Paul explains the symbol of *beautiful feet* and its application as the feet of those who bring the Gospel. Identifying the correct literary form, such as a decadal list, is an important tool in explaining symbolic literature. It is also interesting to note that Solomon wrote about *beautiful feet* as a symbol before Isaiah and Nahum wrote about *beautiful feet* as a prophecy.

There is no direct reference in the Old or New Testament to the existence of meter in the text, as observed by Meir Sternberg in the previous chapter. Yet we see meticulously constructed patterns in the Old Testament repeated in the New Testament. Since nothing is said about them, or any other figure of speech in the Bible, they cannot be a matter of doctrine or confession of faith. These patterns are preserved in their original form simply by preserving the original text. The only words that give us a clue that patterns are related to events in the text are Christ's cryptic words to the apostles in Mark 8:18-21, and even here we cannot be certain that He is actually speaking about biblical number symbolism:

---

[16] Mitchell, p. 1097.

18 Having eyes, see ye not? and having ears, hear ye not? and do ye not remember?
19 When I brake the five loaves among five thousand, how many baskets full of fragments took ye up? They say unto him, Twelve.
20 And when the seven among four thousand, how many baskets full of fragments took ye up? And they said, Seven.
21 And he said unto them, How is it that ye do not understand? (Mark 8:18-21)

No church body has formulated a doctrinal position on the above text. And if they did, what would it be? On the other hand, there is no question that God is interested in maintaining visible patterns. Primary examples would be patterns in the descriptions of the 12 stones on the breast plate worn by Aaron, the priests' robes, rituals for temple worship, and design for the Tabernacle, the temple, the visionary temple in Ezekiel, and the New Jerusalem in Revelation.

Bullinger writes,

> We are told that both Moses and David ordered all things connected with the Tabernacle and Temple worship by direct revelation from God, and as a copy of things in the heavens, Heb. viii. 5; I Chron. xxviii. 12, 19. And the sevenfold phrase (in Exod. xl.) "as the Lord commanded Moses" witnesses to the Divine ordering of all. It was so with the twenty-four courses of priests in the earthly Temple; these were formed on the "pattern of things in the heavens."[17]

Bullinger could have gone on to mention that the 24 courses of priests established by David in 1 Chronicles 24:7-18 are a divine pattern described by John in his vision of the 24 elders around God's throne.

The phrase, *pattern of things in the heavens*, is a reference to Hebrews 8:5. The *New American Standard Bible* and *New International Version* usually translate the first word of the phrase as *model* or *plan*, but in the KJV *pattern* is preferred. If Hebrews 8:5, 1 Chronicles 28:12, 19, Exodus 25:9, and other verses teach that God gave Moses, David, Solomon, and Ezekiel a divine pattern modeled after the order of heaven, why should we not assume the same is true for the text? A divine pattern is necessarily a pattern from heaven.

Metered Phrases and Words in Song of Solomon

Dorsey's observations about Song of Solomon led this author to a reexamination of Hebraic meter in the text. The following is a brief

---

[17] Ethelbert William Bullinger, *Number in Scripture*, Eyre & Spottiswoode, London, 1894, p. 264.

selection of metered words and phrases in Song of Solomon. Notice that Solomon includes his name in the book 7 times. Song of Solomon 6:8 reads, "There are sixty queens and eighty concubines, and maidens without number," which totals 140, or twice 30 queens and twice 40 concubines, for a double 3-4 division. Some of Solomon's adaptation of Hebraic meter is more clever than that of other writers, such as in his heptadic use of *breasts* and decadal use of *beloved/love* in the lists below. This is similar to the use of *not erase* instead of *written* in Revelation 3:5, and *no night there* instead of *day* in Revelation 21:25, as seen in Chapter Five.

Daughters of Jerusalem 7 times in Song of Solomon
    O ye daughters of Jerusalem......... בְּנוֹת יְרוּשָׁלָ͏ִם (Song 1:5)
    O ye daughters of Jerusalem......... בְּנוֹת יְרוּשָׁלַ͏ִם (Song 2:7)
    O ye daughters of Jerusalem......... בְּנוֹת יְרוּשָׁלַ͏ִם (Song 3:5)
    For daughters of Jerusalem......... מִבְּנוֹת יְרוּשָׁלָ͏ִם (Song 3:10)
    O ye daughters of Jerusalem......... בְּנוֹת יְרוּשָׁלָ͏ִם (Song 5:8)
    O ye daughters of Jerusalem......... בְּנוֹת יְרוּשָׁלָ͏ִם (Song 5:16)
    O ye daughters of Jerusalem......... בְּנוֹת יְרוּשָׁלָ͏ִם (Song 8:4)

Beloved/Love: 40, דּוֹד (*dowd*, dode) or (shortened) דֹּד (*dod*, dode), *beloved*, 1:13, 14, 16; 2:3, 8, 9, 10, 16, 17; 4:16; 5:1, 2, 4, 5, 6 (x2), 8, 9 (x4), 10, 16; 6:1 (x2), 2, 3 (x2); 7:10, 11, 12, 14 (x2); 8:5, 14; *love*, 1:2, 4; 4:10 (x2); *mandrake/love apple*, דּוּדַי (*duwday*, doo-dah'-ee) contains word stem for *love*, 7:13;
Breasts: 7/8, שַׁד (*shad*, shad) 1:13; 4:5; 7:3, 7, 8; 8:1, 8, 10; *Breasts* repeats 8 times, but 8:8 says *no breasts*, therefore there are 7;
Eyes: 7, עַיִן (`*ayin*, ah'-yin) 1:15; 4:1, 9; 5:12; 6:5; 7:4; 8:10;
Lebanon: 7, לְבָנוֹן (*Lebanown*, leb-aw-nohn') 3:9; 4:8 (x2), 11, 15; 5:15; 7:4;
Mother: 7, אֵם (`*em*, ame) 1:6; 3:4, 11; 6:9; 8:1, 2, 5;
Sister: 7, אָחוֹת (`*achowth*, aw-khoth') 4:9, 10, 12; 5:1, 2; 8:8 (x2);
Solomon: 7, שְׁלֹמֹה (*Shelomoh*, shel-o-mo') 1:1, 5; 3:7, 9, 11; 8:11, 12;
My Soul: 7, נַפְשִׁי (*nepheshee*, neh-fesh-ay') 1:7; 3:1, 2, 3, 4; 5:6; 6:12;
Spices: 7, בֶּשֶׂם (*besem*, beh'-sem) 2:3; 4:13, 16; 6:11; 7:13; 8:11, 12;
Vineyard: 10, כֶּרֶם (*kerem*, keh'-rem) 1:6 (x2), 14; 2:15 (x2); 7:13; 8:11 (x2), 12; word stem in *Carmel*, כַּרְמֶל (*Karmel*, kar-mel') 7:6;
Wine: 7, יַיִן (*yayin*, yah'-yin) 1:2, 4; 4:10; 5:1; 7:2, 9; *mixed wine*, מֶזֶג (*mezeg*, meh'-zeg) 8:2.

Chapter Eight
Repetition in Genesis and Exodus

Genesis is the origin and the template of Hebraic repetition in the Bible, as displayed in the first 5 chapters of this book. In Chapter One the choice was made to present the data in the New Testament first, and explain its source, purpose, and configuration later. This chapter:

1. Analyzes the Hebraic genre of repetition in Genesis;
2. Gives a more detailed explanation of the methodology used to gather the data;
3. Presents theories on the purpose of this literary style; and
4. Addresses the implications of metered repetition in the Bible.

Chiasm: A Form of Repetition

The first and second editions of *In Search of the Biblical Order* viewed repetition in the Bible through the prism of Revelation. Eyal Rav-Noy's *Who Really Wrote the Bible?* was the first publication this writer encountered in 33 years of research that corroborated the existence of noncontiguous metered repetition in the Bible. Shortly after that, James B. Jordan introduced this writer to *The Literary Structure of the Old Testament* by David A. Dorsey, and *The Shape of Biblical Language* by John Breck. Both writers expound on chiasm in the Bible, which is also an important part of Rav-Noy's book on the Old Testament. Diana Jill Kirby's dissertation, *Repetition in the Book of Revelation*, left little doubt that Umberto Cassuto had found the same repetition in Genesis as published in his 1944 commentary. These writers were helpful in arriving at the conclusion that Revelation is actually the culmination of 1,600 years of Hebraic literary genre, and not a unique literary form in itself.

This book does not focus on chiasm, a form of Hebrew parallelism. However, the existence of chiasm confirms the biblical writers' intent to use repetition and meter in their texts. Chiasm intentionally doubles ordered lists of concepts. When preparing to write a chiasm, the writer must count out the order and number of key words or thoughts and then double them, usually in reverse order. Therefore, chiasm in itself is proof that numeric order is woven into the biblical text. Chiastic structure confirms the authenticity and accuracy of the biblical text, and negates the possibility that more than one writer is responsible for each book in the Bible. Surely a committee or a series of unknown redactors could not have rewritten, edited, or pieced together the biblical text without dismembering chiasms embedded in the text.

Just 2 examples of chiasm from the Gospel of John and Revelation will suffice. They are typical of hundreds of chiasms in the Old and New Testament. Chiastic structure is based on key words or thoughts that are repeated in the text, usually in an inverted order, such as A B C D C B A. Thus, the primary focus of the chiasm is in the middle and not the beginning or the end of the text. Hence, the Bible often engages in circular progression rather than linear reasoning, and readers arrive back at the place they began. Key words in the following example of chiasm are bolded. The word or thought in A is repeated in A', and so forth, until the reader arrives at the middle, which is the central thought of the text.

Chiasm in John 6:48-58
A (48): I am that **bread of life**.
  B (49): Your fathers did **eat manna** in the wilderness,
    and are dead.
    C (50a): **This is the bread which cometh down from heaven**,
      D (50b): that a man may **eat thereof**, and **not die**.
        E (51a): I am the **living** bread which came down from heaven:
          F (51b): **if any man eat** of this bread, he shall live for ever:
            G (51c): and the bread that I will give is **my flesh**,
              which I will give for the life of the world.
              H (52): The Jews therefore strove among themselves,
                saying, How can this man give us
                his flesh to eat?
                I (53): **Then Jesus said unto them, Verily, verily,**
                  I say unto you, Except ye eat the flesh
                  of the Son of man, and drink his blood,
                  ye have no life in you.
              H' (54): Whoso **eateth my flesh**, and drinketh my blood,
              hath eternal life; and I will raise him
              up at the last day.
            G' (55): For **my flesh** is meat indeed,
            and my blood is drink indeed.
          F' (56): **He that eateth** my flesh, and drinketh my blood,
          dwelleth in me, and I in him.
        E' (57): As the living Father hath sent me, and **I live** by the Father:
      D' (57c): so he that **eateth me**, even **he shall live** by me.
    C' (58a): **This is that bread which came down from heaven**:
  B' (58b): not as your fathers did **eat manna, and are dead**:
A' (58c): he that eateth of this **bread shall live for ever**.

Breck published the above example.[1] Hundreds of additional examples of longer chiasm, shorter chiasm, and various forms of chiasm could be reproduced from Rav-Noy, Dorsey, Breck, and many others. These verses were quoted from the *King James Version* because it follows the Greek more closely than most modern translations. The time and logic necessary to write in this fashion is beyond the patience and interest found in Western literary tradition, including that of the ancient Greeks and Romans.

Texts written in chiasm, at times quite lengthy, cannot be evaluated by the standards of Western literature. Nothing like this was encountered in 30 undergraduate semester hours of English literature classes surveying the works of Chaucer, Shakespeare, Bunyan, Milton, Samuel Johnson, Hawthorne, Coleridge, Byron, Shelley, Poe, Carlyle, Dickens, or Joyce. A student essay with John's redundancy would have been marked with red ink by the professor, who would have included a note about getting to the point. One can only imagine the professor's reaction were it explained that the main point was in the middle of the essay.

Breck published this chiasm from John, but seems to have been unaware that, as a single chiastic expression, it also contains at least 4 examples of Hebraic meter. Within the above chiasm there are 2 different Greek words for *eat* that repeat 10 times. The Greek word for *bread* repeats 7 times. *Flesh* or *blood* repeat 10 times, and the verb and noun for *life* or *live* repeats a total of 10 times. The same Hebrew genre that doubles key words and thoughts, repeating them in inverted order, also selects key words for Hebraic repetition.

> **Bread: 7**, ἄρτος (*artos*, ar'-tos) 6:48, 50, 51 (x3), 58 (x2);
> **Eat: 10**, φάγω (*phago*, fag'-o) from ἐσθίω (*esthio*, es'-thi-o) 6:49, 50, 51, 52, 53, 58; τρώγω (*trogo*, tro'-go) 6:54, 56, 57, 58;
> **Flesh/Blood: 10**, σάρξ (*sarx*, sarx) 6:51, 52, 53, 54, 55, 56; αἷμα (*haima*, hah'-ee-mah) 6:53, 54, 55, 56;
> **Life/Live: 10**, ζωή (*zoe*, dzo-ay') 6:40, 47, 48, 51, 53, 54; ζάω (*zao*, dzah'-o) 6:51 (x2), 57, 58.

The second example of chiasm is a different form that follows a pattern of A B C D A' B' C' D'. Instead of the second half being inverted, it follows the same order as the first half. Like the previous example, it is copied verbatim from the KJV. This chiasm was found when it was noticed that the text repeats the same thoughts. This is also called recapitulation. Phillip Giessler identified this form of chiasm as

---
[1] Breck, p. 181.

Stairlike Parallelism.[2] In this case the main point is in both the middle and the end of the text. Why *another angel* initiates the recapitulation of Christ's action in the second half is unknown. We can surmise it is related to the concept of witness, of which numerous examples are displayed in the second edition.[3] As Joseph tells Pharaoh, "And for that the dream was doubled unto Pharaoh twice; it is because the thing is established by God, and God will shortly bring it to pass" (Genesis 41:32).

Chiasm in Revelation 14:14-19A

A And I looked, and behold a **white cloud**, and upon the cloud *one* sat like unto the Son of man, having on his head a golden crown,
  B and in his hand **a sharp sickle**.
    C **And another angel came out** of the temple,
      D **crying with a loud voice** to him that sat on the cloud,
        E **Thrust in thy sickle,**
          F **and reap**: for the time is come for thee to reap;
            G **for the harvest of the earth is ripe**.
              H **And he that sat on the cloud thrust in his sickle on the earth**;
                I **and the earth was reaped.**

A' And another angel came out of the temple which is in **heaven**,
  B' he also having **a sharp sickle**.
    C' **And another angel came out** from the altar, which had power over fire;
      D' and **cried with a loud cry** to him that had the sharp sickle, saying,
        E' **Thrust in thy sharp sickle,**
          F' **and gather** the clusters of the vine of the earth;
            G' **for her grapes are fully ripe.**
              H' **And the angel thrust in his sickle into the earth,**
                I' **and gathered the vine of the earth,**

The above chiasm contains 7 repetitions of the Greek word for *sickle*:

Sickle: 7, δρέπανον (*drepanon*, drep'-an-on) Rev. 14:14, 15, 16, 17, 18 (x2), 19.

Moses wrote the first 5 books of the Bible more than 3,500 years ago. Chiasm in the Bible was not discovered until the 18th century by Bishop Robert Lowth of Oxford, who published his first book on the

---

[2] *God's Word to the Nations: New Evangelical Translation*, 3rd printing, Biblion Publishing, Cleveland, 1990, Appendix 12, pp. 562-63.
[3] Cascione, 2012, pp. 55-70.

subject in 1753.[4] It is only within the last 40 years that Lowth's observations, which were rejected by Rudolf Bultmann, have received limited acceptance.

Cassuto: A Primary Source for This Chapter

According to Eyal Rav-Noy, the existence of chiasm in the Pentateuch discredits the Documentary Hypothesis. Rav-Noy's recommendation to read the works of rabbinic scholar Umberto Cassuto led to an epiphany. Many of Cassuto's observations about Genesis parallel more than 35 years of research into Revelation. It was surprising to see the same metered repetition at opposite ends of the Bible. But who would think to study the structure of Revelation by reading Genesis? The key difference between Cassuto and this writer's approach to repetition is that Cassuto not only recorded noncontiguous lists of words and phrases in Genesis and Exodus, he recorded the repetition of word stems and entire phrases. He also identified repetition within individual paragraphs, accounts, chapters, and sections, an approach that proved highly successful in the 4 Gospels.

Whether one agrees or disagrees with his theology or conclusions, Cassuto is a knowledgeable and astute expounder of the Hebrew text. He identifies Hebraic meter in Genesis where it is far more difficult to locate than in Revelation, particularly without access to a computer.

Cassuto's research unintentionally confirms that the New Testament writers thought and wrote like Moses, and in many cases copied Moses. Thus, by permission of his publisher, this chapter quotes the following 4 volumes by Cassuto, in order to establish Moses as the source for all metered phrases in the Bible:

The Documentary Hypothesis and the Composition of the Pentateuch;
A Commentary on the Book of Genesis: Part I from Adam to Noah;
A Commentary on the Book of Genesis: Part II from Noah to Abraham; and
A Commentary on the Book of Exodus.

However, a thorough understanding of Cassuto's work demands that one read him directly. These volumes, totaling about 1,350 pages, were translated from their original Hebrew into English in the early 1960s. As an Orthodox Jew, Cassuto is convinced that God's word has eternal power. In the first sentence he writes: "THE PURPOSE of the

---

[4] Bishop Robert Lowth, *De Sacra Poesi Hebraeorem, Praelectiones Academicae Oxonii Habitae*, Oxford, Clarendon, 1753, translated into English as *Lectures on the Sacred Poetry of the Hebrews*, J. Johnson, London, 1787.

Torah in this section is to teach us that the whole world and all that it contains were created by the word of the One God, according to His will, which operates without restraint."[5]

The Documentary Hypothesis

Cassuto's primary goal was to defend the integrity of Mosaic authorship from attacks by the proponents of the Documentary Hypothesis. Briefly, the hypothesis asserts that, beginning in 1100 or 1000 B.C., 4 successive committees of writers, known as J E P D (Yahwist, Elohist, Priestly Code, and Deuteronomist), edited, rewrote, and expanded the Hebrew Bible until the time of Jeremiah and the Diaspora in 586 B.C. Cassuto lists a number of scholars who developed the Documentary Hypothesis, beginning with Witter in 1711, and culminating in the writings of Julius Wellhausen published in 1878, with a second edition in 1883.[6]

While numerous rebuttals against the Documentary Hypothesis appear in Cassuto's 3 commentaries, his series of 8 lectures, published as *The Documentary Hypothesis* in 1941, offers the most insightful and scholarly refutation of the hypothesis available in print. Relying on internal evidence, Cassuto consistently cites numerically-ordered repetition in the Hebrew text. His observations relegate the Documentary Hypothesis to the annals of German mythology. *And they shall turn away their ears from the truth, and shall be turned unto fables* (2 Timothy 4:4). It would not be possible for successive committees to edit the text without disturbing the Hebraic meter woven throughout the text. Hence, Cassuto's refutation of the J E P D compelled him to present the most astonishing array of Hebraic meter ever published, in order to establish the authenticity of Mosaic authorship and the biblical text. His research on Genesis and Exodus stands as a biblical hallmark.

University departments of Hebrew Studies around the globe have ignored or forgotten Cassuto's work, but their denial of Mosaic authorship does not change the facts. The age of computers and the proliferation of Hebrew and Greek Bible software make it inevitable that Cassuto will one day be recognized as one of the greatest Hebrew scholars of the 20th century, and perhaps the most innovative of all time. His heroic defense of the text is more significant than Cassuto himself may have realized.

---

[5] Cassuto, *Genesis: Part I*, p. 7.
[6] Umberto Cassuto, *The Documentary Hypothesis and the Composition of the Pentateuch*, Magnes Press, Jerusalem, 1941, translated by Israel Abrahams, Shalem Press, Jerusalem, 2006, pp. 11-14.

Cassuto on Heptadic Repetition

Cassuto takes the reader from the pinnacle of his remarkable discoveries, to his struggle to unravel biblical mysteries. He does not engage in prophecy, numerology, millennialism, Gematria, Notarikon, Kabala, allegory, mysticism, spiritualism, or speculation about the future, as so many others have done. Rather, he is a linguist and ancient Semitic language scholar whose interests lie in the plain meaning of the text. His years of employment as the Vatican archivist of Semitic scrolls gave him access to the most important collection in the world. Work on his catalogue was interrupted by the Nazis in 1938, and he fled to Jerusalem. His son Nathan was killed in a death camp, his daughter-in-law Anna Di Gioacchino was killed in the war for Israeli independence, and his grandson, Dr. Dave Cassuto, became Deputy Mayor of Jerusalem. Cassuto was also a linguistic genius who worked with Akkadian, Arabic, Aramaic, Babylonian, Greek, hieroglyphics, Hittite, Latin, Sumerian, Syriac, and Ugarit. He presents his understanding of *seven* in Genesis, the most commonly used number in the Bible, as a philosophical concept where the text and the numbers merge into one unified communication.

All Hebrew quotations in this chapter are from the Masoretic Text (found in Codex Leningradensis, as published in *Biblia Hebraica Stuttgartensia*, and identified in *BibleWorks 8* as WTT), or they are from Cassuto's writings. An examination of heptadic structure in Genesis and Exodus presents few references to variant readings, unless there is a comparison with the Greek Septuagint. The Dead Sea Scrolls suggest a limited number of corrections.

Cassuto writes most of his observations about repetition as he comments on a particular verse or paragraph in Genesis or Exodus. He locates heptads within a paragraph, a series of paragraphs, a chapter, or longer sections of the text. The reader has already observed the same distribution of repeated words and phrases in the 4 Gospels and Revelation. Cassuto's data published here has also been scanned for accuracy with the *BibleWorks 8* program. Limiting attention to Cassuto's research on heptadic, decadal, or dodecadal repetition does him a disservice by interrupting the continuity and depth of his writing. It also overlooks his remarkable insights into the text. Yet, he does present a formidable display of irrefutable evidence.

In every way imaginable, Cassuto demonstrates the repetition of 7 in the manner in which Moses wrote Genesis: 7 thoughts, 7 things, 7 phrases, 7 concepts, 7 events, 7 actions, multiples of 7, 7 periods of time,

7 descriptions, or 7 divisions. Moses sets the norm for sacred writing. He is named 36 times in the Gospels, and approximately 80 times in the entire New Testament. Moses' heptadic meter permeates every book in the Bible. Cassuto's research compels the Western mindset, obsessed with the majesty of its accumulated wisdom, to admit, "These people did not think in our terms." Therefore, the writing of the prophets should **not** be evaluated solely by the standards of Western literary criticism. The Bible should be assessed with an appreciation and a regard for its own literary conventions, rather than have a foreign set of standards and expectations imposed upon it.

Heptadic Repetition in the Creation Account

Cassuto addresses one of the most often-raised arguments for multiple authors of Genesis by explaining that it was Semitic practice to restate or repeat the same event or history. This practice extends into the New Testament with 4 Gospels. In the beginning of his Genesis commentary, Cassuto writes:

> As for the repetition of the story of man's creation, which is told both in the preceding [Genesis 1:1-2:3] and in the present section [Genesis 2:4-3:24], it should be noted that such duplications, although they may seem strange to those who are accustomed to the Hellenic process of thought, are not at all incongruous to the Semitic way of thinking. When the Torah made use of the two ancient poetic sagas, both of which describe man's creation—the one in brief, general outline, as an account of making of *one of the creatures* of the material world, and second at length and in detail, as the story of the creation of the *central being* of the moral world—it had no reason to refrain from duplicating the theme, since such repetition was consonant with the stylistic principle of presenting first a general statement and thereafter the detailed elaboration, which is commonly found not only in Biblical literature but also in the literary works of the rest of the ancient East.[7]

Cassuto's discussion of repetition in the Genesis creation accounts continues for many fascinating pages, with references from ancient Semitic cultures and quotations from 1,000-year-old sources. His range is encyclopedic.

Cassuto notes that the first verse in the Bible comprises exactly 7 Hebrew words, and the second verse consists of exactly 14 Hebrew

---

[7] Cassuto, *Genesis: Part I*, pp. 90-91.

words.[8] The chapter and verse numbers were added to the text many centuries after Moses, according to the natural flow, content, and rhythm of the text.

> In the beginning God created the heavens and the earth.
> 2 And the earth was without form, and void; and darkness was upon the face of the deep. And the Spirit of God moved upon the face of the waters. (Gen. 1:1-2 KJV)
>
> בְּרֵאשִׁית בָּרָא אֱלֹהִים אֵת הַשָּׁמַיִם וְאֵת הָאָרֶץ
> וְהָאָרֶץ הָיְתָה תֹהוּ וָבֹהוּ וְחֹשֶׁךְ עַל־פְּנֵי תְהוֹם וְרוּחַ אֱלֹהִים מְרַחֶפֶת (Gen. 1:1-2 WTT)

Coincidently, the first verse of Revelation, as divided by those who created the verse numbers, is 28 words.

Cassuto writes, "The structure of our section [Genesis 1:1-2:3] is based on a system of numerical harmony. Not only is the number seven fundamental to its main theme, but it also serves to determine many of its details."[9]

Cassuto lists a series of heptadic repetitions in the beginning of Genesis. He writes, "After the introductory verse (i 1), the section [Genesis 1:1-2:3] is divided into seven paragraphs, each of which appertains to one of the seven days."[10] John parallels the format of the 7 days of creation in Genesis with the 7 letters in the beginning of Revelation, which includes a number of references to Genesis 1-3.

> Each of the three nouns that occur in the first verse and express the basic concepts of the section [chapter 1:1-2:3], viz. *God* [אֱלֹהִים *'Elōhīm*], *heaven* [שָׁמַיִם *šāmayim*], *earth* [אֶרֶץ *'ereṣ*], are repeated in the section a given number of times that is a multiple of *seven*: thus the name of God occurs thirty-five times, that is five times seven (on the fact that the Divine Name, in one of its forms, occurs seventy times in the first four chapters, see below); earth is found twenty-one times, that is three times seven; similarly *heavens* (or *firmament*, רָקִיעַ *rāqīa'*) appears twenty-one times.[11]

There are 10 repetitions of God speaking in the first chapter of Genesis. The first 7 are commands, and the last 3 address the creation of man.

---

[8] Ibid., p. 14.
[9] Ibid., p. 12.
[10] Ibid., p. 13.
[11] Ibid., p. 14.

And God said 7 times concerning the world in Genesis
    And God said, Let there be light (Gen. 1:3)
    And God said, Let there be a firmament in the midst of the waters (Gen. 1:6)
    And God said, Let the waters under the heaven be gathered together
        unto one place (Gen. 1:9)
    And God said, Let the earth bring forth grass (Gen. 1:11)
    And God said, Let there be lights in the firmament of the heaven (Gen. 1:14)
    And God said, Let the waters bring forth abundantly the moving creature
        that hath life (Gen. 1:20)
    And God said, Let the earth bring forth the living creature
        after his kind (Gen. 1:24)

And God said 3 times concerning man in Genesis
    And God said, Let us make man in our image, after our likeness (Gen. 1:26)
    And God said unto them, Be fruitful, and multiply (Gen. 1:28)
    And God said, Behold, I have given you every herb bearing seed (Gen. 1:29)

Among many examples in the first section of Genesis (1:1-2:3), Cassuto lists:
    Beast or *living being* 7 times in the fifth and sixth paragraphs; Gen. 1:24 (x3), 25, 28, 30 (x2);
    Heavens and Firmament, 21 times in the first section; Gen. 1:1, 9, 14, 15, 17, 20, 26, 28, 30; 2:1; and Gen. 1:6, 7 (x3), 8, 14, 25, 17, 20;
    It was good 7 times in the chapter (see example below);
    Light and *day* 7 times in the first section; Gen. 1:5, 8, 13, 19, 23, 31; 2:3;
    Water 7 times in the second and third paragraphs; Gen. 1:6 (x3), 7 (x2), 9, 10;[12]

More examples in the first section not listed by Cassuto include:
    And there was 20 times in the first section; 1:3, 5 (x2), 6, 7, 8 (x2), 9, 11, 13 (x2), 15, 19 (x2), 23 (x2), 24, 30, 31 (x2);
    Day(s) 14 times in the first section; Gen. 1:5 (x2), 8, 13, 14 (x2), 16, 18, 19, 23, 31; 2:2 (x2), 3;
    Kind (species) 10 times in the first section; Gen. 1:11, 12 (x2), 21 (x2), 24 (x2), 25 (x3);
    The heavens 10 times in the first section; Gen. 1:1, 9, 14, 15, 17, 20, 26, 28, 30; 2:1;
    Waters 11, *Firmament* 9 = 20 times in the first section; Gen. 1:2, 6 (x3), 7 (x2), 9, 10, 20, 21, 22; and 1:6, 7 (x3), 8, 14, 15, 17, 20.

And God saw that it was good 7 times in Genesis
    And God saw the light, that *it was* good (Gen. 1:4)
    And God saw that *it was* good (Gen. 1:10)
    And God saw that *it was* good (Gen. 1:12)
    And God saw that *it was* good (Gen. 1:18)

---

[12] Ibid.

And God saw that *it was* good (Gen. 1:21)
And God saw that *it was* good (Gen. 1:25)
And God saw every thing that he had made, and, behold,
it was very good (Gen. 1:31)

(Gen. 1:4) וַיַּרְא אֱלֹהִים אֶת־הָאוֹר כִּי־טוֹב
(Gen. 1:10) וַיַּרְא אֱלֹהִים כִּי־טוֹב
(Gen. 1:12) וַיַּרְא אֱלֹהִים כִּי־טוֹב
(Gen. 1:18) וַיַּרְא אֱלֹהִים כִּי־טוֹב
(Gen. 1:21) וַיַּרְא אֱלֹהִים כִּי־טוֹב
(Gen. 1:25) וַיַּרְא אֱלֹהִים כִּי־טוֹב
(Gen. 1:31) וַיַּרְא אֱלֹהִים אֶת־כָּל־אֲשֶׁר עָשָׂה וְהִנֵּה־טוֹב מְאֹד

Notice how the first and seventh Hebrew lines, above, bracket the other five. It is interesting to note that the heptadic phrase, *and God saw that it was good*, does not line up with the 6 days of creation. The statement is not made on the second or the seventh day, but twice on the third day and the sixth day, though we are certain it was all good. As it often does, the Septuagint attempts to fill in the gaps and repeats the phrase 8 times. The Hebrew genre is not tied to a mechanical order, but can follow a syncopated rhythm, thus further demonstrating intentionality. Perhaps this was an effort to make the heptadic repetition less obvious. Intentional concurrent asymmetry and symmetry is a hallmark of Hebraic meter, an aesthetic that runs counter to the mechanical rote predominant in cultures that surrounded the Hebrews.

In the 7th paragraph (Genesis 2:1-3) Cassuto observes there are 35 words. In the middle of the paragraph there are 3 consecutive statements, each with 7 words, bolded below. The repetition is only in the Hebrew words.[13]

Thus the heavens and the earth were finished, and all the host of them.
And on the seventh day God ended his work which he had made;
and he rested on the seventh day from all his work which he had made.
And God blessed the seventh day, and sanctified it:
because that in it he had rested from all his work which God created and made.

וַיְכֻלּוּ הַשָּׁמַיִם וְהָאָרֶץ וְכָל־צְבָאָם׃
וַיְכַל אֱלֹהִים בַּיּוֹם הַשְּׁבִיעִי מְלַאכְתּוֹ אֲשֶׁר עָשָׂה
וַיִּשְׁבֹּת בַּיּוֹם הַשְּׁבִיעִי מִכָּל־מְלַאכְתּוֹ אֲשֶׁר עָשָׂה׃
וַיְבָרֶךְ אֱלֹהִים אֶת־יוֹם הַשְּׁבִיעִי וַיְקַדֵּשׁ אֹתוֹ
(Gen. 2:1-3) כִּי בוֹ שָׁבַת מִכָּל־מְלַאכְתּוֹ אֲשֶׁר־בָּרָא אֱלֹהִים לַעֲשׂוֹת׃ פ

---

[13] Ibid.

Cassuto summarizes the above lists by stating, "To suppose that all this is mere coincidence is not possible."[14] It is also hardly a coincidence that the repetition of the phrases *and God said* and *and God saw that it was good* follow the identical meter found in the 4 Gospels and Revelation. The goal here is to establish a unity of thought and literary paradigm unique to the Bible.

Heptadic Structure: An Eastern View of Order

In addition to refuting the Documentary Hypothesis, Cassuto also wanted to establish the difference between the ancient Greek and modern view of order versus the ancient Hebrew understanding of order. The following quotations explain that the Torah never intended to present an account or a text driven by the Western view of historical causes and linier thought, as follows:

> In this very analysis, and in the titles that I have given the parts, sections and paragraphs, there is to be found, as it were, a general commentary and an elucidation of the architectonic structure of the work. In annotating the details of the passages, I have endeavored to clarify the way in which the literary techniques of the ancient Orient have been applied, explaining the Eastern concept of 'order', which is unlike Greek and modern concepts, the principles underlying the sequence of the sections, the repetitions (of words, phrases, paragraphs or complete sections), the numerical symmetry, the symbolism of the numbers according to the sexagesimal and heptadic systems, and so forth.[15]

> In the first instance, we must bear in mind that the Torah does not seek to provide us with an objective itinerary of the journeying of the Israelites in the wilderness, nor does it record history for its own sake. Its aim is purely didactic, and for this purpose it utilizes the traditions that were current among the Israelites.[16]

> This [incorrect] expositional approach [an approach that interprets the Bible according to Greek aetiology or the search for historical causes] does not take into account the difference between the Semitic way of thinking and the Greek. The Hellene had a natural bent for abstract speculation, and conse-

---

[14] Ibid., p. 15.
[15] Cassuto, *Exodus*, p. 3.
[16] Ibid., p. 187.

quently he was eager to know the causes of things; this knowledge, unrelated to any practical purpose—knowledge for its own sake—he deemed of great importance. To the Semite, on the other hand, the desire for knowledge that has no practical value was mere dilettantism.[17]

The evidence speaks for itself. The higher critics are challenged to find similar repetition in Shakespeare, Goethe, Cicero, Plato, or editorials in *The New York Times*. They ignore fundamental differences between the Western and Hebrew style, and interpret the supposedly post-Neanderthal Torah with Darwinian hermeneutics. For them, the possibility that Western literature has devolved from superior ancient documents is incomprehensible.

Heptadic Unity in the Creation Accounts

Lowth was the first to write about chiasm, and Cassuto was the first to catalogue heptadic meter in Genesis. In keeping with his goal to demonstrate the unity of numerical symmetry in Genesis, and debunk the Documentary Hypothesis, Cassuto writes:

> I shall add only this one point here, that a clear indication of unity of the section [Genesis 2:4-3:24] (and at the same time of the connection between it and the preceding section [Genesis 1:1-2:3]) is to be seen in the numerical symmetry based on the number *seven* that we find in this section just as we encountered it in the story of creation. Here, too, the words that express the fundamental concepts of the passage recur a given number of times—*seven* times, or a multiple of *seven*. The name Eden occurs, together with קֶדֶם *qedhem* ['east'], seven times; the names אָדָם *'ādhām* ['Adam'] and אִישׁ *'īš* [both mean 'man'] appear altogether twenty-eight times, that is four times *seven*; the word אִשָּׁה *'iššā* ['woman'] and its synonyms עֵזֶר *'ēzer* ['helper'] and צֵלָע *ṣēla'* ['rib'] are used twenty-one times, that is three times *seven*; so, too, we find twenty-one examples of words derived from the root אָכַל *'akhal* ['eat'] (*seven* in the very paragraph describing the sin, iii 1-7). Likewise, the verb לָקַח *lāqaḥ* ['take'], which is given special emphasis in a number of verses—e.g., *because she was taken out of man; for out of it you were taken; from whence he was taken* (ii 23; iii 19, 23)—occurs, all told, *seven* times in the course of the section. And when I sought to break up the section into para-

---

[17] Cassuto, *Genesis: Part I*, p. 139.

> graphs according to the logical division of the contents, there naturally emerged *seven* paragraphs.[18]

In the above quotation, Cassuto summarizes his observations of heptadic repetition in the first 2 sections of Genesis, 1:1-2:3 and 2:4-3:24. He lists 8 examples of key words in heptadic meter that overlap the first and second sections or are located within the second section. His point is that it would not be possible for different committees, who were unaware of this meter, not to disrupt the cadence while editing the text. Therefore, we must have the original sacred text that was written by one, and only one, author. Today, different committees are fictitiously credited as the authors of different sections that were sandwiched together. The fallacy of this scheme, as Cassuto shows, is that some words and phrases set in Hebraic meter overlap adjacent sections. Hence, the same author must have written both sections. The translators of the Septuagint, beginning in 300 B.C., were obviously not aware of most of this Hebraic meter in the text because they did not translate the meter accurately. The only other possibility is that they purposely chose not to translate the meter because they felt it was untranslatable. Others will argue the preposterous theory that there were multiple editions of the Hebrew text, some with meter and others without meter. Obviously the apostles preferred the metered Hebrew to the unmetered Septuagint style. After another 100 pages, Cassuto writes the following excellent summary for the third section (Genesis 4:1-26), as follows:

> The names listed in Cain's family, counting from Adam and Eve to Naamah, total 14—twice times *seven*. Apart from the reminiscences occurring in the utterances of Lamech and Eve at the end of the section [section three, Gen. 4:1-26], Cain's name is mentioned fourteen times—twice *seven*—and Abel's name *seven* times, in the actual narration of events; so too, the word אָח *'āh* ['brother'], in relation to Cain and Abel, is used *seven* times in the section, and likewise the word שֵׁם *shēm* ['name'] is found there *seven* times. Also the nouns אֶרֶץ *'eres* ['earth'] שָׂדֶה *śādhe* ['field'] אֲדָמָה *'ădāmāh* ['ground'] appear, severally, in the combined compass of the two sections comprising the stories of the Garden of Eden and Cain and Abel (chapters 2-4), a given number of times conforming to the same patterns: אֶרֶץ *'eres* ['earth']—*seven* times; שָׂדֶה *śādhe* ['field']—*seven* times; אֲדָמָה *'ădāmāh* ['ground']—14 times;

---
[18] Ibid., p. 94.

that is, twice *seven*. Likewise the words גַּן *gan* ['garden'], עֵדֶן *'edhen* ['Eden'] and קֶדֶם *qedhem* ['east'] occur collectively in the two sections 21 times—thrice *seven*. The Divine names *YHWH* ['Lord'], *'Elōhim* ['God'] and *YHWH'Elôhim* ['Lord God'] are found, in the two sections taken together, 35 times—five times *seven*, the exact number of times that אֱלֹהִים *'Elōhim* ['God'] occurs in the story of Creation. Altogether the Divine names in the three sections [Gen. 1-4:26] number *seventy*. אֱלֹהִים *'lō-him* alone appears 40 times; ה׳ אֱלֹהִים *YHWH 'Elōhim* twenty times; ה׳ *YHWH* by itself ten times....And precisely at the seventieth reference it is solemnly announced: *At that time men began to call upon the name of the Lord*; with these words the section comes to an end. It is inconceivable that all this should be pure coincidence.[19]

In the above summary, Cassuto lists more than 10 heptadic patterns found in the third section of Genesis (Genesis 4:1-26), or that overlap into the previous section or sections. This is a considerable amount of repetition for just 26 verses. In the last 2 sentences above, he identifies 70 repetitions of אֱלֹהִים *'Elōhim* ['God'], ה׳ *YHWH* ['Lord'] and *YHWH'Elōhim* ['Lord God'] that span Genesis 1:1-4:26, a truly amazing discovery. Moses is counting words in heptadic repetition, and we have all of the words. This is an astonishing level of accuracy for 3,500 year-old text.

The fourth section of Genesis (Genesis 5:1-6:8) has more decadal repetition than heptadic. Concerning heptadic repetition in the fourth section, Cassuto writes:

> The word אָדָם *'ădām* ['Adam', 'man'] which expressed the principal theme of *the book of the history of Adam* [Gen. 5:1-6:8], occurs fourteen times in the section—twice times *seven*. The name אֱלֹהִים *'Elōhim* ['God'] is mentioned *seven* times; so, too, the synonymous verbs בָּרָא *bārā'* ['created'] and עָשָׂה *'ăsā* ['made'] appear jointly *seven* times.[20]

Cassuto states that according to rabbinic tradition, "All sevenths are favored...of the generations, the seventh is favoured."[21] Hence, Enoch, the seventh generation from Adam, walks with God. Notice how sevenness integrates literary structure, events, and history in the text.

---

[19] Ibid., p. 192.
[20] Ibid., p. 271.
[21] Ibid., p. 282.

Heptadic Repetition in the Flood

In his second volume on Genesis, Cassuto renumbers the divisions beginning with Genesis 6 – 9:17, which he identifies as the first section. He writes:

> In this section, just as in the preceding, numerical harmony is noticeable. The number *seven*, which, as we have seen, is the number of perfection, is mentioned explicitly in the text many times; periods of seven days (vii 4, 10; viii 10, 12); seven pairs of clean animals, and likewise of the birds of the air (vii 2-3); and if we count the number of times that God spoke to Noah, we shall find that they total exactly seven (vi 13; vii 1; viii 15; ix 1, 8, 12, 17). Similarly the second paragraph, in connection with the construction of the ark, the stem עשׂה *'āsā* ['made'] occurs seven times; in paragraphs 3-5, in regard to the entrance into the ark, the stem בוא *bō* ['come'] is found seven times; the verb שחת *šht*, ['corrupt'] which appears, as I have stated, at the beginning and the end of the section, is used in all seven times; in the last two paragraphs, with reference to the covenant, the word *covenant* occurs seven times; the word *water* is employed twenty-one times—seven times three; the word *flesh* appears fourteen times—seven times two; Noah's name, which occurs also in the continuation of the pericope thirty-five times—seven times five.[22]

In a remarkable paragraph, Cassuto explains that the number of 7 things, such as 7 days and 7 pairs of animals, is accompanied by repetitions of 7 in the text. Thus, the numbers and metered words become a unified communication, a hallmark of Mosaic genre. More will be said about Cassuto's frequent references to 7 as a *number of perfection* in Chapter Nine, a concept which lacks biblical support.

After the Flood, the word *covenant* is repeated 7 more times in Genesis 9:11-17. Cassuto writes, "The word *covenant*, which is common in the present and the preceding paragraphs and forms their principal theme, occurs seven times [Genesis 9:11-17]."[23]

In the following quotation, Cassuto places in capital letters the key words in the section in order to emphasize noncontiguous rhythm in the text. Hence, the concept of 7 is expressed throughout the text in contiguous lists, noncontiguous lists, actions, and numbers, in addition

---

[22] Cassuto, *Genesis: Part II*, p. 32.
[23] Ibid., pp. 134-35.

to other expressions of heptadic format. This is the manner in which Moses records sacred literature. In this context Cassuto comments: "If we dismember the section, this symmetry is destroyed."[24] Thus, the presence of meter in the text certifies that we possess the original words penned by Moses. Why should we not believe the author, who incorporated this heretofore unidentified meter in the text, when he says his name is Moses? The mythological committees known as J E P D are fantasies promulgated by scholars who despise and denigrate the text with extreme bias under the guise of academic inquiry. Moses was more intelligent than his critics imagined. A laptop computer with Bible software exposes their error.

Cassuto becomes so enthused about his findings that he diagrams the heptadic meter in the following quotation. This is further enhanced by dividing the text after the semicolons.

> Now here the word אֶרֶץ *'eres* ['earth', 'land'], which is the keyword in the section whose aim is to describe how the descendants of Noah spread abroad over the face of the whole earth, occurs fourteen times in the section [Genesis 9:19-11:9]—twice times *seven*. Furthermore, it occurs precisely *seven* times in the account of the distribution of Noah's offspring and their division and dispersal
> (ix 19: and from these the whole EARTH was peopled;
> x 5: From these the coastland peoples spread
> in their LANDS [same Hebrew word as earth];
> x 25: the EARTH was divided;
> x 32: and from these the nations spread abroad on the EARTH;
> xi 4: lest we be scattered abroad upon
> the face of the whole EARTH;
> xi 8: So the Lord scattered them abroad from there
> over the face of all the EARTH;
> xi 9: and from there the Lord scattered them abroad
> over the face of all the EARTH).
> If we dismember the section, this symmetry is destroyed.[25]

The following heptad was located by searching for the phrase *over the face of all the earth* that happens to repeat 3 times in the above quotation. This is the same format copied by Matthew, Mark, Luke, and John.

---

[24] Ibid., pp. 147, 248.
[25] Ibid., pp. 147, 248-49.

Over the face of all the earth 7 times in Genesis
Over the face of all the earth............	עַל־פְּנֵי כָל־הָאָרֶץ	(Gen. 1:29)
Over the face of all the earth............	עַל־פְּנֵי כָל־הָאָרֶץ	(Gen. 7:3)
Over the face of all the earth............	עַל־פְּנֵי כָל־הָאָרֶץ	(Gen. 8:9)
Over the face of all the earth............	עַל־פְּנֵי כָל־הָאָרֶץ	(Gen. 11:4)
Over the face of all the earth............	עַל־פְּנֵי כָל־הָאָרֶץ	(Gen. 11:8)
Over the face of all the earth............	עַל־פְּנֵי כָל־הָאָרֶץ	(Gen. 11:9)
Over all the face of the earth............	עַל כָּל־פְּנֵי הָאָרֶץ	(Gen. 41:56)

In this next quotation, Cassuto addresses heptadic repetition in genealogies, which is the subject of Chapter Ten.

> A note should possibly be added on the number of times that characteristic words [usually called keywords] occur in the chapter [Genesis 10:1-32]. The most typical word (וּ)בְנֵי (ū)bᵉnē ['(and) sons of'] is found *seven* times in the first part, vv. 1-7, and another *seven* in the last part, from v. 20 to the end; in all fourteen times. If we add to these the other terms that are characteristic of a genealogy, אֲבִי 'ăbhī ['the father of'], בָּנִים bānīm ['sons'], תּוֹלְדוֹת tōlᵉdhōth ['generations of', 'history of'] and the forms of the verb יָלַד yāladh ['born', 'beget'] we obtain twenty-eight—four times *seven*. Possibly this is not fortuitous. But certainly the sum total of the peoples and the detailed numbers of their families are not coincidental.[26]

Note Cassuto's words *four times seven* in reference to the *sum total of the peoples* in the last sentence. This is the exact same arrangement that John lists for the genealogies of the world in Revelation with the 7 lists of *nation, tribe, people, and language* for a total of 28. How did John know this? He most certainly did not learn it from the Septuagint. It is comments like the above that lead this writer to marvel at Cassuto's analysis of the text.

Rev. 5:9	Rev. 7:9	Rev. 10:11	Rev. 11:9	Rev. 13:7	Rev. 14:6	Rev. 17:15
tribe	nation	peoples	peoples	tribe	nation	peoples
language	tribes	nations	tribes	people	tribe	multitudes
people	peoples	languages	languages	language	language	nations
nation	languages	kings	nations	nation	people	languages
peoples	peoples	people	peoples	peoples	peoples	peoples
nations	nations	nation	nations	nations	nations	nations
languages	languages	language	languages	languages	languages	languages
Dan. 3:4	Dan. 3:7	Dan. 3:29	Dan. 4:1	Dan. 5:19	Dan. 6:25	Dan. 7:14

---

[26] Ibid., p. 179.

Like Cassuto's lists, these lists from Revelation are not contiguous, and are repeated randomly throughout Revelation and Daniel. These lists are separated by 6 centuries, 2 languages, and 2 authors. We have already seen noncontiguous lists in Genesis 1-2:3 interspersed within the ordered progression of the 7-day creation as the first example of concurrent asymmetry and symmetry in the Bible.

Heptadic Blessings Given to Abraham, Isaac, and Jacob

Cassuto identifies heptadic structure in the repetition of events. In total, as He did with Noah, God speaks 7 times with Abraham in Genesis, as follows:[27]

7 Divine Communications to Abraham
1. God speaks to Abram at Haran and gives seven blessings (Gen. 12:2-3)
2. God gives Promised Land to descendants (Gen. 12:7)
3. God gives more information about the Promised Land
    for descendants (Gen. 13:14-7)
4. God's covenant spoken in a dream predicts the acquisition
    of the Promised Land (Gen. 15)
5. God commands circumcision (Gen. 17)
6. God promises birth of son to Sarah within a year (Gen. 18)
7. God gives more promises to Abraham
    after the near sacrifice of Isaac (Gen. 22:16-18)

About 10 pages later, Cassuto points out the heptadic cadence in God blessing Abraham. This is the origin of the 7 blessings in Revelation, as seen in Chapter Five.

> The blessing bestowed by the Lord on Abraham in *vv*. 2-3 comprises seven expressions of benison, as we shall explain in detail later, and it is evident that the Bible intended by this formulation to set before us a form of blessing that was perfect in every respect. It should also be observed that each of the keywords in this section [Genesis 12:1-9]—*Abraham* and *land*—occurs, as usual, seven times in the section.[28]

Cassuto could have gone further. The 7 blessings precede the 7 promises shown above. After the last promise there is another heptadic statement from God. Therefore, the 7 promises begin with a heptad subset after the first promise, and end with a heptad subset after the last promise, for a total of 3 heptads on blessing according to the KJV, as follows:

---
[27] Ibid., pp. 296-97.
[28] Ibid., p. 306.

Seven Blessings on Abraham
    1. God's blessings on Abraham at Haran. (Gen. 12:2-3)
        1. And I will make of thee a great nation,
        2. and I will bless thee,
        3. and make thy name great;
        4. and thou shalt be a blessing:
        5. and I will bless them that bless thee,
        6. and curse him that curseth thee:
        7. and in thee shall all families of the earth be blessed.
    2. God promises to give the land to Abraham's descendants. (Gen. 12:7)
    3. God promises to give the land to Abraham's descendants. (Gen. 13:14-17)
    4. God promises to give the land to Abraham's descendants in 400 years. (Gen. 15)
    5. God makes a covenant to give the land through Sarah's son before circumcision. (Gen. 17)
    6. God promises a son to Sarah in one year. (Gen. 18)
    7. God blesses Abraham and makes him a great nation. (Gen. 22:16-18)
        1. And said, By myself have I sworn, saith the LORD,
        2. for because thou hast done this thing,
        3. and hast not withheld thy son, thine only son:
        4. That in blessing I will bless thee,
        5. and in multiplying I will multiply thy seed as the stars of the heaven, and as the sand which is upon the sea shore;
        6. and thy seed shall possess the gate of his enemies;
        7. And in thy seed shall all the nations of the earth be blessed; because thou hast obeyed my voice.

Cassuto observes that Isaac and Jacob also receive heptadic blessings similar to Abraham's, as follows:

> Similarly we find seven expressions of *benison* in the benedictions bestowed upon Isaac and Jacob. To Isaac God said (Gen. xxvi 3-4; here, too, the verbs, which signify future actions, have to be counted)....[29]

Seven Blessings on Isaac
    Sojourn in this land,
    1. **and** I will be with thee,
    2. **and** will bless thee;
    3. **and** unto thee, and unto thy seed, I will give all these countries,
    4. **and** I will perform the oath which I sware unto Abraham thy father;
    5. **And** I will make thy seed to multiply as stars of heaven,
    6. **and** will give unto thy seed all these countries;
    7. **and** in thy seed shall all nations of earth be **blessed**; (Gen. 26:3-4 KJV)

---

[29] Ibid., pp. 312-13.

Seven Blessings on Jacob
1. Therefore God **give** thee
    of the dew of heaven,
    and of the fatness of the earth,
    and plenty of corn and wine:
2. Let people **serve** thee,
3. and nations **bow** down to thee:
4. **be lord over** thy brethren,
5. and let thy mother's sons **bow** down to thee:
6. **cursed** *be* every one that curseth thee,
7. and **blessed** *be* he that blesseth thee. (Gen. 27:28-29 KJV)

Cassuto concludes:
> This is certainly no coincidence, but a preconceived scheme; it follows that all the conjectures that have been advanced [by advocates of the Documentary Hypothesis] regarding the division of these blessings among the sources and the assignment of some of them to one source and of others to another are incorrect.[30]

Jacob also receives a second heptadic blessing not mentioned by Cassuto, found in the next chapter of Genesis. The first blessing on Jacob was from Isaac, and the following blessing on Jacob was from God. Notice the 7 verbs bolded in the text.

Seven Blessings on Jacob
1. And God Almighty **bless** thee,
2. and **make** thee fruitful,
3. and **multiply** thee,
4. and that you may **be a multitude** of people;
5. And **give** thee the blessing of Abraham, to thee, and to thy seed with thee;
6. that thou mayest **inherit** land wherein you are a stranger,
7. which God **gave** unto Abraham. (Gen. 28:3-4)

The following is another example of heptadic blessing that was found with the aid of a computer, something unavailable to Cassuto. The precision of the Hebrew is remarkable. Again we see that Matthew, Mark, Luke, and John are not following Q, but Moses. The higher critics had to invent a myth to replace the reality they discarded. This is the same repetition for blessing found in Revelation and the Gospel of Mark.

Blessed them 7 times in Genesis
    And God blessed them................ וַיְבָרֶךְ אֹתָם אֱלֹהִים (Gen. 1:22)
    And God blessed them................ וַיְבָרֶךְ אֹתָם אֱלֹהִים (Gen. 1:28)

---
[30] Ibid., p. 313.

And He blessed them	וַיְבָרֶךְ אֹתָם	(Gen. 5:2)
And he blessed them	וַיְבָרֶךְ אֶתְהֶם	(Gen. 31:55)
And he blessed them	וַיְבָרְכֵם	(Gen. 48:20)
And he blessed them	וַיְבָרֶךְ אוֹתָם	(Gen. 49:28)
he blessed them	בֵּרַךְ אֹתָם	(Gen. 49:28)

In the last section (Genesis 13:5-18), on which he comments the day before his death in Jerusalem on December 19, 1951, Cassuto writes:

> The focal point of the section [Genesis 13:5-18] is the corroboration of the promise regarding the acquisitions of the land, which is given to Abram in vv. 14-17 with an elaboration of detail that is certainly not accidental. Similarly, we cannot regard as fortuitous the fact that the word אֶרֶץ *'eres* ['land', 'earth'] occurs seven times in this section, which is a customary distinction for the key-word of the section in the stylistic technique that I have discussed so often in the course of my annotations.[31]

Heptadic Events in Genesis

Cassuto points out that there are 7 manifestations of God in dreams or visions in Genesis.

7 Visions of God in Genesis: [32]

1. After these things the word of the LORD came unto Abram in a vision, (Gen. 15:1)
2. But God came to Abimelech in a dream by night, (Gen. 20:3)
3. And the LORD appeared unto him [Isaac], (Gen. 26:2)
4. And he dreamed, and behold a ladder set up on the earth, (Gen. 28:12)
5. that I [Jacob] lifted up mine eyes, and saw in a dream, (Gen. 31:10)
6. And God came to Laban the Aramean in a dream of the night, (Gen. 31:24)
7. And God spake unto Israel in the visions of the night, and said, Jacob, Jacob. And he said, Here *am* I. (Gen. 46:2)

There are also 3 sets of double dreams without God mentioned in the dreams: 2 given to Joseph, 1 each to the Baker and the Cup Bearer, and 2 given to Pharaoh. Hence, there are 7 dreams or visions with God speaking, and 3 more double dreams in Genesis, for a 7-3 division. Pharaoh's vision of 7 fat cattle consumed by 7 thin cattle, and 7 full heads of grain consumed by 7 thin heads of grain, resulting in 7 years of plenty and 7 years of famine, is filled with 7s. The Hebrew word for 7, שֶׁבַע (*sheba`*, sheh'-bah), is repeated 50 times in Genesis 5:7, 25, 31; 11:21;

---

[31] Ibid., pp. 367-68.
[32] Cassuto, *The Documentary Hypothesis*, pp. 72-74.

21:14, 28, 29, 30, 31, 32, 33; 22:19 (x2); 26:23, 33; 28:10; 29:18, 20, 27 (x2), 28, 30; 33:3; 37:2; 41:2, 3, 4, 5, 6, 7, 18, 19, 20, 22, 23, 24, 26 (x3), 27 (x2), 29, 30, 48, 53, 54; 46:1, 5; 47:28 (x2). To confirm the data, all one need do is to type these 3 Hebrew letters and search the entire book of Genesis, and the answer is 50 repetitions. It is really quite remarkable. Was it J, E, P, or D who supposedly made sure there were 50 repetitions that were not disturbed by the 3 other committees, and who devised it so that no one knew they were in the text until the advent of computers? No translation in Greek, Latin, or English contains this exact number. It is only in the Hebrew.

Heptadic Phrases in Genesis
The Children of Israel / That Creeps on the Earth / Over the Earth / The Land of Goshen / And Called His Name / The House of My Father / Seven Years / To My Lord

Cassuto was unaware of the following 20 examples of phrases from Genesis set in heptadic meter. As stated earlier, Cassuto identified the first example. These additional heptadic phrases were found with the aid of a computer. Likely there are more to be discovered. Each one of them establishes the format that is followed by Matthew, Mark, Luke, and John, and John's Revelation. Without a doubt, the apostles considered themselves biblical writers in the tradition of Moses, and the Gospels are thoroughly Hebrew documents written in Greek.

The children of Israel 7 times in Genesis
    The children of Israel............... בְּנֵי־יִשְׂרָאֵל (Gen. 32:32)
    Over the children of Israel................. לִבְנֵי יִשְׂרָאֵל (Gen. 36:31)
    The children of Israel............... בְּנֵי יִשְׂרָאֵל (Gen. 42:5)
    The children of Israel............... בְּנֵי יִשְׂרָאֵל (Gen. 45:21)
    The children of Israel............... בְנֵי־יִשְׂרָאֵל (Gen. 46:5)
    The children of Israel............... בְּנֵי־יִשְׂרָאֵל (Gen. 46:8)
    The children of Israel............... בְּנֵי יִשְׂרָאֵל (Gen. 50:25)

That creeps on the earth 7 times in Genesis
    That creeps on the earth.......... הָרֹמֵשׂ עַל־הָאָרֶץ (Gen. 1:26)
    That creeps on the earth.......... הָרֹמֶשֶׂת עַל־הָאָרֶץ (Gen. 1:28)
    That creeps on the earth.......... רוֹמֵשׂ עַל־הָאָרֶץ (Gen. 1:30)
    That creeps on the earth.......... הָרֹמֵשׂ עַל־הָאָרֶץ (Gen. 7:14)
    That creeps on the earth.......... הָרֹמֵשׂ עַל־הָאָרֶץ (Gen. 7:21)
    That creeps on the earth.......... הָרֹמֵשׂ עַל־הָאָרֶץ (Gen. 8:17)
    That creeps on the earth.......... רוֹמֵשׂ עַל־הָאָרֶץ (Gen. 8:19)

Over the earth 7 times in Genesis Chapter 1
    Over the earth..................... עַל־הָאָרֶץ (Gen. 1:11)
    Over the earth..................... עַל־הָאָרֶץ (Gen. 1:15)

Over the earth...................... עַל־הָאָרֶץ (Gen. 1:17)
Over the earth...................... עַל־הָאָרֶץ (Gen. 1:20)
Over the earth...................... עַל־הָאָרֶץ (Gen. 1:26)
Over the earth...................... עַל־הָאָרֶץ (Gen. 1:28)
Over the earth...................... עַל־הָאָרֶץ (Gen. 1:30)

The land of Goshen **7 times in Genesis**
    In the land of Goshen............... בְּאֶרֶץ־גֹּשֶׁן (Gen. 45:10)
    The land of Goshen............... אַרְצָה גֹּשֶׁן (Gen. 46:28)
    In the land of Goshen............... בְּאֶרֶץ גֹּשֶׁן (Gen. 46:34)
    In the land of Goshen............... בְּאֶרֶץ גֹּשֶׁן (Gen. 47:1)
    In the land of Goshen............... בְּאֶרֶץ גֹּשֶׁן (Gen. 47:4)
    In the land of Goshen............... בְּאֶרֶץ גֹּשֶׁן (Gen. 47:6)
    In the land of Goshen............... בְּאֶרֶץ גֹּשֶׁן (Gen. 50:8)

And called his name **7 times in Genesis**
    And she bore a son and called his name..... וַתֵּלֶד בֵּן וַתִּקְרָא אֶת־שְׁמוֹ (Gen. 4:25)
    And called his name..... וַתִּקְרָא אֶת־שְׁמוֹ (Gen. 30:11)
    And called his name..... וַתִּקְרָא אֶת־שְׁמוֹ (Gen. 30:13)
    And called his name..... וַתִּקְרָא אֶת־שְׁמוֹ (Gen. 30:20)
    And called his name..... וַתִּקְרָא אֶת־שְׁמוֹ (Gen. 30:24)
    And she bare a son and called his name..... וַתֵּלֶד בֵּן וַתִּקְרָא אֶת־שְׁמוֹ (Gen. 38:4)
    And she bare a son and called his name.... וַתֵּלֶד בֵּן וַתִּקְרָא אֶת־שְׁמוֹ (Gen. 38:5)

The house of my father **7 times in Genesis**
    From the house of my father........ מִבֵּית אָבִי (Gen. 20:13)
    From the house of my father........ מִבֵּית אָבִי (Gen. 24:7)
    To the house of my father........ אֶל־בֵּית־אָבִי (Gen. 24:38)
    And from the house of my father........ וּמִבֵּית אָבִי (Gen. 24:40)
    To the house of my father........ אֶל־בֵּית אָבִי (Gen. 28:21)
    All the house of my father........ כָּל־בֵּית אָבִי (Gen. 41:51)
    And the house of my father........ וּבֵית־אָבִי (Gen. 46:31)

In the following repetitions, note that the 7 shorter phrases in Hebrew are called constructs. There are 12 in the plural absolute without a prefix. There are 14 phrases in the plural absolute.

Seven years **21 times in Genesis**
    Seven years........................... שֶׁבַע שָׁנִים (Gen. 5:7)
    Seven years........................... שֶׁבַע שָׁנִים (Gen. 11:21)
    And seven years........................... וְשֶׁבַע שָׁנִים (Gen. 23:1)
    And seven years........................... וְשֶׁבַע שָׁנִים (Gen. 25:17)
    Seven years...................... שֶׁבַע שָׁנִים (Gen. 29:18)
    Seven years........................... שֶׁבַע שָׁנִים (Gen. 29:20)
    Seven years........................... שֶׁבַע־שָׁנִים (Gen. 29:27)
    Seven years........................... שֶׁבַע־שָׁנִים (Gen. 29:30)
    Seven years........................... שֶׁבַע שָׁנִים (Gen. 41:26)

Seven years............................ שֶׁבַע שָׁנִים (Gen. 41:26)
Seven years............................ שֶׁבַע שָׁנִים (Gen. 41:27)
Seven years............................ שֶׁבַע שְׁנֵי (Gen. 41:27)
Seven years............................ שֶׁבַע שָׁנִים (Gen. 41:29)
Seven years............................ שֶׁבַע שְׁנֵי (Gen. 41:30)
....In seven years...................... בְּשֶׁבַע שְׁנֵי (Gen. 41:34)
..For seven years...................... לְשֶׁבַע שְׁנֵי (Gen. 41:36)
....In seven years...................... בְּשֶׁבַע שְׁנֵי (Gen. 41:47)
Seven years............................ שֶׁבַע שָׁנִים (Gen. 41:48)
Seven years............................ שֶׁבַע שְׁנֵי (Gen. 41:53)
Seven years............................ שֶׁבַע שְׁנֵי (Gen. 41:54)
Seven years............................ שֶׁבַע שָׁנִים (Gen. 47:28)

To my Lord 7 times in Genesis
To my Lord......................... אֶל־אֲדֹנָי (Gen. 18:27)
To my Lord......................... אֲדֹנָי (Gen. 18:31)
To my lord......................... אֶל־אֲדֹנִי (Gen. 24:39)
To my lord......................... אֶל־אֲדֹנִי (Gen. 33:14)
To my lord......................... אֶל־אֲדֹנִי (Gen. 44:20)
To my lord......................... אֶל־אֲדֹנִי (Gen. 44:22)
To my lord......................... אֶל־אֲדֹנִי (Gen. 47:18)

Metered Introduction to Conversation: Anaphoric Phrases
And...Said / These Things / Between You and Me / Eyes

The following 12 examples were set in heptadic meter and are also the template for many similar phrases that were published in the first 5 chapters. It is clear that the Gospel writers incorporated Hebraic meter as they learned it from Moses.

And he said to him 7 times in Genesis (God speaking)
And he said to him................ וַיֹּאמֶר לוֹ (Gen. 3:9)
And he said to him................ וַיֹּאמֶר לוֹ (Gen. 4:15)
And he said to him................ וַיֹּאמֶר לוֹ (Gen. 15:5)
And he said to him................ וַיֹּאמֶר לוֹ (Gen. 20:3)
And he said to him................ וַיֹּאמֶר לוֹ (Gen. 31:24)
And he said to him................ וַיֹּאמֶר־לוֹ (Gen. 35:10)
And he said to him................ וַיֹּאמֶר לוֹ (Gen. 35:11)

And answered...and said 7 times in Genesis
And answered Abraham and said............ וַיַּעַן אַבְרָהָם וַיֹּאמַר (Gen. 18:27)
And answered Isaac and said................ וַיַּעַן יִצְחָק וַיֹּאמֶר (Gen. 27:37)
And answered Isaac his father and said... וַיַּעַן יִצְחָק אָבִיו וַיֹּאמֶר (Gen. 27:39)
And answered Jacob and said............... וַיַּעַן יַעֲקֹב וַיֹּאמֶר (Gen. 31:31)
And answered Jacob and said............... וַיַּעַן יַעֲקֹב וַיֹּאמֶר (Gen. 31:36)
And answered Laban and said.............. וַיַּעַן לָבָן וַיֹּאמֶר (Gen. 31:43)
And answered Joseph and said............. וַיַּעַן יוֹסֵף וַיֹּאמֶר (Gen. 40:18)

And said Laban 7 times in Genesis
>   And said Laban to Jacob……. וַיֹּאמֶר לָבָן לְיַעֲקֹב (Gen. 29:15)
>   And said Laban…………………... וַיֹּאמֶר לָבָן (Gen. 29:19)
>   And said Laban…………………... וַיֹּאמֶר לָבָן (Gen. 29:26)
>   And said Laban…………………... וַיֹּאמֶר לָבָן (Gen. 30:34)
>   And said Laban to Jacob……. וַיֹּאמֶר לָבָן לְיַעֲקֹב (Gen. 31:26)
>   And said Laban…………………... וַיֹּאמֶר לָבָן (Gen. 31:48)
>   And said Laban to Jacob……. וַיֹּאמֶר לָבָן לְיַעֲקֹב (Gen. 31:51)

And said Judah 7 times in Genesis
>   And said Judah……………… וַיֹּאמֶר יְהוּדָה (Gen. 37:26)
>   And said Judah……………… וַיֹּאמֶר יְהוּדָה (Gen. 38:8)
>   And said Judah……………… וַיֹּאמֶר יְהוּדָה (Gen. 38:11)
>   And said Judah……………… וַיֹּאמֶר יְהוּדָה (Gen. 38:23)
>   And said Judah……………… וַיֹּאמֶר יְהוּדָה (Gen. 38:24)
>   And said Judah……………… וַיֹּאמֶר יְהוּדָה (Gen. 43:8)
>   And said Judah……………… וַיֹּאמֶר יְהוּדָה (Gen. 44:16)

And Israel said 7 times in Genesis
>   And Israel said to Joseph….. וַיֹּאמֶר יִשְׂרָאֵל אֶל־יוֹסֵף (Gen. 37:13)
>   And Israel said…………………… וַיֹּאמֶר יִשְׂרָאֵל (Gen. 43:6)
>   And Israel said to them………. וַיֹּאמֶר אֲלֵהֶם יִשְׂרָאֵל (Gen. 43:11)
>   And Israel said…………………… וַיֹּאמֶר יִשְׂרָאֵל (Gen. 45:28)
>   And Israel said to Joseph….. וַיֹּאמֶר יִשְׂרָאֵל אֶל־יוֹסֵף (Gen. 46:30)
>   And Israel said to Joseph….. וַיֹּאמֶר יִשְׂרָאֵל אֶל־יוֹסֵף (Gen. 48:11)
>   And Israel said to Joseph….. וַיֹּאמֶר יִשְׂרָאֵל אֶל־יוֹסֵף (Gen. 48:21)

And Pharaoh said to Joseph 7 times in Genesis
>   And Pharaoh said to Joseph….. וַיֹּאמֶר פַּרְעֹה אֶל־יוֹסֵף (Gen. 41:15)
>   And Pharaoh said to Joseph….. וַיְדַבֵּר פַּרְעֹה אֶל־יוֹסֵף (Gen. 41:17)
>   And Pharaoh said to Joseph….. וַיֹּאמֶר פַּרְעֹה אֶל־יוֹסֵף (Gen. 41:39)
>   And Pharaoh said to Joseph….. וַיֹּאמֶר פַּרְעֹה אֶל־יוֹסֵף (Gen. 41:41)
>   And Pharaoh said to Joseph….. וַיֹּאמֶר פַּרְעֹה אֶל־יוֹסֵף (Gen. 41:44)
>   And Pharaoh said to Joseph….. וַיֹּאמֶר פַּרְעֹה אֶל־יוֹסֵף (Gen. 45:17)
>   And Pharaoh said to Joseph….. וַיֹּאמֶר פַּרְעֹה אֶל־יוֹסֵף (Gen. 47:5)

And he said to them 14 times in Genesis
>   And he said to them………………… וַיֹּאמֶר אֲלֵהֶם (Gen. 24:56)
>   And he said to them………………… וַיֹּאמֶר אֲלֵהֶם (Gen. 26:27)
>   And he said to them………………… וַיֹּאמֶר אֲלֵהֶם (Gen. 37:22)
>   And he said to them………………… וַיֹּאמֶר אֲלֵהֶם (Gen. 40:8)
>   And he said to them………………… וַיֹּאמֶר אֲלֵהֶם (Gen. 42:7)
>   And he said to them………………… וַיֹּאמֶר אֲלֵהֶם (Gen. 42:9)
>   And he said to them………………… וַיֹּאמֶר אֲלֵהֶם (Gen. 42:12)
>   And he said to them………………… וַיֹּאמֶר אֲלֵהֶם (Gen. 42:14)
>   And he said to them………………… וַיֹּאמֶר אֲלֵהֶם (Gen. 42:18)
>   And he said to them………………… וַיֹּאמֶר אֲלֵהֶם (Gen. 42:36)

And he said to them..........................	וַיֹּאמֶר אֲלֵהֶם	(Gen. 43:11)
And he said to them..........................	וַיֹּאמֶר אֲלֵהֶם	(Gen. 45:24)
And he said to them..........................	וַיֹּאמֶר אֲלֵהֶם	(Gen. 49:29)
And he said to them..........................	וַיֹּאמֶר אֲלֵהֶם	(Gen. 50:19)

These things 14 times in Genesis, 10 times with article

After these things.........	אַחַר הַדְּבָרִים הָאֵלֶּה	(Gen. 15:1)
According to these things.........	אֶת־כָּל־הַדְּבָרִים הָאֵלֶּה	(Gen. 20:8)
After these things..........	אַחַר הַדְּבָרִים הָאֵלֶּה	(Gen. 22:1)
After these things..........	אַחֲרֵי הַדְּבָרִים הָאֵלֶּה	(Gen. 22:20)
According to these things........	כַּדְּבָרִים הָאֵלֶּה	(Gen. 24:28)
All these things.........	כָּל־הַדְּבָרִים הָאֵלֶּה	(Gen. 29:13)
After these things.........	אַחַר הַדְּבָרִים הָאֵלֶּה	(Gen. 39:7)
According to these things........	כַּדְּבָרִים הָאֵלֶּה	(Gen. 39:17)
According to these things.........	כַּדְּבָרִים הָאֵלֶּה	(Gen. 39:19)
After these things..........	אַחַר הַדְּבָרִים הָאֵלֶּה	(Gen. 40:1)
These things.........	הַדְּבָרִים הָאֵלֶּה	(Gen. 43:7)
These things.........	אֶת־הַדְּבָרִים הָאֵלֶּה	(Gen. 44:6)
According to these things........	כַּדְּבָרִים הָאֵלֶּה	(Gen. 44:7)
After these things........	אַחֲרֵי הַדְּבָרִים הָאֵלֶּה	(Gen. 48:1)

The phrase *between you and me* is arranged in a chiastic pattern of A B B C B B A. The word for *between*, בֵּין (bên), appears 12 times, once in the first phrase, twice in the next 5 phrases, and once in the last phrase. There are 2 different words for *judge*, which demonstrates an intentional chiastic progression. The shape of this chiasm appears to illustrate the heap of rocks on which Laban and Jacob sat, and ate, and made their covenant. Notice the first and last lines bracket the other verses.

Between you and me 7 times in Genesis 31 between Jacob and Laban

Judge between us both............................	וְיוֹכִיחוּ בֵּין שְׁנֵינוּ	(Gen. 31:37)
A witness between me and between thee......	לְעֵד בֵּינִי וּבֵינֶךָ	(Gen. 31:44)
A witness between me and between thee......	עֵד בֵּינִי וּבֵינֶךָ	(Gen. 31:48)
LORD watch between me and between thee......	יִצֶף יְהוָה בֵּינִי וּבֵינֶךָ	(Gen. 31:49)
God *is* witness between me and between thee.....	אֱלֹהִים עֵד בֵּינִי וּבֵינֶךָ	(Gen. 31:50)
God *is* witness between me and between thee.....	יָרִיתִי בֵּינִי וּבֵינֶךָ	(Gen. 31:51)
Judge between us God............................	יִשְׁפְּטוּ בֵינֵינוּ אֱלֹהֵי	(Gen. 31:53)

The word *eyes*, used here as a Hebrew metaphor for opinion or attention, appears in 3 anaphoric phrases in Genesis, each of them in double heptadic meter:

Grace in...eyes 14 times in Genesis

But Noah found **grace in the eyes** of the LORD (Gen. 6:8)
If now I have found **grace in your eyes** (Gen. 18:3)
Your servant hath found **grace in your eyes** (Gen. 19:19)
If I have found **grace in your eyes** (Gen. 30:27)
That I may find **grace in your eyes** (Gen. 32:6)

To find **grace in the eyes** of my lord (Gen. 33:8)
If now I have found **grace in your eyes** (Gen. 33:10)
Let me find **grace in the eyes** of my lord (Gen. 33:15)
Let me find **grace in your eyes** (Gen. 34:11)
And Joseph found **grace in his eyes** (Gen. 39:4)
And gave him **grace in the eyes** (of the jailer) (Gen. 39:21)
Found **grace in the eyes** of my lord (Gen. 47:25)
If now I have found **grace in your eyes** (Gen. 47:29)
If now I have found **grace in your eyes** (Gen. 50:4)

וְנֹחַ מָצָא חֵן בְּעֵינֵי יְהוָה (Gen. 6:8)
אִם־נָא מָצָאתִי חֵן בְּעֵינֶיךָ (Gen. 18:3)
מָצָא עַבְדְּךָ חֵן בְּעֵינֶיךָ (Gen. 19:19)
אִם־נָא מָצָאתִי חֵן בְּעֵינֶיךָ (Gen. 30:27)
לִמְצֹא־חֵן בְּעֵינֶיךָ (Gen. 32:6)
לִמְצֹא־חֵן בְּעֵינֵי אֲדֹנִי (Gen. 33:8)
אִם־נָא מָצָאתִי חֵן בְּעֵינֶיךָ (Gen. 33:10)
אֶמְצָא־חֵן בְּעֵינֵי אֲדֹנִי (Gen. 33:15)
וְאֶל־אַחֶיהָ אֶמְצָא־חֵן בְּעֵינֵיכֶם (Gen. 34:1)
וַיִּמְצָא יוֹסֵף חֵן בְּעֵינָיו (Gen. 39:4)
וַיִּתֵּן חִנּוֹ בְּעֵינֵי (Gen. 39:21)
נִמְצָא־חֵן בְּעֵינֵי אֲדֹנִי (Gen. 47:25)
אִם־נָא מָצָאתִי חֵן בְּעֵינֶיךָ (Gen. 47:29)
אִם־נָא מָצָאתִי חֵן בְּעֵינֵיכֶם (Gen. 50:4)

Lift up eyes 14 times in Genesis
And Lot **lifted up** his eyes (Gen. 13:10)
lift up now thine eyes (Gen. 13:14)
And he **lift up** his eyes (Gen. 18:2)
Abraham **lifted up** his eyes (Gen. 22:4)
And Abraham **lifted up** his eyes (Gen. 22:13)
and he **lifted up** his eyes (Gen. 24:63)
And Rebekah **lifted up** her eyes (Gen. 24:64)
I **lifted up** mine eyes (Gen. 31:10)
lift up now thine eyes (Gen. 31:12)
And Jacob **lifted up** his eyes (Gen. 33:1)
And he **lifted up** his eyes (Gen. 33:5)
and they **lifted up** their eyes (Gen. 37:25)
and **lifted up** the master's wife her eyes (Gen. 39:7)
And he **lifted up** his eyes (Gen. 43:29)

וַיִּשָּׂא־לוֹט אֶת־עֵינָיו (Gen. 13:10)
שָׂא נָא עֵינֶיךָ (Gen. 13:14)
וַיִּשָּׂא עֵינָיו (Gen. 18:2)
וַיִּשָּׂא אַבְרָהָם אֶת־עֵינָיו (Gen. 22:4)
וַיִּשָּׂא אַבְרָהָם אֶת־עֵינָיו (Gen. 22:13)
וַיִּשָּׂא עֵינָיו (Gen. 24:63)

וַתִּשָּׂא רִבְקָה אֶת־עֵינֶיהָ (Gen. 24:64)
וָאֶשָּׂא עֵינַי (Gen. 31:10)
וַיֹּאמֶר שָׂא־נָא עֵינֶיךָ (Gen. 31:12)
וַיִּשָּׂא יַעֲקֹב עֵינָיו (Gen. 33:1)
וַיִּשָּׂא אֶת־עֵינָיו (Gen. 33:5)
וַיִּשְׂאוּ עֵינֵיהֶם (Gen. 37:25)
וַתִּשָּׂא אֵשֶׁת־אֲדֹנָיו אֶת־עֵינֶיהָ (Gen. 39:7)
וַיִּשָּׂא עֵינָיו (Gen. 43:29)

In the eyes of 14 times in Genesis (7 with *my lord* or *Lord*)
In the eyes of the Lord.......... בְּעֵינֵי יְהוָה (Gen. 6:8)
In the eyes of.......................... בְּעֵינֵי (Gen. 19:14)
In the eyes of.......................... בְּעֵינֵי (Gen. 21:11)
In the eyes of.......................... בְּעֵינֵי (Gen. 28:8)
In the eyes of my lord........... בְּעֵינֵי אֲדֹנִי (Gen. 31:35)
In the eyes of my lord........... בְּעֵינֵי אֲדֹנִי (Gen. 33:8)
In the eyes of my lord........... בְּעֵינֵי אֲדֹנִי (Gen. 33:15)
In the eyes of.......................... בְּעֵינֵי (Gen. 34:18)
In the eyes of the Lord.......... בְּעֵינֵי יְהוָה (Gen. 38:7)
In the eyes of the Lord.......... בְּעֵינֵי יְהוָה (Gen. 38:10)
In the eyes of.......................... בְּעֵינֵי (Gen. 39:21)
In the eyes of.......................... בְּעֵינֵי (Gen. 41:37)
In the eyes of.......................... בְּעֵינֵי (Gen. 45:16)
In the eyes of my Lord.......... בְּעֵינֵי אֲדֹנִי (Gen. 47:25)

Cassuto on Exodus: Heptadic Meter in God's Call to Moses

Cassuto interrupted writing his commentaries on Genesis after the first 2 volumes in order to complete his commentary on Exodus. He approaches Exodus in the same manner in which he wrote his commentaries on Genesis. At the beginning of his commentary he again enumerates heptadic rhythm in Exodus chapter 1. The next 11 paragraphs quote Cassuto's observations on Exodus chapters 1-4. In order to understand Cassuto, it is recommended that one read the first 4 chapters of Exodus.

> Seven expressions for increase are used in this verse [Exodus 1:7], a number indicative of perfection: (1) *were fruitful*; (2) *and teemed*; (3) *and multiplied*; (4) *and grew mighty*; (5) *with strength* [בִּמְאֹד *bim^e'ōdh*]; (6) *strongly* [מְאֹד *m^e'ōdh*]; (7) *so that the land was filled with them.*[33]

Cassuto identifies Exodus 1:1-7 as the first paragraph, and Exodus 1:8-14 as the second paragraph. He finds 7 more key words in the second paragraph:

---

[33] Cassuto, *Exodus*, p. 9.

The words derived from the stem עבד *'bd* ['serve', 'service', 'work'] and follow one another in these verses like hammer blows; and the word *rigour*, which also occurs twice, reverberates like an echo that strengthens and deepens the impression: ...These recurring words number seven; here, as well as in the preceding paragraph, the key words of the paragraph occur *seven* times.[34]

Concerning the third paragraph (Exodus 1:15-21) Cassuto writes, "In this paragraph, too, the key-word *midwife* occurs, in the singular and in the plural, seven times."[35]

Cassuto also notes that the Masoretes observed the heptadic cadence in the first chapter of Exodus: "After the three paragraphs, each of which is divided by the Masoretes into seven verses, comes a single, concluding verse."[36]

In the second chapter, Moses meets the 7 daughters of Reuel (also known as Jethro), the priest of Midian, at the well. Cassuto says the word *daughter* (singular) is a key word and repeats 7 times. He does not list them, but after checking the chapter, the references are Exodus 2:1, 5, 7, 8, 9, 10, and 21.[37]

Cassuto also writes about chapter 2: "The keyword in this paragraph [Exodus 2:10-21] is *child*, which occurs seven times. Also emphasized in the paragraph, by being used three times, are the words *took, called, went* and *suckled*."[38]

The following is Cassuto at his best:

> The first paragraph speaks of the daughter of Levi and the daughter of Pharaoh, and the third tells of the seven daughters of Reuel and, in particular, of his daughter Zipporah; and the number of the daughters, which is expressly stated in the text to be seven, corresponds [to] the number of times that the word *daughter* in the singular occurs throughout the section [Exodus 2:1-22]. With the interconnecting links between the three paragraphs, as well as the threefold iterations in each of them, for the sake of emphasis, we have already dealt.[39]

---

[34] Ibid., p. 12.
[35] Ibid., p. 15.
[36] Ibid., p. 16.
[37] Ibid., p. 17.
[38] Ibid., p. 21.
[39] Ibid., p. 27.

Here Cassuto makes a connection between the word *daughter* appearing 7 times in chapter 2 and the number of Reuel's 7 daughters stated in the text. In other words, the Bible often states a number in the text that corresponds to the repetition in the text.

At the beginning of Exodus chapter 3 Moses goes to see God. God sees Moses, and Moses sees God, and then God says He has seen His people's affliction. The word for *see* is found 7 times in Exodus 3:2 (x2), 3, 4 (x2), 7, and 9. Cassuto counts the infinitive absolute, a double verb for emphasis, in verse 7 as one unit. He writes:

> Following upon six words from the stem רָאָה *rā'ā* ['see'], there occurs a seventh time [in section 3, Exodus 3:1-15], and with special emphasis, a final twofold echo thereof in the utterance of God: 'I have surely seen,' [רָאֹה רָאִיתִי *rā'ō rā'īthī*, literally, 'seen I have seen'] (*v.* 7).[40]

> The stem דבר *dbr* ['speak'] which is characteristic of the verses pertaining to Moses' third doubt and to God's answer thereto (*vv.* 10-17), occurs seven times in this passage. The compound expression [another infinitive absolute] דַּבֵּר יְדַבֵּר *dabbēr yᵉdhabbēr* ['he can speak well'] in *v.* 14 is counted, as usual, as a single unit. The word *mouth*, which is also a feature of Moses' third objection, is likewise found in these verses seven times.[41]

Cassuto finds just as much precision in Exodus as he does in Genesis. The writer of Genesis is obviously the writer of Exodus. Cassuto's ability to keep track of multiple key words in his head as he reads them in Hebrew is quite amazing. He reads and writes about the text like none before him.

In the sixth paragraph (Exodus 4:27-31), Cassuto identifies 7 more occurrences of *see*, as he did in Exodus 3:7:

> We have already noted above (p. 32) that the stem רָאָה *rā'ā* ['see'], used to describe the Lord's perception of the affliction of the children of Israel and His manifestation to Moses at Horeb, occurs repeatedly at the beginning of the section, and at the seventh occurrence it is emphasized by the addition of the absolute infinitive. Thereafter it is employed another seven times, and in the summary verse of the concluding pas-

---
[40] Ibid., p. 32.
[41] Ibid., p. 52.

sage a final echo of it is heard in the sentence, *and that He had seen their affliction.* The stem שָׁלַח *šālah* ['send'], which refers to the mission, is found seven times in iii 10-20, another seven times in iv 4-23, and finally once more in the summary paragraph, iv 28….The verb הָלַךְ *hālakh* ['go'], which plays a significant role in the last paragraph not only in recalling what had previously been stated, but also in the narration of new events mentioned there for the first time, is used fourteen times, twice times seven, in the entire section [Exodus 1:1- 4:31].[42]

The integration of key words in Heptadic meter found by Cassuto in the first 4 chapters of Exodus is sufficient evidence to conclude that we possess the original document penned by the original author. No university department of Hebrew Studies in the world today acknowledges what Cassuto has accomplished. The discovery of the Dead Sea Scrolls verifies that the Masoretes did not insert repetition into the text 600 to 1,000 years after Christ. It can be assumed that this heptadic meter is not found in the Septuagint, because in 300 B.C. the translators did not know this meter was in the text.

Those who may argue that the Septuagint is following an older version of the Hebrew text necessarily imply the unlikely possibility that meter was added to every book in the Old Testament after 300 B.C. Such an assumption would also reverse numerous instances where Cassuto identifies errors in the Septuagint's translation and paraphrases of difficult verses, as discussed in Chapter Six. It is not possible that the Gospel writers included meter from a Hebrew text that was more recent than the Septuagint. At this time no university even acknowledges the presence of heptadic, decadal, and dodecadal meter in either Testament. Another possibility is that the Septuagint translators were aware that there was meter in the Hebrew text, but not knowing to what extent, they made no attempt to claim they had reproduced the meter in their translation. Therefore, they would have understood that a translation can never replace the original document.

Heptadic Events in the 10 Plagues

Cassuto writes about God's 7 promises to free Israel from Egypt, as follows:

> The Divine actions for the benefit of Israel is described in seven clauses, each of which begins with a verb in the first

---
[42] Ibid., pp. 63-64.

person, the verbs being linked together by the Wāw consecutive [a repetition of *and*, as follows Exodus 6:6-8]:[43]

Wherefore say unto the children of Israel,
I *am* the LORD,
and I will bring you out from under the burdens of the Egyptians,
and I will rid you out of their bondage,
and I will redeem you with a stretched out arm, and with great judgments:
and I will take you to me for a people,
and I will be to you a God: and ye shall know that I *am* the LORD your God,
which bringeth you out from under the burdens of the Egyptians.
And I will bring you in unto the land,
concerning the which I did swear to give it
to Abraham, to Isaac, and to Jacob;
and I will give it you for an heritage: I *am* the LORD. Exodus 6:6-8

The number seven, which is expressly mentioned in *v.* 25 (*seven days*), serves also to emphasize the principal word in the paragraph, namely, *Nile*, which occurs fourteen times in the course of the paragraph—twice times seven[44] [Exodus 7:15, 17, 18 (x3), 19, 20 (x2), 21 (x3), 24 (x2), 25].

In the account of the plague of hail and its consequences אֶרֶץ מִצְרַיִם *'eres Misrayim* ['land of Egypt'] occurs five times [Exodus 9:22-26], once we find the word אַרְצָה *'ārsā* ['to the earth'], and in the seventh reference [to אֶרֶץ *'eres* 'land', 'earth'] mention is made of אֶרֶץ גֹּשֶׁן *'eres Gōšen* ['land of Goshen'], enjoying quiet and security, a picture that recalls the Seventh Day, the day of rest, which comes after the six days of hard work imposed on mankind.[45]

It should now be added that in the entire paragraph [Exodus 9:13-35] שָׂדֶה *śādhe* ['field'] occurs seven times [Exodus 9:3, 19, 21, 22, 25 (x3)] and בָּרָד *bārādh* ['hail'] fourteen times, twice seven[46] [Exodus 9:18, 19, 22, 23 (x2), 24 (x2), 25 (x2), 26, 28, 29, 33, 34].

In several paragraphs of this section [Exodus 7:8-11:10] we have already observed a numerical schematism that finds expression in the mention of the name of a plague seven times (swarms of flies, locusts), or fourteen times (hail)....In the first cycle the names of the plagues occur 21 times—three times

---
[43] Ibid., p. 80.
[44] Ibid., p. 100.
[45] Ibid., p. 120.
[46] Ibid., p. 122.

seven (blood 5 times, frogs 11, gnats 5) and with the paragraph pertaining to the crocodile (3 times), 24—twice times twelve; in the second cycle 12 times (swarms of flies 7, pest 1, boils 4); in the third cycle 24 (hail 14, locusts 7, darkness 3): in all 60 times. All this can hardly be fortuitous.[47]

Upon examination, *swarms of flies*, or *insects*, repeats 7 times in Exodus 8:21 (x2), 22, 24 (x2), 29 and 31. *Locust* also repeats 7 times in Exodus 10:4, 12, 13, 14 (x2), and 19 (x2). Cassuto says that, according to the text, Moses' rod, called the rod of God in 4:17, became a snake, and Aaron's rod (a different rod) changed into a crocodile, תַּנִּין (*tanniyn*, tan-neen'), in 7:9-10.[48] Exegetically there is strong support for his interpretation. The KJV overly influenced recent translations on the interpretation of the word תַּנִּין (*tanniyn*), which means *dragon* or *sea monster* in 27 other locations in the Hebrew text. In other words, the KJV translators didn't know what a crocodile was. Even the Septuagint says *dragon* instead of *serpent* in 7:9-10. Cecil B. DeMille's *Ten Commandments* appears to have made *serpent* the only possible translation.

Cassuto identifies the word for *eat* 7 times in connection with the first Passover: "Note should be taken of the poetic parallelism in v. 2 [Exodus 12:1-13], and also of the occurrence, seven times, of references to *eating*—an important aspect of the sacrificial rite."[49] After checking Cassuto's data, repetition of the word *eat* was found in Exodus 12:4, 7, 8 (x2), 9, and 11 (x2).

As Cassuto points out, the festival of Passover was to last a full 7 days.[50] There was the thought of finding something Cassuto had missed, but he ends the paragraph on page 142 with the statement, "*You shall eat nothing leavened; in all your dwelling places you shall eat unleavened cakes.* In this paragraph, too [Exodus 12:14-20], there are seven references to eating." The locations are Exodus 12:15 (x2), 16, 18, 19, and 20 (x2).

So the section draws to a close [Exodus 12:1-12:42], with a twofold repetition of the expression for 'watching' or 'observance' [שִׁמֻּרִים *šimmūrīm*], which we have already encountered [the words are different, but the stem is the same] once at the beginning (v. 6 לְשָׁמְרְתָּם lᵉmišmereth [literary 'charge'; rendered,

---

[47] Ibid., p. 135.
[48] Ibid., p. 94.
[49] Ibid., p. 140.
[50] Ibid., p. 141.

'*you shall* keep it']); then twice in *v.* 17 (וּשְׁמַרְתֶּם *ūšᵉmartem* ['and you shall observe']); and twice again in *vv.* 24-25 (in this case, too, שִׁמֻּרִים *šimmūrīm*); in all there are seven references, which are intended to emphasize the principal thought that the Lord is the keeper of Israel. Similarly, the expressions *this (that) day* and *(this) that night* occur seven times in the section; and fourteen times we find the word *house (household),* referring to the houses of the Israelites over which the Keeper of Israel kept watch. Proof that this is not fortuitous is found in the text itself, which expressly mentions the number seven and its multiples a number of times (*vv.* 15, 19: 'seven days'; *vv.* 15, 16: 'seventh day'; *vv.* 6, 18: 'the fourteenth day'; *v.* 18: 'the twenty-first day')....[51]

Day repeats 7 times in Exodus 12:6, 17 (x2), 24, 25, and 42 (x2), and *Night* repeats 7 times in Exodus 12:8, 12, 29, 30, 31, and 42 (x2), a pattern also found in Genesis and Revelation, as shown in Chapter Five. One must also admire Cassuto's ability to make associations between the meter and the meaning of the text. In the following he contrasts *waters of death* with *waters of life*.

Furthermore, in the first verse of the paragraph we find the word מִיָּם *miyyam* ['from the Sea'], and thereafter six times (in all seven times) the same letters with different vocalization: מַיִם *mayim* or מָיִם *māyim* ['water']; as though to say: from the peril of the Sea of Reeds to the safe dwelling-place by the waters of the wells of Elim.[52]

Reeds in Exodus is the same word as the *weeds* that wrapped around Jonah in the belly of the fish. Yet, reeds only grow in fresh water. Pharaoh's daughter takes Moses out of the reeds of the Nile (2:5). Obviously, the correct meaning of the word is not known. For lack of comparison, words for colors, plants, and animals are difficult to translate from Hebrew. It is also possible that it was known as the *Reed Sea* on the Egyptian side and *Red Sea* on the other side where Exodus was written. *Reeds* repeats 7 times in Exodus, and *Red Sea* repeats 12 times in the Pentateuch (Exod. 10:19; 13:18; 15:4, 22; 23:31; Num. 14:25; 21:4; 33:10, 11; Deut. 1:40; 2:1; 11:4).

The Hebrew words for *Reed Sea* may allude to the Hebrew word for the oasis of Elim אֵילִם (*'Eylim,* ay-leem'), which means *terebinth*

---

[51] Ibid., p. 149.
[52] Ibid., p. 185.

trees. The Hebrew mind could not help but associate the waters of Elim as waters dyed red. The Hebrew word for *rams* is a homograph for *Elim*, and repeats 10 times in Exodus 15:27; 16:1 (x2); 25:5; 26:14; 29:1, 3; 35:7, 23; 39:34. The rams' skins were dyed red, sewn together, and used like a tarp to cover the Holy of Holies in the Tabernacle. The exact phrase, *And for a sacrifice of peace offerings, two oxen, five rams, five he goats, five lambs of the first year: this was the offering*, וּלְזֶבַח הַשְּׁלָמִים בָּקָר שְׁנַיִם אֵילִם חֲמִשָּׁה עַתּוּדִים חֲמִשָּׁה כְּבָשִׂים בְּנֵי־שָׁנָה חֲמִשָּׁה זֶה קָרְבַּן, repeats 10 times in Numbers, in 7:29, 35, 41, 47, 53, 59, 65, 71, 77, and 83. It repeats 2 more times with a slight variation in 17:17 and 17:23. This is an amazing repetition of 14 consecutive Hebrew words in exact order including vowel points, the longest metered phrase found thus far in the Bible. There is meticulous counting in the text.

The Septuagint followed by Acts 7:36 and Hebrews 11:29 translates *Reed Sea* as *Red Sea*, a larger region than the *Reed Sea*, thus presenting an image of baptism in the blood of Christ. *For I do not want you to be unaware, brethren, that our fathers were all under the cloud, and all passed through the sea; and all were baptized into Moses in the cloud and in the sea* (1 Co 10:1-2 NASB). They all passed through the waters and arrived at the image of the Elim/rams waters which historically remind them of skins dyed red.

Heptadic Repetition in the Sinai Desert

After the children of Israel cross the Red Sea, the heptadic meter focuses on the people and their activities in the desert, including the Sabbath, the Tabernacle, and descriptions of God. With more time Cassuto would have noticed that Moses goes up and down the mountain 7 times. He writes, "It is possibly not fortuitous that the word *hand* occurs in this paragraph [Exodus 17:8-16], in both its meanings, seven times."[53] The following are the verses in which *hand* is repeated 7 times: Exodus 17:9, 11 (x2), 12 (x3), and 16. In English translations verse 16 reads *sworn* instead of *hand*.

> The mention of the third new moon is not unintentional. Since the exodus from Egypt, the last two weeks of Nissan and the four weeks of Iyyar had passed, and we are now in the seventh week. Since seven was considered the number of perfection, seven days constituted, according to the customary conception of the ancient East, a given unit of time, while seven weeks formed a still higher unit; and just as after six

---

[53] Ibid., p. 207.

days of labour the seventh day brought rest and enjoyment of the results of that labour, so after six weeks of the travails of journeying the seventh week brought a sense of exaltation and of drawing nearer to the world Divine[54] [Exodus 19:1].

At this point a series of seven categories of living beings is listed, which serves to underscore the number seven, on which the sabbath is based [Exodus 20:10]: (i) *you*, (ii) or *your son*, (iii) *your daughter*, (iv) *your bondman*, (v) *your bondmaid*, (vi) *your cattle*; or even one who, although not actually dependent on you, is nevertheless bound to you because he dwells with you, namely, the seventh in the series: (vii) *or your sojourner who is in your gates*—within your gates—that is, within your cities.[55]

The number of things that may not be coveted, like the list of those who are obliged to rest on the sabbath, totals seven.[56]

Anyone familiar with Shakespeare's sonnets knows that he wrote them in 14 lines. There is no mystery, conspiracy, or guarded secret about it. However, if anyone dares to say that Moses wrote in heptadic repetition, every major university faculty of Hebrew Studies views such a claim as a heretical attack on their sacred Documentary Hypothesis.

God invented the Sabbath, a unique feature of Israel's heptadic cycles of ceremonial time. Cassuto calls Moses' Sabbath cycles *the Sacred Seasons*:

> The first precepts of the group appertain to the seventh year and seventh day ([Exodus 23] *vv.* 10-12), and the verses in which they are formulated conclude with the mention of the *sojourner*....The importance attached by the peoples of the ancient Orient to sequences of seven units of time, and the innovation introduced in Israel with regard to resting on the seventh period, we have already discussed above, in our commentary on xvi 5, xix 1, and xx 8.[57]

Cassuto sees 7 attributes of God in Exodus 36:6-7 as God pronounces His name when He passes by Moses on the mountain.[58]

---

[54] Ibid., p. 224.
[55] Ibid., p. 245.
[56] Ibid., p. 249.
[57] Ibid., p. 300.
[58] Ibid., pp. 439-40.

1. Compassionate and gracious
2. Slow to anger
3. Abounding in loving kindness and truth
4. Keeping lovingkindness for the thousands
5. Forgiving iniquity and transgression and sin
6. But who will by no means clear the guilty
7. Visiting the iniquity of the fathers upon the children and the children's children

When discussing worship prohibitions pertaining to the covenant, Cassuto writes, "The verbs used in picturing this development are seven in number: *play the harlot—slaughter—calls—eat—take—play the harlot—make play the harlot*"[59] (Exodus 34:15-16).

The paragraph of Exodus 35:21-29 gives information on contributions. Cassuto writes, "The fact that the word *brought* occurs seven times in this paragraph is not without significance."[60]

From the beginning of the section [Exodus 35:1] up to this point [Exodus 36:7] the word תְּרוּמָה *terūmā* ['contribution'] has occurred seven times. Likewise the verb בּוֹא *bō* ['come'], in the *Qal* or *Hiphʿīl*, is used seven times, quite apart from the seven occurrences of the word הֵבִיאוּ *hēbhīʾū* ['they brought'] in the preceding paragraph.[61]

On the erection of the Tabernacle (Exodus 40:17-33), Cassuto counts the number of times God commands Moses in this paragraph: "At the end of each passage is reiterated, like an echo reverberating seven times, *as the Lord commanded Moses*."[62]

After meeting with God on the mountain in Exodus 3:1-14, Moses returns to Mount Sinai/Horeb a year later with the children of Israel, and climbs it a total of 7 times, as found by Phillip Giessler:

> Trip 1 described at Exodus 19:3-6 (up); 19:7-8a (down)
> Trip 2 described at Exodus 19:8b-13 (up); 19:14-20 (down)
>   (Fear laid on people; basis of Hebrews 12:18-21; God's voice is heard.)
> Trip 3 described at Exodus 19:21-24 (up); 19:25–20:20 (down)
>   (Moses' first reception & verbal recitation of Ten Commandments.)
> Trip 4 described at Exodus 20:21–24:2 (up); 24:3-14 (down)
>   (Moses in dark cloud; more rules; leaders eat & drink with a vision

---

[59] Ibid., p. 444.
[60] Ibid., p. 457.
[61] Ibid., p. 461.
[62] Ibid., p. 481.

of God.)
Trip 5 described at Exodus 24:15–32:14 (up); 32:15-30 (down)
  (40 days on Horeb; Tabernacle data; two stone tablets; golden calf.)
Trip 6 described at Exodus 32:31–33:3 (up); 33:4–34:3 (down)
Trip 7 described at Exodus 34:4-28 (up); 34:29–40:38 (down)
  (*YHWH* spoke; 40 days & tablets again; face shines; veil; festivals.)

Cataloguing all of the heptadic meter in the Bible (if it were possible) would fill volumes. One of the more interesting heptadic repetitions in the Bible is the 77 questions that God asks Job in Job 38-42, as published on the internet by Jason Duff and many others. In conversation with Duff, he was not aware of who was the first to publish the list of 77 questions, though he had seen it in a few commentaries.[63]

Single Words in Heptadic Meter in Genesis and Exodus

In addition to the above phrases, Genesis has numerous series of single words in heptadic meter. This chapter has already reviewed more than 100 examples of heptadic repetition from Cassuto within paragraphs, chapters, sections, and multiple sections, and the repetition of 7 blessings, events, things, etc. More than 20 examples of heptadic phrases also seen in Matthew, Mark, Luke, and John have been published in this chapter, most of which span the entire book of Genesis. Without the benefit of computers, it would have been difficult for Cassuto to find heptadic repetition of individual words that span the entire book of Genesis, some of which are as follows:

(All citations are from Genesis unless otherwise indicated.)
And if/when: 14, וְכִי (*ūkî*, oo'-kee) Exod. 3:11; 4:31; 12:48; 21:7, 14, 18, 20, 22, 26, 28, 33, 35; 22:13, 15;
Arise: 7, imperative, קוּם (*quwm*, koom) 13:17; 19:15; 27:19; 28:2; 31:13; 35:1; 44:4; see also list of decads;
Baker: 7, אֹפֶה (*'aphah*, aw-faw') 40:1, 2, 5, 16, 20, 22; 41:10;
Blessings: 7, בְּרָכֹת (*berakoth*, ber-aw-koth') noun common feminine plural construct homonym 1, Gen. 28:4; 39:5; 49:25 (x3), 26 (x2);
Blood: 7, דָּם (*dam*, dawm) only this form, Gen. 9:6; 37:22; Exod. 7:19 (x2); 23:18; 24:8; 34:25;
Brother: 21, Chapter 37, אָח (*'ach*, awkh) 37:2, 4 (x2), 5, 8, 9, 10 (x2), 11, 12, 13, 14, 16, 17, 19, 23, 26 (x2), 27 (x2), 30;
Your brother: 7, Chapter 42, אֲחִיכֶם (*āhē'-kĕm*, law-kakh'-kem) 42:15, 16, 19, 20, 33, 34 (x2);
Covenant: 7, Chapter 9, בְּרִית (*beriyth*, ber-eeth') in 9:9, 11, 12, 13, 15,

---

[63] Jason Duff, "The Whole Counsel of God—Job 38-42," sermon notes, March 27, 2013, http://media.calvaryvista.com/library/duff-jason/studies-books/18-JOB-2013/18-JOB-038-001.pdf (7/2015).

16, 17;

Be Fruitful: 7, Spoken by God, פָּרָה (*parah*, paw-raw') 1:22, 28; 8:17; 9:1, 7; 17:6, 20;

The Garden: 7, הַגָּן (*hagan*, ha'-gan) 2:9, 10, 16; 3:1, 2, 3, 8;

Garden: 14, גַּן (*gan*, gan) all cases, 2:8, 9, 10, 15, 16; 3:1, 2, 3, 8 (x2), 10, 23, 24; 13:10;

And the God of: 7, וֵאלֹהֵי (*vē-el- ō -heem'*, ve-el-ō-heem') 24:3; 28:13; 31:5, 29, 53; 32:10; 43:23;

Hurry: 14, מָהַר (*mahar*, maw-har') 18:6 (x2), 7; 19:22; 24:18, 20, 46; 27:20; 34:12; 41:32; 43:30; 44:11; 45:9, 13;

In order that: 7, לְמַעַן (*lᵉma`an*, lᵉmah-an) 12:13; 18:19 (x2), 24; 27:25; 37:22; 50:20;

In order that: 14, לְמַעַן (*lᵉma`an*, lᵉmah-an) Exod. 1:11; 4:5; 8:6, 18; 9:29; 10:1; 11:7, 9; 13:9; 16:4, 32; 20:12; 23:12; 33:13;

Interpretation: 14, Chapters 40 and 41, פִּתְרוֹן (*pithrown*, pith-rone') or פִּתְרֹן (*pithron*, pith-rone') 40:5, 8, 12, 18; 41:11; Interpret פָּתַר (*pathar*, paw-thar') 40:8, 16, 22; 41:8, 12 (x2), 13, 15 (x2);

Locust(s): 7, אַרְבֶּה (*'arbeh*, ar-beh') Exod. 10:4, 12, 13, 14 (x2), 19 (x2);

Lord God: 7, plural construct, יְהוָה אֱלֹהֵי *YHWH'Elōhi*, 9:26; 24:7, 12, 27, 42, 48; 28:13;

Magicians: 7, חַרְטֹם (*chartom*, khar-tome') Exod. 7:11, 22; 8:7, 18, 19; 9:11 (x2);

Midwives: 7, Chapter 1, מְיַלֶּדֶת (*mᵉee-lᵉ-dōth*, mᵉyee'-lᵉ-dōth) Exod. 1:15, 17, 18, 19 (x2), 20, 21;

Nile: 14, יְאֹר (*yᵉ`or*, yeh-ore') Exod. 7:15, 17, 18 (x3), 20 (x2), 21 (x3), 24 (x2), 25, 28;

Nine Hundred: 7, תֵּשַׁע (*tesha`*, tay'-shah) מֵאָה (*me›ah*, may-aw›) 5:5, 8, 11, 14, 20, 27; 9:29;

And Nine: 7, וּתְשַׁע (*wᵉtesha`*), or (masc.) 5:8, 11, 14, 20, 27; 17:1, 24;

Pit: 7, Chapter 37, בּוֹר (*bowr*, bore) 37:20, 22, 24 (x2), 28, 29 (x2);

Prosper: 7, צָלַח (*tsalach*; tsaw-lakh') or צָלֵחַ (*tsaleach*, tsaw-lay'-akh) 24:21, 40, 42, 56; 39:2, 3, 23;

Reeds: 7, סוּף (*cuwph*, soof) Exod. 2:3, 5; 10:19; 13:18; 15:4, 22; 23:31;

Sack: 7/20, 7 in Chapter 42, כְּלִי (*keliy*; kel-ee') 42:25; שַׂק (*saq*, sak) 42:25, 27, 35 (x2); אַמְתַּחַת (*'amtachath*; am-takh'-ath) 42:27, 28; **6** in Chapter 43, אַמְתַּחַת (*'amtachath*, am-takh'-ath) 43:12, 18, 21 (x2), 22, 23; **7** in Chapter 44, אַמְתַּחַת (*'amtachath*, am-takh'-ath) 44:1 (x2), 2, 8, 11 (x2), 12;

Signs: 7, אוֹת (*'owth*, oth) Exod. 4:9, 17, 28, 30; 7:3; 10:1, 2;

Spies: 7, Chapter 42, רָגַל (*ragal*, raw-gal') 42:9, 11, 14, 16, 30, 31, 34;

Surely: 7, adverb, אֲבָל (*'abal*, ab-awl') 17:19; 27:41; 37:35; 42:21; 50:10, 11 (x2);

Tent(s): 7, Chapter 31, אֹהֶל (*'ohel*, o'-hel) 31:25, 33 (x5), 34;

They, There, Here: 14, הֵנָּה (*hennah*, hane'-naw) 6:2; 15:16 (x2); 21:23, 29; 33:6; 41:26 (x2), 27; 42:15; 44:28; 45:5, 8, 13.

Seventy: An Expression of Heptadic Completion

There are at least 62 examples of *70* in the Old Testament, not to mention lists of words and phrases that are repeated 70 times. Ten times 7 is the symbol of heptadic completion. The Hebrew numeric system, like the Egyptian numeric system,[64] is based on 10. The Babylonian, Mesopotamian, and Sumerian systems were sexagesimal, which is base 60.[65] Hebrew also exhibits an augmentation of 7 as observed by Cassuto, which he credits to the influence of the Sabbath. How much influence the Egyptian decimal system had on the Bible is debatable. However, there is no question that ancient Hebrews, including Moses, counted in multiples of 10. In addition to heptads, Cassuto pays particular attention to the repetition of 70.

> The number of seventy nations enumerated in chapter x [Genesis 10] was, without doubt, purposely contrived (it will suffice to recall the allusion of Deut. xxxii 8), yet it is not expressly mentioned in the text. Similarly the number of bulls offered up during the Festival of Tabernacles was clearly fixed at seventy by deliberate design, nevertheless it is only by computation that we are able to arrive at the figure.[66]

Cassuto is also wise to say, "...we must pay particular attention to the *divergences* between the Babylonian and Biblical traditions."[67] In the following quote, Cassuto enumerates the tradition of 70 in the Bible and in pagan cultures in proximity with Israel. There is clearly a common heritage that begins with Noah after the Flood, and which is emulated by other nations.

> ...for it is in keeping with the customary practice obtaining in the ancient East generally, and among the Israelites in particular, of using the number seventy—seven times ten—for the purpose of indicating the abundance of children of a family blessed with fertility. Thus, for example, according to the concepts of the Canaanites concerning the origin and genealogy of the deities in their pantheon, the family of gods—the sons of El and sons of Asherah—comprised seventy souls (*seventy sons of Asherah* in the Ugaritic Tablet II AB, vi, 46). We do not actually possess a list of the names of the seventy gods,

---

[64] Dirk J. Struik, *A Concise History of Mathematics*, rev. 4th ed., Dover Publications, Mineola, NY, 1987, p. 15.
[65] Ibid., pp. 26-27.
[66] Cassuto, *Genesis: Part I*, pp. 261-62.
[67] Ibid., p. 262.

and possibly there existed records that differed from one another in some particulars, except for the total of seventy, which remained unchanged. This usage was also to be found among the Israelites. The number of sons of Jacob who went down to Egypt was fixed at seventy persons (Gen. xlvi 27; Exod. i 5; Deut. x 22); and although there are some divergences between the list in Gen. xlvi and other Biblical lists, and an element of doubt attaches to some of the details of the calculation, the total seventy is considered the essential factor from which there can be no deviation....

Similarly, the Book of Judges (viii 30; ix 2) speaks of the seventy sons of Gideon, and the figure is still adhered to even when it is subsequently stated (*ibid.* ix 5) that one of them slew his brothers, seventy men, and yet another of them Jotham, remained alive for he hid himself. This shows that the number seventy is not exact, but serves, according to the traditional system, to indicate a numerically ideal family. In the same way, in ii Kings x 1, 6, 7, reference is made to the seventy sons of Ahab. Even the Canaanite traditions concerning the seventy sons of El and Asherah has a sequel in Israel's literature....In view of all this, if we find in our chapters, too, that the descendants of Shem, Ham and Japheth total exactly seventy...we must not regard this figure as a mere coincidence but as an additional example of the aforementioned use of the traditional number seventy. The family of the children of Noah is depicted as perfect in the number of its sons, and all mankind, which comprises the seventy nations that issued from these sons, is represented as an ideal creation in the number of its part[s]. Nor may we suppose that sum of seventy peoples is the result of later redaction, for the Ugaritic parallels prove that the system is old.[68]

Stating that 70 sons of Gideon were killed, while 2 of them were still alive, is similar to John 20:24, which speaks about *the twelve* disciples when there are only 11. Cassuto's astute observation paralleling the Ugaritic and Mosaic systems leaves origination an open question. Hebraic meter predates the supposed editorial changes of J E P D. Did the Hebrews copy an earlier Mesopotamian genre, or are both cultures preserving a tradition established before Babel, as indicated by Moses in the genealogy of 70 nations descended from Shem, Ham, and Japheth?

---

[68] Cassuto, *Genesis: Part II*, pp. 175-77.

The latter is selected.

The following are additional quotes from Cassuto's observation of 70 repetitions in Genesis and Exodus.

> Nor is it to be objected that the number seventy is not expressly mentioned in the text, for commonly the numerical symmetry is not explicitly stressed, and only the careful reader discovers it as a result of his study.[69]

> The Torah was concerned only to complete the number of seventy names [Genesis 5:31], and to incorporate therein the names of the principal nations that were near to Israel, or were in some way connected with the Israelites, or were in some manner known to them.[70]

Also within his intriguing discussion on the subject, Cassuto says 2 names, Havilah and Sheba, occur twice in Genesis 10 in order to arrive at 70 nations that descend from Noah.[71]

> Just as the nations of the entire world number seventy, according to Genesis X, so the children of Israel total seventy; they form a small world that parallels the great world, a microcosm corresponding to the macrocosm.[72]

> After encamping at Marah, the children of Israel again journeyed, and they came to Elim—this time it is not stated that Moses led them, and apparently we are to understand that they came there under the Lord's guidance in the manner described in (Exodus) xiii 21—where there were twelve springs of water and seventy palm trees—the Lord brought them to one of the desert oases that are blessed with an abundance of water and fertility....[73]

Cassuto describes the 70 elders in Exodus 24 as, "...a perfect representation of the people by a number that symbolizes perfection...."[74]

As in these quotations about the 70 in Genesis and Exodus, the Old Testament simultaneously presents numbers as reality, symbol, and tradition, such as the 7 days of creation, the 10 Commandments and the

---

[69] Ibid., pp. 177-78.
[70] Ibid., p. 180.
[71] Ibid., p. 182.
[72] Cassuto, *Exodus*, p. 8.
[73] Ibid., p. 185.
[74] Ibid., p. 310.

12 Tribes. The Hebrew words for 60, 70, 80, and 90 repeat in the entire Bible as words and word stems, as follows:

(repetition limited to Genesis appears in parentheses)
60 שִׁשִּׁים *shishshiym*, (shish-sheem')......59 (8) times;
70 שִׁבְעִים *shib'iym*, (shib-eem')..........103 (8) times;
80 שְׁמֹנִים *shemoniym*, (shem-o-neem')....30 (4) times;
90 תִּשְׁעִים *tish'iym*, (tish-eem')............20 (6) times.

Clearly, 70 predominates as a number chosen for symbolic, ceremonial, and traditional use. In Genesis, 60 appears to repeat as many times as 70. However, 60 repeats 6 times within the ages of the antediluvian patriarchs in chapter 5 as part of a larger number, where 70 is only found twice in their ages.

Cassuto points out that God is named 70 times in Genesis 1-4. This is a number of God's blessing on His people, or as in the 70 years of the Babylonian captivity, His judgment on His people.

> Altogether the Divine names in the three sections [Genesis 1-4:26] number *seventy*. אֱלֹהִים *'Elōhim* alone appears 40 times; הָ־אֱלֹהִים *YHWH 'Elōhim* twenty times; ה *YHWH* by itself ten times....And precisely at the seventieth reference it is solemnly announced: *At that time men began to call upon the name of the Lord*; with these words the section comes to an end.[75]

Hebraic Meter Spanning Adjacent Books in the Bible

This book makes no claim to fully comprehend or explain the data that is collected. The first 5 books of the Bible, known as the Pentateuch, are written by the same author, Moses. While searching these books for Hebraic meter, it was observed that some of the meter bridges one or more books of the Pentateuch, just as Cassuto observed some meter overlapping paragraphs, chapters, and sections. This is particularly apparent in longer rhythms of 70 or more repetitions. Longer rhythms usually include Hebraic subsets that verify the accuracy of the total. The assumption is that the same author chose to establish his identity as the author of all 5 books. There is nothing comparable to this genre in any other literature. Imagine Shakespeare or Dickens incorporating numeric patterns that connected 2 or more of their plays or novels. Yet, this is exactly what is found in the Pentateuch, a phenomenon for which there is no adequate explanation. Such a reality removes any possible validity of J E P D, known as the Documentary Hypothesis.

---

[75] Cassuto, *Genesis: Part I*, p. 192.

And the Lord Spoke unto Moses Saying

The phrase *And the Lord spoke unto Moses saying,* וַיְדַבֵּר יְהוָה אֶל־מֹשֶׁה לֵּאמֹר, repeats in Exodus, Leviticus, and Numbers 70 times, just as Moses wrote them. This also reminds us of:

> And the LORD came down in a cloud, and spake unto him, and took of the spirit that *was* upon him, and gave *it* unto the **seventy** elders: and it came to pass, *that*, when the spirit rested upon them, they prophesied, and did not cease. (Numbers 11:25)

> After these things the Lord appointed other **seventy** also, and sent them two and two before his face into every city and place, whither he himself would come. (Luke 10:1)

There are other ways in which the phrase *And the Lord spoke unto Moses saying* is expressed, but this particular Hebrew word order repeats exactly 70 times. The variations in which this phrase repeats masks the fact that 70 of them are exactly the same. It appears as if the writer was attempting to camouflage the fact that 70 are identical and others are merely close, but not exact. After 3,500 years, not one phrase is missing. This is obviously not a mnemonic device, but a means for those with knowledge of the meter to verify the authenticity and accuracy of the text, notwithstanding the significance of 70, as stated above. Legends about such meter in the text may have led to Gnostic speculation and heresy. There will be more on this subject in Chapter Nine and the Conclusion. How will the proponents of J E P D explain the presence of such a pattern in a text they claim was edited by 4 committees? They have no current theory to address this phenomenon in the text. They do not even know there is meter in the text.

And the Lord spoke unto Moses saying 70 times in Exodus, Leviticus, Numbers

Exodus 6:10	וַיְדַבֵּר יְהוָה אֶל־מֹשֶׁה לֵּאמֹר:	Exodus 6:29	וַיְדַבֵּר יְהוָה אֶל־מֹשֶׁה לֵּאמֹר:
Exodus 13:1	וַיְדַבֵּר יְהוָה אֶל־מֹשֶׁה לֵּאמֹר:	Exodus 14:1	וַיְדַבֵּר יְהוָה אֶל־מֹשֶׁה לֵּאמֹר:
Exodus 16:11	וַיְדַבֵּר יְהוָה אֶל־מֹשֶׁה לֵּאמֹר:	Exodus 25:1	וַיְדַבֵּר יְהוָה אֶל־מֹשֶׁה לֵּאמֹר:
Exodus 30:11	וַיְדַבֵּר יְהוָה אֶל־מֹשֶׁה לֵּאמֹר:	Exodus 30:17	וַיְדַבֵּר יְהוָה אֶל־מֹשֶׁה לֵּאמֹר:
Exodus 30:22	וַיְדַבֵּר יְהוָה אֶל־מֹשֶׁה לֵּאמֹר:	Exodus 31:1	וַיְדַבֵּר יְהוָה אֶל־מֹשֶׁה לֵּאמֹר:
Exodus 40:1	וַיְדַבֵּר יְהוָה אֶל־מֹשֶׁה לֵּאמֹר:	Leviticus 4:1	וַיְדַבֵּר יְהוָה אֶל־מֹשֶׁה לֵּאמֹר:
Leviticus 5:14	וַיְדַבֵּר יְהוָה אֶל־מֹשֶׁה לֵּאמֹר:	Leviticus 5:20	וַיְדַבֵּר יְהוָה אֶל־מֹשֶׁה לֵּאמֹר:
Leviticus 6:1	וַיְדַבֵּר יְהוָה אֶל־מֹשֶׁה לֵּאמֹר:	Leviticus 6:12	וַיְדַבֵּר יְהוָה אֶל־מֹשֶׁה לֵּאמֹר:
Leviticus 6:17	וַיְדַבֵּר יְהוָה אֶל־מֹשֶׁה לֵּאמֹר:	Leviticus 7:22	וַיְדַבֵּר יְהוָה אֶל־מֹשֶׁה לֵּאמֹר:

וַיְדַבֵּר יְהוָה אֶל־מֹשֶׁה לֵּאמֹר: Leviticus 8:1	וַיְדַבֵּר יְהוָה אֶל־מֹשֶׁה לֵּאמֹר: Leviticus 7:28
וַיְדַבֵּר יְהוָה אֶל־מֹשֶׁה לֵּאמֹר: Leviticus 14:1	וַיְדַבֵּר יְהוָה אֶל־מֹשֶׁה לֵּאמֹר: Leviticus 12:1
וַיְדַבֵּר יְהוָה אֶל־מֹשֶׁה לֵּאמֹר: Leviticus 18:1	וַיְדַבֵּר יְהוָה אֶל־מֹשֶׁה לֵּאמֹר: Leviticus 17:1
וַיְדַבֵּר יְהוָה אֶל־מֹשֶׁה לֵּאמֹר: Leviticus 20:1	וַיְדַבֵּר יְהוָה אֶל־מֹשֶׁה לֵּאמֹר: Leviticus 19:1
וַיְדַבֵּר יְהוָה אֶל־מֹשֶׁה לֵּאמֹר: Leviticus 22:1	וַיְדַבֵּר יְהוָה אֶל־מֹשֶׁה לֵּאמֹר: Leviticus 21:16
וַיְדַבֵּר יְהוָה אֶל־מֹשֶׁה לֵּאמֹר: Leviticus 22:26	וַיְדַבֵּר יְהוָה אֶל־מֹשֶׁה לֵּאמֹר: Leviticus 22:17
וַיְדַבֵּר יְהוָה אֶל־מֹשֶׁה לֵּאמֹר: Leviticus 23:9	וַיְדַבֵּר יְהוָה אֶל־מֹשֶׁה לֵּאמֹר: Leviticus 23:1
וַיְדַבֵּר יְהוָה אֶל־מֹשֶׁה לֵּאמֹר: Leviticus 23:26	וַיְדַבֵּר יְהוָה אֶל־מֹשֶׁה לֵּאמֹר: Leviticus 23:23
וַיְדַבֵּר יְהוָה אֶל־מֹשֶׁה לֵּאמֹר: Leviticus 24:1	וַיְדַבֵּר יְהוָה אֶל־מֹשֶׁה לֵּאמֹר: Leviticus 23:33
וַיְדַבֵּר יְהוָה אֶל־מֹשֶׁה לֵּאמֹר: Leviticus 27:1	וַיְדַבֵּר יְהוָה אֶל־מֹשֶׁה לֵּאמֹר: Leviticus 24:13
וַיְדַבֵּר יְהוָה אֶל־מֹשֶׁה לֵּאמֹר: Numbers 3:5	וַיְדַבֵּר יְהוָה אֶל־מֹשֶׁה לֵּאמֹר: Numbers 1:48
וַיְדַבֵּר יְהוָה אֶל־מֹשֶׁה לֵּאמֹר: Numbers 3:44	וַיְדַבֵּר יְהוָה אֶל־מֹשֶׁה לֵּאמֹר: Numbers 3:11
וַיְדַבֵּר יְהוָה אֶל־מֹשֶׁה לֵּאמֹר: Numbers 5:1	וַיְדַבֵּר יְהוָה אֶל־מֹשֶׁה לֵּאמֹר: Numbers 4:21
וַיְדַבֵּר יְהוָה אֶל־מֹשֶׁה לֵּאמֹר: Numbers 5:11	וַיְדַבֵּר יְהוָה אֶל־מֹשֶׁה לֵּאמֹר: Numbers 5:5
וַיְדַבֵּר יְהוָה אֶל־מֹשֶׁה לֵּאמֹר: Numbers 6:22	וַיְדַבֵּר יְהוָה אֶל־מֹשֶׁה לֵּאמֹר: Numbers 6:1
וַיְדַבֵּר יְהוָה אֶל־מֹשֶׁה לֵּאמֹר: Numbers 8:5	וַיְדַבֵּר יְהוָה אֶל־מֹשֶׁה לֵּאמֹר: Numbers 8:1
וַיְדַבֵּר יְהוָה אֶל־מֹשֶׁה לֵּאמֹר: Numbers 9:9	וַיְדַבֵּר יְהוָה אֶל־מֹשֶׁה לֵּאמֹר: Numbers 8:23
וַיְדַבֵּר יְהוָה אֶל־מֹשֶׁה לֵּאמֹר: Numbers 13:1	וַיְדַבֵּר יְהוָה אֶל־מֹשֶׁה לֵּאמֹר: Numbers 10:1
וַיְדַבֵּר יְהוָה אֶל־מֹשֶׁה לֵּאמֹר: Numbers 15:17	וַיְדַבֵּר יְהוָה אֶל־מֹשֶׁה לֵּאמֹר: Numbers 15:1
וַיְדַבֵּר יְהוָה אֶל־מֹשֶׁה לֵּאמֹר: Numbers 17:1	וַיְדַבֵּר יְהוָה אֶל־מֹשֶׁה לֵּאמֹר: Numbers 16:23
וַיְדַבֵּר יְהוָה אֶל־מֹשֶׁה לֵּאמֹר: Numbers 17:16	וַיְדַבֵּר יְהוָה אֶל־מֹשֶׁה לֵּאמֹר: Numbers 17:9
וַיְדַבֵּר יְהוָה אֶל־מֹשֶׁה לֵּאמֹר: Numbers 20:7	וַיְדַבֵּר יְהוָה אֶל־מֹשֶׁה לֵּאמֹר: Numbers 18:25
וַיְדַבֵּר יְהוָה אֶל־מֹשֶׁה לֵּאמֹר: Numbers 25:16	וַיְדַבֵּר יְהוָה אֶל־מֹשֶׁה לֵּאמֹר: Numbers 25:10
וַיְדַבֵּר יְהוָה אֶל־מֹשֶׁה לֵּאמֹר: Numbers 28:1	וַיְדַבֵּר יְהוָה אֶל־מֹשֶׁה לֵּאמֹר: Numbers 26:52
וַיְדַבֵּר יְהוָה אֶל־מֹשֶׁה לֵּאמֹר: Numbers 34:1	וַיְדַבֵּר יְהוָה אֶל־מֹשֶׁה לֵּאמֹר: Numbers 31:1
וַיְדַבֵּר יְהוָה אֶל־מֹשֶׁה לֵּאמֹר: Numbers 35:9	וַיְדַבֵּר יְהוָה אֶל־מֹשֶׁה לֵּאמֹר: Numbers 34:16

That I Am the Lord

There are additional phrases that repeat 70 times that are outside the scope of this book, such as *that I am the Lord*, כִּי־אֲנִי יְהוָה, which repeats exactly 70 times in Ezekiel, shown below. Within the 70 repetitions there is a longer phrase, *and they shall know that I am the Lord*, וְיָדְעוּ כִּי־אֲנִי יְהוָה, which repeats 28 times (7 x 4). There is an even longer phrase, *and ye shall know that I am the Lord*, וִידַעְתֶּם כִּי־אֲנִי יְהוָה, which repeats 21 times (7 x 3). Thus there is a 3-4-3 division of 10s of heptads. Ezekiel writes about a vision of a wheel within a wheel. He also arranges his text with meter inside meter.

That I am the Lord 70 times in Ezekiel
    That I am the Lord כִּי־אֲנִי יְהוָה
        repeats 21 times (7 x 3)
    And they shall know that I am the Lord וְיָדְעוּ כִּי־אֲנִי יְהוָה
        repeats 28 times (7 x 4) (italicized citations)
    And ye shall know that I am the Lord וִידַעְתֶּם כִּי־אֲנִי יְהוָה
        repeats 21 times (7 x 3) (bolded citations)

וְיָדְעוּ כִּי־אֲנִי יְהוָה *Ezek. 5:13*	וִידַעְתֶּם כִּי־אֲנִי יְהוָה **Ezek. 6:7**
וְיָדְעוּ כִּי־אֲנִי יְהוָה *Ezek. 6:10*	וִידַעְתֶּם כִּי־אֲנִי יְהוָה **Ezek. 6:13**
וְיָדְעוּ כִּי־אֲנִי יְהוָה *Ezek. 6:14*	וִידַעְתֶּם כִּי־אֲנִי יְהוָה **Ezek. 7:4**
וִידַעְתֶּם כִּי אֲנִי יְהוָה **Ezek. 7:9**	וְיָדְעוּ כִּי־אֲנִי יְהוָה *Ezek. 7:27*
וִידַעְתֶּם כִּי־אֲנִי יְהוָה **Ezek. 11:10**	וִידַעְתֶּם כִּי־אֲנִי יְהוָה **Ezek. 11:12**
וְיָדְעוּ כִּי־אֲנִי יְהוָה *Ezek. 12:15*	וְיָדְעוּ כִּי־אֲנִי יְהוָה *Ezek. 12:16*
וִידַעְתֶּם כִּי־אֲנִי יְהוָה **Ezek.12:20**	כִּי אֲנִי יְהוָה Ezek. 12:25
וִידַעְתֶּם כִּי־אֲנִי יְהוָה **Ezek. 13:14**	כִּי־אֲנִי יְהוָה Ezek. 13:21
כִּי־אֲנִי יְהוָה Ezek. 13:23	וִידַעְתֶּם כִּי־אֲנִי יְהוָה **Ezek. 14:8**
וִידַעְתֶּם כִּי־אֲנִי יְהוָה **Ezek. 15:7**	כִּי אֲנִי יְהוָה Ezek. 16:62
וִידַעְתֶּם כִּי־אֲנִי יְהוָה **Ezek. 17:21**	כִּי אֲנִי יְהוָה Ezek. 17:24
כִּי אֲנִי יְהוָה Ezek. 20:12	כִּי אֲנִי יְהוָה Ezek. 20:20
וִידַעְתֶּם כִּי־אֲנִי יְהוָה **Ezek. 20:38**	וִידַעְתֶּם כִּי־אֲנִי יְהוָה **Ezek. 20:42**
וִידַעְתֶּם כִּי־אֲנִי יְהוָה **Ezek. 20:44**	כִּי אֲנִי יְהוָה Ezek. 21:4
כִּי אֲנִי יְהוָה Ezek. 21:10	כִּי אֲנִי יְהוָה Ezek. 21:37
כִּי־אֲנִי יְהוָה Ezek. 22:16	וִידַעְתֶּם כִּי־אֲנִי יְהוָה **Ezek. 22:22**
וְיָדְעוּ כִּי־אֲנִי יְהוָה *Ezek. 24:27*	וִידַעְתֶּם כִּי־אֲנִי יְהוָה **Ezek. 25:5**
כִּי־אֲנִי יְהוָה Ezek. 25:7	וְיָדְעוּ כִּי־אֲנִי יְהוָה *Ezek. 25:11*
וְיָדְעוּ כִּי־אֲנִי יְהוָה *Ezek. 25:17*	וְיָדְעוּ כִּי־אֲנִי יְהוָה *Ezek. 26:6*
כִּי אֲנִי יְהוָה Ezek. 26:14	כִּי־אֲנִי יְהוָה *Ezek. 28:22*
וְיָדְעוּ כִּי־אֲנִי יְהוָה *Ezek. 28:23*	וְיָדְעוּ כִּי אֲנִי יְהוָה *Ezek. 28:26*
כִּי אֲנִי יְהוָה Ezek. 29:6	וְיָדְעוּ כִּי־אֲנִי יְהוָה *Ezek. 29:9*
וְיָדְעוּ כִּי־אֲנִי יְהוָה *Ezek. 29:21*	וְיָדְעוּ כִּי־אֲנִי יְהוָה *Ezek. 30:8*
וְיָדְעוּ כִּי־אֲנִי יְהוָה *Ezek. 30:19*	וְיָדְעוּ כִּי־אֲנִי יְהוָה *Ezek. 30:25*
וְיָדְעוּ כִּי־אֲנִי יְהוָה *Ezek. 30:26*	וְיָדְעוּ כִּי־אֲנִי יְהוָה *Ezek. 32:15*
וְיָדְעוּ כִּי־אֲנִי יְהוָה *Ezek. 33:29*	וְיָדְעוּ כִּי־אֲנִי יְהוָה *Ezek. 34:27*
וְיָדְעוּ כִּי אֲנִי יְהוָה Ezek. 34:30	כִּי־אֲנִי יְהוָה Ezek. 35:4
וִידַעְתֶּם כִּי־אֲנִי יְהוָה **Ezek. 35:9**	כִּי־אֲנִי יְהוָה Ezek. 35:12
וְיָדְעוּ כִּי־אֲנִי יְהוָה *Ezek. 35:15*	וִידַעְתֶּם כִּי־אֲנִי יְהוָה **Ezek. 36:11**
כִּי־אֲנִי יְהוָה Ezek. 36:23	כִּי אֲנִי יְהוָה Ezek. 36:36

וְיָדְע֖וּ כִּֽי־אֲנִ֥י יְהוָֽה *Ezek. 36:38*	וְיָדְע֗וּ כִּֽי־אֲנִ֥י יְהוָֽה **Ezek. 37:6**
וִידַעְתֶּ֖ם כִּי־אֲנִ֣י יְהוָ֑ה **Ezek. 37:13**	וִידַעְתֶּ֖ם כִּי־אֲנִ֣י יְהוָ֑ה **Ezek. 37:14**
כִּ֥י אֲנִ֖י יְהוָֽה Ezek.37:28	וְיָדְע֖וּ כִּֽי־אֲנִ֥י יְהוָֽה *Ezek. 38:23*
וְיָדְע֖וּ כִּֽי־אֲנִ֥י יְהוָֽה *Ezek. 39:6*	כִּ֥י אֲנִ֖י יְהוָֽה Ezek. 39:7
כִּ֥י אֲנִ֖י יְהוָֽה Ezek. 39:22	וְיָדְע֖וּ כִּ֥י אֲנִ֖י יְהוָֽה *Ezek. 39:28*

And He Saw or *And God Saw / The Land of Egypt / The Seventh Day / And the Word of the Lord Came to Me Saying*

The verb *to see*, רָאָה (*ra'ah*, raw-aw'), with *and*, ו (*wāw*), in front of it looks like וַיַּרְא, and is translated as *and he saw*. This Hebrew phrase appears 70 times in Genesis and Exodus. This is another example that indicates the 2 books were written by the same author.

And he saw 70 times in Genesis and Exodus
> Genesis 1:4, 10, 12, 18, 21, 25, 31; 6:5, 12; 8:13; 9:22; 12:7; 13:10; 17:1; 18:1, 2 (x2); 19:1, 2 (x2), 28; 22:4, 13; 24:63; 26:2, 8, 24; 28:6, 8; 29:2, 31; 31:2; 32:26; 33:1, 5; 34:2; 35:9; 38:2; 39:3; 40:6, 16; 42:1, 7, 27; 43:16, 29; 45:27; 46:29; 48:8, 17; 49:15; 50:11, 23; Exod. 2:11 (x2), 12, 25; 3:2 (x2), 4; 8:11; 9:34; 14:30, 31; 18:14; 20:18; 32:1, 5, 19, 25; 34:30; 39:43.

Longer repetitions, like the above, usually contain subsets. In the following example there are 7 repetitions of the phrase *and God saw* in Genesis 1, as shown at the beginning of this chapter. Those 7 repetitions also include the phrase *it was good*. Later in Genesis there are 2 more repetitions of *and God saw* that do not complete a Hebraic cadence. However, there is 1 more repetition in Exodus, the only remaining repetition in the entire Bible, that completes the decad.

And God saw 10 times in Genesis and Exodus
And God saw the light, that **it was good**.... וַיַּ֧רְא אֱלֹהִ֛ים אֶת־הָא֖וֹר כִּי־טֽוֹב (Gen. 1:4)
And God saw that **it was good**.......................... וַיַּ֥רְא אֱלֹהִ֖ים כִּי־טֽוֹב (Gen. 1:10)
And God saw that **it was good** .... וַיַּ֥רְא אֱלֹהִ֖ים כִּי־טֽוֹב (Gen. 1:12)
And God saw that **it was good** .... וַיַּ֥רְא אֱלֹהִ֖ים כִּי־טֽוֹב (Gen. 1:18)
And God saw that **it was good** .... וַיַּ֥רְא אֱלֹהִ֖ים כִּי־טֽוֹב (Gen. 1:21)
And God saw that **it was good** .... וַיַּ֥רְא אֱלֹהִ֖ים כִּי־טֽוֹב (Gen. 1:25)
And God saw every thing that he had made, and, behold, **it was very good**
.... וַיַּ֤רְא אֱלֹהִים֙ אֶת־כָּל־אֲשֶׁ֣ר עָשָׂ֔ה וְהִנֵּה־ט֖וֹב מְאֹ֑ד (Gen. 1:31)
And God saw .... וַיַּ֥רְא אֱלֹהִ֖ים (Gen. 6:12)
And God saw (appeared)............................... וַיֵּרָ֤א אֱלֹהִים֙ (Gen. 35:9)
And God saw .... וַיַּ֖רְא אֱלֹהִֽים (Exod. 2:25)

The 2 subsets above add further evidence of the author's intent to use the phrase *and he saw* in Hebraic meter. It is rather surprising that of the five books of Moses, the only example of *and God saw* outside of Genesis is found in Exodus 2:25.

There are a number of meters that encompass all 5 books of the Pentateuch. For example, the phrase *the land of Egypt*, מִצְרָיִם אֶרֶץ, repeats exactly 50 times in the Pentateuch, and the phrase *the seventh day* repeats exactly 40 times. This is further evidence pointing to a single author for all 5 books.

The land of Egypt, מִצְרָיִם אֶרֶץ 50 times in the Pentateuch
    Gen. 21:21; 45:19; 47:15; Exod. 6:13, 26; 7:4; 12:17, 41, 42, 51; 13:18; 16:1, 6, 32; 19:1; 20:2; 29:46; 32:1, 4, 7, 8, 11, 23; 33:1; Lev. 11:45; 19:36; 22:33; 23:43; 25:38, 42, 55; 26:13, 45; Num. 1:1; 9:1; 15:41; 26:4; 33:1, 38; Deut. 1:27; 5:6; 6:12; 8:14; 9:7; 13:6, 11; 16:3 (x2); 20:1; 29:24.

The seventh day, הַשְּׁבִיעִי יוֹם 40 times in the Pentateuch
    Gen. 2:2 (x2), 3; Exod. 12:15; 12:16; 13:6; 16:26, 27, 29, 30; 20:10, 11; 23:12; 24:16; 31:15, 17; 34:21; 35:2; Lev. 13:5, 6, 27, 32, 34, 51; 14:9, 39; 23:3, 8; Num. 6:9; 7:48; 19:12 (x2), 19 (x2); 28:25; 29:32; 31:19, 24; Deut. 5:14; 16:8.

The phrase *and the word of the Lord came to me saying*, וַיְהִי דְבַר־יְהוָה אֵלַי לֵאמֹר, is found 40 times in Ezekiel. Ezekiel 12:8 adds one Hebrew word and says, *the word of the Lord came to me in the morning saying*, וַיְהִי דְבַר־יְהוָה אֵלַי בַּבֹּקֶר לֵאמֹר.

And the word of the Lord came to me saying 40 times in Ezekiel
    Ezekiel 3:16; 6:1; 7:1; 11:14; 12:1, 8, 17, 21, 26; 13:1; 14:2, 12; 15:1; 16:1; 17:1, 11; 18:1; 20:2; 21:1, 6, 13, 23; 22:1, 17, 23; 23:1; 24:15; 25:1; 27:1; 28:1, 11, 20; 30:1; 33:1, 23; 34:1; 35:1; 36:16; 37:15; 38:1.

The Angel of the Lord

A similar relationship in heptadic meter between Genesis and Exodus is found in the phrase *the angel of the Lord*.

The angel of the Lord 7 times in Genesis and Exodus
    The angel of the Lord................ מַלְאַךְ יְהוָה (Gen. 16:7)
    The angel of the Lord................ מַלְאַךְ יְהוָה (Gen. 16:9)
    The angel of the Lord................ מַלְאַךְ יְהוָה (Gen. 16:10)
    The angel of the Lord................ מַלְאַךְ יְהוָה (Gen. 16:11)
    The angel of the Lord................ מַלְאַךְ יְהוָה (Gen. 22:11)
    The angel of the Lord................ מַלְאַךְ יְהוָה (Gen. 22:15)
    The angel of the Lord................ מַלְאַךְ יְהוָה (Exod. 3:2)

This phrase only appears 1 time in Exodus. There are none in Leviticus and Deuteronomy. There are 10 in Numbers (another decad) in chapter 22, the account of Balaam and his donkey. In total, there are 17 repetitions in the Pentateuch, arranged in a 7-10 division. This study avoids displaying metered repetition in Numbers, simply because it contains too many examples. Critics might have claimed the data was skewed by relying too heavily on a book with such an obvious title.

As Had Spoken the Lord

The following is a reverse arrangement from the previous example, in that there is 1 repetition from Genesis and 6 repetitions from Exodus. Also notice there are 3 more in Numbers, for a total of 10 in the Pentateuch in a 7-3 division.

As had spoken the Lord 7 times in Genesis and Exodus
    As had spoken the Lord...... כַּאֲשֶׁר דִּבֶּר יְהוָה (Gen. 24:51)
    As had spoken the Lord...... כַּאֲשֶׁר דִּבֶּר יְהוָה (Exod. 7:13)
    As had spoken the Lord...... כַּאֲשֶׁר דִּבֶּר יְהוָה (Exod. 7:22)
    As had spoken the Lord...... כַּאֲשֶׁר דִּבֶּר יְהוָה (Exod. 8:11)
    As had spoken the Lord...... כַּאֲשֶׁר דִּבֶּר יְהוָה (Exod. 8:15)
    As had spoken the Lord...... כַּאֲשֶׁר דִּבֶּר יְהוָה (Exod. 9:12)
    As had spoken the Lord...... כַּאֲשֶׁר דִּבֶּר יְהוָה (Exod. 9:35)
    As had spoken the Lord...... כַּאֲשֶׁר דִּבֶּר יְהוָה (Num. 5:4)
    As had spoken the Lord...... כַּאֲשֶׁר דִּבֶּר יְהוָה (Num. 17:5)
    As had spoken the Lord...... כַּאֲשֶׁר דִּבֶּר יְהוָה (Num. 27:23)

God / Lord God (plural construct)

One of the first places to search for Hebraic meter is in the names of God. The distinction between the plural and plural construct of *God* in Hebrew does not translate into English. Both appear as *God*. *God,* אֱלֹהֵי (*'Elōhiy*, El-o-hee'), repeats 60 times as a plural construct of אֱלֹהִים (*'Elōhiym*, El-ō-heem') in Genesis and Exodus. Thus, the writer maintains a cadence across 2 books:

God / Lord God (plural construct) 60 times in Genesis and Exodus
    Genesis 9:26; 24:3 (x2), 7, 12, 27, 42, 48; 26:24; 28:13 (x2); 31:5, 29, 30, 42 (x2), 53 (x3); 32:10 (x2); 33:20; 35:2, 4; 43:23; 46:1, 3; 50:17;

    Exodus 3:6 (x4), 13, 15 (x4), 16 (x2), 18; 4:5 (x4); 5:1, 3; 7:16; 9:1, 13; 10:3; 12:12; 15:2; 18:4; 20:23 (x2); 24:10; 32:27, 31; 34:17, 23.

In keeping with longer Hebraic meter, there is a subset of 7 using the Hebrew plural construct *'Elōhiy* with the word *Lord* for the phrase *Lord God, YHWH 'Elōhiy*. Later in this chapter the reader will see that *YHWH 'Elōhiym, Lord God,* is predominant, and repeats 20 times in Genesis with just 1 more repetition in Exodus, for a total of 21, or 3 x 7. Thus, multiple meters are intertwined within each other, and the genre is

The Lord God 7 times with plural construct in Genesis
- The Lord God .... יְהוָה אֱלֹהֵי (Gen. 9:26)
- The Lord God .... יְהוָה אֱלֹהֵי (Gen. 24:7)
- The Lord God .... יְהוָה אֱלֹהֵי (Gen. 24:12)
- The Lord God .... יְהוָה אֱלֹהֵי (Gen. 24:27)
- The Lord God .... יְהוָה אֱלֹהֵי (Gen. 24:42)
- The Lord God .... יְהוָה אֱלֹהֵי (Gen. 24:48)
- The Lord God .... יְהוָה אֱלֹהֵי (Gen. 28:13)

Cassuto observes, "One thing appears to me to be beyond doubt, namely, that the variations in the choice of the divine names did not come about accidently but by design."[76]

Decadal Meter in Genesis

And It Came to Pass / And He Said to Him / And Said Behold / And Were All the Days / Fowl of the Air / That It Was Good / Fruitful and Multiply / In His Hand

As stated earlier, Cassuto deals with repetition as it occurs in the text. But the approach of this book is to categorize his information according to meter. The focus will now turn to decadal meter (10 repetitions) and its multiples. Cassuto reports that there are 10 generations from Adam to Noah;[77] 10 generations from Shem to Abraham;[78] 10 plagues over Egypt; and the 10 Commandments. These are just a few of the decadal events in Genesis and Exodus.

The following are examples of decadal phrases and words in Genesis.

And it came to pass 10 times in Genesis
- And it came to pass .... וַיְהִי כַּאֲשֶׁר (Gen. 12:11)
- And it came to pass .... וַיְהִי כַּאֲשֶׁר (Gen. 20:13)
- And it came to pass .... וַיְהִי כַּאֲשֶׁר (Gen. 24:22)
- And it came to pass .... וַיְהִי כַּאֲשֶׁר (Gen. 25:52)
- And it came to pass .... וַיְהִי כַּאֲשֶׁר (Gen. 27:30)
- And it came to pass .... וַיְהִי כַּאֲשֶׁר (Gen. 29:10)
- And it came to pass .... וַיְהִי כַּאֲשֶׁר (Gen. 30:25)
- And it came to pass .... וַיְהִי כַּאֲשֶׁר־בָּא (Gen. 37:23)
- And it came to pass .... וַיְהִי כַּאֲשֶׁר (Gen. 41:13)
- And it came to pass .... וַיְהִי כַּאֲשֶׁר (Gen. 43:2)

---

[76] Cassuto, *The Documentary Hypothesis*, p. 21.
[77] Cassuto, *Genesis: Part I*, pp. 254-60.
[78] Cassuto, *Genesis: Part II*, pp. 250, 253, 291, 294, 306.

And he said to him 10 times in Genesis (man speaking)
    And he said to him .... וַיֹּאמֶר לוֹ (Gen. 20:9)
    And he said to him .... וַיֹּאמֶר לוֹ (Gen. 27:32)
    And he said to him .... וַיֹּאמֶר לוֹ (Gen. 28:1)
    And he said to him .... וַיֹּאמֶר לוֹ (Gen. 29:14)
    And he said to him .... וַיֹּאמֶר לוֹ (Gen. 37:10)
    And he said to him .... וַיֹּאמֶר לוֹ (Gen. 37:13)
    And he said to him .... וַיֹּאמֶר לוֹ (Gen. 37:14)
    And he said to him .... וַיֹּאמֶר לוֹ (Gen. 40:9)
    And he said to him .... וַיֹּאמֶר לוֹ (Gen. 40:12)
    And he said to him .... וַיֹּאמֶר לוֹ (Gen. 47:29)

And said behold 10 times in Genesis
    And he said behold................. וַיֹּאמֶר הִנֵּה (Gen. 18:9)
    And he said behold................. וַיֹּאמֶר הִנֵּה (Gen. 18:27)
    And he said behold................. וַיֹּאמֶר הִנֵּה (Gen. 18:31)
    And he said behold................. וַיֹּאמֶר הִנֵּה (Gen. 19:2)
    And he said behold................. וַיֹּאמֶר הִנֵּה (Gen. 22:7)
    And he said behold................. וַיֹּאמֶר הִנֵּה (Gen. 27:2)
    And she said behold................ וַתֹּאמֶר הִנֵּה (Gen. 30:3)
    And he said behold................. וַיֹּאמֶר הִנֵּה (Gen. 37:9)
    And he said behold................. וַיֹּאמֶר הִנֵּה (Gen. 42:2)
    And he said behold................. וַיֹּאמֶר הִנֵּה (Gen. 48:2)

And were all the days 10 times in Genesis
    And were all the days................. וַיִּהְיוּ כָּל־יְמֵי (Gen. 5:5)
    And were all the days................. וַיִּהְיוּ כָּל־יְמֵי (Gen. 5:8)
    And were all the days................. וַיִּהְיוּ כָּל־יְמֵי (Gen. 5:11)
    And were all the days................. וַיִּהְיוּ כָּל־יְמֵי (Gen. 5:14)
    And were all the days................. וַיִּהְיוּ כָּל־יְמֵי (Gen. 5:17)
    And were all the days................. וַיִּהְיוּ כָּל־יְמֵי (Gen. 5:20)
    And were all the days................. וַיְהִי כָּל־יְמֵי (Gen. 5:23)
    And were all the days................. וַיִּהְיוּ כָּל־יְמֵי (Gen. 5:27)
    And were all the days................. וַיְהִי כָּל־יְמֵי (Gen. 5:31)
    And were all the days................. וַיִּהְיוּ כָּל־יְמֵי (Gen. 9:29)

Fowl of the air 10 times in Genesis
    Fowl of the air...................... וְעוֹף הַשָּׁמַיִם (Gen. 1:20)
    Fowl of the air...................... וּבְעוֹף הַשָּׁמַיִם (Gen. 1:26)
    Fowl of the air...................... וּבְעוֹף הַשָּׁמַיִם (Gen. 1:28)
    Fowl of the air...................... עוֹף הַשָּׁמַיִם (Gen. 1:30)
    Fowl of the air...................... עוֹף הַשָּׁמַיִם (Gen. 2:19)
    Fowl of the air...................... וּלְעוֹף הַשָּׁמַיִם (Gen. 2:20)
    Fowl of the air...................... עוֹף הַשָּׁמַיִם (Gen. 6:7)
    Fowl of the air...................... מֵעוֹף הַשָּׁמַיִם (Gen. 7:3)
    Fowl of the air...................... עוֹף הַשָּׁמַיִם (Gen. 7:23)
    Fowl of the air...................... עוֹף הַשָּׁמַיִם (Gen. 9:2)

That it was good 10 times in Genesis

That it was good...................... כִּי־טוֹב (Gen. 1:4)
That it was good...................... כִּי־טוֹב (Gen. 1:10)
That it was good...................... כִּי־טוֹב (Gen. 1:12)
That it was good...................... כִּי־טוֹב (Gen. 1:18)
That it was good...................... כִּי־טוֹב (Gen. 1:21)
That it was good...................... כִּי־טוֹב (Gen. 1:25)
That it was good...................... כִּי טוֹב (Gen. 3:6)
That it was good...................... כִּי טוֹב (Gen. 40:16)
That it was good...................... כִּי־טוֹב (Gen. 45:20)
That it was good...................... כִּי טוֹב (Gen. 49:15)

Fruitful and multiply 10 times in Genesis

Be fruitful and multiply (Gen. 1:22)
Be fruitful and multiply (Gen. 1:28)
And be fruitful and multiply (Gen. 8:17)
Be fruitful and multiply (Gen. 9:1)
Be fruitful and multiply (Gen. 9:7)
And I will make him fruitful and multiply him (Gen. 17:20)
And make you fruitful and multiply you (Gen. 28:3)
Be fruitful and multiply (Gen. 35:11)
And they were fruitful and they multiplied (Gen. 47:27)
Behold I will make you fruitful and multiply you (Gen. 48:4)

פְּרוּ וּרְבוּ (Gen. 1:22)
פְּרוּ וּרְבוּ (Gen. 1:28)
וּפְרוּ וְרָבוּ (Gen. 8:17)
פְּרוּ וּרְבוּ (Gen. 9:1)
פְּרוּ וּרְבוּ (Gen. 9:7)
וְהִפְרֵיתִי אֹתוֹ וְהִרְבֵּיתִי (Gen. 17:20)
וְיַפְרְךָ וְיַרְבֶּךָ (Gen. 28:3)
פְּרֵה וּרְבֵה (Gen. 35:11)
וַיִּפְרוּ וַיִּרְבּוּ (Gen. 47:27)
הִנְנִי מַפְרְךָ וְהִרְבִּיתִךָ (Gen. 48:4)

In his hand 10 times in Genesis

In his hand........................... בְּיָדוֹ (Gen. 19:16)
In his hand........................... בְּיָדוֹ (Gen. 22:6)
In his hand........................... בְּיָדוֹ (Gen. 24:10)
In his hand........................... בְּיָדוֹ (Gen. 32:14)
In his hand........................... בְּיָדוֹ (Gen. 39:3)
In his hand........................... בְּיָדוֹ (Gen. 39:4)
In his hand........................... בְּיָדוֹ (Gen. 39:23)
In his hand........................... בְּיָדוֹ (Gen. 40:13)
In his hand........................... בְּיָדוֹ (Gen. 44:16)
In his hand........................... בְּיָדוֹ (Gen. 44:17)

Most of the decadal meter in Genesis is not stated and is not apparent until it is identified. However, there are times when it is expressly stated. The following are examples of 10 things counted in Genesis:

1. Abraham living *10 years* in the land of Canaan (Gen. 16:3);
2. Abraham pleads with God to spare Sodom for the sake of *10 faithful people* (Gen. 18:32);
3. Eliezer takes *10 camels* on a trip to find Isaac a wife (Gen. 24:10);
4. Eliezer gives Rebecca a gift of *10 shekels* (Gen. 24:10);
5. Laban wants Rebecca to stay at least *10 more days* (Gen. 24:55);
6. Jacob complains to his wives that Laban changed his wages *10 times* (Gen. 31:7);
7. Jacob complains to Laban that he changed his wages *10 times* (Gen. 31:41);
8. Jacob sends Esau *10 bulls* and *10 male donkeys* among other gifts (Gen. 32:15);
9. *10 brothers*, who deceived their father about Joseph's death, travel to Egypt (Gen. 42:3); and
10. 2 sets of *10 donkeys* with gifts for Jacob from Joseph (Gen. 45:23).

In Genesis, 12 separate things are counted 10 times. In Genesis 18:32 the same group of 10 is named twice. It is also interesting to note that 2 of these 12 things are grouped together in the same verse because of their similarity, namely livestock in 32:15 and more livestock in 45:23. This results in 10 separate enumerations of 10. This is hardly coincidental. Time constraints would not allow such a search without the aid of a computer. We can only imagine what Cassuto would have accomplished had he similar access. In addition to 10 things counted, the Hebrew masculine form of 10 (*ten*), עֲשָׂרָה (*asara*, aw-saw-ra'), repeats a total of 20 times in Genesis: 5:8, 10; 7:20; 11:25; 14:4 (x2), 5; 17:25; 18:32 (x2); 24:10, 22; 31:41; 32:16 (x2); 37:2; 42:3; 45:23; 46:18; 47:28.

Exodus repeats 10 things 9 times, while the inconsistent Septuagint repeats 10 things 10 times. A repetition is missing from the Septuagint at 36:21, including the entire verse, but 2 more are added to 27:13 that are not found in the Hebrew text. The Septuagint error may indicate a desire by the translators to make the repetition of 10 things also occur 10 times in Exodus. Even though the Septuagint translators rarely translate Hebraic meter into the Greek, this does not mean they did not attempt to create some of their own meter. In other words, they appear to have had some understanding of the concept, but did not know where most of the meter was located in the Hebrew text, or it was too complicated to translate the meter correctly.

In all, the number of 10 things or events is repeated 50 times in the Pentateuch. There are 12 in Genesis, 9 in Exodus, 4 in Leviticus, 17 in Numbers, and 5 in Deuteronomy for a total of 47. Again, notice the asymmetric distribution. There are also 3 directives to count captains by 10s in Exodus 18:21, 25; and Deuteronomy 1:15. In these 3 verses, the text not only counts by 10s, but literally directs counting by 10s. Thus a pattern of 10 things numbered 50 times has been preserved in the Pentateuch for 3,500 years. Evidently, the Septuagint writers were not aware of this longer meter, as illustrated by their addition to Exodus 27:13. The arrangement of these numbers in the Pentateuch is obviously contrived. It points to a single author who maintained decadal meter throughout his 5 books, who should be acknowledged as the original and only writer of the Pentateuch. Hollywood gives more credence to Moses than do the scholars. As shown in Chapter Five, the number 10 repeats 10 times in Revelation. One of the 10, Revelation 11:4, is encrypted as an acrostic.

Cassuto writes:
The ten sayings with which, according to the Talmud, the world was created (Aboth v 1; in B. Rosh Hashana 32a and B. Megilla 21b only nine of them are enumerated, the one in i 29, apparently, being omitted)—that is, the ten utterances of God beginning with the words, *and...said*—are clearly divisible into two groups: the first group contains *seven* Divine fiats enjoining the creation of the creatures, to wit, "Let there be light" ... the second group comprises three pronouncements that emphasize God's concern for man's welfare....[79]

The 10 phrases from Genesis 1, a Hebraic meter we have already seen in the 4 Gospels, as well as at the beginning of this chapter, set the paradigm for metered pronouncements throughout the Bible. These 10 pronouncements foreshadow the 10 Commandments.

In order to arrive at 10 repetitions above, Cassuto does not mention that the 2 Hebrew words for *said God* are intentionally set in reverse order in Genesis 1:28. Only 9 statements are in identical order. Yes, there are 10 Hebrew phrases meaning *And God said*, or *And said God,* in the first section (Genesis 1:1-2:3)—7 commands followed by 3 statements about the creation of man—but in 1:28 the Hebrew phrase is in reverse order. However, Cassuto was not aware that there are 20 repetitions of *and said God* (וַיֹּאמֶר אֱלֹהִים) in identical order in the entire book of Genesis, as seen below, if 1:28 is not included in the list.

---

[79] Cassuto, *Genesis: Part I*, p. 14.

And said God 20 times in Genesis

And said God	וַיֹּאמֶר אֱלֹהִים	(1:3)
And said God	וַיֹּאמֶר אֱלֹהִים	(1:6)
And said God	וַיֹּאמֶר אֱלֹהִים	(1:9)
And said God	וַיֹּאמֶר אֱלֹהִים	(1:11)
And said God	וַיֹּאמֶר אֱלֹהִים	(1:14)
And said God	וַיֹּאמֶר אֱלֹהִים	(1:20)
And said God	וַיֹּאמֶר אֱלֹהִים	(1:24)
And said God	וַיֹּאמֶר אֱלֹהִים	(1:26)
And said God	וַיֹּאמֶר אֱלֹהִים	(1:29)
And said God	וַיֹּאמֶר אֱלֹהִים	(6:13)
And said God	וַיֹּאמֶר אֱלֹהִים	(9:8)
And said God	וַיֹּאמֶר אֱלֹהִים	(9:12)
And said God	וַיֹּאמֶר אֱלֹהִים	(9:17)
And said God	וַיֹּאמֶר אֱלֹהִים	(17:9)
And said God	וַיֹּאמֶר אֱלֹהִים	(17:15)
And said God	וַיֹּאמֶר אֱלֹהִים	(17:19)
And said God	וַיֹּאמֶר אֱלֹהִים	(21:12)
And said God	וַיֹּאמֶר אֱלֹהִים	(35:1)
And said God	וַיֹּאמֶר אֱלֹהִים	(43:29)
And said God	וַיֹּאמֶר אֱלֹהִים	(46:2)

The words in 1:28 appear to have been reversed in order to simultaneously maintain 10 repetitions in the first chapter and 20 phrases in exact order in Genesis. Cassuto might have been pleasantly surprised to see further confirmation that his theories about the text encompass the entire book of Genesis. The complexity and design employed in this genre exceeds expectations.

Cassuto notes a lengthy integration of meter and text when he states: "The name of the Lord [*YHWH*] is mentioned in the section *six* times; the verb יָלַד *yāladh* ['bore, begot'], *thirty* times – five times *six* [in Genesis 5:1-6:8]."[80] The English reader can find all 30 in the KJV with the Hebrew verb translated variously as *begot, begat, born, bore,* and *bare.*

The Lord God

Perhaps one of the most enigmatic repetitions in Genesis is the phrase *the Lord God*, which occurs 20 times in the exact form listed below, but only in the second section (Genesis 2:4-3:24), as stated earlier by Cassuto.[81] This repetition, found with the aid of a computer, confirms Cassuto's accuracy in identifying the correct sections in Genesis, and

---

[80] Ibid., p. 271.
[81] Ibid., p. 192.

explodes the Documentary Hypothesis and J E P D. Why is the phrase *the Lord God* only in the second section? Why would the supposed editors of J and E, the Yawist and Elohist traditions, only use it in one section? The answer is, there never was a J or an E, unless the second section, which also happens to include the so-called *Second Creation Myth*, was an insertion by an unknown fifth committee. This is all impossible when tested against the fanciful claims of the Documentary Hypothesis. Quite frankly, there is no explanation for the following numeric series other than that it exists. The phrase *the Lord God* is found 7 more times in the second section in the plural construct for *God*, as shown previously. Cassuto's explanation for changes of style in various sections of the text is simple but profound. "In a word, change of style depends on change of subject matter, not on difference of sources."[82]

The Lord God 20 times in Genesis

The Lord God	יְהוָה אֱלֹהִים	(Gen. 2:4)
The Lord God	יְהוָה אֱלֹהִים	(Gen. 2:5)
The Lord God	יְהוָה אֱלֹהִים	(Gen. 2:7)
The Lord God	יְהוָה אֱלֹהִים	(Gen. 2:8)
The Lord God	יְהוָה אֱלֹהִים	(Gen. 2:9)
The Lord God	יְהוָה אֱלֹהִים	(Gen. 2:15)
The Lord God	יְהוָה אֱלֹהִים	(Gen. 2:16)
The Lord God	יְהוָה אֱלֹהִים	(Gen. 2:18)
The Lord God	יְהוָה אֱלֹהִים	(Gen. 2:19)
The Lord God	יְהוָה אֱלֹהִים	(Gen. 2:21)
The Lord God	יְהוָה אֱלֹהִים	(Gen. 2:22)
The Lord God	יְהוָה אֱלֹהִים	(Gen. 3:1)
The Lord God	יְהוָה אֱלֹהִים	(Gen. 3:8)
The Lord God	יְהוָה אֱלֹהִים	(Gen. 3:8)
The Lord God	יְהוָה אֱלֹהִים	(Gen. 3:9)
The Lord God	יְהוָה אֱלֹהִים	(Gen. 3:13)
The Lord God	יְהוָה אֱלֹהִים	(Gen. 3:14)
The Lord God	יְהוָה אֱלֹהִים	(Gen. 3:21)
The Lord God	יְהוָה אֱלֹהִים	(Gen. 3:22)
The Lord God	יְהוָה אֱלֹהִים	(Gen. 3:23)

In the Land of Canaan / Which Is Beyond the Jordan

The phrase *in the land of Canaan* repeats 20 times in Genesis in exactly the same Hebrew form. If this is a human effort, the writers had a thorough understanding of concurrent symmetry and asymmetry, an aesthetic genre not found in other cultures of the era. The writer took an apparently random text of 50 chapters and dispersed a precise

---

[82] Cassuto, *The Documentary Hypothesis*, p. 64.

list of 20 identical phrases within the text. One will not find a similar, conscious approach to an art form until the advent of 20th century Abstract Expressionism that splattered paint within the boundaries of a precisely measured rectangular canvas. The archeologists and art historians are challenged to name any culture with an aesthetic that intentionally combines order and disorder. Perhaps the appreciation for abstract art among Jewish people today is a subliminal response to the abstraction they encounter through immersion in their own Hebrew text. Of course, this is an apparent abstraction. No artist or mathematician is able to create anything that is purely random, which is why mathematicians rely on random number generators. The ability to integrate abstraction and order is a reflection of life itself, the ability to deal with and not fantasize about reality. The human experience with time, the known, and the unknown is a constant that the wise learn to embrace as the natural order created by God. This is the epitome and superiority of Hebrew versus Western thought.

In the land of Canaan 20 times in Genesis

In the land of Canaan.................... בְּאֶרֶץ־כְּנַעַן (Gen. 13:12)
In the land of Canaan.................... בְּאֶרֶץ כְּנַעַן (Gen. 16:3)
In the land of Canaan.................... בְּאֶרֶץ כְּנַעַן (Gen. 23:2)
In the land of Canaan.................... בְּאֶרֶץ כְּנַעַן (Gen. 23:19)
In the land of Canaan.................... בְּאֶרֶץ כְּנַעַן (Gen. 33:18)
In the land of Canaan.................... בְּאֶרֶץ כְּנַעַן (Gen. 35:6)
In the land of Canaan.................... בְּאֶרֶץ כְּנַעַן (Gen. 36:5)
In the land of Canaan.................... בְּאֶרֶץ כְּנַעַן (Gen. 36:6)
In the land of Canaan.................... בְּאֶרֶץ כְּנַעַן (Gen. 37:1)
In the land of Canaan.................... בְּאֶרֶץ כְּנַעַן (Gen. 42:5)
In the land of Canaan.................... בְּאֶרֶץ כְּנַעַן (Gen. 42:13)
In the land of Canaan.................... בְּאֶרֶץ כְּנַעַן (Gen. 42:32)
In the land of Canaan.................... בְּאֶרֶץ כְּנַעַן (Gen. 46:6)
In the land of Canaan.................... בְּאֶרֶץ כְּנַעַן (Gen. 46:12)
In the land of Canaan.................... בְּאֶרֶץ־כְּנַעַן (Gen. 46:31)
In the land of Canaan.................... בְּאֶרֶץ כְּנַעַן (Gen. 47:4)
In the land of Canaan.................... בְּאֶרֶץ כְּנַעַן (Gen. 48:3)
In the land of Canaan.................... בְּאֶרֶץ כְּנַעַן (Gen. 48:7)
In the land of Canaan.................... בְּאֶרֶץ כְּנַעַן (Gen. 49:30)
In the land of Canaan.................... בְּאֶרֶץ כְּנַעַן (Gen. 50:5)

The text also contains some rather unexpected anomalies, such as the following 2 examples. As shown above, *In the land of Canaan* repeats 20 times in Genesis. It is also found 10 more times, 5 times in Numbers and 5 times in Joshua and Judges. The same arrangement is found in the phrase *which is beyond the Jordan*. It appears 5 times in the

Pentateuch and 5 more times in Joshua and Judges. In each case there are 4 repetitions in Joshua and 1 in Judges, as follows:

In the land of Canaan 10 times in Numbers, Joshua, and Judges

In the land of Canaan	בְּאֶרֶץ כְּנָעַן	(Num. 26:19)
In the land of Canaan	בְּאֶרֶץ כְּנָעַן	(Num. 32:30)
In the land of Canaan	בְּאֶרֶץ כְּנָעַן	(Num. 33:40)
In the land of Canaan	בְּאֶרֶץ כְּנָעַן	(Num. 34:29)
In the land of Canaan	בְּאֶרֶץ כְּנָעַן	(Num. 35:14)
In the land of Canaan	בְּאֶרֶץ כְּנָעַן	(Josh. 14:1)
In the land of Canaan	בְּאֶרֶץ כְּנָעַן	(Josh. 21:2)
In the land of Canaan	בְּאֶרֶץ־כְּנָעַן	(Josh. 22:9)
In the land of Canaan	בְּאֶרֶץ כְּנָעַן	(Josh. 22:10)
In the land of Canaan	בְּאֶרֶץ כְּנָעַן	(Jdg. 21:12)

Which is beyond the Jordan 10 times in Pentateuch, Joshua, and Judges

Which is beyond the Jordan	אֲשֶׁר בְּעֵבֶר הַיַּרְדֵּן	(Gen. 50:10)
Which is beyond the Jordan	אֲשֶׁר בְּעֵבֶר הַיַּרְדֵּן	(Gen. 50:11)
Which is beyond the Jordan	אֲשֶׁר בְּעֵבֶר הַיַּרְדֵּן	(Deut. 3:8)
Which is beyond the Jordan	אֲשֶׁר בְּעֵבֶר הַיַּרְדֵּן	(Deut. 3:25)
Which is beyond the Jordan	אֲשֶׁר בְּעֵבֶר הַיַּרְדֵּן	(Deut. 4:47)
Which is beyond the Jordan	אֲשֶׁר בְּעֵבֶר הַיַּרְדֵּן	(Josh. 2:10)
Which is beyond the Jordan	אֲשֶׁר בְּעֵבֶר הַיַּרְדֵּן	(Josh. 5:1)
Which is beyond the Jordan	אֲשֶׁר בְּעֵבֶר הַיַּרְדֵּן	(Josh. 9:1)
Which is beyond the Jordan	אֲשֶׁר בְּעֵבֶר הַיַּרְדֵּן	(Josh. 9:10)
Which is beyond the Jordan	אֲשֶׁר בְּעֵבֶר הַיַּרְדֵּן	(Jdg. 10:8)

How was this accomplished? The following is a possible explanation for these and similar anomalies not presented in this book. From a perspective of aesthetic analysis, the tradition of Hebraic meter in the text was a highly developed genre by the time Moses completed the Pentateuch. Incomplete meters were intentionally placed in the text on the assumption that future writers would complete the meter in their own books. Hence, the 2 sets of 5 phrases above in the Pentateuch were intentionally left open ended. Joshua added 4 more repetitions to each set, leaving the final repetition, or possible repetitions, for the next writer to complete in his own book. The next writer had the option of rounding off the meter with a repetition of 1 for a total of 10, or adding 11 for a total of 20, or however he chose to complete the meter. With this kind of aesthetic approach to the text, the possibilities are endless. Yes, this is a theory, but let us remember we are dealing with another culture's art form for which there is no comparison. We are also observing the finished product and not the process. Art analysis examines the work of art and looks for an explanation of how the art can be reproduced. This is only a theory, but this theory attempts to incorporate the breadth of the data as it has been presented in this chapter. If the limits of credulity are being stretched, there is only one other explanation: God talked to Moses, and when we open the Bible we are on the same holy ground on which Moses stood. In this case we are wise to speak respectfully about the text.

Decadal Events in Genesis

Cassuto explains that the genealogies from Adam to Abraham are listed in multiples of 10 from Adam to Noah,[83] and from Shem to Abraham.[84] There is also the well-known phrase *these are the generations* that repeats 10 times in Genesis. This phrase indicates that decadal repetition does indeed encompass the entire book of Genesis. Where there is one all-encompassing meter, there will be more, as has already been demonstrated.

These are the generations of 10 times in Genesis
    These are the generations of .... אֵלֶּה תוֹלְדוֹת (Gen. 2:4)
    These are the generations of .... אֵלֶּה תּוֹלְדֹת (Gen. 6:9)
    And these are the generations of .... וְאֵלֶּה תּוֹלְדֹת (Gen. 10:1)
    These are the generations of .... אֵלֶּה תּוֹלְדֹת (Gen. 11:10)
    And these are the generations of .... וְאֵלֶּה תּוֹלְדֹת (Gen. 11:27)
    And these are the generations of .... וְאֵלֶּה תֹּלְדֹת (Gen. 25:12)
    And these are the generations of .... וְאֵלֶּה תּוֹלְדֹת (Gen. 25:19)
    And these are the generations of .... וְאֵלֶּה תֹּלְדוֹת (Gen. 36:1)
    And these are the generations of .... וְאֵלֶּה תֹּלְדוֹת (Gen. 36:9)
    These are the generations of .... אֵלֶּה תֹּלְדוֹת (Gen. 37:2)

The phrase *This is the book of the generations of Adam* (Genesis 5:1) is not included above because it lacks *these* (וְאֵלֶּה) and adds *this is the book of*. However, according to Lessing and Steinmann in *Prepare the Way of the Lord*, the 11 *generations* mark 12 divisions in Genesis.[85] This will be addressed in the next chapter. The following is a chiasm published by Cassuto, where he lists the 10 tests of Abraham's faith. He writes, "Note should also be taken of the chiastic parallelism between the ten episodes."[86]

Ten Tests of Abraham's Faith in Chiastic Order
    A. God's command to leave Haran and live as an alien in Canaan. (Gen. 12:1-4)

---

[83] Cassuto, *Genesis: Part I*, p. 260.
[84] Cassuto, *Genesis: Part II*, p. 294.
[85] R. Reed Lessing and Andrew E. Steinmann, *Prepare the Way of the Lord*, Concordia Publishing House, St. Louis, 2014, p. 49.
[86] Cassuto, *Genesis: Part II*, pp. 294-96.

- **B.** Drought that led to Pharaoh's arrest of Sarah in Egypt. (Gen. 12:1-13:4)
- **C.** Abraham takes second choice when he must divide the land with Lot. (Gen. 13:5-18)
- **D.** Abraham must rescue Lot's family and the Sodomites from 5 kings. (Gen. 15)
- **E.** Strife between Sarah and Hagar who is pregnant with Abraham's first son. (Gen. 16)
- **E'.** God commands circumcision for Abraham, and his first son. (Gen. 17:1-15)
- **D'.** Abraham pleads with God to spare Sodom and Lot's family. (Gen. 17:17-19:28)
- **B'.** Drought that led Abimelech to abduct Sarah in Gerar. (Gen. 20:1-21:7)
- **C'.** Sarah makes Abraham choose between his two sons. (Gen. 21:1-34)
- **A'.** God's command to leave his home and sacrifice Isaac on Mount Moriah. (Gen. 22:2-18)

In a similar format as above, Zechariah chapter 8 lists 10 promises from God; the 10th promise in verse 23 refers to 10 men speaking every language, a reversal of the Babel account.

Decadal Meter in Exodus

There are numerous examples of decadal meter in Exodus. This study will only focus on a few. Obviously, the 10 Plagues and the 10 Commandments are well-known decadal events. The Greek word for *plagues* repeats 10 times in Revelation. In Numbers 14:22 God says the Israelites tempted Him 10 times. The decadal repetition of *horns* originates in Exodus, and is copied by Daniel and Revelation.

Exod. 27:2 horns upon the four corners	Dan. 7:7 a fourth beast…had ten horns.
Exod. 27:2 his horns…overlay with brass.	Dan. 7:8 I considered the horns
Exod. 29:12 upon the horns of the altar	Dan. 7:8 three…horns plucked by roots
Exod. 30:2 the horns shall be of the same.	Dan. 7:20 ten horns that were in his head
Exod. 30:3 horns thereof;…crown of gold	Dan. 7:24 ten horns out of this kingdom
Exod. 30:10 atonement upon the horns	Dan. 8:3 a ram which had two horns:
Exod. 37:25 the horns were of the same.	Dan. 8:3 the two horns were high
Exod. 37:26 horns of it…crown of gold	Dan. 8:6 the ram that had two horns
Exod. 38:2 horns on the four corners	Dan. 8:7 and brake his two horns
Exod. 38:2 horns…he overlaid with brass.	Dan. 8:20 two horns are the kings

Rev. 5:6 Lamb…having seven horns
Rev. 9:13 four horns of the golden altar
Rev. 12:3 seven heads and ten horns
Rev. 13:1 seven heads and ten horns
Rev. 13:1 upon his ten horns ten crowns

Rev. 13:11 he had two horns like a lamb
Rev. 17:3 seven heads and ten horns.
Rev. 17:7 seven heads and ten horns.
Rev. 17:12 the ten horns...are ten kings
Rev. 17:16 ten horns...hate the whore

The 10 Commandments

The theme of the 10 Commandments is also reflected in, and associated with, other decadal statements throughout Exodus. Most readers are not aware that Moses wrote 2 lists of the 10 Commandments in the Pentateuch. The second list is usually called 10 Precepts, not commandments, and they are a little different. There are also a number of decadal lists that divide one commandment into 10 statutes regarding the same law. Cassuto writes as follows:

> Numerical schematism has special character in this section [Exodus 18:1-27]; it is now mainly based on the number ten. The word דָּבָר *dābār* ['word', 'thing', 'matter'] occurs again and again in different meanings, particularly in the dialogue between Moses and Jethro, and finally even in the narrative; in all it is found ten times in the singular and once in the plural. Possibly this decade is to be regarded as a preliminary allusion to the *Decalogue*[87] which is to form the main theme of the next section. Other sets of ten are also discernible in the section: the verb עָשָׂה *'āśā* ['do'] occurs ten times, beginning with 'that God had done' in *v.* 1; likewise the verb בּוֹא *bō'* ['come'], commencing with 'And Jethro...came' in *v.* 5. Since *Jethro's* name appears seven times, as is usual in the case of characteristic words [he also calls them keywords] of a given section or paragraph, and the designation *Moses' father-in-law* is found thirteen times, we arrive at a total of twenty references—twice times ten.[88]

Groups of precepts, containing ten commandments each, are found in other parts of the Pentateuch. And that has given rise to a problem that has occupied an important place in Biblical study. Many exegetes have held the view that the original Decalogue is not that of chapter xx, but a different series of ten commandments, namely, the practical precepts in ch. xxxiv 14-26. This view, after being alluded to in ancient times, in a Greek book dating from the end of the fifth century C.E.,

---

[87] The *10 Words*, also called the *10 Commandments* עֲשֶׂרֶת הַדְּבָרִים, *'ăsereth hadd*ᵉ*bhārīm*.
[88] Cassuto, *Exodus*, pp. 222, 251.

was advanced in a youthful work of Goethe's; and since Wellhausen agreed with it and gave it a scientific basis, it enjoyed popularity, and until recently was entirely accepted among Biblical scholars. Its primary basis was the theory held by historians of religions and culture that ritualism antedated the development of ethical principles. Seeing that the ten precepts in ch. xxxiv are entirely ritualistic, while the commandments of ch. xx are also wholly of a moral character, it followed that the Decalogue of ch. xxxiv was the earlier.[89]

The precepts are preceded by the Decalogue in the form of an address by God to the entire people. Thus the Ten Words [see footnote 87] are not the substance of the covenant, nor its conditions, but the introduction to it. Before the particulars and terms of the covenant are conveyed by the intermediary, God Himself makes a prefatory declaration that established the basic principles on which the covenant will be founded.[90]

After Exodus 20:1-17, Deuteronomy 5:6-21 restates the entire 10 Commandments. Cassuto writes, "As we know, there is more than one recension of the Decalogue. In Deut. v 6-21 [Hebrew 6-18], there occurs a version that differs somewhat from that recorded here in the Book of Exodus."[91] Cassuto continues with a fascinating and informative discussion of other ancient copies of the 10 Commandments, those recorded in the Septuagint, the order of the 10 Commandments, and how they should be divided. God says there are 10 Commandments; therefore we know there are 10. However, anyone who examines the Hebrew will see wording that suggests at least 11 Commandments, if not 12.

Cassuto observes how the text following the 10 Commandments in Exodus 20 divides up the application of some of the commandments into 10 laws for each commandment.

This paragraph [Exodus 21:7-11], which has been placed here, after the paragraph dealing with the Hebrew slave, on account of the similarity of themes, also begins by stating a principal case, commencing with the word וְכִי w^{e}khī ['And when'], and thereafter there are cited here, too, four secondary cases, introduced by the word אִם 'im ['if'] or w^e'im ['and if']. In all there are ten subsections on the laws of slavery in

---

[89] Ibid., p. 237.
[90] Ibid., pp. 238-39.
[91] Ibid., pp. 249-50.

these two paragraphs [Exodus 21:2-6 and 21:7-11], a number that aids memorization, like the number of the Ten Words [Decalogue].[92]

Beginning with Exodus 21:12 through verse 27, Cassuto points out that there are 10 laws pertaining to bodily injury and murder divided into 5 and 5. In the third paragraph on capital offences (Exodus 21:12-17), Cassuto writes:

> In this paragraph are enumerated five cases carrying the penalty of death, beginning with the gravest crime; (a) whoever strikes a man so that he dies; (b) the law applies even if the assailant seeks refuge in the precincts of the sanctuary; (c) whoever strikes his father or mother; (d) whoever steals a man; (e) whoever dishonors his father or mother. In the next paragraph five cases of bodily injury will be cited, the first of which is connected with the present paragraph, namely, the case of the one who strikes another and the victim does not die but keeps his bed [i.e., is disabled]. [93]

> The [fourth] paragraph contains five cases of bodily injury caused by beating (*vv.* 18-19; 20-21; 22-25; 26; 27), just as in the previous paragraph comprised of capital offences. In all they constitute a series of ten cases, a number intended to assist the memory, as we stated before.[94]

The 9th law pertaining to bodily injury (above) contains the well-known heptad of injuries following murder.

> And if *any* mischief follow, then thou shalt give life for life,
> 1 Eye for eye,
> 2 tooth for tooth,
> 3 hand for hand,
> 4 foot for foot,
> 5 Burning for burning,
> 6 wound for wound,
> 7 stripe for stripe. (Exod. 21:24-25)

Leviticus 24:20, Deuteronomy 19:21, and Matthew 5:28 all quote this verse beginning with *eye for an eye*.

---

[92] Ibid., p. 269.
[93] Ibid., p. 271.
[94] Ibid., p. 278.

In Chapter Four, the following meter was listed with the word *commandment* repeated 10 times in the Gospel of John. We can see here how John adapts the Mosaic tradition as a judicial paradigm.

Commandment 10 times in the Gospel of John
    This **commandment** have I received of my Father (John 10:18)
    Now both chief priests and Pharisees had given a **commandment** (John 11:57)
    He gave me a **commandment** (John 12:49)
    And I know that His **commandment** is eternal life (John 12:50)
    A new **commandment** I give unto you (John 13:34)
    Keep my **commandments** (John 14:15)
    He that hath my **commandments** (John 14:21)
    If ye keep my **commandments** (John 15:10)
    Even as I have kept my Father's **commandments** (John 15:10)
    This is my **commandment** (John 15:12)

In 1 Corinthians 9:19-23 Paul uses the Greek word stem for *law* 10 times.

νόμ: **10**, law, νόμος (*nomos*, nom'-os) verse 20, ἐγε**νόμ**ην, **νόμ**ον, **νόμ**ον, **νόμ**ον; 21, ἀ**νόμ**οις, ἄ**νομ**ος, ἄ**νομ**ος, ἔ**ννομ**ος, ἀ**νόμ**ους; and 22, ἐγε**νόμ**ην (BYZ, GOC, SCR, STE).

It appears that Paul and John were aware of Moses' decadal cadence in the Pentateuch, and they incorporated it in their New Testament books.

Nouns and Derivative Verbs in the Creation Account

There is a rather fascinating formation of cognate phrases in the first creation account in Genesis 1-2:3. Cognate words are words that are similar, like *race* and *racing*. They become more apparent after one has read through Genesis in Hebrew and then reads it again. In English we often use verbs that are derived from nouns, which are called cognates, such as *runners run* or *swimmers swim*. Try this sentence: The runners ran, the swimmers swam, the jumpers jumped, the vaulters vaulted, and the sprinters sprinted. There are many other ways to write this in English, but obviously this sentence is arranged to play on the noun-verb relationship. The same thing occurs in Genesis 1-2:3 exactly 10 times, where the noun-verb derivative is not required in Hebrew. For example, the phrase *fruit trees making fruit*, עֵץ פְּרִי עֹשֶׂה פְּרִי (Genesis 1:11), simply says *make* and does not use the verb *to be fruitful*. Obviously the author intended to write with panache. Liberties are taken with the following translation, with considerable loss of meaning, in order to emphasize the matching sounds of these cognates in Hebrew.

10 Noun-Verb Phrases in Genesis 1–2:3

    Sprout the earth sprouts............ תַּדְשֵׁא הָאָרֶץ דֶּשֶׁא (Gen. 1:11)
    Seeding seed..................…..... מַזְרִיעַ זֶרַע (Gen. 1:11)
    Seeding seed...............…......... מַזְרִיעַ זֶרַע (Gen. 1:12)
    Lights…to give light................. לִמְאוֹרֹת בִּרְקִיעַ הַשָּׁמַיִם לְהָאִיר (Gen. 1:15)
    Swarm the sea with swarmers.... יִשְׁרְצוּ הַמַּיִם שֶׁרֶץ (Gen. 1:20)
    Flyers flying......................…..... וְעוֹף יְעוֹפֵף (Gen. 1:20)
    Creepers creeping..........…....... הָרֶמֶשׂ הָרֹמֵשׂ (Gen. 1:26)
    Seeding seed...................…..... זֹרֵעַ זֶרַע (Gen. 1:29)
    Seeding seed...................…..... זֹרֵעַ זֶרַע (Gen. 1:29)
    Sabbathed on the Sabbath day… וַיִּשְׁבֹּת בַּיּוֹם הַשְּׁבִיעִי (Gen. 2:2)

Single Words in Decadal Meter in Genesis and Exodus
  (All citations are from Genesis unless otherwise indicated.)

    And there was: 20, Chapter 1, וַיְהִי (*wᵉy'hēy*, veye-hee') 1:3, 5 (x2), 6, 7, 8 (x2), 9, 11, 13 (x2), 15, 19 (x2), 23 (x2), 24, 30, 31 (x2);

    Appearance: 10, מַרְאֶה (*mar'eh,* mar-eh') 2:9; 12:11; 24:16; 26:7; 29:17; 39:6; 41:2, 3, 4 (x2);

    Boil: 10, שְׁחִין (*shechiyn*, shekh-een') Exod. 9:9, 10 (x2), 11; Lev. 13:18, 19, 20, 23; Deut. 28:27, 35;

    Butler: 10, שָׁקָה (*shaqah*, shaw-kaw') 40:1, 2, 5, 9, 13, 20, 21 (x2), 23; 41:9;

    Circumcised: 10, מוּל (*muwl*, mool) 17:10, 11, 12, 13, 14, 23, 24, 25, 26, 27; not counted in this list: *uncircumcised* at 17:14, and infinitive absolute at 17:13 is one repetition;

    Cloud: 20, עָנָן (*'anan*, aw-nawn') Exod. 13:21, 22; 14:19, 20, 24; 16:10; 19:9, 16; 24:15, 16 (x2), 18; 33:9, 10; 34:5; 40:34, 35, 36, 37, 38; 14 include article;

    Cup: 10, Chapters 40 and 44, גְּבִיעַ (*gebiya`*, gheb-ee›-ah) 40:11 (x3), 13, 21; 44:2 (x2), 12, 16, 17;

    Day: 10, Chapter 1 singular, יוֹם (*yowm*, yome)1:5 (x2), 8, 13, 14, 16, 18, 19, 23, 31;

    Earth: 20, Chapter 1, אֶרֶץ (*'ereṣ,* eh›-rets) 1:1, 4, 10, 11 (x2), 12, 15, 17, 20, 22, 24 (x2), 25, 26 (x2), 28 (x2), 29, 30 (x2);

    Egypt, Egypt's, Egyptian(s): 100, מִצְרַיִם (*Mitsrayim*, mits-rah'-yim) Genesis;

    Evening: 10, עֶרֶב (*'ereb*, eh'-reb) 1:5, 8, 13, 19, 23, 31; 8:11; 24:11, 63; 44:32;

    Firstborn: 20, 15 male, 5 female בְּכוֹר (*bekowr*, bek-ore') 10:15; 19:31, 33, 34, 37; 22:21; 25:13; 27:19, 32; 29:26; 35:23; 36:15; 38:6, 7; 41:51; 43:33; 46:8; 48:14, 18; 49:3;

    Firstborn: 20, בְּכוֹר (*bekowr*, bek-ore') Exod. 4:22, 23; 6:14; 11:5 (x4); 12:12, 29 (x4); 13:2, 13, 15 (x4); 22:29; 34:20;

    Frogs: 10, צְפַרְדֵּעַ (*tsephardea`*, tsef-ar-day'-ah) plural, Exod. 7:27, 28, 29; 8:1, 3, 4, 5, 7, 8, 9; a singular form is found in 8:2 that maintains 10 plural forms;

From him: 10, מִמֶּנּוּ (*mēmĕ'noo*, mi-me'-noo) particle preposition suffix 3rd person masculine singular, 2:17 (x2); 3:3, 5, 11, 17, 22; 23:6; 26:16; 48:19;
From the presence of: 10, מִפְּנֵי (*mipaniy*, mi-paw-nee') 3:8; 7:7; 16:8; 27:46; 35:1, 7; 36:6, 7; 41:31; 47:13;
Go: 10, לֵךְ (*leek*, leekh) imperative masculine singular, Exod. 3:16; 4:12, 18, 19, 27; 7:15; 10:28; 19:10; 32:34; 33:1;
God and Lord: 300, אֱלֹהִים (*'Elōhim*, el-ō-heem') 156 + יְהוָה (Yehovah, yeh-ho-vaw›) 144 = 300;
The God of: 20, אֱלֹהֵי (*'Elōhiy*, el-ō-hee') 9:26; 24:3, 7, 12, 27, 42, 48; 26:24; 28:13; 31:30, 42 (x2), 53 (x2); 32:10; 33:20; 35:2, 4; 46:3; 50:17;
Goshen: 10, גֹּשֶׁן (*Goshen*, go'-shen) 45:10; 46:28 (x2), 29, 34; 47:1, 4, 6, 27; 50:8;
Head of grain: 10, Chapter 41, שִׁבֹּל (*shibbol*, shib'-bole) 41:5, 6, 7 (x2), 22, 23, 24 (x2), 26, 27;
Heavens: 40, שָׁמַיִם (*shamayim*, shaw-mah'-yim) 1:1, 8, 9, 14, 15, 17, 20, 26, 28, 30; 2:1, 4 (x2), 19, 20; 6:7, 17; 7:3, 11, 19, 23; 8:2 (x2); 9:2; 11:4; 14:19, 22; 19:24; 21:17; 22:11, 15, 17; 24:3, 7; 26:4; 27:28, 39; 28:17; 42:21; 49:25; 7 without article, 10 in Chapter 1;
Sons of Heth: 10, בְּנֵי־חֵת (*benee'- cheth*, benee'-khayth) 23:3, 5, 7, 10 (x2), 16, 18, 20; 25:10; 49:32;
Horns: 10, קֶרֶן (*qeren*, keh'-ren) plural form, Exod. 27:2 (x2); 29:12; 30:2, 3, 10; 37:25, 26; 38:2 (x2);
In the field: 10, בַּשָּׂדֶה (*bᵃsadeh*, ba-saw-deh') Exod. 1:14; 9:3, 19 (x2), 21, 25; 16:25; 22:4, 30; 23:16; there are 12 in Genesis;
Kind: 10, Chapter 1, מִין (*miyn*, meen) 1:11, 12 (x2), 21 (x2), 24 (x2), 25 (x3);
Kiss: 10, נָשַׁק (*nashaq*, naw-shak') 27:26, 27; 29:11, 13; 31:28, 55; 33:4; 45:15; 48:10; 50:1;
Light: 10, Chapter 1, אוֹר (*'owr*, ore) 1:3 (x2), 4 (x2), 5, 18; Luminary: מָאוֹר (*ma'owr*, maw-ore') 16 (x2), Give Light: 15, 17;
Mamre: 10, מַמְרֵא (*Mamre'*, mam-ray') 13:18; 14:13, 24; 18:1; 23:17, 19; 25:9; 35:27; 49:30; 50:13;
Morning: 20, בֹּקֶר (*boqer*, bo'-ker) 1:5, 8, 13, 19, 23, 31; 19:27; 20:8; 21:14; 22:3; 24:54; 26:31; 28:18; 29:25; 31:55; 40:6; 41:8; 44:3; 49:27; שַׁחַר (*shachar*, shakh'-ar) 19:15; in the morning 12;
Murmer: 10, וּל (*luwn*, loon) Exod. 15:24; 16:2, 7, 8; 17:3; הַנּוּלֹת (*teluwnah*, tel-oo-naw') 16:7, 8 (x2), 9, 12;
Not let go/Not sent out, 10: לֹא־שָׁלַח (*low-shalach*, low-shaw-lakh') Gen. 42:4; Exod. 8:28; 9:7, 35; 10:20; 11:10; 22:7, 10; 24:11; Num. 22:37;
Offering: 10, מִנְחָה (*minchah*, min-khaw') 4:3; 32:14, 19, 21, 22; 43:11, 15, 25, 26; 49:15;
On account of: 10, בַּעֲבוּר (*'abuwr*, aw-boor') or בַּעֲבֶר (*'abur*, aw-boor') with preposition, 8:21; 18:29, 31, 32; 21:30; 26:24; 27:4, 19, 31; 46:34;
Sent, Shelah, Three: 10, Chapter 38, Word Stem, Sent שָׁלַח (*shalach*, shaw-lakh') 38:17 (x2), 20, 23, 38; Shelah שֵׁלָה (*Shelah*, shay-law') 38:5,

11, 14, 26; Three שָׁלוֹשׁ (*shalowsh*, shaw-loshe') 38:24;

Seven: 50, שֶׁבַע (*sheba`*, sheh'-bah) this form only, 5:7, 25, 31; 11:21; 21:14, 28, 29, 30, 31, 32, 33; 22:19 (x2); 26:23, 33; 28:10; 29:18, 20, 27 (x2), 28; 30; 33:3; 37:2; 41:2, 3, 4, 5, 6, 7, 18, 19, 20, 22, 23, 24, 26 (x3), 27 (x2), 29, 30, 48, 53, 54; 46:1, 5; 47:28 (x2);

Sodom and **Gomorrah: 30**, 21 סְדֹם (*Cedom*, sed-ome') 10:19; 13:10, 12, 13; 14:2, 8, 10, 11, 12, 17, 21, 22; 18:16, 20, 22, 26; 19:1 (x2), 4, 24, 28; עֲמֹרָה. (*`Amorah*, am-o-raw') 10:19; 13:10; 14:2, 8, 10, 11; 18:20; 19:24, 28;

Tamar/Timnath/Signet Ring: 10, Chapter 38, Word Stem, Tamar תָּמָר (*Tamar*, taw-mawr') 38:6, 11 (x2), 13, 24; Timnath תִּמְנָה (*Timnah*, tim-naw') 38:12, 13, 14; Signet Ring חוֹתָם (*chowtham*, kho-thawm') 38:8, 25;

Ten: 20, עֲשָׂרָה (*`asara*, aw-saw-ra') this form only, 5:8, 10; 7:20; 11:25; 14:4 (x2), 5; 17:25; 18:32 (x2); 24:10, 22; 31:41; 32:16 (x2); 37:2; 42:3; 45:23; 46:18; 47:28;

To Pharaoh: 10, אֶל־פַּרְעֹה (*el Par`oh*, el par-o') 12:15; 40:14; 41:14, 25, 28, 32, 55; 47:3, 4, 9;

To the Lord: 10, לַיהוָה Gen. 4:3; 8:20; 12:7, 8; 13:13, 18; 24:26, 48, 52; 25:21;

Wilderness: 10, מִדְבָּר (*midbar*, mid-bawr') 14:6; 16:7; 21:14, 20, 21; 29:9; 31:29; 36:24; 37:22; 45:12.

Dodecadal Meter in Genesis

The following are examples of dodecadal cadence in the text. The number 12 in Genesis is most often associated with genealogies. Cassuto cites the 12 sons of Canaan in Genesis 10.[95]

He also writes:

> The numerical harmony is discernible, as stated, also in the details of our chapter [Genesis 10:1-32]. Other numbers, too, are very prominent there, although they are not expressly mentioned: *seven*, which as we know, is the number of perfection, and *twelve*. The latter, likewise, when it appertains to peoples or tribes, indicates perfection, for the peoples and tribes of antiquity were accustomed, both in the East and the West, to unite in amphictyonic councils or leagues of twelve branches [including ancient Greece prior to the 7th century B.C.]. The union of the twelve tribes is only one example of this system. We observe, moreover, that the total remains unchanged even when the composition is altered. If Joseph is reckoned as one tribe, then the tribe of Levi is also counted; but if the sons of Joseph are regarded as two tribes, then the

---

[95] Cassuto, *Genesis: Part I*, pp. 179, 216.

Repetition in Genesis and Exodus

Levites are excluded. Similarly, we find in the Bible twelve princes of Ishmael (xvii 20; xxv 13-16), twelve sons of Nahor (*ibid.* xxii 20-24) and two lists of chiefs of Edom, which appear to be based essentially on the number twelve. The first (*ibid.* xxxvi 15-18) actually contains thirteen names, but the chief of Amelek (who is descended from the son of Eliphaz by his concubine) was added to the basic group of twelve chiefs; and the second (*ibid. vv.* 40-43) comprises eleven names, partly different from those given in the first, but this list likewise rests on a basic organization of twelve chiefs, only one of them for some reason disappeared or left the league. If we may add to this roll the name Zepho, which is found in the Septuagint in place of Iram, then in this case, too, there will be exactly twelve in all.[96]

Cassuto's reference to *Zepho* in the Septuagint leads to the question of whether Septuagint translators noticed the same problem of an incomplete meter, and the Hebrew is actually the original list. The Septuagint translators were not under the same constraints of inviolable accuracy when creating a Greek text as were copyists who were producing a Hebrew manuscript. More will be said on this subject in the following chapters.

Cassuto points out that the Hebrew words for *sons* and *daughters* repeat 24 times in the Genesis 5 genealogy:

> ...the nouns בֵּן *bēn* ['son'], בָּנִים *bānīm* ['sons'], בָּנוֹת *bānōth* ['daughters'], – apart from the figurative usage, *son of five hundred years* [i.e., 'five hundred years old'] – occur twenty-four times, that is twice twelve. And the number of paragraphs into which the section [Genesis 5:1-6:8] is clearly and unmistakably divisible is precisely *twelve*.[97]

Earlier we mentioned the 12 male descendants of Adam named in Genesis 4.[98] When Israel entered Egypt they numbered 12 sons and 70 people. When Israel exited Egypt they camped by 12 springs and 70 palm trees according to Exodus 15:23 and Numbers 33:9. Cassuto writes:

> After encamping at Marah, the children of Israel again journeyed, *And they came to Elim*—this time it is not stated

---

[96] Cassuto, *Genesis: Part II*, p. 178.
[97] Cassuto, *Genesis: Part I*, p. 271.
[98] Ibid., pp. 192-93.

that Moses led them, and apparently we are to understand that they came there under the Lord's guidance in the manner described in xiii 21—*where there were twelve springs of water and seventy palm trees*....[99]

All Flesh / Seven Years

Thus far only the following dodecadal phrases were found in Genesis.

All flesh 12 times in Genesis

    All flesh...................... כָּל־בָּשָׂר (Gen. 6:12)
    All flesh...................... כָּל־בָּשָׂר (Gen. 6:13)
    All flesh...................... כָּל־בָּשָׂר (Gen. 6:17)
    From All flesh.............. מִכָּל־בָּשָׂר (Gen. 6:19)
    From All flesh.............. מִכָּל־בָּשָׂר (Gen. 7:16)
    All flesh...................... כָּל־בָּשָׂר (Gen. 7:21)
    From All flesh.............. מִכָּל־בָּשָׂר (Gen. 8:17)
    All flesh...................... כָּל־בָּשָׂר (Gen. 9:11)
    In all flesh................... בְּכָל־בָּשָׂר (Gen. 9:15)
    All flesh...................... כָּל־בָּשָׂר (Gen. 9:15)
    In all flesh................... בְּכָל־בָּשָׂר (Gen. 9:16)
    All flesh...................... כָּל־בָּשָׂר (Gen. 9:17)

Seven years (absolute form, no prefix) 12 times in Genesis

    Seven years.................. שֶׁבַע שָׁנִים (Gen. 5:7)
    Seven years.................. שֶׁבַע שָׁנִים (Gen. 11:21)
    Seven years.................. שֶׁבַע שָׁנִים (Gen. 29:18)
    Seven years.................. שֶׁבַע שָׁנִים (Gen. 29:20)
    Seven years.................. שֶׁבַע־שָׁנִים (Gen. 29:27)
    Seven years.................. שֶׁבַע־שָׁנִים (Gen. 29:30)
    Seven years.................. שֶׁבַע שָׁנִים (Gen. 41:26)
    Seven years.................. שֶׁבַע שָׁנִים (Gen. 41:26)
    Seven years.................. שֶׁבַע שָׁנִים (Gen. 41:27)
    Seven years.................. שֶׁבַע שָׁנִים (Gen. 41:29)
    Seven years.................. שֶׁבַע שָׁנִים (Gen. 41:48)
    Seven years.................. שֶׁבַע שָׁנִים (Gen. 47:28)

Seven years (all forms) 12 times in Genesis Chapter 41

    Seven years.................. שֶׁבַע שָׁנִים (Gen. 41:26)
    Seven years.................. שֶׁבַע שָׁנִים (Gen. 41:26)
    Seven years.................. שֶׁבַע שָׁנִים (Gen. 41:27)
    Seven years.................. שֶׁבַע שְׁנֵי (Gen. 41:27)
    Seven years.................. שֶׁבַע שָׁנִים (Gen. 41:29)
    Seven years.................. שֶׁבַע שְׁנֵי (Gen. 41:30)

---

[99] Cassuto, *Exodus*, p. 185.

In seven years	בְּשֶׁבַע שְׁנֵי	(Gen. 41:34)
For seven years	לְשֶׁבַע שְׁנֵי	(Gen. 41:36)
In seven years	בְּשֶׁבַע שְׁנֵי	(Gen. 41:47)
Seven years	שֶׁבַע שָׁנִים	(Gen. 41:48)
Seven years	שֶׁבַע שְׁנֵי	(Gen. 41:53)
Seven years	שֶׁבַע שְׁנֵי	(Gen. 41:54)

In the phrase *all flesh* there is a subset of 7 phrases that are not introduced by a preposition. There are 2 sets of *seven years*, above. Earlier in this chapter, all 21 repetitions of *seven years* were displayed. The first set above spans the entire book of Genesis for exactly the same form with no prefix. The second set repeats (in all forms) 12 times in Genesis 41. Again, we see a relationship between 7 and 12.

One of the goals of this chapter was to give the reader some understanding of the shape and origin of Hebraic meter viewed previously in the 4 Gospels and Revelation. Repetition in the Bible has its own unique application. Beyond establishing its existence in the text and its application, we are left with the enigma of its origin and purpose. The study of repetition in the text actually raises as many questions as it answers. The next 2 chapters will delve deeper into the mysteries of this linguistic phenomenon.

Single Words in Dodecadal Meter in Genesis

And answered: 12, וַיַּעַן (*'anah*, aw-naw') 18:27; 23:10, 14; 24:50; 27:37, 39; 31:31, 36, 43; 40:18; 41:16; 42:2;

Behold: 12, הִנְּנִי (*hinne*, hin-nee') particle interjection suffix 1st person common singular, 6:17; 9:9; 22:1, 7, 11; 27:1, 18; 31:11; 37:13; 41:17; 46:2; 48:4;

Behold: 12, הֵן (*hen*, hane) 3:22; 4:14; 11:6; 15:3; 19:34; 27:11, 37; 29:7; 30:34; 39:8; 44:8; 47:23; note 2 forms of *behold*, each 12 times; there are 8 more in Exodus for a total of 20;

Bethel: 12, בֵּית־אֵל (*Beyth-'El*, bayth-ale') 12:8 (x2); 13:3 (x2); 28:19; 31:13; 35:1, 3, 6, 8, 15, 16; Elbethel, אֵל בֵּית־אֵל, in Gen. 35:7 is excluded;

Blood: 12, הַדָּם with article (*hadam*, hā-dawm) Exod. 7:21; 12:7, 13 (x2), 22, 23; 24:6 (x2), 8; 29:12, 20, 21;

Brother: 12, Chapter 45, אָח (*'ach'*, awkh) 45:1, 3 (x2), 4 (x2), 12, 14, 15 (x2), 16, 17, 24;

Chariot: 12, רֶכֶב (*rekeb*, reh'-keb) Exod. 14:6, 7 (x2), 9, 17, 18, 23, 25, 26, 28; 15:4, 19; there are 10 in chapter 14;

Cows: 12, פָּרָה (*parah*, paw-raw') 32:16; 41:2, 3 (x2), 4 (x2), 18, 19, 20 (x2), 26, 27;

Flood: 12, מַבּוּל (*mabbuwl*, mab-bool') 6:17; 7:6, 7, 10, 17; 9:11 (x2), 15, 28; 10:1, 32; 11:10;

In the field: 12, בַּשָּׂדֶה (*bᵉsadeh*, ba-saw-deh') 4:8; 23:17; 24:63, 65; 29:2; 30:14; 34:5, 28; 36:35; 37:15; 49:29, 30;

Pillar: 12, noun, מַצֵּבָה (*matstsebah*, mats-tsay-baw') 28:18נְצִיב, 22; 31:13, 45, 51, 52 (x2); 35:14 (x2), 20 (x2); verb, מַצָּב (*netsiyb*, nets-eeb') 28:12; all 12 are only associated with Jacob; there is subset of 7 מַצֵּבָה;

Twenty: 12, עֶשְׂרִים (*`esriym*, es-reem') 6:3; 8:14; 11:24; 18:31 (x2); 23:1; 31:38, 41; 32:15 (x2), 16; 37:28.

Single Words Repeated 17 Times

Hail: 17, בָּרָד (*barad*, baw-rawd') in the account of the 10 plagues, Exod. 9:18, 19, 22, 23 (x2), 24 (x2), 25 (2x), 26, 28, 29, 33, 34; 10:5, 12, 15; includes 7 with article and no other prefix;

Month: 17, חֹדֶשׁ (*chodesh*, kho'-desh) Exod. 12:2 (x3), 3, 6, 18 (x2); 13:4, 5; 16:1; 19:1; 23:15; 34:18 (x2); 40:2, 17 (x2).

Chapter Nine
A Deeper Look into Genesis and Exodus

The study of repetition in Genesis and Exodus led to intriguing questions, related subjects, and unintended areas of inquiry about the nature and ramifications of repetition in the Bible. Not limited to an isolated genre, repetition is found in narrative, prophecy, symbolism, poetry, history, genealogy, and chronology. Time itself is arranged in Hebraic meter.

Do these concepts originate with the Bible, or do they have another source? The debate is whether biblical numerics are rooted in antediluvian, Hebrew, or Babylonian culture. The numeric system of early Hebrew worship in the Tabernacle appears to have its origin in the dimensions of Noah's Ark. There is also the paradox of meticulous order juxtaposed to intentional random order.

Genesis may be an introduction to the genre, as Hebraic meter becomes more complex in Exodus. Current views of Genesis range from higher critical to conservative, with Eyal Rav-Noy being one of the few authors who supports or even acknowledges Cassuto's historic observations about meter in the text.

Hebraic Meter in Time

Time and how it is recorded are 2 different subjects. The tradition of 10 generations, as discussed in the previous chapter, is also found in other ancient cultures. Cassuto writes:

> A tradition concerning *ten* heads of primeval generations is found among many peoples of the ancient Orient: the Babylonians, the Egyptians, the Persians, the Indians and others. The closest parallel to the Biblical tradition is the Babylonian concerning the ten kings who reigned before the Flood.[1]

According to the births of the antediluvian patriarchs and the ages of their fathers, the Flood took place 1,656 years after the creation of Adam, when Noah was 600 years old. Cassuto compares the Genesis record of 1,656 years with Julius Oppert's report that the Babylonians

---

[1] Cassuto, *Genesis: Part I*, p. 254.

recorded 432,000 years before the Flood.[2] He notes that Oppert found a relationship between these 2 numbers, indicating a common tradition. Many writers have quoted Julius Oppert, a noted Assyriologist, from his paper delivered in 1874 at the International Congress of Orientalists in London.[3] Oppert quotes Berossus, 324-262 B.C., a contemporary of Alexander the Great, who dedicated his history of Babylon to Antiochus I.[4]

Genesis 2 sets a precedent by measuring the first week. Oppert found that the Babylonian record of 432,000 years before the Flood is 5 times 86,400.[5] Cassuto observes, "In other words, the Babylonian source has 86,400 lustrums as against 86,400 weeks in the Bible."[6] This writer experimented with the number of weeks, multiplying 1,656 by 365.25 days in a year, less 12 days for the century correction, divided by 7 for the number of days in a week, and arrived at a total of exactly 86,406 weeks. The exact number of 86,400 weeks would require 365.223 days in a year, instead of 365.25, or a reduction of about 40 minutes a year. According to Cassuto, both the Bible and the Babylonians rounded numbers, hence the Babylonians most likely rounded the number to 86,400. Thus, it appears that at one time both Genesis and the early Babylonians were dealing with the same basic number of 1,656 before the Flood.

According to Oppert, the Babylonian unit of time known as the lustrum is 60 months, or 5 years. It appears that the earliest Babylonians were aware of the 86,400 weeks before the Flood, which they later increased to years and multiplied by 5. The number 86,400 is divisible by 12 for a quotient of 7,200. One lustrum, or 60 months, times 7,200 equals 432,000.[7]

Cassuto quotes some well-known Sumerian tablets, as follows: "The antediluvian kings numbered only eight according to W.B. 444, but according to W.B. 62 there were actually *ten*, as Berossus states."[8]

---

[2] Ibid., p. 255, "*GGN*, 1877, pp. 205-209, 214-220, and also in *The Jewish Encyclopaedia*, s. v. 'Chronology.'"

[3] Julius Oppert, "Restoration of the Berosus Canon" and "On a Case of Singular Literary Forgery," in Robert K. Douglas (ed.), *Transactions of the Second Session of the International Congress of Orientalists*, Trübner & Co., London, 1876, pp. 48, 51.

[4] John M. G. Barclay, *Flavius Josephus: Translation and Commentary, Volume 10: Against Apion*, Brill, Leiden, The Netherlands, 2007, p. 81.

[5] Cassuto, *Genesis: Part I*, p. 255.

[6] Ibid.

[7] Ibid.

[8] Ibid., p. 257.

Berossus was the only source for Babylonian culture until Babylonian history was interpreted from Sumerian language tablets written around 2200 to 1800 B.C., and published in 1923 by Langdon in the Weld-Blundell collection.[9]

Cassuto dedicates 23 pages to this thoroughly documented and fascinating discussion.[10] Examples of the ages of the Sumerian postdiluvian kings are 12,000, 1,560, 1,200, 960, 900, 840, 720, and 600 years.[11]

Cassuto has proven more than he states. Moses does not count the number of years or weeks before the Flood. The total of 1,656 years, or 86,400 weeks, or 7,200 multiplied by Babylonian 60 lustrums, or 432,000 years are all calculations based on Genesis, but not stated in Genesis. Therefore, Moses' source without any of these calculations is most likely older than the Babylonian source!

The history of counting 12 months in a year is found in nearly every ancient culture. The year was divided into the number of full moons. *Moon* and *month* are cognates. Counting time by hours can be traced to the division of daylight by the number of moons in a year, and then repeating the same division for the night. Based on their calculations of the number of weeks before the Flood, the Babylonians were practicing the 7-day week far earlier than the 6th century B.C. date accepted by today's scholars. According to Genesis 2, the Hebrews and the Babylonians were counting by weeks before Moses wrote Genesis.

The Babylonians were responsible for dividing hours into one lustrum, or 60 minutes, and dividing minutes into one lustrum, or 60 seconds. They also divided the degrees in a circle into 6 lustrum, or 360 degrees. In other words, the Babylonians invented our division of time. They could have chosen any number, such as 24, 30, 36, 40, or 50 for the division of hours and minutes, but they chose 60. Yet, their eagerness to establish themselves as the original civilization before the Flood appears to be reflected in their division of time. It can hardly be a coincidence that the number of seconds in a day is 86,400, the same as their sacred number of weeks before the Flood, as derived from Genesis. The irony is that the worldwide Flood was followed by worldwide Babylonian time, which incorporates the weeks before the Flood every day on every watch, clock, cell phone, and computer in the world. The counting continues.

---

[9] Ibid., p. 256.
[10] Ibid., pp. 249-72.
[11] Cassuto, *Genesis: Part II*, pp. 253-54.

There is much debate about how many days were in a year before the Flood. In Chapter Ten, incontrovertible evidence will show that the ages of the 10 antediluvian patriarchs were chosen for a specific purpose. Therefore, Enoch's predetermined age of 365 years (Gen. 5:23) is most likely a reflection of the days in a year before the Flood. The reader is requested to examine the evidence before coming to a conclusion.

Genesis counts time and events in the sense of a complete number, that which is divisible by 10. There are 10 generations from Adam to Noah, 10 generations from Shem to Abraham, and 10 generations from Perez to David. Therefore, we see the concept of 10 generations and multiples of 10 in Hebrew, Babylonian, Sumerian, and other traditions. If we assume that these traditions originate from a common antediluvian heritage, the question remains as to which is the most accurate source. Claims that Moses exaggerated ages and numbers before the Flood pale by comparison with the exaggerations in other traditions. This would further support the assumption that Moses is recording the older and original numbers.

The concept that people could possibly have lived longer at a particular time in human history than they do today is generally discounted out of hand, based on the modern paradigm of uniformitarianism. Uniformitarianism is the scientific observation that the same natural laws and processes that currently operate in the universe have always operated in the universe, and apply everywhere in the universe. In other words, if it does not happen now, it did not happen then. Thus, a concept of infinity and perpetual stability is projected onto the universe, which in itself is impossible. An example of this paradigm in our day is the astonishment of meteorologists at the occasional breaking of meteorological records set 150 or more years ago.

Origins of the Bible's Number System: Sexagesimal or Antediluvian?

Cassuto reviews 3 major cadences in Hebraic meter: heptadic, decadal, and dodecadal. He was highly influenced by the discovery and publication of Babylonian texts in 1922 and 1923. They include a number of ancient accounts similar to the Genesis accounts of creation, Adam and Eve, Noah, the Flood, and more.

The questions that Cassuto attempted to answer were: "Where did Hebraic numerical meter originate?" "What is entirely Mosaic and what did the early Hebrews incorporate from other cultures into their literature?" Cassuto was of the opinion that the Bible incorporates 3 number systems:

1. The Egyptian decimal system also found in some Canaanite cultures;
2. The Hebrew heptadic system based on the creation account, the Sabbath, and Sabbath laws; and
3. The Babylonian sexagesimal system.

Cassuto writes that all 3 number systems are in the Hebrew text, as follows:

> I do not wish to convey thereby that the text is in any sense allegorical; all the numerous and varied proposals that have been advanced with a view to interpreting the construction of the Tabernacle allegorically have no value in so far as the plain meaning of the Scriptural passages is concerned. I merely desire to indicate that, in order to attain its goal, the Torah utilized various means conformable to the spirit of ancient times, and that *inter alia* it employed the principle of numerical symmetry, which greatly appealed to those generations. These sections [Exodus 25:1-31:18] cite figures that are mentioned only for the sake of achieving such symmetry, which is based partly on the decimal system and partly on the number seven and the sexagesimal system, as will be explained in detail further on.[12]

If there is any question that Cassuto was proposing that Moses incorporated 3 number systems in the text, the above quotation should resolve it. However, this writer does not agree with his view that these 3 systems originated from 3 different cultures. Rather, the evidence suggests there is only one biblical number system which existed before the Flood. This system functioned with 3 bases: namely, heptadic, decadal, and dodecadal, and any one of the 3 was applied whenever and for whatever reason Moses chose. In this 3-base system, numbers can be "rounded" to the nearest 7, 10, or 12.

Cassuto was the first to identify 3 different cadences in the text. His observation proved to be entirely accurate when compared to similar cadences found in Revelation and the 4 Gospels, as published in the first and second editions of *In Search of the Biblical Order*, a point already established in this book. However, advances in the translation of Babylonian texts in his day led Cassuto to conclude that these 3 number systems had 3 different sources. On this perspective, he writes:

---

[12] Cassuto, *Exodus*, p. 320.

After the Flood, too, the basic elements of the chronology are the same as those that we found in connection with the antediluvian generations both in the Pentateuch and in the Mesopotamian tradition: primarily the *sexagesimal system*, augmented by the use of the numbers *seven* or *multiples of seven*. In the aforementioned register of the kings of the first dynasty of Kish [first dynasty of Sumerian kings after the Flood] only the numbers based on the sexagesimal system appear; for example, 1,200, 960, 900, 840, 720, 600.[13]

Cassuto Favors the Babylonian Sexagesimal System

Obviously, the ages of the Babylonian kings before the Flood are all sexagesimal numbers because the Babylonians invented the numbers. Cassuto makes this comment while also promoting the concept of 10 antediluvian and 10 postdiluvian patriarchs. He notes that the Ark is 300 cubits long, 50 cubits wide and 30 cubits high. He says the first and third numbers follow the sexagesimal system, and the second number follows the decimal system. Cassuto's understanding of a sexagesimal system meant a base 60 system and any number divisible by 6 or 12. For example, he writes, "The number 300 is one of the round figures in the sexagesimal system being half 600, which is 10x60."[14] Cassuto is actually claiming that 2 of the 3 measurements of the Ark were influenced by a postdiluvian civilization.

It is not possible for both the antediluvian and postdiluvian eras to have followed the Sumerian-Babylonian number system, unless the postdiluvian era was basically a continuation of the antediluvian culture and number system. This implies that Babylonian history is more accurate and authentic than the Genesis accounts. This would also mean that the decimal system and the Mosaic *augmentation of seven* were both innovations to a supposedly foundational antediluvian/Babylonian sexagesimal system, something with which Cassuto would not agree. Also, Cassuto does not take into consideration that we do not know how the antediluvian numbers were recorded before Moses translated the antediluvian numbers into the context of the base 10 Hebrew decimal system, unless Hebrew is the original language.

Rather, according to the ages of the patriarchs in Genesis 5 and 11, there were 3 number systems functioning simultaneously before the Flood and Babel. After Babel, various cultures each chose to follow one

---

[13] Cassuto, *Genesis: Part II*, pp. 255-56.
[14] Ibid., pp. 62-63.

of these number systems, but the Bible kept all 3. Hence, the Sumerian-Babylonian number system is sexagesimal, and the Egyptian-Canaanite number system is decimal, but Moses maintained the original antediluvian heptadic-decimal-sexagesimal system. It also appears that the Talmud's preference for the sexagesimal system is influenced by Babylonian culture during the captivity.

Cassuto correctly understood that Babylonian accounts of antediluvian history on cuneiform tablets predate Moses' writing of Genesis. The similarity between Babylonian and biblical accounts is the result of a shared common history.

James J. Becker and Joshua J. Becker come to a similar conclusion that chronology in the Old Testament is based on 3 different and concurrent measurements of time. They write, "All this is to illustrate that understanding ancient chronology is not just a matter of being able to count correctly. It also entails figuring out how an ancient culture counted time and how it used the three units of time measurement."[15]

Numbers before the Flood
Cassuto provides a great deal of interesting reading describing the confusion of tongues at Babel, but for some reason he does not consider that this must also include the confusion of number systems. Were this not the case, then Cassuto would have inadvertently proven that the number system in Genesis changed after Babel. However, even though the world changed, he notes above that the number system in Genesis remained the same after the Flood and Babel. All 30 numbers in Genesis 5 associated with the first 10 patriarchs predate Babylonian culture. Therefore, it is not possible that the ages of the antediluvian patriarchs reflect a limited influence from the Babylonian number system, because the Babylonian civilization did not come into existence until after Babel. To suggest otherwise is to conclude that Babylonian culture is the original culture that existed before the Flood.

In the previous quote from Cassuto, he demonstrated perfect harmony between the number system in the Bible before and after the Flood, which predates all cultures. He does not appear to be consistent here. Therefore, how can he conclude that the Pentateuch and the Mesopotamian tradition are the same in regards to the antediluvian generations, when by his own admission the Babylonian system did not include a heptadic or a decimal base? In answer to the question, "Which is more

---

[15] James J. Becker and Joshua J. Becker, *Unexpected Treasures: Finding Value in Bible Names, Dates, and Genealogies*, Northwestern Publishing House, Milwaukee, 2014, p. 22.

accurate, the Babylonian or the Genesis antediluvian numbers?" Cassuto would most certainly agree with Genesis.

We can't imagine 3 concurrent number systems functioning in one culture at the same time. But evidently this was the antediluvian tradition. In some respects we still maintain this ancient system. Moses directed the Israelites to follow heptadic Sabbaths, 7 days of the Passover, 7 year cycles, and 49 year Jubilees. Today we count by Israelite weeks, holidays, and 4 phases of the moon (28 days) in 7s;[16] we organize currency, mathematics, and metrics by 10s; and we count seconds, minutes, hours, months, feet, yards, dozens, gross, and degrees of the compass by 12's or Babylonian lustrums (5x12), without giving it much thought. This does not include counting by ounces, cups, pints, quarts, and gallons, and buying carbonated beverages in liters, which all made first and second grade challenging. However, the Bible applies a far more intricate and simultaneous integration of inter-computation between these 3 cadences. The key to further research in this area is found in the ages of the patriarchs before the Flood and their unity with the 10 patriarchs after the Flood. In the next chapter it will be shown that, unknown to Cassuto, 7, and not 12, predominates in the ages of the antediluvian patriarchs.

This writer's conclusion is that, rather than incorporating 3 different number systems, the Bible has one numeric system that functions simultaneously with 3 different meters. These 3 meters are based on:

7, which the Bible divides into 3 and 4 or 3½;
10, which the Bible divides into 5 and 5 or 7 and 3; and
12, which the Bible divides into 6 and 6 or 3 and 4 (where 12 = 3 x 4).

Note how the number 2 divides these 3 cadences. This results in a paucity of 8s, 9s, and 11s in biblical numbers unless they are multiples of 7, 10, and 12. This also explains the historic confusion accompanying numerous attempts to find some logic in biblical numbers and the apparent inconsistency in biblical number sequence. There never was one exclusive sequence because there are at least 3.

Cassuto's Proof for a Sexagesimal System

Even though there is disagreement, it is important to understand Cassuto's position on the sexagesimal system in the Bible, described in his commentary on Genesis, as follows:

---

[16] Cassuto, *Genesis: Part I*, p. 66.

Nor is it possible to regard as fortuitous the use, which also finds a place in our section [Genesis 4:1-26], of numbers belonging to the *sexagesimal system*, the Sumerian method of numeration, which has left its mark to this day on the habits of our life (the division of the circle into three hundred and sixty degrees, of the hour into sixty minutes and the minute into sixty seconds etc., counting by the dozen and multiples of *twelve*, and so forth), and on which are based many round figures in Biblical as well as in Talmudic and Midrashic literature. The male descendants of Adam mentioned in the section number *twelve*; and the stem ילד *yld* (the verb יָלַד *yāladh* ['to bear (a child)'] and the noun יֶלֶד *yeledh* ['child']) occurs *twelve* times in the section [Genesis 4:1-26]. The paragraphs of the section, which are naturally separable by their content and the parallels between them, total *six*. The name אֱלֹהִים *'Elōhīm*, by itself or in conjunction with ה YHWH, occurs sixty times, counting from the beginning of the book to the end of this section; whilst the name ה YHWH, alone or in combination with אֱלֹהִים *'Elōhīm*, appears half that number of times, that is, thirty times, or five times six.[17]

Both in the two ancient Sumerian documents and in Berossus, the chronology is founded on the Sumerian *sexagesimal system*. According to this method of reckoning, sixty years constitute a time-unit called *šūš*; 10 šūš, that is, 600 years, equal a *nēr*; sixty *šūš*, that is, 3,600 years, equal a *šar*; sixty *šar*, that is 216,000 years, equal a great *šar* [*šūšar*]....According to Berossus, the sum of all the individual reigns is exactly *one hundred and twenty šar* (i.e. 432,000 years). Thus in all three documents we find a round number of *šars*—either *sixty* or a *hundred and twenty* (twice *sixty*)—with the addition, in the case of two of them, of the sacred number *seven*.

These two elements, the *sexagesimal system* and the number *seven*, are common also to the Israelite way of reckoning. I have already indicated above [p. 192, quoted above] that many round figures based on the sexagesimal system occur very frequently in Biblical literature and in Talmudic and Midrashic works; for example, one hundred and twenty, three hundred, six hundred, one thousand and two hundred, three thousand, six thousand, twelve thousand, thirty thousand, sixty thousand,

---

[17] Ibid., pp. 192-93.

six hundred thousand or sixty myriads, and so forth. They all signify: a great number or an exceedingly great number.[18]

The *addition of seven* to round numbers of the sexagesimal system, such as we observed in the two aforementioned Sumerian documents, also obtained among the Israelites. *One hundred and twenty*, for example, means a *large number*; when *seven* is added it connotes *an even greater number*. Thus the years of Sarah's life not only reached the round number of *one hundred and twenty*, but exceeded it by *seven* (xxxiii 1). The number of provinces in the Persian kingdom, which is given as *a hundred and twenty* in the Book of Daniel (vi 2), totals *one hundred and twenty seven* in the Book of Esther (i 1; viii 9; ix 30).... It clearly follows that the chronology of the Book of Genesis as a whole is also founded on the dual principle of the *sexagesimal system* and the *addition of seven*....[19]

Cassuto demonstrates that many of the antediluvian patriarchs' ages, and numbers computed from their ages, end in 7 or are multiples of 5 or 6.[20] He views numbers ending in 0 as rounded sexagesimal numbers, particularly if they are divisible by 6, as seen earlier. Therefore, numbers divisible by 10 are also divisible by 5, and are sexagesimal, as well.[21] He believes a 7 at the end of a number in Genesis indicates a Hebrew augmentation of the Babylonian sexagesimal system. Cassuto goes so far as to see a sexagesimal number in the Tabernacle pillars that are 5 cubits high, because 5 is half of 10.[22] He even associates 60 repetitions of אֱלֹהִים *'Elōhīm* with Babylonian influence.

Sexagesimal System Not Supported by the Text

Cassuto's archeological rather than prophetic interests in the origin of the biblical number system are unexpected, to say the least. He writes about sexagesimal numbers with his designation of *Hebrew augmentation* as the equivalent of a heptadic suffix.[23] The question is, "How could there be Hebrew augmentations to sexagesimal numbers before the Flood, before there were Hebrews or Babylonians?" Hence, for Cassuto, any number that ends in 7, or that is divisible by 5, 6, or 12, or their

---

[18] Ibid., pp. 258-59.
[19] Ibid., p. 259.
[20] Ibid., pp. 260-71.
[21] Ibid., p. 259.
[22] Cassuto, *Exodus*, pp. 354-55.
[23] Cassuto, *Genesis: Part I*, pp. 258-59, 260-62, 271; *Genesis: Part II*, pp. 2, 135, 147, 148, 162, 317; *Exodus*, p. 422.

multiples, that is rounded with a 0, is sexagesimal or a Hebrew augmentation of the sexagesimal system. He points out that Sarah lived to be 127. However, he does not mention that in Genesis and Exodus Cainan lived to be 910 or 7x130, Lamech lived to be 777, Jacob lived to be 147 (7x21), Levi 137 years, and Amram 137 years, none of which indicates a sexagesimal base. He also does not mention that Abraham's 175 years is evenly divisible by 7.

Of the 30 numbers associated with the 10 antediluvian patriarchs,[24] which include the years lived at the time of procreation, years lived after procreation, and total years lived, 25 are sexagesimal according to Cassuto's classification. On the other hand, one could easily argue for a decimal system based on the same data, since 20 of the 30 antediluvian numbers end in 0 or 5. The point is that his category is so broad it ceases to be convincing.

This writer's position is that Mesopotamian culture as we know it did not exist until after Babel, let alone before the Flood. Cassuto's observation of a sexagesimal system before Babel only considers 1 of the 3 antediluvian meters he identifies, to the neglect of the other 2 also present in the text.

Whether or not the reader has been convinced that we are dealing with the integration of 3 antediluvian meters in the text, Cassuto would certainly agree they are present in the text, whatever their origin may be. More of this will be addressed in the next chapter on genealogies, with new data based on Cassuto's methodology.

The Tabernacle

Like Mosaic Law, most of the dimensions of the Tent and the Tabernacle, the center of Hebrew worship, are divisible by 10. The Bible is so vast in its scope and depth that it is hardly possible for one man to be an expert in all areas of inquiry. This writer is unfamiliar with the extensive amount of research that has been focused on the Tabernacle and the first temple. On the other hand, as a rabbinic scholar, Cassuto is completely at ease in describing the Tabernacle and the many nuances of its dimensions. Cassuto writes:

> Numerical schematism based on the decimal system is manifest in this paragraph [Exodus 26:1-14]: the curtains of the tabernacle number 10; their loops 100, their clasps 50, and each set of the tabernacle curtains is 20 cubits wide; the tent

---

[24] Cassuto, *Genesis: Part I*, p. 260.

curtains are 10+1, their loops 100, and their clasps 50, whilst the width of the western set is 20 cubits.[25]

The numbers recorded in this paragraph [Exodus 26:15-30], or those deducible from it directly or indirectly, evince in most cases signs of numerical symmetry based on the decimal system. The length of the boards and the height of the tabernacle are 10 cubits. The length of the tabernacle is 30 cubits, and its width 10 cubits. The length of the walls made of boards is altogether 70 cubits (seven times ten), whilst the entire perimeter of the tabernacle measures 80 cubits. The boards of the south side total 20, and their pedestals 40; the same obtains on the north side. The number of bars on each side are half of 10. The pedestals, if we include also the four silver pedestals mentioned in *v.* 32, come to 100 (see xxxviii 27).[26]

Numerical schematism and fundamental symmetry are manifest through the whole of this description [chapters 25-31]. The decimal system is the primary basis of the measurements: the length of the court is 100 cubits; the entire perimeter is 300 cubits; there are 20 pillars on each of the longer sides, and 10 on each of the shorter sides, totaling 60 in all (on this number see above); the height of the pillars and the hangings is five cubits, that is half of 10 cubits. Possibly there are here also elements of the sexagesimal system in the aggregate of the pillars and in the extent of the perimeter.[27]

The 3 paragraphs on the dimensions of the Tabernacle quoted above are replete with decadal numbers. However, Cassuto views nearly every number beginning with or divisible by 6 or 5 as the Bible's adaptation of the Babylonian sexagesimal number system, an assertion not supported by the data. There is also the question of divine communication. Moses tells us that the dimensions, like the 10 Commandments, were given to him by God. Is God accommodating Himself to a human number system, or are these divine numbers? The assumption is that if these dimensions were given to Moses, this is not an accommodation. Cubits are a human measurement, but the text is telling us the proportions are divine. In Revelation 21:17 we are told that a cubit is also an angelic measurement: "And he measured the wall thereof, an hundred and forty

---

[25] Cassuto, *Exodus*, p. 354.
[26] Ibid., p. 358.
[27] Ibid., p. 368.

and four cubits, according to the measure of a man, that is, of the angel." Suddenly there is a profound purpose for this seemingly obscure comment in the second-to-last chapter in the Bible.

As stated earlier, the Ark is 300 cubits long, 50 cubits wide and 30 cubits high. Cassuto says the first and third numbers follow the sexagesimal system, and the second number follows the decimal system.[28] All of the numbers in the Ark are in the Tent and Tabernacle. Note that the perimeter of the courtyard is the same as the length of the Ark. This cannot be a coincidence. The concept that measurements in both the antediluvian Ark and the postdiluvian Tabernacle are influenced by the Babylonian sexagesimal system is rejected. Why would they be Babylonian when the Hebrews had just spent more than 400 years in Egypt practicing a decimal system? Cassuto would have been well advised to look for all 3 number systems rather than focus on 1.

Order in the Bible

After presenting numerous examples of Hebraic repetition, it should be noted that the Bible is not bound to repeat any specific number of words in any particular order. The repetition we have thus far witnessed in Genesis and Exodus is applied at the writer's discretion like any other figure of speech.

The lists of the 7 nations was published in the first edition, and expanded in the second edition.[29] The unique and challenging aspect of the 7 nations is that they appear only in narrative literature and their pattern is irregular, or asymmetric. Of the 21 lists of the heathen nations, only 4, or possibly 5, actually list 7 nations. We know they are 7 nations because Deuteronomy 7:1 and Acts 13:19 say they are 7 nations, just as we know there are 10 Commandments because the text says there are 10, even though we count at least 11. Once the fact of 7 is established, the Bible has no compulsion to publish exactly 7 names. As seen below, there may be 5, 6, 8, or 10 names given in no particular order; but we know there are 7 nations. This is a little like Big Ten Football that increased to 12 teams, and then to 14 teams.

Each author of the lists appears to know when to vary the length of the list and change the word order. There is nothing like this in pagan literature, which is blindly predisposed to maintain mechanical repetition. Most human beings will straighten a crooked picture on the wall. The lists of 7 nations are another example of Hebraic concurrent symmetry and asym-

---

[28] Cassuto, *Genesis: Part II*, pp. 62-63.
[29] Cascione, 2012, pp. 153-55.

metry, the integration of abstraction and order. Another way of saying this is that the natural order incorporates disorder. This occurs in nature, but in these lists the asymmetry is intentional. Lists in the Bible with the same order may actually indicate scribal error or intentional alteration by a copyist. Thus, the extra nation (Girgashites) in the Septuagint at Deuteronomy 20:17 may be the correct reading so that it does not duplicate Joshua 12:8.

Kenites	Canaanites	Canaanites	Canaanites	Amorites	Canaanite
Kenizzites	Hittites	Hittites	Hittites	Hittites	Amorite
Kadmonites	Amorites	Amorites	Amorites	Perizzites	Hittite
Hittites	Perizzites	Perizzites	Hivites	Canaanites	Perizzite
Perizzites	Hivites	Hivites	Jebusites	Hivites	Hivite
Rephaims	Jebusites	Jebusites		Jebusites	Jebusite
Amorites					
Canaanites					
Girgashites					
Jebusites					
Gen. 15:19-21	Exod. 3:8*	Exod. 3:17**	Exod. 13:5***	Exod. 23:23	Exod. 33:2

Amorite	Amalekites	Hittites	Hittites	Canaanites	Hittite
Canaanite	Hittites	Girgashites	Amorites	Hittites	Amorite
Hittite	Jebusites	Amorites	Canaanites	Hivites	Canaanite
Perizzite	Amorites	Canaanites	Perizzites	Perizzites	Perizzite
Hivite	Canaanites	Perizzites	Hivites	Girgashites	Hivite
Jebusite		Hivites	Jebusites	Amorites	Jebusite
		Jebusites	(Girgashites)	Jebusites	
Exod. 34:11	Num. 13:29	Deut. 7:1	Deut. 20:17	Josh. 3:10	Josh. 9:1

Canaanite	Hittites	Amorites	Canaanites	Egyptians	Amorites
Amorite	Amorites	Perizzites	Hittites	Amorites	Hittites
Hittite	Canaanites	Canaanites	Amorites	Ammon	Perizzites
Perizzite	Perizzites	Hittites	Perizzites	Philistines	Hivites
Jebusite	Hivites	Girgashites	Hivites	Zidonians	Jebusites
Hivite	Jebusites	Hivites	Jebusites	Amalekites	
		Jebusites		Maonites	
Josh. 11:3	Josh. 12:8	Josh. 24:11	Judges 3:5	Judges 10:11-12	1 Kings 9:20

Hittites	Canaanites	Canaanites
Amorites	Hittites	Hittites
Perizzites	Perizzites	Amorites
Hivites	Jebusites	Perizzites
Jebusites	Ammonites	Jebusites
	Moabites	Girgashites
	Egyptians	
	Amorites	
2 Chron. 8:7	Ezra 9:1	Neh. 9:8

*The Septuagint reads: Canaanites, and the Hittites, and the Amorites, and the Perizzites, and the Girgashites, Hivites, and the Jebusites (Exod. 3:8).

**The Septuagint reads: Canaanites, and the Hittites, and the Amorites, and the Perizzites, and the Girgashites, and Hivites, and the Jebusites, unto a land flowing with milk and honey (Exod. 3:17). Both Exod. 3:8 and 3:17 lists are the same in the Hebrew and the Septuagint. Because they are both identical, copyists may be attempting to make the lists repeat when they should be different. Most likely, Girgashites should be in one of the two lists.

***The Septuagint reads: And it shall be when the LORD shall bring thee into the land of the Canaanites, and the Hittites, and the Amorites, and the Hivites, and the Jebusites, and the Girgashites, and the Perizzites (Exod. 13:5).

The following quotations from Cassuto on this issue also demonstrate his understanding that he is not cataloguing Moses' slavish compulsion to pagan repetition. Genesis is not bound to Western or pagan sequence.

> ...that the fact that a given writer once uses the word-sequence *the heavens and the earth* does not exclude the possibility that another writer may also employ this order of words, which is assuredly not a unique character nor does it imply that the former is never permitted to reverse the word-order and say, *the earth and the heavens*;[30]

> The fondness for variation, which is discernible, as we have noted, in the Biblical style, is also noticeable in the work of the Masoretes who fixed at a later period the spelling of the text.[31]

> ...*to the place of the Canaanites, the Hittites, the Amorites, the Perizzites, the Hivites, and the Jebusites* [Exodus 3:8]. This land is now the 'dwelling-place' of six peoples; the Israelites could therefore settle there in their thousands and myriads. The list of nations comprises here and in other passages six names, a round number based on the sexagesimal system that obtained in the ancient East. But there are also verses that list five or seven or ten names; this is solely due to the fondness for diversification, which is a common feature of Biblical style. On the various names, see my commentary on the Book of Genesis.[32]

Cassuto is inconsistent here, because he knows that Deuteronomy 20:17 states there are 7 nations, even though 11 of the 21 lists name 6 nations. He is attempting to explain the paradox by saying that 6s predominate, even though the text says 7 nations. Therefore, Cassuto concludes it is a Babylonian sexagesimal list. However, he is consistent in numbering the 10 Commandments, even though the list given by Moses describes 11, if not 12 commandments. It does not matter if we read 11; the text tells us there are 10.

Diversification, Variation, and Asymmetry

What Cassuto calls *diversification* and *variation* is the paradox of intentional concurrent symmetry and asymmetry. As shown in Chapter Six, Sternberg came to the same conclusion when he wrote: "One

---
[30] Cassuto, *Genesis: Part I*, p. 98.
[31] Cassuto, *Genesis: Part II*, pp. 70, 74, 89, 117. On pp. 70-71, Cassuto offers 3 paragraphs of spelling errors by the Masoretes.
[32] Cassuto, *Exodus*, p. 35.

must then recognize the principle of semantic variation in all its forms and degrees, from a near-equivalence to head-on collision and mutual incompatibility."[33] Cassuto is interested in cataloguing numerical tradition, while this writer is concerned with aesthetic analysis. Throughout the Bible we find the paradox of repetition juxtaposed to asymmetry. Of the 21 lists of the 12 tribes, 9 contain 11, 13, or 14 names. None of the 21 lists are in the same order except Numbers 7:12ff. and 10:16ff. The 5 lists of the 12 apostles in the New Testament are all in a different order.[34]

The 2012 edition addresses this paradox at length in Chapters One and Eleven. The paradox is the Bible's integration of abstraction and order. In the fine arts, a painting labeled as abstract is really a misnomer. It is not possible for an artist to produce true abstraction any more than a mathematician can make a list of 100 random numbers. This is why they rely on books of random numbers and computer-driven random number generators. It is remarkable that Cassuto recognizes this Hebrew aesthetic of *diversification* and *variation* as a biblical genre, and he may be the first to do so.

This raises the question as to which is more ordered, the apparent abstraction or the apparent order. These concepts are not imagined in pagan rote. The very fact that Cassuto is comfortable with such *variation* in the text illustrates the Hebrew mind's subconscious affinity for abstract thinking. Where the Western mind seeks the necessity of order, the Hebrew mind is comfortable with the integration of order and abstraction. Where the Western mind delves into abstraction as a distinct category, the Hebrew mind views abstraction as a necessary variable within reality. The human experience is not the planned event the world would have it to be.

The painting on the back cover of this book illustrates this point. The illusion may appear rather realistic, but all the motifs, such as the repetition in the rocks, saguaro cactus, grass, stripes, hair curls, prickly pear, brush, large rocks, dress emblems, and skin tones, are random and of unknown number and order. Nothing in the painting is counted except the 10 motifs.

Cassuto on Perfection versus Blessing

Associating perfection with the number 7 is a consistent theme in Cassuto's writings, as seen in the following excerpts, on which topic more could have been quoted. Notice how many times Cassuto uses

---

[33] Sternberg, p. 387.
[34] Cascione, 2012, pp. 117-18.

blessing, benison, or *increase* (bolded below), in order to describe perfection. The Hebrew text is talking about blessing, but Cassuto continues to describe it as perfection. It should also be noted that the Hebrew word for *perfection* does not appear in the book of Genesis. In Genesis 9:6 God calls Noah *blameless*, and in 17:1 God tells Abraham to be *blameless*, תָּמִים (*tamiym*, taw-meem'), but this hardly supports Cassuto's understanding of *perfection*. There is no heptadic pattern with *blameless* in Genesis. *Blameless* repeats 12 times in Leviticus in reference to an animal sacrifice without blemish. Yet Cassuto writes again and again about perfection (also bolded) in the following:

> …seven expressions of **benison**: one in xxvii 28 and six in xxvii 29 (every verb constituting a separate benediction). Seven is the number of **perfection**, and each of the three patriarchs received a **perfect blessing**, a sevenfold **benison**.[35]

> Not only is the number seven fundamental to its main theme, but it also serves to determine many of its details. Both to the Israelites and to the Gentiles, in the East and also in the West—but especially in the East—it was the number of *perfection* and the basis of ordered arrangement; and particular importance attached to it in the symbolism of numbers.[36]

> The number *seven*, which, as we have seen, is the number of **perfection**….[37]

> The family of the children of Noah is depicted as **perfect** in the number of its sons and all mankind, which comprises the seventy nations….[38]

> Other numbers too are very prominent there, although they are not expressly mentioned: seven, which as we know, is the number of **perfection**, and *twelve*.[39]

> The **blessing** bestowed by the Lord on Abraham in *vv.* 2-3 comprises seven expressions of **benison**, as we shall explain in detail later, and it is evident that the Bible intended by this formulation to set before us a form of **blessing** that was **perfect** in every respect.[40]

---

[35] Cassuto, *The Documentary Hypothesis*, p. 116.
[36] Cassuto, *Genesis: Part I*, p. 12.
[37] Cassuto, *Genesis: Part II*, p. 32.
[38] Ibid., pp. 176-77.
[39] Ibid., p. 178.
[40] Ibid., p. 306.

This number—seventy—commonly indicates the perfection of a family **blessed** with offspring, both in the pre-Israelitic and the Israelitic traditions....Similarly Jacob's family was **perfect** in the number of its children. [41]

Seven expressions for **increase** are used in this verse [Exodus 1:7], a number indicative of **perfection**: (1) were fruitful; (2) and teemed; (3) and multiplied; (4) and grew mighty; (5) with strength [בִּמְאֹד, bime'ōdh]; (6) strongly [מְאֹד, m e'ōdh]; (7) so that the land was filled with them.[42]

Since seven was considered the number of **perfection**, seven days constituted, according to the customary conception of the ancient East....[43] (Exodus 19:1)

Cassuto describes the 70 elders in Exodus 24 as, "a **perfect** representation of the people by a number that symbolizes **perfection**."[44]

Cassuto even uses the phrase *perfect blessing* above as if God's blessing by itself is not perfect. His concept of *perfection* follows a 2,500-year-old tradition of number symbolism that is traced back to Pythagoras and explained in detail in the books of the great Jewish scholar, Philo of Alexandria, a contemporary of Jesus Christ. The 2012 edition dedicates 2 full chapters to Philo's errors and his accuracy in identifying biblical number symbolism. These chapters are titled, *An Introduction to Biblical Number Symbolism*,[45] and *The Pythagorean Seduction of Western Christendom*.[46] Philo's main thesis is to prove that Pythagoras was following Mosaic number symbolism. In 2013 Ronald Hendel corroborated this opinion when he wrote, "In part he [Philo] wanted to show that Jewish thought is every bit as sophisticated as Greek, and that Moses anticipated Plato's philosophy."[47] This led Eusebius in the 4th century to canonize Philo as part of his effort to discredit Gnosticism, with which he also associated the book of Revelation. Philo may be the only Jew ever recognized as an Early Church Father.

Philo is primarily responsible for Western Christendom's error in associating 7 with perfection. In his writings, Cassuto unavoidably

---

[41] Cassuto, *Exodus*, p. 8.
[42] Ibid., p. 9.
[43] Ibid., p. 224.
[44] Ibid., p. 310.
[45] Cascione, 2012, p. 187.
[46] Ibid., p. 201.
[47] Hendel, p. 91.

talks about perfection in terms of blessing. As displayed in Chapter Eight, Cassuto lists numerous heptadic blessings, including those given to Abraham, Isaac, Jacob, and others. All of God's actions are judgments. His judgments are either blessings or curses. The antithesis of perfection is imperfection, something with which God is not associated. Hence, perfection lacks a dynamic antithetic equivalent consistent with God's nature, whereas the antithetic equivalent of cursing is blessing. "And I will bless them that bless thee, and curse him that curseth thee: and in thee shall all families of the earth be blessed" (Genesis 12:3). Deuteronomy 28:2-6 lists 7 divine blessings followed by 7 divine curses in 28:15-20. More importantly, perfection is a theological concept rooted in tradition, while *blessing* is an actual word in the text. Therefore 7 is the symbolic number of blessing and not perfection. This is why Genesis says, "and God blessed the seventh day, and sanctified it" (Genesis 2:3). It does not say He perfected it or improved it. It was already perfect because everything God does is by necessity perfect. Therefore, blessing is God's judgment, a statement of His continued and sustaining approval.

Increased Complexity in Exodus

This book's primary focus in the Hebrew Bible is repetition in Genesis. Based solely on observation, Hebraic meter in Exodus appears to be more complex than it is in Genesis, though future research may prove otherwise. The next 6 examples demonstrate that Exodus and succeeding books of the Hebrew Bible follow the same genre found in Genesis.

Moses and Aaron 14 times in Exodus

Moses and Aaron	מֹשֶׁה וְאַהֲרֹן	(Exod. 4:29)
Moses and Aaron	מֹשֶׁה וְאַהֲרֹן	(Exod. 5:1)
Moses and Aaron	מֹשֶׁה וְאַהֲרֹן	(Exod. 5:4)
Moses and Aaron	מֹשֶׁה וְאַהֲרֹן	(Exod. 6:27)
Moses and Aaron	מֹשֶׁה וְאַהֲרֹן	(Exod. 7:6)
Moses and Aaron	מֹשֶׁה וְאַהֲרֹן	(Exod. 7:10)
Moses and Aaron	מֹשֶׁה וְאַהֲרֹן	(Exod. 7:20)
Moses and Aaron	מֹשֶׁה וְאַהֲרֹן	(Exod. 8:8)
Moses and Aaron	מֹשֶׁה וְאַהֲרֹן	(Exod. 10:3)
Moses and Aaron	מֹשֶׁה וְאַהֲרֹן	(Exod. 12:28)
Moses and Aaron	מֹשֶׁה וְאַהֲרֹן	(Exod. 12:43)
Moses and Aaron	מֹשֶׁה וְאַהֲרֹן	(Exod. 16:6)
Moses and Aaron	מֹשֶׁה וְאַהֲרֹן	(Exod. 24:9)
Moses and Aaron	מֹשֶׁה וְאַהֲרֹן	(Exod. 40:31)

And said the Lord to Moses, stretch out your hand 7 times in Exodus
    And said the Lord to Moses…stretch out your hand (Exod. 7:19)
    And said the Lord to Moses…stretch out your hand (Exod. 8:1)

And said the Lord to Moses, stretch out your hand (Exod. 9:22)
And said the Lord to Moses, stretch out your hand (Exod. 10:12)
And said the Lord to Moses, stretch out your hand (Exod. 10:21)
And said the Lord to Moses…stretch out your hand (Exod. 14:15-16)
And said the Lord to Moses, stretch out your hand (Exod. 14:26)

וַיֹּאמֶר יְהוָה אֶל־מֹשֶׁה...וּנְטֵה־יָדְךָ (Exod. 7:19)
וַיֹּאמֶר יְהוָה אֶל־מֹשֶׁה נְטֵה אֶת־יָדְךָ (Exod. 8:1)
וַיֹּאמֶר יְהוָה אֶל־מֹשֶׁה נְטֵה אֶת־יָדְךָ (Exod. 9:22)
וַיֹּאמֶר יְהוָה אֶל־מֹשֶׁה נְטֵה יָדְךָ (Exod. 10:12)
וַיֹּאמֶר יְהוָה אֶל־מֹשֶׁה נְטֵה יָדְךָ (Exod. 10:21)
וַיֹּאמֶר יְהוָה אֶל־מֹשֶׁה...וּנְטֵה אֶת־יָדְךָ (Exod. 14:15-16)
וַיֹּאמֶר יְהוָה אֶל־מֹשֶׁה נְטֵה אֶת־יָדְךָ (Exod. 14:26)

Chariots and horsemen **7 times in Exodus**

Chariots of Pharaoh, and his horsemen	(Exod. 14:9)
On his chariots, and on his horsemen	(Exod. 14:17)
On his chariots, and on his horsemen	(Exod. 14:18)
His chariots, and his horsemen	(Exod. 14:23)
On their chariots, and on their horsemen	(Exod. 14:26)
the chariots, and the horsemen	(Exod. 14:28)
With his chariots and with his horsemen	(Exod. 15:19)

רֶכֶב פַּרְעֹה וּפָרָשָׁיו (Exod. 14:9)
בְּרִכְבּוֹ וּבְפָרָשָׁיו (Exod. 14:17)
בְּרִכְבּוֹ וּבְפָרָשָׁיו (Exod. 14:18)
רִכְבּוֹ וּפָרָשָׁיו (Exod. 14:23)
עַל־רִכְבּוֹ וְעַל־פָּרָשָׁיו (Exod. 14:26)
אֶת־הָרֶכֶב וְאֶת־הַפָּרָשִׁים (Exod. 14:28)
בְּרִכְבּוֹ וּבְפָרָשָׁיו (Exod. 15:19)

And spoke the Lord to Moses **14 times in Exodus**

And spoke the Lord to Moses	וַיְדַבֵּר יְהוָה אֶל־מֹשֶׁה	(Exod. 6:10)
And spoke the Lord to Moses	וַיְדַבֵּר יְהוָה אֶל־מֹשֶׁה	(Exod. 6:13)
And spoke the Lord to Moses	וַיְדַבֵּר יְהוָה אֶל־מֹשֶׁה	(Exod. 6:29)
And spoke the Lord to Moses	וַיְדַבֵּר יְהוָה אֶל־מֹשֶׁה	(Exod. 13:1)
And spoke the Lord to Moses	וַיְדַבֵּר יְהוָה אֶל־מֹשֶׁה	(Exod. 14:1)
And spoke the Lord to Moses	וַיְדַבֵּר יְהוָה אֶל־מֹשֶׁה	(Exod. 16:11)
And spoke the Lord to Moses	וַיְדַבֵּר יְהוָה אֶל־מֹשֶׁה	(Exod. 25:1)
And spoke the Lord to Moses	וַיְדַבֵּר יְהוָה אֶל־מֹשֶׁה	(Exod. 30:11)
And spoke the Lord to Moses	וַיְדַבֵּר יְהוָה אֶל־מֹשֶׁה	(Exod. 30:17)
And spoke the Lord to Moses	וַיְדַבֵּר יְהוָה אֶל־מֹשֶׁה	(Exod. 30:22)
And spoke the Lord to Moses	וַיְדַבֵּר יְהוָה אֶל־מֹשֶׁה	(Exod. 31:1)
And spoke the Lord to Moses	וַיְדַבֵּר יְהוָה אֶל־מֹשֶׁה	(Exod. 32:7)
And spoke the Lord to Moses	וַיְדַבֵּר יְהוָה אֶל־מֹשֶׁה	(Exod. 33:1)
And spoke the Lord to Moses	וַיְדַבֵּר יְהוָה אֶל־מֹשֶׁה	(Exod. 40:1)

A Deeper Look into Genesis and Exodus

And said the Lord to Moses 42 times in Exodus

(Exod. 4:4) וַיֹּאמֶר יְהוָה אֶל־מֹשֶׁה   (Exod. 4:19) וַיֹּאמֶר יְהוָה אֶל־מֹשֶׁה
(Exod. 4:21) וַיֹּאמֶר יְהוָה אֶל־מֹשֶׁה   (Exod. 6:1) וַיֹּאמֶר יְהוָה אֶל־מֹשֶׁה
(Exod. 7:1) וַיֹּאמֶר יְהוָה אֶל־מֹשֶׁה   (Exod. 7:8) וַיֹּאמֶר יְהוָה אֶל־מֹשֶׁה
(Exod. 7:14) וַיֹּאמֶר יְהוָה אֶל־מֹשֶׁה   (Exod. 7:19) וַיֹּאמֶר יְהוָה אֶל־מֹשֶׁה
(Exod. 7:26) וַיֹּאמֶר יְהוָה אֶל־מֹשֶׁה   (Exod. 8:1) וַיֹּאמֶר יְהוָה אֶל־מֹשֶׁה
(Exod. 8:12) וַיֹּאמֶר יְהוָה אֶל־מֹשֶׁה   (Exod. 8:16) וַיֹּאמֶר יְהוָה אֶל־מֹשֶׁה
(Exod. 9:1) וַיֹּאמֶר יְהוָה אֶל־מֹשֶׁה   (Exod. 9:8) וַיֹּאמֶר יְהוָה אֶל־מֹשֶׁה
(Exod. 9:13) וַיֹּאמֶר יְהוָה אֶל־מֹשֶׁה   (Exod. 9:22) וַיֹּאמֶר יְהוָה אֶל־מֹשֶׁה
(Exod. 10:1) וַיֹּאמֶר יְהוָה אֶל־מֹשֶׁה   (Exod. 10:12) וַיֹּאמֶר יְהוָה אֶל־מֹשֶׁה
(Exod. 10:21) וַיֹּאמֶר יְהוָה אֶל־מֹשֶׁה   (Exod. 11:1) וַיֹּאמֶר יְהוָה אֶל־מֹשֶׁה
(Exod. 11:9) וַיֹּאמֶר יְהוָה אֶל־מֹשֶׁה   (Exod. 12:1) וַיֹּאמֶר יְהוָה אֶל־מֹשֶׁה
(Exod. 12:43) וַיֹּאמֶר יְהוָה אֶל־מֹשֶׁה   (Exod. 14:1) וַיֹּאמֶר יְהוָה אֶל־מֹשֶׁה
(Exod. 14:26) וַיֹּאמֶר יְהוָה אֶל־מֹשֶׁה   (Exod. 16:4) וַיֹּאמֶר יְהוָה אֶל־מֹשֶׁה
(Exod. 16:28) וַיֹּאמֶר יְהוָה אֶל־מֹשֶׁה   (Exod. 17:5) וַיֹּאמֶר יְהוָה אֶל־מֹשֶׁה
(Exod. 17:14) וַיֹּאמֶר יְהוָה אֶל־מֹשֶׁה   (Exod. 19:9) וַיֹּאמֶר יְהוָה אֶל־מֹשֶׁה
(Exod. 19:10) וַיֹּאמֶר יְהוָה אֶל־מֹשֶׁה   (Exod. 19:21) וַיֹּאמֶר יְהוָה אֶל־מֹשֶׁה
(Exod. 20:22) וַיֹּאמֶר יְהוָה אֶל־מֹשֶׁה   (Exod. 24:12) וַיֹּאמֶר יְהוָה אֶל־מֹשֶׁה
(Exod. 30:34) וַיֹּאמֶר יְהוָה אֶל־מֹשֶׁה   (Exod. 31:12) וַיֹּאמֶר יְהוָה אֶל־מֹשֶׁה
(Exod. 32:9) וַיֹּאמֶר יְהוָה אֶל־מֹשֶׁה   (Exod. 32:33) וַיֹּאמֶר יְהוָה אֶל־מֹשֶׁה
(Exod. 33:5) וַיֹּאמֶר יְהוָה אֶל־מֹשֶׁה   (Exod. 33:17) וַיֹּאמֶר יְהוָה אֶל־מֹשֶׁה
(Exod. 34:1) וַיֹּאמֶר יְהוָה אֶל־מֹשֶׁה   (Exod. 34:27) וַיֹּאמֶר יְהוָה אֶל־מֹשֶׁה

To the sons of Israel 14 times in Exodus

    To the sons of Israel...... אֶל־בְּנֵי יִשְׂרָאֵל (Exod. 3:13)
    To the sons of Israel...... אֶל־בְּנֵי יִשְׂרָאֵל (Exod. 3:15)
    To the sons of Israel...... אֶל־בְּנֵי יִשְׂרָאֵל (Exod. 6:9)
    To the sons of Israel...... אֶל־בְּנֵי יִשְׂרָאֵל (Exod. 6:13)
    To the sons of Israel...... אֶל־בְּנֵי יִשְׂרָאֵל (Exod. 14:2)
    To the sons of Israel...... אֶל־בְּנֵי־יִשְׂרָאֵל (Exod. 14:15)
    To the sons of Israel...... אֶל־בְּנֵי יִשְׂרָאֵל (Exod. 19:6)
    To the sons of Israel...... אֶל־בְּנֵי יִשְׂרָאֵל (Exod. 20:22)
    To the sons of Israel...... אֶל־בְּנֵי יִשְׂרָאֵל (Exod. 25:2)
    To the sons of Israel...... אֶל־בְּנֵי יִשְׂרָאֵל (Exod. 25:22)
    To the sons of Israel...... אֶל־בְּנֵי יִשְׂרָאֵל (Exod. 31:13)
    To the sons of Israel...... אֶל־בְּנֵי־יִשְׂרָאֵל (Exod. 33:5)
    To the sons of Israel...... אֶל־בְּנֵי יִשְׂרָאֵל (Exod. 34:34)
    To the sons of Israel...... אֶל־בְּנֵי יִשְׂרָאֵל (Exod. 35:30)

To the sons of Israel 10 times in Genesis and Exodus

    To the sons of Israel...... לִבְנֵי יִשְׂרָאֵל (Gen. 36:31)

To the sons of Israel...... לִבְנֵי יִשְׂרָאֵל (Exod. 3:14)
To the sons of Israel...... לִבְנֵי־יִשְׂרָאֵל (Exod. 6:6)
To the sons of Israel...... לִבְנֵי יִשְׂרָאֵל (Exod. 9:4)
To the sons of Israel...... לִבְנֵי יִשְׂרָאֵל (Exod. 14:3)
To the sons of Israel...... לִבְנֵי יִשְׂרָאֵל (Exod. 19:3)
To the sons of Israel...... לִבְנֵי יִשְׂרָאֵל (Exod. 28:12)
To the sons of Israel...... לִבְנֵי יִשְׂרָאֵל (Exod. 29:43)
To the sons of Israel...... לִבְנֵי יִשְׂרָאֵל (Exod. 30:16)
To the sons of Israel...... לִבְנֵי יִשְׂרָאֵל (Exod. 39:7)

The verb for *harden* in Exodus 7:3 is different than the other 6 verbs in the list below. Its first meaning is *harden*. The first meaning of the other 6 verbs is actually *strong* or *strengthen*, but *harden* appears in nearly all Bible translations for these other 6 verbs. Obviously, the Lord is not improving Pharaoh's heart, so *strengthen* would not be appropriate. The assumption is that the first verb explains how to interpret the following 6 verbs. It illustrates that the progression is repeating 7 actions without necessarily using the same word. Also, when there is a pattern shift, its purpose may be to preserve the correct meter in other words or phrases of which we are not aware, as seen in the first 5 chapters of this book. This heptadic meter is located in the Hebrew text by searching for the last 3 words, which are all identical.

Harden the heart of Pharaoh 7 times in Exodus
    I will harden the heart of Pharaoh..... וַאֲנִי אַקְשֶׁה אֶת־לֵב פַּרְעֹה (Exod. 7:3)
    The Lord hardened the heart of Pharaoh..... יְחַזֵּק יְהוָה אֶת־לֵב פַּרְעֹה (Exod. 9:12)
    The Lord hardened the heart of Pharaoh..... וַיְחַזֵּק יְהוָה אֶת־לֵב פַּרְעֹה (Exod. 10:20)
    The Lord hardened the heart of Pharaoh..... וַיְחַזֵּק יְהוָה אֶת־לֵב פַּרְעֹה (Exod. 10:27)
    The Lord hardened the heart of Pharaoh..... וַיְחַזֵּק יְהוָה אֶת־לֵב פַּרְעֹה (Exod. 11:10)
    I will harden the heart of Pharaoh...... וְחִזַּקְתִּי אֶת־לֵב־פַּרְעֹה (Exod. 14:4)
    The Lord hardened the heart of Pharaoh..... וַיְחַזֵּק יְהוָה אֶת־לֵב פַּרְעֹה (Exod. 14:8)

Man and beast 10 times in Exodus
    In **man** and in beast....... בָּאָדָם וּבַבְּהֵמָה (Exod. 8:13)
    In **man** and in beast....... בָּאָדָם וּבַבְּהֵמָה (Exod. 8:14)
    Upon **man** and upon beast... עַל־הָאָדָם וְעַל־הַבְּהֵמָה (Exod. 9:9)
    In **man** and in beast....... בָּאָדָם וּבַבְּהֵמָה (Exod. 9:10)
    Every **man** and beast.......... כָּל־הָאָדָם וְהַבְּהֵמָה (Exod. 9:19)
    Upon **man** and upon beast... עַל־הָאָדָם וְעַל־הַבְּהֵמָה (Exod. 9:22)
    Both **man** and beast.......... מֵאָדָם וְעַד־בְּהֵמָה (Exod. 9:25)
    Both **man** and beast.......... מֵאָדָם וְעַד־בְּהֵמָה (Exod. 12:12)
    In **man** and in beast....... בָּאָדָם וּבַבְּהֵמָה (Exod. 13:2)
    Both...**man** and...beast......... מִבְּכֹר אָדָם וְעַד־בְּהֵמָה (Exod. 13:15)*

*Full text reads: Both the first born of man and the first born of beast.

The Book of Numbers may contain the most metered phrases of any book in the Bible, as its name would seem to indicate. The following is one selection. Many phrases overlap and intertwine, presenting more Hebraic meter than there is time to unravel.

The continual burnt offering, meat offering, and drink offerings 10 times in Numbers

and the continual burnt offering, and the meat offering of it, and their drink offerings (Num. 29:6)
and the continual burnt offering, and the meat offering of it, and their drink offerings (Num. 29:11)
    the continual burnt offering,   the meat offering of it, and its   drink offerings (Num. 29:16)
    the continual burnt offering, and the meat offering of it, and their drink offerings (Num. 29:19)
    the continual burnt offering, and the meat offering of it, and its   drink offerings (Num. 29:22)
    the continual burnt offering,   the meat offering of it, and its   drink offerings (Num. 29:25)
    the continual burnt offering, and the meat offering of it, and its   drink offerings (Num. 29:28)
    the continual burnt offering,   the meat offering of it, and its   drink offerings (Num. 29:31)
    the continual burnt offering,   the meat offering of it, and its   drink offerings (Num. 29:34)
    the continual burnt offering, and the meat offering of it, and its   drink offerings (Num. 29:38)

(Num. 29:6) וְעֹלַת הַתָּמִיד וּמִנְחָתָהּ וְנִסְכֵּיהֶם
(Num. 29:11) וְעֹלַת הַתָּמִיד וּמִנְחָתָהּ וְנִסְכֵּיהֶם
(Num. 29:16) עֹלַת הַתָּמִיד מִנְחָתָהּ וְנִסְכָּהּ
(Num. 29:19) עֹלַת הַתָּמִיד וּמִנְחָתָהּ וְנִסְכֵּיהֶם
(Num. 29:22) עֹלַת הַתָּמִיד וּמִנְחָתָהּ וְנִסְכָּהּ
(Num. 29:25) עֹלַת הַתָּמִיד מִנְחָתָהּ וְנִסְכָּהּ
(Num. 29:28) עֹלַת הַתָּמִיד וּמִנְחָתָהּ וְנִסְכָּהּ
(Num. 29:31) עֹלַת הַתָּמִיד מִנְחָתָהּ וּנְסָכֶיהָ
(Num. 29:34) עֹלַת הַתָּמִיד מִנְחָתָהּ וְנִסְכָּהּ
(Num. 29:38) עֹלַת הַתָּמִיד וּמִנְחָתָהּ וְנִסְכָּהּ

The following example is one of the more fascinating heptadic phrases. This order of colors is associated with ceremonial law and temple ritual. *Blue, purple,* and *scarlet* are always in the same order 26 times in Exodus. *Blue, purple, scarlet,* and *linen* appear together 24 times, with *linen* implied in 39:24. There are other possible arrangements with *gold*. After a number of attempts over the years to find the primary meter, it appears to be the following double heptad. The question may be asked, "With so many possibilities, how do we know the following example is the primary meter?" Internal evidence is needed to support this conclusion. Notice the 7th and the 14th lines. There is a change of word sequence. These 2 verses mark the end of each heptad. Unrelated to this meter, it is also of interest to note the missing *and* in 28:6. There is no variant reading. The Septuagint does not record the verse correctly, and is of no value here. However, the Vulgate is also missing this *and*. In other words, this particular *and* is purposely left out of the meter. Its absence also maintains a total of 4,900 *and*s in Exodus and Numbers. This arrangement is a work of art. There will be further discussion on this example in the Conclusion.

Blue and purple and scarlet and fine linen twisted 14 times in Exodus
    Blue and purple and scarlet and fine linen twisted (Exod. 26:31)
    Blue and purple and scarlet and fine linen twisted (Exod. 26:36)
    Blue and purple and scarlet and fine linen twisted (Exod. 27:16)
    Blue and purple,   scarlet and fine linen twisted (Exod. 28:6)
    Blue and purple and scarlet and fine linen twisted (Exod. 28:8)
    Blue and purple and scarlet and fine linen twisted (Exod. 28:15)
    Fine linen twisted and blue and purple and scarlet (Exod. 36:8)
    Blue and purple and scarlet and fine linen twisted (Exod. 36:35)
    Blue and purple and scarlet and fine linen twisted (Exod. 36:37)
    Blue and purple and scarlet and fine linen twisted (Exod. 38:18)
    Blue and purple and scarlet and fine linen twisted (Exod. 39:2)
    Blue and purple and scarlet and fine linen twisted (Exod. 39:5)
    Blue and purple and scarlet and fine linen twisted (Exod. 39:8)
    Fine linen twisted and blue and purple and scarlet (Exod. 39:29)

    תְּכֵלֶת וְאַרְגָּמָן וְתוֹלַעַת שָׁנִי וְשֵׁשׁ מָשְׁזָר (Exod. 26:31)
    תְּכֵלֶת וְאַרְגָּמָן וְתוֹלַעַת שָׁנִי וְשֵׁשׁ מָשְׁזָר (Exod. 26:36)
    תְּכֵלֶת וְאַרְגָּמָן וְתוֹלַעַת שָׁנִי וְשֵׁשׁ מָשְׁזָר (Exod. 27:16)
    תְּכֵלֶת וְאַרְגָּמָן תּוֹלַעַת שָׁנִי וְשֵׁשׁ מָשְׁזָר (Exod. 28:6)
    תְּכֵלֶת וְאַרְגָּמָן וְתוֹלַעַת שָׁנִי וְשֵׁשׁ מָשְׁזָר (Exod. 28:8)
    תְּכֵלֶת וְאַרְגָּמָן וְתוֹלַעַת שָׁנִי וְשֵׁשׁ מָשְׁזָר (Exod. 28:15)
    שֵׁשׁ מָשְׁזָר וּתְכֵלֶת וְאַרְגָּמָן וְתוֹלַעַת שָׁנִי (Exod. 36:8)
    תְּכֵלֶת וְאַרְגָּמָן וְתוֹלַעַת שָׁנִי וְשֵׁשׁ מָשְׁזָר (Exod. 36:35)
    תְּכֵלֶת וְאַרְגָּמָן וְתוֹלַעַת שָׁנִי וְשֵׁשׁ מָשְׁזָר (Exod. 36:37)
    תְּכֵלֶת וְאַרְגָּמָן וְתוֹלַעַת שָׁנִי וְשֵׁשׁ מָשְׁזָר (Exod. 38:18)
    תְּכֵלֶת וְאַרְגָּמָן וְתוֹלַעַת שָׁנִי וְשֵׁשׁ מָשְׁזָר (Exod. 39:2)
    תְּכֵלֶת וְאַרְגָּמָן וְתוֹלַעַת שָׁנִי וְשֵׁשׁ מָשְׁזָר (Exod. 39:5)
    תְּכֵלֶת וְאַרְגָּמָן וְתוֹלַעַת שָׁנִי וְשֵׁשׁ מָשְׁזָר (Exod. 39:8)
    שֵׁשׁ מָשְׁזָר וּתְכֵלֶת וְאַרְגָּמָן וְתוֹלַעַת שָׁנִי (Exod. 39:29)

Thus saith the Lord 10 times in Exodus
    Thus saith the Lord.................... כֹּה אָמַר יְהֹוָה (Exod. 4:22)
    Thus saith the Lord.................... כֹּה־אָמַר יְהֹוָה (Exod. 5:1)
    Thus saith the Lord.................... כֹּה אָמַר יְהֹוָה (Exod. 7:17)
    Thus saith the Lord.................... כֹּה אָמַר יְהֹוָה (Exod. 7:26)
    Thus saith the Lord.................... כֹּה אָמַר יְהֹוָה (Exod. 8:16)
    Thus saith the Lord.................... כֹּה־אָמַר יְהֹוָה (Exod. 9:1)
    Thus saith the Lord.................... כֹּה־אָמַר יְהֹוָה (Exod. 9:13)
    Thus saith the Lord.................... כֹּה־אָמַר יְהֹוָה (Exod. 10:3)
    Thus saith the Lord.................... כֹּה אָמַר יְהֹוָה (Exod. 11:4)
    Thus saith the Lord.................... כֹּה־אָמַר יְהֹוָה (Exod. 32:27)

    The following phrases are addressed to Pharaoh by God. The first phrase refers to Israel as *God's son* instead of *my people*. The Hebrew words for *Let My...go* are repeated in this order 10 times in Exodus. Therefore, it seems correct in this context to assume that *son* in 4:23 and *people* are the same group. Notice the heptadic subset with אֶת־עַמִּי. The first word is the untranslatable sign of the direct object, and the second word translates to *My people*.

Let My people go 10 times in Exodus
    Let My son go............... שַׁלַּח אֶת־בְּנִי (Exod. 4:23)
    Let My people go.......... שַׁלַּח אֶת־עַמִּי (Exod. 5:1)
    Let My people go.......... שַׁלַּח אֶת־עַמִּי (Exod. 7:16)
    Let My people go.......... שַׁלַּח אֶת־עַמִּי (Exod. 7:26/8:1)
    Let My people go............... שַׁלַּח עַמִּי (Exod. 8:16/8:20)
    Let My people go.......... מְשַׁלֵּחַ אֶת־עַמִּי (Exod. 8:17/8:21)
    Let My people go.......... שַׁלַּח אֶת־עַמִּי (Exod. 9:1)
    Let My people go.......... שַׁלַּח אֶת־עַמִּי (Exod. 9:13)
    Let My people go............... שַׁלַּח עַמִּי (Exod. 10:3)
    To let My people go............ לְשַׁלֵּחַ אֶת־עַמִּי (Exod. 10:4)

In all the land of Egypt 12 times in Exodus
    In all the land of Egypt........ בְּכָל־אֶרֶץ מִצְרָיִם (Exod. 5:12)
    In all the land of Egypt...... בְּכָל־אֶרֶץ מִצְרָיִם (Exod. 7:19)
    In all the land of Egypt...... בְּכָל־אֶרֶץ מִצְרָיִם (Exod. 7:21)
    In all the land of Egypt...... בְּכָל־אֶרֶץ מִצְרָיִם (Exod. 8:12)
    In all the land of Egypt...... בְּכָל־אֶרֶץ מִצְרָיִם (Exod. 8:13)
    In all the land of Egypt...... בְּכָל־אֶרֶץ מִצְרָיִם (Exod. 9:9)
    In all the land of Egypt...... בְּכָל־אֶרֶץ מִצְרָיִם (Exod. 9:22)
    In all the land of Egypt...... בְּכָל־אֶרֶץ מִצְרָיִם (Exod. 9:24)
    In all the land of Egypt...... בְּכָל־אֶרֶץ מִצְרָיִם (Exod. 9:25)
    In all the land of Egypt...... בְּכָל־אֶרֶץ מִצְרָיִם (Exod. 10:15)
    In all the land of Egypt...... בְּכָל־אֶרֶץ מִצְרָיִם (Exod. 10:22)
    In all the land of Egypt...... בְּכָל־אֶרֶץ מִצְרָיִם (Exod. 11:6)

The following heptadic phrase in bold type is layered with what appears to be irregular phrases in plain type that are actually lines from other overlapping metered phrases. They appear as concurrent asymmetry and symmetry. There is an internal 3-4 division with *the Lord God of the Hebrews*. The English and Hebrew texts do not all follow the same verse numbers below.

That they may serve me 7 times in Exodus
    And thou shalt say unto Pharaoh,
    Thus saith the LORD…and I say unto thee,
    ***Let my son go*, that he may serve me**: (Exod. 4:22-23)
    And thou shalt say unto him, *The LORD God of the Hebrews*
    hath sent me unto thee, saying,
    ***Let my people go*, that they may serve me** (Exod. 7:16)
    And the LORD spake unto Moses, Go unto Pharaoh,
    and say unto him, Thus saith the LORD,
    ***Let my people go*, that they may serve me.** (Exod. 8:1)

Thus saith the LORD,
Let my people go, that they may serve me. (Exod. 8:20)
Then the LORD said unto Moses, Go in unto Pharaoh, and tell him,
Thus saith *the LORD God of the Hebrews*,
Let my people go, that they may serve me (Exod. 9:1)
Thus saith *the LORD God of the Hebrews*,
Let my people go, that they may serve me. (Exod. 9:13)
Thus saith *the LORD God of the Hebrews*,...
Let my people go, that they may serve me. (Exod. 10:3)

וְאָמַרְתָּ אֶל־פַּרְעֹה כֹּה אָמַר יְהוָה (Exod. 4:22-23)
וָאֹמַר אֵלֶיךָ שַׁלַּח אֶת־בְּנִי וְיַעַבְדֵנִי
וְאָמַרְתָּ אֵלָיו יְהוָה אֱלֹהֵי הָעִבְרִים (Exod. 7:16)
שְׁלָחַנִי אֵלֶיךָ לֵאמֹר שַׁלַּח אֶת־עַמִּי וְיַעַבְדֻנִי
וַיֹּאמֶר יְהוָה אֶל־מֹשֶׁה בֹּא אֶל־פַּרְעֹה (Exod. 7:26)
וְאָמַרְתָּ אֵלָיו כֹּה אָמַר יְהוָה שַׁלַּח אֶת־עַמִּי וְיַעַבְדֻנִי
וְאָמַרְתָּ אֵלָיו כֹּה אָמַר יְהוָה שַׁלַּח עַמִּי וְיַעַבְדֻנִי (Exod. 8:16)
וַיֹּאמֶר יְהוָה אֶל־מֹשֶׁה בֹּא אֶל־פַּרְעֹה וְדִבַּרְתָּ אֵלָיו כֹּה־אָמַר (Exod. 9:1)
יְהוָה אֱלֹהֵי הָעִבְרִים שַׁלַּח אֶת־עַמִּי וְיַעַבְדֻנִי
וְאָמַרְתָּ אֵלָיו כֹּה־אָמַר יְהוָה (Exod. 9:13)
אֱלֹהֵי הָעִבְרִים שַׁלַּח אֶת־עַמִּי וְיַעַבְדֻנִי
וַיֹּאמְרוּ אֵלָיו כֹּה־אָמַר יְהוָה אֱלֹהֵי הָעִבְרִים...שַׁלַּח עַמִּי וְיַעַבְדֻנִי (Exod. 10:3)

Various meters, some displayed earlier in this chapter, overlay and intertwine the above heptad, such as:

Say to Pharaoh 30 times (7-23 division) in Genesis and Exodus;
Let My people go 10 times in Exodus;
That they may serve Me 7 times in Exodus;
Thus saith the Lord 10 times in Exodus.

Such coordination seems beyond the realm of human ability. One gets the sense we are climbing the mountain to join Moses in the cranny of the rock.

There are 9 consecutive repetitions of Moses asking Pharaoh, Pharaoh refusing, or Pharaoh agreeing to let Israel sacrifice to the Lord. In the 10th phrase, in reference to Pharaoh, before Israel crosses the Red Sea, Moses says, "I sacrifice to the LORD the males, the first offspring of every womb, but every first-born of my sons I redeem" (13:15). Earlier, in Exodus 10:26, Moses tells Pharaoh he does not know what the sacrifice will be. Exodus 29:28, which is 16 chapters after the last verse of the decad, and is not listed below, speaks about a sacrifice described as a wave offering, and is not a reference to Pharaoh. Notice that 5 of the phrases include *our* or *your God*. The English and Hebrew texts do not all follow the same verse numbers below.

Sacrifice to the Lord 10 times in Exodus

                And **sacrifice** to the LORD our God (Exod. 3:18)
                And **sacrifice** to the LORD our God (Exod. 5:3)
                Sacrifice to the LORD (Exod. 5:17)
                And **sacrifice** to the LORD (Exod. 8:8)
            For we shall **sacrifice** to the LORD our God (Exod. 8:26)
                And **sacrifice** to the LORD (Exod. 8:27)
         And you may **sacrifice** to the LORD your God (Exod. 8:28)
                To **sacrifice** to the LORD (Exod. 8:29)
        And make whole **sacrifices** to the LORD our God (Exod. 10:25)
                I **sacrifice** to the LORD (Exod. 13:15)

וְנִזְבְּחָה לַיהוָה אֱלֹהֵינוּ (Exod. 3:18)
וְנִזְבְּחָה לַיהוָה אֱלֹהֵינוּ (Exod. 5:3)
נִזְבְּחָה לַיהוָה (Exod. 5:17)
וְיִזְבְּחוּ לַיהוָה (Exod. 8:4)
נִזְבַּח לַיהוָה אֱלֹהֵינוּ (Exod. 8:22)
וְזָבַחְנוּ לַיהוָה (Exod. 8:23)
וּזְבַחְתֶּם לַיהוָה אֱלֹהֵיכֶם (Exod. 8:24)
לִזְבֹּחַ לַיהוָה (Exod. 8:25)
זְבָחִים וְעֹלוֹת לַיהוָה אֱלֹהֵינוּ (Exod. 10:25)
זֹבֵחַ לַיהוָה (Exod. 13:15)

    The predetermined selection of words to arrive at the desired meter is rather apparent in the decadal phrase *stretch out* with a heptadic subset of *your hand*. Exodus 3:20 and 4:4 (x2) (not shown) use שָׁלַח (*shalach*, shaw-lakh') for *stretch out*. The text then introduces 10 repetitions of נָטָה (*natah*, naw-taw') for *stretch out*, and then returns to שָׁלַח (*shalach*, shaw-lakh') in 24:11. Even 9:15 (not shown below), *For now I will stretch out my hand*, switches to שָׁלַח (*shalach*, shaw-lakh'), as does 4:4, *and so he stretched out his hand* (the additions of which would alter the heptadic subset of *hand*), in order to maintain 10 נָטָה (*natah*, naw-taw') with *hand* or *staff*.

Stretch out 10 times, *your hand* 7 times in Exodus

                When I stretch out my hand...... בִּנְטֹתִי אֶת־יָדִי (Exod. 7:5)
                And stretch out **your hand**.......... וּנְטֵה־יָדְךָ (Exod. 7:19)
                Stretch out **your hand**....... נְטֵה אֶת־יָדְךָ (Exod. 8:1)
                Stretch out your staff........ נְטֵה אֶת־מַטְּךָ (Exod. 8:16)
                Stretch out **your hand**....... נְטֵה אֶת־יָדְךָ (Exod. 9:22)
                Stretch out **your hand**............. נְטֵה יָדְךָ (Exod. 10:12)
                Stretch out **your hand**............. נְטֵה יָדְךָ (Exod. 10:21)
                And stretch out **your hand**....... וּנְטֵה אֶת־יָדְךָ (Exod. 14:16)
                Stretch out **your hand**....... נְטֵה אֶת־יָדְךָ (Exod. 14:26)
                Thou didst stretch out thy right hand........... נָטִיתָ יְמִינְךָ (Exod. 15:12)

Decadal Meter in the *Waw* Consecutive (repetition of *and*s)

The repetition of *and* in decadal meter is found in entire chapters of Revelation, and is called *polysyndeton*, meaning *many ands*.[48] The first and second editions list 7 divisions of 1,120 *and*s (or *kai*s) in Revelation. Polysyndeton is actually the Greek version of the Hebrew *waw consecutive,* which is a repetition of *and* (*wāw*, ו). In the first chapter of Genesis *and* repeats 101 times. The extra *and*, if not added as the result of a variant reading, is part of a larger meter. Similar sequences also occur in Revelation. The second chapter in Genesis has 61 *and*s (*waw*s). Again there is an extra *and*. The third chapter has 65 *and*s, which indicates the need for a second 5. The fourth chapter has 68 *and*s, and the fifth chapter has 105, for a total of 400 *and*s in the first 5 chapters. These first 5 chapters complete a natural division in Genesis, culminating with the genealogy of the 10 antediluvian patriarchs from Adam to Noah. The last *waw* in the meter is in the last verse of Genesis chapter 5.

The next natural division in the text, Genesis 6-10, contains 330 *waw*s, and concludes with the Flood account and the generations after Noah. Therefore, every one of the original 730 *waw*s is preserved in the Hebrew text. Those who follow astral numbers, such as James B. Jordan, will note that 730 is twice Enoch's age of 365, the number of days for the earth to revolve around the sun. One can only guess that the number 730 indicates that time before and after the Flood remained the same. The next 5 chapters, 11-15, also contain 330 *waw*s.

The existence of *and* set in Hebraic decadal meter in Genesis is further evidence that we possess the unedited, unaltered, and unredacted original words of Moses. As in Revelation and Genesis, the same Hebraic meter using the word *and* is found in Daniel. Steinmann addresses the 2,300 evenings and mornings in Daniel, as published in the second edition.

> Another approach is to interpret the 2,300 evenings and mornings as 2,300 evening and morning sacrifices, which would take place over 1,150 days, since one evening sacrifice and one morning sacrifice were performed each day. This would explain the unusual syntax of "evening, morning" in 8:14. Moreover, this is confirmed by 8:26, which calls this, literally, "the vision of the evening and the morning." In addition, the vision is about הַתָּמִיד [hātāmîd, the continuity] (8:11-13), which is a term for "the continual sacrifice" offered twice daily.[49]

---

[48] Cascione, 2012, p. 142.
[49] Andrew E. Steinmann, *Daniel: Concordia Commentary*, Concordia Publishing House,

Steinmann would be surprised to know that there are exactly 1,150 *waw*s preserved in the Hebrew manuscript of Daniel in Codex Leningradensis (WTT in *BibleWorks 8*). Leningradensis is arguably the single most important manuscript on earth. For more than 175 years, critical scholars have taught that the last chapters in Daniel were added to his book to make it appear that Daniel prophesied the future. The Hebraic meter in *waw*s demonstrates that the entire book of Daniel was written by one author at the same time.

There is much speculation on the meaning of 1,150 days. Many see Daniel 8:13-14 as a prophecy of Antiochus Epiphanes, who is a type of antichrist. He desecrated the temple in Jerusalem by slaughtering a pig on the altar and initiating pagan worship. It was not cleansed until approximately 1,150 days later by Judas Maccabeus on December 25, 171 B.C. (2 Maccabees 10:1-5). However, this prophecy is most likely the literal number of days of Christ's ministry, the daily sacrifice being taken away forever, and the entire world cleansed by the sacrifice of Christ on Good Friday. If we add the 50 days of Pentecost, the total is 1,200 days, an appropriate number for the beginning of the New Testament Church.

There are 3,005 *waw*s in Exodus and 1,895 *waw*s in Leviticus, for a total of 4,900. The word *Jubilee*, which begins the day after the 49th year, appears 20 times in Leviticus.

> And thou shalt number seven sabbaths of years unto thee, seven times seven years; and the space of the seven sabbaths of years shall be unto thee forty and nine years. Then shalt thou cause the trumpet of the jubilee to sound on the tenth day of the seventh month, in the day of atonement shall ye make the trumpet sound throughout all your land. (Leviticus 25:8-9)

Remember, this is about *and*, the most common word in the Bible, which, if added or deleted, usually does not change the meaning of the text. But it does affect meter. Since higher critics claim that none of the mythical committees known as J E P D are responsible for the entire text of Genesis, what is the explanation for the Hebraic meter of *waw*s, not to mention all of the other Hebraic meter in the text? Each of the major Hebraic meters (7, 10, and 12) found in Revelation and listed in the 2012 edition in Chapters Eight, Nine, and Ten, are found in Genesis; namely, heptads, decads, and dodecads.

St. Louis, 2008, p. 405.

Contemporary Authors' Views on Genesis 75 Years after Cassuto
A Contemporary View of Genesis
Contemporary is a relative term. In this context, it means books published in 2013 and 2014. Little has changed in scholars' views of Genesis since 1941 when Cassuto wrote *The Documentary Hypothesis*, followed by his Genesis and Exodus commentaries.

Ronald Hendel published *The Book of Genesis: a Biography* in 2013. Hendel is a professor of the Hebrew Bible and Jewish Studies at the University of California, Berkeley. He is one of the leading spokesmen and advocates for the J E P D theory.[50] Instead of Genesis being written in 1500 B.C., he dates its authorship 500 to 600 years later. He writes:

> There are several versions of the Babylonian Flood story, all of which are older than Genesis—the oldest Babylonian version is from around 1800 BCE, roughly a thousand years earlier than the J source. Most scholars agree that the biblical versions are descended from the Babylonian version presumably mediated by oral tradition.[51]

Hendel believes the concept of a *messiah* was introduced into the Bible through the misreading of Genesis 49:10, when Jacob prophesies, "The scepter shall not depart from Judah, Nor the staff from between his feet, So that tribute may come to him, And the obedience of the nations shall be his."[52]

Hendel correctly concludes that Philo is the primary influence in the Early Church's understanding of Genesis. "Even though Philo is largely forgotten today, his legacy—philosophical religion over the ages—still looms large."[53]

Hendel credits Philo with introducing the concept of *the ascent of the soul* into Jewish and, consequently, Christian thought.

> Philo consolidated the efforts of his predecessors (mostly Alexandrian Jews) in reading the Bible through the lens of Greek philosophy. In part he wanted to show that Jewish thought is every bit as sophisticated as Greek, and that Moses anticipated Plato's philosophy.[54]

---

[50] Hendel, pp. 17-24, 174.
[51] Ibid., p. 26.
[52] Ibid., p. 52.
[53] Ibid., p. 91.
[54] Ibid.

Hendel explains a progression of thought about Genesis, from Philo to Augustine to Rashi to Luther. For example, he writes:

> Augustine makes abundant use of this hierarchy of knowledge in his interpretation of Genesis. Like Philo, Augustine harmonized Greek philosophy with Genesis through his exposition of the sensible and figural senses of Scripture.[55]

He sees Rashi and Luther as later advocates favoring a literal interpretation over allegory.

Hendel credits Spinoza as the first critic to claim Moses did not write Genesis. "From all this it is plainer than the noonday sun that the Pentateuch was not written by Moses but by someone else who lived many generations after Moses."[56]

Hendel states the current academic view of Genesis when he writes: "By the late eighteenth century, many people—and most biblical scholars—came to view the early stories of Genesis as ancient fables or myths."[57]

Hendel is comfortable in labeling Genesis the Jewish 'Greek mythology':

> We live on the far side of tradition, and the stories of Genesis have become legends. Yet, the advantage of exile is that we can read these legends with new eyes, unencumbered by the burden of ecclesiastical authority.[58]

At the close of his book, Hendel regrets that many people are no longer reading Genesis because it lacks relevance. Hendel is acknowledging that both the advocates of J E P D and Darwinian evolution have discredited Genesis. Hence, there are fewer people interested in learning about Genesis from scholars like Hendel. The higher critics are achieving their ultimate goal of making themselves as irrelevant as they attempt to make Genesis.

A Conservative View of Genesis

On the other side of the spectrum, Concordia Publishing House published a 660-page introduction to the Old Testament titled, *Prepare the Way of the Lord*, by R. Reed Lessing and Andrew E. Steinmann.

---

[55] Ibid., p. 155.
[56] Ibid., p. 173.
[57] Ibid., p. 182.
[58] Ibid., p. 241.

Pages 13-74 are dedicated to the Pentateuch and Genesis. Lessing and Steinmann oppose the J E P D theory, and they advocate a conditional Mosaic authorship. However, they do not explicitly state that Moses wrote the Pentateuch. They write about Moses:

> While more conservative Christians have maintained that these books are essentially the work of Moses, for the past 250 years critical scholars have searched for other ways to explain the origin of the Pentateuch.[59]

> Several passages in the Pentateuch itself indicate that Moses wrote at least a few passages.[60]

> Perhaps the most comprehensive statements about the authorship of the Pentateuch are found in Deut 31, where twice we are told that Moses wrote "this Torah" (Deut 31:9, 24).[61]

> The NT recognized Moses as the author of the Pentateuch. It refers to the "law of Moses" nine times.[62]

> Since Genesis is entirely about events before Moses was born, the case for Mosaic authorship of this book is more vulnerable to challenge than the other books of the Pentateuch. Yet Jesus confidently asserted Moses' writing of the first book of the Torah.[63]

> Scholars who accept the Bible's attribution of the Pentateuch to Moses commonly agree that these small changes in the text were made after his day. Nevertheless, they affirm that the Torah, as it has come down to us, is essentially the work of Moses.[64]

Lessing and Steinmann write 20 pages refuting the arguments and exposing the flaw of the Documentary Hypothesis:

> The higher critical search for the origin of the Pentateuch that occupied scholars in Europe for two centuries and resulted in the Documentary Hypothesis has a checkered history. Even so, it has become the dominant theory in critical scholarship.[65]

---

[59] Lessing and Steinmann, p. 13.
[60] Ibid., p. 14.
[61] Ibid., p. 15.
[62] Ibid., pp. 15-16.
[63] Ibid., p. 16.
[64] Ibid., p. 19.
[65] Ibid., p. 39.

For whatever reason, these two authors are not as certain, nor as adamant about their position as Ronald Hendel is about his position. Do they or do they not agree with Jesus' "confident assertion," that Moses wrote the Torah?

The Tôledôth [Generations] Formulas

Lessing and Steinmann do not suggest that Moses has organized his writing with some kind of literary meter. However, they do reference a few instances of meter in the text. For example, they note that the phrase *these are the generations of* repeats 10 times, as quoted in Chapters Two and Eight. They also note that there is an 11th phrase, *the book of the generations of Adam*, and then state that the purpose of these 11 phrases may be to divide Genesis into 12 parts. In the process they disagree with Wiseman, who argues for 11 divisions of Genesis.[66] Wiseman may have been influenced indirectly by Cassuto, who wrote 2 years before Wiseman, in 1934, a work titled *La questione della Genesi*, while he was the archivist of Semitic scrolls at the Vatican.

Lessing and Steinmann conclude:

> Yahweh's choice of Jacob's twelve sons and their descendants as his special people is also underscored by the eleven tôledôth [generations] formulas, which serve to divide the book into twelve sections but also link those sections into one unified history leading to the survival of the twelve clans of Israel in Egypt.[67]

This writer suggests that the identification of multiple sets of decadal phrases in Genesis, in addition to the tôledôth [generations] formulas, must necessarily change the current understanding of this phrase. The following example includes the tôledôth [generations] formulas and the unique formula at Genesis 5:1.

These are the generations of 10 times in Genesis, plus *This is the book of the generations of* at 5:1

    These are the generations of the heavens (Gen. 2:4)
This is the book of the generations of Adam (Gen. 5:1)
    These are the generations of Noah (Gen. 6:9)
And these are the generations of the sons of Noah (Gen. 10:1)
    These are the generations of Shem (Gen. 11:10)
And these are the generations of Terah (Gen. 11:27)
And these are the generations of Ishmael (Gen. 25:12)

---

[66] Ibid., p. 47.
[67] Ibid., p. 49.

> And these are the generations of Isaac (Gen. 25:19)
> And these are the generations of Esau (Gen. 36:1)
> And these are the generations of Esau (Gen. 36:9)
>> These are the generations of Jacob (Gen. 37:2)

Lessing and Steinmann's position may actually be more a point of emphasis than division. On page 41, Wiseman creates 12 divisions, but he only speaks about 11 repetitions.[68] In art this is called viewing the positive versus the negative space. Every positive creates a negative, every foreground creates a background. Therefore 11 phrases create 12 spaces or divisions.

Henry Morris reverses Lessing and Steinmann by seeing 11 phrases that create 9 divisions, or negative spaces.[69] Like Lenski,[70] he connects Genesis 5:1 with Matthew 1:1, *The book of the generation of Jesus Christ*, portraying Christ as the New Adam.[71] Matthew uses the same Greek as the Septuagint in Genesis, Βίβλος γενέσεως. This writer also notes that Matthew may have been fully aware of the 11 phrases in Genesis, and added the 12th phrase 1,500 years later.

James J. Becker and Joshua J. Becker write, "However, Moses actually divided his book into 10 chapters of unequal length."[72] The Beckers' comment is important because they admit to "unequal length," a characteristic of concurrent asymmetry and symmetry. The Beckers also conflate 36:1 and 36:9 into one repetition because Esau is named twice in the chapter.

Ron Hendel writes, "The formula 'These are the generations of …' occurs roughly ten times in Genesis, creating an internal structure within the book."[73] He says *roughly* because he knows there are 10 identical repetitions of the phrase and an 11th variation of the phrase, and that 36:1 and 36:9 could also be counted as 1 repetition, depending on how one views the text.

---

[68] P. J. Wiseman, *New Discoveries in Babylonia about Genesis*, Marshall, Morgan, & Scott, Ltd., London, Edinburgh, 4th ed., 1946, http://www.biblemaths.com/pdf_wiseman.pdf (7/2015), p. 41.

[69] Henry M. Morris, *The Genesis Record: A Scientific and Devotional Commentary on the Book of Beginnings*, Baker Book House, Grand Rapids, MI, 1976, pp. 27-30.

[70] R. C. H. Lenski, *The Interpretation of St. Matthew's Gospel*, Wartburg Press, 1943, Augsburg Publishing House, Minneapolis, 1961, p. 26.

[71] Morris, p. 152.

[72] Becker and Becker, p. 43.

[73] Hendel, p. 57.

So which is it, 9, 10, 11, or 12 divisions? Lessing and Steinmann say 12 because, "The major drawback of Wiseman's proposal is that the text that follows each of these tôledôth [generations] formulas more naturally belongs with the notice than the material that precedes it."[74] This is true, except for *the material that precedes* Gen. 2:4 and Gen. 5:1. If we begin at 5:1, the lone variation, there are 10 and not 12 divisions with 10 names matching each of the 10 phrases. There is no name applied to the first 2 sections as Lessing and Steinmann divide them, only the sections after Adam.

There is an even more obvious solution, as has already been demonstrated in the previous chapter, where some metered phrases actually cross from one book into another. We know that Moses wrote the Pentateuch. Since he wrote 11 phrases in Genesis, why not look at the 12th phrase that Moses wrote in Numbers 3:1, which clearly states: *"And these are the generations of Aaron and Moses in the day that the LORD spoke with Moses in Mount Sinai."* The Hebrew is identical to the Hebrew in Genesis 10:1; 11:27; 25:12, 19; 36:1 and 9, which creates a subset of 7.

This writer's suggestion is to observe the strange manner in which the 10 Commandments are listed. There could just as well be 11 Commandments if God had not said there are 10, in which case there would be 11 Commandments dividing 12 sections of the law, just as Lessing and Steinmann propose with the tôledôth [generations] formulas. However, numerous examples in this and the previous chapter demonstrate that the meter of tôledôth is not unique to Genesis. The arrangement of other decadal phrases in Genesis must also be given consideration in the analysis of the tôledôth [generations] formulas.

The second observation is that Lessing and Steinmann associate the 12 sons of Jacob with 12 divisions of Genesis. Yet, if anything, the hundreds of examples of metered phrases in this book have shown there are overlapping metered phrases and subsets in this genre, particularly in dodecadal phrases, suggesting multiple themes in the Genesis genealogy. For example, Lessing and Steinmann do not mention that Jacob himself, the last name on the list, is the 12th generation after the Flood.

Based on their analysis of the data, this author sees some merit in the conclusions of Lessing, Steinmann, Wiseman, Morris, Hendel, and the Beckers. Aesthetic analysis also demonstrates the presence of concurrent asymmetry and symmetry in the tôledôth [generations] formulas.

---

[74] Lessing and Steinmann, p. 47.

This is not systematic theology that requires one concise meaning. This is aesthetics that exhibits multiple overlapping meters. The first verb in the Bible states, *God created*. This is a Hebrew art form, or else how do we explain the variation in 5:1, the irregular, optional, and enigmatic 11th tôledôth [generations], the significance of which Wiseman, Lessing, Steinmann, Morris, the Beckers, and Hendel do not mention, other than Morris saying it anticipates Christ in Matthew 1:1. Why are Ishmael and Terah included in the list, and why is Abraham missing from the list while Esau is repeated twice?

The entire genre is far more complex than can be resolved by dwelling on a single solution, as if this were a question of systematic theology instead of aesthetics. Dodecadal meter usually includes subsets of decadal and heptadic sequence. The subset of 10 older sons versus 2 younger sons in the 12 sons of Jacob changed the world, not to mention subsets among his 4 wives with 3 not loved as much as the other. There is also a heptadic subset in the tôledôth [generations] formulas. Adam, Noah, Shem, Terah, Isaac, Jacob, plus the Messiah in Matthew 1:1, make 7. Noah's 2 other sons—Ishmael, named once, and Esau, named twice—are not ancestors of Christ.

Wiseman wrote an entire book of 132 pages to describe the significance of the tôledôth [generations] formulas. Lessing, Steinmann, Morris, the Beckers, and Hendel all speak about it. By comparison, this and the previous chapter virtually skim through 16 examples of decadal phrases in Genesis similar to the tôledôth [generations] formulas. These decadal phrases create numerous overlapping divisions, the significance of which is yet to be determined.

Lessing and Steinmann Locate Limited Hebraic Meter

Lessing and Steinmann provide an outline of Genesis. For an outline to be accurate it should reflect the Hebraic cadence that Moses used when writing Genesis. The authors do not state any numbers, but they divide their outline of Genesis into 12 parts with 12 Roman numerals,[75] and they divide Exodus into 12 parts with 12 letters of the alphabet.[76] One must count them to see that there are 12 parts.

Lessing and Steinmann list 7 citations of *create* in Genesis chapter 1, but do not count them. They list 7 statements where God says what He creates *is good*, without counting them. They also cite 7 verses from the Book of Isaiah about God being the only Creator, again without

---

[75] Ibid., pp. 49-53.
[76] Ibid., pp. 76-77.

counting them.[77] Either they do not wish to deal with the implications of saying there is heptadic meter in the text, or they did not bother to count the repetition in their own lists. They do state that God made 7 promises to Abraham, as previously quoted from Cassuto in Chapter Eight.[78] They also identify 7 categories of promises to the patriarch[79] without addressing meter in the text.

Their writing is reminiscent of Cassuto when they describe God hardening Pharaoh's heart 10 times. Cassuto may be the indirect source for this information.

> Two verbs are used to describe the hardening of Pharaoh's heart, חָזַק [*chazaq*, khaw-zak'] (Qal e.g., Exod. 7:13, 22; 8:19; Piel, e.g., Exod. 4:21; 9:21; 11:10) and כָּבֵד [*kabed*, kaw-bade'] (Qal e.g., Exod. 9:7; Hiphil, e.g., Exod. 9:34; 10:1). Both verbs indicate varying degrees of obstinacy, single-mindedness, stubbornness, and lack of regard. Ten times Yahweh is the subject of these verbs, but ten times Pharaoh (or Pharaoh's heart) is the subject.[80]

When speaking about God's 7 instructions to Moses about building the Tabernacle, they write:

> …Yahweh's directions to Moses come in seven movements (Exod. 25-31) which correspond to seven acts of Moses (Exod. 40:17-33), and these "sevens" are parallel to the seven days of creation (Gen. 1:2-2:3)….[81]

The authors add this insight from Luke 9:31, showing that the Greek word for *Exodus* spoken by Jesus on the top of the mount of transfiguration is also used by the Greek Septuagint to describe Israel's Exodus: "In the third month, when the children of Israel were gone forth out of the land of Egypt, the same day came they *into* the wilderness of Sinai (Exod. 19:1)." Their point is that Jesus was the cloud and pillar of fire that led them out of Egypt, and now in the flesh at the mount of transfiguration He will lead His people out of sin.

> It is no coincidence, then, that when Jesus was transfigured on the mountain and was conversing with Moses and Eli-

---

[77] Ibid., p. 58.
[78] Ibid., p. 63.
[79] Ibid., p. 68.
[80] Ibid., p. 84.
[81] Ibid., p. 90.

jah, he was speaking about "his *Exodus* which he was about to fulfill in Jerusalem" (τὴν *ἔξοδον* αὐτοῦ, ἣν ἤμελλεν πληροῦν ἐν Ἰερουσαλήμ, Luke 9:31). In Jerusalem through his death on the cross and resurrection, Jesus would lead his people out of the bondage of sin and death just as he had led them out of Egypt's slavery.[82]

---

[82] Ibid., p. 71.

Chapter Ten
Repetition in the Genesis Genealogy

Hebraic Meter in the Genesis Genealogy

Over the centuries, scholars have published excellent studies on biblical genealogy and chronology. This chapter's examination of genealogy is primarily focused on repetition in Genesis. In addition to narrative, the Bible applies the paradigm of Hebraic meter to events, genealogy, prophecy, theology, chronology, and symbolism. Every person's age recorded in the Pentateuch serves a prophetic purpose. It will be shown that repetition in the Genesis genealogy became the paradigm for genealogy in Exodus, Ruth, Ezra, Nehemiah, Matthew, and Luke.

Genesis 4 and 5 record 2 lines of descent: Adam through Cain and Adam through Seth. After the Flood and the genealogy in Genesis 10, the most important genealogy is Shem through Abraham, found in Genesis 11.

There are remarkable similarities and differences between the 4 genealogies in Figure 1, below. Each list contains 10 names. Similar names appear in the first 2 lists, but God does not use Cain's genealogy to record time. Cain's genealogy also includes Lamech's 3 sons, Jabal, Jubal, and Tubalcain. These are all the names given for Cain's male descendants.

As demonstrated in Chapters Eight and Nine, the predominant numerical cadences in the Genesis genealogies are 7, 10, 12, and their multiples, which are the same as the meter in the text.

Lamech—the 7th generation from Adam through Cain—is cursed, and says, "If Cain shall be avenged sevenfold, truly Lamech seventy and sevenfold" (Genesis 4:24). Note the 3 7s in verse 24. The other Lamech through Shem's genealogy lives 777 years. Lamech through Cain is a confessed murderer. Enoch—the favored 7th generation in the line of Seth—lives 365 years and ascends to God in heaven without death: "And Enoch walked with God: and he *was* not; for God took him" (Genesis 5:24). Enoch is a living prophecy of eternal life, while Lamech, Cain's descendant, delights in murder. The New Testament Book of Jude reminds us that Enoch is the favored 7th generation from Adam (Jude 1:14). God tells Noah—the 10th generation from Adam—to build the Ark and leave the old world. God tells Abram—the 10th generation from Shem and the 20th generation from Adam—to leave Haran and go to Canaan. Eber in Shem's genealogy is the favored 7th generation from Abraham in reverse, or chiastic, order, and is the patriarch from whom the name *Hebrew* is derived. In Pharez' genealogy, Boaz, the redeemer in the Book of Ruth, is the favored 7th generation. In Ruth, Boaz repeats 20 times, Ruth 12 times, and Naomi 21 times, or 3 times 7.

Figure 1

Adam	930	Adam	600	Shem	Pharez
Cain	912	Seth	438	Arpachshad	Hezron
Enoch	905	Enosh	433	Shelah	Ram
Irad	910	Cainan	464	Eber	Amminadab
Mehujael	895	Mahalalel	239	Peleg	Nahshon
Methusael	962	Jared	239	Reu	Salmon
Lamech	365	Enoch	230	Serug	Boaz
Jabal	969	Methuselah	148	Nahor	Obed
Jubal	777	Lamech	205	Terah	Jesse
Tubalcain	950	Noah	175	Abram	David
Gen. 4		Gen. 5		Gen. 11	Ruth 4

There is a sublime unity of words and numbers in the text that communicates one meaning. Lamech, in Seth's genealogy, lives 777 years. Noah, the son of Lamech, is the 7th living patriarch at his birth 1,056 years after the creation. It is also important to observe that 7 of the 10 antediluvian patriarchs lived more than 900 years, and 3 did not. Likewise, in the 10 generations from Shem to Abraham, the first 7 lived longer than the last 3.

Before the Flood, the names of only 4 women are recorded—Eve, the wife of Adam; Adah and Zillah, the wives of Lamech; and Naamah, the sister of Tubalcain. Sarai, the wife of Abram, is the first woman named in the Bible after the Flood, just as Eve was the first woman named before the Flood. Also, Sarah is the only wife named from the 10 postdiluvian patriarchs, just as Eve is the only wife named from the antediluvian patriarchs. Sarah is the only woman whose full age is given in the Bible. In the New Testament, Anna lived 84 years (7 x 12) after the death of her husband, to whom she was married 7 years (Luke 2:36). Her full age is estimated at 105.[1] Eve tempts Adam with the fruit, and Sarah tempts Abraham with Hagar. Sarah and Abraham, like Adam and Eve, both speak with God. She could be described as the 21st patriarch,

---

[1] R. C. H. Lenski, *The Interpretation of St. Luke's Gospel*, Wartburg Press, 1946, Augsburg Publishing House, Minneapolis, 1961, p. 156. This writer recalls officiating at the funeral of 105-year-old Anna Panich on Oct. 6, 2006, who could easily have fit Anna of Phanuel's description.

or rather, matriarch. Sarah is the first person to laugh in the Bible, and Hagar is the first person to weep in the Bible.

The phrase *begat sons and daughters* has particular significance in Genesis. There are 17 repetitions of the phrase *years, begat sons and daughters* in the entire Bible, all of which are found in Genesis chapters 5 and 11.

Years, begat sons and daughters 17 times in Genesis
- years, begat sons and daughters......... שָׁנָה וַיּוֹלֶד בָּנִים וּבָנוֹת (Gen. 5:4)
- years, begat sons and daughters......... שָׁנָה וַיּוֹלֶד בָּנִים וּבָנוֹת (Gen. 5:7)
- years, begat sons and daughters......... שָׁנָה וַיּוֹלֶד בָּנִים וּבָנוֹת (Gen. 5:10)
- years, begat sons and daughters......... שָׁנָה וַיּוֹלֶד בָּנִים וּבָנוֹת (Gen. 5:13)
- years, begat sons and daughters......... שָׁנָה וַיּוֹלֶד בָּנִים וּבָנוֹת (Gen. 5:16)
- years, begat sons and daughters......... שָׁנָה וַיּוֹלֶד בָּנִים וּבָנוֹת (Gen. 5:19)
- years, begat sons and daughters......... שָׁנָה וַיּוֹלֶד בָּנִים וּבָנוֹת (Gen. 5:22)
- years, begat sons and daughters......... שָׁנָה וַיּוֹלֶד בָּנִים וּבָנוֹת (Gen. 5:26)
- years, begat sons and daughters......... שָׁנָה וַיּוֹלֶד בָּנִים וּבָנוֹת (Gen. 5:30)
- years, begat sons and daughters......... שָׁנָה וַיּוֹלֶד בָּנִים וּבָנוֹת (Gen. 11:11)
- years, begat sons and daughters......... שָׁנָה וַיּוֹלֶד בָּנִים וּבָנוֹת (Gen. 11:13)
- years, begat sons and daughters......... שָׁנָה וַיּוֹלֶד בָּנִים וּבָנוֹת (Gen. 11:15)
- years, begat sons and daughters......... שָׁנָה וַיּוֹלֶד בָּנִים וּבָנוֹת (Gen. 11:17)
- years, begat sons and daughters......... שָׁנָה וַיּוֹלֶד בָּנִים וּבָנוֹת (Gen. 11:19)
- years, begat sons and daughters......... שָׁנָה וַיּוֹלֶד בָּנִים וּבָנוֹת (Gen. 11:21)
- years, begat sons and daughters......... שָׁנָה וַיּוֹלֶד בָּנִים וּבָנוֹת (Gen. 11:23)
- years, begat sons and daughters......... שָׁנָה וַיּוֹלֶד בָּנִים וּבָנוֹת (Gen. 11:25)

There is little doubt that the number 1,656, the years before the Flood, is selected for some unique characteristics. It is divisible by 2, 3, 4, 6, 8, 12, 18, 23, 24, 36, 46, 69, 72, 92, 138, 414, and more numbers than we wish to calculate. The year that Noah stepped on dry land in 1657 or 2347 B.C. (according to Ussher) is a prime number and is not divisible by any whole number.

Each of the 10 patriarchs in Seth's genealogy appears 5 times in Genesis chapter 5, except for Noah, who is named 4 times. Noah's death is not recorded until Genesis chapter 9, which completes a total of 50 names and 30 numbers for the antediluvian patriarchs.

Some authors, such as James B. Jordan, place Noah at the beginning of the third list in Figure 1 instead of at the end of the second.[2] Jordan's arrangement offers its own unique set of patterns, substantiating the hypothesis that one particular arrangement does not exhaust the possibility of additional patterns layered in the text. According to pattern

---

[2] Jordan, *A Chronological and Calendrical Commentary on the Pentateuch*, pp. 58-60.

theory, if a numeric pattern is present in the genealogies, the search for more patterns is justified. Jordan and other chronologists extend their search for patterns and accurate dating to include the calendar year, lunar days, months, and years, the solar year, the Jubilee and its multiples, and astral numbers of the planets (the number of days for a planet to circle the sun). Enoch's age is an astral number. Rather than experiment with various patterns, this chapter's focus is limited to numbers that are expressly stated or based on the text.

Unity of Numbers in the Patriarchs

It is not known if Moses needed to translate antediluvian numbers in Figure 2 from a different base, such as 7 or 12, or however they were written, into the Hebrew decimal system after the confusion of tongues at Babel. The confusion of tongues must have included a confusion of numbers—not the numbers themselves, but the base in which their mathematics was arranged. The relationship between the 30 numbers in the genealogy of the antediluvian patriarchs is the only known example of antediluvian mathematics (Figure 2).

In Figure 2, 21 of the 60 numbers end with a zero, 3 times the number of probability, and obvious evidence of a decimal system. The following is a chart listing the ages of the patriarchs, their ages at the birth of their notable sons, and the years they lived after the birth of their notable sons, as found in Genesis 5 and 11.

Figure 2 Ages of the Patriarchs

Patriarch	Total age	At son's birth	After son's birth	Patriarch	Total age	At son's birth	After son's birth
	A	B	C	D	E	F	G
Adam	930	130	800	Shem	600	100	500
Seth	912	105	807	Arpachshad	438	35	403
Enosh	905	90	815	Shelah	433	30	403
Cainan	910	70	840	Eber	464	34	430
Mahalalel	895	65	830	Peleg	239	30	209
Jared	962	162	800	Reu	239	32	207
Enoch	365	65	300	Serug	230	30	200
Methuselah	969	187	782	Nahor	148	29	119
Lamech	777	182	595	Terah	205	(70)	135
Noah	950	500	450	Abraham	175	100	75
	8575	1556	7019		**3171**	490	2681

The ages of the 10 patriarchs from Adam to Noah total 8,575 years. This total is divisible by 7. Seven of the 10 patriarchs lived more than 900 years. The ages of the 7 oldest patriarchs total 6,538 years, which is also divisible by 7. When the 17 numbers that comprise 6,538 and 8,575 are added together, the total is 15,113 years, which is divisible by 17. The probability of such a coincidence is 119 to 1.

The same numerical relationship is found in the second list of patriarchs from Shem to Abraham, whose ages total 3,171 years. This number is divisible by 7. When the 7 largest numbers, totaling 2,643, are added to 3,171, the total of the 17 numbers is 5,814. This number is divisible by 17. The probability of both lists exhibiting these same properties is 14,161 to 1. The requirement that all of these numbers must have 3 digits lowers the probability even further.

The fact that 2 lists of 10 patriarchs share these identical properties indicates that they are governed by the same mathematical formula. Before proceeding any further, adventuresome readers may want to solve the following problem on their own: "What is the mathematical formula necessary to create a list of 10 numbers that are divisible by 7, and when the 7 largest numbers in the list are added to the original 10 numbers, the total of the 17 numbers is divisible by 17?"

If these lists were humanly devised, what would the formula look like to arrive at these lists of 10 numbers? With this question in mind, assistance was requested from a Ph.D. candidate (now a Ph.D.) in engineering at Iowa State University. After a number of attempts, he recommended a 4th-year math major, Matt Swanson (matthewjohnswanson@gmail.com) for a solution to the problem. After examining the problem, Swanson consulted a Ph.D. candidate in mathematics. She and Swanson were able to get close, but they could not find the exact solution, which they determined was based in modular mathematics.

They both recommended that this writer locate a theoretical mathematician at another university, because Iowa State excels in statistical and scientific mathematical research. Swanson also provided 3 pages of mathematical equations to help present the problem to a doctor of theoretical mathematics.

After contacting one of this nation's largest universities in another state, the secretary of the mathematics department suggested 2 of the 8 doctors of theoretical mathematics on their faculty who were available in June of 2014. Before explaining the mathematical problem, one of the professors graciously volunteered his time, but requested that his name not be published. By chance, he is an Orthodox Jew familiar with Hebrew, and he was intrigued by the prospect of a mathematical problem of this nature in Genesis. Later that day he solved the problem and sent me the solution via email.

The professor was asked at what time in history this form of mathematics was first discovered. He then consulted an expert in the history of mathematics, who wrote the following reply from his cell phone:

> It is my understanding that the Chinese Remainder Theorem was unknown in the Mediterranean basin prior to when they learned it from the Chinese. Quotient and remainders were important to the Babylonians, and the Euclid algorithm, as a method for finding common measures, is probably even older. But there are Chinese instruments and tables for using the CRT for counting after 520 AD, but I am pretty sure no middle or European counterparts [are] identified as such. If they did use it, there should at least be tables that make it [a] practice. Calculating using an algorithm would not have [been] practical for everyday problems.

According to this response, Moses appears to be the most advanced mathematician of the ancient world by at least 2,000 years; or someone else rewrote these numbers in the Hebrew text at least 520 years after Christ; or Moses had help from another source.

The calculations received from the anonymous professor were sent to Swanson for verification. Swanson stated that the calculations are correct, and the anonymous professor had found the solution.[3]

By coincidence, the key number that must be present in the antediluvian list for the formula to work is 969, which happens to be the age of Methuselah. A key number that must be in the algorithm to solve the problem for both lists is 119, the number of years Nahor lived after the birth of Terah.

Genesis Mathematics Superior to Cuneiform Tablets

There is now absolute proof that the ages in Genesis are not random numbers collected from ancient nomadic fables; collated by a mythical committee of Yawists between 1100 and 1000 B.C.; and edited by successive committees of Elohists, Priestly Code, and Deuteronomists at intervals of 100 to 150 years, until Jeremiah in the early 6th century B.C., as is proclaimed according to the hallowed Documentary Hypothesis.

Far from primitive, the writer of Genesis was working with a higher level of mathematics than anyone on earth had seen at the time

---

[3] See Appendix A following the Conclusion for the professor's explanation of the calculations. See Appendix B for Swanson's correction of his own calculations after viewing the professor's solution.

of its writing. This writer consulted Eyal Rav-Noy, sent him the calculations, and asked if he was aware of such mathematics in Genesis. He was not.

A noted archeologist and expert in Hebrew, cuneiform tablets, and cuneiform mathematics was consulted at another major university. He was asked if he had any knowledge of Hebraic meter in the ages of the Genesis patriarchs, and whether it was possible that modular mathematics was used to create these lists. Nearly a year earlier he had recommended Ronald Hendel's *The Book of Genesis, A Biography*, which was quoted a number of times at the end of Chapter Nine. All communication with the archeologist on this topic transpired via email.

The first contact with the archeologist on this subject involved sending him the numerical relationships in the ages of the Genesis patriarchs and the mathematical calculations in Appendix A.

Reply from the Archeologist:

> I prefer not to render such cursory judgments, but this looks better suited to a conspiracy website than a serious monograph. I'd strongly advise you to steer clear of this stuff. There are indeed some numerical patterns here and there in the MT [Masoretic Text], but you must understand they creep into the text during the editorial phases. We see this clearly in the Qumran variants. So you may indeed be seeing patterns (although I'd dispute many of them), but they are late period (Persian to Roman) conceits.

Reply to the Archeologist:

> I deeply appreciate your opinion as a true professional.
>
> Actually, I came up with all [of] this on my own. I consulted two PhDs at a very large university. One worked out the math necessary to create the two lists in Genesis 5 and 11 with these properties, and [the] other is an expert in the history of math.
>
> These are the same numbers everyone sees in Genesis.
>
> Obviously, I don't know when the numbers were put in the text. However, anyone with a hand calculator can see that the total of both lists [is] divisible by 7, and that when the 7 largest numbers in each list are added to each list, both lists are divisible by 17. The random probability of two consecutive

lists with these properties is 14,161 to 1. It is not as if I experimented. I simply followed Cassuto's theory and it worked on first try.

There is no question that the math necessary to create such lists with these properties did not exist till 520 A.D. in China.

Could you please tell me why you "dispute" the numbers that anyone can check with a hand calculator?

Thank you again,

Reply to the Archeologist:
I forgot to add that the numbers in MT are the same numbers as in the Vulgate which is 4th century A.D.

The point of the replies to the archeologist is that it was not possible for the Masoretes to change the patriarchal ages because Jerome's Vulgate, written at least 300 years before the Masoretes, uses the same numbers we all see in our English translations today.

The archeologist defended his position by writing that today's version of Genesis resulted from a long tradition of numerical patterns edited into the Hebrew text by the Masoretes. However, Harvard PhD graduate, Dr. Nathan Jastram, stated in 2009 that the observation of patterns in the Hebrew text was the product of this writer's own creative imagination. On the other hand, if the archeologist is correct, why are scholars not writing about metered sequences in the Hebrew text? This would also be a contradiction to J E P D and the Documentary Hypothesis in support of Cassuto and Rav-Noy.

The archeologist was informed that the computations in Appendix A of this book were the work of 2 mathematicians from a major university.

Reply from the Archeologist:
This arithmetic is clearly developed by the early second millennium BCE in Babylonia (and likely at least as early as Ur III), where scribes are already performing advanced quadratics. I'd have to check, but I'm sure it presents in Egypt before the Late Kingdom period. I'm not familiar with the contention that the Chinese originated it.

Who did you consult?

The archeologist's second reply was in direct contradiction to the university historian of mathematics by a spread of 3,500 to 2,500 years.

This led to the conclusion that the archeologist had not worked with modular mathematics, and didn't really understand the calculations he received in Appendix A, or what the mathematicians were saying. Dirk J. Struik of MIT reports that the first use of modular mathematics appeared in China no earlier than 625 A.D. in a book written by Wang Xiatong. The Chinese Remainder Theorem was not fully developed until 1247 in a book by Qin Jiushao.[4] This theorem was not proven to be accurate until 1801 by Fredrik Gauss in his *Disquisitiones Arithmeticae*.

Reply to the Archeologist:

    You are asking just the right question I hoped you would ask.

    I promised the Professor and I think the other [Professor] who is the Chairman of the Math Department (the first worked out the equation and the second who is an expert in and teaches the history of mathematics both at a very large American university) that I would not publish their names. There are no records of modular mathematics prior to 520 A.D. in China and certainly not in Babylon. These professors tell me there is no other way to construct these lists than with modular mathematics. There must be an equation, because there are two consecutive lists with the same properties. I asked for a formula that could generate such lists....I would be pleased to ask if I can identify them to you, if I can tell them who you are. I know of your expertise, credentials, and international reputation in ancient languages, but I doubt your expertise in modular mathematics and that you [are] able to read the formulas they published. I, for one, am not able to follow their calculations.

    When they learn who it is who is asking, my guess is that they will be open to communication. Thank you so much for asking the question. Now I have a reason to approach them again over the importance of their work. As I told the Professor, he is the first man to have produced a formula that can generate the lists in Genesis 5 and 11. He doesn't grasp its significance. Of course, no one knew that the lists were governed by an equation.

---

[4] Struik, pp. 73-74.

Reply from the Archeologist:
> My expertise includes cuneiform mathematics.
>
> I have to level with you. If they don't want to be identified, it's because they were humoring you and don't want to be associated with this kind of work. I would be very surprised if they allowed you to reveal their names to me. I'm sure your colleague understands the significance as you presented it to him. He merely rejects the premise.

Reply to the Archeologist:
> Many have humored me before. Can I tell them who is asking for their names?
>
> Cuneiform mathematics is about as rare a specialty as I've heard. Actually, the professor who worked out all the math was quite serious. I had his [work] checked out by another mathematician. You can see it at the bottom of this thread. I also doubt that the Babylonians knew anything about modular math, which involves imaginary numbers. I'm really interested in what they have to say.

Reply from the Archeologist:
> Modular arithmetic is not necessary to arrive at these multiples. Everything you describe is discernible and explicable within the Mesopotamian scribal tradition, of which numerous problem texts exist with extant remainder formulae from the OB [Old Babylonian] to Seleucid periods. We don't have the pedagogical tables, but we have the texts (a) which depended on such primers and (b) in which the scribes "show their work." Your source is speaking of tables as one kind of evidence of usage, but we have other evidence.
>
> But all of this is a red herring in any case. You are trying to make sense of editorial retro-engineering. These are no more real numbers of real lifespans than those of the Sumerian King List on which genre the generation lists of Genesis are based. I don't understand what this has to do with Moses.
>
> Feel free to pass along my name.

Reply to the Archeologist:
> Thank you for the opportunity to talk to the professors about you and your excellent reply. It is not every day that I

have the privilege to converse with someone who studies cuneiform mathematics in the original language.

My thoughts:

1. Genesis says Moses is the one who recorded the ages of the patriarchs, and that is the only name we have.

2. There is no question that the tablets recording the ages of the Sumerian Kings are older than Genesis. However, the assumption is that Moses was working from older documents.

3. There is no pattern in the ages of the Sumerian Kings, or for that matter, the list of any other kings. You were not aware of the patterns in the ages of the Genesis patriarchs until I brought them to your attention.

4. Both cultures are recording a common heritage.

5. Cassuto, an expert in cuneiform, claims that heptadic numeric patterns are Hebraic, not Babylonian.

6. As a former professor of art at Indiana State University [now University of Southern Indiana] and an expert in visual genre, the patterns in the patriarchal numbers are consistent with the entire OT and NT tradition. Genre does not retrograde or retro-engineer the past. Genre progresses. Yes, there are revivals, but they are always modified. In other words, those who wrote after Moses in the Hebrew tradition are copying Moses, just like Cubists copy Picasso. Picasso does not copy them. The Romans copied and improved on the Greeks, but they did not retro-engineer Greek ruins. Why is the OT the exception to genre?

What if the Babylonians did not know there were any patterns in the Gen. 5 and 11 lists, which is why there are no patterns in their lists? Hence, it was not their genre. Cubists paint like Cubists.

One of the reasons mathematicians at both universities used modular math is because the total ages of the patriarchs in Gen. 5 and 11 are both less than 14,161 or (7 x 17 x 7 x 17), hence there is no common denominator. The second list was more challenging because it is a smaller total than the first. My challenge to them was asking them to produce an equation that creates lists with the same properties as Gen. 5 and 11 and still small enough for Gen. 5 and 11.

Please tell me what kind of math they were using in the Mesopotamian scribal tradition (beginning in the Old Babylonian 2000-1600 BC) to produce these lists if it wasn't modular math? If they could do it, we should be able to do it. I would like to ask the professor to try that method.

The university professor and the archeologist did communicate with each other. The university professor sent me the archeologist's last reply to him about me.

Reply of the Archeologist to the Mathematician:
> The math is fine. The problem is Jack's *a priori* assumption that a divine equation generated the fictional numbers. I can create multiples of 7 and 17 after the fact, as you know, without a modulus. So could (and did) the editors of the MT. This is a straw-man poser, I'm afraid.

This writers' comment, which was not sent to the archeologist, is that at no time was the archeologist told this was a "divine equation." We really do not know how the numbers were generated. The goal was to see if it is humanly possible to create lists like these, which is why the mathematician was consulted. It is doubtful that the archeologist could create such a list using any method he chose. The mathematicians at Iowa State could not. Also note that the archeologist was not aware of these numerical relationships in the ages of the Genesis patriarchs until they were brought to his attention. Additionally, the archeologist insists that Masoretic Text editors created the numbers, even though the numbers appear at least 300 years earlier in Jerome's Vulgate. Did the MT editors retro-engineer their text by copying the Catholic Church's translation of the Vulgate? More important is that the Gospel writers were using Hebraic meter 600 years before the Masoretes supposedly retro-engineered their text.

Final Reply from the Archeologist:
> I'm flying out of town to film this NatGeo thing. Try to touch base later. Meanwhile, Moses wrote Genesis? Come on, Jack. That tradition doesn't even begin until the Hellenistic period (at the earliest). You know better than that.

The purpose of taking the reader through this dialogue is to give some insight into the academic world's resistance to any evidence confirming that Moses wrote the first 5 books of the Bible, that Moses even existed, or that Hebraic meter exists in the Old and New Testaments.

Even verifiable evidence from the science of mathematics is rejected if it doesn't support the Documentary Hypothesis. Essentially, the Documentary Hypothesis functions as a religion invented by scholars, similar to Scientology, in order to avoid the reality of the text. For "believers" in the Documentary Hypothesis, motive negates facts.

Additional Hebraic Meter in the Ages of the Patriarchs

There are more numeric relationships in the patriarchal ages than listed in the previous discussion. The first list from Adam to Noah totals 8,575, and is not only divisible by 7, but is also divisible by 7 cubed, or 7^3. When divided by 7, the quotient is 1,225, which also divides evenly by 7 for a quotient of 175, which also divides evenly by 7 for a quotient of 25. This means that 7 cubed, that is 343, divides evenly 25 times into 8,575. As a Hebraic symbol, 7^3 can also be viewed as $7 + 3 = 10$, and 343 can be viewed as $3 + 4 + 3 = 10$. The age of Lamech, Noah's father, is 777, which may also be viewed as 21, or 7 x 7 x 7, or 7^3.

How did the writer of Genesis arrive at 2 numbers where the addition of the exponent (7^3) or resulting cubed number ($3 + 4 + 3$) both total 10? Euclid, known as the father of geometry (c. 365-275 B.C.), discovered the concept underlying exponents in his book *Elements*, calling the area of a square a power of the length of a single side. Archimedes later generalized the idea of powers or exponents in his work, *The Sand Reckoner*.[5] He discovered and proved the law of exponents in the same work. This would be 1,200 years after Moses wrote Genesis. The Septuagint cannot be the source of this mathematics because it does not record the numbers correctly from the Hebrew, and adds 1,466 years to the age of the world. This will be addressed later in this chapter.

Further evidence of meter in the ages of the patriarchs is that Eber is the favored 7th generation in reverse (chiastic) order from Abraham. The total ages of the patriarchs from Abraham to Eber is 1,700 (175, 205, 148, 230, 239, 239, and 464 = 1,700). Remember that the total of the 10 numbers in this list plus the addition of the 7 largest numbers is divisible by 17.

The number of years before the Flood is calculated by adding the total of column B in Figure 2 to the first number in column F, for a total of 1,656 years. Also, the list of 10 numbers in column F totals 490, which is 7 x 7 x 10, a multiple of the Jubilee.

---

[5] Archimedes, *The Sand Reckoner of Archimedes*, translated by Thomas Heath, Cambridge University Press, 1897, Forgotten Books, www.forgottenbooks.org, 2008.

The total number of years the antediluvian patriarchs lived after the births of their notable sons before the Flood is 7,019 years (Figure 2, column C), and the years the postdiluvian patriarchs lived after the birth of their notable sons is 2,681 years (column G) for a total of 9,700 years. The significance is that this number is divisible by 100, even if its meaning is unknown.

The age of the world at the death of Abraham is calculated by adding the 20 ages in columns B and F, plus the 75 years Abraham lived after the birth of Isaac, listed in column G. These 21 numbers total 2,121, which is divisible by 21 a total of 101 times. It is also divisible by 7 303 times. The significance of 9,700 and many of these numbers is yet to be determined. However, they are obviously arranged to emphasize a series of Hebraic symbols.

Had one of these ages in the Hebrew text been incorrect, it would not have been possible to trace the above relationships. Yet, the proponents of the Documentary Hypothesis at Harvard, Yale, Oxford, and Cambridge would tell us that these numbers were passed down as legends recited around the campfire by nomadic tribes, which were later edited and rewritten by successive committees named J, then E, then P, and then D. They apparently know nothing of the mathematical relationships in Genesis, or if they do, they will not acknowledge them when presented with the data.

How many additional patterns of 7, 10, and 17 are to be found in these numbers? In the previous chapter, Cassuto, Steinmann, and Lessing all commented on the Hebrew tradition of the honored 7th generation. But what if the relationship between the antediluvian and postdiluvian numbers is also chiastic? There are certainly enough correlations between Adam and Eve and Abraham and Sarah to establish this theory. In this case, Enoch is the 7th generation from Adam, and Eber is the 7th generation from Abraham. A numerical check on this theory proves that the total ages of the last 7 postdiluvian patriarchs is an even 1,700. In more ways than can be determined, the text demonstrates a unity of repetition between the numbers, events, chronology, genealogy, symbols, and theology. However, the purpose and the meaning of the unity between the ante- and postdiluvian patriarchs is yet to be determined.

Dates for the Exodus, Abraham, and the Flood

Lessing and Steinmann's date for the birth of Abraham is no later than 2166 B.C., and is based on biblical reasoning. Although other scholars may disagree, they arrive at this number by placing the Exodus in 1446 B.C., 430 years after Jacob entered Egypt (Exodus 12:40-41).[6] They identify Thutmose III as the ruler of Egypt during the Exodus[7] when Israel departed Egypt in 1446 B.C. in the month of Nissan (Exodus 12:2, Numbers 33:3).

Lessing and Steinmann's date of 2166 B.C. for the birth of Abraham leads us to a hypothetical (though unstated) date for the creation of at least 110 years earlier than Bishop Ussher's date of 4004 B.C. Therefore, according to Lessing and Steinmann, Christ was born 4,114 years after the creation.[8] Yet, according to Genesis 5, and assuming that Arphachshad is born 2 years after Noah entered the Ark, Abraham is born 292 years after the Flood began, or 1,948 years after the creation. This means that Noah died when Abraham was 158 and Isaac was 58. But if we count backwards from 2166 B.C., Abraham is born 182 years after the Flood; hence, Lessing and Steinmann require an additional 100 years, which is a reasonable adjustment. Theoretically, this would still leave time for Abraham's encounter with Melchizedek, whom Luther clearly states is Shem.[9] Lessing and Steinmann do not discuss Babel, or the possibility of a gap in the genealogy after Babel.

Gaps in the Genealogy: Yes and No

The Bible is not compelled to list every name in a genealogy. *Begat* may refer to a son, grandson, or skip even more generations. In the Gospel of Matthew, Christ is called *the Son of David* (9:27), as traced through His stepfather Joseph, with a gap of 28 (4x7) generations (1:6-16). In the Gospel of Luke, Christ is called *the Son of David* (1:32), as traced through His mother Mary, with a gap of 42 (6x7) generations (3:23-31). A difference of 14 generations between Matthew and Luke for David's genealogy to Christ indicates significant and intentional editing. The next quotation by Lessing and Steinmann could have been written by Cassuto. They come to the same conclusion as Cassuto, namely, that some gaps in the genealogies are created in order to round off the list to a symbolic number. Based on previous chapters, that rounding could be to the nearest 7, 10, or 12.

> This can be seen in the genealogy of ten generations from Perez to David in Ruth 4:18-22, where ילד [begat] is also used. There has to be more than ten generations in this span, given

---

[6] Lessing and Steinmann, p. 57.
[7] Ibid., p. 78.
[8] Ibid., p. 57.
[9] *Luther's Works, Vol. 2, Lectures on Genesis, Chapters 6-14*, translated by George V. Schick, Concordia Publishing House, St. Louis, 1960, p. 382.

the 837 years between Perez and David. It appears that the author of Ruth purposely omitted some generations so that Boaz would be listed as the honored seventh person in the genealogy, and David would be the tenth generation.[10]

Like Cassuto, Lessing and Steinmann observe that there are 10 generations from Adam to Noah, and 10 more from Shem to Abraham, followed by 10 generations from Pharez (Perez) to David, as seen in Figure 1. Here they correctly conclude that some generations have been left out between Pharez and David in order to make the count come out to 10, with subdivisions of 7 and 3. The elapsed time from Pharez to David is 837 years, and will be addressed later in this chapter. This is nearly 3 times the 292 years between the 10 generations from Shem and Abraham, when the patriarchs were living an average of 310 years, while David lived 70 years (See Figure 2). After Moses, there is no record in the Bible of anyone living longer than 120 years. Hence, if there is one gap in the genealogies listed by Luke, there are probably more. Therefore, genealogies in the Bible are literal and accurate, but not necessarily complete, and do not claim to be complete according to Western criteria. At the same time, we must assume there is no gap in a given genealogy unless there is evidence in the text that indicates otherwise.

This writer disagrees with Lessing and Steinmann's certainty of gaps in the generations between Adam and Noah.[11] They claim Genesis 7:1 means Noah must be the only living patriarch in order to be the only righteous man in his generation.[12] The fact that Enos, Cainan, Mahalalel, Jared, Methuselah, and Lamech lived during Noah's lifetime does not negate Noah's status as the *only righteous man of his time*. First, where does it say *only*? Second, what about Noah's 3 sons? The understanding of the phrase *righteous man* must be in this context. Third, all of the other patriarchs died before God told Noah to enter the Ark, saying, "...for thee have I seen righteous before me in this generation" (Genesis 7:1).

It is also difficult to explain Abraham's interaction in a populated world 367-392 years after the Flood when he was 75-100 years old. Construction began on the Great Pyramid in 2470 B.C. with an estimated workforce of 30,000 men. According to Genesis, Abraham was born 1,948 years after the creation, or in 2056 B.C. based on Ussher's numbers.

---

[10] Lessing and Steinmann, p. 56.
[11] Ibid.
[12] Ibid., p. 57.

A simple estimated population of the world 300 years after the Flood when Abraham was 8 years old might look as follows. This chart assumes the optimum conditions that every man and wife produced 10 children by the time they were 50 years old; that there are no deaths, disease, or deformities; and that the marriage rate was 100% for 300 years. Yet, we are fairly certain that some women such as Hagar and Sarah only produced 1 child, and four wives were required to produce Jacob's 12 sons.

Estimated Population Projection after the Flood

Years	People	Couples
0 years	6	3 couples
50 years	30	15 couples
100 years	150	75 couples
150 years	750	375 couples
200 years	3750	1,875 couples
250 years	18,750	9,375 couples
300 years	93,750	
	117,188	plus 2 for Noah

Genesis 10 lists the 70 nations that descended from Noah, and states that the division at Babel took place in the days of Peleg, who was born 131 years after the Flood and died when Abraham was 72. According to the above progression, and assuming the division at Babel took place 175 years after the Flood, there were about 3,000 people on the earth, or approximately 43 people per nation. Following this progression, there were probably less than 750 able-bodied men to build the tower of Babel—if they were not farming, building homes, or herding animals for the survival of their 10 children. Additionally, when Abraham was born, the 70 nations had already scattered around the globe. Contrast all of this with the estimated number of men required to build the Great Pyramid, as stated above. The point of this speculation is to demonstrate that there are intentional gaps in the genealogy after the Flood. This is not an error or a discrepancy in the text. This is how the Bible always intended to record genealogy in the Pentateuch.

This writer is of the opinion that Bishop Ussher's number of 4,004 years from the creation to the birth of Christ is the total number of years the reader is supposed to calculate. The Bible never intended to give a precise number of years from Adam to Christ. If anything, Christ was born 3 years earlier, in what would be 3 B.C., and our calendar today is short by 3 years. This would set up a possible and interesting heptadic 4,000-3,000 division for the history of the world. In actual time the 4,000 years would be expanded, and the 3,000 would probably be a lesser number. There are 2 concurrent histories, one prophetic and the other chronological.

How Genesis Records Numbers

Ancient Hebrew has 10 words for the 10 cardinal numbers, plus words for 100 and 1,000. There are no digits in Genesis to represent numbers, only words. There are no ancient Hebrew words for the numbers 11, 12, 19, etc. To express the number 19, Moses wrote in Hebrew the phrase *nine and ten*. Numbers such as 30, 40, 50, through 90 are expressed as plurals of 3, 4, 5, etc. To express the number 119, Moses wrote *nine and ten and a hundred*. The plural of 10 (literally *tens*) and the plural of 100 (literally *hundreds*) express 20 and 200, respectively. The number 300 is *three times a hundred* when the Hebrew word for 100 is singular.

This method of recording numbers is cumbersome, to say the least, but it led to an integration of numbers and literary thought. Moses' numbers in Genesis were probably ceremonial, or a formal method of writing numbers, similar to our use of Roman numerals today. Whatever the reason, Moses' method of recording numbers lends itself to numeric thought unique to the Bible. Before proceeding further with this line of inquiry, let us examine the manner in which Moses recorded the numbers for Shem's genealogy. In Figure 3, column A lists the 10 postdiluvian patriarchs. Column B lists the total years lived. Column C lists anomalies in the manner in which Moses records Terah's and Abraham's ages. Column D lists the protracted style in which Moses records the ages of the patriarchs when their notable sons were born (although in this and other columns numbers are substituted for the word equivalents in the text). Note that Terah's years are not actually listed by Moses, but are deduced by subtraction of 70 from 205. Column F is the protracted style in which Moses records the years the patriarchs lived after the birth of their notable sons. Columns E and G list the Western style of recording the numbers in D and F.

Figure 3

A	B	C	D	E	F	G
Shem	600		100	100	5 x 100	500
Arpachshad	438		5 and 3s	35	3 and 4 x 100	403
Shelah	433		3s	30	3 and 4 x 100	403
Eber	464		4 and 3s	34	3s and 4 x 100	430
Peleg	239		3s	30	9 and 100s	209
Reu	239		2 and 3s	32	7 and 100s	207
Serug	230		3s	30	100s	200
Nahor	148		9 and 10s	29	9 and 10 and 100	119
Terah	205	100s-5	7s	70	(5 and 3s and 100)	(135)
Abraham	175	100-7s-5	100	100	5 and 7s	75

Note that patriarchal ages exhibit patterns of 3, 4, or 7, except for Shem and Nahor. Jordan comments on this repetition when he writes, "...most of these 3s are visibly and inescapably linked to 4s, to make symbolic 7s."[13] In column F, Arpachshad, Shelah, and Eber each contain a 3-4 sequence; Reu has a 7; Nahor can be viewed as 2 consecutive 1s subtracted from 9, which thus equals 7, also 119 is divisible by 7 exactly 17 times; and Abraham has a 7 in his age and is also divisible by 7. Abraham's age equals the total ages of the 10 antediluvian patriarchs divided by 7^2. In column D, Terah's age is 7s, or 10 times 7. The 7 ages of the 7 oldest patriarchs subdivide into a pattern of 3 and 4.

Adam, Noah, and Abraham are each directed by God to move from their current location. Adam is expelled from the perfect world. Noah and Shem leave and arrive in a new world. Abraham is called to the Promised Land. This is a chiastic progression of A B B A. Arpachshad is born when Shem is 100 years old, and Isaac is born when Abraham is 100 years old.[14] This is a chiastic history.

Like Adam's and Noah's ages,[15] in Shem's genealogy only the total ages of Terah and Abraham are published in a different order, as shown in Column C. Perhaps this is because they were on a journey. This reverse order in recording ages can only be observed in the Hebrew text.

Cassuto observed definite rules for how compound numbers are recorded in the Bible. He writes, "Upon investigating all the compound numbers in the Bible, I discovered that the ascending and descending orders are used according to definite rules that hold good for all books."[16] Technical or statistical data is recorded in ascending order, and numbers in narrative speech or poetry are arranged in descending order.

Questions about Terah's Age at Abraham's Birth

There is an apparent contradiction in the genealogy of Terah, Abraham's father. Genesis 11:26 says Terah was 70 years old when Abraham was born, and lived to be 205 (11:32) when Abraham was 75 years old (12:4). Many scholars, including Lessing and Steinmann, use this apparent contradiction to support false assumptions about genealogy in Genesis.[17] Hervey points out this apparent discrepancy in the age of

---

[13] Jordan, *A Chronological and Calendrical Commentary on the Pentateuch*, p. 63.
[14] Ibid., p. 260.
[15] Adam's age in Moses' record is "nine hundreds year and threes year" (Gen. 5:5). Noah's age in Moses' record is "nine hundreds year and fives year" (Gen. 9:29).
[16] Cassuto, *The Documentary Hypothesis*, pp. 62-63.
[17] Lessing and Steinmann, p. 56.

Terah when Abraham was born. "If then we understand from Gen. xi. 26, that Terah was 70 years old at the birth of Abram, here is an obvious contradiction. For 70 + 75 = 145. And as Abram did not leave Haran till his father's death, his father could not have lived 205 years."[18] We read in Genesis:

> "And Terah lived seventy years, and begat Abram, Nahor, and Haran" (Genesis 11:26).

> "And the days of Terah were two hundred and five years: and Terah died in Haran" (Genesis 11:32).

> "So Abram departed, as the LORD had spoken unto him; and Lot went with him: and Abram was seventy and five years old when he departed out of Haran" (Genesis 12:4).

According to these verses, Terah was 130 when Abraham was born and not 70 years old, and Abraham left Haran when his father Terah died at 205 (Acts 7:4). Hervey points out that the solution is we should not assume that Abraham was the oldest son. Genesis 5:32 states Noah was 500 when he *begat Shem, Ham, and Japheth*, but according to Genesis 10:21 Japheth was the oldest. There is no reason to believe that Noah produced all 3 sons in the same year with one wife unless they were triplets. Shem was 100 years old when Arpachshad was born 2 years after the Flood (11:10), and yet, he appears to be Shem's 3rd son. Only the first of 21 lists of the 12 Tribes is in the correct birth order because the first list is recorded in the history of their births over 5 chapters. Twice the Bible says *Jacob and Esau*, but Esau was the oldest. Also, the Bible speaks about Ephraim and Manasseh 7 times (Genesis 48:5; Deuteronomy 34:2; 1 Chronicles 9:3; 2 Chronicles 15:9; 2 Chronicles 30:1, 10, 18), but Manasseh, according to Genesis 41:52, was the oldest. There is no reason to assume that any genealogy in the Bible gives the correct birth order unless specifically stated. Note that Terah does not take Nahor with him when he travels (11:31), but Abraham, who could be 60 years younger than Nahor, if not Haran.

Therefore, if Abraham was born when Terah was 130, this would explain the apparent nearness in age between Abraham and his nephew Lot. Thus, 60 years could be added to 292, placing the birth of Abraham at 352 years after the Flood.

---

[18] Lord Arthur Hervey, *The Genealogies of Our Lord and Saviour Jesus Christ, As Contained in the Gospels of Matthew and St. Luke*, Macmillan and Co., Cambridge, London, 1853, https://archive.org/stream/genealogiesourl01hervgoog#page (7/2015), pp. 82-83.

This kind of investigation illustrates how complicated the study of chronology really is, and why this chapter focuses on the significance of the given ages without delving into details that have spawned numerous and exhaustive scholarly books on the subject of chronology. For the purpose of maintaining genealogical symmetry, this book deals with the numbers stated in the text. It says Terah was 70, therefore that is the number we work with.

Genesis Genealogy Symbolized as World Government in Revelation

Locating 3-4 sequences in Genesis 11 led to comparisons with similar 3-4 sequences in Revelation chapters 4, 6, 7, 8, 9, 18, 19, and 21, as discussed in Chapter Five. The Genesis genealogies are literal accounts and numbers. Revelation adopts this same sequence and presents it in the context of a symbolic vision. Verifying such a relationship indicates:

1. John is fully aware that Moses had set the precedent for Hebraic meter in Genesis. Thus, the genre in Genesis is repeated in Revelation.
2. John adapted the 3-4 sequence in Genesis as a poetic device to symbolize God's deconstruction of the earth in Revelation. In other words, John takes the same 3-4 heptadic meter Moses used to describe the origin of humanity in Genesis 5 and 11, and applies it as a chiastic symbol of humanity's destruction in Revelation.
3. Biblical history is arranged in chiastic order.

In addition to the 3-4 division in 7, there is also a similar 3-7 division in 10, and a 7-10 division, the symbol for judgment and completion, to form 17, the number of complete power or final judgment. Hence, the dragon in Revelation has 7 heads, 10 horns, and 7 crowns (Revelation 12:3); the beast has 7 heads, 10 horns, and 10 crowns (Revelation 13:1); and the scarlet beast has 7 heads and 10 horns (Revelation 17:3, 7). These 3 beasts are named 4 times, comprising another 3-4 division. There are 4 beasts that come out of the sea in Daniel 7—a lion, bear, leopard, and one with iron teeth. The beast that comes out of the sea in Revelation 13 looks like a lion, bear, and leopard—another 4-3 division between beasts in Daniel and Revelation. Revelation uses 10 and 7 as symbols that can be added for a total of 17, multiplied for a total of 70, or arranged with 7 as a subset of 10, the same relationships seen in the Genesis genealogies.

The numerical symbolism in Revelation leads us back to the reality in Genesis from which it originated. Again and again we see that the future in Revelation is predicated on the past in Genesis and leads us back to Genesis, which is a decidedly Eastern chiastic view of history. The future was already established in the past. The Flood begins on the 17th day (Genesis 7:11), and the Ark lands on Ararat on the 17th day (Genesis 8:4), as pointed out by Cassuto.[19] The earth is dry on the 17th day (Genesis 8:14). This same number (17) is symbolized in Revelation by beasts with 7 heads and 10 horns (Revelation 12:3; 13:1; 17:3, 7). Another chiastic event is found in the comparison of the confusion of tongues at Babel and the 17 nations that hear the apostles speak in their own language at Pentecost.[20]

The numbers 7, 10, and 17, as seen above in the patriarchs before the Flood, are the numbers associated with world government in Revelation. Full authority began with Adam after Eden and with Shem after the Flood. However, 10 generations later, Noah and Abraham were both outcasts from mainstream society in a world with people who abandoned the true God. There is a subset of 7 in the 10 ages of the antediluvian and postdiluvian patriarchs. The world government established by God under the 10 patriarchs, and then again by Noah's 3 sons, is reordered by the devil's 3 beasts in a sequence of 7, 10, and 17 at the end of the world. Thus human history begins and ends in a chiasm with the same numerical sequence: 10, 7, 3, 3, 7, and 10.

Repetition of Prophetic Images

A unity of theology is evident in the repetition of corresponding themes and the fulfillment of these themes throughout the Bible. For example:

1. The tree of life is named 3 times in Genesis and 3 times in Revelation, if we follow the KJV at Revelation 22:19.[21]
2. Genesis 3:3 says, *Ye shall not eat of it, neither shall ye touch it, lest ye die*. John writes, *and our hands have handled, of the Word of life* (1 John 1:1); and again, *Except ye eat the flesh of the Son of man, and drink his blood, ye have no life in you* (John 6:53).
3. The tree to be desired in Genesis 3:6 (*and that it was pleasant to the eyes, and a tree to be desired*) becomes the tree we could not look at in Isaiah 53:2 (*he hath no form nor comeliness; and when we shall see him, there is no beauty that we should desire him*).

---

[19] Cassuto, *Genesis: Part II*, p. 103.
[20] Galileans, Parthians, Medes, Elamites, Mesopotamia, Judaea, Cappadocia, Pontus, Asia, Phrygia, Pamphylia, Egypt, Libya Cyrene, Rome, Cretes, and Arabians (Acts 2:7-11).
[21] Cascione, 2012, pp. 143, 235, 241.

4. The Spirit hovers over the waters in Genesis 1:2, and the Holy Spirit descends as a dove at the baptism of Christ in the Jordan River (John 1:32).
5. Adam and Eve become ashamed of their nakedness in Genesis 3, but in nakedness Christ *endured the cross, despising the shame* (Hebrews 12:2).

Metered Genealogy in the Gospels

Most readers skip over the genealogy in the first 17 verses of Matthew chapter 1, which states:

> So all the generations from Abraham to David *are* **fourteen generations**;
> and from David until the carrying away into Babylon *are* **fourteen generations**;
> and from the carrying away into Babylon unto Christ *are* **fourteen generations**.

When these generations are displayed as 6 columns of 7 names in Figure 4, the arrangement can be viewed as 42, or 3 times 14, or 6 times 7. Figure 4 illustrates the only place where the Old Testament symbol of 42 is found in the New Testament other than in Revelation. More information on this subject is presented in the 2012 edition.[22] As discussed in Chapter Four, Christ could be called the "Son of" anyone of the patriarchs in Figure 4. He is regularly called the *Son of David* in the Gospel of John, but is actually separated from David by 28 generations. *Son of Man* is usually a Hebraism for *Son of Adam*. As Cassuto points out, the Hebrews did not speculate in Aristotelian philosophical categories, such as *Son of Man*, without a primary designation (namely Adam), versus a predicated substance (humanity).

Figure 4

Abraham	Amminadab	Solomon	Joatham	Jechonias	Achim
Isaac	Naasson	Roboam	Achaz	Salathiel	Eliud
Jacob	Salmon	Abia	Ezekias	Zorobabel	Eleazar
Judah	Boaz	Asa	Manasses	Abiud	Matthan
Phares	Obed	Josaphat	Amon	Eliakim	Jacob
Esrom	Jesse	Joram	Josias	Azor	Joseph
Aram	David	Ozias	(Jehoiachim)*	Sadoc	Jesus

*Lenski, *The Interpretation of St. Matthew's Gospel*, pp. 31-32: Lenski explains that Matthew's phrase *and his brothers* (2 Kgs. 23:30-25:7 and 1 Chron. 3:15-16) omits the names of Josias' 3 faithless sons who all held the throne at Jerusalem after him and during the Babylonian captivity. Josias' second son, Jehoiachim, is the father of Jechonias. In other words, Josias is Jechonias' grandfather, and we added Jehoiachim in parentheses to Matthew's list to give the full 14 generations he intended with the phrase *and his*

---

[22] Ibid., pp. 154-58.

brothers. Matthew assumed his readers understood that *and his brothers* recalled the confusion on the Davidic throne just before and during the Babylonian captivity.

Luke 3:23-38 presents a second genealogy of Christ, as traced through Mary (Figure 5). There are 11 lists of 7 for a total of 77 generations, making God number 77, the source of blessings and curses. The assumed 12th list of 7 includes all of the descendants of Christ by faith, which is symbolized by the 7 churches addressed by Paul in his epistles and by John in Revelation. In Matthew, Jesus' genealogy through Joseph is 6 lists that become 7 lists, and in Luke, Jesus' genealogy through Mary is 11 lists that become 12 lists.

Figure 5

Jesus	Joseph	Mattathias	Salathiel	Jose	Joseph
Joseph	Mattathias	Semei	Neri	Eliezer	Jonan
Heli,	Amos	Joseph	Melchi	Jorim	Eliakim
Matthat	Naum	Judah	Addi	Matthat	Melea
Levi	Esli	Joanna	Cosam	Levi	Menan
Melchi	Nagge	Rhesa	Elmodam	Simeon	Mattatha
Janna	Maath	Zorobabel	Er	Judah	Nathan
David	Aram	Thara	Cainan	Jared	
Jesse	Esrom	Nachor	Arphachshad	Maleleel	
Obed	Phares	Saruch	Sem	Cainan	
Booz	Judah	Ragau	Noah	Enos	
Salmon	Jacob	Phalec	Lamech	Seth	
Naasson	Isaac	Heber	Mathusala	Adam	
Amminadab	Abraham	Sala	Enoch	God	

As shown above, these genealogical patterns in Figures 4 and 5 are not unique to the Gospels. In both examples, Matthew and Luke have not included all the possible names in their genealogies. In other words, they may have been more interested in presenting heptadic meter than the full genealogy.

Chronological Order Not a Priority in the Bible

One of the challenges of chronological order in the Bible is that accurate chronology as the Western mind understands it is not a priority in the Bible. We should also be aware, as Cassuto points out, that chronological order does not take precedence in ancient Eastern cultures.

> The arrangement of narratives in the Torah is certainly not in the 'sequence' required by the Greek ways of thinking to which we are accustomed today. Rather it does follow the thought processes of the ancient East, which are not generally in accord with those of the Greek and modern writers. Chronological order, for instance, which takes precedence in the techniques of Greek and modern literature, is not of such

importance in the ancient Eastern writings; the rabbinic sages, already, noted that there is no 'early and late' in the Torah. But this does not mean that the Pentateuchal arrangement is arbitrary; there are rules and methods. I have already shown (in my lecture at the Congress of Jewish Studies, Jerusalem 1947, and elsewhere) that one of the methods is to arrange the subject-matter on the basis of association—both thematic and verbal association.[23]

Cassuto makes this observation in regard to non-sequential events in the Bible, in this case Exodus 16 through 17. However, as a general principle this pertains to the entire Torah. He writes: "Neither the place nor the time is important, only the theme is significant."[24] This same approach is evident in genealogy. The point is that biblical genealogy is designed to tell us more than names, places, and ages. Genealogy also tells us about history, theology, prophecy, symbols, and events.

Earlier references were made to meter in the genealogy found in Genesis 5, 10, and 11. This writer has yet to encounter a genealogy in the Bible that is not recorded in the Hebraic cadence of 7, 10, 12, and their multiples.

In Genesis chapter 10, there are 14 groups of sons and grandsons, and the last group has 14 names from Joktan to Jobab. This is the same cadence as the 42 names divided into 3 groups of 14 in Matthew 1. The genealogies in Matthew 1:1-17, Luke 3:23-38, Exodus 1:1-5, and Genesis 10:26-29, along with the numbers of those returning from Babylon in Ezra 2:3-67 and Nehemiah 7:8-67, all exhibit Hebraic meter.

The genealogy in Exodus chapter 6 names exactly 40 males divided into 12 groups. Some wives are also listed, but not the daughters. We read that Levi, who lives 137 years, begets Kohath, who lives 133 years; Kohath begets Amram, who lives 137 years; Amram begets Aaron, who is 83 years old at the time of the Exodus, for a total of 490 years, 10 times the Jubilee. The Jubilee begins the day after the 49th year. It should also be noted that in the Gospel of John, Christ enters the temple in the 46th year of its construction (John 2:20), and then 3 years later in the 49th year (John 12), the week of His crucifixion and resurrection.

---

[23] Cassuto, *Exodus*, p. 187.
[24] Ibid., p. 188.

Problem of the Second Cainan

Lessing and Steinmann claim that the inclusion of the second Cainan in Luke 3:35-36 between Shem and Abraham is an error because the second Cainan is not found in the Hebrew. This writer disagrees because the earliest manuscripts of the Septuagint and Luke do not contain the second Cainan. Cassuto correctly says that the addition of the second Cainan after Arphachshad is an error in the Septuagint.[25]

Meter in the genealogy presents an unintended problem. Copyists not familiar with the Bible's propensity to repeat or delete names in order to maintain Hebraic meter are tempted to correct the genealogies. The biblical genre that maintains a Mosaic cadence of 7, 10, or 12 may be mistaken as a scribal error when names are abridged. Cassuto, Lessing, and Steinmann previously illustrated this rounding out of genealogies. However, in regard to the second Cainan in Luke's Gospel, the supposed son of Arphachshad, there is a much more difficult issue. The second Cainan is missing from the Hebrew text, as is the supposed 130 years he lived before begetting Sala. Lessing and Steinmann blamed this discrepancy on an error in Luke 3:35-36.[26]

Most commentaries on Luke, including Lenski's, do not address this issue. In Alford's commentary, revised in 1871, there is a reference to Hervey's *The Genealogies of Our Lord*.[27] Hervey dedicates an entire chapter to the question of the second Cainan in Luke's Gospel.[28] He begins his chapter with the arguments for and then against the validity of the second Cainan in Luke's Gospel.

Arguments Given by Walton, Yardley, Jackson, Dr. Mill, and Others for the Second Cainan[29]

1. "All the MSS. [manuscripts] and printed editions of St. Luke's Gospel do contain the second Cainan, except the Cambridge MS. presented by Beza to that University, and the editions printed from it."[30] Hervey describes Codex Beza, also known as "D," as "somewhat impaired."[31]

---

[25] Cassuto, *Genesis: Part II*, p. 251.
[26] Ibid.
[27] Henry Alford, *The New Testament for English Readers*, Vol. II, 1852, revised 1871, 7th ed. 1877, Rivingtons, London, Oxford, Cambridge, Guardian Press, Grand Rapids, MI, 1976, p. 474.
[28] Hervey, pp. 168-203.
[29] Ibid., pp. 168-71.
[30] Ibid., p. 168.
[31] Ibid.

2. "All the old versions of the Gospel of St. Luke, the Italic, the Coptic, the Syriac, the Persian, the Arabic, the Æthiopic, the Gothic, and the Vulgate, do agree with our present copies, and do insert the second Cainan."[32]
3. "The Fathers, from the end of the fourth century and downwards, as Epiphanius, Gregory Nazianzen, Jerome, Augustine, &c. did all find him in their copies, and make mention of him expressly, or by implication."[33]
4. "All existing MSS. and editions of the Septuagint version, as the Complutensian, the Aldine, and the Alexandrian, and the Vatican *edition*, do make Cainan the son of Arphaxad in Gen. x. 24, and xi. 12; and all, except the Vatican MS. and edition, which omit the whole passage, in 1 Chron. i. 18, likewise. It must however be noted, that the Vatican *MS.*, most unfortunately, is deficient in the first forty-six chapters of Genesis; and that it, in common with the Alexandrian and other MSS., makes Sala the son of Arphaxad (omitting Cainan) in 1 Chron. i. 24."[34]
5. According to Procopius Gazaeus, who wrote after A.D. 500, Origen's *Hexapla* contained the second Cainan.[35]
6. The second Cainan is found in the Septuagint used by Augustine and the African Church.[36]
7. "Demetrius, the historian, who lived under the Ptolemies, about B.C. 170, in a fragment quoted by Alexander Polyhistor, who wrote about B.C. 86, in a passage preserved to us by Eusebius, (*Praep. Evang.* Lib. ix. cap. 21), follows exactly the Septuagint chronology, reckoning with the Seventy [Septuagint] 3624 years from Adam—and 1360 years from the Flood, or rather, from the birth of Shem,—to Jacob's going down into Egypt: to make up which the 130 years of Cainan must needs be reckoned. From whence it should appear that Cainan was in the Septuagint within one hundred years of that translation being made."[37]
8. Many church Fathers contemporary with Origen and Africanus, including Labbe, Gregory Nazianzen, Epiphanius, and

---

[32] Ibid., p. 169.
[33] Ibid.
[34] Ibid., pp. 169-70.
[35] Ibid., p. 170.
[36] Ibid.
[37] Ibid.

Augustine, quote the Septuagint containing the second Cainan.[38]

Arguments against the Inclusion of the Second Cainan

1. "The Hebrew MSS., and editions which form the authoritative text of Scripture, do not contain, nor ever did contain, Cainan, either in the tenth and eleventh chapters of Genesis, or in 1 Chron. i."[39]
2. "The Samaritan Pentateuch, which represents the state of the Hebrew text prior to the captivity, and which in many important points agrees with the Septuagint, when the Septuagint disagrees with the Hebrew, does not acknowledge Cainan."
3. "Onkelos, in his Chaldee Targum, which is thought to have been made or compiled from older versions, about the time of our Saviour, does not acknowledge Cainan."[40]
4. "The Syriac version made from the Hebrew, very early, as is thought, in the Christian era, does not acknowledge Cainan, neither do the Arabic, nor the Vulgate, nor any version made from Hebrew."[41]
5. "But, further, there are very strong grounds for asserting that the intrusion of Cainan into the Septuagint version is of comparatively modern date. For,"[42]
    i. "In the Vatican MS. of the Septuagint, Cainan is omitted in the first chapter of 1 Chronicles altogether, where the genealogy of Shem is given thus in ver. 24: 'Arphaxad, Sala, Heber, Phaleg, &c.' From the 17th to the 24th verse are omitted. Hence it is obvious to conclude, that neither did it contain Cainan in Genesis, the first forty-six chapters of which are unhappily wanting. And since this MS. is thought to have been written before the time of St. Jerome, (Walton's *Proleg.* ix.), it affords most important evidence that the older and genuine MSS. of the Septuagint did not contain Cainan."
    ii. "The Armenian version of the Old Testament, which was made from the Septuagint, in the fourth century, has no Cainan in Genesis x. or xi., or in 1 Chron. i. 24, though they express him in 1 Chron. i. 18. (Dr. Mill, on

---

[38] Ibid., pp. 170-71.
[39] Ibid., p. 171.
[40] Ibid.
[41] Ibid., pp. 171-72.
[42] Ibid., p. 172.

The Geneal. p. 146)."

iii. "It is certain that Josephus knew nothing of [the second] Cainan." He does not include the second Cainan in his genealogy. In his *Jewish Antiquities*, Lib. I. cap. vi. 4, where he gives a detailed genealogy, he does not mention the second Cainan, though he uses the Septuagint's number of years and forms of names. "Moreover he both himself makes Abraham the tenth generation after Noah and quotes Berosus and Eupolemus as doing so likewise: a calculation which necessarily excludes Cainan. Whence it results, *certainly*, that the version of the Septuagint which Josephus used did not contain [the second] Cainan, neither that from whence Eupolemus derived his information, and that he was not in the Scriptures which Berosus had access to."[43]

iv. "Philo, who habitually follows the Septuagint, was equally ignorant of the second Cainan."[44]

v. Theophilus, Bishop of Antioch A.D. 168, leaves the second Cainan out of his genealogy in *ad Autolycum*, though he follows the Septuagint numbering of years. "Yet, as Archbishop Usher says, he leaves out Cainan and makes Arphaxad the father of Sala."

vi. "Julius Africanus, the contemporary of Origen, who always follows the Septuagint, and does not appear to have ever seen a Hebrew Bible, who at all events quotes from the Septuagint in the very passage under consideration...omits Cainan." He falls short in his Septuagint computation of the years from the Flood to Abraham by exactly 130 years. Therefore Procopius Gazaeus' alleged testimony that the second Cainan was listed in Origen's *Hexapla* is discredited.

vii. Eusebius does not record the second Cainan from his copies of the Septuagint. "...and all doubt on this point is now removed by the valuable discovery of his *Canones Chronici*, in the Armenian language, of which a Latin translation with the Greek fragments preserved by Georgius Syncellus and others, was published at Milan, A.D. 1818." On page 51 Eusebius gives a detailed account of Noah's descendants, and makes no mention

---
[43] Ibid., pp. 172-73.
[44] Ibid., pp. 173-74.

of the second Cainan. Eusebius lists the chronologies from Adam, as listed in the Septuagint, the Hebrew Scripture, and the Samaritan Hebrew copy, and comments on the differences between the 3 texts. Eusebius ascribes willful alteration of the text by the Jews—who were anxious to encourage early marriages.[45]

6. Epiphanius omits the second Cainan from his genealogy. It is obvious he is quoting the Septuagint numbers and is ignorant of the Hebrew text. The Septuagint mistakenly writes that Arphaxad was 135 years old when he begat Cainan, but the copy that Epiphanius possessed says Arphaxad was 135 years old when he begat Selah, as published in the Hebrew.[46] Epiphanius also writes that there are 21 generations from Adam to Abraham, evidence that someone tampered with Epiphanius' text, the one who altered the text being inconsistent in making all the necessary changes.[47] Hervey's lengthy discussion on this is evidence of his excellent scholarship, and it is recommended for further reading.

7. Jerome did not include the second Cainan in his Vulgate, or read him in the Septuagint.[48] "Jerome says distinctly in his Epistle to Pope Damasus, 'Ab Adam usque ad Christum generationes septuaginta septem', which although incorrect, and very likely therefore copied from some other writer, yet certainly shews that St. Luke's Gospel then contained the same names that it does now, including Cainan, a conclusion which Jerome's Latin version of St. Luke, in which Cainan is found, fully confirms. And hence we have a very remarkable confirmation of the opinion to which the other evidence leads, that Cainan was in St. Luke's Gospel before he got into the Septuagint. For the facts of the case go distinctly to this, that he was in St. Luke as read by Jerome, but was not in the Septuagint."[49] (Hervey's point here is that Jerome had a later copy of Luke and an earlier copy of the Septuagint, which is quite an astute observation.)

---

[45] Ibid., pp. 174-77.
[46] Ibid., p. 180.
[47] Ibid., p. 182.
[48] Ibid., pp. 188-89.
[49] Ibid., pp. 189-90.

Hervey reports that Yardley and Georgius Syncellus, who believe the evidence favors the second Cainan, both insinuate that Eusebius intentionally falsified his chronology.[50]

Hervey gives a detailed explanation of how part of Epiphanius' account had obviously been altered to agree with the insertion of the second Cainan, but those who inserted Cainan neglected to continue all the necessary alterations throughout the document.[51]

In addition to Beza's manuscript, which excludes the second Cainan from Luke's Gospel, Irenaeus only counts 72 generations in Luke's Gospel. "But we know from Africanus and Eusebius, that some copies in their time omitted Matthat and Levi, making Melchi the father of Heli. If then they were omitted in Irenaeus' copy, and Rhesa also, there would be exactly 72 remaining, without Cainan."[52]

Hervey gives convincing evidence that the insertion of the second Cainan was due to a copyist error, and illustrates the slight change necessary to make the new word.[53] Also he writes, "The number of years ascribed to the second Cainan before he begat Salah, is precisely the same as the number ascribed to Arphaxad before he begat Cainan."[54]

Hervey believes that early church fathers, particularly Augustine, could hardly resist the temptation to speak about 77 generations.[55] If Hervey were alive today, he most certainly would have placed the discovery of P75, the oldest known copy of Luke (175-225 A.D.) as his primary witness that the second Cainan was not in Luke's Gospel.[56]

The confirmation of P75 substantiates Hervey's thorough examination of the question about the second Cainan. Most likely it was a copyist's error in the Septuagint that led later copyists to make Luke's Gospel agree with the error in the Septuagint. Of course there is also the enigmatic comment in Dr. Harold Buls' notes, where the esteemed doctor suggests the possibility that both Genesis and the Septuagint are

---

[50] Ibid., p. 179.
[51] Ibid., pp. 185-88.
[52] Ibid., p. 193.
[53] Ibid., p. 197.
[54] Ibid., p. 201.
[55] Ibid., pp. 169, 190, 202.
[56] Reuben J. Swanson (ed.), *New Testament Greek Manuscripts: Variant Readings Arranged in Horizontal Lines against Codex Vaticanus: Luke*, Sheffield Academic Press, Sheffield, England, William Carey International University Press, Pasadena, CA, 1995, p. 60.

correct.[57] This means there was an intentional gap in the Genesis genealogy, and Luke added the missing Cainan from the temple records. This is rather implausible because the oldest manuscripts, including P75 that Buls praised highly, do not contain the second Cainan. On this issue we agree with Hervey's conclusion.

One would now think the matter has been fully investigated, but there is yet more confusion of which Hervey was unaware, or more likely chose not to address.

Admin Missing from the Septuagint and the Old Testament

Luke's genealogy, from his investigation of the temple records, includes Admin, but Admin's name does not appear in the Hebrew or Greek Old Testament. This is not an error in Luke or Genesis.

In his 1996 commentary, Dr. Arthur Just writes,

> Luke signals his theological intent in the frame of the text, by beginning with Jesus and ending with Adam and God, and in the structure of eleven lists of seven names (seventy-seven names in all). Significant names begin some of the lists, i.e., David, Abraham, and Enoch, and the final seventy-eighth name is God. (Following variants in various manuscripts results in a shorter genealogy of anywhere from seventy-two to seventy-six names.) [58]

A number of manuscripts followed by BNT, GNT, TIS, and VST add Admin between Amminadab and Ram, for a total of 78 instead of 77 names. This additional name is not found in the Old Testament or the Septuagint. Just includes the second Cainan in his list, and thus arrives at 78 names. The names Admin and Amminadab are so close they could be a copyist's error. Nestle-Aland's text shows that unlike Cainan, Admin is found in P75. Thus it appears that more than one copyist was going to make sure there were 77 names, which led to both names being copied into some manuscripts.

On the other hand, James B. Jordan suggests that Admin was removed from the abridged list in Ruth 4, discussed earlier.[59] Jordan's hypothesis is as follows:

---

[57] Harold Buls, *Notes on the Gospel of Luke*, Concordia Theological Seminary Press, Fort Wayne, IN, 1977, p. 12.

[58] Arthur Just, *Concordia Commentary, Luke 1:1-9:50*, Concordia Publishing House, St. Louis, 1996, p. 165.

[59] James B. Jordan, "The Second Cainan Question," *Biblical Chronology*, Vol. II, No. 4, Nice, FL, 1990, p. 2.

My preliminary conclusion is that originally Luke did not have the name Cainan in his list, but did have five names in [Luke 3] verse 33. At some later date, the name Cainan was added to verse 36 in order to square it with the revised LXX [Septuagint], and so a name had to be dropped out of verse 33. This led to several versions of verse 33 floating around, and caused the Church Fathers to express reservations about the second Cainan.[60]

Thus it appears that Luke searched temple records to find the actual genealogical list, including many names not listed in the Bible after 400 B.C., and found the name Admin there, but not in the Old Testament. In this case Dr. Harold Buls' opinion would be correct, namely that the Old Testament, the original copy of the Septuagint, and the earliest versions of Luke, as found in P75, were all correct. It could well be that the writer of Ruth wanted to express 10 names in Pharez's genealogy, but the temple records had a longer list.

The result is that even though Hervey may have proved that the second Cainan was not in the oldest copies of the Septuagint and Luke, other questions about the list of names in Luke make it impossible to come to a firm decision. There could be 77 names and there could be 72 names, which would make 12 lists of 6 instead of 11 lists of 7 in Luke. James B. Jordan's theory also sounds plausible.

Finally, there are 77 names according to the list in P75, the oldest known copy of Luke, and this is the best estimation.

Hebraic Meter in Ezra and Nehemiah's Postexilic Records

Ezra 2:3-67 (Figure 6) has the same pattern as Matthew's genealogy in Figure 4. By family head and member count, Ezra lists 42 groups returning to Jerusalem after 70 years of captivity in Babylon. He then lists King Cyrus' 7 gifts for the temple. In a rather unexpected summary, Ezra includes the total number of those returning to Jerusalem, 42,360, in his list. These census numbers for 42 families, below, are a parallel pattern to the 42 generations in Matthew chapter 1 (Figure 4). This list ends with Jesus and assumes the formation of 7 churches in the New Testament, which also parallels the additional 7 gifts from Cyrus.

---

[60] Ibid.

Figure 6

2,172	642	323	42	1,254	1,247	**42,360**
372	623	112	743	320	1,017	**7,337**
775	1,222	223	621	725	74	**200**
2,812	666	95	122	345	128	**736**
1,254	2,056	123	223	3,630	139	**245**
945	454	56	52	973	392	**435**
760	98	128	156	1,052	652	**6,720**

Ezra 2:3-67

In Figure 7, Nehemiah 7:8-69 presents the same list as Ezra, but with 40 groups instead of 42. The number 40 symbolizes a complete list of people or earthly quantities such as time, events, animals, objects, actions, and measurements. It is one of the most common numbers in the Bible and is found more than 150 times in the Old and New Testament.

Just like Ezra, Nehemiah ends with the same 7 gifts to the temple. The first 42 numbers in Ezra total 29,818 and the first 40 numbers in Nehemiah total 31,089. According to the Septuagint, rather than 40 numbers, Nehemiah lists 42 numbers with a total of 31,101, and follows the same pattern as Ezra. Note that Ezra and the Septuagint translation of Nehemiah exhibit the same pattern found in Matthew.

Those who defend the discrepancies in the genealogy of the Septuagint patriarchs will have difficulty explaining discrepancies in the Septuagint lists in Nehemiah. They certainly cannot blame it on a rabbinical plot to encourage Jewish men to marry at an earlier age.

The total number from Ezra is evenly divisible by 17 for a quotient of 1,754, and the total number from Nehemiah in the Septuagint is evenly divisible by 7 for a quotient of 4,443. There is obvious awareness of Hebraic meter in Ezra, Nehemiah, and the Septuagint, and intentional pattern arrangement in these lists. However, the Septuagint total in Nehemiah being divisible by 7 may be coincidental.

Figure 7

2,172	628	112	123	1,052	**42,360**
372	2,322	95	52	1,247	**7,337**
652	667	188	1,254	1,017	**245**
2,818	2,067	128	320	74	**736**
1,254	655	42	345	148	**245**
845	98	743	721	138	**435**
760	328	621	3,930	392	**6,720**
648	324	122	973	642	

Nehemiah 7:8-69

2,172	648	328	128	**1,252**	1,247	**42,360**
372	628	324	42	320	1,017	**7,337**
652	2,322	112	743	345	74	**245**

2,618	667	**223**	621	721	148	**736**
1,254	2,067	95	122	3,930	138	**245**
845	655	**123**	123	973	392	**435**
760	98	**56**	52	1,052	642	**6,720**

Nehemiah 7:8-69 Septuagint

The lists in Ezra and Nehemiah appear as random numbers. However, the significant aspect of their lists is not in the numbers themselves, but in the number of groups that returned to Jerusalem.

Both Ezra and Nehemiah state that the total number of those returning to Jerusalem is 42,360. We are not told about the other groups that are added into the numbers listed in order to total 42,360. In other words, none of the lists of numbers from Ezra and Nehemiah in the Hebrew or the Greek add up to 42,360, which is divisible by 10, 12, 20, 30, 40, 60, 120 and more. They do not intend to give the whole list of those who returned. Rather, they select a portion of the list in order to arrive at 40 and 42 numbers. Again, notice that the goal is to arrive at the correct meter by editing the lists.

The discrepancy in the census numbers between Ezra and Nehemiah is perhaps explained by a difference in numbers at departure versus arrival after a long, arduous journey. In chapter 2, Ezra repeats the phrase *the children of* exactly 100 times, and in the entire book, 153 times, the same number as the fish in John 21:11, which some consider a symbolic number of the elect. In Nehemiah chapter 7, the phrase *the children of* repeats 88 times, a repetition of the number 8 for the elect (see Chapter Four, page 122), and 12 less than 100.

Every knowledgeable Jew at the time of Christ was aware of the postexilic lists in Ezra and Nehemiah. Thus, every knowledgeable Jew at the time of Christ would also be aware of the meter in the genealogical lists in Matthew and Luke as having been derived from the Old Testament. Those returning from Babylon to Israel would necessarily include the ancestors of Mary and Joseph.

Septuagint Inaccuracies in the Patriarchal Ages

There is a significant divergence between the Masoretic Text and the Septuagint in the ages of the antediluvian and postdiluvian patriarchs. Additionally, while a remarkable numeric symmetry based on the patriarchal numbers exists in the Masoretic Text, as seen earlier, the patriarchal ages in the Septuagint do not exhibit any symmetry or internal relationships.

Figure 8 Septuagint Patriarchs

Patriarch	Total age	Years after son's birth	Patriarch	Total age	Years after son's birth	Patriarch
Adam	930	230-700	Shem	600	100-500	Pharez
Seth	912	205-707	Arpachshad	535	135-400	Hezron
Enosh	905	190-715	Cainan	460	130-330	Ram
Cainan	910	170-740	Shelah	460	130-330	Amminadab
Mahalalel	895	165-730	Eber	404	134-270	Nahshon
Jared	962	162-800	Peleg	339	130-209	Salmon
Enoch	365	165-200	Reu	339	132-207	Boaz
Methuselah	969	167-802	Serug	330	130-200	Obed
Lamech	753	188-565	Nahor	304	179-125	Jesse
Noah	950	500-100-350	Terah	205	70-135	David
			Abraham	175	100-75	

A popular explanation for this discrepancy, circulated in the 1800s and as far back as Eusebius, is the preposterous theory that Jewish scholars altered their own Hebrew text sometime after the Septuagint was translated, and before the birth of Christ, in order to encourage fathers to have children at an earlier age. Actually, the opposing theory would be more correct, namely, that Septuagint copyists added more years to the postdiluvian patriarchs before they produced their significant sons in order to make them appear more distinguished.

The Septuagint increases time before the Flood by 586 years, from 1,656 to 2,242 years (Figure 8). The Septuagint actually makes Lamech, the son of Methuselah, 24 years younger. It also adds 880 years to the period between the end of the Flood and the birth of Abraham, for a total addition of 1,466 years to the Old Testament. This would mean that Bishop Ussher's date for the creation at 4004 B.C. is off by 1,466 years, and the world was created in 5470 B.C. Try to tell this to Luther and many others, whose chronologies follow the Masoretic Text, and not the Septuagint.

Also according to the Septuagint, Methuselah died 802 years after Lamech was born: 1,454 + 802 = 2,256 years after creation. Or we could say Methuselah died 969 years after he was born in the year 1287 after the creation. This means Methuselah lived 2,256 years after the creation. According to the Greek Septuagint, the Flood took place 2,242 years after creation. Therefore, the Septuagint tells us Methuselah died 14 years after the Flood. There is no record of Methuselah being on the Ark. The high credibility some scholars hold for the Septuagint is beyond this writer's understanding.

If the Septuagint is accurate, there should be 12 more repetitions of the Hebrew word for *hundred* added to the Hebrew text, in addition to other words. The Masoretic Text contains a form of the word *hundred* as a subset exactly 40 times in Genesis, which coincidently is the exact total Bishop Ussher calculated for the number of years Christ was born after the creation, concluding that He was probably born in 3 B.C.

In the Masoretic Text, the 3 consonants for the word *hundred* appear together 40 times in Genesis without the long hōlem: מְאַת (*meʿaʾat*, may-at') Genesis 5:3, 4, 6, 18, 25, 28, 30; 7:24; 8:3, 8; 11:10, 19, 21, 23, 25, 32; 17:27; 19:24; 21:5; 23:15, 20; 25:7, 10, 17; 26:27, 31; 27:30; 32:15 (x2); 35:28; 38:1; 42:24; 43:34; 44:28; 47:9, 22, 28; 49:30, 32; 50:13.

Another result of alterations in the Septuagint would be the change in Lamech's age from 777 years to 753 years, which also removes one repetition of the phrase *and seven* from the text. This phrase appears in the Masoretic Text 7 times, וּשֶׁבַע (*ūshebaʿ*, ū-sheh'-bah) Genesis 5:26, 31; 23:1; 25:17; 41:26, 27 (x2). More examples could be given.

This is not to suggest that 4,001 is the literal number of years between Adam and Christ. There are intentional gaps in the genealogy, such as in Ruth. The numbers in the genealogy are arranged according to Hebraic meter, although each name given in the Hebrew text is literally accurate, as are the ages. Every intended gap in the genealogy creates a corresponding intended total age of the antediluvian and postdiluvian world. One must only calculate what the text presents, even though we know there are intentional gaps.

In some instances the Bible symbolizes time, and in other instances it means exactly what it says. It is like knowing the difference between a parable and a clear text. For example, what is the precise time of *seven seasons* in Daniel? What is the meaning of 1,260 days in Revelation 12:3? Context matters. Christ's *3 days and 3 nights* in the tomb was not 72 hours, but closer to 36 hours if we count from sundown on Friday until sunrise on Sunday. Any part of the Hebrew day was considered a whole day. Queen Esther asked the Jews to fast and pray 3 days and 3 nights, but went to see the King on the 3rd day. We do not question that Christ was tempted 40 days in the desert, but theoretically the actual time could have been 23 hours and 58 minutes less than 40 days as the Hebrew mind understands time.

In numerous places the Septuagint generalizes and is paraphrastic, while the Vulgate is a more accurate translation. The Vulgate lists the same ages for the patriarchs as the Masoretic Text and does not follow the Septuagint. However, it is doubtful that Jerome would have been able to translate the Hebrew text without the Septuagint.

The assumption must be that the Hebrew text was also designed to communicate more meaning with its arrangement of meter and numbers, but the temple records were keeping what they felt was a more accurate chronology. It appears that, as the opportunity arose, the Septuagint translators opted to give readers the amended chronology from the temple records, without disturbing the Hebrew text. With this approach in mind, Luke may have chosen to take one more name such as *Admin* from the temple records in order to complete his metered arrangement of names. Thus he followed the same approach as the writer of Ruth's genealogy, and Ezra and Nehemiah's postexilic lists.

Repetition throughout the Genealogies

There is a great deal of evidence supporting the claim that biblical genealogies, beginning with Moses, are recorded in Hebraic meter in the text. Cassuto identifies considerable Hebraic repetition in the genealogies. He states that the Bible lists 70 sons of Gideon (Judges 8:30; 9:2), although it is obviously a rounded number, as shown in Chapter Eight. Ahab has 70 sons in 2 Kings 10:1, 6, and 7. Nahor has 12 sons; Ishmael has 12 sons; there are 2 lists of the 12 chiefs of Edom if Amelek is not counted (because he is the son of a concubine in the first list) and Zepho is added to the second list; and Jacob has 12 sons.[61]

At no place does the Bible say there are 70 names in Genesis chapter 10, yet there are 70 names listed. Cassuto enumerates the 70 descendants of Noah, which predates the 70 descendants of Jacob, as follows:

> Japheth has *seven* sons (Gomer, Magog, Madai, Javan, Tubal, Meshech, and Tiras), and his grandsons also number *seven*, (Askenaz, Riphath, Togarmah, Elishah, Tarshish, Kittim, and Dodanim); in all *fourteen*. In the pedigree of the Sons of Ham, the sons and grandsons of Cush are *seven*, (Seba, Havilah, Sabtah, Raamah, Sabteca, Sheba, and Dedan); the sons of Egypt are *seven* (Ludim, Anamin, Lehabim, Naphtuhim, Pathrusim, Casluhim, and Caphtorim), to whom have been added the Philistines, who were descended from Casluhim; Canaan's sons total *twelve* (Sidon, Heth, the Jebusites, the Amorites, the Girgashites, the Hivites, the Arkites, the Sinites, the Arvadites, the Zemarites, the Hamathites, and

---

[61] Cassuto, *Genesis: Part II*, p. 178.

the Canaanites). Thus altogether the sons of Ham number: Cush and his sons and grandsons, *eight*; Egypt and his seven sons and the Philistines, *nine*; Put, having no sons, *one*; the tribes of the Canaanites, *twelve*; in all, *thirty*. The sons and grandsons of Shem, up to Peleg, are *twelve*; the sons of Joktan are *thirteen*, and with Joktan *fourteen*—twice times seven. All told, the sons of Shem are *twenty-six*. Thus all the sons of Shem and Ham and Japheth mentioned in the chapter come to: 14+30+26=70.[62]

Cassuto reminds us that the Bible intentionally rounds numbers to the nearest total that allows the list to arrive at the desired number. He presents an outstanding 12-page defense of Genesis chapter 10 against the Documentary Hypothesis.[63] He addresses the fact that there are 70 names of 70 nations listed in Genesis 10, but the Bible does not specifically say there are 70. In order to arrive at 70 names, Moses rounds out the list by repeating *Sheba* twice in Genesis 10:7 and 28, and *Havilah* twice in Genesis 10:7 and 29, as discussed in Chapter Eight.[64] Variant readings in the Septuagint do not change the total. The fact that some of Israel's pagan neighbors follow a tradition of 70 descendants indicates they shared a common history and tradition that originates with Noah, and predates Moses.

> The Torah was concerned only to complete the number of 70 names, and to incorporate therein the names of the principal nations that were near to Israel, or were in some way connected with the Israelites, or were in some manner known to them.[65]

> Nor should we be surprised at the fact that in this chapter the boundaries between an individual and a tribe (or people) and a city (or state) are blurred. The scholars who attribute to this chapter naïve and primitive conceptions, as though it intended to tell us that a man named Egypt begot a man called Ludim and a man called Anamim and other people with similar names, or that a person called Canaan begot a man called Sidon and a man called Heth and a man named the Jebusite and the like, fail to understand the nomenclature of the passage.

---

[62] Ibid., pp. 178-79.
[63] Ibid., pp. 172-82.
[64] Ibid., p. 182.
[65] Ibid., p. 180.

In this way it is possible to understand the duplication of the names Havilah and Sheba, which occur twice in the chapter (... compare Gen. xxxvi 23), and half of Salma (i Chron. ii 54). Needless to say, the two different elements are counted as two in the total of seventy nations.[66]

In addition to Cassuto's observations, there is the list of 40 men in Exodus 6 divided into 12 groups.

There is even a repetition of romance. Eliezer finds Isaac's wife Rebecca by a well. Jacob meets Rachel by a well, and Moses meets Zippora by a well.[67] Christ's encounter with the woman at the well is a demonstration of God's love for His church.

Repetition of Names in Genesis
Abimelech 24;
Abraham 133 + Sarah 37 = 170 (italic *Abraham* not counted in 21:33);
Abram/Abraham 14, Chapter 17, אַבְרָהָם, '*Abraham* (ab-raw-hawm') 17:1 (x2), 3, 5 (x2), 9, 15, 17, 18, 22, 23 (x2), 24, 26;
Cain 14, Chapter 4;
Hagar 12, 16:1, 3, 4, 8, 15 (x2), 16; 21:9, 14, 17 (x2); 25:12;
Ham 10;
Isaac 80, Rebecca 30 = 110;
Ishmael 17;
Jacob 180 (Hebrew has "supplant," the meaning of Jacob's name, at 27:36); the KJV has 181 but 45:26 is not in Hebrew;
Jacob 180, Rachel 44, Bilhah 9, Zilpah 7 = 240;
Joseph 14, Chapter 37:2 (x2), 3, 5, 13, 17, 23 (x2), 28 (x3), 29, 31, 33;
Joseph 10, Chapter 40;
Joseph 20, Chapter 41;
Joseph 12, Chapter 42;
Joseph 10, Chapter 43;
Joseph 14, Chapter 45;
Joseph 12, Chapter 48;
Judah 28, 4 times 7;
Judah 40, in Pentateuch without prefix or suffix;
Leah 33 + Zilpah 7 = 40;
Lot 30;
Rachel 44, Bilhah 9, Zilpah 7 = 60;
Rebecca 30;
Shem 14.

---

[66] Ibid., p. 182.
[67] Cassuto, *Exodus*, p. 23.

Conclusion

The Preface states that this book intends to give the reader an understanding of the Bible's unique concept and application of repetition. Initially the word *pattern* was used to describe repetition, but *pattern* is more visual than literary. Eventually the word *meter* was considered a more accurate description. Poetic meter, such as iambic pentameter or dactylic hexameter, carries the sense of numerics in meter, but is also associated with rhyme and feet. At this time there is no adequate definition that describes repetition in the Bible. Hence, the term *Hebraic meter* was borrowed by this writer to define a literary style which previously had no definition.

Currently, scholars admit that the term *Hebraic meter* is rather vague. William Watters comments: "Now it must be said at the outset of our discussion on meter, that we are not sure at all what constitutes an 'Hebraic meter'."[1] Watters is clear that *Hebraic meter*, as it is understood before the publication of this book, has nothing to do with anything similar to poetic measure in classical Greek. Since *Hebraic meter* is a term in need of clarification, this book has hopefully supplied an appropriate definition. In the future, it is hoped that biblical scholars with more expertise than this writer will arrive at the same conclusion. The reader has essentially been introduced to a literary form that is, thus far, found only in the Bible.

The order and structure of this repetition in the book is more closely related to aesthetics than mathematics. The choice of words and phrases, their arrangement, positioning of subsets within sets, and the juxtaposition and counterbalance of linguistic symmetry and asymmetry are aesthetic choices, illustrating a highly refined and elaborate literary genre.

The subject of repetition is of such enormity, this summation is hardly adequate. There are numerous areas worthy of further investigation, such as a thorough examination of the entire Bible, the Apocrypha, the Old Testament Pseudepigrapha, the Gnostic writings, and possible repetition in Egyptian tomb paintings, to name a few. This conclusion is limited to 4 subjects related to *Repetition in the Bible*:

---

[1] William R. Watters, *Formula Criticism and the Poetry of the Old Testament*, Beihefte zur Zeitschrift für die alttestamentliche Wissenschaft 138, De Gruyter, Berlin, New York, 1976, p. 99.

1. Repetition in the Gnostic Gospels
2. The Quackery of Q
3. How Was Meter Placed in the Text?
4. Three Impossibilities

Repetition in the Gnostic Gospels

Over the years this writer has searched for evidence from the ancient world suggesting recognition or acknowledgment of Hebraic meter in the Bible. At this point there is no evidence that any prophet or apostle in the history of the Bible knew they were writing phrases in metered repetition into the text. As quoted in Chapter Six, Sternberg states similar frustration in not finding one self-explanatory quote on repetition in the Hebrew Bible. To our knowledge, there is no comment about metered repetition in the biblical text in the 38-volume set of writings of the Ante-Nicene, Nicene, and Post-Nicene church fathers.

Examination of other ancient literature has not produced phrases set in Hebraic meter as found in the Old and New Testaments. The Septuagint; *The Old Testament Pseudepigrapha* (falsely ascribed writings) edited and translated by Charlesworth, which includes 64 books from the ancient world;[2] the Apocrypha's 16 books as listed in the *BibleWorks King James Apocrypha*; and other Gnostic writings have thus far failed to exhibit the same metered cadence found in the Pentateuch and the Gospels.

Pagan literature and fraudulent texts are filled with repetition, but not with the genre of Hebraic meter. Lists of events or things that imitate the 7 days of creation, 12 tribes and apostles, or the 7 letters, seals, bowls, and trumpets of Revelation are found in many pseudepigraphal and Gnostic writings. But these are examples of obvious superficial mimicry. However, the Gnostic Gospel titled the *Secret Book of John*, more correctly called the *Apocryphon of John* (AOJ) in a volume titled *The Secret Teachings of Jesus*, appears to replicate aspects of Hebraic meter found in Revelation with surprising precision.[3]

Gnosticism is a second-century Christian heresy whose advocates promoted asceticism, abstinence, and celibacy; claimed secret wisdom, knowledge, and doctrine; and taught from so-called secret books about God. This Coptic book from the Nag Hammadi library, written some-

---

[2] *The Old Testament Pseudepigrapha*, 2 vols., Ed. by James H. Charlesworth, Doubleday & Company, Garden City, NY, 1983.
[3] Marvin W. Meyer, *The Secret Teachings of Jesus: Four Gnostic Gospels*, Random House, New York, 1984.

time between 125 and 175 A.D., is an obvious attempt to write a counterfeit apocalypse.

The following is a quote from *The Secret Teachings of Jesus: Four Gnostic Gospels*, translated by Marvin W. Meyer.

> The fourth and final text translated in this volume, the *Secret Book of John* [*Apocryphon of John*], also consists of disclosures and discourses of Jesus set within the framework of a dialogue between Jesus and a disciple. The content of this text differs substantially from that of the other three documents [the *Secret Book of James*, *Gospel of Thomas*, and *Book of Thomas*], however, and the *Secret Book of John* contains very little, if anything, that can be considered as coming from the historical Jesus. Rather, this text is an overtly mythological account of the creation, fall, and salvation of the world and the people within the world.[4]

Revelation is the first book to publish Hebraic meter in a widely-read language. No other book in the New Testament is arranged with Revelation's integration of heptadic sequences, symbols, numbers, and visions. It is evident that the AOJ's primary source for the Old Testament is the Septuagint. The writer gives no indication that he is aware of meter derived from the Pentateuch. It should also be noted that there is no evidence of any writer attempting to imitate repetition found in the 4 Gospels, as seen in the first 4 chapters. Rather, the Gnostics gravitate to apocalyptic scenarios, fanciful stories about Jesus, and dialogue filled with an affected tone of lofty, patronizing omniscience.

This writer does not read Coptic, and is relying on 2 different English translations of the AOJ by Marvin Meyer and Frederik Wisse. Wisse's translation was searched online and cross checked with the translation in Meyer's book.

The following is a sample of noncontiguous words and phrases set in Hebraic meter found in the AOJ, with 4 examples of metered words in Revelation:

Repetition in the AOJ　　　*Repeated from Revelation*
　　Adam: 7 times
　　Christ: 7 times……..............Jesus Christ: 7 times
　　Holy Spirit: 7 times…...…........Spirits: 7 times
　　John: 14 times………...….....Jesus: 14 times

---

[4] Ibid., p. xx.

Lord: 12 times singular.......Lord: 24 times
Sevenness: 14 times
(Seven, Seventh)
Virginal Spirit: 10 times

Notice how closely the writer of the AOJ duplicates noncontiguous words set in Hebraic meter, as found in Revelation, such as *Lord*, *Jesus Christ*, *spirits*, and *Jesus*. It appears the writer of the AOJ had access to a copy of Revelation when he wrote his book.

As a corrupted commentary on Revelation, it is interesting to note that the AOJ understands *seven spirits* in Revelation 1:4, 3:1, 4:5, and 5:6 as referring to the Holy Spirit. The following are noncontiguous decadal phrases from Wisse's translation,[5] which are also found in Meyer.

And I said…Lord or *Savior* 10 times in the AOJ
    And I said, "Lord,
    And I said to the savior, "Lord,
    And I said to the savior
    And I said to the savior, "Lord,
        I said to him, "Lord,
    And I said, "Lord,
    And I said, "Lord,
    And I said, "Lord,
    And I said, "Lord,
    And I said, "Lord,

Archons (*Archangels* or *Angels*) 7 named in the AOJ
    And the archons created seven powers for themselves, and the powers created for themselves six angels for each one until they became 365 angels. And these are the bodies belonging with the names:
        the **first** is Athoth, he has a sheep's face;
        the **second** is Eloaiou, he has a donkey's face;
        the **third** is Astaphaios, he has a hyena's face;
        the **fourth** is Yao, he has a serpent's face with seven heads;
        the **fifth** is Sabaoth, he has a dragon's face;
        the **sixth** is Adonin, he had a monkey's face;
        the **seventh** is Sabbede, he has a shining fire-face.
    This is the sevenness of the week.

---

[5] "The Apocryphon of John," translated by Frederik Wisse, in James M. Robinson (ed.), *The Nag Hammadi Library*, rev. ed., HarperCollins, San Francisco, 1990, http://gnosis.org/naghamm/apocjn.html (7/2015).

There are 2 more lists in the AOJ that count out 7 things like the above, followed by a list that counts out 12 things. This is followed by a list of 72 body parts, including uvula, tonsils, marrow, and testicles. The 7 deities in charge of these 72 body parts are listed next, followed by 30 body parts in which other angels work. This is followed by a list of 7 archons beginning with Michael, and then 5 more powers, for a total of 12.

After observing the reference to *seven angels* (*archons*) (9:24) in the AOJ,[6] Revelation was searched for the phrase *seven angels*, which is found 12 times. This example of dodecadal meter was added to Chapter Five at the occasion of this writing. In order to arrive at a dodecad of *seven angels* (*archons*), the AOJ writer must have followed the variant in Revelation 16:17, which is only found in Textus Receptus (see Chapter Five, *seven angels*). This indicates that the AOG contains the earliest known reference to Revelation, as evidenced by the inclusion of this metered phrase from Textus Receptus, or more likely from an early manuscript on which Receptus relies. The AOJ writer's effort to duplicate repetition in Revelation also led to a search for the plural of *spirit* in Revelation. *Spirits* repeats 7 times in Revelation, and this heptad was also added to Chapter Five of this book.

The AOJ lists set in Hebraic meter record ridiculous detail and fantasy. The AOJ divides *Lord God* into *YHWH* (Lord) who is good, and *Eloim* (God) who is evil, a heretical distortion of the Old and New Testament. The AOJ writer is obsessed with recounting events of sexual depravity among the demigods, though he personally advocates Gnostic celibacy. It is not difficult to understand the early church fathers' revulsion against Gnosticism. The AOJ writer peddles salacious stories about semi-deities in the name of religion.

From a limited view of the original text through 2 English translations, the AOJ lacks understanding of:

1. Hebraic meter in polysyndeton (many ands);
2. Subsets within noncontiguous phrases;
3. Concurrent symmetry and asymmetry;
4. Repetition outside of Revelation; and
5. Differences between pagan rote and Hebraic meter.

In other words, meter in the AOJ is a clumsy counterfeit of the Hebrew genre found in Revelation. What is fascinating is the writer's recognition of metered repetition in Revelation, and his attempt to imi-

---

[6] Meyer, p. 73.

tate John's style in his own book. Who would have guessed it was possible to study the structure of Revelation through the AOJ's mimicry of John's style? This is like the FBI hiring a check forger to study banking.

In terms of deep structure, the AOJ writer does not comprehend the Hebraic aesthetic of concurrent asymmetric and symmetric meter. Rather, like one who doesn't let the carrots touch the peas on his plate, he isolates his metered literary elements, a clear indication of biblical forgery. He does not integrate abstraction and order.

In her book, *The Gnostic Gospels*, Elaine Pagels introduces the following heptad from a bizarre text that borders on the ridiculous. She offers only one comment, and we assume she has divided the text correctly, which is a question in her work.

> Another text, mysteriously entitled *The Thunder, Perfect Mind*, offers an extraordinary poem spoken in the voice of a feminine divine power:
>
>> For I am the first and the last.
>> I am the honored one and the scorned one,
>> I am the whore and the holy one,
>> I am the wife and the virgin....
>> I am the barren one, and many are her sons....
>> I am the silence that is incomprehensible...
>> I am the utterance of my name.[7]

Pagels offers no comment about heptadic meter, repetition, Genesis, the Gospel of John, or Revelation, nor any reference to Umberto Cassuto. The writer of *The Thunder, Perfect Mind* is clearly copying Revelation, as follows:

> I am the First
> and the Last:
> and the Living One,
> and I was dead;
> and, behold, I am alive for evermore, Amen;
> and I have the keys of death
> and Hades. (Rev. 1:17b-18)

---

[7] Elaine Pagels, *The Gnostic Gospels*, Vintage Books, Random House, New York, 1979, p. xvi.

In view of the above poem, and a clear heptad later in the text,[8] a search was made for *I Am* (ἐγώ εἰμι) in Revelation. This phrase also repeats 24 times in the Gospel of John, as shown in Chapter Four. Only Textus Receptus has 7 repetitions of ἐγώ εἰμι: Rev. 1:8, 11, 17; 2:23; 21:6; 22:13, 16. Revelation 1:11 is a variant rejected in the 2012 edition, including the phrase that follows it. In Revelation 1:18, as seen above, Christ refers to Himself as *I am* with just the verb εἰμι. This makes 7 references where Christ speaks about Himself as *I am*, another example of concurrent asymmetry and symmetry that apparently eluded the writer of *The Thunder, Perfect Mind*.

Approximately 1,850 years after it was written, the counterfeit apocalypse known as *The Apocryphon of John* serves an unexpected purpose. In his attempt to write a forgery purportedly written by the Apostle John, the AOJ writer proves that at least some were aware of meter in Revelation. This also means the AOJ writer, in his attempt to generate readership, inadvertently proved himself to be a rather expert textual critic, more astute than those who claim to have found the lost gospel of Q. Look at his accomplishment. The AOJ writer actually reproduces noncontiguous meter found in Revelation. Now 1,850 years later, professors who claim to have found Q show they lack the skill of the AOJ writer in their forgery. They have no concept of Hebraic meter in Matthew, Mark, Luke, and John.

The Quackery of Q

The so-called gospel of Q was referenced in the first 4 chapters of this book. One of the major advocates for Q is Burton L. Mack, author of *The Lost Gospel: The Book of Q & Christian Origins*.[9] The higher critics reject Cassuto's hard evidence of meter in Genesis, which is also found in the Gospels, yet they believe in Q. The name Q comes from the German word *Quelle*, which means *source*. Mack writes that Matthew, Mark, and Luke each copied Q independently. Matthew and Luke also copied Mark. Q is also said to be the part of Matthew and Luke that they copied directly from Q in addition to Mark.[10] In seeming contradiction, Mark is thought to be the first Gospel that copied Q.[11]

---

[8] *The Thunder, Perfect Mind*, translated by George W. MacRae, in James M. Robinson (ed.), *The Nag Hammadi Library*, rev. ed., HarperCollins, San Francisco, 1990, http://gnosis.org/naghamm/thunder.html (7/2015): "For I am knowledge and ignorance. I am shame and boldness. I am shameless; I am ashamed. I am strength and I am fear. I am war and peace. Give heed to me."
[9] Burton L. Mack, *The Lost Gospel: The Book of Q & Christian Origins*, HarperCollins, San Francisco, 1993.
[10] Ibid., p. 4.
[11] Ibid., p. 172.

Mack claims that the Q document has been discovered, even though there is not one fragment that proves there ever was a Q. He says Q is found in bits and pieces layered in the 4 Gospels, and in recently discovered ancient books, such as *The Epistle of Barnabas* in 1859, the *Didache* in 1875, the Coptic-Gnostic *Nag Hammadi Library* in 1945, and many books in the Dead Sea Scrolls in 1948. Since there is no copy of Q, Mack can claim it is in every document that references anything that hints at the message of the Gospels.

Mack says Q is about 225 verses long. He published 2 editions of Q in his book: the first edition is pure Q, or the original Q, and is 7 pages long;[12] the longer edition of Q, or the complete Q, is 21 pages.[13] To the average reader it is a rather disorganized jumble to which Mack has added numerous headings and subheadings in an attempt to make sense of it.

Burton Mack cites numerous 19th and 20th-century authors whose books contributed to the process of discovering Q, such as:

Karl Lachmann 1835	B. H. Streeter 1924
Christian Wilke 1838	Vincent Taylor 1933
Christian Weisse 1838	Siegfried Schulz 1972
H. J. Holtzmann 1863	Wolfgang Schenk 1981
Albert Schweitzer 1906	Athanasius Polag 1982
Adolf von Harnack 1907	Dieter Zeller 1984
Martin Dibelius 1919	Ivan Havener 1987
Rudolf Bultmann 1921	John Kloppenborg 1988

Mack approaches the subject as an investigative reporter writing an exposé on the Jesus myth. He reduces the Gospels to a collection of moralistic teachings and sayings.

The AOJ writer understands that a good forger must also copy the structure of the text. Basic principles of fine art make a distinction between form and content. Distortion of the form in the Gospels by Mack and his pantheon of Q hunters makes the content unintelligible. The following are a series of quotes from Mack's *The Lost Gospel, the Book of Q*. Notice his affinity for words like *fiction* and *myth*.

> The Jesus movement was attractive as a place to experiment with novel social notions and life-styles.[14]

---

[12] Ibid., pp. 73-80.
[13] Ibid., pp. 81-102.
[14] Ibid., p. 9.

> Upon a closer reading of the Gospels, [Protestant scholars] had to agree that the gospels contained a good bit of mythology and too many miracles for comfort.[15]
>
> In spite of knowing that Mark's gospel was a fiction, the setting and logic of his story still served as the frame of reference for understanding the sayings and themes in Q^2....[16]
>
> Mythmaking in the Jesus movement at the Q^2 stage was an act of creative borrowing and the clever rearrangement of fascinating figures from several other vibrant mythologies of the time.[17]
>
> [Q] achieved this unified mythology by merging all the earlier mythological concepts in the single figure of the son of God.[18]
>
> The Christ myth created a much more fantastic imaginary universe than anything encountered in the Jesus traditions.[19]
>
> ...it was Q that the authors of the narrative gospels used as a foundation upon which to build their own novel myths of origin.[20]

Mack speaks about 7 clusters of rhetorical units in Q that all address a coherent set of issues to the same audience. Of course, he is the one who organizes the sayings into 7 clusters. The 7 clusters are now recognized as the remains of the earliest collection of sayings in the Q tradition, the layer of material called Q^1.[21] In other words, in the absence of meter in the text, Mack arranges the clusters into his own heptadic outline. He then arranges the material in Q^2 into 14 blocks, or a double heptad.[22] This is rather ironic. He rejects the concept of Hebraic meter in the Gospels as they exist today, factors out data from Matthew, Mark, and Luke according to his own theory, and then imposes heptadic outlines on this data as if Q were originally written in Hebraic meter.

---

[15] Ibid., p. 17.
[16] Ibid., p. 47.
[17] Ibid., p. 149.
[18] Ibid., p. 174.
[19] Ibid., p. 219.
[20] Ibid., p. 245.
[21] Ibid., pp. 106-7, 109.
[22] Ibid., pp. 132-33.

Mack tells us, "In order to be certain about seams [in the text], a mastery of Greek syntax is required, but even in English translations thematic shifts are easily seen...."[23] He does not mention the Hebraic origin of heptadic division, or say anything about the need to master Hebrew syntax, while ignoring voluminous evidence that the Gospels often follow Hebrew syntax written in Greek. His entire research is conducted as if the Gospels were written in a vacuum isolated from the Old Testament. The word *Hebrew* does not even appear in his index.

Hundreds of examples of heptadic, decadal and dodecadal meter published in this book prove that Matthew, Mark, Luke, and John are following Moses, not Q. The complex Hebraic meter from Matthew that is published later in this conclusion is an example of a genre that could not possibly have been copied from the mythological Q.

Hundreds of universities spend enormous sums of money funding faculty, maintaining facilities, and publishing materials that promote academic quackery and voodoo exegesis as serious textual study endorsing Q. Without a physical scrap of evidence, Mack tallies up—as historical 'fact'—175 years of canonized fantasies about the New Testament, because enough people have said it was so. That which he claims the most, is that which he has the least, namely, analytical skills.

How Was Meter Placed in the Text?

The reader cannot bridge the chasm. If there is meter in the text, the text cannot possibly be the product of collated, edited, redacted, conflated, or expanded myths. Intricate meter in the text could not have survived the editorial juggernaut of the J E P D committees without disturbing the work of the original author. The Masoretes could not have retro-engineered meter found in the Gospels back into the Hebrew text 600 years later. Paisley is not an accident.

A few observations on the purpose of these metered words have already been offered in this book. However, this writer has refrained from directly addressing the following questions until now. "How were these metered phrases placed in the text?" "Is their origin human or divine?"

The Doctrine of Divine Inspiration views the text as the verbally transmitted, inspired, infallible, inerrant, plenary words of the Holy Spirit, written through the hands of the prophets and the apostles. This

---

[23] Ibid., p. 107.

doctrine also teaches that the Holy Spirit accommodated Himself to adopt the language, style, vocabulary, traditions, and vernacular of the individual authors. In other words, Moses wrote in a style according to his own unique personality, and Matthew wrote according to his own personality. According to this doctrine, if the meter was initiated by Moses, this was the manner in which God allowed him to communicate according to his own Hebraic genre. If the meter is a distinct characteristic of divine inspiration, it was incorporated by the Holy Spirit as He guided the author in writing the text.

Bullinger lists 217 figures of speech found in the Bible that are also found in human language, such as simile, metaphor, irony, hendiadys, metonymy, peristasis, polysyndeton, etc. The Doctrine of Divine Inspiration allows us to assume the prophets and apostles were aware that they were using these figures of speech in the text, if they had the education to recognize them. But, were they aware of the Hebraic meter they were writing in the text when they wrote it?

The Bible itself does not name any of the 217 figures of speech used in its texts. Likewise, it does not tell us which words are nouns, verbs, adjectives, adverbs, prepositions, participles, or infinitives, nor does it explain its own grammar. All of this must be discerned by the reader. So also the Bible does not tell us that the apostles and prophets incorporated a myriad of metered words and phrases in their books. The Bible gives little or no explanation about the process of its own creation, other than stating that its pages are the written word of God. Essentially, the critics have invented their own mythology for the creation of the Bible that does not resemble the artifact at hand.

The questions remain: "How were these metered phrases placed in the text?" "Is their origin human or divine?" The answers must be found in the text itself. To address these questions, let us examine the following 2 examples, one from Exodus and the other from Matthew:

Blue and purple and scarlet and fine linen twisted 14 times in Exodus
    Blue and purple and scarlet and fine linen twisted (Exod. 26:31)
    Blue and purple and scarlet and fine linen twisted (Exod. 26:36)
    Blue and purple and scarlet and fine linen twisted (Exod. 27:16)
    Blue and purple,   scarlet and fine linen twisted (Exod. 28:6)
    Blue and purple and scarlet and fine linen twisted (Exod. 28:8)
    Blue and purple and scarlet and fine linen twisted (Exod. 28:15)
    Fine linen twisted and **blue** and purple and scarlet (Exod. 36:8)
    Blue and purple and scarlet and fine linen twisted (Exod. 36:35)
    Blue and purple and scarlet and fine linen twisted (Exod. 36:37)
    Blue and purple and scarlet and fine linen twisted (Exod. 38:18)

Blue and purple and scarlet and fine linen twisted (Exod. 39:2)
Blue and purple and scarlet and fine linen twisted (Exod. 39:5)
Blue and purple and scarlet and fine linen twisted (Exod. 39:8)
Fine linen twisted and **blue** and purple and scarlet (Exod. 39:29)

(Exod. 26:31) תְּכֵלֶת וְאַרְגָּמָן וְתוֹלַעַת שָׁנִי וְשֵׁשׁ מָשְׁזָר
(Exod. 26:36) תְּכֵלֶת וְאַרְגָּמָן וְתוֹלַעַת שָׁנִי וְשֵׁשׁ מָשְׁזָר
(Exod. 27:16) תְּכֵלֶת וְאַרְגָּמָן וְתוֹלַעַת שָׁנִי וְשֵׁשׁ מָשְׁזָר
(Exod. 28:6) תְּכֵלֶת וְאַרְגָּמָן תּוֹלַעַת שָׁנִי וְשֵׁשׁ מָשְׁזָר
(Exod. 28:8) תְּכֵלֶת וְאַרְגָּמָן וְתוֹלַעַת שָׁנִי וְשֵׁשׁ מָשְׁזָר
(Exod. 28:15) תְּכֵלֶת וְאַרְגָּמָן וְתוֹלַעַת שָׁנִי וְשֵׁשׁ מָשְׁזָר
(Exod. 36:8) שֵׁשׁ מָשְׁזָר וּתְכֵלֶת וְאַרְגָּמָן וְתוֹלַעַת שָׁנִי
(Exod. 36:35) תְּכֵלֶת וְאַרְגָּמָן וְתוֹלַעַת שָׁנִי וְשֵׁשׁ מָשְׁזָר
(Exod. 36:37) תְּכֵלֶת וְאַרְגָּמָן וְתוֹלַעַת שָׁנִי וְשֵׁשׁ מָשְׁזָר
(Exod. 38:18) תְּכֵלֶת וְאַרְגָּמָן וְתוֹלַעַת שָׁנִי וְשֵׁשׁ מָשְׁזָר
(Exod. 39:2) תְּכֵלֶת וְאַרְגָּמָן וְתוֹלַעַת שָׁנִי וְשֵׁשׁ מָשְׁזָר
(Exod. 39:5) תְּכֵלֶת וְאַרְגָּמָן וְתוֹלַעַת שָׁנִי וְשֵׁשׁ מָשְׁזָר
(Exod. 39:8) תְּכֵלֶת וְאַרְגָּמָן וְתוֹלַעַת שָׁנִי וְשֵׁשׁ מָשְׁזָר
(Exod. 39:29) שֵׁשׁ מָשְׁזָר וּתְכֵלֶת וְאַרְגָּמָן וְתוֹלַעַת שָׁנִי

There was a rather detailed explanation of meter in the above example in Chapter Nine. It should be noted that the Hebrew word for *scarlet*, תּוֹלַעַת (tôla›at), can also be written as תלעת (Exodus 26:1) with the same pronunciation and meaning, but one has the full hōlem ו (which looks like a *waw* ו with a dot above it) and the other has the hōlem as a dot over the consonant. The computer search for the above example does not work if the full hōlem ו is not used. In fact, the entire meter in all 3 related phrases is lost if the full hōlem is not used in *scarlet*. This point is made in order to demonstrate the precision with which the meter in the text is arranged.

Let us assume Moses was fully aware of this process. How might he have included this Hebraic repetition in Exodus? Aesthetically speaking, other related words orbit around the double heptad. If we were going to duplicate this style, we could start by recording the above double heptad on a separate piece of parchment, while making sure that the correct number of the Hebrew words for *scarlet* with the full hōlem are used, instead of the words for *scarlet* with the hōlem. Then each of the 14 lines could be inserted intermittently as the text was written. In the process, related words and phrases, including 12 variations of phrases with *blue and purple and scarlet*, would be written between and around the 14 lines in order to disguise the entire arrangement from the perception of the uninformed reader. The entire double heptad in Exodus covers 13 chapters. No one would be aware of this meter except an inner circle of priests and/or scribes. As a Hebrew genre, this approach in the hands of Moses could be incorporated into the text, just like any other figure of speech, under the guidance of the Holy Spirit in accord with the understanding of the Doctrine of Divine Inspiration.

As seen in the 11 tôledôth [generation] formulas in Genesis, there are 11 repetitions in Exodus of the formula *And the LORD spake unto Moses, saying*, וַיְדַבֵּר יְהוָה אֶל־מֹשֶׁה לֵּאמֹר. One of them has a slightly different setting. Exodus is divided into 12 sections by these 11 phrases (6:10, 29; 13:1; 14:1; 16:11; *25:1; 30:11, 17, 22; 31:1*; 40:1). The italicized verse numbers are the 5 sections that contain the 26 repetitions of *blue and purple and scarlet*. They are all found between 25:1 and 39:43. The number of *and*s (Hebrew *waw*s) in these 5 divisions of Exodus is 1,260, the same as the number of days in Daniel's *times, time, and half a time* (12:7), and Revelation's *time, times, and half a time* (12:14)—1,260, and 42 months.[24] The addition of *and* before *scarlet* at Exodus 28:6 in the example above would disrupt numerous overlapping and related Hebraic meters that would reverberate through the Bible. It should also be noted that discovery of the tôledôth [generation] formulas generated an entire book by Wiseman in 1936, while this equally significant phrase in Exodus is given one paragraph in this chapter. There is simply too much data.

Now, let us take a look at the following decad from Matthew:

Spoken…through…the prophet saying 10 times in the Gospel of Matthew
That which was fulfilled spoken…through…the prophet saying 7 times

In order that **might be fulfilled** that which was spoken by the Lord **through** the prophet saying (Matt. 1:22)
In order that **might be fulfilled** that which was spoken by the Lord **through** the prophet saying (Matt. 2:15)
In order that **might be fulfilled** what was spoken **through** Isaiah the prophet, saying (Matt. 4:14)
That it **might be fulfilled** which was spoken **through** Isaiah the prophet (Matt. 8:17)
In order that **might be fulfilled** what was spoken **through** Isaiah the prophet, saying (Matt. 12:17)
That it **might be fulfilled** which was spoken **through** the prophet, saying (Matt. 13:35)
In order that **might be fulfilled** that which was spoken **through** the prophet saying (Matt. 21:4)
Then that which **was spoken through** Jeremiah the prophet was fulfilled, saying (Matt. 2:17)
For this is he that **was spoken** of **through** the prophet Isaiah, saying (Matt. 3:3)
Then that which **was spoken through** Jeremiah the prophet was fulfilled, saying (Matt. 27:9)

ἵνα **πληρωθῇ** τὸ ῥηθὲν ὑπὸ κυρίου **διὰ** τοῦ προφήτου λέγοντος (Matt. 1:22 BNT)
ἵνα **πληρωθῇ** τὸ ῥηθὲν ὑπὸ κυρίου **διὰ** τοῦ προφήτου λέγοντος (Matt. 2:15 BNT)
ἵνα **πληρωθῇ** τὸ ῥηθὲν **διὰ** Ἠσαΐου τοῦ προφήτου λέγοντος (Matt. 4:14 BNT)
ὅπως **πληρωθῇ** τὸ ῥηθὲν **διὰ** Ἠσαΐου τοῦ προφήτου λέγοντος (Matt. 8:17 BNT)
ἵνα **πληρωθῇ** τὸ ῥηθὲν **διὰ** Ἠσαΐου τοῦ προφήτου λέγοντος (Matt. 12:17 BNT)

---

[24] Daniel 4:16, 23, 25, 32, and 12:7 expresses the concept of 3½ years, seven seasons, times, time, and 1/2 a time, 720 + 360 + 180 days = 1,260 days, or 42 months. The middle of the week in Dan. 9:27 is fulfilled in Christ's crucifixion and expressed symbolically in 1,260 days (Rev. 12:6). In Rev. 12:14, time, times, and half a time symbolizes the entire era of the Church on earth for the gathering of souls for heaven, from the time of Christ until the end of the world. Christ is the 42nd person in Matthew's genealogy. Theoretically, the second half of the week is completed and symbolized in the 42 months of the beast's power (Rev. 13:5).

ὅπως **πληρωθῇ** τὸ ῥηθὲν **διὰ**   τοῦ προφήτου λέγοντος (Matt. 13:35 BNT)
ἵνα **πληρωθῇ** τὸ ῥηθὲν **διὰ**   τοῦ προφήτου λέγοντος (Matt. 21:4 BNT)
τότε ἐπληρώθη τὸ ῥηθὲν **διὰ** Ἰερεμίου τοῦ προφήτου λέγοντος (Matt. 2:17 BNT)*
οὗτος γάρ ἐστιν ὁ ῥηθεὶς **διὰ** Ἠσαΐου τοῦ προφήτου λέγοντος (Matt. 3:3 BNT)**
τότε ἐπληρώθη τὸ ῥηθὲν **διὰ** Ἰερεμίου τοῦ προφήτου λέγοντος (Matt. 27:9 BNT)
The following have ὑπὸ (by) instead of διὰ (through).
*Τότε ἐπληρώθη τὸ ῥηθὲν ὑπὸ Ἰερεμίου τοῦ προφήτου, λέγοντος (Matt. 2:17 BYZ, GOC, SCR, STE).
**ὁ ῥηθεὶς ὑπὸ Ἠσαΐου τοῦ προφήτου, λέγοντος (Matt. 3:3 BYZ, GOC, SCR, STE).

There are 3 different repeated phrases in this metered text. The longest phrase (a heptad) is *in order that might be fulfilled that which was spoken...through the prophet saying*. Notice the bold type to the left in Greek and English above. There are 7 verbs in the same tense. There is a shorter decad which states, *that which was spoken through... the prophet saying*. The shortest phrase (a dodecad) reads, *through...the prophet saying*, as seen below:

Through...the prophet 12 times in the Gospel of Matthew
    Through   the **prophet saying** (Matt. 1:22)
    Through   the **prophet**   (Matt. 2:5)
    Through   the **prophet saying** (Matt. 2:15)
    Through **Jeremiah** the **prophet saying** (Matt. 2:17)
    Through **Isaiah**   the **prophet saying** (Matt. 3:3)
    Through **Isaiah**   the **prophet saying** (Matt. 4:14)
    Through **Isaiah**   the **prophet saying** (Matt. 8:17)
    Through **Isaiah**   the **prophet saying** (Matt. 12:17)
    Through   the **prophet saying** (Matt. 13:35)
    Through   the **prophet saying** (Matt. 21:4)
    Through **Daniel**   the **prophet**   (Matt. 24:15)
    Through **Jeremiah** the **prophet saying** (Matt. 27:9)

    διὰ............τοῦ **προφήτου λέγοντος** (Matt. 1:22 BNT)
    διὰ............τοῦ **προφήτου**............ (Matt. 2:5 BNT)
    διὰ............τοῦ **προφήτου λέγοντος** (Matt. 2:15 BNT)
    διὰ Ἰερεμίου τοῦ **προφήτου λέγοντος** (Matt. 2:17 BNT)
    διὰ Ἠσαΐου τοῦ **προφήτου λέγοντος** (Matt. 3:3 BNT)
    διὰ Ἠσαΐου τοῦ **προφήτου λέγοντος** (Matt. 4:14 BNT)
    διὰ Ἠσαΐου τοῦ **προφήτου λέγοντος** (Matt. 8:17 BNT)
    διὰ Ἠσαΐου τοῦ **προφήτου λέγοντος** (Matt. 12:17 BNT)
    διὰ............τοῦ **προφήτου λέγοντος** (Matt. 13:35 BNT)
    διὰ............τοῦ **προφήτου λέγοντος** (Matt. 21:4 BNT)
    διὰ Δανιὴλ....τοῦ **προφήτου**............ (Matt. 24:15 BNT)
    διὰ Ἰερεμίου τοῦ **προφήτου λέγοντος** (Matt. 27:9 BNT)

In the example from the Greek, all 3 meters are present at the same time. The word *through* (διὰ) appears 12 times; there are 7 names of the prophets; the word *prophets* (προφήτου) appears 12 times; and there are 10 participles for *saying* (λέγοντος).

Conclusion

As in the example from Exodus, there is pattern within pattern within pattern. It is in the mind of the writer to integrate a variety of meter within a larger, more complex meter. This could be compared to various melodies coordinated in a work by Bach.

There is a fair amount of certainty that this is the first time these examples of Hebraic meter in Exodus and Matthew have been published. This repetition in Exodus was not translated into the Septuagint, thus revealing the inaccuracy and paraphrastic nature of the Septuagint. There is also the possibility that the Septuagint translators understood how much meter is actually in the Hebrew text, and realized that it would not be possible to translate the meter into another language. The Vulgate is more accurate than the Septuagint and follows much of the repetition from the Hebrew.[25] Therefore, we can assume the only way for Matthew to have actually seen meter in any text, and to have learned how to incorporate it into his Greek Gospel, would have been his familiarity with the Hebrew. However, we are often told by scholars, incorrectly it now appears, that the apostles could not read Hebrew.

Humanly speaking, it could be assumed that Matthew also created this list of phrases on a separate piece of parchment, and wrote the lines into the text as he proceeded through his Gospel. This is an attempt to offer a plausible explanation for these 2 examples in the text.

Three Impossibilities

Credulity reaches its limits, not with the existence of the above examples from Exodus and Matthew, or a few more, but with the vast number and complexity of metered phrases recorded in this book from Genesis, Exodus, Song of Solomon, Daniel, Matthew, Mark, Luke, John, Revelation and other parts of Scripture.

> First, "How did these writers keep track of all of the metered phrases, and so many more that permeate the Old and New Testaments?" This book records no more than 1% of the repetition in the Bible.

---

[25] It would be interesting to compare Codex Amiatinus, the oldest copy of the Vulgate from 716 A.D., with Vulgata Clementina (revised in 1598) and the Septuagint. But at this time the Codex Amiatinus is not available for examination except for a purchase fee of $20,000 for a facsimile. A copy of the Vulgate from 1535 contains the same numbers in Genesis 5 as the Hebrew text. Sacrae bibliae. in quo continentur quinque libri Moysi, libri Iosue, et Iudicum, liber Psalmorum, Prouerbia, Salomonis, liber Sapientie, et Nouum Testamentum Iesu Christi. Tomus primus Tomus primus. Londini: Excudebat Thomas Betheletus, 1535.

Second, "How does anyone explain that this Hebraic genre crosses 2 languages but is not recorded from the Hebrew into the Septuagint?"

Third, "Why is there no historical record of this meter or reference to it?"

Fourth, "How did each writer in the Bible know they were supposed to write metered phrases in heptads, decads, and dodecads into the text?"

The only rebuttal from the archeologist cited in the last chapter is that the Masoretes retro-engineered meter into their own Hebrew text, but he had no explanation for why they would happen to copy the genre of metered phrases found in the Gospels. He also had no explanation for how the ages of the patriarchs in the Masoretic Text were the same as in the Vulgate, which predates the Masoretes by at least 300-600 years.

This writer's opinion is that the complexity, extent, coordination, and permeation of Hebraic meter in the Bible is beyond the capabilities of human writers. This also means the texts were copied accurately by hand. Many of the examples in this book could not have been identified without a computer, let alone created without a computer. Logic leads to 3 impossible conclusions:

1. The biblical writers did not know they were writing in heptadic, decadal, or dodecadal meter until they had written their text and examined their own writing – if they were aware of it at all.
2. The biblical writers are responsible for all of the metered words and phrases in the Bible.
3. There is no Hebraic meter in the Old and New Testaments, and all of the data in this book is contrived by the creative mind of the author.

After point 3 was typed, it was noticed that the Hebrew phrase for *fruitful and multiply* repeats 10 times in Genesis, and *stretch out your hand* or *staff* with the same verb repeats 10 times in Exodus. In addition, 70 repetitions of complex phrases in the Pentateuch and Ezekiel is beyond the realm of probability. Anyone can check this data for themselves, as found in Chapter Eight. There is simply too much data to support the third conclusion.

The second choice is equally impossible. The capability of the apostles to reproduce Hebraic meter with such accuracy in their Gospels defies credulity, and the preservation of this meter in the text after all these millennia is astonishing.

Humanly speaking, the first choice is also impossible. It broaches the subject of the divine style, which cannot be proven. There is no point of comparison. Therefore, the origin and preservation of the biblical text is as mysterious as the message it records. This book has raised far more questions than it has answered about the origin of the Bible. Let the reader decide which of the 3 choices is correct, unless there are more reasonable possibilities. The Bible remains a book of miracles. The text itself becomes a paradigm for the 2 natures of Christ, simultaneously human and divine. No one could observe that He was divine by watching Him walk the streets of Jerusalem.

Many of those who witnessed miracles in the Old Testament, and Christ's miracles in the New Testament, no matter how verifiable, remained skeptics. Faith is required to believe a miracle, even when witnessed with one's own eyes. Pharaoh's chariots pursued the Israelites through the canyon of divided Red Sea water, even though they knew that water does not form walls. Many who saw, heard, and experienced Jesus' miracles responded without faith, such as 9 of the 10 lepers; the 5,000 who were fed in the desert; and the man who continued to arrest Jesus after his ear was restored. Faith is required to believe miraculous events in the Bible, even by eyewitnesses, including the soldiers guarding Christ's tomb, and the High Priest who plotted to kill Lazarus in order to get rid of the evidence. The God who was rejected to His face at Eden is now only believed by faith. The conclusion is that agreement with the Bible is an act of faith, regardless of how many computer programs prove there is meter in the text.

The grass withers, the flower fades:
but the word of our God shall stand for ever (Isaiah 40:8)

Appendix A

Calculations From A University Mathematician

I worked a bit on the problem, and realized that my initial thought was not quite right. I think that the student you talked with was on the right track. So far this is what I can do:

If you specify 9 numbers, and look for a 10th which satisfies your rules about divisibility, and where the 10th number is not among the 3 smallest numbers in the set of ten, then you can find the 10th number using this formula:

76*(the sum of the 9 numbers) + 42*(the sum of the 6 largest numbers of the 9 you specify) - 119*n where n is a whole number. In your case for the antediluvian ages, the sum of the 9 smallest ages is 7606, and the sum of the larger 6 of those is 5569, so the formula is 76*7606+42*5569-n*119=811954-119*n. The remainder of 811954 modulo 119 is 17. You get that with n=6823. However, if we need our number to be among the 7 largest ones, it must be at least 895. With n=6815, we get 969. With n=6816, we get 850 which is too small. 969 is the smallest solution that satisfies both the divisibility constraints and also is at least 895. Of course we can keep adding 119 to 969 and we will get an infinite number of additional solutions 1088, 1207, 1326,...

When I try the same rule with the postdiluvian numbers, I get 76*2571+42*2043-119*n=281202-119*n. Possible values that show up are 243, 362, 481, 600, 719, 838 etc. The desired value of 600 shows up, but, it is not the first solution that is sufficiently large. Even if we had specified that our missing number had to be the largest age, the constraint would have been satisfied by the value of 481.

I have also looked at the case where the missing number is one of the 3 smaller ones. In that case, you get a different formula, but the solution is not so special.

The formula is:
118*(sum of the 9 specified numbers)+84*(sum of the 7 largest specified numbers)-119*m where m is a whole number. You can check that this works with the antediluvian numbers if you exclude 365. In that case you get the sum of the 9 numbers as 8210 and of the 7 larger numbers as 6538. The formula becomes 1517972-119*m. Using

m=12753 we recover the value of 365, but, other possible values are 8, 127, 246, 484, 603, and 722.

If you want to allow the missing number to be either in the set of the 3 smallest or in the 7 largest, I do not have a single formula that I can use. I suspect that the unknown n's and m's in my formulas could be defined a bit better if I can use some more complicated functions in the formula (the floor function or some other sort of rounding function).

Here is how the formula 76*(the sum of the 9 numbers) + 42*(the sum of the 6 largest numbers of the 9 you specify) - 119*n is arrived at.

We are looking for a number (call it X) so that when it is added to the sum of the 9 numbers (call that sum S) is divisible by 7, and when twice that number (2X) is added to S and also to the sum of the 6 larger numbers of the 9 specified (call that sum L) is divisible by 17. We can write that as X+S = 0 modulo 7 and 2X+S+L=0 modulo 17.

We can rewrite those modular equalities as X=-S mod 7 and 2X=-S-L mod 17.

Now we need to use a very neat trick that allows us to effectively divide through by 2 when we work modulo 17. Since 2*9=18=1 modulo 17, multiplying by 9 modulo 17 accomplishes the same thing as dividing by 2. That allows us to write X=9*2*X=-9(S+L) mod 17.

That means we are looking for a number X which is -S modulo 7 and which is -9(S+L) modulo 17.

There is a famous theorem called the Chinese remainder theorem first published in the 3rd to 5th centuries by Chinese mathematician Sun Tzu (according to Wikipedia) . It says that if you have two simultaneous congruences, and the moduli do not share any common factors (in this case that is that 7 and 17 have no factors in common), then you can find a unique solution modulo the product of the moduli (in this case modulo 119). Say we have congruences X=A mod 7 and X=B mod 17. If we find numbers c and d so that 7c=1 modulo 17 and 17d=1 modulo 7, then setting X=A*(17*d)+B*(7*c), we see that modulo 7, X=A*(17*d)=A*1=A, and modulo 17, X=B*(7*c)=B*1=B. It is also true that adding or subtracting any multiple of 7*17=119 will not change this result.

In our case, it is easy to check that 7*5=35=1+2*17=1 modulo 17, and 17*5=85=1+12*7=1 modulo 7 so we can use c=d=5. (There is a that can be used to find the right values for c and d). To get the congruences we need for our X, we use X=-S(17*5)-9(S+L)(7*5) modulo 119.

APPENDIX A

I want to simplify this a bit, so I group together all the terms involving S to get X=(-17*5-9*7*5)S-(9*7*5)L modulo 119.

Finally I reduce the coefficients modulo 119 using that -17*5-9*7*5=-400=76-4*119=76 modulo 119, and -9*7*5=-315=42-3*119=42 modulo 119.

This gives the formula X=76*S+42*L mod 119 or equivalently X=76*S+42*L-119*n for some whole number n.

It does all seem pretty complicated, but, each step just relies on the properties of modular arithmetic. Most of the ordinary things that you can do with algebraic equations also work for arithmetic modulo some number (called the modulus). Division is the operation that is a bit tricky, but as you saw, we replaced dividing by 2 by multiplying by 9 modulo 17. That kind of trick can always be worked providing the number you want to invert shares no factors with the modulus.

If you prefer, you can just produce the formula and verify directly that it produces the desired results:

We can check that the calculation works directly by adding X to S X+S=76*S+42*L-119*n+S=77*S+42*L-119*n=7(11*S+6*L-17*n) and of course that is divisible by 7. Adding 2X to S+L we get 2X+S+L=154*S+84*L-2*119*n+S+L=153*S+85*L-2*119*n=17(9*S+5*L-14*n) and that is divisible by 17.

Your other constraint for the 10th number is that it should be larger than the smallest 3 numbers from your original 9 in the sum S. (If it were not, then the new number would not need to be added twice, and the calculation would change.) This can always be arranged by adding multiples of 119 to X (i.e. making the value of n smaller in the formula for X).

Regarding the math that the Hebrews or other ancients knew, you may want to consult a math historian to get more depth. Sometimes special cases or more cumbersome variants of algorithms or theorems may have been known, and those may not make it into Wikipedia etc. I would like to ask one of my colleagues about this issue if that is OK with you. I do not need to describe your observations, but, I would need to explain the question of whether the ancients might have been able to solve this sort of divisibility problem.

Appendix B

Calculations From Mathematician Matthew Swanson

I agree entirely with your math contact who worked this through. Here is my re-write of the process, attempting to smooth it out.

First, here is the equation when you are looking to find which numbers (variable D) would work if you are trying to pick the final number in the set to make our constraints hold. Remember the number must not be one of the three smallest in our set of 9 (or 10).

> $A = $ Sum of **nine** (out of the ten) numbers in our set
> $B = $ Sum of the **six** largest numbers of those nine
> $C = $ Any Integer
> $D = $ Our final number to meet all of our constraints
> Our equation is as follows: $D = 76A + 42B - 119C$

Here is a table to show this for your two lists, antediluvian and postdiluvian. I took Methuselah (969) from the first and Shem (600) from the second. However, remember that we could remove any one of the 7 largest from our list(s) and this formula would still find us possible answers for our number we removed. Our smallest D is the smallest positive number our formula gives while still being one of the 7 largest numbers in our set of ten. You can take the smallest D and add 119 as many times as you want and it still satisfies our set constraints and equation.

Names	A	B	76A	42B	76A+42B	D=?	Smallest D
Ante-D	7606	5569	578056	233898	811954	811954 – 119C	969
Post-D	2571	2043	195396	85806	281202	281202 – 119C	243

Now, here is the equation when you are looking to find which numbers (variable D) would work if you are trying to pick the final number in the set to make our constraints hold. However, now the number must be one of the three smallest in our set of 9 (or 10).

> $X = $ Sum of **nine** (out of the ten) numbers in our set
> $Y = $ Sum of the **Seven** largest numbers of those nine
> $Z = $ Any Integer
> $W = $ Our final number to meet all of our constraints
> Our equation is as follows: $W = 118X + 84Y - 119Z$

Here is a table to show this for your two lists, antediluvian and postdiluvian. This time I took Enoch (365) from the first and Nahor (148) from the second. However, remember that we could remove any one of the 3 smallest from our list(s) and this formula would still find us possible answers for our number we removed. "Possible values for W" lists **all** possible values that would complete our set and still be one of the 3 smallest elements. The one I removed is highlighted, demonstrating that this equation does hold for our two lists.

Names	X	Y	118X	84Y	118X+84Y	W=?	Possible values for W
Ante-D	8210	6538	968780	549192	1517972	1517972 – 119Z	8; 127; 246; **365**; 484; 603; 722; 841
Post-D	3023	2643	356714	222012	578726	578726 – 119Z	29; 148;

Interestingly enough, it is impossible for the equation to create a number that works for my set. Obviously it produces outputs; however the closest ones were -15 and 104. One is not a possible age while the other is too large to be one of the 3 smallest ones. The reason that this does not work is simply because of how limiting my example set is, not because the equation is flawed.

[As] you have said, each of these sets can really be treated as a single variable, because no matter what 9 numbers you start with, it is possible to create a 10th number that makes our constraints (the divisibility) hold. In fact, to test that, here is an example of 9 random numbers and we will try to cook up a tenth number, first that is one of the 7 largest, and then one that is one of the 3 smallest.

Example: The {1, 8, 19, 37, 68, 94, 112, 125, 160}

Names	A	B	76A	42B	76A+42B	D=?	Smallest D
Matt ex.	624	596	47424	25032	72456	72456 – 119C	104

So if we add a number to our set, it must be 104 +119C. So 104, 223, 342,... up to infinity. Now let's try to find a number that is the smallest.

Names	X	Y	118X	84Y	118X+84Y	W=?	Possible values for W
Matt ex.	624	615	73632	51660	125292	125292 – 119Z	**None**

Interestingly enough, it is impossible for the equation to create a number that works for our set. Obviously it produces outputs, however the closest ones were -15 and 104. One is not a possible age while the other is too large to be one of the 3 smallest ones.

Conclusion:

So what does this all mean? Honestly I'm not 100% sure. However, this equation confirms that at most one out of every 119 numbers satisfies this equation, at least when you are looking for a large number to add to the set. When you try to find a number to add that is one of the 3 smallest in the set, it limits us even more, sometimes making the set impossible to complete in the way that we would want. However, these equations do prove that for any set you can find a 10th number that completes it with the divisibility constraints that we wanted (related to 7 and 17).

The notes you sent me said that he thought the first equation for finding large numbers is more interesting. However, I personally am more intrigued by the second equation, as its outputs are even more limiting, and make fudging one of the three smallest numbers a bit more difficult, especially with small numbers.

Sorry I don't have much more for you, but all in all, I think these equations are very useful (and correct) while still supporting how unlikely it is to be able to construct one of these sets with just basic mathematics.

Good luck with your meetings and continued work.

Best Regards,
Matt Swanson
matthewjohnswanson@gmail.com

WORKS CITED

Achtemeier, Paul J., *"Omne Verbum Sonat*: The New Testament and the Oral Environment of Late Western Antiquity," *Journal of Biblical Literature*, Vol. 109, No. 1, 1990.

Alford, Henry, *The New Testament for English Readers*, Vol. II, 1852, revised 1871, 7th ed. 1877, Rivingtons, London, Oxford, Cambridge, Guardian Press, Grand Rapids, MI, 1976.

"The Apocryphon of John," translated by Frederik Wisse, in James M. Robinson (ed.), *The Nag Hammadi Library*, rev. ed., HarperCollins, San Francisco, 1990, http://gnosis.org/naghamm/apocjn.html (7/2015).

Archimedes, *The Sand Reckoner of Archimedes*, translated by Thomas Heath, Cambridge University Press, 1897, Forgotten Books, www.forgottenbooks.org, 2008.

Aune, David E., *Revelation*, 3 vols., World Biblical Commentary 52, Thomas Nelson, Nashville, 1997.

Barclay, John M. G., *Flavius Josephus: Translation and Commentary, Volume 10: Against Apion*, Brill, Leiden, The Netherlands, 2007.

Barclay, William, *The Gospel of Luke*, 3rd ed., The Westminster Press, Philadelphia, 1977.

Beale, Gregory K., *The Book of Revelation*, Eerdmans, Grand Rapids, MI, 1999.

Becker, James J. and Joshua J. Becker, *Unexpected Treasures: Finding Value in Bible Names, Dates, and Genealogies*, Northwestern Publishing House, Milwaukee, 2014.

Becker, Siegbert W., *Revelation: The Distant Triumph Song*, Northwestern Publishing House, Milwaukee, 1985.

BibleWorks 8, DVD-ROM, BibleWorks, LLC, Norfolk, VA, 2008.

Boismard, M. E., "'L'Apocalypse', ou 'les Apocalypses' de S. Jean," *Revue Biblique*, 56, 1949.

Breck, John, *The Shape of Biblical Language: Chiasmus in the Scriptures and Beyond*, reprint of St. Vladimir's Seminary Press, Crestwood, NY, 1994, Kaloros Press, Wadmalaw Island, SC, 2008.

Brighton, Louis, *Concordia Commentary, Revelation*, Concordia Publishing House, St. Louis, 1999.

Bullinger, Ethelbert William, *Figures of Speech Used in the Bible*, reprint of Eyre and Spottiswoode, London, 1898, Baker Book House, Grand Rapids, MI, 1968.

———, *Number in Scripture*, Eyre & Spottiswoode, London, 1894.

Buls, Harold, *Notes on the Gospel of Luke*, Concordia Theological Seminary Press, Fort Wayne, IN, 1977.

Cascione, Gioacchino Michael, *In Search of the Biblical Order: Patterns in the Text Affirming Divine Authorship from Revelation to Genesis*, RedeemerPress.org, Saint Clair Shores, MI, 2012.

———, J. M., *In Search of the Biblical Order*, Biblion, Fairview Park, OH, 1987.

Cassuto, Umberto Moshe David, *A Commentary on the Book of Exodus*, Jerusalem, 1951, translated by Israel Abrahams, Varda Books, Skokie, IL, 2005.

———, *A Commentary on the Book of Genesis: Part I from Adam to Noah, Genesis I-VI 8*, Jerusalem, 1944, translated by Israel Abrahams, Varda Books, Skokie, IL, 2005.

———, *A Commentary on the Book of Genesis: Part II from Noah to Abraham, Genesis VI 9-XI 32*, Jerusalem, 1949, translated by Israel Abrahams, Varda Books, Skokie, IL, 2005.

———, *The Documentary Hypothesis and the Composition of the Pentateuch*, Magnes Press, Jerusalem, 1941, translated by Israel Abrahams, Shalem Press, Jerusalem, 2006.

Charles, R. H., *A Critical and Exegetical Commentary on the Revelation of St. John*, Scribner's, New York, 1920.

Collins, Adela Yarbro, *The Combat Myth in the Book of Revelation*, Scholars Press, Missoula, MT, 1976.

Demoss, Matthew S., *Pocket Dictionary for the Study of New Testament Greek*, InterVarsity Press, Downer's Grove, IL, 2001.

Dorsey, David A., *The Literary Structure of the Old Testament: A Commentary on Genesis–Malachi*, Baker Academic, Grand Rapids, MI, 1999.

Works Cited

Duff, Jason, "The Whole Counsel of God—Job 38-42," sermon notes, March 27, 2013, http://media.calvaryvista.com/library/duff-jason/studies-books/18-JOB-2013/18-JOB-038-001.pdf (7/2015).

Farstad, Arthur L. and Zane C. Hodges, *The Greek New Testament According to the Majority Text*, Thomas Nelson, Nashville, 1982.

Franzmann, Martin H., *Follow Me: Discipleship According to Saint Matthew*, Concordia Publishing House, St Louis, 1961.

God's Word to the Nations: New Evangelical Translation, 3rd printing, Biblion Publishing, Cleveland, 1990.

Hendel, Ronald, *The Book of Genesis: a Biography*, Princeton University Press, Princeton, NJ, 2013.

Hervey, Lord Arthur, *The Genealogies of Our Lord and Saviour Jesus Christ, As Contained in the Gospels of Matthew and St. Luke*, Macmillan and Co., Cambridge, London, 1853, https://archive.org/stream/genealogiesourl01hervgoog#page (7/2015).

Jordan, James B., *A Chronological and Calendrical Commentary on the Pentateuch, Studies in Biblical Chronology No. 3*, Biblical Horizons, Niceville, FL, 2001.

———, "The Second Cainan Question," *Biblical Chronology*, Vol. II, No. 4, Nice, FL, 1990.

Just, Arthur, *Concordia Commentary, Luke 1:1-9:50*, Concordia Publishing House, St. Louis, 1996.

Kirby, Diana Jill, *Repetition in the Book of Revelation*, Ph.D. diss., ProQuest, Ann Arbor, MI, 2009.

Kuske, David P., *Biblical Interpretation: The Only Right Way*, Northwestern Publishing House, Milwaukee, 1997.

———, *1, 2 Thessalonians (The People's Bible)*, Northwestern Publishing House, Milwaukee, 2000.

———, *A Commentary on Romans 1-8*, Northwestern Publishing House, Milwaukee, 2007.

———, *A Commentary on Romans 9-16*, Northwestern Publishing House, Milwaukee, 2014.

———, *A Commentary on 1 & 2 Peter, Jude*, Northwestern Publishing House, Milwaukee, 2015.

Lenski, R. C. H., *The Interpretation of St. John's Revelation*, Wartburg Press, 1943, Augsburg Publishing House, Minneapolis, 1963.

———, *The Interpretation of St. Luke's Gospel*, Wartburg Press, 1946, Augsburg Publishing House, Minneapolis, 1961.

———, *The Interpretation of St. Matthew's Gospel*, Wartburg Press, 1943, Augsburg Publishing House, Minneapolis, 1961.

Lessing, R. Reed and Andrew E. Steinmann, *Prepare the Way of the Lord*, Concordia Publishing House, St. Louis, 2014.

Lowth, Bishop Robert, *De Sacra Poesi Hebraeorem, Praelectiones Academicae Oxonii Habitae*, Clarendon, Oxford, 1753, translated into English as *Lectures on the Sacred Poetry of the Hebrews*, J. Johnson, London, 1787.

Luther's Works, Vol. 2, *Lectures on Genesis, Chapters 6-14*, translated by George V. Schick, Concordia Publishing House, St. Louis, 1960.

Luther's Works, Vol. 15, *Ecclesiastes, Song of Solomon, Last Words of David, 2 Samuel 23:1-7*, Concordia Publishing House, St. Louis, 1972.

Luther's Works, Vol. 35, *Word and Sacrament I*, translated by E. Theodore Bachmann, Muhlenberg Press, Philadelphia, 1960.

Mack, Burton L., *The Lost Gospel: The Book of Q & Christian Origins*, HarperCollins, San Francisco, 1993.

Metzger, Bruce M., *The Text of the New Testament: Its Transmission, Corruption, and Restoration*, 2d ed., Oxford University Press, New York and Oxford, 1968.

Meyer, Marvin W., *The Secret Teachings of Jesus: Four Gnostic Gospels*, Random House, New York, 1984.

Mitchell, Christopher, *Concordia Commentary, The Song of Songs*, Concordia Publishing House, St. Louis, 2003.

Morris, Henry M., *The Genesis Record: A Scientific and Devotional Commentary on the Book of Beginnings*, Baker Book House, Grand Rapids, MI, 1976.

The Old Testament Pseudepigrapha, 2 vols., Ed. by James H. Charlesworth, Doubleday & Company, Garden City, NY, 1983.

Oppert, Julius, "Restoration of the Berosus Canon" and "On a Case of Singular Literary Forgery," in Robert K. Douglas (ed.), *Transactions of the Second Session of the International Congress of Orientalists*, Trübner & Co., London, 1876.

Pagels, Elaine, *The Gnostic Gospels*, Vintage Books, Random House, New York, 1979.

Pitts, M., "Gerald Hawkins: Astronomer who claimed Stonehenge was a computer," *The Guardian*, London, July 24, 2003. http://www.theguardian.com/news/2003/jul/24/guardianobituaries.highereducation (7/2015).

Rav-Noy, Eyal, and Gil Weinreich, *Who Really Wrote the Bible?*, Richard Vigilante Books, Minneapolis, 2010.

Schussler-Fiorenza, Elizabeth, *The Book of Revelation: Justice and Judgment*, Fortress Press, Philadelphia, 1985.

Soulen, Richard N. and R. Kendall Soulen, *Handbook of Biblical Criticism*, 3d ed., revised and expanded, Westminster John Knox Press, Louisville, KY, 2001.

Steinmann, Andrew E., *Daniel: Concordia Commentary*, Concordia Publishing House, St. Louis, 2008.

Sternberg, Meir, *The Poetics of Biblical Narrative: Ideological Literature and the Drama of Reading*, Indiana University Press, Bloomington, 1985.

Struik, Dirk J., *A Concise History of Mathematics*, rev. 4th ed., Dover Publications, Mineola, NY, 1987.

Swanson, Reuben J. (ed.), *New Testament Greek Manuscripts: Variant Readings Arranged in Horizontal Lines against Codex Vaticanus: Luke*, Sheffield Academic Press, Sheffield, England, William Carey International University Press, Pasadena, CA, 1995.

Theological Word Dictionary of the Old Testament, Ed. by Harris, Archer, and Waltke, Moody Bible Institute, Chicago, 1980.

The Thunder, Perfect Mind, translated by George W. MacRae, in James M. Robinson (ed.), *The Nag Hammadi Library*, rev. ed., HarperCollins, San Francisco, 1990, http://gnosis.org/naghamm/thunder.html (7/2015).

Watters, William R., *Formula Criticism and the Poetry of the Old Testament*, Beihefte zur Zeitschrift für die alttestamentliche Wissenschaft 138, De Gruyter, Berlin, New York, 1976.

Wiseman, P. J., *New Discoveries in Babylonia about Genesis*, Marshall, Morgan, & Scott, Ltd., London, Edinburgh, 4th ed., 1946, http://www.biblemaths.com/pdf_wiseman.pdf (7/2015).

IN SEARCH OF THE BIBLICAL ORDER, 2012

The assumptions, theories, and methodology of *Repetition in the Bible* are largely based on the research and opinions of authors quoted in the 2012 edition. In a number of respects, this current volume is a continuation and development of works cited in the 2012 edition that are not listed above.

Allen, Diogenes, *Philosophy for Understanding Theology*, Westminster John Knox Press, Louisville, 1985.

Baillie, John, *The Idea of Revelation in Recent Thought*, Columbia University Press, New York, 1956.

Barth, Karl, *Church Dogmatics*, Vol. II: *The Doctrine of God*, Scribner, New York, 1957, quoted by John Frame, "God and Biblical Language: Transcendence and Immanence," in John Warwick Montgomery (ed.), *God's Inerrant Word: An International Symposium on the Trustworthiness of Scripture*, Bethany Fellowship, Inc., Minneapolis, 1973.

———, *Kirchliche Dogmatik*, I, 2, quoted by Cornelius Van Til, *The New Modernism*, Presbyterian & Reformed, Philadelphia, 1946, quoted by Edward J. Young, *Thy Word Is Truth*, Eerdmans, Grand Rapids, MI, 1957.

Bonhoeffer, Dietrich, *No Rusty Swords: Letters, Lectures and Notes, 1928-1936*, Harper and Row, New York, 1965.

Brunner, Emil, *The Mediator*, Lutterworth, London, 1934.

———, *The Theology of Crisis*, Charles Scribner's Sons, New York, 1929, quoted by J. T. Mueller, "The Holy Spirit and the Scriptures," in Carl F. Henry (ed.), *Revelation and the Bible: Contemporary Evangelical Thought*, Baker Book House, Grand Rapids, MI, 1958.

Works Cited

Bultmann, Rudolf, "The New Testament and Mythology," translated by R. H. Fuller in H. W. Bartsch (ed.), *Kerygma and Myth*, Harper, New York, 1961.

———, *Theology of the New Testament*, Vol. I, translated by Kendrick Grobel, Charles Scribner's Sons, New York, 1955.

———, *Theology of the New Testament*, Vol. II, translated by Kendrick Grobel, Charles Scribner's Sons, New York, 1955.

Burke, Kenneth, *On Human Nature: A Gathering While Everything Flows*, University of California Press, Berkeley, 2003.

Calvin, John, *Institutes of the Christian Religion*, quoted by Kenneth S. Kantzer, "Calvin and the Holy Scriptures," in John W. Walvoord (ed.), *Inspiration and Interpretation*, Evangelical Theological Society, Eerdmans, Grand Rapids, MI, 1957.

Carnell, Edward John, "Reinhold Niebuhr's View of Scripture," in John W. Walvoord (ed.), *Inspiration and Interpretation*, Evangelical Theological Society, Eerdmans, Grand Rapids, MI, 1957.

Chemnitz, Martin, *The Two Natures in Christ*, translated by J. A. O. Preus, Concordia Publishing House, St. Louis, 1971.

Drosnin, Michael, *The Bible Code*, Simon and Schuster, New York, 1997.

Eusebius Pamphilus (339 A.D.), *The Ecclesiastical History of Eusebius Pamphilus*, translated by C. F. Cruse, published with Isaac Boyle, *A Historical View of The Council of Nice*, T. Mason and G. Lane, New York, 1839.

The Formula of Concord. Thor. Decl. VIII. Of the Person of Christ, Concordia Triglotta, Concordia Publishing House, St. Louis, 1921.

Friedman, Richard Elliott, *Who Wrote the Bible?*, Prentice Hall, Englewood Cliffs, NJ, 1987.

Harrison, James, *The Pattern & The Prophecy: God's Great Code*, Isaiah Publications, Peterborough, Ontario, 1994.

Henry, Carl F. H., *Divine Revelation and the Bible*, in John W. Walvoord (ed.), *Inspiration and Interpretation*, Evangelical Theological Society, Eerdmans, Grand Rapids, MI, 1957.

Hodge, A. A., *Outlines of Theology*, edited by W. H. Goold, London, Edinburgh, 1863, quoted by John Baillie, *The Idea of Revelation in Recent Thought*, Columbia University Press, New York, 1956.

Hopper, Grace M., *The Ungenerated Seven as an Index to Pythagorean Number Theory*, The American Mathematical Monthly, Vol. 43, No. 7, August-September 1936, pp. 409-13.

Hopper, Vincent Foster, *Medieval Number Symbolism*, republication of Columbia University Studies in English and Comparative Literature No. 132, Columbia University Press, New York, 1938, Cooper Square Publishers, Inc., New York, 1969.

Johnshoy, Joseph Walter, *The Masterkey to the Revelation of St. John the Divine: A Method of Interpretation*, The Author, Moorhead, MN, 1934.

Kantzer, Kenneth S., "Calvin and the Holy Scriptures," in John W. Walvoord (ed.), *Inspiration and Interpretation*, Evangelical Theological Society, Eerdmans, Grand Rapids, MI, 1957.

Kerr, David W., *Augustine of Hippo*, in John W. Walvoord (ed.), *Inspiration and Interpretation*, Evangelical Theological Society, Eerdmans, Grand Rapids, MI, 1957.

Liddell, Henry George, and Robert Scott, *A Greek-English Lexicon*, reprint of 9th edition, Oxford University Press, Oxford, 1978.

Luther's Works, Vol. 1, Lectures on Genesis, Chapters 1-5, Concordia Publishing House, St. Louis, 1999 (1958).

Luther's Works, Vol. 4, Lectures on Genesis, Chapters 21-25, Concordia Publishing House, St. Louis, 1964.

Luther's Works, Vol. 5, Lectures on Genesis, Chapters 26-30, Concordia Publishing House, St. Louis, 1968.

Luther's Works, Vol. 9, Lectures on Deuteronomy, Concordia Publishing House, St. Louis, 1999 (1960).

Luther's Works, Vol. 54, Table Talk, Fortress Press, Philadelphia, 1967.

Meeter, Henry, *Calvinism, An Interpretation of its Basic Ideas*, Zondervan, Grand Rapids, MI, 1939, quoted by Kenneth S. Kantzer, "Calvin and the Holy Scriptures," in John W. Walvoord (ed.), *Inspiration and Interpretation*, Evangelical Theological Society, Eerdmans, Grand Rapids, MI, 1957.

Montgomery, John Warwick (ed.), *God's Inerrant Word: An International Symposium on the Trustworthiness of Scripture*, Bethany Fellowship, Inc., Minneapolis, 1973.

Mueller, Theodore, "Luther and the Bible," in John W. Walvoord (ed.), *Inspiration and Interpretation*, Evangelical Theological Society, Eerdmans, Grand Rapids, MI, 1957.

Natan, Yoel, *The Jewish Trinity*, CreateSpace.com United States, Edition 1.0.1, 2003.

Niebuhr, Helmut Richard, *The Meaning of Revelation*, Macmillan Co., New York, 1941.

Payne, J. Barton, "The Biblical Interpretation of Irenaeus," in John W. Walvoord (ed.), *Inspiration and Interpretation*, Evangelical Theological Society, Eerdmans, Grand Rapids, MI, 1957.

Pieper, Francis, *Christian Dogmatics, Vol. I*, Concordia Publishing House, St. Louis, 1950.

Poellot, Luther, *Revelation: The Last Book in the Bible*, Concordia Publishing House, St. Louis, 1962.

Preus, Robert, *The Inspiration of Scripture*, reprint of 1955 first edition, Concordia Heritage Series, Concordia Publishing House, St. Louis, 1981.

———, *The Theology of Post-Reformation Lutheranism, Vol. I: A Study of Theological Prolegomena*, Concordia Publishing House, St. Louis, 1970.

———, *The Theology of Post-Reformation Lutheranism, Vol. II: God and His Creation*, Concordia Publishing House, St. Louis, 1972.

Pritchard, James B., *Ancient Near Eastern Texts Relating to the Old Testament*, Princeton University Press, Princeton, NJ, 1950.

Richardson, John Adkins, *Art the way it is*, Prentice-Hall, Englewood Cliffs, NJ, 1973.

Roberts, Alexander, and James Donaldson (eds.), *The Ante-Nicene Fathers*, rev. Vol. V, Charles Scribner's Sons, New York, 1919.

Sanday, W., *Inspiration: Eight Lectures*, Longmans, Green, and Co., London, 1896.

Sanford, J. C., *Genetic Entropy*, FMS Publications, Waterloo, NY, 2008.

Smith, Andrew Phillip, *The Lost Sayings of Jesus*, Skylight Paths Publishing, Woodstock, VT, 2005.

Synod of Bishops, XII Ordinary General Assembly, The Word of God in the Life and Mission of the Church, *Instrumentum Laboris*,

Vatican City, 2008.

Tappert, Theodore G. (trans. and ed.), *The Book of Concord: The Confessions of the Evangelical Lutheran Church*, Fortress Press, Philadelphia, 1959.

Tenney, Merrill C., *Interpreting Revelation*, Eerdmans Publishing, Grand Rapids, MI, 1957.

"Vide" [Fide], in H. J. D. Denzinger and Clemens Bannwart, *Enchiridion symbolorum definitionum et declarationum de rebus fidei et morum*, 21st ed., 1937, quoted by John Baillie, *The Idea of Revelation in Recent Thought*, Columbia University Press, New York, 1956.

Voelz, James W., *What Does This Mean?*, Concordia Publishing House, St. Louis, 1994.

Weikart, Richard, "Scripture and Myth in Dietrich Bonhoeffer," *Fides et Historia* 25, 1, University of Iowa, 1993.

Woolford, P. M., *The Genesis Grid*, AuthorHouse UK Ltd, Central Milton Keynes, 2010.

Wordsworth, Chr., *Lectures on the Apocalypse; Critical, Expository, and Practical*, Herman Hooker, Philadelphia, 1852.

Yonge, Charles Duke (trans.), "The Special Laws, II," in *The Works of Philo Judaeus, The Contemporary of Josephus*, Vol. III, H. G. Bohn, London, 1854-1890.

―――, "A Treatise on the Account of the Creation of the World, as Given by Moses," in *The Works of Philo Judaeus, The Contemporary of Josephus*, Vol. I, H. G. Bohn, London, 1854-1890.

Young, Edward J., *Thy Word Is Truth*, Eerdmans, Grand Rapids, MI, 1957.

INDEX

1 Peter, 122

Aaron, 210, 246, 303, 319, 347
Abimelech, 234, 273, 362
Abraham, 28, 37, 79, 97, 103, 130, 217, 231-33, 237, 240, 245, 263, 266, 272-73, 288, 295, 301, 303, 320-21, 323-24, 326-27, 335-42, 344-46, 348, 351-52, 354, 358, 362. *See also* Abram.
Abram, 97, 231, 234, 324, 342, 362. *See also* Abraham.
Abstract Expressionism, 91, 270
Achtemeier, Paul J., 187
Acts, 68, 74, 248, 297, 342, 344 n. 20
Admin, 354-55, 360
Aesthetic Hermeneutics, 24, 195
Aesthetics, i, 1, 16, 24, 78, 131, 192-93, 195-98, 223, 269-71, 300, 319-20, 363, 368, 370, 374
Aetiology, 224
Africanus, 349, 351, 353
Akkadian, 219
Aland, Kurt, 13. *See also* Nestle-Aland's Greek New Testament
Aldine, 349
Alexander the Great, 286
Alexandrian, 8, 23, 51, 76, 314, 349
Alford, Henry, 348
Algorithm, 328, 383
Allegory, 119, 202, 206, 219, 289, 315
Amiatinus, Codex, 377 n. 25
Amphictyonic League, 280
Anaphoric Phrases, 15-16, 27, 49, 54-55, 61, 71, 97, 158, 187, 237, 239
Angel of the Lord, 261
Antediluvian, 1, 194, 256, 285-86, 288, 290-92, 294-95, 297, 312, 324-26, 328, 336, 341, 344, 357, 359, 381, 384-85
Ante-Nicene, 364
Antiochus I, 286
Apocalyptic Literature, 4, 6, 90, 130, 133, 146, 165, 180, 182, 189, 194, 365, 369
Apocrypha, iii, 363, 364
Apocryphon of John, 162, 182, 364-70
Aramaic, 35, 219
Archimedes, 335
Aristotle, 196 n. 49
Arithmetic, 330-32, 383
Ark, 122, 228, 285, 290, 297, 324, 337-38, 344, 358
Arphachshad, 337, 346, 348
Asceticism, 364
Assyriologist, 286
Astral numbers, 312, 326
Asymmetry, 16, 84, 91, 131, 146, 163, 182-84, 190-92, 194, 202, 223, 231, 267, 269, 297-300, 309, 318-19, 363, 367-69. *See also* Symmetry.
Atkinson, Richard, 196
Atonement, 273, 313
Augustine, 315, 349-50, 353
Aune, David E., 181, 183-85, 191

Babel, 254, 273, 290-91, 295, 326, 337, 339, 344
Babylon, 183, 200-201, 286, 331, 345, 347, 355, 357
Babylonian, 71, 146, 202, 219, 253, 256, 285-92, 294, 296-97, 299, 314, 328, 332-34, 345-46
Baptism, 37, 43, 46, 106, 122, 207, 248, 345
Barclay, William, 129

Barnabas, Epistle of. *See* Epistle of Barnabas.
Bauckham, Richard, 189
Beale, Gregory K., 181, 185-86
Becker, James J., 291, 318-20
Becker, Joshua J., 291, 318-20
Becker, Siegbert W., 144, 167, 208
Benison, 231-32, 301
Berossus or Berosus, 286-87, 293, 351
Beza, Codex, 348
Beza, Theodore, 348, 353
BibleWorks 8, 4, 8 n. 10, 11-12, 219, 313, 364
Biblia Hebraica Stuttgartensia, 219
Biblical Number Symbolism, 23, 78, 130, 194, 209, 224, 285, 301-2, 323, 343
Blessing, 10, 38, 59, 78-79, 83, 144, 147, 162-63, 166, 223, 231-34, 251, 253, 255-56, 300-303, 346
Boaz, 324, 338, 345, 358
Boismard, M.E., 180
Book of Life, 138-39, 169
Breck, John, ii, 3, 184, 208, 213, 215
Brighton, Louis, 207-8
Bullinger, Ethelbert William, i, 187, 210, 373
Buls, Harold, 353-55
Bultmann, Rudolf, 217, 370
Byzantine, 8, 13, 22, 44, 51

Cain, 226, 323-24, 362
Cainan, 295, 324, 326, 338, 346, 348-55, 358. *See also* Second Cainan.
Canaanite, 253-54, 289, 291, 298-99, 361
Cassuto, Umberto Moshe David, ii, 3-5, 7-8, 22, 27, 37, 42, 47, 51, 71, 77, 81, 106, 133, 137, 175, 179, 182-85, 189, 191-92, 194, 201-2, 208, 213, 217-35, 241-44, 246-51, 253-56, 263, 266-69, 272, 274-76, 280-82, 285-92, 294-97, 299-303, 314, 317, 321, 330, 333, 336-38, 341, 344-48, 360-62, 368-69
Catholic Church, 10, 334
Ceremonial Law, 194, 307
Chaldee Targum, 350
Charles, R. H., 180-83, 189
Charlesworth, James H., 364
Chiasm, ii, 184, 194, 200, 203-4, 213-17, 225, 239, 272, 324, 335-36, 341, 343-44
China, 330-31
Chinese Remainder Theorem, 328, 331, 382
Christ. *See* Jesus Christ.
Chronology, 285, 290-91, 293-94, 323, 326, 336, 340, 343, 346, 349, 352-53, 358, 360. *See also* Minutes; Seconds; Time.
Church Fathers, i, 119, 349, 353, 355, 364, 367
Circumcision, 122, 231-32, 273, 278
Cognates, 277, 287
Collins, Adela Yarbro, 181, 183-85, 191
Commandment, 13, 37, 104, 142-44, 277. *See also* Ten Commandments.
Complutensian, 349
Contiguous, 9, 187, 228, 231. *See also* Noncontiguous.
Coptic, 12, 349, 364-65, 370
Covenant, 228, 231-32, 239, 250-51, 275
Crocodile, 246
Crucifixion, 347, 375 n. 24
Cubists, 333
Cubit, 290, 294-97
Cuneiform, 291, 328-29, 332-33
Curse, 164, 232-33, 303, 323, 346
Cyrus, 355

INDEX 399

Daniel, iv, 33, 82-83, 146-49, 152, 162-63, 185-86, 201-2, 206, 208, 230-31, 273, 294, 312-13, 343, 359, 375-77
Darwinian, 186, 225, 315
David, 23, 28-31, 47, 59, 79, 95-96, 120-21, 153, 199-200, 210, 288, 324, 337-38, 345-46, 354, 358
Dead Sea Scrolls, 219, 244, 370
Decad, iv, 4, 21-27, 30-31, 35-36, 38, 42, 47-48, 59, 68, 70, 73, 76, 78-79, 95, 104, 106, 119, 124-25, 129, 133-34, 139-40, 149-52, 155, 159-61, 169, 179-80, 189-91, 202, 204-5, 207-9, 211, 219, 227, 244, 251, 260-61, 263, 266-67, 272-74, 277-78, 288-89, 296, 310-13, 317, 319-20, 366, 372, 375-76, 378
Demon, 9-10, 39, 44-45, 47, 58, 64-65, 123, 129
Demon-Possessed, 10-11, 37, 45, 64-65, 129
Deuteronomist, 218, 328
Deuteronomy, 43, 61, 247, 253-54, 261, 267, 271, 275-76, 278, 297-99, 303, 342
Didache, 370
Disquisitiones Arithmeticae, 331
Doctrine, 4, 10, 41, 89, 163, 208-10, 364, 372-73, 375
Dodecad, iv, 4, 26-27, 31, 33, 35-36, 39, 44, 50, 53, 56, 59, 62, 68, 70-71, 78-79, 95, 121, 125, 133-34, 161, 173, 179-80, 189, 191, 219, 244, 280, 282-83, 288-89, 313, 319-20, 367, 372, 376, 378
Dorsey, David A., ii, 3, 144, 202-4, 208, 210, 213, 215
Duff, Jason, 251

East, 9, 48, 51, 70, 76, 84, 92, 133, 156, 184, 220, 224-25, 227, 248, 253, 280, 299, 301-2, 344, 346-47
Eber, 324, 326, 335-36, 340-41, 358
Eden, 225-27, 344, 379
Egypt, 97, 244-45, 248, 254, 260-61, 263, 266, 273, 278, 281, 297, 309, 317, 321-22, 330, 337, 344 n. 20, 349, 360-61
Egyptian, 34, 194, 198, 245, 247, 253, 278, 285, 289, 291, 298, 363
Elim, 247-48, 255, 281
Elohim, 221, 227, 256, 279, 293-94
Elohist, 218, 269, 328
Enoch, 227, 288, 312, 323-24, 326, 346, 354, 358, 385
Ephraemi Rescriptus, Codex, 13
Ephraim, 342
Epiphanius, 349, 352-53
Epistle of Barnabas, 370
Erasmus, 13
Eternal, 58, 82-83, 104, 146, 149, 214, 217, 277, 323
Eternity, 122, 148
Euclid, 328, 335
Eusebius, 10, 302, 349, 351-53, 358
Eve, 226, 288, 324, 336, 345
Everlasting Life, 82
Evolution, 315
Exodus, ii, iv, 4, 37, 43, 61, 77, 131, 153-54, 175, 194, 210, 217-19, 241-52, 254-5, 257, 260-63, 266-67, 273-76, 278-79, 281, 283-85, 289, 295-99, 302-11, 313-14, 320-23, 336-37, 347, 362, 373-75, 377-78
Expressionism, 91. *See also* Abstract Expressionism.
Ezekiel, iv, 153, 210, 258-61, 378
Ezra, 298, 323, 347, 355-57, 360

Farstad, Arthur L., 13
Flood, 228, 253, 283, 285-92, 294-95, 312, 314, 319, 323-25,

335-39, 342, 344, 349, 351, 358
Forever, 78, 82-83, 147-49,
Formulae, 43, 188-90, 317-20, 327-28, 331-32, 375, 381-85
Franzmann, Martin H., 129

Gauss, Fredrik, 331
Gematria, 219
Genealogy, 79, 230, 253-54, 272, 280-81, 285, 295, 312, 319, 323-26, 336-43, 345-48, 350-52, 354-57, 359-60, 375 n.24
Generation, 34, 42, 61, 199, 227, 230, 263, 272, 285, 288-91, 312, 315, 317-20, 323-24, 332, 335-38, 344-46, 351-53, 355, 375
Genesis, ii, iv, 3-4, 7, 15-16, 30-31, 34-35, 37, 41-43, 47, 49, 51-53, 57-58, 65, 71, 75-78, 82, 97-98, 102-3, 106-8, 120, 122, 126, 130-31, 133-34, 142, 144-47, 151-53, 158, 175, 179, 181-83, 185, 191, 194, 196-97, 200, 213, 216-23, 225-41, 243, 247, 251, 253-56, 260-273, 277-83, 285-88, 290-95, 297-99, 301, 303, 305, 310, 312-21, 323-45, 347, 349-50, 353-54, 359-62, 368-69, 375, 377-78
Genre, i-ii, 1, 43, 47, 52, 75, 78, 81, 91, 96, 98, 102-3, 116-17, 120, 131, 133-34, 179-82, 184, 186, 188, 191-92, 194-96, 198, 206, 213, 215, 223, 228, 254, 256, 262, 268-69, 271, 285, 300, 303, 319-20, 332-33, 343, 348, 363-64, 367, 372-74, 378
Giessler, Phillip, 215, 250
Gnostic Gospels, iii, 364-65, 368
Gnosticism, iii, 182, 257, 302, 363-65, 367-68, 370
God, 10, 28-31, 41-43, 46-47, 51-52, 57, 67-68, 75-76, 82-83, 89 n. 1, 94-97, 104, 107-8, 114, 116, 118, 130, 136-37, 141-44, 146-47, 151-55, 161, 163-64, 171-72, 174-75, 190, 200, 202, 205-6, 208, 210, 216-18, 221-24, 227-28, 231-34, 237, 239, 241, 243-46, 248-52, 256, 260-63, 266-70, 272-75, 279, 296, 301-3, 308-11, 319-21, 323-24, 338, 341, 343-44, 346, 354, 362, 364, 367, 371, 373, 379. *See also* Son of God.
God the Father, 6-7, 18-20, 36, 47, 89, 104, 110-11, 114, 117-21, 153, 207, 214, 277
Gospel of Thomas, 365
Gospels, Synoptic. *See* Synoptic Gospels.
Greek New Testament, 5, 12-13, 197
Greek Text, Nestle-Aland's Greek New Testament. *See* Nestle-Aland's Greek New Testament.
Greek Text of the Greek Orthodox Church, 13
Greek Text, United Bible Society. *See* United Bible Society Greek Text.

Ham, 254, 342, 360-62
Haran, 231-32, 272, 324, 342
Hawkins, Gerald, 196
Hebraic Meter, ii, iv, 1-2, 4-5, 8-9, 11, 13, 15, 17, 18-20, 22-25, 27, 30-32, 34-35, 37, 44, 46-51, 55, 58, 62-63, 66, 68, 70, 73-75, 77-78, 81-82, 84, 86-87, 95, 97, 99, 102, 106, 108, 113, 118-19, 122, 127, 129-30, 133-34, 137, 149, 160-61, 165, 175, 179, 189-91, 194, 198, 202, 210-11, 215, 217-18, 223, 226, 237, 244, 254, 256, 260, 262, 266-67, 271, 283, 285, 288, 303, 307, 312-13, 320, 323, 329, 334-35, 343, 347-48, 355-56,

INDEX 401

359-60, 363-67, 369, 371-73, 375, 377-78. *See also* Decad; Dodecad; Heptad.
Hebraism, 95, 345
Hebrew, i, iii-iv, 1, 3-5, 7-8, 13, 22-23, 27, 34-35, 51-53, 65, 76, 83, 97, 102, 121, 136, 152, 154, 175, 184, 190-95, 200, 204, 213, 215, 217-20, 223-26, 229, 233-36, 239, 243-44, 246-49, 253-54, 256-57, 260-62, 266-70, 275, 277, 281, 285, 287-90, 294-95, 297-98, 300-301, 303, 306, 308-10, 312-14, 319-20, 324, 326-30, 333, 335-36, 340-41, 345, 348, 350-52, 354, 357-60, 362, 364, 367, 372, 374-75, 377-78, 383
Hellene, 220, 224, 334
Hendel, Ronald, 41-43, 302, 314-15, 317-20, 329
Heptad, iv, 4-6, 8, 12-21, 23-25, 27, 33-37, 43-46, 48-52, 54, 56, 59, 61-63, 65-68, 71, 73, 75-76, 78, 82-83, 87, 89-92, 95, 99-102, 106, 110, 112, 114-15, 119-22, 129, 133-34, 137-42, 144, 146-47, 149-51, 155, 162, 165, 179-80, 182, 189, 191, 211, 219-21, 223-35, 237, 239, 241-42, 244, 248-49, 251, 253, 258, 261, 276, 288-89, 291-92, 294, 301, 303, 306-7, 309-11, 313, 320-21, 333, 339, 343, 346, 365, 367-69, 371-72, 374, 376, 378
Hermeneutics, 24, 195, 197, 225. *See also* Aesthetic Hermeneutics.
Hervey, Lord Arthur, 341-42, 348, 352-55
Hexapla, 349, 351
Hieroglyphics, 219
High Priest, 16-17, 72, 79, 379
Hodges, Zane C., 13
Holy Spirit, 4, 14, 19, 40, 52, 70-71, 75, 81, 97, 130, 174, 345, 365-66, 372-73, 375
Horeb, 243, 250-51. *See also* Mount Sinai.
Hort, Fenton John Anthony, 13, 51
Hoskier Table of Manuscripts, 197

Impressionism, 195
In Search of the Biblical Order, i-ii, 2, 122, 133, 175, 202, 213, 289
Inerrancy, 372
Inspiration, ii, 2, 206, 372-73, 375
Iowa State University, 327, 334
Isaac, 97, 103, 231-34, 237, 245, 266, 273, 303, 318, 320, 336-37, 341, 345-46, 362
Isaiah, 23, 33, 199-200, 206, 209, 320, 344, 375-76, 379
Israel, 43, 61, 70, 154, 181, 200, 224, 234-35, 238, 243-45, 247-50, 253-55, 273, 281, 292-94, 299, 301-2, 305-6, 308, 310, 317, 321, 337, 357, 361, 379

J E P D, iii, 182, 218, 229, 254, 256-57, 269, 313-16, 330, 372
Jacob, 97, 103, 231-34, 237-40, 245, 254, 266, 284, 295, 302-3, 314, 317-20, 337, 339, 342, 345-46, 349, 360, 362
James, Secret Book of. *See* Secret Book of James.
Japheth, 254, 342, 360-61
Jared, 324, 326, 338, 346, 358
Jeremiah, 23, 33, 200-201, 218, 328, 375-76
Jerome, 330, 334, 349-50, 352, 360
Jerusalem, 3, 6, 43-44, 61-63, 183, 203-4, 210-11, 219, 234, 313, 322, 345, 347, 355, 357, 379
Jesse, 324, 345-46, 358
Jesus Christ, 7, 9-11, 13, 16-18, 20-21, 23, 28-29, 34-35, 43, 48, 52-56, 59, 61, 66-68, 70-73, 79, 81, 83-84, 87, 89-92,

94-96, 98, 100-104, 106-16, 120-21, 123, 125, 127-30, 135-37, 140, 142-43, 153-55, 163, 167, 170, 180, 190, 199-200, 202, 204-9, 214, 216, 244, 248, 302, 313, 316-18, 320-22, 328, 337, 339, 345-47, 352, 354-55, 357-59, 362, 364-66, 369-71, 375 n. 24, 379
Jethro, 242, 274. See also Reuel.
Jewish, 130, 136, 152, 185, 270, 302, 314-15, 347, 351, 356, 358. See also Jews.
Jewish Antiquities, 351
Jews, 91, 104-5, 214, 270, 314, 352, 359. See also Jewish.
John the Apostle, i, iv, 2, 12, 24, 27, 31, 34, 36, 44, 51, 56-57, 61, 63-64, 66, 70, 74-75, 78, 81-85, 87-102, 104-22, 126-27, 129-30, 133-34, 137, 140, 142, 146-49, 152, 158-59, 162, 173, 177, 180, 182-86, 189-91, 197, 200-202, 206, 208, 210, 214-15, 221, 229-30, 233, 235, 251, 254, 277, 343-47, 357, 364-65, 368-69, 372, 377
John the Baptist, 5, 28, 46, 71, 80, 93
Jordan, James B., ii, 3, 213, 312, 325-26, 341, 354-55
Joseph, Husband of Mary, 28, 38, 337, 345-46, 357
Joseph, Son of Jacob, 103, 216, 234, 237-38, 240, 266, 280, 362
Josephus, Flavius, 351
Joshua, iv, 270-71, 298
Jubilee, 146, 292, 313, 326, 335, 347
Judah, 97, 238, 314, 345-46, 362
Judges, iv, 254, 270-71, 298, 360
Just, Arthur, 354
Justification, 167

Kabala, 219
Key Words, 1, 5, 37, 63, 108, 110, 112, 117, 141, 159, 213-215, 226, 228, 234, 241-44
King James Version, iv, 5, 8, 10-11, 13, 27, 29, 51, 73, 75, 114, 138, 153-54, 156, 158, 171, 203-4, 210, 215, 221, 231-33, 246, 268, 344, 362
Kirby, Diana Jill, ii-iii, 3, 5, 133, 137, 142, 170, 179-195, 197-98, 208, 213
Kohath, 347
Kuske, David P., ii, 3

Lamech, 226, 295, 323-24, 326, 335, 338, 346, 358-59
Langdon, Stephen Herbert, 287
Lazarus, 79, 379
Leningradensis, Codex, 52, 219, 313. See also Masoretic Text.
Lenski, R. C. H., 208, 318, 345, 348
Lessing, R. Reed, 272, 315-20, 336-38, 341, 348
Levi, 242, 280, 295, 346-47, 353
Levite, 281
Leviticus, 257-58, 261, 267, 276, 278, 301, 313
Lord, 6, 22-23, 35-36, 43, 61, 74-75, 79, 103-4, 113, 115, 122-23, 137, 174, 200, 205, 208-10, 227, 229, 231-35, 237, 239-41, 243, 245, 247, 250, 255-62, 268, 272, 279-80, 282, 298, 301, 303-6, 308-11, 319, 342, 366-67, 375
Lord God, 97, 151, 227, 252, 262-63, 268-69, 309-10
Lord God Almighty, 142-43, 151, 155
Lowth, Bishop Robert, 216-17, 225
Lunar days, 326
Lustrum, 286-87, 292
Luther, Martin, 13, 158, 199, 202, 205-6, 315, 337, 358
Lutheran, 10, 113, 196
LXX, 154, 355. See also Septuagint.

Maccabeus, Judas, 313
Mack, Burton L., 369-72
Macro-Patterns, 163-64, 174
Mahalalel, 324, 326, 338, 358
Majority Text, 8, 13
Manasseh, 342
Manuscript P52, 12
Manuscript P75, 126, 128, 353-55
Manuscripts, 1-2, 6, 8, 12-14, 19, 22, 28, 44, 49, 51, 54-55, 73, 119, 126, 128, 134, 147, 156, 159, 176, 194, 197, 281, 313, 348, 353-54, 367
Markan Priority, iii, 24, 46, 48
Mary, Mother of Jesus, 20, 80, 337, 346, 357
Masoretes, 192, 242, 244, 299, 330, 334, 372, 378
Masoretic Text, 52, 192, 219, 329-30, 334, 357-60, 378. *See also* Leningradensis, Codex.
Mathematics, 131, 164, 270, 292, 300, 326-36, 363, 381-84, 386. *See also* Modular Mathematics.
Mediterranean, 328
Melchizedek, 337
Mesopotamian, 253-54, 290-91, 295, 332, 334, 344 n. 20
Methuselah, 324, 326, 328, 338, 358, 384
Metzger, Bruce M., 13, 51
Meyer, Marvin W., 365-66
Midrashic, 293
Millennialism, 219
Minutes, 286-87, 292-93, 359
Mitchell, Christopher, 205, 207-9
Modular Mathematics, 327, 329, 331-34, 381-83
Moon, 248, 287, 292
Morris, Henry M., 318-20
Moses, i-ii, 1, 8, 13, 21, 23, 27, 31, 35, 38, 42, 46-47, 49, 51-52, 54-55, 57-58, 65, 67-68, 70, 75-76, 78-79, 81, 87, 96-98, 102, 104, 106-8, 115-16, 119, 126-28, 133-34, 142, 150, 154-55, 158, 182, 184, 186, 191-93, 197, 210, 216-18, 219-21, 227-29, 233, 235, 237, 241-43, 246-50, 253-57, 261, 267, 271-72, 274, 277, 282, 287-92, 295-96, 299, 302-5, 309-10, 312, 314-21, 326, 328, 332-35, 338, 340-341 n. 15, 343, 348, 360-62, 372-75
Motif, 35, 91, 106, 149, 181, 188, 195, 300
Mount Moriah, 204, 273
Mount Sinai, 250, 319. *See also* Horeb.
Mount Zion, 204
Mouth, 159-60, 172, 203-6, 243
Mysticism, 219
Mythology, 9, 180, 218, 315, 365, 370-73

Nag Hammadi Library, 364, 370
Nahor, 281, 324, 326, 328, 340-42, 358, 360, 385
Nebuchadnezzar, 146, 163, 202
Nehemiah, 83, 298, 323, 347, 355-57, 360
Nestle, Eberhard, 13
Nestle-Aland's Greek New Testament, 5, 13, 51, 133-34, 191, 197, 354
New American Standard Bible, iv, 5, 8, 10-11, 13, 27, 32, 51, 73, 86, 204, 209-10, 248
New Gregory, 197
Nicene, 364
Nile, 245, 247, 252
Nissan, 248, 337
Noah, 107, 228-29, 231, 239, 253-55, 263, 272, 285, 288, 301, 312, 317, 320, 323-26, 335, 337-39, 341-42, 344, 346, 351, 358, 360-61
Noncontiguous, 187, 213, 217, 228, 231, 365-67, 369. *See also* Contiguous.
Notarikon, 219

Number System, 288-92, 294, 296-97
Numerology, 219

Oppert, Julius, 285-86
Orientalists, 286
Origen, 349, 351
Orthodox Jew, 217, 327

Pagan, 41, 91, 146, 182, 184, 192, 202, 253, 297, 299-300, 313, 361, 364, 367
Pagels, Elaine, 368
Papyrus P52. *See* Manuscript P52.
Papyrus P75. *See* Manuscript P75.
Parallelism, 187, 194, 213, 246, 272
Parallelism, Antithetic, 35, 188
Parallelism, Stairlike, 216
Paraphrase, 11, 65, 192, 244, 359, 377
Passover, 78, 124, 246, 292
Patriarchs, 256, 285, 288, 290-92, 294-95, 301, 312, 321, 324-27, 329-30, 333-36, 338, 340-41, 344-45, 356-58, 360, 378
Pattern, ii, 24, 27, 34-36, 43, 52, 61, 64-65, 67, 91-92, 99, 117, 119, 121, 127, 137, 140, 150, 153, 155, 162-65, 173-74, 182, 185, 187, 193-94, 202, 206, 208-10, 215, 226-27, 239, 247, 256-57, 267, 297, 301, 306, 325-26, 329-30, 333, 336, 341, 346, 355-56, 363, 377
Pentateuch, ii, iv, 149, 184, 191, 198, 217, 247, 256, 261-62, 267, 271, 274, 277, 290-91, 315-16, 319, 323, 339, 347, 350, 362, 364-65, 378
Perfection, 10, 228, 241, 248, 255, 280, 300-303
Persian, 285, 294, 329, 349
Peter (Simon Peter) 3, 28-29, 39, 59, 78-80, 96-97, 122, 129
Pharaoh, 154, 163, 216, 234, 238, 242, 247, 273, 280, 304, 306, 308-10, 321, 379
Pharez, 288, 324, 337-38, 355, 358
Philistines, 298, 360-61
Philo, 10, 302, 314-15, 351
Philosophy, 219, 302, 314-15, 345
Picasso, Pablo, 333
Pitts, Mike, 196
Plato, 225, 302, 314
Polysyndeton, 312, 367, 373
Postdiluvian, 287, 290, 297, 324, 336, 340, 344, 357-59, 381, 384-85
Post-Nicene, 364
Priest, 16-17, 37, 66, 72, 79, 123, 127, 167, 205, 210, 242, 277, 374, 379. *See also* High Priest.
Priestly Code, 218, 328
Procopius Gazaeus, 349, 351
Pseudepigrapha, iii, 363-64
Ptolemies, 349
Pyramid, Great, 338-39
Pythagoras, 10, 302

Q Source, iii, 24, 27, 46, 48, 52, 57-58, 65, 102, 149, 233, 364, 369-72
Qin Jiushao, 331
Questione della Genesi, La, 317
Qumran, 329

Rashi, 315
Rav-Noy, Eyal, ii, 2-3, 208, 213, 215, 217, 285, 329-30
Rebecca, 97, 266, 362
Received Text, 13, 197. *See also* Textus Receptus.
Red Sea, 247-48, 310, 379
Redaction, iii, 179-80, 214, 254, 312, 372
Redeemer, 324
Resurrection, 109, 121, 322, 347
Retro-engineering, 332-34, 372, 378
Retrograde, 333
Reuel, 242-43. *See also* Jethro.

28, 155, 196, 210, 216, 295, 307, 313, 347, 354-56, 360
Ten Commandments, 43, 79, 104, 130, 246, 250, 255, 263, 267, 273-76, 296-97, 299, 319. *See also* Commandment.
Terah, 317, 320, 324, 326, 328, 340-43, 358
Textus Receptus, 8, 13, 75, 85, 87, 133-35, 138, 147, 171, 367, 369. *See also* Received Text.
Thunder, Perfect Mind, The, 368-69
Thutmose III, 337
Time, 71, 147, 165, 169, 216, 219, 248-49, 270, 285-88, 291-93, 312, 323, 337-39, 356, 358-59, 371, 375. *See also* Chronology; Minutes; Seconds.
Tischendorf, Lobegott Friedrich, Constantin (von), 13, 99-101
Tōlᵉdhōth, 230, 317, 319-20, 375
Torah, 75, 175, 218, 220, 224-25, 255, 289, 316-17, 346-47, 361
Transfiguration, 207, 321
Tree of Life, 138-39, 169, 344
Trinity, 89 n. 1, 125, 128, 153, 200
Tubalcain, 323-24
Two Natures of Christ, 95, 379

Ugarit, 219, 253-54
Uniformitarianism, 288
United Bible Society Greek Text, 31, 51
University of Southern Indiana, iii, 333
Ur, 330
Usher or Ussher, Bishop, 325, 337-39, 351, 358-59

Vatican, ii, 3, 219, 317, 349-50
Verily, 37, 66, 82-87, 103-4, 214
Voice, 92-94, 159-60, 162, 174, 200-201; 204-6, 216, 232, 250, 368

Vulgata Clementina 1598, 377 n. 25
Vulgate, iii, 65, 307, 330, 334, 349-50, 352, 359, 377-78
Vulgate 1535, 377 n. 25

Wang Xiatong, 331
Water, 37-38, 106-8, 122, 125, 175, 203-4, 206, 221-22, 228, 247-48, 255, 282, 345, 379
Waw, 52, 245, 260, 312-13, 374-75
Weld-Blundell Collection, 287
Wellhausen, Julius, 218, 275
West, 1, 9, 31, 34, 44, 48-49, 51, 70, 91-92, 136, 184, 186, 195-97, 215, 220, 224-25, 270, 280, 296, 299-302, 338, 340, 346
Westcott, Brooke Foss, 13, 51
Wiseman, P. J., 317-20, 375
Wisse, Frederik, 365-66
Word Stem, iv, 2, 4, 7, 114, 136, 149, 175-76, 190, 211, 217, 228, 242-44, 246, 256, 277, 279-80, 293

Yahwist, 218
Yardley, 348, 353
YHWH, 227, 251-52, 256, 262, 268, 293, 367

Zechariah, 273
Zippora, 242, 362

Revelation, ii, iv, 3-5, 7, 15-16, 23, 30, 32, 37, 47, 51-52, 58, 61, 67, 70, 78-84, 97, 129-131, 133-65, 175-76, 179-91, 193-94, 196-202, 204-8, 210-11, 213-14, 216-17, 219, 221, 224, 230-31, 233, 235, 247, 267, 273-74, 283, 289, 296, 302, 312-13, 343-46, 359, 364-69, 375, 377
Righteous, 34-35, 37-38, 61, 338
Roman, 186, 194, 320, 329, 333, 340
Rome, 3, 344 n. 20
Ruth, iv, 323-24, 337-38, 354-55, 359, 360

Sabbath, 39, 79, 129, 248-49, 253, 278, 289, 292, 313
Sacrament, 209
Saint, 167-68, 174-75
Sand Reckoner of Archimedes, The, 335
Sarah, 97, 231-32, 273, 294-95, 324-25, 336, 339, 362. *See also* Sarai.
Sarai, 324. *See also* Sarah.
Satan, 65
Schussler-Fiorenza, Elizabeth, 181, 184
Scrivener, F. H. A., 13
Second Cainan, 348-55
Seconds, 287, 292-93
Secret Book of James, 365
Seleucid, 332
Septuagint, iii, 27, 34-35, 44, 51-52, 62, 65, 68, 76-77, 102, 146, 152, 192, 219, 223, 226, 230, 244, 246, 248, 266-67, 275, 281, 298, 307, 318, 321, 335, 348-361, 364-65, 377-78. *See also* LXX.
Seth, 323-26, 346, 358
Sexagesimal, 224, 253, 288-97, 299
Shem, 254, 263, 272, 288, 317, 320, 323-24, 326-27, 337-38, 340-42, 344, 348-50, 358, 361-62, 384

Sinaiticus, Codex, 13
Soden, Hermann von, 13
Sodom and Gomorrah, 86, 266, 273, 280
Solar year, 326
Solomon, 202-4, 206-7, 209-11, 345
Son of David, 23, 28-31, 47, 95-96, 337, 345
Son of God, 28-31, 67-68, 95-96, 136-37, 371
Son of Man, 28, 30-31, 47-48, 68-70, 95-96, 136-37, 204-6, 214, 216, 344-45
Song of Solomon, iv, 106, 199, 202-11, 377
Song of Songs. *See* Song of Solomon.
Spinoza, Baruch, 315
Spiritualism, 219
Steinmann, Andrew E., 272, 312-13, 315-20, 336-38, 341, 348
Stephanus, 13
Sternberg, Meir, iii, 76, 191-93, 208-9, 299, 364
Stonehenge, 196
Sumerian, 219, 253, 286-88, 290-91, 293-94, 332-33
Swanson, Matthew, 327-28, 384, 386
Symmetry, 16, 84, 91, 131, 146, 163, 182-83, 190, 192, 194, 202, 223-25, 229, 231, 255, 269, 289, 296-97, 299, 309, 318-19, 343, 357, 363, 367-69. *See also* Asymmetry.
Synoptic Gospels, 57, 61
Syriac, 12, 219, 349-50

Tabernacle, 168, 210, 248, 250-51, 253, 285, 289, 294-97, 321
Tablets, 251, 253, 286-87, 291, 328-29, 333
Talmud, 267, 291, 293
Taxonomy, 179, 181, 186-88, 191, 194-95, 198
Temple, 31, 63, 87-88, 123, 125, 127-